THE GREAT DEPRESSION OF THE 1930s

The Great Depression of the 1930s

Lessons for Today

HB
3711
G684
2013
WEB

Edited by
NICHOLAS CRAFTS & PETER FEARON

OXFORD
UNIVERSITY PRESS

OXFORD
UNIVERSITY PRESS

Great Clarendon Street, Oxford, OX2 6DP,
United Kingdom

Oxford University Press is a department of the University of Oxford. It furthers the University's objective of excellence in research, scholarship, and education by publishing worldwide. Oxford is a registered trade mark of Oxford University Press in the UK and in certain other countries

© Oxford University Press 2013

The moral rights of the authors have been asserted

First published 2013
First published in paperback 2016

All rights reserved. No part of this publication may be reproduced, stored in a retrieval system, or transmitted, in any form or by any means, without the prior permission in writing of Oxford University Press, or as expressly permitted by law, by licence or under terms agreed with the appropriate reprographics rights organization. Enquiries concerning reproduction outside the scope of the above should be sent to the Rights Department, Oxford University Press, at the address above

You must not circulate this work in any other form
and you must impose this same condition on any acquirer

Published in the United States of America by Oxford University Press
198 Madison Avenue, New York, NY 10016, United States of America

British Library Cataloguing in Publication Data
Data available

Library of Congress Cataloging in Publication Data
Data available

ISBN 978–0–19–966318–7 (Hbk.)
ISBN 978–0–19–878278–0 (Pbk.)

Links to third party websites are provided by Oxford in good faith and for information only. Oxford disclaims any responsibility for the materials contained in any third party website referenced in this work.

Contents

List of Figures

List of Tables

List of Contributors

Michael Bordo is Professor of Economics and Director of the Center for Monetary and Financial History at Rutgers University. He has been a Visiting Professor at the University of California Los Angeles, Carnegie Mellon University, Princeton University, Harvard University, and was Pitt Professor of American History and Institutions at Cambridge University. Professor Bordo has been a Visiting Scholar at the IMF, the Federal Reserve Banks of St Louis and Cleveland, the Federal Reserve Board of Governors, the Bank of Canada, the Bank of England, and the Bank for International Settlements. He is also a Research Associate of the National Bureau of Economic Research. He has published many articles in leading journals and ten books in monetary economics and monetary history.

Charles W. Calomiris is Henry Kaufman Professor of Financial Institutions at Columbia Business School, a Professor at Columbia's School of International and Public Affairs, and a Research Associate of the National Bureau of Economic Research. He is a member of the Advisory Scientific Committee of the European Systemic Risk Board, the Shadow Financial Regulatory Committee, the Shadow Open Market Committee, the Financial Economists Roundtable, the Task Force on Property Rights at the Hoover Institution, the Federal Reserve Centennial Advisory Council, and the World Economic Forum Agenda Council on Fiscal Crises. He has held other positions at the Council on Foreign Relations, the American Enterprise Institute, and the Pew Trusts. In 2011, he was the Houblon–Norman Senior Fellow at the Bank of England.

Forrest Capie is Professor Emeritus of Economic History at the CASS Business School, City University, London. He has also taught at the London School of Economics, the University of Warwick, and the University of Leeds. He has been a British Academy Overseas Fellow at the National Bureau, New York, a Visiting Professor at the University of Aix-Marseille and at the London School of Economics, and a Visiting Scholar at the IMF. He was head of Department of Banking and Finance at City University from 1989 to 1992 and Editor of the *Economic History Review* from 1993 to 1999. He has published widely on money, banking, trade, and commercial policy. He has recently completed the commissioned history, *The Bank of England: 1950s to 1979* (Cambridge University Press, 2010), and his most recent book (with G. E. Wood) is *Money over Two Centuries. Selected Topics in British Monetary History, 1870–2010* (Oxford University Press, 2012).

Nicholas Crafts is Professor of Economic History and Director of the ESRC Research Centre, Competitive Advantage in the Global Economy, at the University of Warwick. He is a Fellow of the British Academy, a former President of the Economic History Society, and a former Editor of the *Economic History Review*. His publications include *Economic Growth in Europe Since 1945*

(Cambridge University Press, 1996, edited with Gianni Toniolo) and *Delivering Growth while Reducing Deficits: Lessons from the 1930s* (CentreForum, 2011).

Barry Eichengreen is George C. Pardee and Helen N. Pardee Professor of Economics and Political Science at the University of California, Berkeley, Research Associate of the National Bureau of Economic Research, and Research Fellow of the Centre for Economic Policy Research. Among his books are: *Golden Fetters: The Gold Standard and the Great Depression 1919–1939* (Oxford University Press, 1992) and *Exorbitant Privilege: The Rise and Fall of the Dollar and the Future of the International Monetary System* (Oxford University Press, 2011).

Peter Fearon is Emeritus Professor of Modern Economic History at the University of Leicester. He has held visiting positions at the universities of Cambridge, Kansas, and La Trobe University, Australia. He has published extensively on the Great Depression and his most recent monograph is *Kansas in the Great Depression. Work Relief, the Dole and Rehabilitation* (University of Missouri Press, 2007). His current research interests include the economics of the New Deal and money lending in the UK during the interwar period.

Alexander J. Field is the Michel and Mary Orradre Professor of Economics at Santa Clara University. After graduating from Harvard University, he received his MSc from the London School of Economics and his PhD from the University of California, Berkeley. Between 2004 and 2012 he served as executive Director of the Economic History Association. He is the author of *Altruistically Inclined? The Behavioural Sciences, Evolutionary Theory, and the Origins of Reciprocity* (University of Michigan Press, 2001) and *A Great Leap Forward: 1930s Depression and US Economic Growth* (Yale University Press, 2011).

Price Fishback is the Thomas R. Brown Professor of Economics at the University of Arizona. He is a Research Associate of the National Bureau of Economic Research. His books include *Soft Coal, Hard Choices: The Economic Welfare of Bituminous Coal Miners, 1890 to 1930* (New York: Oxford University Press, 1992), *Prelude to the Welfare State: The Origins of Workers' Compensation* (with Shawn Kantor. University of Chicago Press, 2000), and *Government and the American Economy: A New History* (University of Chicago Press, 2007, co-authored). Since 2000 he has been publishing widely on the creation and the impact of New Deal programmes.

Timothy J. Hatton is Professor of Economics at the University of Essex and at the Australian National University. He is also a Research Fellow of the Centre for Economic Policy Research. His principle research interests are in labour market history, including unemployment, wage determination, poverty, and the welfare state. Recently he has focused on the socioeconomic determinants of trends in the health and stature of children in the UK during the interwar period. He has also published widely on the economics of international migration, past and present. His work on asylum seekers and asylum policy has appeared in *Seeking Asylum in the OECD: Trends and Policies* (CEPR, 2011)

John Landon-Lane, an Associate Professor of Economics at Rutgers University, has published numerous journal articles and chapters in edited volumes in the areas of time series and Bayesian econometrics, macroeconomics, and macroeconomic history. He has also published a number of papers on the economic history of the United States and his current research agenda includes the comparison of the recent global financial crisis to past global financial crises.

Joseph R. Mason is Professor of Finance, Hermann Moyse Jr/Louisiana Bankers Association Chair of Banking at the Ourso School of Business, Louisiana State University, and Senior Fellow at the Wharton School. His research focuses primarily on business cycle persistence, financial and economic crises, and structured finance. He emphasizes the role of regulation in achieving market efficiency and liquidity in thinly traded assets and illiquid market conditions, as well as the efficiency of bailout and resolution policies through the history of financial markets. Joseph Mason has been a visiting scholar at the Federal Reserve Bank of Atlanta, the Federal Deposit Insurance Corporation, and the Federal Reserve Bank of Philadelphia.

Roger Middleton, Professor of the History of Political Economy and Head of the School of Humanities at the University of Bristol, is an economic historian who has written extensively in the areas of modern British economic history and the history of economics and economic policy. His most recent book is *Inside the Department of Economic Affairs: Samuel Brittan, the diary of an 'irregular', 1964–1966* (Oxford University Press, 2012). He is currently working as general editor of the British Historical Statistics Project, a major initiative which will lead to the publication of a new multi volume print and an online edition of British Historical Statistics.

Kris James Mitchener is the Robert and Susan Finocchio Professor of Economics at Santa Clara University and Research Associate of the National Bureau of Economic Research. His research focuses on international economics, macroeconomics, and economic history and he has published widely in leading journals including the *Journal of Political Economy*, *The Economic Journal*, the *Journal of Money, Credit and Banking* and *The Journal of Economic History*. Kris Mitchener has held visiting positions at the Bank of Japan, the St Louis Federal Reserve Bank, UCLA, Stanford, and CREi at Universtat Pompeu Fabra.

Albrecht O. Ritschl is Professor of Economic History at the London School of Economics. He is a Fellow at the Centre for Economic Policy Research (CEPR), the Centre for Economic Performance (CEP), and at CESinfo. He is also a member of the Scientific Advisory Board to the German Ministry of Economics and is currently speaker of an expert commission researching the history of the German Ministry of Economics and its predecessors since 1919. He has published extensively on twentieth century German economic history with an emphasis on the Great Depression and the 1930s.

Peter Temin is Elisha Gray 11 Professor Emeritus at the Massachusetts Institute of Technology (MIT). He was a Junior Fellow of the Society of Fellows at Harvard University, Pitt Professor of American History and Institutions at Cambridge University, Head of the Economics Department at MIT, and President of the

Economic History Association. Professor Temin's research interests include macroeconomic history, the Great Depression, industry studies in both the nineteenth and the twentieth centuries, and ancient Rome. His most recent books are *The Roman Market Economy* (Princeton University Press, 2013) and *Prometheus Shackled: Goldsmith's Banks and England's Financial Revolution after 1700* (Oxford University Press, 2013, with Hans-Joachim Voth).

Mark Thomas is Professor of History and Economics at the University of Virginia and Leverhulme Visiting Professor of Economics at the University of Warwick (2011–12). He is the author or co-author of five books and numerous journal articles and book chapters on the economic history of Britain, Australia, and the USA. His dissertation was awarded at the inaugural Alexander Gerschenkron Prize of the Economic History Association. He is the recipient of the T. S. Ashton Prize (Economic History Society) and, with J. A. James, the Arthur H. Cole Prize (Economic History Association). He is currently working on a project comparing the British and American economies between 1850 and 1940 from a social accounting perspective.

John Joseph Wallis is Professor of Economics at the University of Maryland and a Research Associate at the National Bureau of Economic Research. He is an economic historian and institutional economist whose research focuses on the dynamic interaction of political and economic institutions over time. As an American historian, he has collected large data sets on government finances and on state constitutions and used them to study how political and economic forces changed American institutions in the 1830s and 1930s. In the last decade his research has expanded to cover a longer period, wider geography, and more general questions of how societies use economic and political institutions to solve the problem of controlling violence and, in some situations, sustaining economic growth.

Nikolaus Wolf is Professor of Economic History in the Department of Economics, Humboldt University of Berlin, Germany. He has also held academic posts at the London School of Economics, the University Pompeu Fabra, Barcelona, the Free University, Berlin, and the University of Warwick. His research is centred on special economic development, especially patterns of trade and industrial location and the macroeconomics of Europe in the interwar period. He is a research affiliate at CEPR (London), CESinfo (Munich), GEP (Nottingham), and CAGE (Warwick).

1

Depression and Recovery in the 1930s: An Overview

Nicholas Crafts and Peter Fearon

1.1. INTRODUCTION

The Great Depression deserves its title. The economic crisis that began in 1929 soon engulfed virtually every manufacturing country and all food and raw materials producers. In 1931, Keynes observed that the world was then '. . . in the middle of the greatest economic catastrophe . . . of the modern world . . . there is a possibility that when this crisis is looked back upon by the economic historian of the future it will be seen to mark one of the major turning points' (Keynes, 1931). Keynes was right. Table 1.1 illustrates the movement of key variables in the most

Table 1.1. The Great Depression vs. Great Recession in the advanced countries

	Real GDP	Price level	Unemployment (%)	Trade volume
1929	100.0	100.0	7.2	100.0
1930	95.2	90.8	14.1	94.8
1931	89.2	79.9	22.8	89.5
1932	83.3	73.1	31.4	76.5
1933	84.3	71.7	29.8	78.4
1934	89.0	75.3	23.9	79.6
1935	94.0	77.6	21.9	81.8
1936	100.6	81.4	18.0	85.7
1937	105.3	91.5	14.3	97.4
1938	105.4	90.4	16.5	87.0
2007	100.0	100.0	5.4	100.0
2008	100.0	102.0	5.8	101.9
2009	96.4	102.8	8.0	90.2
2010	99.5	103.8	8.3	101.2
2011	101.1	105.3	7.9	106.5

Sources: 1929–38

Real GDP: Maddison (2010); western European countries plus western offshoots.

Price Level: League of Nations (1941); data are for wholesale prices, weighted average of 17 countries.

Unemployment: Eichengreen and Hatton (1988); data are for industrial unemployment, unweighted average of 11 countries.

Trade volume: Maddison (1985), weighted average of 16 countries.

Source: 2007–11

IMF, World Economic Outlook Database, April 2012.

important economies during the downturn of the early 1930s and in the recovery which followed. Real GDP (gross domestic product) reached a trough in 1932 and did not regain pre-Depression levels until 1936. Industrial unemployment also reached a trough in 1932 but even in 1937, the best year of the decade, the jobless total remained extraordinarily high. The Great Depression caused a major decline in world trade; it was a time of tariff increases, quotas, competitive devaluations, and the promotion of bilateral at the expense of multilateral trade. It is also important to note that the depression was a time of deflation. On average, prices fell by 28.3 per cent between 1929 and 1933. Even by the end of the decade, prices had not returned to their pre-Depression level. The persistent deflation increased the real burden of debt, raised real interest rates, and caused consumer and investor uncertainty. Deflation was a major destabilizing feature which policy makers were forced to address. Finally, the data shows that the path to recovery was checked in 1937 when a brief but severe recession in the US affected the world economy.

If we move from the aggregate picture to examine the fortunes of the UK, the USA, and Germany it is clear that their experiences differed. A study of Table 1.2 shows that the UK fall in real GDP reached a trough in 1931, a modest contraction compared with the fall experienced by the US (trough in 1933) and Germany (trough in 1932). Stock market prices declined in all three countries but least in the UK. It is also apparent that the early recovery from the depression was more robust in the UK than in either the US or Germany, though we can note the surge in real GDP during the late 1930s as the Nazi economy became more heavily engaged in preparations for war.

There are other important features of this international crisis which will be analysed in this volume. In the early 1930s, major financial crises caused panic not just in stock markets but also in banking systems. In the US, for example, clusters of bank failures, especially in 1931 and during the winter of 1932–33, had a devastating effect on the real economy. Across the world, bank failures became the norm rather than the exception. The UK was the only major country where the commercial banking system was robust and the possibility of bank failure remote. In most other countries, credit markets ceased to function effectively and depositors rushed to withdraw their savings as they lost faith in financial institutions. Banks ceased to lend and tried instead to bolster their reserves as an insurance against depositor runs. Business bankruptcies and cutbacks in output inevitably caused job losses and also led to a steep decline in investment. As the depression worsened, all governments faced a decline in tax revenue at a time when the need for welfare spending increased. Reductions in public spending in order to achieve budget balance served to worsen the economic decline and intensify misery, which in some countries led to serious political unrest. The severe unanticipated economic crisis made it difficult, and finally impossible, for many countries to meet payment on their debts which had been accumulated during the 1920s. Consequently, in 1931 and 1932 there were a large number of sovereign debt defaults.

What are the key questions that we should ask about the Great Depression? Asking why did the crisis begin in 1929 is an obvious start, but more important questions are why it was so deep and why it lasted so long? Sustained recovery did not begin in the United States until the spring of 1933, though the UK trough

Table 1.2. Depression and recovery in Germany, United Kingdom, and United States

	Real GDP	GDP Deflator	Unemployment (%)	Stock Market Prices
UK				
1929	100.0	100.0	8.0	100.0
1930	99.9	99.6	12.3	80.5
1931	94.4	97.2	16.4	62.8
1932	95.1	93.7	17.0	60.2
1933	96.0	92.5	15.4	74.3
1934	102.8	91.7	12.9	90.3
1935	106.6	92.6	12.0	100.0
1936	109.9	93.1	10.2	115.9
1937	114.7	96.6	8.5	108.0
1938	118.2	99.3	10.1	88.5
USA				
1929	100.0	100.0	2.9	100.0
1930	91.4	96.4	8.9	69.4
1931	85.6	86.3	15.6	35.8
1932	74.4	76.2	22.9	30.8
1933	73.4	74.2	20.9	46.2
1934	81.3	78.4	16.2	45.8
1935	88.6	79.9	14.4	63.1
1936	100.0	80.7	10.0	79.8
1937	105.3	84.1	9.2	50.5
1938	101.6	81.7	12.5	61.7
Germany				
1929	100.0	100.0	10.4	100.0
1930	93.3	99.6	17.2	79.1
1931	82.6	93.8	25.5	53.8
1932	74.7	84.6	31.5	38.5
1933	80.3	80.6	27.2	50.5
1934	88.8	81.3	15.7	58.4
1935	99.6	80.7	12.1	68.0
1936	110.8	80.5	9.6	80.3
1937	123.2	81.0	5.0	90.7
1938	135.0	82.3	2.2	89.6

Sources: UK—Real GDP: Feinstein (1972); GDP deflator: Feinstein (1972); Unemployment: Boyer and Hatton (2002); Stock market prices: Mitchell (1988)
Sources: USA—Carter et al. (2006)
Note: Unemployment based on the whole-economy series constructed by Weir (1992)
Sources: Germany—Real GDP: Ritschl (2002); GDP deflator: Ritschl (2002); Unemployment: Institut fur Konjunkturforschung, Wochenbericht, various issues.
Stock market prices: Ronge (2002).

occurred in late 1931 and in Germany during the following year. Why and how did the depression spread so that it became an international catastrophe? What role did financial crises play in prolonging and transmitting economic shocks? How effective were national economic policy measures designed to lessen the impact of the depression? Did governments try to coordinate their economic policies? If not, then why not? Why did the intensity of the depression and the recovery from it vary so markedly between countries? Why did the eradication of unemployment prove to be so intractable? In 1937–38 a further sharp depression hit the US economy increasing unemployment and imposing further deflation.

What caused this serious downturn and what lessons did policy makers draw from it? In short, how can economies be rehabilitated after they have been subject to a major economic contraction intensified by financial disorder?

By the late twentieth century, the memory of international financial seizure in the US and Europe, mass unemployment, and severe deflation had receded. Indeed, many policy makers assumed that markets, free from the restraints of regulation, would be sufficiently robust to avoid another Great Depression. However, during 2007–08, an astonishing and unexpected collapse occurred which caused all key economic variables to fall at a faster rate than they had during the early 1930s. As Eichengreen and O'Rourke (2010 and 2012) report, the volume of world trade, the performance of equity markets, and industrial output dropped steeply in 2008. Table 1.1 indicates that the decline in real GDP 2008–09 was steep but soon arrested. Trade volume declined more rapidly in 2008 than it did in the early phase of the Great Depression, but the decline was only brief. Unemployment rose, but fortunately the problem has not become as serious as it did during the early 1930s. However, the aggregate figures for unemployment mask very serious problems amongst particular groups in a number of countries. For example, the jobless totals in Greece and Spain are a disturbing echo of the 1930s. In sharp contrast with the Great Depression, gentle price rises rather than deflation were a feature of the post 2007 international economy.

However, like the Great Depression, a full blown financial crisis quickly emerged. In 2007, the US housing boom collapsed and subprime mortgages which had been an attractive investment both at home and abroad now became a millstone round the necks of those financial institutions that had eagerly snapped them up. The crisis was not confined to the US. In August 2007, the French bank, BNP Paribus, suspended three investment funds worth 2bn. euros because of problems in the US subprime sector. Meanwhile, the European Central Bank (ECB) was forced to intervene to restore calm to distressed credit markets which were badly affected by losses from subprime hedge funds. On 14 September 2007, the British public became aware that Northern Rock had approached the Bank of England for an emergency loan. Frantic depositors rushed to withdraw their savings. The run on Northern Rock was an extraordinary event for the UK. During the Great Depression no British financial institution failed, or looked like failing, but in 2007 there was immediate depositor panic. It was clear that, without some assurance on the security of deposits, other institutions were at risk. In 2009, UK GDP contracted by 4.8 per cent, the steepest fall since 1921.

Contrary to the experience in the Great Depression, central banks were quick to respond to the 2008 crisis both nationally and, by cooperation, internationally. Interest rates were slashed, massive quantitative easing was used as a tool to provide liquidity to distressed banking systems, and coordinated monetary expansion provided an additional boost. Indeed, both historically low interest rates and a commitment to quantitative easing have been retained by the US Federal Reserve and the Bank of England in order to sustain recovery. Fortunately, there was no resort to the trade war policies that bedevilled the international economy during the 1930s. Although monetary policy has been expansionary, after an initial phase of stimulus, fiscal policy has trodden a different path. Concern over the level of sovereign debt has led many governments to embrace fiscal austerity in the belief that the policy of budgetary consolidation would reduce the burden of debt and also assist economic expansion. In 2008, there seemed a real possibility that the world would be plunged into another Great Depression. Clearly that did not happen, but the problem that the world now confronts is that the expansion evident in 2010 has stalled. There is a danger that the budgetary squeeze, severe for countries such as Greece, Ireland, and Spain constrained by the fixed exchange rate of the eurozone, will cause more pain but not cure the disease. Sustained fiscal consolidation may even transform a world economy now languishing in stagnation into one sliding towards depression (Eichengreen and O'Rourke, 2012).

What lessons, if any, did policy makers learn from the economic and financial debacle of 1929–33? Is the fact that the recession that began in 2007 has not, at least so far, descended into mass unemployment, waves of bank failure, trade wars, and destabilizing deflation the result of the implementation of monetary and fiscal policies that were not employed during the Great Depression? Has enlightened international cooperation replaced the intransigent self interest evident 80 years ago? Is there a unified view amongst policy makers striving to promote economic growth in today's sluggish economies? In order to answer these questions we must first analyse the course and causes of the Great Depression.

1.2. DISGUISED INSTABILITY: THE INTERNATIONAL ECONOMY IN THE 1920S

It is sensible to begin an investigation of the Great Depression with an analysis of the world's most powerful economy, the USA. During the 1920s, America became the vital engine for sustained recovery from the effects of the Great War and for the maintenance of international economic stability. Following a rapid recovery from the post-war slump of 1920/21, until the end of the decade, Americans enjoyed a great consumer boom which was heavily dependent upon the automobile and the building sectors. Low interest rates, high levels of investment, significant productivity advances, stable prices, full employment, tranquil labour relations, high wages, and high company profits combined to create buoyant optimism in the economy and perfect conditions for a stock market boom (Field, 2011). Many contemporaries believed that a new age of cooperative capitalism had dawned in sharp contrast to the weak economies of class ridden Europe (Barber, 1985).

America was linked to the rest of the world through international trade as the world's leading exporter and was second, behind the UK, as an importer. Furthermore, after 1918 America replaced Britain as the world's leading international lender. The First World War imposed an onerous and potentially destabilizing indebtedness on many of the world's economies. Massive war debts accumulated by Britain and France were owed to both the US government and to US private citizens. Britain and France, but not the United States, sought punitive damages from Germany in the form of reparations (Ritschl, 2013). But the post-war network of inter-government indebtedness was complex and eventually involved 28 countries with Germany the most heavily in debt and the US owing 40 per cent of total receipts (League of Nations, 1931; Wolf, 2013). There was strong public support in the US for the view that both Britain and France should pay their war debts in full and begin the repayment immediately. This insistence provided an extra incentive, if one was needed, for Britain and France to collect the maximum in reparations payments from Germany.

Between 1924 and 1931 the US was responsible for about 60 per cent of total international lending, about one third of which was absorbed by Germany. American investors, attracted by relatively high interest rates and the apparent security of an economy which had been stabilized by US financiers who constructed the Dawes Plan (1924), eagerly sent short term funds to Germany. This inflow enabled the world's most indebted economy to borrow sufficient funds to discharge not only its reparations responsibilities but also to fund considerable improvements in living standards which were quite unjustified in the light of domestic economic performance. Short term foreign borrowing made it possible for Germany to maintain a large and persistent current account surplus and to fund wage increases that far outstripped productivity growth (Ritschl, 2003; Schuker, 1988). Austria, Hungary, Greece, Italy, and Poland, together with several Latin American countries, were also considered attractive opportunities by US investors. American promoters actively sought foreign borrowers and some borrowers also shared the increasingly irrational exuberance of the lenders. Indeed, as the decade progressed and confidence grew, rashness on the part of both borrowers and lenders increased (Lewis, 1938; Mintz, 1951). By paying for imports, and by investing overseas, the US was able to send abroad a stream of dollars which enabled other countries not only to import more goods but also to service their international debts. The decision by the Federal Reserve (the Fed) to adopt a low interest rate policy encouraged US investors to seek higher returns overseas. However, countries wishing to attract foreign capital had to maintain relatively high interest rates, thus ensuring that the real cost of their domestic credit was high. The fact that a high proportion of the borrowing was short term did not disturb the recipients (Feinstein et al., 1997).

The majority of the world's economies were linked to each other by the gold standard, which had been suspended during the First World War but its restoration was considered a priority by virtually all the major economic powers. It is easy to understand the appeal of the gold standard to contemporaries. The frightening inflations which intensified after 1918, and the severe deflation of 1920–21, made policy makers yearn for a system that would provide international economic and financial stability. In particular, the hyperinflation that tore at the very fabric of German society, until currency stabilization brought it to a halt in 1924, served as a warning to policy makers everywhere of the dangers of monetary laxity. Even today, the actions of German bankers and politicians are conditioned by the spectre of runaway inflation. To policy makers during the post-war decade, the gold standard represented a state of normality for international monetary relations; support for it was a continuation of the mindset that had become firmly established in the late nineteenth century (Eichengreen and Temin, 2013). There was a widespread belief that the rules of the gold standard had imposed order within a framework of economic expansion during the 40 years before 1914, and order was certainly required in the post-war world. In particular, contemporaries believed that the discipline of the gold standard would curb excessive public spending by politicians who would fear the subsequent loss of bullion, an inevitable consequence of their profligacy.

Once countries had squeezed war-induced inflation from their economies they began to go back to the gold standard. But monetary stability was achieved at different times and, as a result, the return to gold was accomplished in an uncoordinated fashion. France and Belgium, for example, had to cope with destabilizing inflation during 1924–26 and their delay in returning to gold enabled both countries to adopt exchange rates that were not only significantly below their 1913 levels, but also provided a distinct competitive advantage. The temptation, to which several countries succumbed, was to consider other exchange rates when setting one's own. France eventually returned to gold at an exchange rate for the franc that was only one fifth of the 1913 level (Eichengreen and Temin, 2013).

UK policy makers did not go down this route. In 1925 sterling returned to gold at the 1913 exchange rate, after a deflationary squeeze had made this just possible. In general, financiers and bankers supported the return to gold at the pre-war exchange rate but industrialists were apprehensive. Choosing the 1913 exchange rate meant that sterling was overvalued, not only in comparison to France and Belgium but also to the US and Germany which also had undervalued currencies (Redmond, 1984). Britain's export industries were disadvantaged but, once chosen, the exchange rate had to be maintained and, if necessary, defended. Even Keynes, who argued for a return to gold at a lower exchange rate, was firm in his support for £1 = US$4.86 once it had been chosen. Monetary policy was the responsibility of an independent Bank of England whose principle policy aim was sustaining exchange parity and the restrictions that inevitably flowed from that choice. For example, the bank had to ensure that UK interest rates were in line with foreign rates, especially those in the United States. Britain's attempt to achieve international competitiveness through deflation was the dominant force determining domestic economic policy during the 1920s.

Unfortunately, UK exports suffered from war-induced disruption, which overvaluation exacerbated. Markets which had been readily exploited before 1914 offered much reduced opportunities after 1918. UK difficulties would have been more manageable if the bulk of Britain's exports had been in categories that were expanding rapidly in world markets. Unfortunately coal, cotton and woollen textiles, and shipbuilding, which had provided the foundations for nineteenth century prosperity, faced severe international competition. Over capacity led to high and persistent structural unemployment in the regions where these industries were dominant. During the 1920s, UK unemployment was double the pre-1913 level and also higher than in all the other major economic powers. On average, each year between 1923 and 1929, almost 10 per cent of the UK insured workforce was unemployed. The jobless were concentrated in the export oriented staple industries. In those parts of the economy not exposed to foreign competition, unemployment was closer to pre-war levels. Although the fixed exchange rate of the gold standard gave financiers and merchants confidence about the terms on which international accounts would be settled, there was a downside. Gold standard countries surrendered the right to an independent monetary policy. Changes in gold reserves drove monetary policy not domestic economic concerns.

During the 1920s, US industrialists led by Henry Ford believed that high wages would lead to improved worker motivation, productivity growth, high profits, and full employment (Barber, 1985; Raff and Summers, 1987). The evidence appeared to confirm their belief. In the UK, on the other hand, many employers were convinced that lowering wages was a necessary route to increasing sales, lower unemployment, and balance of payments equilibrium. However, attempts to lower wages were not cost free. The General Strike of 1926 showed that the determination of some workers could create a formidable barrier against attempts to reduce their nominal wages.

A further problem for Britain, and for most other countries too, was the uneven distribution of gold stocks. The US was gold rich throughout the 1920s but after the stabilization of the franc in 1926 the Bank of France began to sell its foreign exchange in order to purchase bullion (Clarke, 1967; Irwin, 2010, 2012). By 1929, the US and France had accumulated nearly 60 per cent of the world's gold stock and their central banks sterilized much of their bullion so that it did not inflate the money supply. Under the rules of the game, countries receiving gold should have inflated their economies through domestic monetary expansion. The expectation was that eventually gold would flow from the inflating countries to those who had experienced deflation. In that way the forces of inflation and deflation would be moderated and the risk of instability minimized. However, neither the United States nor France played by the traditional rules of the game. As both countries sterilized their gold holdings, their central banks kept a high proportion of the world's gold stock secure in their vaults and withdrawn from circulation. As a result, other countries were forced to deflate in order to compensate for a shortage of reserves. Unfortunately, the gold standard imposed penalties on countries which lost gold while the few which gained did so with impunity (Irwin, 2012).

Gold shortages compelled UK policy makers to impose relatively high interest rates in order to attract foreign funds—hot money—which bolstered the country's inadequate bullion reserves. Unfortunately, potential domestic investors suffered as the real cost of credit rose. The decision taken by the Fed during the mid-1920s to adopt relatively low interest rates helped the UK and also Germany, the world's major borrower. Had US interest rates been higher, countries that wanted to secure American funds would have had to impose punitively high rates in order to attract it. Contemporaries seemed oblivious to the weaknesses in the operation of the gold standard that are so obvious with the benefit of hindsight. Faith in the gold standard was so ingrained that there was a widespread belief that merely by adopting it, stability would be guaranteed. As the membership of the gold standard club grew in the 1920s, policy makers congratulated themselves that all major trading countries were bound together in a system that was dedicated to the maintenance of economic stability. As events soon demonstrated, this confidence was seriously misplaced.

It is clear now that the international economy was in a potentially precarious position in 1929. Continuing prosperity was dependent upon the capacity of the US economy to absorb imports and to maintain a high level of international lending on which many countries had become dependent. If a financial crisis struck the US banking system how would the Federal Reserve deal with it? The Fed, created in 1913, was a relatively untested central bank. Would it act aggressively as lender of last resort if the banking system became stressed? Would its decentralized division into 12 regional reserve banks, with monetary policy formulated by a seven member Board, demonstrate weakness or strength in fighting a depression? And, should a crisis materialize, would the gold standard's rules force contracting economies to deflate, thus worsening their plight rather than providing a supportive international framework?

1.3. FROM BOOM TO SLUMP

In 1928 the US public, and virtually all informed commentators, viewed the economy with a confidence that events soon proved to be mistaken (Reinhart and Rogoff, 2009). The consumer durable boom continued and, although the private housing market had peaked in 1926, the construction industry continued to thrive as the demand for roads and commercial buildings was buoyant. There were no signs of industrial bottlenecks, or the inflationary stresses that one would expect at the peak of a boom with the possible exception of the dramatic increase in share values on the Wall Street stock exchange. In January 1928, the Federal Reserve decided that action was needed to curb volatile stock market speculation which, if uncontrolled, could end in a destabilizing collapse. The Fed changed course and ended several years of easy credit by introducing a tight money policy which began with a sale of government securities and a gradual increase in the discount rate which rose in steps from 3.5 per cent to 5 per cent. The Fed was fully aware that a sudden rise in interest rates could be destabilizing for business and might bring a period of economic prosperity to an unhappy conclusion. To avoid this possibility, the monetary authorities aimed to gently deflate the worrying bubble on Wall Street by making bank borrowing for speculation progressively more expensive. Monetary policy makers believed that by acting steadily rather than suddenly, speculation could be controlled without damaging legitimate business credit demands. It seemed a good idea at the time but, unfortunately, this policy had serious unforeseen domestic and international repercussions. The new higher rates made more funds from non-bank sources available to the ever rising stock market and speculation actually increased. Many corporations used their large balances to fund broker's loans and investors who normally looked overseas found loans to Wall Street a more attractive option. Unfortunately, countries that had become dependent on US capital imports, for example, Germany, were suddenly deprived of an essential support for their fragile economies (League of Nations, 1931). Moreover, the Fed's tight money policy led to an influx of gold which coincided with a drive by France to dramatically increase its bullion holdings (Irwin, 2010, 2012). The accumulation of gold by the US and France put added pressure on other countries as they saw their meagre gold reserves further depleted.

Adversely affected by Fed policies, the US economic boom reached a peak in August 1929. After a few months of continuously poor corporate results, the confidence of investors waned and eventually turned into the panic which became the Wall Street Crash in October 1929 (Hamilton, 1987). After the stock market collapse, the Fed saw the need for monetary ease and embarked on vigorous open market operations and reduced interest rates. The Wall Street crash markedly diminished the wealth of stockholders and could well have adversely affected the optimism of consumers (Flacco and Parker, 1992; Romer, 1990). However, in late 1929 the market seemed to stabilize close to the level it had reached in early 1928. For several months it appeared that the US economy was recovering after a dramatic financial contraction. Overseas lending revived and interest rates throughout the world responded to the Fed's monetary easing. Optimists saw no reason why vigorous economic expansion should not be renewed, as it had been in 1922. However, pessimists noted the substantial growth of indebtedness that had occurred during the 1920s, and which had become a considerable burden to individuals and to businesses (Bernanke, 1983).

The optimists were wrong. From the peak of the 1920s expansion in August 1929 to the trough in March 1933 output fell by 52 per cent, wholesale prices by 38 per cent, and real income by 35 per cent. Company profits, which had been 10 per cent of GNP (gross national product) in 1929, were negative in 1931 and also during the following year. The collapse in demand centred on consumption and investment, which experienced unprecedented falls. Gross private domestic investment, measured in constant prices, had reached $16.2bn in 1929; the 1933 total was only $0.3bn. In 1926, gross expenditure on new private residential construction was $4,920m; in 1933 the figure had fallen to a paltry $290m. Consumer expenditure at constant prices fell from $79.0bn in 1929 to $64.6bn in 1933. Durables were especially affected; in 1929, 4.5m passenger vehicles rolled off assembly lines; in 1932, 1.1m cars were produced by a workforce that had been halved. Automobile manufacture and construction had been at the heart of the 1920s economic expansion but as they fell supporting industries tumbled too. Inventories were run down, raw material purchases reduced to a minimum, and workers laid off. In particular, companies producing machinery, steel, glass, furniture, cement, and bricks faced a collapse in demand. The number of wage earners in manufacturing fell by 40 per cent but many lucky enough to hang on to their jobs worked fewer hours and experienced pay cuts. The producers of non-durable goods such as cigarettes, textiles, shoes, and clothing faced more modest declines in output and employment.

The most dramatic price falls were in agriculture and a fall of 65 per cent in farm income was unsustainable for farm operators, especially if they were in debt. Unlike manufacturers, individual farms did not reduce output in response to low prices. Indeed, their reaction to economic distress was to produce more in a desperate attempt to raise total income. The result was the accumulation of stocks which further depressed prices. Nor could farmers lay off workers as most only employed family members. As banks and other financial institutions foreclosed on farm mortgages, distress auctions caused so much local anger that the governors of some states were obliged to suspend them. Farmers who were unable to pay their debts put pressure on the undercapitalized unit banks that served rural communities. As bank failures spread unease amongst depositors, the natural reaction of institutions was to engage in defensive banking. Loans were called in and lending, even for deserving cases, was curtailed; the banks gained liquidity by bankrupting many of their customers. Rural families were forced to reduce their purchases of manufactured goods, adding to urban unemployment. The bitter irony of starving industrial workers unable to buy food that farmers found too unprofitable to sell helped to undermine faith in the free market economic system and prepared the way for regulation and government intervention.

The slide from mid-1929 to spring 1933 was not smooth and continuous. Periodically, it seemed that the depression had bottomed out and Hoover was able to declare that recovery was under way. A destabilizing fall in consumption occurred during 1930 (Temin, 1976) as households, heavily burdened with instalment debt, reduced consumption expenditure in order to avoid default (Olney, 1999). In spite of consumer uncertainty, it seemed possible that the economy would revive. This expectation was quashed by a wave of bank failures at the end of the year. Although mostly confined to small banks in the south east of the US, the failures gave depositors a warning sign. Indeed, bank failure was a major contributor to the worsening depression and there were two major crises, the first in the autumn of 1931 and the second during the winter of 1932–33. Unlike the UK, where branch banking was the norm, the US banking structure was dominated by thousands of small standalone unit banks. The vast majority of these unit banks could not satisfy the minimum capital requirements for membership of the Fed, but they were an important part of the culture of rural America. In 1929, nearly half the states in the union expressed their distrust for the concentration of financial power by banning branch banking. Small towns, villages, and even hamlets wanted, and actually supported, their own independent banks. Many of these undercapitalized units struggled to survive even in good times; in fact, during the 1920s, approximately 5,000 banks disappeared through mergers or failure. When times were tough, unit banks were the first to fail. Indeed, the monetary authorities, who believed that the country was 'overbanked', welcomed a reduction in the number of undercapitalized banks. The combination of a banking system with many weak units and incompetent bankers, a culture that accepted bank failure, and a depression of unprecedented severity explain much bank mortality. However, US banking problems were not confined to small units. Larger banks who were members of the Fed also succumbed with devastating implications for economic recovery.

For example, during the first half of 1931 the economy revived but hopes were dashed in the aftermath of Britain's abandonment of the gold standard in September when a wave of bank failures served to undermine the diminishing faith of depositors who rushed to withdraw their money, thus making the closure of their banks inevitable. Many kept their withdrawn funds idle rather than trust another bank with their savings. In other words, depositors withdrew their money from the banking system and made it impossible for many banks to conduct business. As a result, credit markets were in disarray and even the requests for loans by sound businesses could not be met (Bernanke, 1983: Bordo and Landon-Lane, 2013; Calomiris and Mason, 2003). Economic expansion in the summer and autumn of 1932 was reversed during the policy vacuum between Roosevelt's electoral victory in November 1932 and his inauguration in March 1933. The uncertainties present during this 'lame duck' period led to a further wave of bank failures which became so serious that by the time Roosevelt delivered his inaugural address in March 1933, the governors of 35 states had declared their banks closed to prevent almost certain failure and strict limitations on the withdrawal of deposits had been introduced by the others (Calomiris, 2013). There was a sharp difference between the British experience where no financial institution failed and the US where financial paralysis was the end result.

Why was the Fed unable or unwilling to ensure banking stability? A central bank would normally offer help at times of crisis by rapidly adopting a low discount rate and by pumping liquidity into the system via engaging in open market operations (quantitative easing). In their classic work, Friedman and Schwartz (1963) emphasized the contraction by one third of the US money stock between 1929 and 1933, a reduction which they believe explains fully the severity of the depression. They accused the Federal Reserve of pursuing perverse monetary policies which transformed a recession into a major depression. It was, however, a combination of monetary and non-monetary causes, varying in intensity during these critical years, which account for the depth of this crisis (Gordon and Wilcox, 1981; Meltzer, 2003). Nevertheless, as Fishback (2013) shows, the judgement of the Fed was at times seriously flawed, although policy errors are sometimes more apparent with the benefit of hindsight.

Because nominal interest rates had been reduced to a very low level, the Fed believed that it was pursuing an appropriate easy money policy. Indeed, the Fed would argue that it was difficult to see how interest rates could be forced lower. However, the monetary authorities failed to take account of the savage deflation which caused real interest rates to rise to punitive levels for borrowers. The central bank never considered the real interest rate and was convinced that it was pursuing an easy money policy when the reverse was the case. Moreover, when faced with a policy choice, the Fed always opted to follow the gold standard rule. As a result, during late 1931, following Britain's exit from the gold standard, the dollar came under speculative pressure and the Fed reacted to gold losses by raising interest rates and pursuing a tight money policy. This was the correct policy if protecting the exchange rate was the priority, but it was exactly the reverse of what was required to support a beleaguered banking system. This action also drained gold from other countries and put enormous pressure on their central banks (Eichengreen and Temin, 2013). During the winter of 1932–33, the Fed again raised interest rates to protect the dollar from external speculation in order to halt gold losses. Little wonder that so many banks, in a system that had been under sustained pressure for over three years, closed their doors. There is no doubt that monetary policy had serious adverse effects during the worst depression years.

Unemployment was one of the great curses of the depression. Widely-accepted estimates show that the percentage of the US civilian labour force without work rose from 2.9 per cent in 1929 to a distressing peak of 22.9 per cent in 1932 (Table 1.2). Many classified as employed were on short time and some had also experienced wage cuts. Unlike Britain, the US had no national system of unemployment benefits; the jobless were subjected to a harsh regime which included dependence on miserly poorly administered local relief. Those most affected included the young, the old, and ethnic minorities whose unemployment rates were relatively high. In addition, social workers stressed that those who had been out of work for long periods became increasingly unattractive to employers. Loss of income and employment uncertainty combined to reduce consumer spending.

Even fortunates who felt secure in their jobs and whose real incomes had risen were deterred from consumption by the persistent deflation. Why buy a motor vehicle, or a house, now when both would be significantly cheaper in a few months time. Deflation increased the burden of existing debt and acted as a warning against the accumulation of new obligations. Deflation also intensified business uncertainty and further undermined the confidence necessary to make investment decisions. Traditionally, price falls were seen as one of the natural self correcting mechanisms of the market economy. Deflation automatically led to a rise in real incomes even with wage cuts, it was argued, and consumers would soon start a purchasing drive that would lift the economy out of recession. The persistent price falls over such a long period, however, brought about a paralysis in both consumption and investment. Potential spenders wanted to wait until the price falls had reached their nadir before they committed themselves to major purchases and new debt.

President Herbert Hoover was hard working, energetic, and intelligent. He probably had a greater grasp of contemporary economics than any twentieth century president and was confident enough to be his own economic advisor (Stein, 1988). He was familiar with the current literature on business cycles and was not a man to stand aside and watch as recession accelerated into depression (Bernstein, 2001). Hoover publicly urged business leaders to share scarce work rather than add to the unemployed and pleaded with them not to cut wage rates, which had been the instant response of employers in 1920–21. In the first two years of the depression the money wage rate in manufacturing industry showed a remarkable resilience. Nominal wages declined only by approximately 10 per cent and workers who retained their jobs secured a significant increase in real income (Field, 2013). This was not the result of concerted trade union pressure as organized labour was weak and ineffective; it was a business rather than a labour led initiative. By their collective action, business leaders hoped to avoid the collapse in demand and the spiralling bankruptcies that had been a destabilizing part of the post-war slump (O'Brien, 1989). Big businesses and their workers preferred reducing hours to cutting pay. Many employers held out against wage cuts until mid-1931 when, faced with overwhelming financial losses, the dam broke and they could resist no more. Nominal wage cuts became common as did mass lay-offs; indeed, wages in manufacturing declined by 25 per cent during the last phase of the depression. In other words, from 1931 wages were not sticky, they were highly flexible. Nevertheless, it is reasonable to believe that wage falls of such magnitude that the labour market would have cleared would have been politically and socially unacceptable. Some critics see Hoover's unwavering commitment to high wages and the maintenance of purchasing power as a serious mistake which caused mounting unemployment and added to the severity of the downturn (Ohanian, 2009; Smiley, 2002). However, the strong resistance shown by employers to wage cutting was widespread in the early part of the depression and recent research has shown that Hoover's urging played a very minor role in their decisions on wage setting (Rose, 2010).

Hoover refused to listen to the pleas of 1,038 American economists who, in 1930, urged him to veto the Smoot–Hawley tariff bill. When it became law, this legislation raised US import duties and ultimately led to retaliatory action throughout the world. Many countries viewed it as an additional barrier for nations trying to repay American debts during a particularly difficult period. Not surprisingly, US foreign trade declined once the depression began to bite. The value of US exports was $7.0bn in 1929 but only $2.5bn in 1932; imports declined from $5.9bn to $2.0bn during the same period. Nevertheless, the US balance of payments remained in surplus. Although the Smoot–Hawley tariff figures prominently in many accounts of the depression, it was not responsible for the internationalization of the economic crisis, it did not unleash a trade war, though one did start in 1931, and its effect on American imports was relatively modest (Eichengreen, 1989). The rapid income decline in countries that wanted to purchase US goods was the most significant factor in causing the contraction in international trade (Irwin, 1998, 2011). Hoover's support for tariff increases demonstrated his consistency. His priority was to protect companies that paid high wages from competition by cheap imported goods (Vedder and Gallaway, 1993).

In early 1932, following Hoover's lead, Congress approved the Reconstruction Finance Corporation (RFC) with a remit to lend to distressed banks, which was the responsibility of the Fed but one that it failed to discharge. The hope that the RFC, acting as lender of last resort, would bring stability to the financial system was compromised by a politically mischievous Congressional decision to publicize the names of all institutions that approached the RFC for financial help. Hoover also authorized a large increase in federal spending on work relief projects but the federal budget, at 4 per cent of GNP, was too small to make a noticeable dent in the growing social distress. Inevitably declining revenue forced the budget into deficit for fiscal 1931. The deficit was too small to exert an expansionary effect on the economy but it did enable Roosevelt to attack Hoover during the election campaign of 1932 for failing to appreciate the necessity of economy in government. Ironically, the budget deficit of 1931 was the most expansionary of the entire decade though no one at the time saw this as a benefit (Brown, 1956). Unfortunately, Hoover soon re-embraced deflationary policies. In 1932 he became so concerned about the domestic and foreign disapproval of the federal budget deficit, which he believed would have led to speculative attacks on the dollar, that spending was reduced and the Revenue Act (1932) introduced a raft of substantial tax increases. In spite of his efforts, the budget remained in the red and, not surprisingly, unemployment remained stubbornly high. It is a misfortune that Hoover's understanding of contemporary economics led him to an unshakeable belief in the gold standard. He shared with many contemporary economists the view that fiscal and monetary policies must be directed to support gold rather than to directly promote domestic economic expansion or bank stability.

1.4. THE TRANSMISSION OF THE DEPRESSION

It is easy to see that the year on year reduction in imports by the main industrial powers and the collapse of international lending placed many economies in great difficulty. In particular, a regular flow of dollars had been crucial to debtor countries, enabling them to buy goods and services and discharge their debt payments. Once the flow dried up, countries were forced to confront balance of payment and debt repayment problems which were entirely unanticipated. Primary producers had to act quickly to reduce imports and boost their exports as the terms of trade moved sharply against them. Desperate to curb gold and foreign exchange loss, they used restrictive monetary and fiscal policies to savagely deflate their economies. They employed every possible means to maintain their exchange rates regardless of the suffering caused. Public spending was slashed, wages were cut, and misery increased but all to no avail. It was impossible to earn sufficient foreign currency, or to attract new international loans. Once the cure of deflation was judged more painful than the disease it was supposed to remedy, default on international loans was inevitable. When this happened foreign investors panicked and repatriated their funds as quickly as possible. In 1931, US lending virtually ceased and did not recover during the rest of the decade.

The key element in the transmission of the Great Depression, the mechanism that linked the economies of the world together in this downward spiral, was the gold standard. It is generally accepted that adherence to fixed exchange rates was the key element in explaining the timing and the differential severity of the crisis. Monetary and fiscal policies were used to defend the gold standard and not to arrest declining output and rising unemployment. It is clear that those countries that abandoned the gold standard early in the depression reaped the benefits of early recovery and were less exposed to banking crises (Bernanke, 1995; Eichengreen, 1992; Eichengreen and Sachs, 1985; Grossman, 1994).

Contemporaries believed that the gold standard imposed discipline on all economies wedded to the system. But in operation the gold standard was not even handed. As we have seen, states accumulating gold were not forced to inflate their currencies but when gold losses occurred, governments and central banks were expected to take immediate action in order to stem the flow. The action was always deflation but never devaluation (Temin, 1993). Between 1927 and 1932 France experienced a surge of gold accumulation which saw its share of world gold reserves increase from 7 per cent to 27 per cent of the total. Since the gold inflow was effectively sterilized, the policies of the Bank of France created a shortage of reserves and put other countries under great deflationary pressure. Irwin (2010) concludes that, on an accounting basis, France was probably more responsible even than the US for the worldwide deflation of 1929–33. He calculates that through their 'gold hoarding' policies the Federal Reserve and the Bank of France together directly accounted for half the 30 per cent fall in prices that occurred in 1930 and 1931. There was no compulsion or inclination for the US and France to recycle their surpluses and this illustrates a serious flaw in the operation of the interwar gold standard (Eichengreen and Temin, 2013).

The year 1931 provided a major turning point in the Great Depression. A devastating financial crisis engulfed many European countries before moving to the US. The crisis exposed the fragility of the gold standard and the weakness of financial institutions; it led to the destruction of multilateral trade and the adoption of protectionist policies. When US capital flows to Germany began to dry up in 1928, the German economy was already experiencing an economic downturn. Under these new circumstances it was clear that the current account deficit that borrowing had made possible was not sustainable. Moreover, the Dawes Plan was about to be replaced by the Young Plan which imposed a higher annual reparations charge. In 1930, the economic situation was so disturbing that democracy was suspended and Germany was governed by a group of unelected technocrats headed by Heinrich Bruning and ruled by emergency decrees issued by President Hindenburg. In fact, democracy would not be restored in Germany until after the Second World War.

Following gold standard rules, Germany was forced to deflate even though already in the early stages of a depression; between 1930 and 1932 central government expenditure was reduced by 20 per cent in real terms. Fiscal policy was directed solely towards balancing the budget and avoiding default under the Young Plan (Ritschl, 2013). Indeed, the fiscal squeeze was successful in significantly reducing the budget deficit (see Table 1.4) between 1930 and 1932 but not without serious social costs. As Table 1.3 shows, in 1931 short term interest rates in Germany reached an extraordinarily high level for an economy experiencing a savage contraction. Soon mounting unemployment, which amounted to 25.5 per cent of the labour force in 1931 (see Table 1.2), and violent political unrest, as Nazi supporters battled with left wing groups, led to growing investor unease. Political violence made it difficult to impose tax increases and although wage cuts were imposed, they were insufficient to arrest the steep rise in real wages. Ritschl (2013) argues that the increase in unit wage costs led to soaring unemployment, lower tax revenues, additional budgetary strains and a further contraction in investment.

In May 1931 Austria's largest bank, the Credit Anstalt, experienced such difficulty that speculators attacked the Austrian schilling. Austria's gold and foreign exchange reserves were inadequate and soon exhausted and the country was forced to introduce exchange controls. Speculators then turned to Germany which faced similar difficulties. The country had a weak economy, a budget deficit, a suspect banking system, a high level of short term debt and worrying political divisions. As speculation gathered force, depositors withdrew their savings from banks and, wherever possible, marks were exchanged for gold. German officials undertook a desperate search for international bank credit to prop up their disintegrating economy.

This growing financial crisis presented an opportunity for decisive coordinated intervention by the major economic powers. A flawed German economy faced the

Table 1.3. Short term interest rates compared (%)

	Germany	UK	USA
1929	7.50	5.26	5.78
1930	4.78	2.46	3.55
1931	7.23	3.83	2.63
1932	6.06	1.67	2.72
1933	5.03	0.66	1.67
1934	4.64	0.80	0.88
1935	3.36	0.59	0.75
1936	2.87	0.58	0.75
1937	2.76	0.58	0.94
1938	2.79	0.68	0.86
	Euro Area	UK	USA
2007	5.00	5.67	4.25
2008	3.00	4.68	0.13
2009	1.75	0.53	0.13
2010	1.75	0.48	0.13
2011	1.75	0.52	0.13

Sources: 1929–38: commercial bill rates, Chadha and Dimsdale (1999). 2007–11: short term policy rates, IMF, International Financial Statistics.

Table 1.4. Budget balances (% GDP)

	Germany		UK		USA	
	Actual	Structural	Actual	Structural	Actual	Structural
1929	1.0	2.9	−0.7	0.4	0.7	1.2
1930	0.0	3.5	−1.4	1.1	0.8	0.9
1931	0.7	7.0	−2.2	2.5	−0.6	−0.5
1932	−0.1	7.2	−0.5	3.0	−4.7	0.9
1933	−0.5	4.9	0.4	4.2	−4.6	1.9
1934	−0.1	4.0	0.5	3.2	−5.5	0.1
1935	−1.6	1.4	−0.3	2.0	−3.8	0.8
1936	−2.9	−1.2	−0.7	0.8	−5.3	−0.6
1937	0.7	0.7	−1.5	−0.1	−3.0	2.8
1938	−2.0	−1.7	−3.7	−1.5	−1.4	2.9
	Euro Area		**UK**		**USA**	
	Actual	Structural	Actual	Structural	Actual	Structural
2007	−0.7	−2.3	−2.7	−4.0	−2.7	−2.8
2008	−2.1	−2.9	−4.9	−6.5	−6.7	−5.0
2009	−6.4	−4.4	−10.4	−9.0	−13.0	−7.5
2010	−6.2	−4.2	−9.9	−7.8	−10.5	−7.8
2011	−4.1	−3.2	−8.7	−6.3	−9.6	−7.2

Sources: 1929–38: Germany, Cohn (1992); UK, Middleton (1996); USA actual, Carter et al. (2006); USA structural, Peppers (1973). 2007–11: IMF World Economic Outlook Database, April 2012.

possibility of a catastrophic financial implosion which, if not contained, could have serious ramifications for others. Who amongst the great powers would help? Britain was too financially enfeebled to offer more than marginal assistance. What of the United States, the world's leading creditor nation? In June 1931, President Hoover intervened by unilaterally proposing a moratorium, for one year only, on reparation and war debts payments. The Hoover Moratorium referred just to inter-government debt. Hoover expected private debts to be honoured. His intervention was opposed by the French, who were furious at the lack of consultation, but more fundamentally they believed that they lost more than they gained from the moratorium. France, with ample gold reserves, was in a position to assist but the political conditions attached to their offer of help made it impossible for Germany to accept. In August 1931, Germany, gold reserves exhausted and unable to pay its debts, abandoned the gold standard, introduced exchange controls, and halted the free flow of gold and marks. German policy makers did not believe that departure from the gold standard gave them the freedom to introduce expansionary fiscal and monetary initiatives. In both the UK and the US, interest rates fell to historically low levels soon after the departure from the gold standard but in Germany, rates remained high (see Table 1.3) and a barrier to recovery. Even though this was a time of falling prices, the horrors of post-war hyperinflation were so fresh in the memory of the German public and policy makers that any action to stimulate the economy was viewed with deep suspicion. Furthermore, Germany's reparations debt had been fixed in gold terms and a devaluation of the mark would significantly increase it (James, 1986). As a result, the mark was not devalued and the government continued with the draconian deflation that had been introduced in accordance with gold standard rules (Eichengreen and Temin, 2013). The government also introduced severe trade restrictions.

The crisis then engulfed sterling. Although there was no destabilizing asset price boom to alarm investors, there had been obvious signs of recession in the UK as early as 1928 when the curtailment of US lending affected UK international trade in services. About 40 per cent of UK overseas trade was with primary producing countries which were forced to immediately restrict their spending when US credit dried up (Solomou, 1996). The crisis worsened in 1929 as world demand collapsed and the UK experienced a sharp fall in the export of goods and services. Unemployment, already high in export oriented industries, rose rapidly (Eichengreen and Jeanne, 1998). Inevitably, tax revenues declined and transfer payments increased, which pushed the budget towards deficit in 1930 and 1931 (see Table 1.4). Following gold standard rules, taxes were raised, real interest rates rose to defend sterling and public expenditure cuts were imposed in an attempt to achieve budget balance. However, adherence to the gold standard was not slavish and the monetary authorities, conscious of the social consequences of a severe contraction, tried to minimize the effects of the deflationary impulse by reducing interest rates and sterilizing gold outflows (Bernanke and Mihov, 2000).

Like Austria and Germany, Britain was faced with the withdrawal of short term foreign deposits—hot money—as the holders of sterling anticipated the potential loss to them from devaluation. The struggle to defend the pound was all to no avail. On 21 September 1931 Britain was forced to leave the gold standard, the first major country to do so, and to devalue sterling (Ahamed, 2009). Perhaps Britain was fortunate that the inadequacy of the Bank of England's reserves forced an early departure from gold thus avoiding a long drawn out and costly defence of the exchange rate. The devaluation was substantial; sterling, once free to float, fell by 25 per cent against the dollar though, of course, it is the multilateral effects of devaluation rather than the bilateral which are the most significant. Some 18 countries, all closely linked by trade and finance to Britain, also abandoned gold (see Table 1.5).

Speculators then attacked the US dollar which, as we have seen, was defended by the Federal Reserve, though at the cost of compromising the banking system and intensifying an already serious depression.

Though relatively mild when compared to the US and to Germany, the UK recession of 1929–31 saw real GDP fall by 5.6 per cent between 1929 and 1931 (see Table 1.2). In other words, the Great Depression contraction in the UK was similar in magnitude to the recession of 2008–09. Once free from the restrictions of the gold standard, the UK gained full control of monetary policy, was also free to reduce interest rates, and no longer needed to deflate prices and wages in order to reduce unemployment. Indeed it was now possible, as well as desirable, to implement policies that would lower real interest rates and change inflationary expectations. Although some policy makers believed that the UK faced a possible sovereign debt crisis, the economy was in a relatively strong position which could have been exploited. The economic contraction between the start of the depression and the abandonment of the gold standard, apart from a rise in unemployment, was severe but it was not as destabilizing as events in Germany or the US. Even in these crisis years, consumption in the UK remained relatively stable. Furthermore, alone amongst advanced industrial

Table 1.5. Dates of changes in gold standard policies

	Return to Gold	Suspension of Gold Standard	Foreign Exchange Control	Devaluation
Argentina	08/1927	12/1929	10/1931	11/1929
Australia	04/1925	12/1929		03/1930
Austria	04/1925	04/1933	10/1931	09/1931
Belgium	10/1926	03/1935	03/1935	03/1935
Bolivia	07/1928	09/1931	10/1931	03/1930
Brazil	01/1927	12/1929	05/1931	12/1929
Bulgaria	01/1927		10/1931	
Canada	07/1926	10/1931		09/1931
Chile	01/1926	04/1932	07/1931	04/1932
Columbia	07/1923	09/1931	09/1931	01/1932
Costa Rica	10/1922		01/1932	01/1932
Cuba	06/1919	11/1933	06/1934	04/1933
Czechoslovakia	04/1926		10/1931	02/1934
Denmark	01/1927	09/1931	11/1931	09/1931
Ecuador	08/1927	02/1932	05/1932	06/1932
El Salvador	01/1920	10/1931	08/1933	10/1931
Estonia	01/1928	06/1933	11/1931	06/1933
Finland	01/1926	10/1931		10/1931
France	08/1926			10/1936
Germany	09/1924		07/1931	
Greece	05/1928	04/1932	09/1931	04/1932
Guatemala				04/1933
Hungary	04/1925		07/1931	
Italy	12/1927		05/1934	10/1936
Japan	12/1930	12/1931	07/1932	12/1931
Latvia	08/1922		10/1931	
Netherlands	04/1925	09/1936		09/1936
Nicaragua	06/1919	11/1931	11/1931	01/1932
Norway	05/1928	09/1931		
New Zealand	04/1925	09/1931		04/1930
Panama	06/1919			04/1933
Paraguay	08/1927		08/1932	11/1929
Peru	05/1928	05/1932		05/1932
Poland	10/1927		04/1936	10/1936
Romania	02/1929		05/1932	07/1935
Spain			05/1931	
Sweden	04/1924	09/1931		09/1931
Switzerland	06/1925			09/1936
United Kingdom	05/1925	09/1931		09/1931
United States	06/1919	03/1933	03/1933	04/1933
Uruguay	01/1928	12/1929	09/1931	04/1929
Yugoslavia	06/1931		10/1931	07/1932

Sources: Bernanke and James (1991); Brown (1940); Wolf and Yousef (2007).

nations, the UK financial system remained strong and had not been undermined by a loss of depositor confidence. No bank or building society failed, or seemed in danger of failing.

The departure from gold gave an initial fillip to the economy but, unfortunately, the devaluation of September 1931 was not followed by sustained economic recovery because policy makers failed to immediately grasp the opportunities

Table 1.6. Banking crises, 1929–38

Argentina	1931, 1934
Austria	1931–2
Belgium	1931, 1934
Brazil	1931, 1937
Denmark	1931
Estonia	1930–2
Finland	1931
France	1930–2
Czechoslovakia	1931
Germany	1931
Greece	1931
Hungary	1931
Italy	1930–1, 1935
Latvia	1931
Norway	1931
Poland	1931
Portugal	1931–2
Romania	1931
Spain	1931
Sweden	1931–2
Switzerland	1931
Turkey	1931
United States	1930–3
Yugoslavia	1931

Sources: Bernanke and James (1991); Bordo et al. (2001); Grossman (2010); Reinhart and Rogoff (2009).

presented to them. After breaking free from gold, there was great uncertainty over the appropriate course of action that should be taken. With the benefit of hindsight it seems extraordinary that, given the state of the economy, the bank rate was actually increased from 4.5 to 6.0 per cent. The best explanation for this perverse move is that policy makers were experiencing a deep psychological shock as they absorbed the enormity of the decision to leave the gold standard (Howson, 1975). In spite of experiencing one of the largest price falls in modern history, they worried about the inflationary effects of devaluation and moved to counter that illusion. Fiscal policy had begun to tighten in 1929–30 and continued to be restrictive until 1933–34. Under the circumstances it is not surprising that the economy slid back into depression in mid-1932. This double dip recession was a clear warning that leaving the gold standard was a necessary, but not a sufficient, action for vigorous sustained recovery.

In 1931, banking crises erupted in a large number of countries and, in some, financial dislocation continued into the following year (see Table 1.6). In 1931 too, eight countries were forced to default on their debts. The sovereign debt crisis enveloped a further seven countries in 1932 and an additional five during the following year (see Table 1.7).

Everywhere they materialized, financial crises added an unwelcome blast of uncertainty and apprehension to the woes that already existed. Without financial stability economic recovery was unattainable but the gold standard, which was supposed to provide stability, was in the process of disintegration (Wolf, 2008). In

Table 1.7. Sovereign debt defaults, 1929–38

Austria	1932
Bolivia	1931
Brazil	1931
Bulgaria	1932
Chile	1931
Colombia	1932
Costa Rica	1937
Cuba	1933
Dominican Republic	1931
Ecuador	1931
El Salvador	1931
Germany	1932
Guatemala	1933
Hungary	1931
Nicaragua	1932
Panama	1932
Paraguay	1932
Peru	1931
Poland	1936
Romania	1933
Uruguay	1933
Yugoslavia	1933

Source: Sturzenegger and Zettelmeyer (2007).

1931, 47 countries were members of the gold standard club. By the end of 1932 the only significant members were Belgium, France, Netherlands, Poland, Switzerland, and the US (see Table 1.5). In fact, 1931 was a dramatic year when a major financial crisis dealt a mortal blow to the gold standard while output and prices continued to decline throughout the world (League of Nations, 1933). Far from providing stability and fulfilling the expectations of its supporters, the gold standard was instrumental in forcing economies to deflate during a period of intense depression. Indeed, departure from gold was a prerequisite for recovery. It is a supreme irony that the gold standard, adopted by so many countries as a bulwark against inflation was overwhelmed by the effects of deflation. It is also worth noting that leaving the gold standard was a lot easier than it is now for a deeply troubled country to severe links with the eurozone.

Between 1929 and 1933 the value of world trade fell by 65 per cent measured in gold dollars. Trade volume shrank by 25 per cent between 1929 and 1932, with manufactured goods being particularly severely affected. However, the price falls in food stuffs and raw materials were steeper than for manufactured goods so the terms of trade moved against primary producing countries. The fracturing of the gold standard in 1931 had a disruptive effect on international trade. Devalued currencies gave exports a competitive edge which trade rivals remaining on gold sought to blunt by the imposition of tariffs, quotas, the promotion of import substitutes, and bilateral trade agreements (Eichengreen and Irwin, 2010). Countries which left gold but did not devalue their currencies also embraced protection (see Table 1.8). In Germany, for example, a drive for greater self-sufficiency was added to strict exchange controls and these policies were accompanied by a

Table 1.8. Tariff rates, 1928, 1935 and 1938 (%)

	1928	1935	1938
Austria	8.1	17.5	14.8
Belgium	3.4	8.3	6.7
Canada	15.9	15.4	13.9
Czechoslovakia	7.8	10.0	7.2
Denmark	5.5	8.2	7.3
France	6.6	16.9	16.6
Germany	7.9	30.1	33.4
Hungary	11.0	7.2	12.0
Italy	6.7	22.2	12.1
Japan	7.1	6.2	6.6
Netherlands	2.1	9.1	6.7
New Zealand	17.1	17.5	16.4
Norway	11.5	14.4	12.2
Spain	24.1	27.9	n/a
Sweden	9.3	10.1	9.5
Switzerland	9.3	23.3	18.1
United Kingdom	10.0	24.5	24.1
United States	13.8	17.5	15.5

Note: Tariff rate is defined as customs revenue/value of imports.
Source: Eichengreen and Irwin (2010).

reliance on bilateral rather than multilateral trade (Obstfeld and Taylor, 1998.) Japan and Italy also provide examples of autarkic imperialism. Liberal internationalism was no more. Individual countries, or groups, strove to minimize their imports and maximise their exports. As one country's imports are another's exports, retaliation was usually swift, but these actions in turn led to further counter measures. Unusually, the recovery in world GDP was more rapid than the revival in trade during the 1930s, and as late as 1940 world trade in manufactures had not returned to its pre-depression peak (Irwin, 2012).

Trade protection could provide a supportive framework for domestic expansion, but not if most trading nations were simultaneously engaged in this activity. Under these circumstances, every country will end up disadvantaged. If international cooperation had been strong and effective, a programme of coordinated devaluations together with appropriate expansionary monetary policies would have generated recovery and revived international trade (Eichengreen and Sachs, 1985). Unfortunately, just as the return to gold during the 1920s had been disorderly, so was the exit from it (see Table 1.5). For many countries it was an unplanned reaction to speculative pressure.

1.5. ECONOMIC POLICY AFTER THE ABANDONMENT OF THE GOLD STANDARD

After leaving the gold standard, monetary and fiscal policy was freed from its obligation to support the exchange rate and could be used as a tool for economic expansion. But how effective would monetary and fiscal policy be in regenerating shattered economies? Would monetary policy be effective when a banking system was in disarray? Or when interest rates are set at the lower bound? Should fiscal policy be used to stimulate demand rather than reduce levels of indebtedness? Recent research (Almunia et al., 2010) provides support for the view that government expenditure had a positive impact on GDP during the interwar period and that both output and employment grew in response to increases in government spending. Furthermore, they found that monetary policy also had a role to play in recovery; for example, central bank discount policy had a positive effect in boosting GDP. The results of this research show that expansionary monetary and fiscal policies were effective in the fight against the Great Depression where they were used. However, would policy makers in Europe and in the US have the courage to fully employ these powerful tools to bring about recovery?

After the downturn caused by the double dip recession in mid-1932, the UK economy recovered strongly. In each year between 1933 and 1937, real GDP grew by at least 3.1 per cent. Indeed, real GDP surpassed its 1929 level as early as 1934 and was 18.2 per cent greater by 1938. A new surge of optimism pushed stock market prices to their pre-depression levels in 1935. Unemployment fell and by 1937 was back to 1929 levels but, absolutely, the total was unacceptably high. The recovery was robust so while it is possible to detect the effects of the 1937–38 US recession in both unemployment and stock market prices, real GDP growth was unaffected (see Table 1.2). The rapidity of the post-depression recovery is evident when compared to both Germany and the US, though both started from a much lower base. How can we explain this economic transformation?

It is clear that the earlier countries abandoned the gold standard and devalued their currencies the sooner they began to recover from the depression. We can start by asking what benefits did the UK gain from the devaluation of sterling? After the exit from gold, sterling fell sharply from its gold standard parity of $4.86 to a low point of $3.24 by late 1931, though an appreciation to $3.80 had taken place by March 1932. At this point the Treasury, which had taken over responsibility for monetary policy from the Bank of England, decided that a devaluation of about 30 per cent was appropriate and moved to peg sterling against the US dollar at $3.40. After the US devaluation in March 1933, sterling was pegged against the French franc at FrF 88 and later at FrF 77 (Howson, 1980). The Exchange Equalisation Account, set up in the summer of 1932, was used to prevent unwanted currency appreciation. The most effective way to measure the effect of sterling's devaluation is to examine the exchange rate against the average of other currencies and consider relative inflation rates rather than track its performance against a single currency. In 1936, the sterling real exchange rate was nearly 20 lower than in 1929 thus boosting the competitiveness of British exports (Dimsdale, 1981). Another crucial element in Treasury policy was a commitment to 'cheap money'. The bank rate was reduced to 2 per cent in June 1932 and nominal interest rates remained low for the remainder of the decade (see Table 1.3).

The crisis also provided the incentive for Britain to turn away from an emotional commitment to Free Trade (Garside, 1998; Williamson, 1992). The Imports Duties Act (1932) imposed a general 10 per cent duty on a range of imports. Within a few months, Imperial Preference instituted agreements between Commonwealth countries and Britain to favour each other's exports. UK tariff rates increased in the early 1930s and remained at a relatively high level throughout the decade. International trade restrictions increased dramatically throughout the world during the 1930s but even when there was some relaxation it was not multinational. With the Reciprocal Trade Agreements Act (1934), the US Congress authorized the president to negotiate bilateral tariff reductions with other countries. By 1939 the US had signed 20 treaties with countries accounting for 60 per cent of its trade (Findlay and O'Rourke, 2007). Unfortunately, during the 1930s, multilateral trade gave way to bilateral arrangements as trading within blocs, of which Imperial Preference was one, grew more common. The outcome was trade diversion rather than creation. As Germany never devalued, high levels of protection were necessary as the mark rendered exports increasingly uncompetitive (see Table 1.8).

Although devaluation assisted trade, its impact on the UK economy was slight as the change in net exports made only a modest contribution to the growth in demand which fuelled recovery. The recovery was not export led. The principal positive effects of devaluation and the exit from gold must be seen in the liberation of monetary and fiscal policy from the shackles of the gold standard. However, in the early stages of recovery between 1933 and 1935, fiscal policy was contractionary rather than expansionary. Fiscal tightening was adopted in 1929/30 and continued after the May Committee Report (1931) forecast a large and potentially destabilizing budget deficit (Middleton, 1985, 2013). Correcting the budget imbalance was seen as the overriding priority and, in spite of the depressed economy, public expenditure cuts and tax increases were imposed to that end. Fiscal consolidation in the financial years 1932/33 and 1933/34 eliminated the budget deficit by 1934 and from this point fiscal policy was eased (see Table 1.4). In other words, the early recovery was not spurred by deficit spending; at this time fiscal policy was clearly deflationary. However, in 1935 the political climate changed dramatically when the government became convinced that the threat of war was too worrying to ignore. A major rearmament programme centred on re-equipping the Royal Air Force and the Royal Navy transformed fiscal policy. Rearmament spending created a budget deficit and stimulated an economy functioning below full capacity. Thomas (1983) argues that between 1935 and 1938, deficit financed rearmament expenditure delivered a powerful fiscal stimulus to the economy of about 3 per cent of GDP. Only after 1935 could fiscal policy be described as 'Keynesian'.

Given the rate of economic expansion, it is clear that monetary policy overcame the deflationary fiscal forces and drove economic growth before defence spending transformed the fiscal stance. In 1932 the Treasury, which had assumed responsibility for monetary policy, quickly provided a coherent strategy which has been described as a 'managed economy' approach (Booth, 1987; Howson, 1975). In 1932 a 'cheap money' policy was introduced and short term interest rates were reduced to historically low levels (see Table 1.3). This was a sensible move, but it did mean that that there would be little scope in the future for further nominal interest rate reductions. However, monetary stimulus could still be provided if real interest rates declined. This was apparent to Treasury policy makers who, with the support of the Chancellor of the Exchequer, worked to change inflationary expectations. The persistent increase in prices reduced real wages and real interest rates, improved profits, and increased business optimism. At the core of the 'managed economy' strategy, so necessary as an antidote to the deflationary fiscal stance, was the adoption of low real interest rates, a commitment to a low exchange rate and the use of protective tariffs. Business responded to lower real interest rates and one indication of changed expectations can be seen in the rapid revival of stock market prices which returned to 1929 levels in 1935 (see Table 1.2).

Low interest rates helped to stimulate house building, which played a vital role in the revival of the economy (Broadberry, 1986; Dimsdale and Horsewood, 1995; Worswick, 1984). The house building sector was a major employer and purchaser of raw materials and it responded positively to low interest rates. According to Broadberry (1987), almost half of the additional housing investment in the 1930s was on account of lower interest rates. The vast majority of the new housing was for the private buyers market rather than for local authorities and construction was concentrated in the midlands and the south east of England. These were the regions of growing prosperity; the regions dominated by the cotton textiles, coal, iron, and steel industries remained centres of unemployment. Unfortunately, the Treasury was too cautious in promoting inflation and even by 1938 the price level was nearly 10 per cent below the 1929 figure (see Table 1.1). Nevertheless, monetary policy must be judged a success. The vigorous growth in private house construction is a vivid example of monetary policy changing inflationary expectations. Between 1933 and 1935 monetary policy provided an antidote to fiscal consolidation. After 1935 both fiscal and monetary policy contributed positively to continuing economic expansion.

The UK and Germany left the gold standard within a few months of each other in 1931. However, the economic experience of both countries differed dramatically during the remainder of the decade. Germany was disadvantaged by the destabilizing effects of a major bank crisis in 1931 and also had a serious sovereign debt problem. Moreover, foreign credit had been vital to fund reparations payments and increased living standards during the 1920s but it was now unavailable. The depression was, therefore, far more acute in Germany than it was in the Britain. Weighed down by a weak banking system, the demands of foreign creditors and, even in an age of deflation, the nagging fear that currency depreciation could see the return of hyperinflation, policy options were not without problems.

Germany did not devalue the mark and was therefore, unlike the UK, unable to enjoy the benefits of a flexible exchange rate. Without devaluation the imposition of exchange controls and trade protection policies was necessary. Although one of the major advantages of leaving gold was that monetary and fiscal policy could be used to stimulate the economy, Germany actually chose to tighten the severe deflationary policy which had been in place since 1930 in an attempt to demonstrate that the continuance of reparations payments was a major priority. The outcome was disastrous. Unemployment soared from 25.5 per cent of the labour force in 1931 to 31.5 per cent during the following year, a higher figure even than the US (see Table 1.2). Nominal short term interest rates were high and, as prices tumbled, real rates were prohibitive (see Table 1.3). The high cost of borrowing was a deterrent for business investment, but so was the high level of real wages which the government found impossible to reduce (Ritschl, 2013). As the economic decline worsened, tax revenues fell but tax payers were highly resistant to attempts to raise more revenue, especially as they believed that the money was destined for reparations payment not the relief of domestic misery. Many of those demonstrating in the streets were convinced that default was a more acceptable option than continued deflation.

Hitler became German Chancellor in January 1933 just a few months before Franklin Roosevelt took the presidential oath in Washington DC, but the economic aims of the two leaders were radically different. Like Keynes, Roosevelt sought to rescue capitalism and raise it from the depths to which it had sunk. The Nazis dismissed the old liberal economic model. Nazi economic policy was designed to make possible the creation of a new empire rather than have as its primary aim the improvement of German living standards. This totalitarian regime was more interested in the production of capital goods than consumer goods. Its foreign trade policy was not determined by buying in the cheapest markets and selling in the dearest. It used bilateral trade agreements and exchange controls in order to favour imports and exports of strategic importance. The Nazis saw the political importance of eradicating unemployment and embarked on a programme of work creation schemes which were remarkably effective in reducing the numbers out of work (see Tables 1.2 and 1.4). The work creation schemes were funded by substantial budget deficits which increased after 1935 by high levels of military spending as the regime tooled up for war.

Nevertheless, starting from a very low base, real GDP had exceeded the 1929 level by 1936 and was 35 per cent greater two years later, though the composition of GNP was determined by the state not the market. Contemporaries noted, and Hitler often reminded them, that the Nazis managed to eliminate unemployment while Roosevelt's New Deal did not. Indeed, the bleak message for the supporters of democratic government was that fascism and communism seemed to offer the only solution for a return to full employment.

In seeking an explanation for the Nazi rise to power it is superficial to rely simply on the severity of the depression in Germany. It is true that persistent severe depression and accompanying mass unemployment can cause great social distress, lead to public disorder and an escalating discontent with the established order. However, economic contraction by itself will not always lead to the rise to power of extremist political movements. The depression was severe in the US but democracy in that country was never seriously challenged. On the other hand, allied to a severe economic and financial collapse, German democracy was not strong. As early as 1930 Germany was governed by presidential decree rather than by an elected parliament. This act compromised a fledgling democracy and may well have undermined the legitimacy of democratic parties. It may also have made street demonstrations and violence more likely but it was the lack of a strong democratic tradition which set the scene for a Nazi takeover not the depression (de Bromhead et al., 2012; Ritschl, 2013).

The impact of the depression in the UK was mild compared with the devastating consequences of the economic collapse in the US. When Roosevelt delivered his stirring inaugural address in March 1933 the US economy was in disarray. The entire banking system was in a state of paralysis and had ceased to function. The confidence of both investors and consumers was at rock bottom. Nearly a quarter of the labour force was unemployed and many of those out of work had been idle for more than 12 months. The fall in farm income led to inevitable economic and social distress in the countryside at a time when migration to urban areas, the traditional escape route for rural hardship, was no longer an option. Persistent deflation had increased the real burden of debt. Mortgage holders were forced to sell their assets on a falling market and few consumers or investors wished to take on new debt. Even if they did, finding lenders was difficult as credit markets were in disarray. Contrary to the views of some contemporaries, falling prices were not a potential stimulus to consumer spending. Deflation, intensified by overproduction and excessive competition, was widely viewed as playing a major role in spreading misery. It is not surprising that there was a general loss of faith in the self generating powers of the free market economy.

Although many of the economic problems were self evident, there was no universal agreement how they should be remedied. There was no consensus amongst bankers, financiers, or economists as to the causes of the economic crisis and therefore none regarding a solution. Roosevelt and his advisors had not developed a coherent recovery strategy at the time of his electoral victory. Indeed, during his campaign he had stressed the need for a balanced budget as an integral part of any recovery strategy, though at the same time he was committed to additional federal spending on relief for the distressed (Barber, 1996). The Democrat Party had captured both the House and the Senate with large majorities. Many elected politicians did not share Roosevelt's fiscal conservatism. They lost no time in supporting ideas to vigorously inflate the economy, to raise consumer purchasing power, or to restrict the working week so that the limited available work could be shared. On the other hand, some bankers, economists, and financiers urged more deflation, an unwavering commitment to the gold standard, and further reductions in public spending. As Meltzer (2003) observes, 'views like these were not just wrong, they were influential'.

Roosevelt promised the American people 'bold persistent experimentation' and, although scholars see in the New Deal continuity with America's past, the public saw decisive action and lots of it (Bordo et al., 1998; Fishback and Wallis, 2013). Immediately on entering office the new president addressed the banking problem. A bank holiday closed all the nation's banks and the president assured the public that they would only be permitted to re-open when an independent examination had declared them sound. The Banking Act (1933) separated investment from commercial banking, imposed maximum interest rates on bank accounts, and introduced federal deposit insurance (FDIC). Roosevelt was opposed to the creation of the FDIC believing that the moral hazard disadvantages outweighed the advantages to depositors (Calomiris and White, 1994). The banking legislation has also been criticized for preserving the unit banking system that was inefficient and potentially unstable (Calomiris, 2013). Nevertheless, a combination of Roosevelt's assurances and the new regulations ushered in a period of banking stability which was a vital prerequisite for recovery. In fact, the banking initiative was not especially radical and Hoover would have been comfortable with the outcome, though whether he could have been as reassuring to depositors as his successor is unlikely. However, there can be little doubt that if Hoover had achieved bank stability as president he would have used this as a means of marshalling further support for the gold standard. Roosevelt, however, was prepared to cast off the golden shackles.

During the dramatic 'first hundred days' of the Roosevelt presidency, Congress accepted a cascade of legislative measures which were intended to generate recovery, reform, and relief. For example, the Agricultural Adjustment Act (AAA 1933) sought to raise farm income by restricting the output of key commodities. The National Industrial Recovery Act (NIRA) introduced a complex bureaucracy intended to introduce minimum wages and maximum hours, encourage the growth of trades unions, and also curb destabilizing price competition by encouraging collusion between companies. It was a misguided attempt to invigorate the economy by producing less. The Federal Emergency Relief Administration (FERA) committed the federal government to work with the states to fund a comprehensive relief programme (Fishback and Wallis, 2013; Wallis, 2010). This first phase of the New Deal shows a radical change from Hoover's policy stance. Roosevelt's administration embraced planned scarcity as a means of raising prices. It sought to raise business confidence by encouraging monopolistic practices and to raise effective demand by increasing wages. In addition, federal expenditure rose dramatically indicating an expanded role for central government and an acceptance of deficit expenditure. Clearly Roosevelt had moved into the inflationist rather than the deflationist camp.

However, the most dramatic way in which Roosevelt departed from the policies of his predecessor came in April 1933 with the decision to leave the gold standard and devalue the dollar. The US departure from gold was even more shocking to conservatives than that of sterling in September 1931. Under intense speculative pressure, the Bank of England struggled to defend the exchange rate but was ultimately forced to concede defeat. The US had ample gold reserves and was under no speculative pressure; the decision to abandon gold was a coolly taken policy initiative. Once free from the restrictions of the gold standard, the Fed had no further need to impose deflationary policies on a stricken economy and was free to implement expansionary monetary and fiscal policies, if it chose to do so. After devaluation, the US became a safe haven for gold, especially from a troubled Europe. The Treasury, not the Fed, allowed the gold flows to generate an expansion of the money supply which played a vital role in stimulating recovery.

These early New Deal policy initiatives, which showed that Congress was committed to high levels of public spending, created an important regime shift which triggered recovery. It was soon clear to consumers, investors, workers, and employers that the New Deal focus was on increasing output and reversing the debilitating curse of deflation (Eggertsson, 2008, 2012; Temin and Wigmore, 1990). In particular, the decision to abandon the gold standard and show that domestic recovery was the priority was crucial in the battle to change expectations and to create an atmosphere of hope for the future. However, as we have seen in our analysis of the UK after the departure from gold, devaluation, though important, was not by itself sufficient to generate recovery. The raft of New Deal policies that clearly signalled Hoover's deflationary stance had been reversed were a vital part of the regime change message. The increase in the money supply from 1934 onwards following the gold influx also contributed to the regime change. Some inflation was essential in order to reduce real interest rates as nominal rates were close to zero and could not be reduced. Inflation was also important as a means of reducing real debt. Prices rose by 8.6 per cent in 1934, 2.4 per cent in 1935, though not at all in 1936. However, Romer (1999) emphasizes the inflationary effect of rapid growth of real output on price increases after 1933 rather than devaluation and changes in expectations. Whatever the cause, within a few months of assuming power, the Roosevelt administration had embarked upon a much-needed inflationary regime change.

Critics of the New Deal often attack its lack of coherence. This is an easy target as the New Deal of 1933–35, with its emphasis on planning, restriction, and cooperation with business, gave way to the New Deal of 1935–38 with its emphasis on competition, support for organized labour, and growing anti-business stance. In 1938 and 1939 Roosevelt called for additional spending to assist recovery and also set in motion a detailed investigation into price fixing by big business. Rapid changes in policy orientation make an evaluation of New Deal programmes very difficult (Fishback, 2007). The picture is certainly one of confusion and a regime of uncertainty which may have adversely affected investment decisions. However, it would be a mistake to view this period as one of unremitting gloom for producers. Some employers may have been adversely influenced by Roosevelt's anti-business rhetoric and frequent changes in policy emphasis, but others seized the opportunity to make their businesses more efficient and profitable (Field, 2003, 2013; Hannah and Temin, 2010).

Any critical appraisal of New Deal policies must take into account the state of economics at the time. Macroeconomics was struggling to emerge during the 1930s. There was no intellectual or political support for the large federal budget deficits that would have been a more powerful aid to recovery than the piecemeal structural initiatives that the New Dealers favoured. The reaction of many contemporaries to the problem of unemployment was to promote polices that would share work, to advocate high wages in order to stimulate purchasing power, to support attempts to remove married women from the workforce, and to institute a compulsory age of retirement. Moreover, although the federal budget was in deficit for every year during Roosevelt's presidency, these deficits were too small and unplanned to be described as Keynesian. Furthermore, while the federal government ran small budget deficits, the state governments countered the expansionary effect by running budget surpluses. The New Deal was not an exercise in Keynesian economics (Brown, 1956; Fishback, 2013; Peppers, 1973).

Critics also highlight what they perceive is a sluggish recovery after 1933, as growth was interrupted by a severe recession in 1937–38 and the economy did not reach its full employment trend until 1942. The post 1933 recovery, however, was extraordinarily rapid. From the exceptionally low base, real GDP grew rapidly at an average of over 8 per cent a year until 1937. After a check, growth between 1938 and 1941 was, at over 10 per cent, even more rapid. Between 1929 and 1933 real GDP fell by 27 per cent; between 1933 and 1937 it rose by 36 per cent (see Table 1.2). In 1937, the best year of the decade, output had just reached 1929 levels and there were as many people at work as there had been in the prosperous year of 1929. Unfortunately, the labour force had grown by 6 million and the unemployment rate, at 9.2 per cent, remained unacceptably high. Private investment failed to revive satisfactorily: total gross private domestic investment (current $) rose from $1.4bn in 1933 to $11.8bn in 1937. The figure for 1929 was $16.2bn. However, as Field (2013) shows, in spite of the failure of investment to reach its pre-depression level, during this period total factor productivity rose impressively. Recovery was cut short by the recession of 1937–38 which was a sudden and devastating blow to an economy functioning far below full capacity. Private investment was driven down to $6.5bn and full recovery was held back for several years. The economy did not reach its long run trend growth path until June 1942.

If fiscal policy was passive, how can we explain the rapid growth between 1933 and 1937, and also between 1938 and 1941? And why did an economy with so many underutilized resources experience a sharp recession during 1937–38? The economy received its stimulus from a rapid growth in the monetary base. The cause of this increase was twofold. The revaluation of gold stocks during 1933–34 increased the value of US holdings by about 70 per cent to which we can add the substantial flow of gold entering the banking system, particularly from troubled Europe (Romer, 1992). In other words, the monetary stimulus was accidental rather than the result of a deliberate attempt by the monetary authorities to stimulate the economy. However, it is important to note that the Treasury took the decision to allow the influx to inflate the money supply rather than sterilize it.

By 1936, the recovery seemed so successful that Roosevelt decided that it was time to balance the budget. Nominal federal spending rose sharply to reach a temporary peak of $8.4bn. Spending cutbacks and tax increases reduced this figure to $6.8bn in 1938. This was a very unwise fiscal retrenchment. At the same time, the Fed became concerned at the potentially inflationary excess reserves held by member banks. Three interventions in 1936 and 1937 doubled reserve requirements and one result was that the banking system reduced lending to businesses; another was that interest rates rose. The latest research suggests that the Fed's action was unwise but not powerful enough to provide the main cause of the 1937–38 recession (Calomiris et al., 2011; Telser, 2001) The major deflationary force was provided by the Treasury which, in December 1936, decided to sterilize the inflow of gold, which turned the rate of monetary growth negative (Velde, 2009). As monetary growth had provided the engine for economic expansion between 1933 and 1937, this change in policy had disastrous effects on the economy.

The combination of restrictive monetary and fiscal policies plunged the economy into a serious year long downturn during which real GDP fell by 10 per cent and unemployment rose to 12.5 per cent. With the benefit of hindsight we can see that the Fed and the Treasury blundered, but at the time actions taken to dampen inflation attracted the support of some prominent economists and captains of industry (Mitchener and Mason, 2013; Roose, 1954). Unfortunately, the federal government was very slow to react once it was clear that a serious contraction was taking place. Roosevelt called for a $3.0bn spending stimulus, but not until April 1938. At the same time, the Fed reduced its reserve requirements and the Treasury desterilized all the gold that it had sterilized since December 1936. The monetary base expanded rapidly, as did the economy and excess bank reserves, though prices continued to fall for another two years (Meltzer, 2003). The 1937–38 recession was a serious, self inflicted wound which held back full recovery by several years. Fortunately, the downturn did not precipitate a banking crisis, which showed that New Deal regulation had created depositor confidence. As Europe moved inexorably towards war, the already substantial gold flow to the US increased. By the close of 1940, the US Treasury owned over 80 per cent of the world's monetary gold (Meltzer, 2003).

Germany and the UK escaped the effects of the 1937–38 contraction because both economies were protected by heavy rearmament expenditure. Indeed, the period 1937–39 saw the most pronounced fiscal stimulus ever experienced in the UK during peacetime (Middleton, 2012).

1.6. UNEMPLOYMENT

Hatton and Thomas (2013) offer an explanation for the mass unemployment in both the US and the UK during the 1930s. Unemployment in the UK during the thirties was similar to that of the 1920s. It was concentrated in the regions where the old staple industries, cotton textiles, coal mining, ship building, and iron and steel industries dominated. However, in other parts of the country, a private housing boom, encouraged by low interest rates and rising real wages, created many jobs and there was employment growth too in the manufacture of consumer durables and in the service sector. By the mid-1930s, UK unemployment was primarily regional and structural.

In contrast, the US had enjoyed low unemployment during the 1920s. The stubborn refusal of unemployment to decline to pre-depression levels as economic recovery got underway ensured that expenditure on relief was a new and a major item in the federal budget. Indeed, by the late 1930s the US committed a higher proportion of its GDP to social spending than any other country; more than Germany, the UK, France, and Sweden (Amenta, 1998).There were other differences between the twenties and the thirties. The Roosevelt administration encouraged the growth of trade unions and in the first New Deal, minimum wages and maximum hours raised both real wages and labour costs. Indeed, the support of both Hoover and Roosevelt for polices designed to prevent wage rates from falling helps to explain the extraordinary growth in money wages during a period of mass unemployment. The employed benefited, but real wages increased above market clearing levels and, as a result, unemployment persisted. In contrast to the UK, the US construction industry did not revive and, as a result, many jobs failed to materialize even though the economy expanded. Moreover, the significant growth of TFP (total factor productivity) enabled output to expand with the minimum of labour (Field, 2013). The US experienced jobless growth.

Unlike British policy makers, the New Dealers were totally opposed to 'dole' payments, which they feared would lead to a dependency culture. Instead, they stressed the benefits of work relief with a cash wage and hourly wage rates identical to those in the private sector. Hours worked were restricted so that take home pay was not so munificent that private sector work would be rejected if it was offered. Unfortunately, limited funding enabled only 40 per cent of workers eligible for work project placements to find employment on them. Rejected applicants were forced to accept relief from their counties, which was far less generous than that provided by Washington.

Mass unemployment was a worldwide phenomenon during the depression. Sweden, Denmark and Norway, like Britain, endured double digit unemployment in both the twenties and the thirties (see Table 1.9). In Germany, the deflationary policies pursued even after the gold standard had been abandoned led to an unemployment total of 6 million in 1933, roughly double that of the

Table 1.9. Unemployment in industry (%)

	1929	1930	1931	1932	1933
Australia	10.2	18.4	26.5	28.1	24.2
Belgium	1.3	3.6	10.9	19.0	16.9
Canada	4.2	12.9	17.4	26.0	26.6
Denmark	15.5	13.7	17.9	31.7	28.8
France	1.0	2.0	6.5	15.4	14.1
Germany	13.3	22.7	34.3	43.8	36.2
Netherlands	2.9	7.8	14.8	25.3	26.9
Norway	15.4	16.6	22.3	30.8	33.4
Sweden	10.2	11.9	16.8	22.4	23.2
United Kingdom	10.4	16.1	21.3	22.1	19.9
United States	5.3	14.2	25.2	36.3	37.6
	1934	1935	1936	1937	1938
Australia	19.6	15.6	11.3	8.4	7.8
Belgium	18.9	17.8	13.5	11.5	14.0
Canada	20.6	19.1	16.7	12.5	15.1
Denmark	22.2	19.7	19.3	21.9	21.5
France	13.8	14.5	10.4	7.4	7.8
Germany	20.5	16.2	12.0	6.9	3.2
Netherlands	28.0	31.7	32.7	26.9	25.0
Norway	30.7	25.3	18.8	20.0	22.0
Sweden	18.0	15.0	12.7	10.8	10.9
United Kingdom	16.7	15.5	13.1	10.8	12.9
United States	32.6	30.2	25.4	21.3	27.9

Source: Eichengreen and Hatton (1988).

UK. The social and political distress in Germany, which played a significant part in the election of Hitler as Chancellor in 1933, was widely seen at the time as one of the unacceptable costs of unemployment. The eradication of unemployment was a Nazi priority and the new government acted swiftly by imposing a 'new deal' on Germany which was radically different from Roosevelt's model. The Nazis abolished German trade unions, and with them collective bargaining. A mass programme of public works financed by budget deficits was begun immediately. Industrial recovery emphasized the production of capital goods not consumer goods. Labour service, and the introduction of military conscription in 1935, helped to reduce the ranks of the jobless so that in 1937 unemployment had been reduced to less than 2 million. A striking feature of the labour market was the very modest growth in real wages which this totalitarian regime was able to control. When the market became tight, and labour shortages appeared, there were no trade unions to help workers exploit their scarcity.

The contribution of Nazi work creation schemes, and the state's ability to control wage growth, explains why the decline of unemployment in Germany appeared a success story when compared to Roosevelt's efforts in the US (Temin, 1989). Depressed commentators in the free world wondered if the only way to eradicate unemployment was to embrace the policies of either Nazi Germany or the Soviet Union. Neither option had great appeal. It was, however, preparation for war which sheltered Britain, France, and Germany from sharing the US experience during 1937–8. Expansionary fiscal policies sustained the European economies as they geared up for conflict and minimized the effects of this contraction.

1.7. COMPARISONS WITH THE GREAT RECESSION

The Great Recession, just like the Great Depression, had its origins in the US. At its heart was a monumental crisis in the housing sector. Home ownership had been vigorously championed by the Bush administration which promoted mortgages for low income purchasers. Low interest rates and easy credit led to a boom in real estate prices which rose, on average, by 50 per cent between 2000 and 2005. However, the housing market peaked in 2006 and the links between mortgages and the financial sector provided the catalyst for a spectacular collapse.

The practice of packaging mortgages together and selling them as collateralized debt obligations began in the 1970s. The aim was to spread the risk on loans, especially residential mortgages, by selling them in the US and overseas. Pension funds, money managers, hedge funds, and other financial institutions—in what became known as the 'shadow' finance sector—found these attractive investments. Even the Federal National Mortgage Association (Fannie Mae) and the Federal Home Loan Mortgage Corporation (Freddie Mac) purchased mortgages from commercial banks and savings and loan associations. It seemed a good idea. Risks were shared, the cost of borrowing was reduced, and the mortgage lenders were liberated to issue more mortgages. During the 1980s, an innovative financial sector began to bundle mortgages into different categories of risk ranging from the secure to the very risky. The latter included the subprime: that is advances to individuals with a questionable ability to pay, and those to individuals whose income status was unverified. The most risky, or 'toxic' mortgages attracted the highest interest returns and these were purchased by some hedge funds as attractive investments for their clients. Banks and mortgage brokers sold their packaged mortgage loans (called securitization) and were thus able to issue even more mortgages. Soon other forms of debt, credit card and commercial debts for example, were packaged and sold in the same way. Confidence was high. The period of expansion since the 1980s had not been checked by a serious setback and this period of stability attracted the description, The Great Moderation. The shock administered by the Great Depression was now a distant memory. Both lenders and investors developed the cavalier attitude to risk that accompanies easy credit and the seductive optimism fuelled by a prolonged economic expansion (Minsky, 1982).

By the turn of the twenty-first century, progressive deregulation had been a feature of financial life for over 30 years. A key moment arrived in 1999 with the repeal of the Glass–Steagall Act (1933) which had separated the activities of commercial and investment banks and curbed the freedom of the former to operate in the securities market. With its repeal, commercial banks were permitted to offer a wide range of services, including the underwriting of securities. In fact, the erasure of the Glass–Steagall Act was symbolic; the most significant change in the provision of financial services was the growth of a large 'shadow' finance sector. These 'shadow' institutions were not only outside the regulatory control of the Federal Reserve, they were also unable to call upon the lender of last resort facility provided by the central bank should the need for it arise. Many 'shadow' institutions borrowed short and lent long on relatively illiquid assets which were highly vulnerable should their risk assessment prove to be poor. Subprime mortgages also became an attractive investment for financial institutions in other countries. As a result, there was a strong possibility that, if a crisis involving the housing sector were to emerge, it could not be contained within the boundaries of the US. Furthermore, if house prices collapsed, household income would decline and demand for goods and services would fall. However, with just a few notable exceptions, academics and bankers expressed great faith in the stability of financial markets, indeed in all markets.

In April 2007, New Century Financial, one of the largest subprime lenders in the US, filed for Chapter 11 bankruptcy. It included Goldman Sachs and Barclays Bank amongst its creditors. In August, Bear Stearns, an international finance house heavily involved in the subprime market, teetered on the verge of bankruptcy. Even though Bear Sterns was a non-deposit institution, the Fed helped finance its sale to JPMorgan Chase during the following year and also took onto its books $30bn of Bear Stearns toxic assets. Up to this point, the credit crisis was worrying but not viewed as particularly serious. The prevailing view was that it could be contained and the effect on the economy would be slight (Mishkin, 2010).

However, from the middle of 2008, the financial crisis developed with a sudden and terrifying force. In July, Freddie Mac and Fannie Mae, which together accounted for half of the outstanding mortgages in the US, were subject to a federal takeover because their financial condition had deteriorated so rapidly. On 15 September, Lehman Brothers, the fourth largest investment bank in the US, a company with 25,000 employees, declared bankruptcy. This was the largest bankruptcy filing in US history. The Fed had concluded that it could not save Lehman Brothers and worked to minimize the impact of the firm's collapse. Nevertheless, the decision to allow Leman Brothers to go bankrupt had serious domestic and international ramifications because of the interconnections between financial institutions. Notwithstanding its decision on Lehman Brothers, on 16 September the Fed decided to support American International Group (AIG), the largest insurance company in the US with customers in 130 countries. AIG was stricken by bad debts which had incurred from insuring mortgage backed securities. The company had engaged in high risk lending which, in spite of its potential to wreck the financial system, had gone unnoticed by regulators (Mishkin, 2010). Eventually the Federal Reserve and the federal government pumped $182bn into AIG, the largest federal bailout in US history.

It seemed as if financial meltdown was not only a possibility, it was a certainty unless drastic action was taken. The Chair of the Fed, Ben Bernanke, is a prominent economic historian of the Great Depression, as the references to his work in this volume testify. He was fully aware of the drastic mistakes made by the Fed before and during the two depressions of 1929–33 and 1937–8 and was determined not to repeat them. Bernanke ensured that there would be no collapse in the money supply as happened during 1929–33 and no destabilizing deflation. The Fed's discount rate was reduced as soon as the crisis first became apparent and by late 2008 interest rates were close to zero. Bernanke stressed that the Fed's discount window would be open for distressed banks and that, unlike the practice Congress obliged the RFC to follow in 1932, any approach would be confidential. In his analysis of the financial disintegration during the Great Depression, Bernanke (1983) has emphasized the significance of credit disintermediation as a factor intensifying the impact on the real economy. Given his convictions, it is not surprising that in 2007 and 2008 the Fed vigorously intervened in a valiant, though not always entirely successful, attempt to make credit constantly available. The Fed also recognized the global dimensions of the crisis and liaised with other central banks to ensure that dollar credits were available to them. Quantitative easing was used on a massive scale from 2008 through to early 2010 and, as a result, the money supply rose dramatically. In other words, the Fed was highly active in dealing with the crisis in sharp contrast to its passivity during the Great Depression (Wheelock, 2010).

US fiscal policy also showed an interventionist vigour that was lacking during the 1930s. The American Restoration and Recovery Act, which became law in early 2009, earmarked $787bn to stimulate the economy and was described by Christina Romer, a distinguished economic historian of the Great Depression and then Chair of the President's Council of Economic Advisors, as 'the biggest and boldest countercyclical action in American History' (Romer, 2009). The effectiveness of these policies can be seen from the following figures: the real GDP decline for 1929–33 was 36.2 per cent, for 1937–8 it was 10.0 per cent, but for 2007–9 that figure was a modest 3.7 per cent (Wheelock, 2010). Unfortunately, the rapid reduction in unemployment which Romer anticipated would follow the implementation of the recovery plan has not materialized and this gave critics of the package a weapon for sustained attack. Furthermore, while the descent into a full blown depression has been halted, the vigorous economic growth that is vital for job creation, increasing tax revenue, and a reduction in government funded transfer payments has proved elusive. It is possible that Romer and her advisors underestimated the extent of the economic collapse facing the new administration in early 2009. It now appears that the big and bold stimulus plan that Congress approved was far short of what was needed. However, it is highly likely that Congress would have rejected a larger fiscal stimulus.

The boom in the UK economy from the 1990s was characterized by a massive rise in bank lending and high levels of consumer borrowing. The banking sector was subject to an increasingly light regulatory touch and it reacted by borrowing recklessly and aggressively expanding lending while disregarding the speculative bubble in the housing market. As in the US, there was an extraordinary rise in house prices which encouraged even more borrowing. The housing boom was not confined to the US and the UK; it was evident in other countries too, most notably Ireland and Spain. By 2007, UK households were heavily in debt, much of it accumulated in the belief that house prices would not only continue to rise, they would do so rapidly.

On 14 September 2007, the British public became aware that Northern Rock, a bank which had vigorously expanded its activities in the mortgage markets, had approached the Bank of England for an emergency loan. Northern Rock started life as a building society (savings and loans) and a high proportion of the bank's assets were tied up in loans to home owners and were highly illiquid. The bank had moved into subprime lending after concluding a deal with Lehman Brothers and was also heavily involved in securitization. Because of the worldwide credit crunch, the bank could no longer borrow to fund its daily operations. As soon as Northern Rock's difficulties became public knowledge, the bank's shares fell by 32 per cent and frantic depositors rushed to withdraw their savings. During the Great Depression no UK financial institution failed; depositor panic was a new and frightening phenomenon, especially as it raised questions about the standing of other banks. Northern Rock was taken over by the government in 2008 and it was clear that some form of national deposit insurance, possibly a UK version of FDIC, would be needed to secure public trust in the banking system. Responding to the crisis, the Bank of England adopted the lowest interest rates since its foundation in 1694, quantitative easing was used aggressively, and bank bailouts were funded where necessary. In October 2007, the guarantee for UK bank deposits was raised to £36,000 per depositor and further increased to £50,000 during the following year. In both the US and the UK, policies were pursued on a scale that would have been unacceptable during the 1930s but, crucially, these bold initiatives prevented financial meltdown. In both countries the objections relating to moral hazard were overwhelmed by the conviction that many troubled financial institutions were too big to fail.

In their prescient volume, Reinhart and Rogoff (2009) stress the particularly destabilizing features of major financial crises. Analysing the impact of financial collapses over many centuries, they concluded that when financial disintegration accompanies an economic downturn the dislocation is so serious that recovery is rarely swift. It is difficult to stimulate consumer demand when the priority is to reduce levels of indebtedness. There can be no doubt about the severity of the crisis that began in 2007. A comparison of the catastrophic Great Depression banking crisis in 1931 with that of 2007/8 shows that the countries involved in 1931 accounted for 55.6 per cent of world GDP, while the figure for the latter period is 33.5 per cent (Reinhart, 2010; Maddison, 2010). This was the most widespread banking crisis since 1931 and it is also the first time since that date that major European countries and the United States have both been involved. The financial tidal wave was totally unexpected and was of such severity that immediate policy action was required to prevent total melt down. For a while it seemed that the world stood at the edge of an abyss, a short step away from an even greater economic disaster than had occurred three quarters of a century earlier.

The big lesson learned from policy failures during the Great Depression is not to be passive in the face of large adverse financial shocks. As we have seen, in the US and the UK, aggressive monetary and fiscal policies were immediately implemented to halt the financial disintegration. Fortunately, neither country was constrained by the oppressive stranglehold of the gold standard. Both monetary and fiscal policies could be used to support economic expansion rather than to impose deflation, or try to restore a balanced budget. The avoidance of deflation has ensured that there has been no rise in real interest rates or in real debts. Flexible exchange rates gave policy makers the freedom to use devaluation as an aid to recovery. The problem for both countries is that, although financial meltdown has been avoided, economic growth, particularly in the UK, has not materialized. But growth is necessary to create more jobs and to lessen the debts burden. The emphasis on fiscal consolidation in order to reduce the UK's structural deficit seems to be inhibiting economic growth.

Problems are even more acute in parts of the eurozone where weak member states, for example, Greece, Spain, Ireland, and Portugal, are being forced to deflate their economies as a price for receiving assistance with their large debts. The deflation has increased unemployment to Great Depression levels, has eroded economic confidence and crushed consumer demand. Indeed, the eurozone does display some worrying similarities to the gold standard. The one size fits all common exchange rate forces debtors like Greece, Ireland, and Spain to deflate but the experience of the 1930s shows that it is very difficult to bring about sharp decreases in wages and prices. Moreover, while it is difficult for just one country to deflate, when several countries are forced to follow this route at the same time the outcome is potentially disastrous for economic growth. Just as in the 1920s we can find examples of rash borrowing but also of rash lending. Moreover, while the debtor countries have to endure misery there is no mechanism for countries that have accumulated great surpluses, for example, Germany, to recycle them. In some ways the eurozone rules are more draconian than those of the gold standard. In the 1930s, it was possible for countries to abandon gold with relative ease; that is not the case for any country which might want to leave the euro and devalue its national currency (Eichengreen and Temin, 2013).

Thus far, the containment of the financial crisis has meant that a repeat of the Great Depression has been avoided (see Figure 1.1 and Figure 1.2). A dramatic financial collapse has been averted and an impressive international economic recovery is progressing, Figure 1.1 shows the precipitous decline in world industrial production, which for a year after the start of the 2007 crisis fell at a faster rate than it did in 1920 and 1930. The persistent rise since then is a tribute to international action to contain the financial crisis as well as the resilience of large economies such as Brazil, China, and India. This recovery is in sharp contrast to the performance of

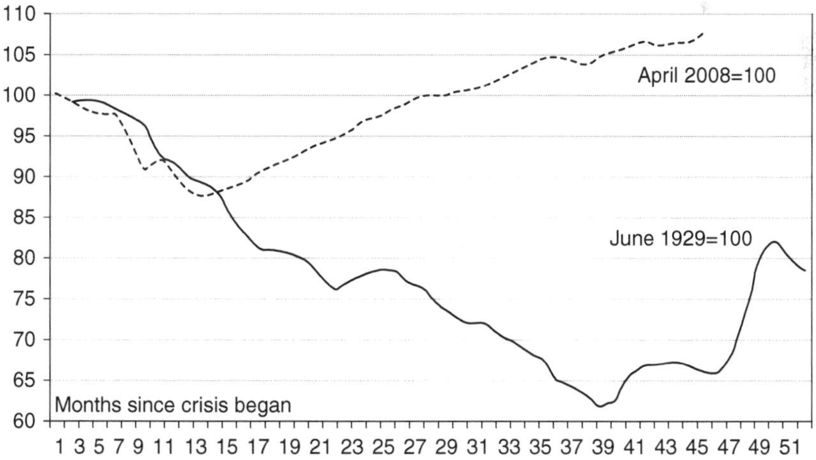

Fig. 1.1. World industrial production

Source: Data kindly supplied by Kevin O'Rourke.

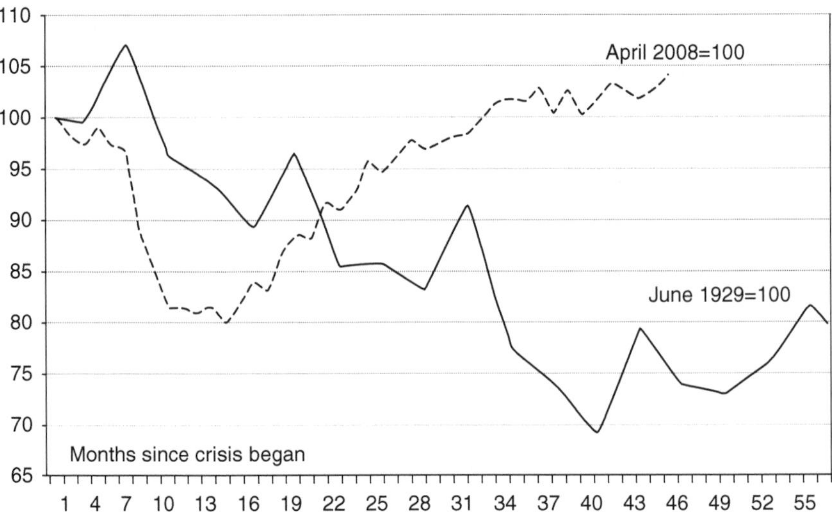

Fig. 1.2. Volume of world trade

Source: data kindly supplied by Kevin O'Rourke.

the international economy during the 1930s when sustained recovery did not commence for over three years after the downturn, and even then there was a check to progress less than a year later. Four and a half years after the start of the depression World Industrial Production was 20 per cent below pre-depression levels.

Another contrast is shown in Figure 1.2. The decline in the volume of world trade from 2007 was dramatic and far more severe than the picture in the early days of the Great Depression. The graph shows a sharp fall for about 12 months, but from that point a rapid recovery so that pre-recession levels were reached in less than three years. The recent economic decline did not result in an outbreak of trade wars, and the rapid recovery of the international economy helped a recovery in international trade. Thus, two important elements of the international economy, industrial production and world trade, have displayed a much stronger recovery during the Great Recession than they did during the Great Depression.

For the economies at the centre of this volume there is no doubt that some important lessons have been learned from the experiences of the Great Depression. It is clear that financial crises are particularly destabilizing and that vigorous monetary and fiscal intervention is necessary to deal with them. One lesson that was forgotten was the significance of regulation of financial services to ensure the stability of the system by minimizing risk. In the boom which preceded the 2007 collapse, reckless bank lending led to an asset price bubble which, like all bubbles, was unsustainable. The experiment with light-touch regulation failed. For all the criticism heaped on New Deal banking regulation (Calomiris, 2013), it did usher in a period of financial stability which lasted for many decades. Regulation and the supervision of the financial sector is a vital prerequisite in the search for stability. It is important to know what policies should be used to counter a financial crisis, but it is wiser to try and avoid one in the first place.

The other lesson that has been neglected is the importance of sustained economic recovery. An emphasis on contractionary fiscal policy which holds back growth is not wise because growth is the key to employment expansion, increasing tax revenues, and a reduction in the GDP debt ratio. In spite of unacceptable high levels of unemployment, too many countries have been condemned to mount the treadmill of austerity. The failure of deflationary policies during the 1930s should serve as a warning to policy makers in the eurozone, but at the moment it seems that debt repayment has been prioritized and the short term disadvantages of this strategy ignored. Outside the eurozone, both the US and the UK economies show that even an effective propping up of the banking system, and hoping for substantial gains from a depreciated currency, is not enough. The low costs of borrowing and persistent unemployment combine to make a powerful case for government investment in much-needed infrastructure improvements even if this leads to a short term increase in sovereign debt. If this route is chosen, the 1937–38 recession in the US provides a stark warning against adopting an exit strategy prematurely. Most countries have absorbed the lessons provided by the Great Depression on how to deal with financial crises. The lessons for sustained recovery are still being learned.

BIBLIOGRAPHY

Ahamed, L. (2009), *Lords of Finance. 1929, The Great Depression, and the Bankers Who Broke the World*. London: Heinemann.

Almunia, M., Benetrix, A., Eichengreen, B., O'Rourke, K. H., and Rua, G. (2010), 'Lessons from the Great Depression', *Economic Policy*, 62, 219–65.

Amenta, E. (1998), *Bold Relief. Institutional Politics and the Origins of Modern American Social Policy*. Princeton: Princeton University Press.

Barber, W. J. (1985), *From New Era to New Deal: Herbert Hoover, the Economist and American Economic Policy, 1921–1933*. London: Cambridge University Press.

Barber, W. J. (1996), *Designs Within Disorder: Franklin D. Roosevelt, the Economists and the Shaping of Economic Policy, 1933–1945*. Cambridge: Cambridge University Press.

Bernanke, B. (1983), 'Non-Monetary Effects of the Financial Crisis in the Propagation of the Great Depression', *American Economic Review*, 73, 257–76.

Bernanke, B. (1995), 'The Macroeconomics of the Great Depression: A Comparative Approach', *Journal of Money, Credit and Banking*, 27, 1–28.

Bernanke, B. and James, H. (1991), 'The Gold Standard, Deflation, and Financial Crisis in the Great Depression: An International Comparison', in R. G. Hubbard (ed.), *Financial Markets and Financial Crises*. Chicago: University of Chicago Press, 33–68.

Bernanke, B. and Mihov, I. (2000), 'Deflation and Monetary Contraction in the Great Depression: An Analysis by Simple Ratios', in B. Bernanke (ed.), *Essays on the Great Depression*. Princeton: Princeton University Press, 108–60.

Bernstein, M. A. (2001), *A Perilous Progress: Economists and Public Purpose in Twentieth Century America*. Princeton: Princeton University Press.

Booth, A. (1987), 'Britain in the 1930s: A Managed Economy?', *Economic History Review*, 40, 499–522.

Bordo, M., Eichengreen, B., Klingbiel, D., and Martinez-Peria, M. (2001), 'Is the Crisis Problem Growing More Severe?', *Economic Policy*, 32, 53–82.

Bordo, M. D. and Landon-Lane, J. (2013), 'The Banking Panics in the United States in the 1930s: Some Lessons for Today', in N. Crafts and P. Fearon (eds), *The Great Depression of the 1930s: Lessons for Today*. Oxford: Oxford University Press.

Bordo, M. D., Goldin, C., and White, E. N. (1998), 'The Defining Moment Hypothesis: The Editors' Introduction', in Bordo, M. D., Goldin, C., and White, E. N. (eds), *The Defining Moment: The Great Depression and the American Economy in the Twentieth Century*. Chicago: University of Chicago Press, 1–20.

Boyer, G. R. and Hatton, T. J. (2002), 'New Estimates of British Unemployment, 1870–1913', *Journal of Economic History*, 62, 643–75.

Broadberry, S. N. (1986), *The British Economy between the Wars: A Macroeconomic Survey*. Oxford: Basil Blackwell.

Broadberry, S. N. (1987), 'Cheap Money and the Housing Boom in Interwar Britain: An Econometric Appraisal', *The Manchester School*, 55, 378–89.

Brown, E. C. (1956), 'Fiscal Policy in the Thirties: A Reappraisal', *American Economic Review*, 46, 857–79.

Brown, W. A. Jr (1940), *The International Gold Standard Reinterpreted, 1914–1934*. New York: National Bureau of Economic Research.

Calomiris, C. W. (2013), 'The Political Lessons of Depression-era Banking Reform', in N. Crafts and P. Fearon (eds), *The Great Depression of the 1930s: Lessons for Today*. Oxford: Oxford University Press.

Calomiris, C. W. and Mason, J. R. (2003), 'Consequences of Bank Distress during the Great Depression', *American Economic Review*, 93, 937–47.

Calomiris, C. W. and White, E. N. (1994), 'The Origins of Federal Deposit Insurance', in C. Goldin and G. Libecap (eds), *The Regulated Economy: A Historical Approach to Political Economy*. Chicago: University of Chicago Press, 145–88.

Calomiris, C., Mason, J., and Wheelock, D. (2011), 'Did Doubling Reserve Requirements Cause the Recession of 1937/8? A Microeconomic Approach', NBER Working Paper No. 16688.

Carter, S. B., Gartner, S. S., Haines, M. R., Olmstead, A. L., Sutch, R., and Wright, G. (2006), *Historical Statistics of the United States*. Cambridge: Cambridge University Press.

Chadha, J. S. and Dimsdale, N. H. (1999), 'A Long View of Real Rates', *Oxford Review of Economic Policy*, 15(2), 17–45.

Clarke, S. V. O. (1967), *Central Bank Cooperation, 1924–31*. New York: Federal Reserve Bank.

Cohn, R. L. (1992), 'Fiscal Policy in Germany during the Great Depression', *Explorations in Economic History*, 29, 318–42.

De Bromhead, A., Eichengreen, B., and O'Rourke, K. (2012), 'Right-wing Political Extremism in the Great Depression', NBER Working Paper No. 17871.

Dimsdale, N. H. (1981), 'British Monetary Policy and the Exchange Rate, 1920–1938', *Oxford Economic Papers*, 33 (2, supplement), 306–49

Dimsdale, N. H. and Horsewood, N. (1995), 'Fiscal Policy and Employment in Interwar Britain: Some Evidence from a New Model', *Oxford Economic Papers*, 47, 369–96.

Eggertsson, G. (2008), 'Great Expectations and the End of the Depression', *American Economic Review*, 98, 1476–516.

Eggertsson, G. B. (2012), 'Was the New Deal Contractionary?', *American Economic Review*, 102, 524–55.

Eichengreen, B. (1989), 'The Political Economy of the Smoot–Hawley Tariff', *Research in Economic History*, 12, 1–43.

Eichengreen, B. (1992), *Golden Fetters: The Gold Standard and the Great Depression, 1919–1939*. New York: Oxford University Press.

Eichengreen, B. and Hatton, T. J. (1988), 'Interwar Unemployment in International Perspective: An Overview', in B. Eichengreen and T. J. Hatton (eds), *Interwar Unemployment in International Perspective*. London: Kluwer Academic Publishers, 1–59.

Eichengreen, B. and Irwin, D. A. (2010), 'The Slide to Protectionism in the Great Depression: Who Succumbed and Why?', *Journal of Economic History*, 70, 871–97.

Eichengreen, B. and Jeanne, O. (1998), 'Currency Crisis and Unemployment: Sterling in 1931', NBER Working Paper No. 6563.

Eichengreen, B. and O'Rourke, K. (2010), 'What Do the New Data Tell Us?', <http://www.voxeu.org/index.php> (accessed 12 September 2012).

Eichengreen, B. and O'Rourke, K. (2012), 'A Tale of Two Depressions Redux', <http://www.voxeu.org/index.php> (accessed 12 September 2012).

Eichengreen, B. and Sachs, J. (1985), 'Exchange Rates and Economic Recovery in the 1930s', *Journal of Economic History*, 45, 925–46.

Eichengreen, B. and Temin, P. (2013), 'Fetters of Gold and Paper', in N. Crafts and P. Fearon (eds), *The Great Depression of the1930s: Lessons for Today*. Oxford: Oxford University Press.

Feinstein, C. H. (1972), *National Income, Expenditure and Output of the United Kingdom 1855–1965*. Cambridge: Cambridge University Press.

Feinstein, C. H., Temin P., and Toniolo, G. (1997), *The European Economy Between the Wars*. Oxford: Oxford University Press.

Field, A. J. (2003), 'The Most Technologically Progressive Decade of the Century', *American Economic Review*, 93, 1399–413.

Field, A. J. (2011), *A Great Leap Forward: 1930s Depression and US Economic Growth*. New Haven: Yale University Press.

Field, A. J. (2013), 'Economic Growth and Recovery in the United States, 1919–1941', in N. Crafts and P. Fearon (eds), *The Great Depression of the 1930s: Lessons for Today*. Oxford: Oxford University Press.

Findlay, R. and O'Rourke, K. H. (2007), *Power and Plenty: Trade, War, and the World Economy in the Second Millennium*. Princeton: Princeton University Press.

Fishback, P. (2007), 'The New Deal', in Fishback, P. (ed.) *Government and the American Economy: A New History*. Chicago: University of Chicago Press, 384–430.

Fishback, P. (2013), 'US Monetary and Fiscal Policy in the 1930s', in N. Crafts and P. Fearon (eds), *The Great Depression of the 1930s: Lessons for Today*. Oxford: Oxford University Press.

Fishback, P. and Wallis, J. J. (2013), 'What Was New about the New Deal?', in N. Crafts and P. Fearon (eds), *The Great Depression of the 1930s: Lessons for Today*. Oxford: Oxford University Press.

Flacco, P. R. and Parker, R. E. (1992), 'Income Uncertainty and the Onset of the Great Depression', *Economic Inquiry*, 30, 154–71.

Friedman, M. and Schwartz, A. (1963), *A Monetary History of the United States, 1867–1960*. Princeton: Princeton University Press.

Garside, W. R. (1998), 'Party Politics, Political Economy and British Protectionism, 1919–1932', *History*, 83, 47–65.

Gordon, R. J. and Wilcox, J. A. (1981), 'Monetarist Interpretations of the Great Depression: An Evaluation and Critique', in K. Brunner (ed.), *The Great Depression Revisited*. The Hague: Martinus Nijhoff Publishing, 49–107.

Grossman, R. (1994), 'The Shoe that Didn't Drop: Explaining Banking Stability During the Great Depression', *Journal of Economic History*, 54, 654–82.

Grossman, R. S. (2010), *Unsettled Account*. Princeton: Princeton University Press.

Hamilton, J. (1987), 'Monetary Factors in the Great Depression', *Journal of Monetary Economics*, 19, 145–69.

Hannah, L. and Temin, P. (2010), 'Long-Term Supply-Side Implications of the Great Depression', *Oxford Review of Economic Policy*, 26, 561–80.

Hatton, T. J. and Thomas, M. (2013), 'Labour Markets in Recession and Recovery: The UK and the USA in the 1920s and 1930s', in N. Crafts and P. Fearon (eds), *The Great Depression of the 1930s: Lessons for Today*. Oxford: Oxford University Press.

Howson, S. K. (1975), *Domestic Monetary Management in Britain, 1919–1938*. Cambridge: Cambridge University Press.

Howson, S. K. (1980), 'The Management of Sterling, 1932–1939', *Journal of Economic History*, 40, 53–60.

Irwin, D. A. (1998), 'From Smoot–Hawley to Reciprocal Trade Agreements: Changing the Course of US Trade Policy in the 1930s', in Bordo, M. D., Goldin, C., and White, E. N., *The Defining Moment: The Great Depression and the American Economy in the Twentieth Century*. Chicago: University of Chicago Press, 325–52.

Irwin, D. A. (2010), 'Did France Cause the Great Depression?', NBER Working Paper No. 16350.

Irwin, D. A. (2011), *Peddling Protectionism: Smoot–Hawley and the Great Depression*. Princeton: Princeton University Press.

Irwin, D. A. (2012), *Trade Policy Disaster: Lessons from the 1930s*. Cambridge, Mass.: MIT Press.

James, H. (1986), *The German Slump: Politics and Economics, 1924–1936*. Oxford: Clarendon Press.

Keynes, J. M. (1931), 'An Economic Analysis of Unemployment', in Q. Wright (ed.), *Unemployment as a World Problem*. Chicago: University of Chicago Press.

League of Nations (1931), *The Course and Phases of the World Economic Depression*. Geneva: Secretariat of the League of Nations.

League of Nations (1933), *World Economic Survey, 1932–33*. Geneva: Secretariat of the League of Nations.

League of Nations (1941), *Statistical Yearbook, 1940/1*. Geneva: Secretariat of the League of Nations.

Lewis, C. (1938), *America's Stake in International Investments*. Washington DC: The Brookings Institution.

Maddison, A. (1985), *Two Crises: Latin America and Asia 1929–38 and 1973–83*. Paris: OECD.

Maddison, A. (2010), *Historical Statistics of the World Economy, 1–2008 AD*. <http://www.ggdc.net/maddison> (accessed September 2012).

Meltzer, A. H. (2003), *A History of the Federal Reserve: Volume 1, 1913–1951*. Chicago: University of Chicago Press.

Middleton, R. (1985), *Towards the Managed Economy*. London: Methuen.

Middleton, R. (1996), *Government versus the Market*. Cheltenham: Edward Elgar.

Middleton, R. (2010), 'British Monetary and Fiscal Policy in the 1930s', *Oxford Review of Economic Policy*, 26, 414–41.

Middleton, R. (2013), 'Can Contractionary Fiscal Policy Be Expansionary? Consolidation, Sustainability, and Fiscal Policy Impact in Britain in the 1930s', in N. Crafts and P. Fearon (eds), *The Great Depression of the 1930s: Lessons for Today*. Oxford: Oxford University Press.

Minsky, H. P. (1982), *Can 'It' Happen Again? Essays on Instability and Finance*. Armonk, New York: M. E. Sharpe.

Mintz, I. (1951), *Deterioration in the Quality of Foreign Bonds Issued in the United States, 1920–1930*. New York: NBER.

Mishkin, F. S. (2010), 'Over the Cliff: From the Subprime to the Global Financial Crisis', NBER Working Paper 16609.

Mitchell, B. R. (1988), *British Historical Statistics.* Cambridge: Cambridge University Press.

Mitchener, K. J. and Mason, J. (2013), '"Blood and Treasure": Exiting the Great Depression and Lessons for Today', in N. Crafts and P. Fearon (eds), *The Great Depression of the 1930s: Lessons for Today.* Oxford: Oxford University Press.

O'Brien, A. P. (1989), 'A Behavioral Explanation for Nominal Wage Rigidity during the Great Depression', *Quarterly Journal of Economics,* 104, 719–35.

Obstfeld, M. and Taylor, A. M. (1998), 'The Great Depression as a Watershed: International Capital Mobility over the Long Run', in Bordo, M. D., Goldin, C., and White, E. N., *The Defining Moment: The Great Depression and the American Economy in the Twentieth Century.* Chicago: University of Chicago Press, 353–402.

Ohanian, L. E. (2009), 'What—or Who—Started the Great Depression?', *Journal of Economic Theory,* 144, 2310–35.

Olney, M. L. (1999), 'The Role of Credit in the Consumption Collapse of 1930', *Quarterly Journal of Economics,* 114, 319–35.

Peppers, L. (1973), 'Full Employment Surplus Analysis and Structural Change: The 1930s', *Explorations in Economic History,* 10, 197–210.

Raff, D. and Summers, L. (1987), 'Did Henry Ford Pay Efficiency Wages?', *Journal of Labor Economics,* 5, S57–86.

Redmond, J. (1984), 'The Sterling Overvaluation in 1925: A Multilateral Approach', *Economic History Review,* 37, 520–32.

Reinhart, C. and Rogoff, K. (2009), *This Time is Different.* Princeton: Princeton University Press.

Reinhart, C. M. (2010), 'This Time is Different Chartbook: Country Histories on Debt, Default, and Financial Crises', NBER Working Paper No. 15815.

Ritschl, A. (2002), *Deutschlands Krise und Konjunktur, 1924–1934.* Berlin: Akademie-Verlag.

Ritschl, A. (2003), '"Dancing on a Volcano": The Economic Recovery and Collapse of Weimar Germany', in T. Balderston (ed.), *The World Economy and National Economies in the Interwar Slump.* Basingstoke: Palgrave Macmillan, 105–42.

Ritschl, A. (2013), 'Reparations, Deficits and Debt Default: The Great Depression in Germany', in N. Crafts and P. Fearon (eds), *The Great Depression of the 1930s: Lessons for Today.* Oxford: Oxford University Press.

Romer, C. (1990), 'The Great Crash and the Onset of the Great Depression', *Quarterly Journal of Economics,* 105, 597–624.

Romer, C. (1992), 'What Ended the Great Depression?', *Journal of Economic History,* 52, 757–84.

Romer, C. (1999), 'Why Did Prices Rise in the 1930s?', *Journal of Economic History,* 59, 167–99.

Romer, C. (2009), 'The Economic Crisis: Causes, Policies and Outlook', Testimony before the Joint Economic Committee, 30 April.

Ronge, U. (2002), *Die Langfriste Rendite Deutcher Standardaktien, 1870 bis 1959.* Frankfurt am Main, New York: Lang.

Roose, K. D. (1954), *The Economics of Recession and Revival: An Interpretation of 1937–38.* New Haven: Yale University Press.

Rose, J. D. (2010), 'Hoover's Truce: Wage Rigidity in the Onset of the Great Depression', *Journal of Economic History,* 70, 843–70.

Schuker, S. (1988), *American Reparations to Germany, 1924–1933.* Princeton: Princeton University Press.

Smiley, G. (2002), *Rethinking the Great Depression.* Chicago: Ivan R. Dee.

Solomou, S. (1996), *Themes in Macroeconomic History.* Cambridge: Cambridge University Press.

Stein, H. (1988), *Presidential Economics: The Making of Economic Policy from Roosevelt to Reagan and Beyond*. Washington DC: American Enterprise Institute for Public Policy Research.

Sturzenegger, F. and Zettelmeyer, J. (2007), *Debt Defaults and Lessons from a Decade of Crises*. Cambridge, Mass.: MIT Press.

Telser, L. G. (2001), 'Higher Member Bank Reserve Ratios in 1936 and 1937 Did Not Cause the Relapse into Depression', *Journal of Post Keynesian Economics*, 24, 205–16.

Temin, P. (1976), *Did Monetary Forces Cause the Great Depression?*. New York: Norton.

Temin, P. (1989), *Lessons from the Great Depression*. London: MIT Press.

Temin, P. (1993), 'Transmission of the Great Depression', *Journal of Economic Perspectives*, 7, 87–102.

Temin, P. and Wigmore, B. A. (1990), 'The End of One Big Deflation', *Explorations in Economic History*, 27, 483–502.

Thomas, M. (1983), 'Rearmament and Economic Recovery in the Late 1930s', *Economic History Review*, 36, 552–79.

Vedder, R. K. and Gallaway, L. E. (1993), *Out of Work: Unemployment and Government in Twentieth Century America*. New York: Holmes & Meier.

Velde, F. R. (2009), 'The Recession of 1937: A Cautionary Tale', *Federal Reserve Bank of Chicago Economic Perspectives*, 4, 16–37.

Wallis, J. J. (2010), 'The Political Economy of the New Deal', *Oxford Review of Economic Policy*, 26, 442–62.

Weir, D. R. (1992), 'A Century of US Unemployment, 1890–1990: Revised Estimates and Evidence for Stabilization', *Research in Economic History*, 14, 301–46.

Wheelock, D. C. (2010), 'Lessons Learned?: Comparing the Federal Reserve's Responses to the Crises of 1932–33 and 2007–2009', *Federal Reserve Bank of St. Louis Review*, 92, March/April, 89–107.

Williamson, P. (1992), *National Crisis and National Government: British Politics, the Economy and Empire, 1926–1932*. New York: Cambridge University Press.

Wolf, H. C. and Yousef, T. M. (2007), 'Breaking the Fetters: Why Did Countries Exit the Interwar Gold Standard?', in T. J. Hatton, K. H. O'Rourke, and A. M. Taylor (eds), *The New Comparative Economic History*. Cambridge, Mass.: MIT Press, 241–65.

Wolf, N. (2008), 'Scylla and Charybdis: Explaining Europe's Exit from Gold, January 1928 to December 1936', *Explorations in Economic History*, 45, 383–401.

Wolf, N. (2013), 'Europe's Great Depression: Coordination Failure after the First World War', in N. Crafts and P. Fearon (eds), *The Great Depression of the 1930s: Lessons for Today*. Oxford: Oxford University Press.

Worswick, G. D. N. (1984), 'The Sources of Recovery in the UK in the 1930s', *National Institute Economic Review*, 110, 85–93.

2

The 1930s: Understanding the Lessons

Nicholas Crafts and Peter Fearon

2.1. INTRODUCTION

Having described the evolution of depression and recovery in the 1930s, we now turn to a more technical analysis framed with a view to deriving lessons for the making of economic policy. The relevance of this for today is underlined by the recent economic crisis and its aftermath together with widespread doubts about the value of modern macroeconomics and its ahistorical character. We organize our analysis on the basis of addressing a series of questions by way of providing a review of the main results in the research literature while at the same time highlighting important points made in the contributions to this volume. From this survey, we then go on to set out the key lessons with regard both to crisis management and returning to growth post-crisis.

2.2. ANALYSIS

2.2.1. What caused the downturn?

Economic historians have traditionally viewed the large falls in real GDP that happened in the Great Depression as the result of large aggregate demand shocks. We think this is still appropriate and will identify the main sources of these shocks.[1] However, the translation of adverse shifts in aggregate demand into an impact on output as well as the price level implies that the aggregate supply curve

[1] Until relatively recently, this was also commonplace among macroeconomists even those of a strong neoclassical persuasion. Since Cole and Ohanian (1999) there have been attempts to explain the Great Depression in a real business cycle (RBC) framework. This would naturally look to adverse TFP shocks as the recessionary impulse. In common with most economic historians, for example Inklaar et al. (2011), Pensieroso (2007) and Temin (2008), we do not believe that this venture has been successful. The strong point of RBC modelling of the 1930s has been to point out and seek to quantify impacts of the New Deal on aggregate supply during the recovery phase (Cole and Ohanian, 2004). Indeed, in that tradition the term 'Great Depression' is applied to the whole of the 1930s for the United States on the grounds that, despite quite a strong recovery after 1933, real GDP remained well below what would have been predicted on the basis of 1920s trend growth.

was non-vertical and the reasons for this need to be explored. Moreover, it is now generally accepted that the shocks which started the downward spiral were greatly amplified by the financial crises which characterized the early 1930s. A further key aspect of the Great Depression is that recessionary impulses were not immediately countered by an effective policy response and this also has to be explained. Here a central role was played by the gold standard, the fixed exchange rate system, of which all the major economies were members at the end of the 1920s.

The most important source of shocks to the world economy from the late 1920s onwards was the United States. This was not only because the collapse in output in the world's largest economy was spectacular but also because other countries responded to deflationary changes in American monetary policy notably at the end of the 1920s (Eichengreen, 2004). At least since Friedman and Schwartz (1963), monetary policy errors have been blamed by many economists; the M1 measure of the money supply fell by over 25 per cent between 1929 and 1933 and it is generally agreed that, notwithstanding the constraints of the gold standard, at least through early 1932 there was scope for the Federal Reserve to reverse this decline by an aggressive response. Instead, adhering to the real bills doctrine, it was believed that monetary policy was loose and expansionary policy was inappropriate, even though real interest rates were very high (Fishback, 2013).

It should be noted that there has been some disagreement as to quite how high ex-ante real interest rates were during the downturn as several estimation methods have been used which give different results. Cecchetti (1992) used time-series econometrics to obtain forecasts of the rate of deflation and found that there was such strong persistence in price movements that there should have been no surprise that prices fell so much; this would imply that ex-ante 3-month real interest rates were very high indeed, peaking at about 20 per cent in late 1931 and early 1932. Econometric analyses of actual market behaviour have found, however, that a substantial part of the deflation was unanticipated (Hamilton, 1992; Klug et al., 2005) such that the peak was in the range 5–10 per cent. Either way, these would be very different from what might be expected of a central bank seeking to use monetary policy to combat a severe downturn.

Econometric analysis has supported the view that declines in the money supply tended to have negative effects on real output in the United States in the interwar period; however, the decline in output in the early 1930s was much bigger than would be predicted simply on the basis of the fall in M1 (Gordon and Wilcox, 1981). A major additional factor was the spate of banking crises that engulfed the United States in the early 1930s when more than 9,000 banks failed (comprising about a seventh of total deposits). In a seminal paper, Bernanke (1983) found that adding changes in deposits of failing banks to an equation to predict output based on money and price shocks substantially improved its predictive power; he interpreted this result as an indication that bank failures implied a loss of services of financial intermediation, a 'credit crunch', in which output fell consequent on an adverse shift in the supply of loans.[2] As we know, investment collapsed and lack of credit may have been an important factor.

[2] A disruption of credit supply might be caused by a reduction in intermediaries capital, or in the acceptable degree of leverage, and be reflected in an increase in interest rate spreads between savers and

Subsequent research has strongly supported this hypothesis. Micro-level research into the consequences of bank failures has shown that profit-maximizing banks, faced by increased costs of equity finance, acted to reduce market fears of default by shrinking loans and holding more reserves (Calomiris and Wilson, 2004), that bank failures were highly correlated with subsequent survey findings of unmet credit needs (Carlson and Rose, 2011), and that, at the state level, changes in bank deposits and loans were causally related to changes in incomes during 1930–32 (Calomiris and Mason, 2003a).

Why did the United States have so many bank failures in the early 1930s? Clearly, banking had structural weaknesses and entered the 1930s with a weak financial system, under-capitalized, taking excessive risks, and based on unit rather than branch banking. The probability that a bank would fail strongly reflected fundamentals and insolvency stemming from ex-ante balance-sheet weakness rather than panic (Calomiris and Mason, 2003b). Moreover, high failure rates reflected weaknesses in regulation, notably with regard to lenient capital adequacy requirements and the prohibition of branch banking, and prudential supervision, in particular because of inadequate standards at the state level. Indeed, Mitchener (2007) estimated that the bank failure rate might have been halved had regulatory and supervisory practices across states improved by one standard deviation.

That said, it must also be recognized that local macroeconomic conditions mattered for bank failures according to the survival model estimated by Calomiris and Mason (2003b), and that the baseline hazard of failure reflected the actions of the Fed as lender of last resort as is suggested by the large fraction of failures attributed to illiquidity rather than insolvency by bank examiners. This is suggested by the pattern of bank failures in Mississippi in 1930/1, a state which was divided between the Atlanta and St Louis Fed districts. At that time, unusually, the Atlanta Fed was an energetic lender of last resort but St Louis was not. Richardson and Troost (2009) found that bank suspension and failure rates were much higher in the St Louis division of the state in 1930/1 whereas at other times there was no difference.

Similarly, Bordo and Landon-Lane (1913) in a VAR (vector auto-regression) analysis of bank failures using the bank examiners' reports find that, had the Fed acted aggressively to supply liquidity, the waves of banking failures of the early 1930s in the United States could have been largely averted, as Friedman and Schwartz (1963) famously claimed. The incorporation of a financial sector into a DSGE (dynamic stochastic general equilibrium) model of the interwar American economy gives similar insights. Christiano et al. (2003) found that shocks that raise liquidity preference (reduce bank deposits relative to currency holdings) lower funds for investment and contribute to a non-neutral debt deflation, but that a monetary policy rule that responded to these money demand shocks could have limited the fall in real GDP in the early 1930s to only about 6 per cent.

Where does the Wall Street Crash fit into this story? To the person in the street, the collapse of stock market prices is surely the iconic aspect of the Great

borrowers leading to a reduction in the volume of lending at any credit spread. This is equivalent to a (perhaps considerable) inward shift of the IS curve (Woodford, 2010).

Depression. The Dow Jones industrial index fell from 381 to 198 between the peak, in early September, and mid-November 1929; while from the peak to the trough in 1932 about 5/6th was wiped off stock market values. The crash in the autumn of 1929 included the infamous Black Thursday and Black Tuesday (24 and 29 October). In contrast, economists and economic historians have generally thought that the Wall Street Crash played, at most, a minor role in the downturn. In part, this is because the fundamental value of a share reflects the discounted present value of future earnings and is thus an endogenous variable. That said, share price indices exhibit 'excess volatility'—they jump about much more than can be explained by an efficient markets hypothesis (Shiller, 2003)—and probably were quite a bit 'too high' ex-ante in 1929.[3] So there is scope to think in terms of an exogenous shock to share prices. The question then is how much effect might this have had on the real economy. The answer is probably a small impact on consumption through wealth effects and postponement of durables as a response to increased uncertainty (Romer, 1990). There is good evidence that increases in uncertainty affected investment quite significantly through increased risk premia, but, that said, this does not seem to result from discrete events like the stock market crash (Ferderer and Zalewski, 1994). So, overall, the impact of the Wall Street Crash on the real American economy was probably quite modest in comparison with that of monetary policy and banking crises.

In sum, the collapse in American economic activity was the result of large shocks, both monetary and IS, to aggregate demand interacting with a fragile financial system so as to magnify the impact. Discretionary policy responses were, at best, too little too late while automatic stabilizers were very weak in an economy with a small federal budget together with low tax rates and transfer payments. Although nominal interest rates fell by several percentage points, ex-post real interest rates rose steeply while bank failures and declining asset prices delivered a credit crunch.

For the typical small open economy in the rest of the world, the big problem, as the depression took hold, was being subjected to deflationary pressure as world output and prices fell while being severely constrained in policymaking by membership of the gold standard. The concept of the macroeconomic trilemma tells us that such a country can only have two of a fixed exchange rate, capital mobility and an independent monetary policy. This last was typically given up while the gold standard prevailed, although in the globalization backlash that ensued capital controls were very widely adopted. It follows that a monetary policy response to the deflationary shocks needed to be coordinated across countries (thereby allowing interest rate differentials to remain unchanged) but, as Wolf (2013) explains, international coordination was out of the question. Indeed, non-cooperative behaviour was the order of the day epitomized by France's accumulation and sterilization of gold reserves (Irwin, 2010).

Besides having no control over monetary policy, staying on the gold standard required reductions in prices and money wages to maintain competitiveness, and,

[3] Whether there was a 'bubble' in the 1929 stock market has been controversial. The most persuasive evidence that there was a substantial bubble comes from the pricing of loans to stock brokers and the valuation of closed-end mutual funds; see Rappoport and White (1993) and De Long and Shleifer (1991).

as adjustment took place, entailed high real interest rates and increases in real labour costs (Newell and Symons, 1988). It is implicit in this discussion that the aggregate supply curve is positively sloped rather than vertical so that aggregate demand shocks have output as well as price-level effects. This seems to be borne out by the evidence. Bernanke and Carey (1996), in a careful panel-data econometric study, found both that there was an inverse relationship between real wages and output and that this reflected incomplete (and indeed quite sticky) nominal wage adjustment in the presence of aggregate demand shocks. The severity and duration of the downturn was increased the longer a country stayed on the gold standard (Bernanke, 1995). Decisions whether to leave the gold standard were influenced by the strength of worries about loss of monetary discipline and the degree of pain in terms of price falls and devaluations by important trading partners (Wolf, 2008).

Staying on the gold standard also increased the risk of a banking crisis as balance sheets deteriorated, although these crises were experienced in many countries and were associated with weaknesses in banking systems as well as the deflationary pressures which stressed them (Grossman, 1994). Banking crises were bad for the real economy and countries which went through them were exposed to much larger decreases in real output; the median banking crisis lasting a year lowered industrial output by 12 per cent according to the estimates in Bernanke and Carey (1996).

These themes have resonance for Britain, which was exposed to a substantial aggregate demand shock after 1929 triggered by big declines in exports leading to falls in both output and prices (Broadberry, 1986a). Interest rates were kept high to safeguard gold standard membership. Against a background of great anxiety about fiscal sustainability in the context of a high public debt to GDP ratio resulting from World War I—worries which were seriously exacerbated by price deflation—the fiscal policy response by 1931 was to override the automatic stabilizers and seek to return towards a balanced budget (Middleton, 2013). An inability to agree on the mix of fiscal consolidation ended in resignation of the minority Labour administration and a new National Government in August 1931, but Britain then experienced a 'second-generation' currency crisis in September 1931 leading to forced exit from the gold standard as markets perceived reluctance to raise interest rates further to defend the pound, given that unemployment was already very high (Eichengreen and Jeanne, 1998). British unemployment was already substantial in the 'good times' of the 1920s as labour market institutions and policies sustained a high NAIRU (non-accelerating inflation rate of unemployment) (Hatton and Thomas, 2013). However, the deflationary shock interacted with the inflexibility of wage and price-setting behaviour to create a difficult adjustment problem during which unemployment rose considerably as real-product wages increased markedly (Dimsdale et al., 1989).

While Britain experienced no more than a severe recession in the early 1930s, the slump in Germany was of American proportions and real GDP fell by 25 per cent between 1929 and 1932. This suggests that, in addition to external shocks, initial conditions in the domestic economy and policy responses were important determinants of the extent of the downturn. The acute difficulties in formulating German macroeconomic policy resulted from reparations, the legacy of the hyperinflation, the weaknesses of German banks, and substantial foreign borrowing in the later

1920s. Germany was exposed to a 'sudden stop' in capital inflows in 1929 in the context of fears about fiscal sustainability and excessive risk taking by German banks, which culminated in the twin banking and currency crisis of 1931 and foreign exchange controls (Ritschl, 2013; Schnabel, 2004). A substantial fiscal consolidation was undertaken between 1929 and 1932 (Cohn, 1992) while the money supply contracted by 30 per cent between 1930 and 1933 (James, 1984).

The ratio of foreign debt to GDP was about 80 per cent in 1929 and 100 per cent in mid-1931 with slightly more than half from reparations liabilities (and less than half from commercial liabilities). Faced with a desperate fiscal position, in which issuing bonds was no longer viable and monetizing the debt was precluded if the terms of the 1924 stabilization were maintained, Germany faced a difficult choice as to whether to default and devalue or to pursue austerity policies and hope reparations would be cancelled; as is well-known, chancellor Brüning opted for the latter approach, a course of action which was defended by Borchardt (1990) as virtually dictated by the pre-history of the Great Depression. As with Britain, the deflationary shock had a large effect on unemployment because of wage inflexibility (Ritschl, 2013).

2.2.2. What drove the recovery?

The decline in economic activity across the world came to an end in 1932/3, although there were substantial output gaps for a long time afterwards. Changes in economic policy played a major role in promoting economic recovery on the demand side and to some extent by inhibiting it on the supply-side. Banking crises became relatively infrequent. Central to the way in which recovery came about was the abandonment of the gold standard which had largely occurred by the spring of 1933 and was complete by the autumn of 1936.

On average, the earlier a country did this the less deep was the downturn and the sooner recovery began, as was first shown in a very influential paper by Eichengreen and Sachs (1985) and has subsequently been confirmed for wider samples of advanced and middle income countries by Bernanke (1995) and Campa (1990).[4] Bernanke (1995) points to leaving gold as permitting monetary expansion and leading to big declines in real interest rates. In principle, going off gold also allowed countries with balance of payments deficits to escape from the deflationary pressures on fiscal policy that, with sterilization of monetary inflows in surplus economies, bore heavily as they tried to prevent a currency crisis (Eichengreen and Temin, 2013). This might have allowed temporary fiscal stimulus to promote recovery but, as Wolf (2013) explains, for a variety of reasons, including continued fear of inflation, many countries were reluctant to follow this path in the first half of the 1930s.

Having left the gold standard at a time when prices were falling, interest rates in countries like the UK and the USA quickly approached the zero lower bound

[4] As Capie (2013) points out, the logic goes even further in that Spain, which did not join the gold standard, was largely protected from the economic crisis.

(ZLB). As is well-known, this is a special situation with important implications for the conduct of macroeconomic policy. Consider inflation targeting as practised by using a Taylor Rule. The central bank raises short-term interest rates if inflation is above target or if the 'output gap' is negative. Conversely, interest rates would be reduced if inflation is below target or if GDP is below the sustainable level.[5]

Inflation targeting using a Taylor Rule runs into difficulties when it requires that the nominal interest rate be negative. This is the ZLB constraint. This is most likely to matter in times of deflation or severe recession, especially if this is associated with a banking crisis and credit crunch which might imply that r^* and α are negative (Woodford, 2010). This suggests either that a strategy has to be devised to lower real interest rates by creating inflationary expectations and/or that it may be necessary to use expansionary fiscal policy. Fiscal stimulus may be expected generally to have a larger multiplier effect when interest rates are held constant at the lower bound, as recent discussions have emphasized. One way in which this may work is when a deficit-financed increase in government spending leads expectations of inflation to increase. Simulated examples of fiscal stimulus in 'great depression' conditions suggest values in excess of two may be observed (Woodford, 2011).

Real interest rates can be negative; the central bank can stimulate the economy by holding its nominal interest rate down while encouraging people to expect inflation. Indeed, this is the classic recipe for escaping the so-called 'liquidity trap'. Reductions in the real interest rate sustained over a period of time can act as an expansionary policy so monetary policy is not impotent when interest rates hit the ZLB.[6] This may be easier said than done, however, since there is a problem of time inconsistency; the central bank has to be seen to be credibly committed to future inflation. One way to do this might be through exchange rate policy. Svensson (2003) suggested that a 'foolproof' way to escape the liquidity trap is to combine a price-level target path with an initial currency devaluation and a crawling exchange rate peg which will require a higher price level in equilibrium and can be underpinned by creating domestic currency to purchase foreign exchange.

In the United States, recovery after 1933 can be characterized as strong but incomplete. In the four years 1933 to 1937, real GDP rose by 36 per cent compared with a fall of 27 per cent in the previous four years, taking the level in 1937 back to about 5 per cent above that of 1929. Assuming trend growth at the pre-1929 rate, however, there was still an output gap of some 25 per cent.

[5] The Taylor Rule can be written as $R_S = \alpha + \beta(\pi - \pi^*) + \gamma(Y - Y^*)$ where π and π^* are the actual inflation rate and the target inflation rate, respectively, and $(Y - Y^*)$ is the difference between real GDP and the sustainable level of real GDP. The standard values for β and γ are 1.5 and 0.5, respectively. The term $\alpha = r^* + \pi^*$ where r^* is the (neutral) real interest rate that is consistent with maintaining aggregate demand at a level consistent with a zero output gap.

[6] The central bank can manipulate short term interest rates, but long term interest rates matter for investment decisions. Given that long term rates must reflect the expected sequence of short term rates through time which it can control, the central bank can also affect long term rates but generally with less certainty because it may be less successful in influencing expectations and markets have to take a view on how the authorities will respond to inflation in future. It follows that the central bank can influence long term real rates but less easily than short term nominal rates. For a review of these topics which concludes that policy matters for both short- and long-term real interest rates, see Allsopp and Glyn (1999).

However, we should remember that the population grew from 121.8m in 1929 to 128.9m in 1937. As a result, real GDP per capita was considerably below its 1929 level in 1937 and did not exceed it until 1941. From 1933, the New Deal swung into action with its alphabet soup of public-spending initiatives. It is natural to assume that this represented a substantial Keynesian fiscal stimulus but, as has been known since the calculations of Brown (1956) and Peppers (1973), this was not the case.

Fishback (2013) points out that the New Deal was largely financed by tax increases and he notes that the direct effects of fiscal stimulus were at most a very small part of the recovery. The federal deficit in 1936 was about 5.5 per cent of GDP and between 1933 and 1936 the discretionary increase probably amounted to around half of this figure. So, fiscal policy was not really tried. Would it have worked? This turns on the value of the fiscal multiplier. Gordon and Krenn (2010) provide a recent estimate of 1.8 based on a VAR analysis but their method may not be reliable, as Ramey (2011) has pointed out.[7] At this point, the size of the multiplier remains unclear.

Romer (1992) argued that the main stimulus to recovery in the United States was in fact monetary not fiscal policy, noting very rapid growth in the monetary base and M1 after 1933. This was driven by (largely-unsterilized) gold inflows after the United States left the gold standard. M1 grew at nearly 10 per cent per year between 1933 and 1937 and Romer estimated that this was sufficient to raise real GDP in 1937 by about 25 per cent compared with what would have happened under normal monetary growth. She found a large reduction in real interest rates from 1933 and concluded that this had favourable impacts on investment spending.[8] By implication, the positive effect of monetary policy on nominal GDP was a major reason why the federal debt to GDP ratio only went up from 16 per cent in 1929 to 44 per cent in 1939.

This account needs to be supplemented by explicitly considering how the United States escaped the liquidity trap, i.e., delivered monetary stimulus despite interest rates at the lower bound. The key here was 'regime change', as was originally stressed by Temin and Wigmore (1990). They argue that leaving the gold standard was a clear signal that the deflationary period was over. Eggertsson (2008), working with a standard DSGE model, built on this and provided some quantification. His argument is that Roosevelt's several actions on taking office, comprising leaving gold, announcing an objective of restoring the prices to pre-depression levels, and implementing New Deal spending, amounted to a credible policy that delivered a major change in inflationary expectations which drove down real interest rates and raised the expected money supply, i.e. the classic recipe for escaping the liquidity trap.[9] Eggertsson's calibration implied that the regime change accounted for about three-quarters of the recovery in output between 1933 and 1937. Subsequently, Eggertsson (2012) has argued that the

[7] Ramey (2011) notes that their method does not control for anticipation of future large increases in government spending, which could explain the observation of large increases in output in response to what seems to be a modest rise in government spending.

[8] It is generally agreed that ex-ante real interest rates fell substantially and that inflation forecasts were much more accurate post-1933, see for example Klug et al. (2005).

[9] So leaving the gold standard was necessary but not sufficient to deliver the 'regime change'.

New Deal also created expectations of an increase in the price level by its impact on market power through the National Industrial Recovery Act (NIRA) (1933) which would have further raised output at the ZLB. Interestingly, this analysis makes the New Deal a major factor in promoting recovery, but via its indirect effects in changing inflationary expectations rather than through a traditional Keynesian fiscal stimulus.

It should be recognized that the conventional wisdom on the New Deal is that it had adverse supply-side effects, notably through its impact on the labour market, and that its overall effect on recovery may well have been negative. The NIRA and later the National Labor Relations Act (1935) were intended to increase the bargaining power of workers vis-à-vis employers and to prevent nominal wage declines. A number of papers using different empirical methodologies have concluded that real wages were increased quite significantly (Bernanke, 1986; Bordo et al., 2000). Hatton and Thomas (2013) suggest that the New Deal may well have raised the equilibrium level of unemployment considerably; they find that the NAIRU was 12 percentage points higher in the American economy in the 1930s compared with the 1920s. Cole and Ohanian (2004), in the RBC tradition, argue that the effect was to raise real wages and unemployment compared with competitive market outcomes and their calibrated model predicts that this could (depending on assumed parameter values) account for a significant part of the shortfall of output in 1937 relative to the pre-1929 trend.[10]

An important ingredient in recovery in the United States was rehabilitation of the banking system to put an end to the waves of bank failures and to ease the credit crunch; this was indeed a major priority for legislators. Both re-capitalization and re-regulation of the banks were required. Following a compulsory closure of all banks for three days for inspection of their books, the Roosevelt administration passed an emergency banking act in March 1933 and this was followed by the banking acts of 1933 (Glass–Steagall) and of 1935. About 4,000 banks were declared insolvent and not allowed to re-open after the 'bank holiday'. Inter alia, these banking acts empowered the Reconstruction Finance Corporation (RFC), a government agency, to buy preferred stock in banks with voting rights that frequently entailed effective control, introduced federal deposit insurance, raised minimum capital for Federal Reserve member banks to US$50,000, separated investment from commercial banking, and imposed interest rate ceilings on bank accounts (regulation Q). However, nationwide branch banking continued to be prohibited.

This approach was successful in part, as Mitchener and Mason (2013) discuss. Deposit insurance, made permanent under the auspices of the Federal Deposit Insurance Corporation (FDIC), was important in ending the threat of further bank runs, as theory suggests it should (Diamond and Dybvig, 1983). The RFC provided substantial capital. By March 1934 it owned stock in nearly half of all commercial banks, and in June 1935 it owned more than a third of the capital ($1.3 billion in 6,800 banks) of the American banking system (Olson, 1988). The RFC imposed conditions on banks which were a good substitute for market

[10] This methodology assumes away any effect of the banking crisis on productive potential either in terms of a levels or a growth rate effect and may well exaggerate the role of the New Deal.

discipline on risk taking (Calomiris and Mason, 2003c) and the RFC made money for the American taxpayer. Bank runs ceased and failures returned to normal low levels; the deposits-to-currency ratio which had fallen from 10.9 to 5.1 between 1929 and 1933 went back above 7. Bank lending, however, remained far below pre-depression levels and deposit-to-reserve ratios continued to fall from 13.0 in 1929 to 8.2 in 1933 to 5.0 in 1937, when loans were a little over half but bank capital was over 80 per cent of the 1929 level. This reflected continued efforts by banks to reduce default risk at a time when they found it costly to raise new equity (Calomiris and Wilson, 2004).

The regulatory response to the banking crises, captured by political interest groups intent on preserving unit banking and imbued with the ideology of the real bills doctrine, was highly unsatisfactory (Calomiris, 2013).[11] Calomiris notes that the legislation was designed to support unit banking, yet this was the main structural weakness of the system which inhibited diversification of risks, prevented coordinated responses to shocks, restricted competition, and was a major source of banking instability. However, the difficulties in addressing the unit bank problem should not be minimized. In 1933, 18 states had no branch banks operating at the national or state level (Board of Governors, 1943). The hostility to branch banking would have delayed the passage of this vital legislation if it had incorporated an attack on unit banking. In contrast, the Glass–Steagall Act mandated the separation of commercial and investment banking whereas the evidence is that banks which did both were better diversified and less likely to fail (White, 1986) and that there were no good investor-protection reasons for this legislation (Kroszner and Rajan, 1994). In the longer term, the downside of deposit insurance in terms of encouragement of greater risk taking was an important concern, (especially as banks became 'too-big-to-fail') but politically it was impossible to remove; this might be seen as a significant cost of the ineffectiveness of the Federal Reserve as lender of last resort.

A key issue with macroeconomic policies to promote recovery is when to withdraw monetary and fiscal stimulus and revert to normal bank policy: too soon and a double-dip recession ensues, too late and inflation takes off. These 'exit-strategy' issues are considered by Mitchener and Mason (2013). For the United States, the former problem materialized in 1937/8 when there was a short but severe recession in which real GDP fell by over 10 per cent from peak to trough (see Table 2.1). This seems to have been consequent on a combination of deflationary fiscal and monetary policies being implemented prematurely, in which the latter was probably more important (Velde, 2009). The literature has traditionally pointed to a rise in the full employment surplus by about 3.4 per cent of GDP (Peppers, 1973) as an attempt was made to re-balance the federal budget in the face of increases in the public debt to GDP ratio, together with a doubling by the Fed of banks' reserve requirements between August 1936 and May 1937, as well as the adoption by the Treasury of a policy of sterilizing gold inflows.

[11] The real bills doctrine held that the Federal Reserve should simply supply credit to meet the needs of trade and should not seek to target monetary growth or inflation; adherents believed in the separation of investment and commercial banking.

Table 2.1. Quarterly real GDP

	UK (1930_{Q1} = 100)		USA (1929_{Q3} = 100)
1929_{Q1}	97.5	1930_{Q3}	86.9
1929_{Q2}	98.9	1930_{Q4}	82.8
1929_{Q3}	99.9	1931_{Q1}	83.0
1929_{Q4}	99.9	1931_{Q2}	84.4
1930_{Q1}	100.0	1931_{Q3}	81.1
1930_{Q2}	99.1	1931_{Q4}	77.0
1930_{Q3}	97.8	1932_{Q1}	74.2
1930_{Q4}	95.9	1932_{Q2}	70.6
1931_{Q1}	93.6	1932_{Q3}	68.1
1931_{Q2}	93.1	1932_{Q4}	67.7
1931_{Q3}	**92.8**	**1933_{Q1}**	**63.8**
1931_{Q4}	93.7	1933_{Q2}	68.4
1932_{Q1}	94.0	1933_{Q3}	73.8
1932_{Q2}	93.4	1933_{Q4}	68.6
1932_{Q3}	92.9	1934_{Q1}	72.4
1932_{Q4}	94.6	1934_{Q2}	76.5
1933_{Q1}	94.4	1934_{Q3}	73.3
1933_{Q2}	96.0	1934_{Q4}	73.3
1933_{Q3}	97.6	1935_{Q1}	77.9
1933_{Q4}	99.1	1935_{Q2}	78.2
1934_{Q1}	101.2	1935_{Q3}	80.4
1934_{Q2}	102.6	1935_{Q4}	84.8
1934_{Q3}	103.5	1936_{Q1}	85.2
1934_{Q4}	104.0	1936_{Q2}	90.6
1935_{Q1}	104.3	1936_{Q3}	93.2
1935_{Q2}	106.2	1936_{Q4}	96.3
1935_{Q3}	107.4	1937_{Q1}	95.9
1935_{Q4}	108.5	1937_{Q2}	98.4
1936_{Q1}	109.7	1937_{Q3}	98.0
1936_{Q2}	111.6	1937_{Q4}	91.0
1936_{Q3}	113.0	1938_{Q1}	87.1
1936_{Q4}	113.1	1938_{Q2}	88.6
1937_{Q1}	113.9	1938_{Q3}	93.7
1937_{Q2}	115.6	1938_{Q4}	97.4

Note: Devaluation was in 1931_{Q3} in the UK and 1933_{Q1} in the USA.
Sources: UK: Mitchell et al. (2011); USA: Balke and Gordon (1986).

Recent research has found that the monetary squeeze came from the sterilization policy rather than the reserve requirements and was felt primarily through the monetary base rather than the banks' money multiplier (Irwin, 2011). Banks held large excess reserves and the new requirements were not binding (Calomiris et al., 2011). Eggertsson and Pugsley (2006) stressed that in early 1937 the Roosevelt administration started to sound very hawkish on inflation and suggested that, at least for a while, the impact of this together with the changes in fiscal and monetary policy meant that expectations were undermined, ex-ante real interest rates surged, and there seemed to be a prospect of reverting to the 'Hoover Regime'.[12]

[12] This would mean that the time-inconsistency problem was not actually removed by the New Deal even though this was the basis of the simulation in Eggertsson (2008).

The United Kingdom is an example of a country that took time effectively to exploit its new policy options after the leaving the gold standard. Unlike the United States in 1933, there was no clear 'regime change' with an end to falling prices in the autumn of 1931. By the time the 'cheap money' policy had been devised and started to be implemented, the economy had slipped back into a double-dip recession in the middle of 1932 (see Table 2.1). However, from this point on there was a credible monetary policy stimulus to offset the deflationary impact of ongoing fiscal consolidation.

Booth (1987) argued that from 1932 there was coherence in the Treasury's thinking which deserved the label of a 'managed-economy' approach. The hallmark was a central objective of a steady increase in the price level—which on the assumption that money wages would not react also amounted to reducing real wages and restoring profits—subject to not letting inflation spiral out of control. The rise in the price level would be promoted through cheap money, a weak pound, tariffs, and encouraging firms to exploit their (enhanced) market power, similar to the implications of the New Deal as argued by Eggertsson (2012), but fears of an inflationary surge would be allayed through balancing the budget and intervening if necessary to prevent a currency crisis. The chancellor announced the objective of raising prices at the British Empire Economic Conference at Ottawa in July 1932 and subsequently reiterated it frequently. The fall in the exchange rate from $3.80 in March 1932 to $3.28 in December 1932 is consistent with escaping the liquidity trap in the 'foolproof way', as is the sustained fall in the value of the pound, and the large increase in foreign exchange reserves over the next four years which reflected intervention by the authorities to keep the pound down (Howson, 1980). So market reactions suggest that the cheap money policy quickly became credible.

The 'managed-economy' strategy was clearly quite similar to a price-level target. There was a big reduction in ex-post real interest rates compared with the start of the decade; the real short rate fell from 9.7 per cent in 1931 to 0.7 per cent in 1933 and −2.9 per cent in 1936.[13] On this measure, monetary stimulus was still being provided after nominal interest rates bottomed out. Obviously, this strategy does not represent an irrevocable commitment but it was a credible policy given that the Treasury and the Chancellor of the Exchequer were in charge.[14] Cheap money and a rise in the price level were clearly in the Treasury's interests from 1932 as a route to recovery, better fiscal arithmetic, and to provide an alternative to the Pandora's Box of jettisoning balanced-budget orthodoxy and adopting Keynesianism (Howson, 1975).

The direct effects of cheap money were felt from mid-1932 onwards with reductions in nominal and real interest rates. Business investment responded to lower interest rates (Broadberry, 1986b) while bank lending was largely maintained in a climate of business as usual in the absence of a banking crisis (Billings and Capie, 2011). House-building was the sector most positively affected by the

[13] Based on the estimates underlying the analysis in Chadha and Dimsdale (1999); data kindly provided by Jagjit Chadha.

[14] This would not have been the case had the Bank of England run monetary policy. Governor Norman plainly disliked cheap money and regarded it as a temporary expedient (Howson, 1975: 95).

cheap money policy but was well positioned for a number of other reasons including the behaviour of building societies, permissive land-use planning rules, and a shortfall of investment in the 1920s (Humphries, 1987; Richardson and Aldcroft, 1968). Broadberry (1987) estimated that about half the additional housing investment was on account of lower interest rates. An increasing ratio of rents to construction costs was also favourable but, as Howson (1975) stressed, the leap in house-building only occurred once it was believed that construction costs had bottomed out. Here may be the most concrete illustration of the importance of monetary policy in changing inflationary expectations.

From 1935, there was a second phase of recovery in the United Kingdom which featured a switch to expansionary fiscal policy associated with rearmament; it is plausible that this stimulus had a sizeable multiplier effect. The budget, which had been balanced in 1934, showed a deficit of 3.7 per cent of GDP in 1938 although, interestingly, the ratio of public debt to GDP slowly continued to decline. The formal announcement that the British government intended to re-arm came in the Defence White Paper of March 1935 (Cmd. 4827) and by the end of the year defence spending had risen 28 per cent compared with a year earlier. The ante was upped considerably in February 1937 when the Defence White Paper (Cmd. 5374) warned of expenditure of £1,500 million over the next 5 years, which would be partly deficit-financed, and the Defence Loans Bill, which authorized borrowing of £400 million over 5 years, was approved. Actual defence expenditure rose from a 'peacetime' level of £118 million (at 1938 prices) to £181 million in 1936 and £353 million in 1938.

It is generally believed that this promoted a substantial increase in GDP and employment. Using a social accounting matrix, Thomas (1983) estimated that the fiscal multiplier was about 1.6 in 1938 and that about 1 million jobs were created over the three years after 1935. However, his technique assumes no crowding out—an assumption which is defended informally by reference to contemporary comment on economic conditions. In fact, the best available estimates of the fiscal multiplier suggest it may have been even larger than this. Dimsdale and Horsewood (1995) estimated a structural model comprising both an aggregate demand side based on income-expenditure and an aggregate supply-side based on wage and price equations. They argued that unemployment was above the natural rate throughout the 1930s and their model exhibited very substantial nominal inertia. In simulations holding short-term interest rates constant, their estimate of the multiplier after one year was 1.9, which would imply that increased defence spending raised GDP by about 6 per cent in 1938.

As Middleton (2013) stresses, even if rearmament was a successful de facto 'Keynesian' policy to promote recovery, this does not imply that a similar solution was available in the early 1930s. Given the debt dynamics at a time of deflation, there was a real risk that any move then to fiscal stimulus would have triggered an adverse reaction that raised interest rates as risk premia rose steeply. Moreover, borrowing to meet a military emergency was very different from announcing to markets that the government no longer believed in balanced budgets in peacetime.

Recovery in Germany took place under the Nazis and was notably rapid and sustained compared with the United States which had suffered a similar drop in real GDP; by 1938 real GDP in Germany was 35 per cent above the 1929 level compared with 2 per cent above in the USA. The German experience has

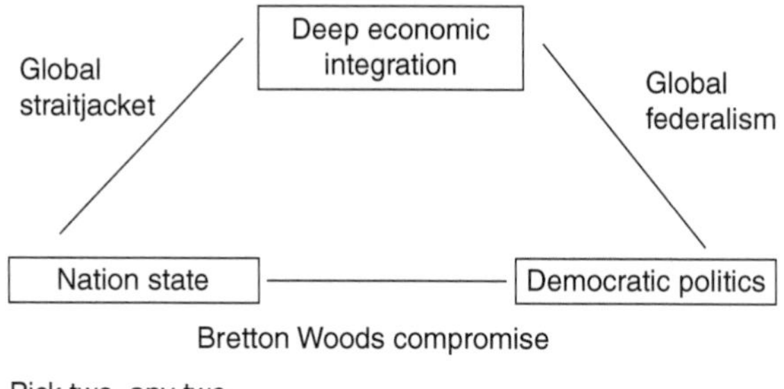

Fig. 2.1. The political trilemma of the world economy (Rodrik, 2000)

sometimes been portrayed as a Keynesian solution to the depression but this is quite misleading. Ritschl (2013) finds a fiscal multiplier of about one and notes that this implies that deficit spending only accounted for a small part of the recovery; indeed the implications of his chapter are that to a large extent recovery in Germany was a spontaneous rebound rather than a policy-driven process. It should also be noted that while deflation ceased and accordingly real interest rates fell, nominal interest rates were not reduced to the ZLB and price inflation was very subdued so the Anglo-American strategy of pushing real interest rates down was not really followed either. The fast-growing component of aggregate demand was investment much of it by government while consumption and real wages were held down. This was 'state-led' growth rather than a Keynesian macroeconomic strategy (Overy, 1982) and took place in an economy that had strong similarities to the Soviet Union in terms of economic coercion and government priorities (Temin, 1991).

2.2.3. Why did the world economy 'disintegrate'?

The 1930s saw a massive 'globalization backlash' as countries introduced policies that reduced the integration of markets. Both trade and capital flows were seriously impaired. Broadly speaking, we can attribute this de-globalization to the pressures on policy makers imposed by the Great Depression, but it is useful to explore the detail of the impetus to devalue, default, or to erect trade barriers. These decisions were, of course, informed by politics and they can be usefully analysed in the context of the political trilemma proposed by Rodrik (2000). This trilemma is that one can have, at most, two of deep economic integration, democratic politics, and the nation state (see Figure 2.1).

The decision to leave the gold standard was analysed by Wolf (2008) who used a probit model to examine the odds of staying on gold. His results were that a country was more likely to leave if its main trading partner did, if it had returned to gold at a high parity, if it was a democracy, or if the central bank was independent. It was less likely to leave if it had large gold reserves, less price deflation, and strong banks. The model predicts departures well and indicates that France was under the least pressure to exit in the early 1930s. This account maps into various generations of currency-crisis models and it also matches the insight of the political trilemma that, in the absence of international coordination, democratic politics would undermine the gold standard. As Eichengreen (1996) underlined, the extension of the franchise had made acceptance of deflationary policies to stay on gold much less acceptable than in the nineteenth century.

The volume of international trade fell dramatically during the Great Depression, both absolutely and relative to GDP, and the period is notable for a surge in protectionism following the Smoot–Hawley Tariff imposed by the United States in 1930. For the advanced countries, real GDP fell by 16.7 per cent between 1929 and 1932 but import volumes fell by 23.5 per cent. Increased barriers to trade clearly played an important role, although estimates of their contribution can be sensitive to methodology. Models based on import demand functions (Madsen, 2001) and on the historical relationship between world production and trade (Irwin, 2012) both suggest that protectionism accounted for around 40 per cent of the fall in trade volumes.

The goals of protectionist policies were typically to safeguard employment, to improve the balance of payments, and to raise prices. Unlike today, there were no constraints from WTO (World Trade Organization) membership. Protectionism is usually thought of as the triumph of special-interest groups but, in this period, it may be more a substitute for a macroeconomic policy response. For example, Eichengreen and Irwin (2010) found that, on average, tariffs were higher in countries that stayed on gold longer and so had less scope to use monetary or fiscal policies to promote economic recovery. Their analysis suggests that the financial crisis of 1931 rather than the Smoot–Hawley Tariff was the real trigger for the 1930s trade war.

Sovereign default was widespread in the 1930s—much more so than in the debt crisis of the 1980s—and was an important part of the world economic crisis and the withdrawal of Latin American countries in particular from the world economy. Debts were owed to private bondholders rather than banks and this was important in permitting a relaxed attitude by lender governments (Eichengreen and Portes, 1989). Default was typically triggered by the increased burden of debt service as the depression intensified and export prices fell while real interest rates rose. Econometric analysis of the decision to default shows that it was more likely the higher the debt to income ratio and the greater the terms of trade shock, but was also made more likely by unwillingness to pursue austerity policies (Eichengreen and Portes, 1986). Eichengreen and Portes also pointed out that default was more likely against lenders who were unable or unwilling credibly to threaten sanctions—American suffered more than British bondholders.

In the 1930s, maintaining debt service tended to be associated with fiscal austerity and measures to improve the current account of the balance of payments, while the decision to suspend payments was often accompanied by fiscal expansion and monetary reflation. An analysis of the implications of default shows that it promoted growth, especially for heavy defaulters (Eichengreen and Portes, 1990). It should also be recognized that undergoing a long and deep contraction in GDP did political damage and was conducive to the rise of extremist political parties, although the link was not automatic and depended on the structure of the electoral system and whether there was a long-standing democratic tradition (de Bromhead et al., 2012).

2.2.4. What were the long-term implications of the Great Depression?

The Great Depression had long-lasting effects on economic policy and performance. In the UK it can be seen as a major step down 'the road to 1945' and the favourable reception in the 1940s and 1950s to the ideas of Beveridge and Keynes, while in the United States there is a widely-held belief that it was the 'defining moment' in the development of the American economy (Bordo et al., 1998). Obviously, there is a danger of attributing to the depression those changes which would have come about anyway, but there is no doubt that the failures of the market economy in the 1930s were game-changing.

Clearly, one implication was a major re-thinking of macroeconomics by the economics profession, which in the Anglo-American world rapidly adopted Keynesian thinking. This had implications for policymaking, although these need to be handled with care. In the United States, the main change was that it became generally accepted that the automatic stabilizers would not be over-ridden in pursuit of a balanced budget, and these were now much more powerful with federal spending considerably bigger, but there was no move to try to fine-tune the economy through Keynesian demand management (De Long, 1998). In the UK, after the war, activist government intervention to prevent shortfalls of aggregate demand did become the norm and by the 1950s and 1960s short-term demand management was very prominent in a way that would have been unthinkable in the early 1930s.[15]

There was also a legacy from the 1930s for the framework of macroeconomic policy in terms of the macroeconomic trilemma. The move to controls on international capital movements proved to be long-lasting; in most countries, they continued throughout the Bretton Woods period with the return to pegged exchange rates and freer international trade. These years were characterized by very small current-account positions, very high correlations of domestic savings and investment, and the insulation of domestic from foreign interest rates, thus allowing independent monetary policy (Obstfeld and Taylor, 2004). This has been portrayed by Rodrik (2000) as the 'Bretton Woods Compromise' in terms of the acceptable limits on globalization required by domestic politics at the level of the nation state after the debacle of the 1930s.

The crisis of the 1930s surely also contributed to the massive increase in social transfers that characterized the OECD (Organisation for Economic Co-operation and Development) countries in the 50 years from 1930 to 1980, during which time the median percentage of GDP rose from a strikingly low 1.66 to 20.09 per cent (Lindert, 2004). Here too, the story should not be over-simplified—many other

[15] The initial stance of the Labour government in the late 1940s was to embrace planning rather than fine-tuning. It should also be noted that there has been a vigorous debate among economic historians about the validity of the concept of a 'Keynesian revolution' in British economic policy-making; see Booth (2001) for an introduction and further references.

factors played a role including population ageing, trends in income distributions, and rising prosperity. Nevertheless, the 'defining moment' hypothesis for the United States is perhaps at its most persuasive in terms of federal social-insurance schemes; Fishback and Wallis (2013) see a fundamental change in terms of fiscal federalism as the New Deal succeeded in putting rules in place that underpinned the political acceptability of inter-state transfers.

The Great Depression also had big implications for microeconomic policy; Hannah and Temin (2010) suggest that the immediate impact can be seen as a serious retreat from the capitalist free market with a new emphasis on government interventions to correct market failures. This implied a greater role for regulation and, in most OECD countries, for state ownership. The short-term implication was undoubtedly a substantial reduction in the extent of competition in product markets, including the rise of cartels encouraged by government and the anti-competitive effects of protectionism. The weakening of competition turned out to be much more pervasive and long-lasting in the UK than in the US (Broadberry and Crafts, 1992; Shepherd, 1981). In the late 1950s, tariffs were still at mid-1930s levels and about 60 per cent of manufacturing output was cartelized. The retreat from competition had adverse effects on productivity performance over several decades and provided the context in which industrial relations problems and sleepy management proliferated (Crafts, 2012).

It is well-known that financial crises can have permanent adverse effects on the level and possibly also the trend growth rate of potential output and this is a major reason why such crises usually have serious fiscal implications including big increases in structural deficits as a percentage of GDP. Thinking in terms of a production function, there will be direct adverse effects on the amount of capital as investment is interrupted, on the amount of labour inputs through hysteresis effects, and on TFP (total-factor productivity) if R&D (research and development) is cut back. Indirect effects—either positive or negative—may also be felt depending on the impact the crisis has on supply-side policy. Furceri and Mourougane (2009) estimate that for OECD countries a severe banking crisis reduces the level of potential output by about 4 per cent while the review of the evidence in IMF (2009), which covers lower-income economies, suggests 10 per cent; in neither case is long-run trend growth thought to be affected.

What does the experience of the United States in the 1930s reveal? One way to address the issue is through time-series econometrics where the shock in the 1930s has been a focal point in debates about deterministic or stochastic trends.[16] Here the evidence is rather inconclusive and the picture is muddied by World War Two. In fact, assuming trend-stationarity and extrapolating the pre-1929 trend of per capita income growth into the long-run gives quite a good approximation to actual experience, but a more careful look suggests a break in trend in 1929 comprising a levels decrease followed by a modest increase in trend growth through 1955 (Ben-David et al., 2003). The pre-1929 trend line was crossed in 1942.

[16] With a deterministic trend, a shock only has a temporary effect and the economy then returns to the previous trend growth path. In contrast, if the trend is a non-stationary stochastic process, shocks have an enduring effect on the future growth path and long-run forecasts are affected by historical events.

Table 2.2. Contributions to labour productivity growth in United States (% per year)

	K/HW growth	HK/HW growth	TFP growth	Y/HW growth
1906–19	0.51	0.26	1.12	1.89
1919–29	0.31	-0.06	2.02	2.27
1929–41	-0.19	0.14	2.97	2.92
1941–48	0.24	0.22	2.08	2.54
1948–73	0.76	0.11	1.88	2.75

Note: estimates are for private non-farm economy.
Source: derived from Field (2013).

More insight may be obtained by considering business cycle, peak-to-peak growth-accounting estimates, as in Table 2.2. The obvious feature of the 1930s is that the financial crisis undermined growth in the capital stock. Had growth of the capital to labour ratio continued at the pre-1929 rate, by 1941 it would have been about 25 per cent larger and, accordingly, potential GDP per hour worked perhaps 8 per cent bigger. Growth of labour inputs was sluggish, impaired by the impact of the New Deal. However, TFP growth was very strong, powered by sustained R&D, and Field (2013) has labelled the 1930s the most technologically progressive decade of the twentieth century in the United States. Overall, the clear impression is that the result of the banking crisis was to lower the level of productive potential rather than its growth rate.

Productive potential was also reduced for a while through the impact of the 1930s downturn on the employability of the labour force, a hysteresis effect. In this case, however, in both Britain and the United States, this was subsequently reversed by the opposite shock of World War Two (Hatton and Thomas, 2013). However, in the 1930s a legacy of the depression was a large rise in the number of long-term unemployed workers and the share of unemployment which was long-term. In Britain, where the impact has been quantified, this was to a large extent the result of job losses in the traditional export industries interacting with the unemployment insurance system to generate a group of workers who would have liked their old jobs back but could survive on the dole. These long-term unemployed workers seem to have experienced declining re-employment probabilities over time as they became discouraged, their human capital deteriorated, and employers regarded them as damaged goods (Crafts, 1987). The plight of these workers scarred the period and, virtually excluded from the labour market, they did not hold down wage pressures (Crafts, 1989). So, at any level of unemployment, wage pressure was greater than in the 1920s or, equivalently, hysteresis effects had raised the NAIRU—perhaps by about 1.5 percentage points.

2.3. POLICY IMPLICATIONS

This section pulls out the strongest policy lessons from the 1930s which have emerged from the above discussion. Some of these are well-understood and, fortunately, in the Great Recession of 2008–09 many of the worst mistakes of 80 years ago were not repeated. The economic history of the Great Depression is, of course, well-known to key players such as Ben Bernanke and Christina Romer, who are distinguished contributors to the literature. We are, of course, aware that some things are different now, for example, there was no European Monetary Union or too-big-to-fail doctrine in the 1930s, and that policy decisions and outcomes were contingent on the circumstances of the time; nevertheless, we believe that there is value in re-visiting the experience of that decade.

Starting with the monetary and fiscal policy responses to a financial crisis, the headlines from the American experience are clear enough and were acted upon this time around. Monetary policy bears a big responsibility for the early-1930s slump; subsequent research has refined rather than refuted the claims of Friedman and Schwartz (1963). Monetary policy errors were both of commission and omission. Inappropriate tightening of policy precipitated the downturn while the subsequent failure to provide greater monetary stimulus allowed recession to develop into depression. In particular, as Bordo and Landon-Lane (2013) show, the Federal Reserve failed in its role as lender of last resort and thus made the financial crisis much more serious.

The 1930s showed us the dangers of a passive response to a banking crisis and the mistakes made then were not repeated in 2008/9 when American monetary policy was aggressively expansionary (Wheelock, 2010). Interest rates were cut further and faster and the monetary base rose rapidly. Free of the constraints of the gold standard, central banks across the world provided much more liquidity to the banking system in 2008/9 (5.5 per cent commercial bank deposits) than in 1931 (1 per cent) (Moessner and Allen, 2011)

Similarly, the early 1930s tightening of American fiscal policy in an attempt to limit budget deficits has not been repeated; the fiscal stabilizers were allowed to operate and a major discretionary stimulus added in 2008/9 (Fishback, 2013). The evidence reviewed earlier suggests that this would have been a better stance to adopt in the early 1930s. Indeed, across major OECD economies the policy response has been similar to that in the United States and seems to suggest a common understanding of the importance of acting to avoid a banking collapse and to inject a stimulus to aggregate demand (Almunia et al., 2010). Thus, we see budget deficits in the euro area, and the UK allowed to increase massively compared with the 1930s, and real interest rates far below those which prevailed in the deflation of the early 1930s.

With regard to recovery, it is clear that the initial phase in both the UK and the USA was driven by monetary rather than fiscal policy (Fishback, 2013; Middleton, 2013). The necessary condition in both cases was exit from the gold standard which allowed nominal and, especially, real interest rates to fall sharply as deflation came to an end. It has long been understood that expansionary monetary policies were central to the strong recovery that was underway in both countries by 1934/5 (Dimsdale, 1981; Romer, 1992). From the perspective of today's policy makers, a very important aspect of this experience was that it took place with interest rates at the ZLB and entailed a major change in inflationary expectations.

The most persuasive account of the American turning point in 1933 is to explain it as a 'regime change' linked to the exit from the gold standard (Temin and Wigmore, 1990). Recent research has clarified and amplified this proposition in the context of the ZLB. Eggertsson (2008) stressed that the key was not devaluation per se but creating inflationary expectations which reduce real interest rates by a credible commitment to raising the price level. The cheap money policy in the UK can be interpreted in a similar way (Howson, 1975), but the failure to implement this quickly exposed the British economy to a double-dip in 1932 as the authorities were initially unsuccessful in changing expectations (Mitchell et al., 2011). This calls into question the wisdom of today's conventional inflation targeting at the ZLB. It could become desirable to go beyond the current version of quantitative easing to a monetary policy that seeks to work by reducing ex-ante real interest rates.[17] Then, in the UK it would be important to abandon formally the 2 per cent CPI (consumer price index) target and replace it with a new mandate for the Bank of England. This could take the form either of raising the target rate of inflation rate or, as in the 1930s, of adopting a price-level target which entails a significant average rate of inflation over a period of years.

In the 1930s recovery in the United States, fiscal policy played, at most, a minor role through traditional Keynesian multiplier effects. It is important not to be misled by the frenetic activity of the New Deal; deficit-financed fiscal policy did not fail, rather it was not really tried (Fishback, 2013). The British experience of rearmament in the later 1930s suggests that fiscal stimulus could be effective while the VAR analysis of the impact after a year of 1930s defence expenditure in 27 countries by Almunia et al. (2010) found a multiplier of 1.2. Bearing in mind the methodological critique in Ramey (2011), this should be treated with caution. Nevertheless, in the depressed conditions of the 1930s at the ZLB, it is quite plausible that the fiscal multiplier was at least 1.0 and that the failure to attempt greater fiscal stimulus was costly.

The evidence suggests that the downturn of the 1930s had significant hysteresis effects. It led to increased long-term unemployment (Hatton and Thomas, 2013), and, especially in the United States, a smaller capital stock. In such circumstances, it is quite possible that 'temporary' increases in government purchases financed by borrowing could improve the long-term fiscal position provided that they did not become permanent and that they could be introduced without seriously raising the interest rates at which the government could borrow (De Long and Summers, forthcoming).[18] It is an interesting issue whether such arguments can be used to justify a postponement of fiscal consolidation at present when the analysis in Guichard and Rusticelli (2010) suggests that the average increase in the NAIRU through hysteresis effects from the crisis, both across the OECD as a whole and also in the UK, could be around 0.75 percentage points.

Whatever the favourable effects of rearmament in the later 1930s, in the context of gold standard membership, and of the very unpleasant budgetary arithmetic arising from wartime borrowing, there was much less room to manoeuvre at the start of the decade in the face of deflation and fears of an adverse reaction from

[17] Quantitative easing could, in principle, work either through portfolio rebalancing or through signalling higher future inflation. It appears that, so far, its main effects have come through the former channel (Joyce et al., 2011). The MPC's commitment to the 2 per cent CPI target makes that unsurprising; the public's medium-term inflationary expectations have changed very little during the crisis.

[18] De Long and Summers (2012) show that there is a future fiscal dividend from deficit-financed fiscal expansion now if the government can borrow at an interest rate $r < g + (\eta\mu T)/(1 - \mu T)$ where g is the growth rate, μ is the multiplier, T is the marginal tax and transfer rate, and η is the hysteresis loss as a fraction of future GDP. For $\eta = 0.5$, a multiplier of 1 and $T = 0.33$, this is satisfied when $r - g < 5$ percentage points.

financial markets (Middleton, 2013).[19] Devaluation allowed an end to deflation, permitted cheap money, and made fiscal consolidation much less painful. Fiscal consolidation is normally deflationary and there is no obvious reason to think that this was not the case in the early-1930s UK, but the severity of its impact typically depends on the extent to which it is offset by the beneficial effects of currency depreciation on net exports and by interest rate reductions (Guajardo et al., 2011) and these mitigating factors were available. The further lessons here are that falling prices greatly magnify worries about fiscal sustainability and that, if fiscal policy is a valuable weapon, it is highly advantageous to enter a crisis with a history of fiscal prudence.

Banking crises were at the heart of the Great Depression in the United States. That experience and the wider evidence base tells us that such crises are typically very expensive in terms of the depth and length of the downturns with which they are associated and the fiscal legacy that they bequeath through increased structural deficits and government debt-servicing. The net present value of the median banking crisis has been estimated at 63 per cent GDP (ICB, 2011). It is clear that although ex-post, as in the 1930s, it is fairly easy to explain bank failures using standard tools of economic analysis (Calomiris and Mason, 2003b), ex-ante forecasting of banking crises is extremely difficult. Economic history points to credit booms based on increased leverage as strong leading indicators (Schularick and Taylor, 2012) but early warning models of threats to financial stability are still far from satisfactory.[20] The policy implication is that it is worth incurring some costs by introducing measures to prevent banking crises, and this was the American response in the 1930s.[21]

Microeconomic analysis incorporating implications of asymmetric information predicts that there is the potential for serious market failures in the banking sector with attendant risks of banking crises; for example, a bank run (a coordination failure) can happen even though agents are rational and banks are solvent (Diamond and Dybvig, 1983). Deposit insurance is a possible solution and can, in principle, be costless if coordination panics are the only problem. However, the American experience in the 1930s was that it was not so much panics but weak balance sheets that led to bank failures (Calomiris and Mason, 2003b) and this makes deposit insurance potentially a costly intervention. Deposit insurance also increases moral hazard (incentivizes excessive risk taking) so that complementary regulation to ensure capital adequacy and sufficient equity to absorb losses is also required (Allen et al., 2011).

[19] Using the standard formula that for fiscal sustainability $b > d(r - g)$ where b is the primary surplus/GDP, r is the interest rate on government debt, and g is the growth rate of nominal GDP with the data set from Middleton (2013), in the late 1920s, $d = 1.7$, $r = 4.6$, and $g = 2.5$, if inflation is zero then $b = 3.6$ per cent but if prices fell at 5 per cent per year, b rose to 12.1 per cent. Conversion of the war debt and gently rising prices in the post gold-standard world changed this so that b fell below 2 per cent. The value of b is quite small in each of these scenarios if d is at the 1913 level of 0.25.

[20] For example, the preferred model in Davis and Karim (2008) gave the probability of a banking crisis in the UK in 2007 as 0.6 per cent.

[21] The costs are likely to come through a rise in the supply price of capital and a reduction in the equilibrium capital stock, and these need to be set against the benefits of a lower crisis risk (Miles et al., 2011).

In 1929, the United States had a badly regulated and under capitalized banking system, an inexperienced and incompetent lender of last resort, and no federal deposit insurance. At the end of the crisis, responses were made both in terms of prudential regulation and crisis management. In 1933, ending the waves of banking crises was both an economic and a political imperative. As today, reliance on market discipline appeared unrealistic. The lender of last resort had failed. So, the solution was deposit insurance plus regulatory reform, and the political attractions of the former meant that it would be a permanent feature of the American banking system (Calomiris, 2013). Many other countries have followed down this path, a choice reinforced by the present crisis. For this solution to work effectively, it is crucial that regulation is well-designed. The lesson from the 1930s is that it may well not be because vested interests are likely to hijack the politics of regulatory design. In particular, it is clear that the Glass–Steagall Act introduced unjustified restrictions on universal banking while failing to address the real structural problem, namely, unit banking.

At the beginning of the current crisis, international trade collapsed and it was widely remarked that there was a chilling parallel with the trade-wars period of the early 1930s with its seriously adverse implications for income levels in the long-term. Subsequently, research has found that the contribution of trade barriers to falling world trade volumes in 2008–9 was very small, perhaps only 2 per cent (Kee et al., 2010), which is well below estimates of 40 per cent or more in the Great Depression. It seems that the structure of world trade has changed in ways that make volumes much more sensitive to demand shocks.

This raises the important question of why we have seen creeping rather than rampant protectionism this time. Research on the interwar period by Eichengreen and Irwin (2010) finds that protectionist policies were less likely to be adopted by countries which left the gold standard early, i.e. where there was more freedom to adopt expansionary monetary and fiscal policies. They argue that this has made protectionism much less likely now because the scope for a macroeconomic policy response is much greater. The countries to which this description does not apply today are eurozone economies with sovereign debt and competitiveness problems. The possible implication is that they will be even more reluctant to implement the European Single Market in services where governments still have considerable discretion to maintain trade barriers notwithstanding the Services Directive (Badinger and Maydell, 2009).

Even so, another big difference from the 1930s may also be relevant, namely, that we now have the trade rules overseen by the WTO, including bound tariff agreements. Evenett (2009) points out that these tariff bindings have held. Unfortunately, it is also true that there is a great deal of leeway for WTO-legal increases in trade barriers, partly because, in many cases, tariffs are well below bound levels and partly because anti-dumping is not well addressed by the rules. This underlines the importance of reducing the scope for governments legally to raise levels of protection, and emphasizes that there could still be real value from concluding the Doha Round (Hoekman et al., 2010).

Within the eurozone there are several countries which have lost international competitiveness, while also having very high ratios of public debt to GDP, and which perhaps should not have joined in the first place (Capie, 2013). The policy responses now needed to address their problems while remaining within the euro seem to imply a long period of slow growth, a 'lost decade'. If competitiveness can only be restored by falling prices, greater fiscal stringency is required to ensure long-run fiscal sustainability. The 1930s experience seems to suggest strongly that a strategy of devaluation and sovereign default is an attractive escape route. In case this is the outcome, it is important that the balance sheets of European banks are strong enough to withstand this shock. The European and IMF loans provided to Greece may have bought time to achieve this outcome. However, the benefit/cost ratio of leaving the gold standard then was very different from that of leaving the eurozone; Eichengreen and Temin (2013) argue that a decision to reintroduce the national currency now would engender 'the mother of all financial crises' through instantaneous capital flight and collapse of the banking system.

If that is the case, then logic points to a solution to the political trilemma problem different from either the 1930s retreat from economic integration or the 1950s 'Bretton Woods Compromise'. The implication is that deep economic integration and democratic politics are chosen by going down the route of 'global federalism' in a 'United States of Europe' rather than deep economic integration combined with the nation state through the 'golden straitjacket'. Wolf (2012, 2013) spells this out; he notes that this would require major political and economic reforms which might allow more effective European fiscal and monetary policy at the ZLB, and political legitimization of a much higher level of transfer payments from an expanded European budget while also finding a way to share burdens of adjustment between surplus and deficit countries. In this regard, Fishback and Wallis (2013) point to the lessons of the New Deal where a politically acceptable way had to be found to expand the role of the central government. They argue that this can only be achieved by imposing strict limits on central administrative discretion.

Germany in 1931 offers a stark reminder of how difficult is the task of economic policy makers, confronted by a sudden stop in capital inflows in an economy with a fragile banking system, where freedom to manoeuvre is constrained by a fixed exchange rate. Public finances are potentially wrecked and austerity beckons. Citizens in some eurozone countries today know the feeling. If the eurozone is to avoid a repeat of the present trauma, the history of the 1930s does suggest that it is important in the medium term to redesign its rules to regulate banks more strictly in recognition of the dangers of credit booms and subsequent crashes in asset prices (Schularick and Taylor, 2012).

Finally, it is worth considering the impact of the current crisis for future European growth prospects. If there is an adverse implication for the future trend growth rate, it will most probably come from policy responses. In this respect, it should be noted that the 1930s crisis led to the adoption of policies that run very much in the opposite direction to the supply-side reforms which it is often argued are required to speed up European growth. For example, they do not bode well for the agenda of completing the single market and making labour markets more flexible and employment-friendly put forward by Sapir (2006). The risk is a world of more state intervention, lower willingness to implement the Single Market, and more expensive social protection. In other words, just the opposite of what the Sapir Report thought was needed in Europe.

BIBLIOGRAPHY

Allen, F., Carletti, E., and Leonello, A. (2011), 'Deposit Insurance and Risk Taking', *Oxford Review of Economic Policy*, 27, 464–78.

Allsopp, C. J. and Glyn, A. (1999), 'The Assessment: Real Interest Rates', *Oxford Review of Economic Policy*, 15(2), 1–16.

Almunia, M., Benetrix, A., Eichengreen, B., O'Rourke, K. H., and Rua, G. (2010), 'Lessons from the Great Depression', *Economic Policy*, 50, 219–65.

Badinger, H. and Maydell, N. (2009), 'Legal and Economic Issues in Completing the EU Internal Market for Services: An Interdisciplinary Perspective', *Journal of Common Market Studies*, 47, 693–717.

Balke, N. S. and Gordon, R. J. (1986), 'Historical Data', in R. J. Gordon (ed.), *The American Business Cycle: Continuity and Change*. Chicago: University of Chicago Press, 781–850.

Ben-David, D., Lumsdaine, R., and Papell, D. H. (2003), 'Unit Roots, Postwar Slowdowns and Long-Run Growth: Evidence from Two Structural Breaks', *Empirical Economics*, 28, 303–19.

Bernanke, B. (1983), 'Non-Monetary Effects of the Financial Crisis in the Propagation of the Great Depression', *American Economic Review*, 73, 257–76.

Bernanke, B. (1986), 'Employment, Hours and Earnings in the Depression: An Analysis of Eight Manufacturing Industries', *American Economic Review*, 76, 82–109.

Bernanke, B. (1995), 'The Macroeconomics of the Great Depression: A Comparative Approach', *Journal of Money, Credit and Banking*, 27, 1–28.

Bernanke, B. and Carey, K. (1996), 'Nominal Wage Stickiness and Aggregate Supply in the Great Depression', *Quarterly Journal of Economics*, 111, 853–83.

Billings, M. and Capie, F. (2011), 'Financial Crisis, Contagion, and the British Banking System between the World Wars', *Business History*, 53, 193–215.

Board of Governors of the Federal Reserve System (1943), *Banking and Monetary Statistics, 1914–1941*. Washington DC: Government Printing Office.

Booth, A. (1987), 'Britain in the 1930s: A Managed Economy', *Economic History Review*, 40, 499–522.

Booth, A. (2001), 'New Revisionists and the Keynesian Era in British Economic Policy', *Economic History Review*, 54, 346–66.

Borchardt, K. (1990), 'A Decade of Debate about Bruning's Economic Policy', in J. von Kruedener (ed.), *Economic Crisis and Political Collapse: The Weimar Republic, 1924–1933*. Oxford: Berg Publishers, 99–151.

Bordo, M. D. and Landon-Lane, J. (2013), 'The Banking Panics in the United States in the 1930s: Some Lessons for Today', in N. Crafts and P. Fearon (eds), *The Great Depression of the 1930s: Lessons for Today*. Oxford: Oxford University Press.

Bordo, M. D., Erceg, C., and Evans, C. (2000), 'Money, Sticky Wages, and the Great Depression', *American Economic Review*, 90, 1447–63.

Bordo, M. D., Goldin, C., and White, E. N. (1998), 'The Defining Moment Hypothesis: The Editors' Introduction', in M. D. Bordo, C. Goldin, and E. N. White (eds), *The Defining Moment: the Great Depression and the American Economy in the Twentieth Century*. Chicago: University of Chicago Press, 1–20.

Broadberry, S. N. (1986a), 'Aggregate Supply in Interwar Britain', *Economic Journal*, 96, 467–81.

Broadberry, S. N. (1986b), *The British Economy between the Wars: A Macroeconomic Survey*. Oxford: Basil Blackwell.

Broadberry, S. N. (1987), 'Cheap Money and the Housing Boom in Interwar Britain: An Econometric Appraisal', *The Manchester School*, 55, 378–89.

Broadberry, S. N. and Crafts, N. F. R. (1992), 'Britain's Productivity Gap in the 1930s: Some Neglected Factors', *Journal of Economic History*, 52, 531–58.

Brown, E. C. (1956), 'Fiscal Policy in the Thirties: A Reappraisal', *American Economic Review*, 46, 857–79.

Calomiris, C. W. (2013), 'The Political Lessons of Depression-era Banking Reform', in N. Crafts and P. Fearon (eds), *The Great Depression of the 1930s: Lessons for Today*. Oxford: Oxford University Press.

Calomiris, C. W. and Mason, J. R. (2003a), 'Consequences of Bank Distress During the Great Depression', *American Economic Review*, 93, 937–47.

Calomiris, C. W. and Mason, J. R. (2003b), 'Fundamentals, Panics, and Bank Distress During the Depression', *American Economic Review*, 93, 1615–47.

Calomiris, C. W. and Mason, J. R. (2003c), 'How to Restructure Failed Banking Systems: Lessons from the US in the 1930s and Japan in the 1990s', NBER Working Paper No. 9624.

Calomiris, C. W. and Wilson, B. (2004), 'Bank Capital and Portfolio Management: The 1930s "Capital Crunch" and the Scramble to Shed Risk', *Journal of Business*, 77, 421–55.

Calomiris, C., Mason, J., and Wheelock, D. (2011), 'Did Doubling Reserve Requirements Cause the Recession of 1937/8? A Microeconomic Approach', NBER Working Paper No. 16688.

Campa, J. (1990), 'Exchange Rates and Economic Recovery in the 1930s: An Extension to Latin America', *Journal of Economic History*, 50, 677–82.

Capie, F. (2013), 'Disintegration of the International Economy between the Wars', in N. Crafts and P. Fearon (eds), *The Great Depression of the 1930s: Lessons for Today*. Oxford: Oxford University Press.

Carlson, M. A. and Rose, J. (2011), 'Credit Availability and the Collapse of the Banking Sector', Federal Reserve Board Finance and Economics Discussion Paper No. 2011–38.

Cecchetti, S. G. (1992), 'Prices During the Great Depression: Was the Deflation of 1930–1932 Really Unanticipated?', *American Economic Review*, 82, 141–56.

Chadha, J. S. and Dimsdale, N. H. (1999), 'A Long View of Real Rates', *Oxford Review of Economic Policy*, 15(2), 17–45.

Christiano, L., Motto, R., and Rostagno, M. (2003), 'The Great Depression and the Friedman–Schwartz Hypothesis', *Journal of Money, Credit and Banking*, 35, 1119–97.

Cohn, R. L. (1992), 'Fiscal Policy in Germany During the Great Depression', *Explorations in Economic History*, 29, 318–42.

Cole, H. L. and Ohanian, L. E. (1999), 'The Great Depression in the United States from a Neoclassical Perspective', *Federal Reserve Bank of Minneapolis Quarterly Review*, 23, 2–24.

Cole, H. L. and Ohanian, L. E. (2004), 'New Deal Policies and the Persistence of the Great Depression: A General Equilibrium Analysis', *Journal of Political Economy*, 112, 779–816.

Crafts, N. (1987), 'Long-Term Unemployment in Britain in the 1930s', *Economic History Review*, 40, 418–32.

Crafts, N. (1989), 'Long-term Unemployment and the Wage Equation in Britain, 1925–1939', *Economica*, 56, 247–54.

Crafts, N. (2012), 'British Relative Economic Decline Revisited: The Role of Competition', *Explorations in Economic History*, 49, 17–29.

Davis, E. P. and Karim, D. (2008), 'Could Early-Warning Systems Have Helped to Predict the Sub-Prime Crisis?', *National Institute Economic Review*, 206, 35–47.

De Bromhead, A., Eichengreen, B., and O'Rourke, K. H. (2012), 'Right-Wing Political Extremism in the Great Depression', NBER Working Paper No. 17871.

De Long, J. B. (1998), 'Fiscal Policy in the Shadow of the Great Depression', in M. D. Bordo, C. Goldin, and E. N. White (eds), *The Defining Moment: The Great Depression and the American Economy in the Twentieth Century*. Chicago: University of Chicago Press, 67–85.

De Long, J. B. and Shleifer, A. (1991), 'The Stock Market Bubble of 1929: Evidence from Closed-End Mutual Funds', *Journal of Economic History*, 51, 675–700.

De Long, J. B. and Summers, L. H. (2012), 'Fiscal Policy in a Depressed Economy', *Brookings Papers on Economic Activity*, 1, 233–97.

Diamond, D. and Dybvig, P. (1983), 'Bank Runs, Deposit Insurance, and Liquidity', *Journal of Political Economy*, 91, 401–19.

Dimsdale, N. H. (1981), 'British Monetary Policy and the Exchange Rate, 1920–1938', *Oxford Economic Papers*, 33 (2, supplement), 306–49.

Dimsdale, N. H. and Horsewood, N. (1995), 'Fiscal Policy and Employment in Interwar Britain: Some Evidence from a New Model', *Oxford Economic Papers*, 47, 369–96.

Dimsdale, N. H., Nickell, S., and Horsewood, N. (1989), 'Real Wages and Unemployment in Britain during the 1930s', *Economic Journal*, 99, 271–92.

Eggertsson, G. B. (2008), 'Great Expectations and the End of the Depression', *American Economic Review*, 98, 1476–516.

Eggertsson, G. B. (2012), 'Was the New Deal Contractionary?', *American Economic Review*, 102, 524–55.

Eggertsson, G. B. and Pugsley, B. (2006), 'The Mistake of 1937: A General Equilibrium Analysis', *Monetary and Economic Studies*, 24, 151–90.

Eichengreen, B. (1996), 'Deja Vu All Over Again: Lessons from the Gold Standard for European Monetary Unification', in T. Bayoumi, B. Eichengreen, and M. Taylor (eds), *Modern Perspectives on the Gold Standard*. Cambridge: Cambridge University Press, 365–87.

Eichengreen, B. (2004), 'Understanding the Great Depression', *Canadian Journal of Economics*, 37, 1–27.

Eichengreen, B. and Irwin, D. (2010), 'The Slide to Protectionism in the Great Depression: Who Succumbed and Why?', *Journal of Economic History*, 70, 871–97.

Eichengreen, B. and Jeanne, O. (1998), 'Currency Crisis and Unemployment: Sterling in 1931', NBER Working Paper No. 6563.

Eichengreen, B. and Portes, R. (1986), 'Debt and Default in the 1930s', *European Economic Review*, 30, 599–640.

Eichengreen, B. and Portes, R. (1989), 'Settling Defaults in the Era of Bond Finance', *World Bank Economic Review*, 3, 211–39.

Eichengreen, B. and Portes, R. (1990), 'The Interwar Debt Crisis and Its Aftermath', *World Bank Research Observer*, 5, 69–94.

Eichengreen, B. and Sachs, J. (1985), 'Exchange Rates and Economic Recovery in the 1930s', *Journal of Economic History*, 45, 925–46.

Eichengreen, B. and Temin, P. (2013), 'Fetters of Gold and Paper', in N. Crafts and P. Fearon (eds), *The Great Depression of the 1930s: Lessons for Today*. Oxford: Oxford University Press.

Evenett, S. J. (2009), 'What Can Be Learned from Crisis-Era Protectionism?: An Initial Assessment', CEPR Discussion Paper No. 7494.

Ferderer, J. P. and Zalewski, D. A. (1994), 'Uncertainty as a Propagating Force in the Great Depression', *Journal of Economic History*, 54, 825–49.

Field, A. J. (2013), 'Economic Growth and Recovery in the United States, 1919–1941', in N. Crafts and P. Fearon (eds), *The Great Depression of the 1930s: Lessons for Today*. Oxford: Oxford University Press.

Fishback, P. (2013), 'US Monetary and Fiscal Policy in the 1930s', in N. Crafts and P. Fearon (eds), *The Great Depression of the 1930s: Lessons for Today*. Oxford: Oxford University Press.

Fishback, P. and Wallis, J. J. (2013), 'What Was New about the New Deal?', in N. Crafts and P. Fearon (eds), *The Great Depression of the 1930s: Lessons for Today*. Oxford: Oxford University Press.

Friedman, M. and Schwartz, A. (1963), *A Monetary History of the United States, 1867–1960*, Princeton: Princeton University Press.

Furceri, D. and Mourougane, A. (2009), 'The Effect of Financial Crises on Potential Output: New Empirical Evidence from OECD Countries', OECD Economics Department Working Paper No. 699.

Gordon, R. J. and Krenn, R. (2010), 'The End of the Great Depression, 1939–1941: Policy Contributions and Fiscal Multipliers', NBER Working Paper No. 16380.

Gordon, R. J. and Wilcox, J. A. (1981), 'Monetarist Interpretations of the Great Depression: An Evaluation and Critique', in K. Brunner (ed.), *The Great Depression Revisited*. The Hague: Martinus Nijhoff Publishing, 49–107.

Grossman, R. (1994), 'The Shoe That Didn't Drop: Explaining Banking Stability during the Great Depression', *Journal of Economic History*, 54, 654–82.

Guajardo, J., Leigh, D., and Pescatori, A. (2011), 'Expansionary Austerity: New International Evidence', IMF Working Paper No. 11/158.

Guichard, S. and Rusticelli, E. (2010), 'Assessing the Impact of the Financial Crisis on Structural Unemployment in OECD Countries', OECD Economics Department Working Paper No. 767.

Hamilton, J. D. (1992), 'Was the Deflation of the Great Depression Anticipated? Evidence from Commodity Futures Markets', *American Economic Review*, 82, 157–77.

Hannah, L. and Temin, P. (2010), 'Long-Term Supply-Side Implications of the Great Depression', *Oxford Review of Economic Policy*, 26, 561–80.

Hatton, T. J. and Thomas, M. (2013), 'Labour Markets in Recession and Recovery: The UK and the USA in the 1920s and 1930s', in N. Crafts and P. Fearon (eds), *The Great Depression of the 1930s: Lessons for Today*. Oxford: Oxford University Press.

Hoekman, B., Martin, W., and Mattoo, A. (2010), 'Conclude Doha: It Matters', CEPR Discussion Paper No. 7788.

Howson, S. (1975), *Domestic Monetary Management in Britain, 1919–1938*. Cambridge: Cambridge University Press.

Howson, S. (1980), 'The Management of Sterling, 1932–1939', *Journal of Economic History*, 40, 53–60.

Humphries, J. (1987), 'Interwar House Building, Cheap Money and Building Societies: The Housing Boom Revisited', *Business History*, 29, 325–45.

Independent Commission on Banking (2011), *Final Report*. London: ICB.

International Monetary Fund (2009), *World Economic Outlook*, October 2009.

Inklaar, R., de Jong, H., and Gouma, R. (2011), 'Did Technology Shocks Drive the Great Depression? Explaining Cyclical Movements in US Manufacturing', *Journal of Economic History*, 71, 827–58.

Irwin, D. (2010) "Did France Cause the Great Depression", NBER Working Paper No.16350.

Irwin, D. (2011), 'Gold Sterilization and the Recession of 1937–1938', NBER Working Paper No. 17595.

Irwin, D. (2012), *Trade Policy Disaster: Lessons from the 1930s*. Cambridge, Mass.: MIT Press.

James, H. (1984), 'The Causes of the German Banking Crisis of 1931', *Economic History Review*, 37, 68–87.

Joyce, M., Tong, M., and Woods, R. (2011), 'The United Kingdom's Quantitative Easing Policy: Design, Operation and Impact', *Bank of England Quarterly Bulletin*, 3, 200–12.

Kee, H. L., Neagu, C., and Nicita, A. (2010), 'Is Protectionism on the Rise?: Assessing National Trade Policies during the Crisis of 2008', World Bank Policy Research Working Paper No. 5274.

Klug, A., Landon-Lane, J. S., and White, E. N. (2005), 'How Could Everyone have been so Wrong? Forecasting the Great Depression with the Railroads', *Explorations in Economic History*, 42, 27–55.

Kroszner, R. S. and Rajan, R. G. (1994), 'Is the Glass–Steagall Act Justified? A Study of the US Experience with Universal Banking before 1933', *American Economic Review*, 84, 810–32.

Lindert, P. H. (2004), *Growing Public.* Cambridge: Cambridge University Press.

Madsen, J. (2001), 'Trade Barriers and the Collapse of World Trade During the Great Depression', *Southern Economic Journal*, 67, 848–68.

Middleton, R. (2013), 'Can Contractionary Fiscal Policy Be Expansionary? Consolidation, Sustainability, and Fiscal Policy Impact in Britain in the 1930s', in N. Crafts and P. Fearon (eds), *The Great Depression of the 1930s: Lessons for Today.* Oxford: Oxford University Press.

Miles, D., Yang, J., and Marcheggiano, G. (2011), 'Optimal Bank Capital', Bank of England External MPC Unit Discussion Paper No. 31 (revised version).

Mitchell, J., Solomou, S., and Weale, M. (2011), 'Monthly GDP Estimates for Interwar Britain', Cambridge Working Paper in Economics No. 1155.

Mitchener, K. J. (2007), 'Are Prudential Supervision and Regulation Pillars of Financial Stability? Evidence from the Great Depression', *Journal of Law and Economics*, 50, 273–302.

Mitchener, K. J. and Mason, J. (2013), '"Blood and Treasure": Exiting the Great Depression and Lessons for Today', in N. Crafts and P. Fearon (eds), *The Great Depression of the 1930s: Lessons for Today.* Oxford: Oxford University Press.

Moessner, R. and Allen, W. A. (2011), 'Banking Crises and the International Monetary System in the Great Depression and Now', *Financial History Review*, 18, 1–20

Newell, A. and Symons, J. (1988), 'The Macroeconomics of the Interwar Years: International Comparisons', in B. Eichengreen and T. J. Hatton (eds), *Interwar Unemployment in International Perspective.* London: Kluwer, 61–96.

Obstfeld, M. and Taylor, A. M. (2004), *Global Capital Markets: Integration, Crisis, and Growth.* Cambridge: Cambridge University Press.

Olson, J. S. (1988), *Saving Capitalism.* Princeton: Princeton University Press.

Overy, R. J. (1982), *The Nazi Economic Recovery, 1932–1938.* London: Macmillan.

Pensieroso, L. (2007), 'Real Business Cycle Models of the Great Depression: A Critical Survey', *Journal of Economic Surveys*, 21, 110–42.

Peppers, L. (1973), 'Full Employment Surplus Analysis and Structural Change: the 1930s', *Explorations in Economic History*, 10, 197–210.

Ramey, V. A. (2011), 'Can Government Purchases Stimulate the Economy?', *Journal of Economic Literature*, 49, 673–85.

Rappoport, P. and White, E. N. (1993), 'Was There a Bubble in the 1929 Stock Market?', *Journal of Economic History*, 53, 549–74.

Richardson, G. and Troost, W. (2009), 'Monetary Intervention Mitigated Banking Panics during the Great Depression: Quasi-Experimental Evidence from a Federal Reserve Border District, 1929–1933', *Journal of Political Economy*, 117, 1031–73.

Richardson, H. W. and Aldcroft, D. H. (1968), *Building in the British Economy between the Wars.* London: George Allen & Unwin.

Ritschl, A. (2013), 'Reparations, Deficits, and Debt Default: The Great Depression in Germany', in N. Crafts and P. Fearon (eds), *The Great Depression of the 1930s: Lessons for Today.* Oxford: Oxford University Press.

Rodrik, D. (2000), 'How Far Will International Economic Integration Go?', *Journal of Economic Perspectives*, 14(1), 177–86.

Romer, C. (1990), 'The Great Crash and the Onset of the Great Depression', *Quarterly Journal of Economics*, 105, 597–624.

Romer, C. (1992), 'What Ended the Great Depression?', *Journal of Economic History*, 52, 757–84.

Sapir, A. (2006), 'Globalization and the Reform of European Social Models', *Journal of Common Market Studies*, 44, 369–90.

Schnabel, I. (2004), 'The German Twin Crisis of 1931', *Journal of Economic History*, 64, 822–71.

Schularick, M. and Taylor, A. M. (2012), 'Credit Booms Gone Bust: Monetary Policy, Leverage Cycles and Financial Crises, 1870–2008', *American Economic Review*, 102, 1029–61.

Shepherd, W. G. (1981), 'Causes of Increased Competition in the US Economy, 1939–1980', *Review of Economics and Statistics*, 64, 613–26.

Shiller, R. (2003), 'From Efficient Markets Theory to Behavioral Finance', *Journal of Economic Perspectives*, 17, 83–104.

Svensson, L. E. O. (2003), 'Escaping from a Liquidity Trap and Deflation: The Foolproof Way and Others', *Journal of Economic Perspectives*, 17(4), 145–66.

Temin, P. (1991), 'Soviet and Nazi Economic Planning in the 1930s', *Economic History Review*, 44, 573–93.

Temin, P. (2008), 'Real Business Cycle Views of the Great Depression and Recent Events: A Review of Timothy J. Kehoe and Edward C. Prescott's *Great Depressions of the Twentieth Century*', *Journal of Economic Literature*, 46, 669–84.

Temin, P. and Wigmore, B. A. (1990), 'The End of One Big Deflation', *Explorations in Economic History*, 27, 483–502.

Thomas, M. (1983), 'Rearmament and Economic Recovery in the Late 1930s', *Economic History Review*, 36, 552–79.

Velde, F. R. (2009), 'The Recession of 1937: A Cautionary Tale', *Federal Reserve Bank of Chicago Economic Perspectives*, 4, 16–37.

Wheelock, D. C. (2010), 'Lessons Learned? Comparing the Federal Reserve's Responses to the Crises of 1932–1933 and 2007–2009', *Federal Reserve Bank of St. Louis Review*, 92, March/April, 89–107.

White, E. N. (1986), 'Before the Glass–Steagall Act: An Analysis of the Investment-Banking Activities of National Banks', *Explorations in Economic History*, 23, 33–55.

Wolf, N. (2008), 'Scylla and Charybdis: Explaining Europe's Exit from Gold, January 1928 to December 1936', *Explorations in Economic History*, 45, 383–401.

Wolf, N. (2012), 'Crises and Policy Responses within the Political Trilemma: Europe, 1929–1936 and 2008–2011', EHES Working Papers in Economic History No. 16.

Wolf, N. (2013), 'Europe's Great Depression: Coordination Failure after the First World War', in N. Crafts and P. Fearon (eds), *The Great Depression of the 1930s: Lessons for Today*. Oxford: Oxford University Press.

Woodford, M. (2010), 'Financial Intermediation and Macroeconomic Analysis', *Journal of Economic Perspectives*, 24(4), 21–44.

Woodford, M. (2011), 'Simple Analytics of the Government Expenditure Multiplier', *American Economic Journal: Macroeconomics*, 3(1), 1–35.

3

Europe's Great Depression: Coordination Failure after the First World War

Nikolaus Wolf

3.1 INTRODUCTION

The Great Depression remains by some margin the most devastating international economic crisis in modern time, especially if measured in terms of collapsing manufacturing output and the ensuing surge in unemployment. Moreover, recovery from the depression was slow, and it was far from universal. As shown in Figure 3.1, manufacturing output in the US and most European economies had reached its trough around mid-1932. However, few countries regained their 1929 output-levels before 1936, some not before 1939. As a general rule, recovery followed about half a year after a country had abandoned the interwar gold exchange standard (Eichengreen, 1992: 393). For example, Britain and the Scandinavian countries that left the gold standard in September or October 1931 recovered much earlier than countries that adhered to the gold standard beyond the London conference in 1933 such as France, Italy (until 1934), or Poland (see Figure 3.1). What it not shown in the figure, however, is the extent to which this 'recovery' was driven from the mid-1930s onwards by armament programmes that foreshadowed the Second World War.

The purpose of this chapter is to survey and re-interpret the extensive literature that tried to explain both the depth of the crisis in Europe and the delay of recovery as a failure to coordinate economic policies. I argue that Europe's Great Depression was more than the result of some misguided economic policy in any particular country. Europe could not exploit her vast economic potential after 1918, because the war had not yet come to an end—indeed it did not end before 1945. Both domestic and international institutions suffered from a lack of reciprocal trust and commitment, which can be clearly illustrated in the realm of monetary policy (Eichengreen, 1992) but affected many other areas of policy making, such as energy or migration policies. These institutions in turn affected expectations and thereby the extent to which, for example, expansionary policies could be effective. Put differently, not all options that would exist in a perfect environment were available to all policy makers at every time, because of serious flaws in the institutional framework that led to coordination failure. The remainder of this chapter elaborates this argument in four sections. In the next section

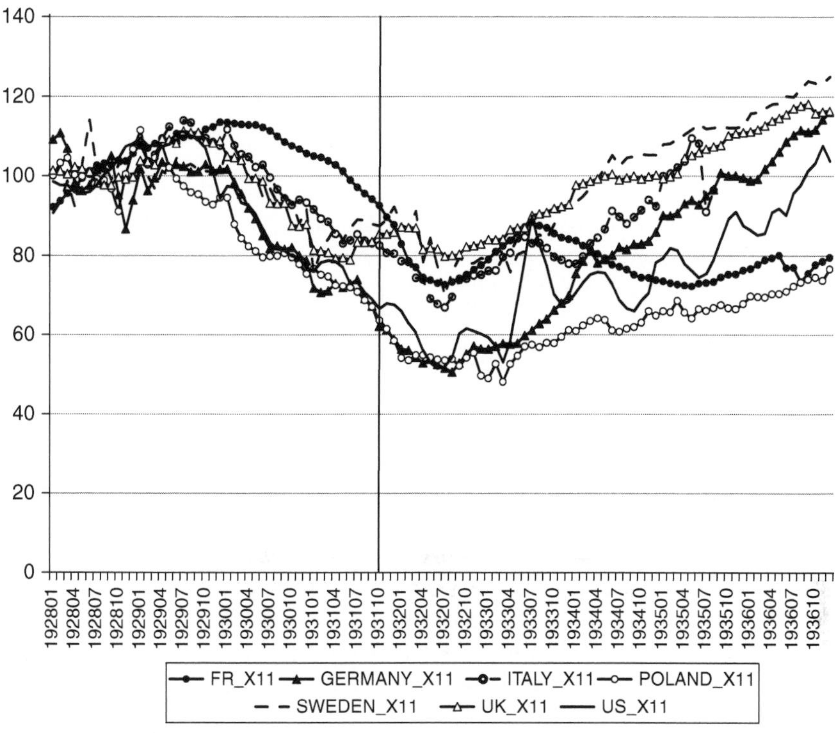

Fig. 3.1. Manufacturing output in various countries, 1928–36 (1928 = 100)

I provide a framework to think about policy coordination in general and its application to the interwar period in particular. Subsequently, I argue that the three most fundamental obstacles to policy coordination were direct consequences of the First World War: the fragility of political institutions after 1918, the problem of war debts and reparations that remained largely unresolved until 1933, and the irritating memory of the 1920s inflation. With this background I will then proceed in section 3.4 to discuss the painfully slow process of Europe's recovery that led from the abandonment of the gold standard to the stepwise implementation of expansionary economic policies. Section 3.5 concludes with remarks on the sustainability of these policies and implications for contemporary economic policy in Europe.

3.2. ECONOMIC POLICY COORDINATION IN THE 1930s: A SIMPLE FRAMEWORK

Europe emerged from the First World War economically and politically weakened. Millions had died in the trenches, from starvation or epidemics, others had survived permanently disabled or traumatized. The war had also caused unprecedented material destruction from France to Russia (Broadberry and

Harrison, 2005). From a long-term perspective the years 1914–18 mark the end of Europe's economic expansion and her decline relative to the rest of the world economy that continued throughout the twentieth century (Roses and Wolf, 2010). An apt example to illustrate the consequences of the war is the decline of the City of London as the world's leading financial centre and the rise of New York (Cassis, 2006; Cochrane, 2009). However, this economic (and political) decline was far from unavoidable. Europe continued to have a vast potential for economic development and growth, driven by technological, organizational, and sectoral change, by the ongoing accumulation of physical capital, and by the formation and accumulation of human capital. The period saw the beginnings of mass-motorization, advances in chemical and electrical engineering, the construction of an extensive road network, the emergence of commercial aviation, and, crucially, the electrification of large parts of the European economy, including some of the most remote rural areas. European industry underwent a broad process of modernization, including many firms that attempted to introduce and adapt new methods of American-style standardized mass-production (Chandler, 1990). The share of agriculture declined in all European economies between 1913 and 1950 with labour moving into the more productive industrial and service sectors, especially in northern and western Europe (Buyst and Franaszek, 2010). The governments of newly created states, which had their rationale in the growing demand for political participation, all aimed for a rapid economic development of their largely backward countries, and the records show rising school enrolment and numbers of students, high, and in some cases rising, participation rates in the labour markets jointly with a steady growth of the European population. But the new technologies and methods of production were capital intensive and required extensive new network infrastructures and large markets to become profitable. Hence, in the context of Europe's political fragmentation, they required more coordination of economic policies across state borders than ever before to facilitate capital flows and trade. It is this coordination that failed during the interwar years, except during a brief period from 1925–28/29. The electrification of Europe's large periphery, for example, was delayed until after 1945 on account of difficulties in agreement on technological standards across borders and because of the perceived risk of investment during the interwar years (Lagendijk, 2008). The latter was largely affected by political instability and unprecedented uncertainty about monetary policies.

To think about the coordination of economic policies more systematically, consider the classic 'macroeconomic policy trilemma' (Obstfeld et al., 2005). Policy makers in a small economy—which would apply to each European economy in the twentieth century—have to face a choice that, of the three typically desirable policies of a stable exchange rate, open capital markets, and autonomous monetary policy, only two can be mutually consistent. We can add that policies that aim for exchange rate stability are tightly related to (but obviously separate from) policies that pursue price stability. When a country credibly and permanently pegs its exchange rate to some base country (or fixes it in gold), and when capital continues to be freely mobile across borders, then simple interest parity will pin down the domestic interest rate to be equal to that in the base country (or to the level in the dominant gold standard economies). Here we take it for granted that policy makers want to engage in active macroeconomic policy over the business

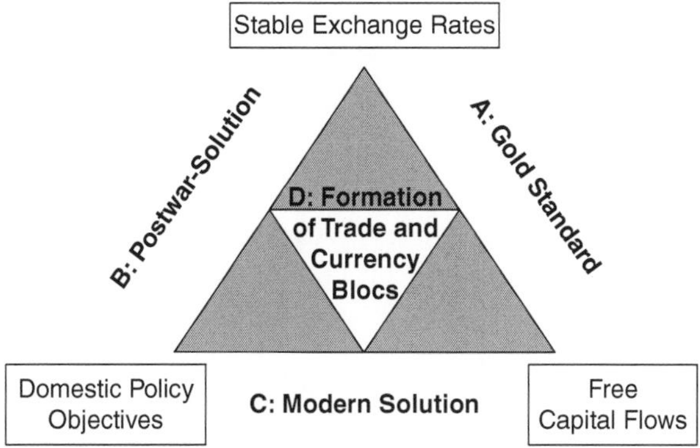

Fig. 3.2. The 'macroeconomic policy trilemma'

cycle, maybe on account of their belief that, with short-run rigidities in wages and prices, such policies can be effective. While the trilemma is a choice between policies or political means, it will be useful to note that it can also be expressed as a choice between policy objectives, namely the objectives of Confidence, Liquidity, and Adjustment—Paul Krugman's 'eternal triangle'. Confidence in this context means the ability to protect the exchange rate from speculation, especially from a currency crisis. Liquidity means access to capital, basically short-term capital mobility, while Adjustment means the ability to pursue macroeconomic stabilization policies. Whether expressed as the 'macroeconomic trilemma' or the 'eternal triangle', policy makers in small economies have to choose one of the following *four* policy regimes as illustrated in Figure 3.2. It is noteworthy that in any case the choices of policy makers will be interdependent. As we will see, policy makers experimented with all four options during the interwar years.

First policy makers can attempt to defend the exchange rate given capital mobility by adjusting monetary policy to this objective. This implies that policy makers are able and willing to sacrifice autonomous monetary policy (Option A). Alternatively, they can attempt to limit capital mobility in order to simultaneously stabilize the exchange rate and gain some room for autonomous monetary policy (Option B). Here an important issue for international policy coordination will be the level at which exchange rates are stabilized in the first place. Third, policy makers can sacrifice the stability of exchange rates to benefit from both open capital markets and autonomous monetary policy geared towards domestic objectives (Option C). The key problem here is clearly the ability of the central bank to fight inflation. Finally, policy makers can opt for the formation of economic blocs, for example by stabilizing the exchange rate with countries that have highly synchronized business cycles. Given that the members self-select into blocks in a way that they face similar shocks and share the objectives of macro-economic policy over the business cycle, they can continue to benefit from unrestricted international capital mobility, pursue autonomous monetary policy within their economic block, and maintain stable exchange rates between each other (Option D). Rodrik (2000) proposed to augment this 'macroeconomic policy trilemma' to a 'political trilemma', where the three typically desirable policy objectives are the defence of national sovereignty (beyond a national currency), economic integration (beyond capital mobility) and democratic politics based on an unrestricted franchise, a high degree of political mobilization, and democratic political institutions (beyond autonomous monetary policy). Let us keep this in mind when discussing the options of European policy makers in the interwar period.

Both in theory and practice, monetary policy in the interwar years was dominated by the gold standard. Governments that adhered to the gold standard regime essentially chose Option A in this framework (Obstfeld et al., 2004), where the value of the national currency was fixed in terms of gold, gold was free to flow between countries, and the quantity of money in each country was essentially determined by the balance of payments. Central banks were expected to follow the 'rules of the game' to support the adjustment of international balances of payments, not to support domestic macroeconomic policies. In a nutshell, these rules provided that, whenever gold flowed into a country, a central bank should increase the supply of national currency, and similarly whenever gold flowed out, the central bank was expected to contract its domestic assets (Nurkse, 1944: 66–67). Eichengreen argued that this regime of monetary policy was not automatic but actually relied on some form of central bank cooperation. If one central bank unilaterally reduced the discount rate but others failed to follow, it would have suffered reserve losses and might have been forced to increase the bank rate in order to defend the gold parity. This is why the Bank of England, as the leading central bank with plenty of resources and credibility prior to 1914, had to play a role as 'conductor of the international orchestra' (Keynes, 1930: 306) by 'signalling the need for coordinated action' (Eichengreen, 1992: 8) that others could follow. In addition, central banks overtly cooperated to increase the resources available to a central bank whenever its gold parity was under attack. Hence, the stability of the gold standard was based on the *joint* commitment of central banks to the rules of the game (Eichengreen, 1992: 8).

The experience of prolonged economic growth with stable prices during the period of the classical gold standard (1870–1913), suggests that this was a highly successful policy regime. After 1918, it was a near-universal aim of policy makers to replicate this success and return to the gold standard. It is debatable to what extent the alternatives to this option were understood (Eichengreen and Temin, 2000), but deviations from Option A were generally considered risky. First, adherence to the gold standard continued to be seen as a 'good housekeeping seal of approval' and hence a precondition for access to international capital markets (Bordo et al., 1999). Second, and related to this, the commitment to defend the gold parity of a currency was generally considered as the most effective mechanism to ensure price stability. But it proved extremely difficult to re-establish the gold standard after the war. The monetary policy regime that emerged during the early 1920s and started to be in full operation around 1927 was considerably less stable for various reasons. The conference at Genoa in April 1922[1] had recommended that countries should stabilize their currencies at the

[1] The Genoa Conference was—after the failed conference at Brussels in 1920—the second attempt to provide a framework for international cooperation after the First World War. It took place in

rates prevailing at that time to ease the transition for countries that had experienced significant inflation during and after the war. Moreover, the conference resolution suggested minimizing the need for gold by 'maintaining reserves in the form of foreign balances, such as the gold exchange standard' (quoted after Eichengreen, 1984: 19). But the conference failed to produce an understanding on central bank cooperation, except the suggestion that the Bank of England should call a meeting of central bankers to prepare a convention on these issues. In hindsight, the conference at Genoa 1922 was a failure, not at least because the US refused to participate. Some countries returned to the gold standard at parities on or close to the pre-war levels (such as Britain in 1925), which proved to put deflationary pressure on the economy. Others, such as France (de facto in 1926, de jure in 1928), returned at much lower parities, which contributed to a sustained balance of payment surplus in the latter. The adoption of a gold exchange standard increased the ratio of central bank liabilities to the gold base which increased the fragility of the system and opened new possibilities for sterilization operations. And finally, the envisaged convention on central bank cooperation had to wait until 1936, when Britain, the USA, and France signed the Tripartite Agreement. The *joint* commitment of central banks to the gold standard, and its rules of the game, had given way to a more limited commitment of individual central banks to defend their *own* gold parity: central banks tended to sterilize inflows of gold or other international assets rather than to reinforce them by concurrent changes in domestic assets. Considering the behaviour of 26 central banks over the period 1922–38 Nurkse (1944: 68ff.) found that, in more than 60 per cent of all cases, central banks were apparently trying to offset changes between their international and domestic assets.

When this new monetary system was put to a test in 1929 it failed and, what is more, it deepened the crisis considerably. Tightening monetary conditions and a collapse in consumer spending in the US hit already weak European economies.[2] Especially capital importers were put between Scylla and Charybdis who, in an attempt to defend their parity and access to foreign capital, put massive deflationary pressure on their economies (Wolf, 2008). Real wages and real interest rates soared, resulting in mass unemployment and a sharp decline in manufacturing output and investment. The political systems in Europe in turn, especially the various new democracies that had emerged after 1918, could not tolerate these policies of monetary tightening for long (Simmons, 1994). What was needed was either a coordinated reflation within the existing system (Eichengreen and Sachs, 1986) or a transition to a new system within the constraints of the trilemma. What happened was that all European countries clung on to the gold exchange standard until one after the other was forced to give it up. By 1932, the European economy

reaction to events that challenged the Paris peace settlements and demands for their revision from Germany, Soviet Russia, and the United States. Hosted by Italy's last democratic government, in 1922 from 10 April to 19 May the representatives of 34 countries convened to discuss the economic reconstruction of Europe, especially of central and eastern Europe and to improve the relationship between European capitalist regimes and Soviet Russia. See Fink (1984).

[2] The explanation for the onset of the Great Depression in the US and in Europe is still the subject of debate and the literature on this is too large to be cited here. Among others see Friedman and Schwartz (1963), Temin (1976), Hamilton (1987), Ohanian (2009), Ebell and Ritschl (2008).

had been fragmented into several currency and trade blocks that already foreshadowed the Second World War. What were the fundamental factors that prevented a coordinated response to the crisis?

3.3. THE SHADOW OF WORLD WAR ONE

In this section I will try to spell out several obstacles to international policy coordination in interwar Europe which proved to be fatal during the years 1930–33. All of them were more or less directly related to World War One. The war had been an inconclusive test for hegemonic power in Europe, and ended not so much with a peace but a transitional period in which states continued to fight the war and prepared to settle accounts—a 'second thirty years war'. The three most important consequences of the war with implications for the coordination of economic policies were the change in character and the fragility of the new political institutions, the unsettled issues of war debts and reparations, and the memories of the 1920s inflation which restricted the options of monetary policy.

Everywhere in Europe, the post-war situation made it necessary for societies to struggle over the distribution of income and war debts. The fundamental issue was 'whether deflation and unemployment would saddle a major share of the load on the working class, as contrasted with the rentier' (Kindleberger, 1986: 323). But the political bargaining power of labour had dramatically increased as a result of political compromises reached during and immediately after the war. Examples include the significant extension of the franchise or the introduction of the eight hour day in many countries. Not least, the political threat posed by the Soviet Union raised the political bargaining power of the moderate left. This undermined the prevailing solution to the macroeconomic policy trilemma under the gold standard: to sacrifice autonomous monetary policy geared towards macroeconomic stabilization. But when deflation in response to an outflow of gold and foreign exchange was no longer a viable option, and unilateral expansion was considered risky unless accompanied by a strict regime of exchange controls, international cooperation became more important than ever before (Eichengreen, 1992: 10).

But the new institutional framework made it more difficult to cooperate. The new political landscape that had emerged after 1918 was significantly more democratic than prior to the war, but also less stable. To start with, there were a number of new states including Poland, the Baltic States, Czechoslovakia, and other successors of the Habsburg Empire, but also the Republic of Irleand whose borders, sovereignty, and included national minorities continued to be the subject of international disputes throughout the interwar years (Wandycz, 1988). A prominent example was the internationalization of Danzig/Gdansk, and its Baltic seaport, and the creation of the so-called 'Polish corridor' that gave Poland access to the Baltic, but separated the German territory of Eastern Prussia from the rest of the German Empire. Polish governments made considerable efforts to use the corridor as a means of reducing the country's economic dependency on Germany. The backbone of these efforts was the development of Gdynia as main seaport to reduce dependency on Danzig/Gdansk, and the construction of a direct railway

Table 3.1. Average cabinet duration (years)

	1870–1913	1923–39
Austria-Hungary	2.3	09. (Austria) 1.5 (Hungary)
Belgium	3.3	1.3
France	1.3	0.6
Germany	1.9	1.4
Italy	1.5	1.4
Netherlands	2.3	2.1
Romania	1.3	0.7
Sweden	2.7	1.7
United Kingdom	1.7	1.3

Source: Banks and Textor (1971).

connection between the Upper Silesian coalfields and this new port. For both enterprises, the Polish government sought to attract foreign, especially French, capital, not least in order to create vested interests in the corridor (see Wolf, 2007). But political instability was by no means limited to the new democracies. Governments in nearly all European countries were less stable after the war than before. Table 3.1 shows the average duration of cabinets for a broad selection of countries.

Not only had the losers of the war, such as Germany or Austria and Hungary, experienced a significant increase in political tribalism and government instability after the war, but so had members of the winning coalition, notably France and Britain. This instability, accompanied in countries like Germany with an increase in the fragmentation of the acting coalition governments, impeded and delayed political decisions within countries and the coordination of policies across countries (Simmons, 1994).

War debts and reparations were a second major consequence of the war with implications for international policy coordination. The war had produced a web of debts between the Allies and massive claims for reparations against the central powers. This, and the rivalry with commercial loans, impeded the recreation of international finance in the 1920s (Kindleberger, 1986: 298). Germany in particular was opposed to reparation claims, but eager to attract commercial loans. In contrast, France wanted to get rid of war debts, had only limited interest in commercial lending, but considered reparations from Germany as necessary both to rebuild the devastated provinces in the north and east, and to repay war debts to Britain and, most importantly, to the United States. Britain, in turn, was, from about 1920 onwards, prepared to cancel out reparations and war debt but was interested in commercial lending. The United States had little interest in reparations. Congress wanted to collect the war debts and American financiers wanted to revitalize commercial lending (Schuker, 1988). Given the extent of the various claims, they significantly distorted the incentives for policy makers in domestic and international decisions. In May 1921, the Reparations Commission announced the London Schedule of Payments that amounted to a reparations bill of 132 billion gold marks, denominated in gold and payable in gold, commodities, or services. Critically, this bill came in two parts. Germany would have to pay interest and amortization on two ('A' and 'B') bond series over about 50 billion gold marks that were meant to cover the Allied war costs and debts, while the remaining 'C' bonds would be issued later depending on Germany's capacity to pay (Schuker, 1988). The former sum was comparable to pre-war experience, notably to the French indemnity of 1871, the 50th anniversary of which happened to coincide with the announcement of the London Schedule, and roughly in line with Keynes' estimation of a payable maximum (Ritschl, 2002: 223ff.). While payment on the second part of the bill was deferred until Germany would have become sufficiently prosperous, it had far-reaching political implications. Internationally, the 'C' bonds served as a strategic asset in inter-allied negotiations on war debts. Within Germany, they undermined the efforts of the so-called 'Weimar coalition' (the social-democrat SPD, the liberal DDP, and the conservative catholic Zentrum) to stabilize the young democracy, because the extent of this claim was considered as excessive even by moderate political forces. What is possibly more important, the link of the 'C' bonds to the condition of the German economy 'diminished the incentive for German policymakers to put their house in order' (Eichengreen, 1992: 128). After the conflict of interest about the settlement of war debts and reparations—especially between France, Germany, and the United States—had contributed to inflation and exchange rate instability in both France and Germany, the London Schedule was replaced by the Dawes Plan in 1924, and that would stay in place until 1929. The Dawes Plan differed from the London Schedule in several ways (Schuker, 1976: 180ff.). First of all, it reflected a new engagement of the US in European affairs, and US interest in European recovery to revitalize commercial lending. The new schedule immediately reduced the required annual payment to 1 billion marks in 1924–25, with a gradual rise to a standard annuity of 2.5 billion marks by 1928–29. After this, it was planned to adjust Germany's obligations according to some 'index of prosperity'. Together with an international loan of 800 million gold marks of foreign currency, this gave the German government some breathing space in 1924. Next, the plan avoided any definite statements about the extent of Germany's total liability, but rather proposed an arrangement that would allow 'to restore confidence, . . . to facilitate a final and comprehensive agreement . . . as soon as circumstances make this possible' (Commission des Réparations, 1924: 35). Finally, it introduced a distinction between Germany's obligation to raise the specified annuity internally on one hand and the problem of transferring the amount to the Allies on the other. To this end, the plan devised a new Bank of Issue in Berlin, where the German government had to deposit the reparation payments, and a special reparations agent. The reparations agent would then, jointly with a Transfer Committee, determine how much Germany could safely transfer to the Allies without causing foreign exchange difficulties. This arrangement essentially introduced a 'transfer protection' that safeguarded the service of commercial over reparation debts (Schuker, 1988: 35). After the very successful placement of the Dawes Loan, this new settlement of the reparations issue unleashed a wave of lending by the United States to Europe, especially to Germany. However, insofar as this flow of investment depended on the existence of US surpluses relative to Europe, and on the still pending issue of war debts and reparations, it produced a precarious equilibrium. A severe downturn of the business cycle, political tensions over the negotiations of the 'final and comprehensive agreement', when the Dawes Plan

Table 3.2. Consumer price indices in Germany and France 1920–26

	1920	1922	1924	1926
Germany (1914 = 100)	990	14602	128	141
France (1914 = 100)	371	315	395	560

Source: Feinstein et al., 2008: 40.

would expire, or doubts about the rising debt-servicing burden in central Europe could easily bring the system to a collapse (Eichengreen, 1992: 152). Apparently, this is what happened when negotiations over the Young Plan in 1929 met with a downturn of the business cycle (see section 3.4.1).

A third consequence of the war was inflation, which in several cases turned into hyperinflation. It is not so much the inflation itself, but the memory of inflation among policy makers and markets that mattered for international economic policy in the 1930s (see section 3.4). The experience of inflation during the 1920s would prove to be one of the best predictors of which countries would allow their currencies to depreciate in the 1930s. Technically, prices rose everywhere in Europe after the war because output was weak, while several factors contributed to an increase in money supply. It is disputed to what extent the increase in money supply was an endogenous response to changes in demand or the result of explicit economic policies, and the answer to this will vary across countries. Let us briefly consider the cases of France, Germany, and Poland. Table 3.2 gives the development of consumer prices 1920–26 in France and Germany.

Clearly, inflation in France never reached the extent of that in Germany (or Poland), but it was high enough to undermine public trust in the country's monetary authorities. After the war, the French expected German reparations to reconstruct the country to the extent that reconstruction expenditures in the extraordinary budget were balanced by reparation receipts that had not yet been collected (Kindleberger, 1986). When German deliveries fell into arrears over the summer of 1922, French and Belgian troops occupied the Ruhr in January 1923 in order to enforce deliveries. The failure of this occupation (not least because of the raging inflation in Germany) shifted attention back to the ability of French governments to balance the budget and raise taxes as opposed to pursuing inflationary policies. In March 1924, it took a significant increase in taxes, and an international effort with a major loan from J. P. Morgan, to counter a speculative attack on the franc (Kindleberger, 1986: 339–43). But this victory was short-lived. Over the year 1924 it became clear that the Banque de France had secretly increased note circulation while several governments struggled to reduce the fiscal deficit. After another *ten* ministers of finance between June 1924 and July 1926, the new Poincaré government used a new American loan and a sharply deflationary budget to stabilize the franc at around 20 per cent of its pre-war gold parity in late 1926. With the monetary reform in June 1928, the French franc returned at this parity, also de jure on the gold standard, and French monetary authorities 'intended to stay there' (Mouré, 2002: 73).

The German hyperinflation over 1921–24 was one of the most extreme cases recorded in history. The debate on it has often been described in terms of a competition between a balance-of-payments school and a fiscal view, but, fundamentally, the origins of inflation in Germany were similar to anywhere else: there was no consensus regarding the distribution of income and tax burdens. While some progress towards such a consensus was made during 1920, this was undermined by the reparations problem. The political situation after 1919 was fragile but the 'Weimar coalition' had implemented far-reaching tax reforms in 1919 and 1920 and organized significant 'interim payments', in anticipation of a formal agreement on reparations, that amounted to some 20 per cent of German national income in 1921 (Eichengreen, 1992: 129). After the Reparations Commission announced a reparations bill of 132 billion gold marks in May 1921, further tax reforms stalled. The mark depreciated dramatically, temporarily halted by a rescheduling of reparations payments in January 1922. With the occupation of the Ruhr, however, the stage was set for hyperinflation. Because of the lag between tax assessment and tax collection, inflation eroded government revues. The government started to print money on an unprecedented scale to cover expenses, and, from January 1923 onwards, to fund striking miners. While it is indisputable that the mounting budget deficits led to money creation, inflation, and depreciation, the fundamental cause of the budget deficit is still debated. German politicians maintained the balance-of-payments view that capital flight weakened the exchange rate, which drove up import prices and triggered domestic inflation, higher money demand, and hence an increase in money supply (Bresciani-Turroni, 1937: 45). While it can be shown that the budget would still have been in deficit in the absence of inflation, the extent of this deficit can be largely explained by reparations payments (Webb, 1989: 37). Hence, reparations can be seen as the ultimate reason why German inflation developed into hyperinflation (Eichengreen, 1992: 141). In turn, hyperinflation could be ended for good only because a radical change in monetary and fiscal policies in November 1923 was supported by the emergence of a new reparation regime: the Dawes Plan (Webb, 1988: 73).

The Polish experience of inflation and hyperinflation was no less dramatic. The government of the new Polish state in late 1918 faced the challenge to create a working fiscal administration and a common currency area out of the five currencies that were in circulation on Polish territory while it still fought a war with the Soviet army in the eastern provinces. The Warsaw government only controlled the Polish mark—a currency that the Germans had introduced after their occupation during the war (Trenkler and Wolf, 2005). It adopted a stepwise strategy to get rid of the competing banknotes. Some months after the introduction of the Polish mark as a parallel currency in the different areas, the other currencies were withdrawn. With the exception of Upper Silesia, this aim was realized in April 1920 (Zbijewski, 1931). While this quick institutional change was a remarkable success, it could not create the necessary revenues to win the ongoing war with the Red Army. However, it opened the way for the Polish government to effectively tax money holders via inflation. The data on Poland's hyperinflation is far from complete, but the general picture is clear. The money supply increased by 519 per cent between 1918 and 1919 and in the following year by another 929 per cent, reaching in 1923 more than 12,000,000 per cent of the 1918 level (Trenkler and Wolf, 2005: 202). Initial gains from seigniorage and the devaluation of the budget deficit were quickly wiped out by the costs of hyperinflation, namely the flight of capital. When Prime Minister Władysław Grabski tried to stabilize the currency in 1924, his strategy was to link the Polish currency with some foreign currency that had successfully restored the gold standard. Indeed, Grabski managed to realize this task with the help of a temporary property tax fixed in Swiss gold francs and several (small) international loans. By mid-January 1924, the nominal exchange rate had been stabilized and a new currency, the zloty ('golden'), was fixed to the Swiss gold franc. After a second wave of devaluations triggered by revelations about secret increases in currency circulation similar to that in France 1924–25, a new right-wing government under Marshall Piłsudski finally succeeded in stabilizing the currency in late 1926. This, and an American stabilization loan, allowed Poland in October 1927 to join the international gold exchange standard (Smith, 1936). The Piłsudski government considered this stabilization as one of its major achievements and was determined to defend the parity at any cost.

3.4. COORDINATION FAILURE: EUROPE'S REACTION TO THE GREAT DEPRESSION 1930–36

With the stabilization of the franc in 1926, and the lira in 1927, Europe had essentially completed the reconstruction of the gold standard. The political situation had also stabilized with the treaties of Locarno in late 1925,[3] some hopes for effective disarmament, and domestic stabilization in many European countries. But the new political and economic stability soon proved to be frail. Germany was at the brink of a recession already in 1927, as indicated by a fall in industrial investment (Temin, 1971: 247) and orders to German machinery industry (Ritschl, 2003a: 116). While the origins of the US depression are still heavily disputed,[4] tightening monetary conditions in the United States started to reduce foreign lending from about summer 1928 onwards. This hit European debtor countries first, which heavily depended on capital imports from America. In order to serve dollar and other foreign loans, borrowers had to shift their current account balances to surplus and tighten monetary and fiscal policies to limit domestic demand. Hence, the monetary tightening in the US and elsewhere produced a deflationary shock to Europe, transmitted by adherence to the gold standard. From mid-1929 onwards, wholesale prices started their long decline. Within the framework of the macroeconomic policy trilemma (see Figure 3.2), policy makers attempted to restore external balance at the expense of macroeconomic stabilization at home

[3] The Locarno treaties were signed in December 1925. The 'Rhineland pact' between France, Belgium, Germany, the UK, and Italy guaranteed Germany's western borders according to the Treaty of Versailles. Instead, Germany signed arbitration conventions with France, Belgium, Poland, and Czechoslovakia to negotiate Germany's eastern borders. Finally, France signed treaties on mutual assistance against Germany with Poland and Czechoslovakia that renewed earlier agreements. The treaties were interpreted as a step towards Franco-German reconciliation but simultaneously as a threat to the new states in Central and Eastern Europe.

[4] See footnote 1, especially the recent work by Ebell and Ritschl (2008) and Ohanian (2009).

(Option A). This in turn was the key transmission mechanism that turned a bad recession into the Great Depression (Temin, 1989: 38). In this section I discuss why it took so long (and so much unemployment) to find a new solution within the trilemma. It might be useful to split this discussion into two parts. First, I discuss the factors that prevented European policy makers from loosening their 'golden fetters' (Eichengreen, 1992), either in terms of devaluation, by imposing capital controls or both. Second, I discuss the related, but distinct, question of what factors prevented policy makers in Europe pursuing expansionary policies after they had been forced to abandon the gold standard.

3.4.1. The decision (not) to abandon the gold standard

The currency crisis of 1931 deepened the crisis but also triggered a first set of effective policy responses to the worldwide depression, when several countries were forced to abandon the gold standard. Notably, there was no single European country that abandoned the gold standard as a matter of choice, in contrast to the US in April 1933 (Temin and Wigmore, 1990: 489). A historical narrative would start with the experience of Europe's four largest short-term debtors Austria, Hungary, Germany, and Britain. In May 1931, the Creditanstalt, Austria's largest deposit bank, had to be rescued by the Austrian government (Schubert, 1991). Given the size of this commitment, the weak position of the Austrian economy, and difficulties over the negotiation of international assistance, the crisis turned into a currency crisis of the schilling, which then spread to Hungary. A different set of events that was ultimately linked to the issue of reparations led, in July 1931, to a crisis in Germany that looked like a 'twin crisis' with a near simultaneous run on bank deposits and the currency (Schnabel, 2004). When Germany was forced off gold in July 1931, the attention of the markets turned to the other large weak gold currency, sterling. From mid-July 1931, the Bank of England was losing gold at an alarming rate. In a situation of already very high unemployment, the incumbent Labour government was unable to agree on spending cuts large enough to calm the markets and it fell in August 1931. The following 'national government' under Ramsay MacDonald had to face the impossibility of further deflationary policies. It suspended convertibility on 19 September 1931, and many European countries followed immediately.

However, there was considerable variation in the pattern of exit from the gold exchange standard during the 1930s. France and Switzerland continued to adhere to the gold standard for another five years until September 1936, Poland until April 1936, Italy left in 1934, while others introduced exchange controls but continued to follow deflationary policies as if they were still on the gold standard. This variation in exit has been the subject of several comparative studies including Wandschneider (2008) and Wolf (2008). The literature on currency crisis that distinguishes between first, second, and third generation models gives useful guidance in understanding this curious pattern and to explore systematically the pressures that European countries on the gold standard faced in the 1930s. These models are not mutually exclusive but stress different aspects of currency crisis, notably all in the framework of the macroeconomic trilemma. The canonical ('first generation') currency crisis model by Krugman (1979) explains such crises as the outcome of a fundamental inconsistency between domestic policies—typically fiscal policies aimed at stabilizing the economy during a downturn—and the attempt to maintain a fixed exchange rate. Insofar as this takes capital mobility for granted, the model reflects the classic macroeconomic trilemma (see Figure 3.2). If the central bank has sufficiently large reserves, this inconsistency can be covered for some time. But there will be a point when these reserves become low enough to trigger a speculative attack that would quickly drive those reserves to zero and force an abandonment of the fixed exchange rate. Second generation models, for example Obstfeld (1986), build on this canonical model but stress that even if the development of fundamental variables is not particularly unfavourable, a currency crisis can occur because of—for example—self-fulfilling expectations, herding behaviour or contagion. The government weights the benefits from adherence to a currency peg (such as the possibility to import credibility to fight inflation) to those against the peg (such as the possibility to pursue a monetary policy according to domestic policy objectives) and these weights will change with the arrival of new information. In Obstfeld (1986), a crisis can occur when the loss arising from maintaining the current regime is considered to be at least as large as the combined loss from discretionary policy *and* the associated loss in credibility. Related to this, Calvo and Reinhart (2001, 2002) have argued that developing countries are reluctant to tolerate much variation in exchange rates because of a 'fear of floating' that mainly stems from a lack of credibility and the fear of losing access to capital markets. In models with coherent self-fulfilling expectations, there are multiple steady states in exchange rates and monetary policy. The arrival of 'bad news' from official statistics or changes in the political conditions can move the economy from one steady state to another. Herding models, in turn, are based on the idea that gathering information is costly. When the majority of participants behave adaptively and follow big participants in their behaviour, small random shocks to the latter can have large effects. Similarly, regional linkages through trade or financial relations can cause crisis contagion, as a crisis in one region will adversely affect the macroeconomic fundamentals—or at least the perception thereof—in the second region (which is not necessarily the geographical neighbour). Finally, third generation models such as McKinnon and Huw (1996) or Krugman (1998) highlight that structural problems in the banking and financial sector can affect the probability that currency crises occur in the first place, but also affect the character and length of the currency crisis. These models allow for the possibility of a simultaneous currency and banking crisis—a 'twin crisis'. For example, in Krugman (1998), the government guarantees investments in companies for banks that are mainly branch offices of foreign banks or whose business strategy relies mainly on borrowing money in international capital markets to extend loans to domestic companies. The incentive for the government to issue guarantees comes from an attempt to attract foreign investment. However, when the government fails to regulate and control financial agents, serious problems of moral hazard can make the country prone to a banking crisis that will turn into a currency crisis as foreign funds are withdrawn. Note that such 'twin crises' could also arise without a failure to regulate banks. In the presence of rigidities, especially nominal wage-stickiness and non-contingent financial contracts, price deflation can cause significant increases in both real wages and

Table 3.3. Discrete time survival models, January 1928–December 1936

	Logit	Logit
Baseline Hazard: constant	18.455 (0.779)	−26.891 (−0.195)
Baseline Hazard: months on gold	**1.607** (2.303)	3.770 (0.529)
Baseline Hazard: months on gold X debtor		**1.988** (4.400)
Whole28	**−2.039** (−1.786)	**−2.821** (−1.987)
Banking	**−0.387** (−2.865)	−1.003 (−0.223)
Banking X debtor		**−1.092** (−1.775)
Devalhist	**0.520** (2.297)	−1.012 (−0.691)
Cover	**−8.152** (−2.194)	**−10.399** (−2.198)
Indep	**10.526** (2.684)	8.557 (1.447)
Polity	**3.103** (2.025)	**0.681** (1.811)
Int_France	**−10.719** (−2.191)	**−9.518** (−1.634)
Tradegold	**−3.426** (−2.482)	**−2.044** (−1.560)
Number of Observations	484	484
McFadden R2	0.811	0.860

Source: Wolf (2008).
(Binary dependent variable = 1 in the month of exit; robust standard errors in parentheses, bold letters indicate significance at 10 per cent or better).

in real debt—Irving Fisher (1933) discussed the latter in the context for the Great Depression as 'Debt Deflation' (see Bernanke, 1995). While a rise in real wages would tend to increase unemployment and hence foster political pressure on monetary policy, debt deflation can trigger a wave of bankruptcies in highly indebted sectors and adversely affect private banks as their main creditors. Together, this might produce a 'twin crisis' with both banks and currency under pressure.

Several of these factors were at play during the 1930s, and their variation over time and across countries can explain the pattern of Europe's long exit from the gold standard that was not completed before the autumn of 1936 (Wolf, 2008: 391–5). Table 3.3 shows the results from a discrete time survival model that explains the timing of exit from the gold standard for a panel of eight European countries based on monthly data 1928–36.

A key factor for European capital importers was the tightening of monetary policy in the US as the main capital exporting country, which changed macroeconomic fundamentals in debtor countries and put pressure on their gold and foreign exchange reserves (Eichengreen, 1992). Spiralling deficits and declining reserves forced one after the other off gold. As the deflationary pressures grew stronger (captured by indices of wholesale prices with 1928 = 100, *Whole28*), countries abandoned the gold standard. Clearly, the lower the cover ratio (of gold and foreign exchange relative to M1), the earlier a country had to leave. Note that several circumstances probably 'conditioned' the fundamentals in some countries during the 1920s, which are not directly captured in this comparative analysis. Examples include the return to gold in the 1920s at unsustainable parities—too low in France but too high in Britain (Keynes, 1972; Redmond, 1982; Sicsic, 1992), the particular role of reparations for the German crisis (Ritschl, 2002), and growing current account deficits on account of exogenous changes in the structure of world trade after the war (Svennilson, 1954) may all have weakened fundamentals of European economies over the course of the 1920s and hastened the collapse of the gold standard. We will come back to some of these factors further below.

Beyond fundamentals, expectations and beliefs of both governments and market participants played a significant role for monetary policy during the 1930s crisis akin to second generation models. We saw earlier that policy makers all over Europe were eager to re-establish the gold standard after 1918 in an attempt to increase the credibility of monetary policy (Bordo et al., 1999). However, both policy makers and their electorates differed in their adhesion to gold standard orthodoxy (their 'mentality') that can be explained by differences in their own recent experience. Everywhere in Europe, but especially in countries which suffered a hyperinflation or a significant depreciation of their currencies relative to the pre-war parities, there prevailed the opinion that only adherence to gold could ensure price stability (Straumann, 2010). This can be captured by the parity at which a country resumed the gold standard in the mid-1920s, expressed as a percentage of its pre-war parity (*devalhist* that varied from 0 to 100). The positive and significant coefficient on this variable indicates that countries which returned to gold below their pre-war parity, because of strong inflation in the 1920s, were less prone to exit gold *ceteris paribus*. Column 2 in Table 3.3 shows that this actually mattered only for capital importers. This suggests that it was indeed a 'fear of floating' that prevented these countries from leaving gold (see also Wandschneider 2008).

Earlier, I argued that the stability and character of domestic institutions mattered for the course of the Great Depression. For example, the perceived risk of expansionary monetary policies to produce hyperinflation may be smaller the less directly a government can affect monetary policy (Kydland and Prescott, 1977). Table 3.3 shows that, as a rule, countries with more independent central banks (captured by *Indep* where a high value indicates high independence) were prone to exit the gold standard earlier. More importantly, Table 3.3 bears out that the political system prevailing in a country strongly affected a country's choice of monetary policy. The extension of the franchise (James, 2001) and political instability (Eichengreen and Simmons, 1995) apparently weakened the ability of governments to commit to the rules of the gold standard. Authoritarian regimes had tools at hand to defend the gold standard and successfully suppress any political quest for expansionary full employment policies that arose under the trilemma. This ability to defend the gold standard at home is measured here by *polity*, which reflects a combined score on a democracy variable (0–10) and an autocracy variable (0–10) based on Marshall and Jaggers (2005). As shown in Table 3.3, and highlighted in the historical literature, less democratic governments, such as Italy or Poland, stayed longer on gold *ceteris paribus*. For example, the French democracy faced significantly lower pressures to leave the gold standard in the early 1930s because of much higher gold and foreign exchange reserves and a belated onset of deflation.

Yet another set of arguments can be linked to the idea of contagion in second generation models: the degree of economic integration between country pairs differed widely during the interwar years. For example, the crisis of the Austrian Creditanstalt in May 1931 is typically seen as the immediate trigger for the Hungarian crisis that led to the exit from gold (see Ellis, 1939: 88) and many argued that there were elements of contagion from Austria into the German banking system (Born, 1967; Schnabel, 2004). In contrast, spill-over effects into Italy were apparently limited, which is partly explained by government intervention (Feinstein et al., 1997) and partly by a more limited degree of financial integration. Similarly, exchange rate stabilization may have dominated other monetary policy goals in the presence of tight trade relations. For example, countries which traded intensively with the UK might have had stronger incentives to follow Britain off gold in 1931 than others, while integration with France may have had the opposite effect (Ritschl and Wolf, 2011). Straumann and Woitek (2009) argue that the monetary policy pursued by the Swedish Riksbank—which has been praised as a predecessor of modern inflation targeting (Fregert and Jonung, 2004)—can be largely explained by the attempt to stabilize the exchange rate with sterling. Table 3.3 clearly shows that the exit decision of major trading partners could force a country to leave as well. Adherence of the major trading partner to gold (*tradegold*), and beyond this the level of trade integration with France in 1928 (*Int_France*), induced countries to stay longer on the gold standard (on the latter see Wolf, 2008: 397).

Finally, it can be shown that the occurrence of a banking crisis affected the course of the currency crisis of 1931, even after taking all the other elements into account as suggested in third generation models. This is captured by a simple monthly index of bank deposits, again indexed to 1928 = 100 (*banking*). While this is arguably a rough proxy—ignoring for example any 'structural' weaknesses of a country's banking sector—it should reflect any banking crises serious enough to threaten the currency of a country. Notably, banking crisis occurred, and therefore mattered, only in debtor countries (see Table 3.3, column 2). This last finding leads us back to the historical narrative of the beginning of this section and the key impediments for international cooperation during the currency crisis of 1931: unstable institutions, war debts and reparations, and the memory of hyperinflation.

The reparations problem had always a domestic and an international dimension, which developed over time. The already fragile Weimar Republic had been further destabilized with a significant rise in unemployment during the winter of 1928/29. A centre-left coalition government fought against communists and an increasingly well-organized right. The best part of 1929 had been dominated by a public referendum against the Young Plan and, in fact, any form of further reparations. This referendum clearly failed in December 1929, but it had helped to focus the disparate parties of the right with Hitler's *NSDAP (National Socialist German Workers' Party)* as the new rising force (Schulze, 1982: 311). On the international dimension, the reparation settlement under the Dawes Plan of 1924 had allowed significant net-capital inflows from the US to Germany between 1924 and 1928, not at least because of a 'transfer protection' clause by which commercial debt had been made de facto senior to reparation debt (Schuker, 1988: 47–53). Under the new Young Plan, the reparations annuity was marked down but the 'transfer protection' had been removed (see section 3.2). This needs to be seen in the context of the Mellon–Bérenger accord of 1926, which committed France to a schedule for the repayment of her inter-allied war debts with the United States. However, the agreement was not ratified before 22 July 1929, because of a dispute over a 'safeguard' clause that would have made payments contingent on the receipt of German reparations (Rhodes, 1969: 802).

German government officials, industrialists, and economists alike realized that this new schedule limited Germany's access to foreign credit not only during the crisis but even more so in good times (Ritschl, 2002: 130). From March 1930 onwards, Germany had no government with a stable parliamentary majority any more, but a series of cabinets that ruled either by presidential decree or by ad hoc majorities. The September election in 1930 showed a massive radicalization of the electorate, when (based on a voter turnout of 82 per cent) only two major parties could increase the share of their votes: the communists from 10.6 per cent to 13.1 per cent and the Nazis from 2.6 per cent in 1928 to a spectacular 18.3 per cent. In this situation, the government under Heinrich Brüning relied more than ever on tangible success in the international arena to secure political support at home, and it was compelled by those around President Hindenburg to look for exactly this. The three most important elements on the foreign policy agenda were, therefore, revisionist in nature: to end reparations, to lift restrictions on Germany's market access to eastern and south-eastern Europe, and to remove restrictions on Germany's military capacity. In March 1931, the German and Austrian governments announced a preliminary agreement to form a customs union (Orde, 1980: 52) that was considered as a serious threat in Czechoslovakia and caused a political confrontation with France. When the Austrian government attempted to secure an international loan in the wake of the deepening crisis of the Creditanstalt in May 1931, the French demanded a renunciation of the customs union. Negotiations over an international loan took more than two weeks and intensified the run on the schilling. The loan that was finally arranged at the end of May 1931 was exhausted within five days (Kindleberger, 1986: 361). Because of the still significant reserves of the Austrian Nationalbank, this process continued for several weeks until September 1931 when the country was forced to introduce exchange controls and hence left the gold standard (Eichengreen, 1992: 269).

The crisis in Austria worsened an already precarious situation in Germany (see Temin 1971; Voth 2003). German financial institutions showed increasing signs of distress. August 1929 saw the collapse of FAVAG, Germany's second largest insurance company, followed by a stock market crash and several bank failures, but with little effect on the currency (Schnabel, 2004: 846). With the effects of the American depression spreading, and German creditworthiness in decline,[5] the Young loan in June 1930 briefly gave some breathing space before the political radicalization with the September elections triggered a significant wave of capital flight. Great branch banks such as Deutsche Bank, Danatbank, and Dresdner Bank experienced large withdrawals of foreign (but not domestic) deposits between June 1930 and March 1931 (Schnabel, 2004: 851). This was clearly related to their deteriorating liquidity positions, but combined with mounting doubts by investors about the Reichsbank's ability to support these banks with foreign exchange in times of crisis. In May 1931 this long heralded crisis had apparently arrived. It was in this situation that the Brüning government attempted to use the

[5] There was actually one successful major international loan to Germany after the Young loan of June 1930, organized by Lee, Higginson, and even with French participation; see Ferguson and Temin (2003: fn. 67). However, the circumstances of this loan were rather particular and included not least French demands for additional securities and further fiscal tightening in Germany; see James (1985, 121ff) and Ritschl (2002: 133–7).

crisis and its very limited room for manœuvre as an opportunity to get rid of reparations once and for all. According to his confidant, state-secretary Hans Schäffer of the Finance Ministry, Brüning was convinced that the issue of reparations could not be resolved once the world economy started to recover.[6] His policy in 1931 can be described as an explicit effort to signal to the Allies that German goodwill was ultimately futile without far-reaching concessions on reparations. Without doubt, this policy involved great risks. But the same applied to potential alternatives as we will see in section 3.4.2. As described earlier, any signal of political 'goodwill' during the crisis of 1931 essentially amounted to the announcement of radically deflationary policies. On the eve of a visit to the British prime minister, the cabinet had decided on another bundle of deflationary measures on an unprecedented scale that appeared to be unacceptable to the majority of the German parliament (Schulz, 1992: 357). During Brüning's stay in Britain, on 6 June 1931 the government published a carefully drafted statement that announced the deflationary measures together with a dramatic appeal that the German people had now reached the limit of their ability to suffer and needed relief from the burden of reparation (Schulz, 1992: 382). The ensuing run on the Reichsmark came to a halt when several parties, including the moderate left, decided not to overturn the new budget on 16 June (Winkler, 1993: 413) and President Hoover proposed a moratorium on war debts and reparations on 20 June to gain time for international negotiations. However, France showed strong resistance against the moratorium until 7 July. In the meantime, news spread about massive losses of Nordwolle, a textile company, which sparked a run on its main creditors, Danatbank and Dresdner Bank (Kindleberger, 1986: 363). The remainder was a repetition of the events in Austria, but now in the setting of a 'twin crisis' (Schnabel, 2004). International efforts to halt the run on the Reichsmark and support the Reichsbank in its attempt to bail out the banks were too little too late, largely because of disputes about reparations and Germany's ability to continue deflation. Between August and September, Germany imposed increasingly stringent exchange controls and thereby defected from the gold standard (Eichengreen, 1992: 276). As described earlier, the crisis spread to Britain and forced a series of other countries off gold. While this in principle opened the way for recovery, the way was only reluctantly taken.

3.4.2 The decision (not) to pursue expansionary policies

The purpose of this section is to discuss the factors that prevented policy makers in Europe from pursuing expansionary policies after they had been forced to abandon the gold standard. Within the trilemma (see Figure 3.2) the wave of exit from gold in autumn 1931 that included Austria, Britain, Czechoslovakia, Germany, Hungary, and all of Scandinavia, should have allowed policy makers to implement policies of fiscal and monetary expansion in order to stabilize their economies. As we will see, this was done only very reluctantly from about summer 1932 onwards.

[6] See the letter by Hans Schäffer to Hans Staudinger, dated 12 July 1952, cited in Schulze (1982: 351).

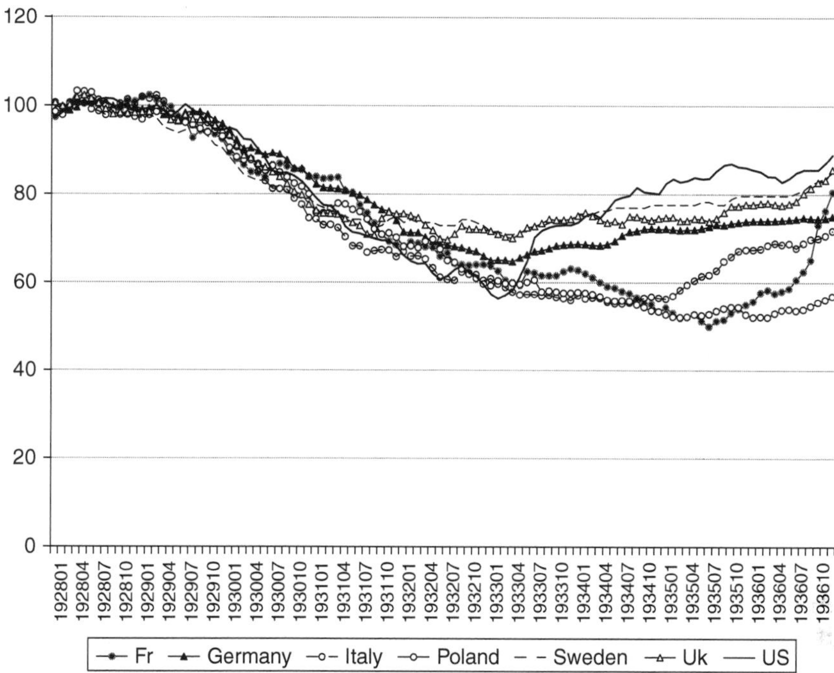

Fig. 3.3. Wholesale prices in various countries, 1928–36 (1928 = 100)
Source: Wolf (2008).

As a rule, policies did not become strongly expansionary before 1935. In the following I will briefly describe three factors at work—a continued fear of inflation in memory of the early 1920s, constraints stemming from international disputes over the final settlement of war debts and reparations, and rearmament—and focus on the experience in Britain, Germany, France, and Poland. In terms of the 'eternal triangle', I argue that governments continued to fear another collapse of the currency (confidence). This was exacerbated by political factors that affected short-run capital flows, namely tensions over war debts and reparations until 1933, to be followed by fears of another war after the rise of Hitler (liquidity). Together, this contributed to a fragmentation of Europe into currency and trade blocs (or Option 'D' in Figure 3.2), where the reluctance to pursue expansionary policies was finally broken by rearmament programmes roughly along the lines of these blocs (adjustment). Figure 3.3 shows the development of wholesale prices (1928 = 100) for various parts of Europe.

Britain suspended gold convertibility and introduced a system of a managed float that allowed a significant devaluation of sterling (Howson, 1980). A group of countries that followed Britain off gold in September and October 1931 (with several currencies pegged to sterling) started to recover from about mid-1932 onwards. Recovery in the US, in turn, was related to Roosevelt's decision to leave the gold standard in April 1933 together with the announcement and implementation of a whole set of new economic policies, the 'new deal' (see Fishback, 2010;

and chapter 10 of this volume). Another group of countries tried to follow France in her policy of strict adherence to the gold standard without imposing exchange controls and at prevailing parities; including Belgium, Czechoslovakia, Italy, the Netherlands, Poland (with Danzig), and Switzerland. All of them experienced a continued deflation, and further economic decline (see Figures 3.1 and 3.3). Finally, there was a group of 'exchange control countries', including Germany, Austria, Hungary, and several other central and eastern European countries, that had openly introduced exchange controls to limit further capital losses, but did not devalue. Instead, they introduced a complex web of clearing agreements to manage trade on a bilateral basis at increasingly inappropriate exchange rates (Nurkse, 1944: 162–89). To some extent, membership in the 'gold bloc', 'exchange control bloc', and even the 'sterling bloc' that emerged around Britain was as much a signal of strategic political orientation as of actual economic policy, which can help to explain why these blocs had little effect on trade (Ritschl and Wolf, 2011). Czechoslovakia, for example, introduced exchange controls in October 1931 but continued to consider itself a member of the gold bloc until early 1934 (Ellis, 1939: 36).

After Britain had to suspend convertibility in September 1931, the Bank of England increased the bank rate to 6.5 per cent accompanied by discussions about the course of future monetary policy. These discussions were 'strongly coloured at the beginning by fears of a dangerous inflation' (Sayers, 1976: 418). Even more so, officials at the Treasury continued the tight fiscal policy stance they had followed during the depression. Fiscal policy did not become expansionary before the extension of Britain's rearmament programme in 1937/38 (Middleton, 1981; Thomas, 1983). What caused the recovery then, visible in price and output data, was the combined effect of devaluation in 1931 and a monetary expansion that started in early 1932. According to Broadberry (1986), the competitive gain of devaluation and growth impulse was particularly large in 1932. Given devaluation elsewhere and a significant reorientation of trade in the wake of a universal rise of trade barriers in terms of tariffs, quotas, and exchange controls, the effective exchange rate increased from 1933 onwards (Cairncross and Eichengreen, 1983: 92). From late February 1932 onwards, the Bank of England started a stepwise reduction of the bank rate. This new policy of 'cheap money' was introduced, despite a fear of inflation, partly in the hope of a domestic economic recovery, partly it was done to reduce the cost of government debt service and help to balance the budget, which was considered crucial to regain confidence in the markets (Howson, 1975: 89). The consequent recovery was visible but not spectacular, at least in terms of unemployment rates that never consistently fell below 10 per cent (Thomas, 1988: 99). The experience in other countries of the 'sterling bloc' was similar. In a broader perspective, Britain, and countries dependent on trade with Britain, moved towards the last option of the trilemma: they continued to maintain relatively stable exchange rates between each other, benefitted from some limited degree of capital mobility, and could still pursue 'autonomous' monetary policy within their economic block that was essentially managed by Britain.

The case of Germany's belated recovery has attracted considerable attention in the literature, not least because German economic policy during and after the crisis of July 1931 apparently contributed to the rise of the NSDAP (Komlos and

Stoegbauer, 2004). I will not attempt to summarize the vast literature, but present a perspective on recent and ongoing research. Let us start with some data. Chancellor Brüning was dismissed in late May 1932; after the von Papen government, Hitler was appointed Chancellor in late January 1933. The data on manufacturing output (see Figure 3.1) shows that the crisis in Germany had reached its low point in July 1932, roughly coinciding with the conference at Lausanne that ended reparations. Orders to German machine builders started to increase in autumn 1932 (Buchheim, 2008: 384) and the German Institut für Konjunkturforschung (IfK) declared on 21 December 1932 that the German economy showed clear signs of recovery (IfK 1932: 151). Similar to the experience elsewhere, this recovery was slow and could result in a reduction in unemployment only with a significant time lag and from an extraordinary level of German unemployment above 40 per cent in 1932 (Galenson and Zellner, 1957).

The focus of the still ongoing debate is on the assessment of Brüning's economic policy between June 1931 and May 1932. Following the logic of the monetary policy trilemma, Germany should have been able to pursue expansionary policies after it had been forced to abandon the gold standard, similar to Britain (from February 1932 onwards). In contrast, the German government continued its deflationary policy after the summer 1931, accompanied by political turmoil and heated discussions about the appropriate course of economic policy (see Borchardt, 1979 and 1990). On 15 and 16 September 1931, several leading German economists discussed the available policy options, including Colm, Eucken, and Roepke (Borchardt and Schoetz 1987). The explicit aim of the meeting, convened by the Reichsbank and the Friedrich-List society, was to discuss a stimulation of the economy, which was considered to be necessary to reduce mass unemployment. The discussion focused on the feasibility of a credit expansion to fund public labour programmes as suggested by Wilhelm Lautenbach, a high-ranking official at the Economics ministry. In summary, the economists warned against any expansionary policy without international consent. Once the international constraints were removed, they recommended implementing expansionary policies without further delay. This paradox double-strategy was apparently also the one followed by Brüning, who prepared, in early 1932, several expansionary programmes that were implemented by his successors von Papen and Hitler (Ritschl, 2002: 172–6; Buchheim, 2008: 391). But the crucial negotiations on reparations (and related to this, war debts) following the Hoover moratorium of June 1931 were delayed, not least by elections in France and the United States, while unemployment and support for the NSDAP rose in Germany. When reparations were finally cancelled at Lausanne in early July 1932 (still subject to US consent on a reduction of war debts), Brüning had already been forced to resign and Hitler was within reach of power.

Hence, the question is whether expansionary economic policies could have succeeded prior to the summer of 1932. The perceived risks of unilateral monetary or fiscal expansion ranged from another uncontrollable inflation, renewed pressures by the Allies such as another occupation of the Ruhr, to forced autarky. Holtfrerich (1982, 1990 and 1996) and Temin (1989) argued that none of the alternatives could have been more risky than the policy pursued: 'even a certain amount of chaos on the way to recovery might well have been preferable to . . . the rise of Hitler' (Temin 1989: 73). While this is certainly true in hindsight, it can hardly do justice to the historical circumstances. First, the international risks of unilateral steps taken by Germany in 1932 were indeed considerable. The government must have weighed the risks based on the experience of the Ruhr occupation ten years earlier, which was followed by the dramatic collapse of the mark. Second, expansionary policy would have been the remedy within our framework of the macroeconomic policy trilemma. But from the perspective of spring 1932 it was far from obvious that any type of expansionary policy would have produced a significant and quick reduction in unemployment. If anything, German economists and policy makers were more optimistic in that respect than most of their European counterparts in Britain—Keynes notwithstanding—and certainly France.[7] Related to this, all parts of Germany's economy that supported the Weimar democracy (the moderate left, centre, and liberals) had an interest in Germany's re-integration into world markets. In contrast, both the traditional and the extreme right argued for protectionism or outright autarky. This helps to explain how Brüning could find a (silent) majority for many of his deflationary measures for so long, even among the moderate left. It also suggests a reason why an initially limited fiscal expansion under a right-wing alliance was so surprisingly effective, and why a Brüning government may not have done it: because German expansionary policy in 1932 under the prevailing reparations settlement essentially implied autarky, only the far-right could provide a credible regime change comparable to that in the US (Eggertsson, 2008; see also Temin 1989: 112–17). This is an area for further research that would have to go beyond the framework of the macroeconomic trilemma.

Let us finally consider the case of Germany's largest neighbours, France in the west and Poland in the east. Both countries are of interest here, because both adhered to the gold standard and deflationary policies until 1936, but under strikingly different circumstances. France was a creditor country, Poland a debtor. France was clearly under less pressure to leave the gold exchange standard in the early 1930s than any other European country (and probably in the world), while Poland experienced the deepest and longest decline of industrial production in Europe. After Britain's exit from gold in 1931, France continued to attract gold; the cover ratio remained steadily high until December 1935. Similarly, after the US devaluation in 1933, this did not immediately weaken the French position. However, it became increasingly clear that France had lost any competitive advantage that it may have had on account of an initially 'undervalued' currency. As argued by Paul Reynaud in his 'devaluation' speech to the Chamber of Deputies in June 1934, France and the gold bloc had become the most expensive countries in the world. And further domestic price deflation apparently hindered recovery, as the contrast with countries that had devalued showed (see Mouré, 1988: 487). Indeed, while industrial production started to recover from the depression in most countries in late 1932, this recovery came to a halt in France in mid-1933, just after the US had left gold. On the other hand, French unemployment was slowly rising, but still markedly below the European average, gold reserves stayed high and the financial sector seemed to be resilient. For example,

[7] Recent studies cast doubts on the effects of fiscal expansion in Germany after 1933 (Ritschl 2003b; Weder, 2006).

the index of bank deposits (1928 = 100) (mentioned in section 3.4.1) still stood at 95.6 in 1934. While there is evidence that some pressure to leave gold was built up over the year 1935, and many signs indicate changes in the public opinion, a real change occurred only in late 1935: the cover ratio started to decline between December 1935 and January 1936, and bank deposits started to be withdrawn. After the Front Populaire, which rejected further deflation (at least in the election programme) had won the elections in May 1936, these pressures increased very sharply with the index of bank deposits declining from 84.5 in April 1936 to 77.8 in July 1936, and the cover ratio plummeting over the same time from 80.3 to 65.2. In addition to this, military considerations may have contributed to France's abandonment of gold in 1936 as recently argued by Hallwood et al. (2007). German rearmament under Hitler was carefully observed throughout Europe. The massive rise in German military spending from 1934 onwards, the reintroduction of conscription in March 1935, but especially the reoccupation of the Rhineland in March 1936 put pressure on French military spending. According to Einzig (1937) the government refused a general mobilization called for by the military because of its budgetary implications. Hallwood et al. (2007) argue that this growing inconsistency between the need to increase military spending and fiscal discipline under the gold standard added to the problem of overvaluation und undermined the credibility of French adherence to gold. They show that short-term interest rates and yield gaps (short-term relative to long-term rates) in France relative to Switzerland reacted to German militarization. When the government announced a new 21 billion franc rearmament programme in early September, partly in response to the lengthening of German military service in late August, capital outflow accelerated. Bank of France reserves were again falling sharply, and France finally devalued on 25 September 1936 (Frankenstein, 1982).

Poland is a closely related case, which has been so far largely neglected in the literature. The country was the only debtor country that joined the gold bloc in 1933 and stands out in comparison to all her neighbours, especially Czechoslovakia and Hungary. As I argue in Wolf (2008), this adherence to gold and the late decision to exit and start an expansionary policy in 1936 was tightly related to Poland's relations with France and military considerations. The Piłsudski regime that had ruled Poland since May 1926 was predominantly concerned with strategies to defend the independence and territorial integrity of the new Polish state against foreign aggression (especially from Germany and the USSR, see Wandycz 1988). The perceived risk that leaving the gold standard can produce monetary instability was in part on account of the Polish experience of hyperinflation until 1923 followed by a second inflation in 1925–26 (as for example argued in the earlier Polish literature, see Knakiewicz, 1967). But in contrast to other central European countries that experienced a hyperinflation in the 1920s (such as Austria or Hungary), the Polish government was afraid of an additional cost of leaving gold: losing access to 'friendly' capital in terms of the political system of Versailles. For example, in August 1931 the Polish chargé d'affaires, Muehlstein, discussed in Paris the possibility of replacing the influence of German banks in Upper Silesia with French capital. 'As long as the situation was normal, the fight with the German banks was very difficult, but now, when the German *krach* had undermined their authority, it would just be a political sin not to use this opportunity and not to try to replace the German capital by French capital'.[8] At the same time, the question of how to finance the urgent modernization of the Polish army came up again because the depression started to produce growing budget deficits and because the government feared the growing political instability in Germany. After a Polish attempt, in July 1929, to negotiate a new French armament credit of over 1.5 billion francs had failed, renewed efforts to at least get the final instalment of the 1921 credit—frozen since Locarno—succeeded in February 1931. The deliveries were scheduled for May 1931 until December 1933 (Ciałowicz, 1970: 162f). After this, the Polish side immediately attempted to discuss a new armament credit via Ambassador Chłapowski in Paris. When this failed, Piłsudski sent a special envoy, Targowski, to Paris in November 1931 to explore the chances for private armament credits (Ciałowicz, 1970: 164) followed by an official request of the Polish General Staff about the price for a large delivery of heavy weapons. In this political environment of 1931 it is hardly surprising that Poland followed neither Germany (still her largest trading partner) nor later Britain off gold. In addition to a possible risk of inflation, the Polish government feared the loss of access to French capital when it felt the need for it most. Polish monetary policy apparently hinged to a large degree on the strategic considerations of the authoritarian regime. This is supported by a private memorandum of late 1935 by W. M. Zawadzki, an eminent Polish economist and founding member of the Econometric Society, who served as minister of finance between 1931 and 1935 (Landau and Tomaszewski, 1965). In the memorandum he recapitulated his monetary policy. Importantly, this memorandum was never meant for publication (see Landau and Tomaszewski, 1965). Zawadzki stressed that his monetary policy was based on two principles: first, to finance the military budget of the Polish state, to which the whole economy must be adapted, and second, to stick to the gold exchange standard. He describes his motivation for the latter as threefold: first, to gain access to foreign capital; second, to avoid domestic turmoil after a destabilization of the currency that could undermine the authority of the regime; and third, Zawadzki mentions the fact that a devaluation of the złoty would 'automatically decrease the military budget', because it would decrease its purchasing power abroad.[9] In addition, he was positively convinced that it was possible to overcome the crisis by a downward adjustment of prices,[10] and he pursued this policy until his demission in October 1935. Among the several effects of the death of Marshall Piłsudski in May 1935 was the political comeback of Kwiatkowski, 'father of the harbour of Gdynia', who stood for the idea of reducing the economic dependency on German trade. In October 1935, Kwiatkowski replaced Zawadzki as minister of finance and, in December 1935, the cabinet decided on a four year investment plan that merged older plans for 'big-push' industrialization with plans for setting up a large-scale Polish armament industry to be concentrated in the 'Security Triangle' formed by Vistula and San (see Strobel, 1975; Landau and Tomaszewski, 1999). In the meantime, the economic pressure to finally release the 'golden fetters' had increased sharply, with a large

[8] Own translation from a Letter of Muehlstein to Polish Foreign Minister Zaleski, 8 August 1931, cited in Landau and Tomaszewski (1964: 315).

[9] Landau and Tomaszewski (1965: 127–51, especially page 134).

[10] Landau and Tomaszewski (1965: 132).

decline in Poland's reserves from mid-1935 onwards, mainly from the imposition of new exchange restrictions in Germany and elsewhere. Poland's membership in the gold bloc had become a mere façade without any economic foundation. The time to act finally came in March 1936 with the remilitarization of the Rhineland, when Germany de facto cancelled the treaty of Locarno: a major threat to Poland. Poland signalled her preparation to support France in an armed conflict in the spirit of the 1921 convention, but France did not react (Ciałowicz, 1970: 216f). Moreover, the changing political climate in France, with an expected success of Blum's Front Populaire, questioned the future of the gold bloc altogether (Mouré, 2002: 209ff.). On 9 April 1936, a National Defence Fund was set up by presidential decree to be equipped with 1 billion złoty over the period 1937–40 in order to finance the modernization of Poland's army (Krzyżanowski, 1976: 146), apparently in anticipation of a radical change in monetary policy. Only two weeks later, on 26 April, another presidential decree introduced exchange controls, and thereby ended Poland's adherence to the gold exchange standard. The half-official Monthly Bulletin of the state-owned Bank Gospodarstwa Krajowego (BGK), published in French, defended this step as follows:

> Therefore, the introduction of exchange controls was not directly determined by economic difficulties. The Polish government saw itself forced to this radical step in the first place in order to fight the currency speculation, which has developed recently and to stop the tendencies of hoarding, encouraged mainly by events from the domain of international politics. The aggravation of the political situation in Europe and the threat of war had a negative impact on all countries and in the first place on the members of the gold bloc . . . (BGK 1936: 2).

Hence, the final decision to leave the gold standard and pursue expansionary policies in Germany's neighbours, France and Poland, was apparently affected not only by increasing economic pressures on the remaining members of the gold bloc, as implied by devaluations elsewhere, but also by pressures to increase military spending.

3.5. CONCLUSION AND SOME IMPLICATIONS FOR EUROPEAN ECONOMIC POLICY

By 1936, the European economy had apparently recovered from the Great Depression as indicated by rising prices, increasing industrial production, and falling levels of unemployment. After an extremely painful and uncoordinated adjustment process, the US and European economies had freed themselves from their 'golden fetters' and had embarked on more expansionary monetary, and in some cases also fiscal, policies. The Tripartite Agreement, reached between Britain, France, and the United States in late 1936, highlighted again the need for cooperation between central banks, and even institutionalized some consultation process under the Gold Agreement Act of October 1936. But cooperation was not regarded as an objective in itself, rather an instrument to avoid negative effects of domestic policies as the Tripartite Agreement had its origins in an effort to avoid another round of competitive devaluations in the wake of the collapsing gold bloc.

Internal balance was explicitly recognized as the ultimate objective of policy, with the maintenance of international stability as 'basically a useful ancillary target' (Eichengreen, 1984: 44). Moreover, the new economic order foreshadowed in several ways the system of the time after 1945. Exchange rates between the US dollar, sterling, and franc were quite stable after 1936 with the dollar emerging as de facto international reserve currency, given its strong gold backing. However, with the US devaluation in April 1933, it was clear that the gold parity of the dollar was in principle adjustable to changing economic conditions (Eichengreen, 1984). Importantly, the Tripartite Agreement had also a political dimension, insofar as the rising threat from German rearmament facilitated negotiations between France, Britain, and the United States (Sayers, 1976: 476; Oye, 1985: 193). The significant role of rearmament for the dynamics of European growth in the late 1930s cast serious doubts on the sustainability of this recovery altogether. While GDP returned to long-run trends after the depression, it can be argued that the European economy lacked a political consensus in the late 1930s, given Nazi-Germany's aggressive preparations for another military confrontation. From this perspective, we might say that the Great Depression had its fundamental origins in the First World War and ended only with the Second World War.

The interwar period provides some general lessons for economic policy, many of which have been spelled out already in Temin (1989) and also in other contributions in this volume. Here, I just want to highlight some general aspects and one more specific 'lesson' for the conduct of economic policy in contemporary Europe. On a general level, an analysis of the Great Depression shows that economic models actually matter (Temin, 1989: 86–7). Policy makers and market participants alike only gradually discovered the various options that were available under the constraints of the monetary policy trilemma during the crisis: the limits of deflationary policies, the possibilities of fiscal and monetary expansion, but also ways to control capital flows. The fact that no government in the world dared to pursue expansionary economic policies before spring 1932 suggests that gold standard orthodoxy mattered. However, it would be misleading to think that expansionary policies had not been considered before Keynes published his General Theory in 1936. Rather, these options were not pursued, because the risks of unilateral action were long considered too high—maybe rightly so—and multilateral action seemed impossible. Put differently, not all options that would exist in a perfect environment were available to policy makers at every time because of a serious lack of institutional stability. Europe could not exploit her vast economic potential after 1918 because the war had not yet come to an end. Both domestic and international institutions suffered from a lack of reciprocal trust and commitment, which can be clearly illustrated in the realm of monetary policy but affected many other areas of policy making. These institutions in turn affected expectations and thereby the extent to which, for example, expansionary policies could be effective. Hence, the second general lesson is that commitment and trust in economic policies are crucial to avoid another Great Depression. A third, quite general, 'lesson' from the interwar years is that failure to deal with an economic crisis can have political side-effects that may prove to be far more damaging than the crisis itself. The rise of the NSDAP to power in 1933 made it hard to avoid the Second World War in 1939.

Finally, the interwar years provide some useful insights for the conduct of economic policy in Europe today. The period can be seen as the (failed) attempt by European policy makers to simultaneously pursue the objectives of liquidity, confidence, and adjustment or, alternatively, the policies of stable exchange rates, free capital flows, and macroeconomic stabilization. The brief period between 1924 and 1929—the 'golden twenties'—suggested that it would be possible to have it all: exchange rates stabilized at the new gold-parities, Europe was in receipt of significant capital inflows from the US, and inflation and unemployment seemed to be under control. The Great Depression proved that this was an illusion. The system of 1929 was based on a fragile institutional framework including domestic institutions that limited the tolerance for domestic adjustment (that is unemployment), and the interim settlement of reparations and war debts with the Dawes Plan in conjunction with the un-ratified Mellon-Bérenger accord of 1926. Crucially, Europe's brief prosperity in the 1920s depended on the continued inflow of capital from the US that had forged ahead of Europe in terms of productivity. The US had a large trade surplus with Europe, and Europe, in turn, provided ample scope for profitable but risky investment. When the US, as the core of the system, suffered a crisis, something had to give—exchange rate stability, capital mobility, or macroeconomic stabilization. In this situation of interdependence and 'fear of floating', bold unilateral action might have shortened the depression, but only some coordinated multilateral action would have prevented the initial downturn from becoming the Great Depression. If central banks and governments had been able to coordinate a change in gold parities, or the introduction of capital controls, the crisis might have been contained earlier (e.g. see Eichengreen and Sachs, 1985).

The eurozone today shows similarities and some important differences when compared to the situation of the 1930s. Let us start with highlighting three differences between the interwar gold exchange standard and the eurozone. First, monetary policy in the eurozone is far more flexible in its ability to react to economic downturns, limited below only by the zero bound for nominal interest rates and above by an average medium term inflation target. Second, the process of modern European integration and interdependence has reached a new quality with the introduction of a common currency in 1999. This happened both because policy makers wanted to foster European integration and because other developments, such as technological change and competition from other parts of the world, increased the costs of fragmentation and the benefits of a large common market. Third, the eurozone as a whole struggles more with internal imbalances than with external imbalances, where some members are in surplus while others are in deficit. This is in contrast to the 1930s, where a key surplus country was politically and geographically abroad: the US. With these differences in mind, the 1930s do provide some 'lessons' for the eurozone today. But as with the interwar situation, it is crucial to distinguish between countries that run a current account deficit (such as Greece or Portugal) and those with a surplus (such as Austria or Germany).

Similar to the 1930s, deficit countries in the eurozone seem to face a choice between two evils: as policy makers now realize, staying in the eurozone puts limits on a country's fiscal policies, largely because of their implications for government bond yields and the cost of servicing government debt. Leaving the eurozone, in turn, would risk capital flight, inflation, and increased foreign debts. However, for several reasons, deficit countries are much more likely to stay in the euro compared to deficit countries staying on gold after 1929. First, monetary policy in the eurozone is clearly countercyclical and reduces the burden on fiscal policy. Second, the cost of any deficit country leaving the euro might be limited for the remaining eurozone members, but is likely to be dramatic for the country that leaves. And importantly, third, no country in the current situation can be forced to leave the eurozone. In contrast to the 1930s gold standard, a breakup of the eurozone is highly unlikely unless a surplus country such as Germany would want to leave.

Therefore, the stability of the eurozone today crucially hinges upon the willingness of surplus countries within the eurozone such as Germany, Austria, or the Netherlands to stabilize the system with a position similar to that of the US in the interwar period (and again immediately after 1945). An important factor is the extent to which surplus countries and voters within these countries benefit from the system. Do they? The current situation of a strong economic 'core' with high levels of productivity running long-run current account surpluses with a predominantly weak periphery was not caused by the introduction of the common currency, but the common currency in 1999 did apparently very little to reduce these structural imbalances. Such a situation of large structural imbalances tends to produce both opportunities and risks for core and periphery. The core has access to an enlarged market with profitable investment opportunities, while the periphery has access to the capital it needs to catch up. Among the systematic risks are asset 'bubbles', government debt crises or combinations of them in the periphery that may emerge when expectations about the growth prospects in the periphery change. Another risk is that the integration itself might undermine convergence and rather lead to a more uneven distribution of economic activity, as argued by Krugman (1991). Given that after 1999 an increasing share of Germany's trade surplus was generated by trade with other members of the eurozone (see Mihram and Wolf 2010), it is likely that the core benefitted from the euro, which should increase political support for the system in times of crisis.

The experience of the interwar period suggests that—at least from the perspective of the periphery—the eurozone needs some institutionalized and automatic adjustment mechanism that is readily available in time of a business cycle downturn. Otherwise, political tensions over appropriate stabilization policies—whether rooted in election cycles, history, or elsewhere—will not only delay recovery but will lead to contagion effects and turn a limited downturn into a major crisis. It needs to be able to act quickly and on a sufficient scale to be credible. The recent agreement on a European Stabilization Mechanism (ESM) does point in the right direction, as has been argued by De Grauwe (2010). However, the implementation of such an automatic adjustment mechanism can go wrong. The design of a currency union without a strong institutionalized adjustment mechanism has always been justified by arguments of moral hazard. The Stability and Growth Pact of 1997 and its followers were meant to ensure that governments would not build up unsustainable levels of debt that could undermine the stability of the common currency. Clearly, in contrast to the gold standard currencies, the stability of the euro as a common currency is not so much threatened by a change in its external value but by the distributional, and hence political, consequences of uncoordinated fiscal policies. The combination of a common monetary policy and open capital markets imply that macroeconomic stabilization policies, especially fiscal policies, need to be coordinated between member states (Uhlig, 2003). It can be argued that the ESM increases the risk of moral hazard, hence the risk that governments use this as an insurance to create excessive deficits and debt levels (Sinn, 2010). Given that the euro is a political project between surplus and deficit countries, this needs to be addressed to ensure political support in all parts of the eurozone, especially in the surplus countries that can leave the union. To build up political support in the core is therefore the main aim of the 'fiscal compact' on which most European countries recently agreed. However, it would be misleading to argue that the crisis of the eurozone had its origins in a general profligacy of national governments. With the exception of Greece, it was private rather than government debt that reached unsustainable level in the wake of an asset bubble driven by poorly regulated financial markets, which, in turn, triggered an increase in government debt (De Grauwe, 2010). Again, there is a parallel here to the banking crisis of 1931 that produced a currency crisis. Hence, another safeguard that is needed to stabilize the eurozone and support the ESM is a tighter regulation of financial markets.

But all these measures fall short of addressing the issue of long-run stability of the eurozone. In the short to medium term, it is necessary to ensure the willingness of the core to support the system. In the long run, European policy makers will have to address the root problems of the eurozone, which are the large structural imbalances between core and periphery in the absence of automatic adjustment mechanisms, for instance large-scale labour mobility. Countries such as Portugal or Greece would need structural reforms that enable them to attract competitive economic activities. For this they need more investment in physical infrastructure and education, and probably a fundamental reform of their public administration. While spending on infrastructure and education will be uncontroversial, especially if the funding comes from the European core, attempts to improve the system of public administration are likely to imply job cuts, and thus to face political resistance. The key issue, therefore, seems to be a political one. European integration involves both opportunities and risks for both core and periphery. The historical experience of the interwar period, and the following post-war growth spurt, strongly suggests that a political consensus to foster economic integration between European countries is a precondition for growth (Roses and Wolf, 2010). As such it has no viable (peaceful) alternative, especially not for the core. The ESM together with the new 'fiscal compact' might provide the adjustment mechanism that was needed, and it still needs to be complemented by some tighter regulation of financial markets. But, more importantly, policy makers have to find a way to improve the competitiveness of Europe's periphery. This will take a lot of time, so they will have to convince their constituencies that the process of European integration, with all its far-reaching implications, is beneficial in the long run for the current core and for Europe's periphery. Otherwise doubts about the political sustainability of the ESM will always tend to undermine the eurozone's economic equilibrium.

BIBLIOGRAPHY

Bank Gospodarstwa Krajowego (BGK), *Revue Mensuelle* 1936, Warsaw: BGK.

Banks, A. and Textor, R. (1971), *A Cross-Polity Survey*. Cambridge, Mass.: MIT Press.

Bernanke, B. (1995), 'The Macroeconomics of the Great Depression: A Comparative Approach', *Journal of Money, Credit and Banking*, 27(1), 1–28.

Borchardt, K. (1979), 'Zwangslagen und Handlungsspielräume in der grossen Wirtschaftskrise der frühen dreissiger Jahre', *Jahrbuch der Bayrischen Akademie der Wissenschaften*, 85–132.

Borchardt, Knut (1990), 'A Decade of Debate about Bruning's Economic Policy', in J. v. Kruedener, *Economic Crisis and Political Collapse: The Weimar Republic 1924–1933*. Oxford: Berg, pp. 99–151.

Borchardt, K. and Schoetz, O. (1987), *Wirtschaftspolitik in der Krise. Die (Geheim-) Konferenz der Friedrich-List-Gesellschaft im September 1931 über die Möglichkeit und Folgen einer Kreditausweitung*. Baden-Baden: Nomos.

Bordo, M., Edelstein, M., and Rockoff, H. (1999), 'Was Adherence to the Gold Standard a Good Housekeeping Seal of Approval during the Interwar Period?', NBER Working Paper No. 7186.

Born, K.-E. (1967), *Die deutsche Bankenkrise*. Munich: Piper.

Bresciani-Turroni, C. (1937), *The Economics of Inflation: A Study of Currency Depreciation in Postwar Germany*. London: Allen & Unwin.

Broadberry, S. N. (1986), *The British Economy between the Wars: A Macroeconomic Survey*. Oxford: Blackwell.

Broadberry, S. N. and Harrison, M. (2005), *The Economics of World War I*. Cambridge: Cambridge University Press.

Buchheim, C. (2008), 'Das NS-Regime und die Überwindung der Weltwirtschaftskrise in Deutschland', *Vierteljahreshefte für Zeitgeschichte*, 56(3), 381–414.

Buyst, E. and Franaszek, P. (2010), 'Sectoral Developments, 1914–1945', in S. N. Broadberry and K. H. O'Rourke (eds), *The Cambridge Economic History of Modern Europe*, Volume 2. Cambridge: Cambridge University Press, pp. 208–31.

Cairncross, A. and Eichengreen, B. (1983), *Sterling in Decline: The Devaluations of 1931, 1949, and 1967*. Oxford: Blackwell.

Calvo, G. and Reinhart, C. (2001), 'Fixing for our Life', in S. Collins and D. Rodrik (eds) *Brookings Trade Forum 2000. Policy Challenges in the Next Millenium*. Washington: Brookings Institution, pp. 1–39.

Calvo, G. and Reinhart C. (2002), 'Fear of Floating', *Quarterly Journal of Economics*, 117(2), 379–408.

Cassis, Y. (2006), *Capitals of Capital: A History of International Financial Centres 1780–2005*. Cambridge: Cambridge University Press.

Chandler, A. D. (1990), *Scale and Scope*. Cambridge, Mass.: The Belknap Press of Harvard University Press.

Ciałowicz, J. (1970), *Polsko-Francuski Sojusz Wojskowy 1921–1939*. Warsaw: Państwowe Wydawnictwo Naukowe.

Cochrane, S. (2009), 'Assessing the Impact of World War I on the City of London', Oxford Department of Economics Discussion Paper Series 456, Oxford.

Commission des Réparations (1924), *Report of the First Committee of Experts*. Paris: Annexe 2075.

De Grauwe, P. (2010), *Fighting the Wrong Enemy*, <http://www.voxeu.org>, published 19 May 2010.

Directorate General for Economic and Financial Affairs (DG ECFIN) (2010), *The Economic Stabilization Mechanism*. Press Release 10 May 2010.

Ebell, M. and Ritschl, A. (2008), 'Real Origins of the Great Depression: Monopoly Power, Unions and the American Business Cycle in the 1920s', *CEP Discussion Paper* 0876. London: Centre for Economic Performance.

Eggertsson, G. B. (2008), 'Great Expectations and the End of the Depression', *American Economic Review*, 98(4), 1476–516.

Eichengreen, B. (1984), 'International Policy Coordination in Historical Perspective: A View from the Interwar Years', NBER Working Paper 1440.

Eichengreen, B. (1992), *Golden Fetters: The Gold Standard and the Great Depression, 1919–1939*. New York: Oxford University Press.

Eichengreen, B. and Sachs, J. (1985), 'Exchange Rates and Economic Recovery in the 1930s', *Journal of Economic History*, 45, 925–46.

Eichengreen, B. and Sachs, J. (1986), 'Competitive Devaluation and the Great Depression. A Theoretical Reassessment', *Economics Letters*, 22, 67–71.

Eichengreen, B. and Simmons, B. (1995), 'International Economics and Domestic Politics: Notes from the 1920s', in C. Feinstein (ed.), *Banking, Currency and Finance in Europe between the Wars*. Oxford: Clarendon Press, pp. 131–49.

Eichengreen, B. and Temin, P. (2000), 'The Gold Standard and the Great Depression', *Contemporary European History*, 9, 183–207.

Einzig, P. (1937), *World Finance 1935–1937*, London: Macmillan.

Ellis, H. S. (1939), 'Exchange Control In Austria and Hungary', *The Quarterly Journal of Economics* 54 (1): 1–185.

Feinstein, C., Temin, P., and Toniolo, G. (1997), *The European Economy between the Wars*. Oxford: Oxford University Press.

Feinstein, C., Temin, P., and Toniolo, G. (2008), *The World Economy between the World Wars*. Oxford: Oxford University Press.

Ferguson, T. and Temin, P. (2003), 'Made in Germany: The German Currency Crisis of July 1931', *Research in Economic History*, 21, 1–53.

Fink, C. (1984), *The Genoa Conference: European Diplomacy, 1921–1922*. Chapel Hill: University of North Carolina Press.

Fishback, P. (2010), 'US Fiscal and Monetary Policy', *Oxford Review of Economic Policy*, 26(3), 385–413.

Fisher, I. (1933), 'The Debt-Deflation Theory of Great Depressions', *Econometrica*, 1 (4), 337–57.

Frankenstein, R. (1982), *Le Prix du Réarmement Français, 1935–1939*. Prais: Publications de la Sorbonne.

Fregert, K. and Jonung, L. (2004), 'Deflation Dynamics in Sweden: Perceptions, Expectations, and Adjustment during the Deflations of 1921–1923 and 1931–1933', in R. Burdekin and P. Siklos (eds), *Deflation: Current and Historical Perspectives*. Cambridge and New York: Cambridge University Press, pp. 91–128.

Friedman, M. and Schwartz, A. J. (1963), *A Monetary History of the United States, 1867–1960*. Princeton: Princeton University Press.

Galenson, W. and Zellner, A. (1957), 'International Comparisons of Unemployment Rates', in NBER *The Measurement and Behavior of Unemployment*. Princeton: Princeton University Press.

Hallwood, P., MacDonald, R., and Marsh, I. (2007), 'Did Impending War in Europe Help Destroy the Gold Bloc in 1936? An Internal Inconsistency Hypothesis', *University of Connecticut, Department of Economics Working Paper 2007–23*.

Hamilton, J. (1987), 'Monetary Factors in the Great Depression', *Journal of Monetary Economics*, 13, 1–25.

Holtfrerich, C.-L. (1982), 'Alternativen zu Brünings Politik in der Weltwirtschaftskrise?', *Historische Zeitschrift*, 235, 605–31.

Holtfrerich, C.-L. (1990), 'Was the Policy of Deflation in Germany Unavoidable?', in J. v. Kruedener, *Economic Crisis and Political Collapse. The Weimar Republic 1924-1933*. Oxford: Berg, pp. 63–80.

Holtfrerich, C.-L. (1996), 'Zur Debatte um die deutsche Wirtschaftspolitik von Weimar zu Hitler', *Vierteljahreshefte fur Zeitgeschichte*, 44, 119–32.

Howson, S. (1975), *Domestic Monetary Management in Britain, 1919–1938*. Cambridge: Cambridge University Press.

Howson, S. (1980), 'Sterling's Managed Float: The Operations of the Exchange Equalisation Account', *Princeton Studies in International Finance* No. 46, Princeton.

IfK (1932), 'Die Weltwirtschaft Ende 1932', *Wochenbericht des Instituts für Konjunkturforschung*. Berlin: Institut für Konjunkturforschung, 21 December.

James, H. (1985), *The Reichsbank and Public Finance in Germany, 1924–1933: A Study of the Politics of Economics during the Great Depression*. Frankfurt am Main: Knapp.

James, H. (2001), *The End of Globalization: Lessons from the Great Depression*. Cambridge, Mass.: Harvard University Press.

Keynes, J. M. (1930), *A Treatise on Money*. London: Macmillan.

Keynes, J. M. (1972 [1925]). 'The Economic Consequences of Mr. Churchill', in *The Collected Writings of John Maynard Keynes*, vol. IX: Essays in Persuasion. London: Macmillan.

Kindleberger, C. (1986), *The World in Depression: 1929–1939* 2nd edition. Berkeley: University of California Press.

Knakiewicz, Z. (1967), *Deflacja Polska 1930–1935*. Warsaw: Panstwowe Wydawnictwo Ekonomiczne.

Komlos, J. and Stoegbauer, C. (2004), 'Averting the Nazi Seizure of Power: A Counterfactual Thought Experiment', *European Review of Economic History*, vol. 8 (02), 173–99.

Krugman, P. (1979), 'A Model of Balance-of-Payment Crisis', *Journal of Money, Credit and Banking*, 11 (3), 311–25.

Krugman, P. (1991), *Geography and Trade*. Cambridge, MA: MIT Press.

Krugman, P. (1998), *What happened to Asia?* mimeo MIT: Boston.

Krzyżanowski, K. (1976), *Wydatki Wojskowe Polski w Latach 1918–1939*. Warsaw: Państwowe Wydawnictwo Naukowe.

Kydland, F. and Prescott, E. (1977), 'Rules Rather than Discretion: The Inconsistency of Optimal Plans', *Journal of Political Economy*, 87, 473–92.

Lagendijk, V. (2008), *Electrifying Europe. The power of Europe in the Construction of Electricity Networks*. Amsterdam: Aksant Academic Publishers.

Landau, Z. and Tomaszewski, J. (1964), *Kapitały Obce w Polsce 1918–1939. Materiały i dokumenty*. Warsaw: Książka i Wiedza.

Landau, Z. and Tomaszewski, J. (1965), 'Memorial Wł. M. Zawadzkiego', *Kwartalnik Historyczny*, 72, 127–51.

Landau, Z. and Tomaszewski, J. (1999), *Zarys Historii Gospodarczej Polski 1918–1939*. Warsaw: Książka i Wiedza.

Marshall, M. G. and Jaggers, K. (2005), *POLITY IV Project. Political Regime Characteristics and Transitions, 1800–2004. Dataset Users' Manual*. Fairfax, Washington, DC: George Mason University.

McKinnon, R. and Huw, P. (1996), 'Credible Economic Liberalizations and Overborrowing', *America Economic Review*, 87, 189–93.

Middleton, R. (1981), 'The Constant Employment Budget Balance and British Budgetary Policy, 1929–39', *Economic History Review*, 34(2), 266–86.

Mihram, F. and Wolf N. (2010), *Ifo-Schnelldienst*. München: Ifo-Inst. für Wirtschaftsforschung, ISSN 0018-974x, ZDB-ID 2185180. - Vol. 63.2010, 24 (22.12.): 6–10.

Mouré, K. (1988), '"Une eventualité absolument exclue": French Reluctance to Devalue, 1933-1936', *French Historical Studies*, 15(3), 479-505.

Mouré, K. (2002), *The Gold Standard Illusion. France, the Bank of France, and the International Gold Standard, 1914-1939*. Oxford: Oxford University Press.

Nurkse, R. (1944), *International Currency Experience. Lessons of the Inter-War Period*. Geneva: League of Nations.

Obstfeld, M. (1986), 'Rational and Self-Fulfilling Balance-of-Payments Crises', *American Economic Review*, 76(1), 72-81.

Obstfeld, M., Shambaugh, J. C., and Taylor, A. M. (2004), 'Monetary Sovereignty, Exchange Rates, and Capital Controls: The Trilemma in the Interwar Period', *IMF Staff Papers*, 51, 75-108.

Obstfeld, M., Shambaugh, J. C., and Taylor, A. M. (2005), 'The Trilemma in History: Tradeoffs among Exchange Rates, Monetary Policies, and Capital Mobility', *Review of Economics and Statistics*, 87(3), 423-38.

Ohanian, L. E. (2009), 'What—or Who—Started the Great Depression?', NBER Working Paper No. 15258.

Orde, A. (1980), 'The Origins of the German-Austrian Customs Union Affair of 1931', *Central European History*, 13(1), 34-59.

Oye, K. A. (1985), 'The Sterling-Dollar-Franc Triangle: Monetary Diplomacy 1929-1937', *World Politics*, 38(1), 173-99.

Redmond, J. (1982), 'The Sterling Overvaluation in 1925: A Multilateral Approach', *Economic History Review*, 37, 520-32.

Rhodes, B. D. (1969), 'Reassessing "Uncle Shylock": The United States and the French War Debt, 1917-1929', *The Journal of American History*, 55(4), 787-803.

Ritschl, A. (2002), *Deutschlands Krise und Konjunktur 1924-1934. Binnenkonjunktur, Auslandsverschuldung und Reparationsproblem zwischen Dawes-Pland und Transfersperre*. Berlin: Akademie Verlag.

Ritschl, A. (2003a), 'Dancing on a Volcano: The Economic Recovery and Collapse of the Weimar Republic, 1924-1933', in T. Balderston (ed.), *World Economy and National Economies in the Interwar Slump*. London: Macmillan, pp. 105-42.

Ritschl, A. (2003b), 'Hat das Dritte Reich wirklich eine ordentliche Beschäftigungspolitik betrieben?', *Jahrbuch für Wirtschaftsgeschichte*, 2003(I), 125-40.

Ritschl, A. and Wolf, N. (2011), 'Endogeneity of Currency Areas and Trade Blocs: Evidence from the Interwar-Period', *Kyklos*, 64 (2), 291-312.

Rodrik, D. (2000), 'How Far will International Economic Integration Go?', *Journal of Economic Perspectives*, 14(1), 177-86.

Romer, C. D. (1992), 'What Ended the Great Depression?', *Journal of Economic History*, 52(4), 757-84.

Roses, J. and Wolf, N. (2010), 'Aggregate Growth, 1913-1950', in S. N. Broadberry and K. H. O'Rourke (eds), *The Cambridge Economic History of Modern Europe* Volume 2. Cambridge: Cambridge University Press, pp. 181-207.

Sayers, R. S. (1976), *The Bank of England, 1891-1944*. Cambridge: Cambridge University Press.

Schnabel, I. (2004), 'The German Twin Crisis of 1931', *Journal of Economic History*, 64(3), 822-71.

Schubert, A. (1991), *The Credit-Anstalt Crisis of 1931*. Cambridge: Cambridge University Press.

Schuker, S. A. (1976), *The End of French Predominance in Europe: The Financial Crisis of 1924 and the Adoption of the Dawes Plan*. Chapel Hill: University of North Carolina Press.

Schuker, S. A. (1988), *American 'Reparations' to Germany, 1919-1933: Implications for the Third-World Debt Crisis*. Princeton: Princeton University Press.

Schulz, G. (1992), *Zwischen Demokratie und Diktatur: Verfassungspolitik und Reichsreform in der Weimarer Republik*. Berlin, New York: de Gruyter.

Schulze, H. (1982), *Weimar. Deutschland 1917–1933*. Berlin: Severin and Siedler.

Sicsic, P. (1992), 'Was the Franc Poincaré deliberately undervalued?', *Explorations in Economic History*, 29, 69–92.

Simmons, B. (1994), *Who Adjusts? Domestic Sources of Foreign Economic Policy during the Interwar Years*. Princeton: Princeton University Press.

Sinn, H.-W. (2010), 'Euro-Krise', *ifo Schnelldienst*, 63 (10). Munich: Institut für Wirtschaftsforschung an der Universität München, 3–9.

Smith, L. (1936), 'The Zloty', *Journal of Political Economy*, 44(2), 145–83.

Straumann, T. (2010), 'Rule Rather than Exception: Brüning's Fear of Devaluation in Comparative Perspective', *Journal of Contemporary History*, 44(4), 603–17.

Straumann, T. and Woitek, U. (2009), 'A Pioneer of a New Monetary Policy? Sweden's Price Level Targeting of the 1930s Revisited', *European Review of Economic History*, 13, 251–82.

Strobel, G. (1975), 'Die Industrialisieruing Polens am Vorabend des Zweiten Weltkriegs zwischen Innen- und Wehrpolitik', *Zeitschrift für Ostforschung*, 24(10), 221–71.

Svennilson, I. (1954), *Growth and Stagnation in the European Economy*. Geneva: United Nations Economic Commission for Europe.

Temin, P. (1971), 'The Beginning of the Great Depression in Germany', *Economic History Review*, 24, 240–8.

Temin, P. (1976), *Did Monetary Forces Cause the Great Depression?* New York: Norton.

Temin, P. (1989), *Lessons from the Great Depression*. Cambridge: MIT Press.

Temin, P. and Wigmore, B. (1990), 'The End of One Big Deflation', *Explorations in Economic History*, 27, 483–502.

Thomas, M. (1983), 'Rearmament and Economic Recovery in the Late 1930s', *Economic History Review*, 36 (4), 552–79.

Thomas, M. (1988), 'Labour Market Structure and the Nature of Unemployment in Interwar Britain', in B. Eichengreen and T. Hatton (eds), *Interwar Unemployment in International Perspective, proceedings of the NATO Advanced Research Workshop on Interwar Unemployment in International Perspective, Harvard University, Cambridge Mass., 7–8 May 1987*. London: Kluwer, pp. 97–148.

Trenkler, C. and Wolf, N. (2005), 'Economic Integration Across Borders: The Polish Interwar Economy 1921–1937', *European Review of Economic History*, 9, 199–231.

Uhlig, H. (2003), 'One money, but many fiscal policies in Europe: What are the consequences?', in M. Buti (ed.), *Monetary and Fiscal Policies in EMU*. Cambridge: Cambridge University Press.

Voth, J. (2003), 'With a Bang, not a Whimper: Germany's "Stock Market Bubble" in 1927 and the Slide into Depression', *The Journal of Economic History*, 63(1), 65–99.

Wandschneider, K. (2008), 'The Stability of the Interwar Gold Exchange Standard—Did Politics Matter?', *Journal of Economic History*, 68, 151–81.

Wandycz, P. S. (1988), *The Twilight of French Eastern Alliances, 1926–1936*. Princeton: Princeton University Press.

Webb, S. B. (1988), 'The German Reparation Experience Compared with the LDC Debt Problem today', *Weltwirtschaftliches Archiv*, 124, 745–74.

Webb, S. B. (1989), *Hyperinflation and Stabilization in Weimar Germany*. New York and Oxford: Oxford University Press.

Weder, M. (2006), 'A Heliocentric Journey into Germany's Great Depression', *Oxford Economic Papers*, 58(2), 288–316.

Winkler, H.-A. (1993), *Weimar 1918–1933. Die Geschichte der Ersten Deutschen Demokratie*. Munich: Beck.

Wolf, N. (2007), 'Should I stay or should I go? Understanding Poland's Adherence to Gold, 1928–1936', *Historical Social Research*, 32(4), 351–68.

Wolf, N. (2008), 'Scylla and Charybdis. Explaining Europe's Exit from Gold, January 1928–December 1936', *Explorations in Economic History*, 45, 383–401.

Zbijewski, W. (1931), 'Waluta Polska', in *Odrodzona Skarbowosc Polska*. Warsaw: Naklad Stowarzyszenia Urzednikow Skarbowych RP, 173–81.

4

Reparations, Deficits, and Debt Default: The Great Depression in Germany

Albrecht O. Ritschl

4.1. INTRODUCTION

Plagued by structural unemployment throughout the 1920s, the German economy went through a sharp contraction after 1929, followed by complete recovery and the restoration of full employment around 1937. Both the timing and the severity of the contraction set Germany apart from European developments at the time, bearing similarities to the US depression instead. Like the US, Germany experienced a strong economic rebound between 1933 and 1936, surpassing growth rates in most European countries. In a significant departure from the US pattern, however, Germany's recovery continued after that year, joining the economies of north-western Europe in avoiding the recession of 1937/38 (see Feinstein et al., 1997).

Between the return to the gold standard in 1924 and the beginning of World War Two, the German economy went through a succession of reparation arrangements, which coincided with balance-of-payment regimes. These were characterized by increasingly tight foreign borrowing constraints and growing levels of debt default. Germany went from being a massive capital importer during the Dawes Plan of 1924–29 to a sudden stop in its current account under the Young Plan of 1929/30, and on to an autarkic command economy with tight capital and foreign exchange controls after the end of the Young Plan in 1932. The timing of these regime switches coincided with the turning points of the German business cycle and defined the limits and scope for domestic macroeconomic policies.

This chapter reviews Germany's macroeconomic performance between 1924 and 1938 with a view to the reversals in its international payments position and their consequences. The main observation is that the quick succession of reparation arrangements, each with its own incentive problems and borrowing constraints, created distinct macroeconomic policy regimes. After the gold-based stabilization under the Dawes Plan of 1924, and a short-lived adjustment crisis, Germany experienced recovery led by large short-term capital inflows. This enabled Germany to pay reparations on credit—an effect soon named the transfer problem, which had been predicted by Keynes and which was discussed controversially with his critics at the time (Keynes, 1922 and 1929; Ohlin, 1929). The same capital inflows also allowed Germany to maintain large current account deficits. With monetary policy largely constrained by the gold standard, fiscal policy adopted a neutral stance. While it avoided major deficits, it also failed to generate the surpluses needed to effect reparation transfers, a fact which Keynes' detractors were quick to point out (see Rueff, 1929; Mantoux, 1946). With tighter terms of reparation payments looming under the Young Plan, and a substantial amount of accumulated foreign debt, Germany experienced a sudden current reversal in early 1929, accompanied by the first of a series of public debt funding crises. As a consequence, fiscal policy switched to austerity and forced deflation in the summer of 1929. This change came at the hand of the Reichsbank, Germany's central bank that had been made independent of the government in 1922 and put under international control in 1924. Violating the letter but arguably not the spirit of its statutory rules, the Reichsbank, in mid-1929, began offering short-term credit to the government but imposed a programme of severe budget cuts, which was adhered to through 1931. The open outbreak of the budget crisis was delayed through an international stabilization loan in connection with the Young Plan, which, however, imposed similar conditions on fiscal policy (see Ritschl, 2002).

At the core of the analysis of this chapter is an incentive-based interpretation of the German transfer problem under the Dawes Plan. Political scientists and diplomatic historians have long agreed that the foreign exchange arrangements under Dawes Plan gave Germany an incentive to borrow abroad excessively, with a view to driving out reparations in a future transfer crisis (see Helbich, 1962; Link, 1970; McNeil, 1986; Schuker, 1988). This mainstream argues that the Young Plan, with its tighter terms of payment, was a response to this incentive problem. As a consequence, the sudden stop in Germany's current account after 1928 was endogenous to Germany's debt levels, restoring an external credit constraint on the German economy that the Dawes Plan had temporarily softened (see the discussion in Ritschl, 2002).

Historians have been in bitter controversies about alternatives to Germany's fiscal policy during the slump since Borchardt's (1979) claim that the government faced a borrowing constraint (see the opposing views in Borchardt, 1990; Holtfrerich, 1990; as well as the restatement of the traditional position in Ferguson and Temin, 2003). The austerity policy pursued seems easier to motivate and explain with reference to Germany's mounting foreign debt problems (Ritschl, 2002). Accounting for the foreign dimension of Germany's debt problem—notably, the reparations issue—also sharpens the focus on policy counterfactuals and their historical feasibility.

Germany's debt crisis and recovery holds a series of lessons in stock for today's attempts to deal with high levels of national debt. The central bank's conditioning of debt monetization on a government austerity programme resembles current attempts to rein in the fiscal policy of debtor countries in the eurozone. Then, as now, it depends for its success on the willingness of other creditors to fall in line, and at the same time is a test of the central bank's own anti-inflationary credibility.

The rest of this chapter is structured as follows. Section 4.2 provides a brief survey of Germany's reparations arrangements, in particular the Dawes and Young Plans. The subsequent sections examine the macroeconomic regimes associated with these plans for key macroeconomic variables, with Section 4.3

looking at monetary policy, Section 4.4 focusing on fiscal policy, and Section 4.5 turning to labour demand and investment. Section 4.6 concludes with implications for the Great Recession after 2008.

4.2. GERMANY'S REPARATION ARRANGEMENTS: A BRIEF REFRESHER

German reparations after World War One were not fixed immediately. The peace conference in Paris ended with compromise formulae on this matter, but without reaching consensus among the Allies on how much to demand from the Germans. The two main building blocks of any reparations were supposed to be indemnities proper, as well as compensation for inter-allied World War One debts. The main instruments of reparation payment were to be confiscation of overseas assets, deliveries out of existing stock, deliveries in kind out of current production, and monetary payments in gold-based foreign exchange. Issuing reparations bonds and floating them on international markets, as France had done with her reparations to Prussia after the war of 1870/71, was considered briefly but discarded. Nevertheless, the concept of denominating reparations in bonds was retained even if flotation in the markets was seen as difficult given the magnitudes involved. During an interim period until the final bill was drawn up, payment consisted largely in confiscations of physical and intellectual property abroad, as well as in deliveries in kind.

Reparations soon came to be seen as odious by much of academia, and indeed by considerable parts of the public. Confronted with rather unrealistic figures on planned reparations, Keynes pulled out in protest from his role as an advisor to the British delegation in Paris and published scathing criticism in his *Economic Consequences of the Peace* (Keynes, 1920). Keynes' approach to the issue provided the framework for most of the future discussion, shaping the views even of his critics. He argued that the envisaged reparations would exceed Germany's capacity to pay, and if ever seriously enforced would cause widespread economic disruption, even famine, and ultimately the rise of a dictatorship bent on waging a war of revenge. In later work, Keynes added that reparation transfers would be near-impossible to effect, on account of both protectionism in the recipient countries and the difficulties of lowering German wages sufficiently. And, if attempted, transfers would be counteracted by capital inflows (on this and the ensuing controversy see Keynes, 1926 and 1929; Ohlin, 1929; Rueff, 1929). The transfer problem in the presence of high capital mobility soon became a standard fixture of open economy macroeconomics (Metzler, 1942; Johnson, 1956).

Reparations as determined by the London ultimatum of 1921 came in three tranches, a net indemnity of 12bn gold marks (A bonds), a compensation of 38bn gold marks for inter-allied war debts (B bonds), and an additional, largely notional, charge of 82bn gold marks (C bonds). Depending on which part of these reparations is included, a wide range of debt-to-GNP ratios can be obtained (see Table 4.1).

Table 4.1. Reparations and German GNP

		1913	1925	1929	1931
Nominal GNP (bn Reichsmarks)		51	71.1	88.4	68.0
Reparations (bn gold marks/Reichsmarks)		—as percentage of nominal GNP—			
(a) London ultimatum					
A bonds (net indemnity)	12	23.5	16.9	13.6	
A + B bonds (38 bn, for inter-allied war debt)	50	98.0	70.3	56.5	
A + B + C bonds (82 bn)	132	258.8	185.5	149.2	
(b) Dawes Plan of 1924	46		59.0	47.5	
(c) Young Plan of 1929/30	37			41.8	54.4

Source: Hardach (1980), Holtfrerich (1990), Ferguson (1998), Ritschl (1996, 2002).

Legally, all three tranches of the 1921 reparations bill were owed, although there is wide consensus that the largest bit, the 82bn gold marks of C bonds, was mostly a political bargaining chip and essentially served for domestic policy purposes in London and Paris (Feldman, 1993).

Taken in isolation, the A bonds amounted to 20 per cent of German GDP of 1913, a burden that was equivalent to France's reparations to Germany in 1871 (Ritschl, 1996). Adding the B bonds generated a reparations burden of 100 per cent of 1913 GDP. Including the C bonds as well raised the reparations burden to over 260 per cent of 1913 GDP. However, it was communicated to the Germans that the C bonds would not have to be paid under any realistic conditions. The Germans had anticipated a burden of 30–40bn gold marks. Hence, the realistic part of the reparation bill was not entirely beyond the imagination of German policy makers (Feldman, 1993; Ferguson, 1998).

News of the reparations bill nevertheless proved toxic for Germany's nascent Weimar Republic. Weimar's new constitution of 1920 had strengthened and centralized tax collection with a view to generating a strong tax base. Tax revenues under the new system initially looked promising and brought post-war inflation to a temporary halt (Dornbusch, 1987). However, when news broke in late 1920 that reparations might be far higher than expected by the German public, a veritable tax boycott developed. Tax collection plummeted, the monetization of short-term government paper resumed, and inflation accelerated again. In a confrontational climate, the finance minister and architect of Weimar's fiscal constitution, Erzberger, was forced to resign and was later assassinated. The government adopted a progressively less cooperative stance vis-á-vis reparations, provoking the French occupation of the Ruhr district in late 1922. A policy of passive resistance against the occupiers was proclaimed, leading to a significant drop in German output, combined with ever-higher hyperinflation in 1923.

Stabilization of the German currency in late 1923 was part of a political settlement that included reparations. Under the Dawes Plan of 1924, reparations were rescheduled but not formally reduced. To assist in the recovery of the German economy, reparation annuities were phased in gradually from a low base to reach a steady state in 1929. Discounted at 5 per cent, the interest rate of the Dawes loan, they amounted to 42bn Reichsmarks in present value in 1924, slightly below the sum of A and B bonds fixed in the London ultimatum. The resulting debt/GDP ratio for 1925 was 68 per cent, marginally down from the 70 per cent debt/GDP ratio implied by the sum of A and B bonds. The ominous C bonds were left out of the Dawes Plan but were formally not off the table.

A burden this size was by no means impossible to bear. There is broad consensus on this issue both internationally (see e.g. Marks, 1978, Ferguson, 1998) and east of the Rhine (Hardach, 1980; Holtfrerich, 1986; Ritschl, 1996). However, while France's and Britain's debts were largely denominated in domestic currency, Germany's reparation burden was owed in foreign currency and to foreign claimants, giving rise to 'Original Sin' (Eichengreen and Hausman, 1999). The sovereign nature of German reparation debt implied willingness-to-pay constraints (see Eaton et al., 1986), which should potentially limit the amount of credit to be obtained from foreign lenders.

Given these debt constraints, Germany's balance of payments during the mid-1920s presents a paradox: on the one hand, the country owed heavy reparations; on the other, it was able to attract major capital inflows. This evidence seems contradictory, and the capital inflows of the 1920s are indeed at the root of a debt crisis. This crisis would break out in full during the Great Depression and culminate in near-complete debt default in 1933 (Klug, 1993).

Indeed, the debt burden implied by the Dawes Plan was higher than just the present value of the Dawes Plan annuities themselves. While excluded from the Dawes Plan payment scheme, the ominous C bonds had not been formally rescinded and still loomed as a risk, all the more so as reparations were a first charge on Germany under the peace treaty. Including the C bonds, the reparations total under the Dawes Plan amounted to 180 per cent of German GDP in 1925. This makes it less than straightforward that Germany was able to attract foreign credit in significant measure after 1924. Even ignoring the C bonds, the Dawes Plan's 68 per cent charge on Germany's 1925 GDP left only limited room for foreign credit if a sovereign debt crisis was to be avoided.

However, the Dawes Plan created a loophole by giving commercial claims on Germany transfer protection against reparations. Transfer protection implied that, at the central bank's foreign exchange window, transfers of dividends and interest on commercial loans would take precedence over transfers of reparations. This had the effect of making reparation recipients the residual claimants on German foreign exchange surpluses. While not repudiating the peace treaty's principle that reparations were first rank, transfer protection for commercial claims reversed seniority in terms of foreign exchange. Thus, reparations were effectively turned into junior debt (Ritschl, 1996 and 2002).

This created a double moral hazard problem. With reparations effectively being of lower rank, the German government had little incentive during the Dawes Plan to stem the inflow of foreign credit. On the contrary, the more funds came in, the less would have to be paid out in reparations. This logic was understood and widely accepted in German government circles. Already in 1924, a memorandum in Germany's foreign office pointed out that foreign debt would turn Germany's commercial creditors into hostages of future editions of the reparations conflict (Link, 1970; McNeil, 1986). Opposition came only from the Reichsbank, which was worried that paying reparations on credit would only perpetuate the reparations conflict. If a crisis of reparations was inevitable, it was preferable to have it

Table 4.2. The German balance of payments (million Reichsmarks)

	Exports[1]	Reparations[1]	Current Account[1]	Long Term Credit (Net)	including: Stabilization Loans[2]	GDP
1924		281	−1664	1000	281	
1925	10257	1057	−3710	1124	519	71151
1926	11519	1191	−763	1376		73830
1927	12211	1584	−5028	1765		83166
1928	13806	1990	−4030	1698		89049
1929	15282	2337	−3476	414		89248
1930	13709	1706	−1317	805	1470	82935
1931	11156	988	647	−85		69153
1932	7197	160	257	14		56444

Notes: [1] Excluding reparations in kind. [2] 1924/25: Proceeds from Dawes Loan; 1930: Proceeds from Young Loan.
Sources: Statistisches Jahrbuch für das Deutsche Reich, various issues; Deutsche Bundesbank (1976); Ritschl (2002).

sooner than later, before Germany's foreign creditworthiness was irreversibly damaged (James, 1985).

Moral hazard existed also on the part of commercial creditors. As long as Germany's commercial debt was small relative to her gains from trade (the ultimate measure of her willingness to continue participating in international credit markets), lending seemed perfectly safe, even if it has the effect of crowding out reparations at the margin. Only if the level of commercial debt threatened to approach the willingness-to-pay constraint (or alternatively, if transfer protection was only imperfectly credible) did commercial creditors have an incentive to take a closer look before they signed up. Matters were not helped by the fact that the Dawes Plan itself was drawn up by New York bankers (Schuker, 1976).

Transfer protection proved quite effective in attracting foreign credit, and created a distinct macroeconomic regime. In all years of the Dawes Plan, the current account was negative, implying that Germany borrowed more than needed to recycle reparations (see Table 4.2).

The current account deficits indeed exceeded reparations in most years; reparations thus only played a secondary role in the build-up of foreign debt. Up until 1928, reparation payments were roughly matched by long-term capital imports. On balance, the current account deficit was financed with short-term capital imports.

This caused concern both among reparation claimants and, once debt levels were high enough, among commercial creditors. An Agent General for Reparations, located in Berlin to monitor German compliance with the Dawes Plan, lobbied against German foreign borrowing. With arguments similar to the Reichs bank, his reports urged that capital inflows into Germany must be stopped and suggested that withdrawing transfer protection of the returns on these investments would be the way forward (Gilbert, 1925–30). However, 1928 was an election year in the US, France, and Germany, and as transfer crisis was seen as the likely outcome of this change, no decisions were taken.

Negotiations over a new reparations deal with tighter terms of payment began in late 1928. The German side hoped that, in return for abandoning transfer protection, it could achieve considerably lower annuities. On the Allied side, the stabilization of the franc in 1928, and the Bérenger–Mellon accord on the resumption of French debt service on inter-allied war credits, aligned the incentives of US and French policy makers and resulted in a hardened position. The new plan envisaged reparations equivalent to the remaining inter-allied war credits still owed to the US by France and Britain. The scheme was deemed final, which removed the remaining uncertainty about the C bonds.

News on this was leaked in March 1929. Under the new scheme, commercial transfers would only be protected for up to one year, after which reparation transfers would regain seniority. Reparation annuities were to decrease only marginally, but a new stabilization loan was to be floated once the plan was ratified. The immediate effect of the news leak was a confidence crisis in money and bond markets in the same month. The central bank lost reserves, a central government bond flotation failed, and a sudden stop in long-term capital inflows ensued: net capital long-term imports in 1929 declined by 75 per cent from the previous year. Commercial debt alone now equalled 30 per cent of GDP; about two thirds of that debt was short term. Including reparations, total foreign debt would reach 80 per cent of GDP in 1929, or 75 per cent under the reduced Young Plan annuities if Germany accepted the new plan (see Table 4.3). The offer included a full withdrawal of French troops from the remaining territories occupied in 1923, as well as an end to international control over the railway system. This, and a threatening budget squeeze, induced Germany to accept the Young Plan, despite the risk of being cut off from international capital markets.

Transition to the Young Plan brought about major political change in Germany. Within a year from the March 1929 crisis, the finance minister, his budget director, the Reichsbank's president, and finally the government itself were out of office. A government of technocrats was appointed and the country ruled by presidential emergency decree, activating the same reserve constitution that had been employed in preparation of currency stabilization during 1923. Political historians tend to agree that this transition marked the end of Weimar as a democracy, almost three years before its final demise.

The stabilization loan floated in 1930 temporarily alleviated the pressure and postponed the current account reversal until 1931. The data in Table 4.2 show that, in the commercial long-term market, Germany became a capital exporter,

Table 4.3. Foreign debts and GDP (million Reichsmarks)

	Commercial	Reparations	GDP	Foreign debt/ GDP (%)
1928	27	40	89.0	75.2
1929	31	46/37	89.2	86.3/76.2
1930	32.6	35	82.9	81.5
1931 (mid-year)	33.6	34	*68.5*	98.7
1931 (end)	26.6	34	*58.1*	104.3
1932	25.9	—	56.4	45.9

Notes: Figures in italics are quarterly, annualized. Reparations 1929: Dawes Plan/Young Plan (NPV).
Sources: Bundesbank (1976), Ritschl (2002).

losing long-term loans for the first time since the stabilization of 1924. With national output in decline, the ratio of foreign debt to national income increased quickly. Failure to win parliamentary approval for the 1930 austerity budget brought about parliamentary elections in September 1930, which saw the extreme right and left increase their combined vote to almost 40 per cent. Foreign credit to the central government after that date was not forthcoming, and further fiscal tightening ensued.

German politics found itself caught between increasing domestic pressure to unilaterally default on the Young Plan and international demands to stay current on her payments if a return to sanctions or military action was to be avoided. By spring 1931, the ratio of foreign debt to GDP approached 100 per cent, and reserve losses accelerated after an Austro-German customs union project failed under foreign pressure, prompting the resignation of the Austrian government and coinciding with the near-collapse of Creditanstalt, Austria's largest commercial bank (James, 1986).

Breaking away from an earlier commitment to fully comply with the Young Plan during its first year, the German government in early June warned publicly that it might not be able to fully transfer both foreign debt service and reparations for the year. With this announcement, the issue of seniority of reparations over commercial foreign debt was open again. A series of negotiations and an international conference in the same month failed to produce clear results. While France was willing to extend short-term credit in exchange for foreign policy concessions from Germany, both Britain and the US were opposed, as injecting fresh money implied a return to recycling reparations through credit.

Under heavy international pressure, Germany refrained from taking unilateral steps and would neither declare default nor leave the gold standard. Instead, the moratorium proposed by the US president, Hoover, introduced a one-year reparations holiday, combined with an offer to negotiate a standstill on short-term debt (see Schuker, 1988, for a detailed account). However, no fresh money would be injected into the German economy this time, and no substantial central bank credit was given to replenish Germany's foreign exchange reserves. The price of this arrangement was a full-fledged banking and payments crisis. Shaken by the fraudulent bankruptcy of a major industrial client, DANAT, a major bank, became insolvent. In response to the banking crisis, credit restrictions were imposed and bank holidays declared. In a rescue operation, four out of five of Germany's largest banks were recapitalized and placed under government control (Schnabel, 2004).

As a consequence of the 1931 crisis, the Young Plan was suspended, though not yet gone. Amidst negotiations about its future, Germany tightened her deflation policy further to demonstrate willingness to pay, while an international commission investigated her capacity to pay. Published in the Beneduce report of November 1931, its findings were that, given the international slump, reparations under the Young Plan should not be resumed (Toniolo, 2005). A political settlement was delayed by parliamentary elections in France, as well as presidential elections in Germany due in the spring of 1932. Reparations were cancelled in August 1932.

August 1932 marked the trough of the depression in Germany. In the following month, the first steps were taken towards expanding domestic credit behind a firewall of foreign exchange controls. However, these controls were still far from complete. For the time being, Germany remained current on her foreign long-debt, while the short-term debt was rolled over in a process of continuous renegotiations, with foreign creditors carefully monitoring every step of German credit policies (Klug, 1993).

Transition to full-fledged capital controls came only after Germany's unilateral debt default in May 1933, and even then with a delay. In a reversal of strategy, Germany now attempted to minimize transfers on long-term debt while staying current and, in cases, resuming debt service on parts of her short-term standstill debt, discriminating among trading partners. This uncooperative approach was initially less than successful, and transfers increased again. A balance of payments crisis threatened in 1934 when credit expansion began in earnest. The response was the establishment of a state monopoly on foreign exchange, which completed Germany's foreign debt default.

4.3. THE REICHSBANK AND THE EFFECTS OF MONETARY POLICY

The various reparations plans translated themselves into distinct macroeconomic policy regimes. Stabilization from the hyperinflation was seen by policy makers and contemporary observers as being primarily a monetary task. Stabilization in late 1923 created new currency units, converted from the inflated paper mark at 10^{12}:1. The new currency was initially based on gold-indexed mortgage bonds and later linked to gold at the pre-war parity without, however, revaluing most of the outstanding public debt. To lend credibility to the stabilization, the Reichsbank was placed under international supervision and received a set of strict rules, including a tight cap on lending to the government. A 40 per cent gold cover for notes in circulation and deposits at the Reichsbank was prescribed.

Even under this strict regime, monetary aggregates in the second half of the 1920s increased faster than real output, making it plausible that the stabilization from the hyperinflation was more fiscal than monetary in nature (Sargent, 1982). The foreign credit boom under the Dawes Plan was reflected by inflows of gold and currency reserves to the central bank. Eager to build up a buffer stock of reserves, the Reichsbank partly sterilized these inflows but still allowed a substantial increase in the monetary base. Owing to a rapid recovery in deposits, the quantity of money increased even faster; real M1 grew by 40 per cent in a matter of five years.

With its hands tied by the gold standard and the transfer protection clause, the central bank relied on indirect means to make its influence felt. These included moral suasion, announcements, and repeated forays into the domain of fiscal policy. The Reichsbank in 1926 began a political campaign to stem the inflow of foreign funds, lobbying in vain to be given control over the foreign borrowing of states and municipalities. In May 1927, it threatened credit rationing in the money market if foreign inflows did not recede. This, and repeated warnings by the reparations agent about German borrowing, helped to cool off the mood of international investors, and both investment and the stock market began a slow decline.

Having acted as a whistle-blower on German borrowing, in late 1928 the Reichsbank became involved in the negotiations over a revised reparations package. The confidence crisis caused by the news of March 1929 gave the Reichsbank sufficient leverage to influence fiscal policy. Under the impression of the bad news on reparations, a major loan flotation planned for the same month failed, leaving government in a scramble for cash. In conflict with its statutes, the Reichsbank stepped in and began providing short-term loans to the government, however, under strict conditionality. These conditions included a sharp turn towards deflationary policy, as well as the creation of a sinking fund with senior claims to the government to ensure the reduction of short-term government debt according to a fixed schedule. Meeting these conditions and continuing debt service to this sinking fund became the basic tenets of government policy until after the end of the Young Plan in 1932.

As output began to fall in mid-1929, monetary aggregates declined as well. GDP in 1930 was 7 per cent below the 1929 level, and M1 declined by the same amount. Initially this decline was driven in equal measure by a loss in deposits and gold reserves. Losses of reserves became massive in the run-up to the crisis of summer 1931, outpacing the loss of deposits. Desperate attempts to secure international central bank credit remained unsuccessful. The crisis grew into a banking panic, to which the Reichsbank responded by imposing bank holidays, closing the stock exchanges, and placing four of the five leading commercial banks under public control. At the same time, it reduced the gold cover to 20 per cent and increased the monetary base to a level beyond the 1929 peak. However, further reserve losses during the spring of 1932, and the attempt to defend the lower gold cover, led to renewed monetary contraction.

Monetary expansion only began in early 1933 when the Reichsbank suspended gold convertibility. The gold parity was not formally abandoned but became increasingly meaningless as foreign exchange controls were tightened progressively. A complex network of bilateral exchange agreements with split exchange rates emerged during 1934. Designed primarily to complete the foreign debt default and minimize its domestic consequences, the transition to foreign exchange control resulted in an average devaluation of 30–40 per cent.

Already, during the gold standard, the Reichsbank relied on a network of public proxy banks to carry out operations not within its own remit. These off-balance-sheet institutions would lend against bills that did not meet the Reichsbank's eligibility standards, and conducted open market and buyback operations. This system of proxy institutions gained importance after 1931 and took a key role in financing the public shadow budgets beginning in 1933. Plans had existed already in 1930 to use this network to finance public borrowing in the money market, given that overt government borrowing would lead to renewed reparation demands. Public banks would be used to accept bills of exchange issued in conjunction with public works. These bills would be formally private and designed to meet the eligibility criteria at the central bank's discount window. Though formally created as three-monthly paper, these bills carried prolongation coupons for up to five years. This gave investors the option value of redeeming the bills at par quarterly horizons. The Reichsbank would receive short-term treasury bills as collateral from the government. It was hoped that in this way, liquid money market assets could be created that were attractive for private investors to hold and would not have to be monetized at the central bank. These plans did not materialize before the end of 1932; an attempt by the Bruening government to finance a first wave of work creation in this way in the spring of 1932—when international, notably French, opposition to domestic credit expansion in Germany was considerably weaker than a year before—was struck down as unconstitutional upon intervention by the Nazi party (Ritschl, 2002).

With the Nazi party in power, work creation between 1933 and 1936 was financed according to the same concept. The central bank received short-term treasury bills as collateral. Instead of floating these in the market directly—which was deemed difficult given the low credibility of the government—its proxy banks accepted an equivalent amount of bills of exchange issued by contractors carrying out the public work projects (Silverman, 1998). As had been hoped, private sector firms were content to keep these work creation bills in their portfolios to maximum maturity. As a consequence, the work creation bills did not flow back to the central bank for rediscounting. This enabled the Reichsbank to tap the money market for public borrowing without inflating the monetary base.

Broadly similar procedures were followed with the Mefo armament programme. An entity very similar to modern special purpose vehicles, Mefo was set up by the Reichsbank in cooperation with industry leaders, and accepted bills of exchange issued by suppliers to the military. In contrast to the work creation programmes, no collateral paper was issued by the government. As a consequence, Mefo debts were effectively hidden from the government debt statistics. Again, these bills were mostly kept to maturity by the original issuer. To preserve secrecy and prevent the bills from circulating within the private sector, the Reichsbank operated a buyback programme on behalf of the government.

The Mefo bills flowed back to the Reichsbank in 1938 when the programme ended but were only partly redeemed through long-term debt. Large scale monetization and a sharp increase in money supply was the immediate consequence. A formal protest submitted by the bank in early 1939 led to the dismissal of its directorate including its president (James, 1986).

With government borrowing siphoning off excess liquidity from the money market, monetary aggregates expanded at a slower rate than nominal income and real output. By the mid-1930s, financial depth, measured crudely as the ratio of M1 to real output, had fallen to the level of 1925. It was still below its 1929 level in 1938 when inflationary war finance was beginning in earnest.

The mostly adaptive role of monetary policy since the stabilization of 1924 is also reflected in the time series evidence. The succession of several monetary regimes paired with deflation and depression suggests the presence of structural breaks in the money/income relationship. To obtain such breaks endogenously, this and the following sections will specify time-varying VARs, which relate the respective policy instrument to outcomes via a plausible transmission mechanism, following related procedures in the literature.

Let $\mathbf{y}_t$ be an $[n.\ 1]$ vector of $i = 1, \ldots, n$ time series y_i, observed at time $t=1, \ldots,$ T. Let $\mathbf{x}_t$ be an $[(n.p+1).1]$ vector that includes the first p lags of the same time series,

(a)

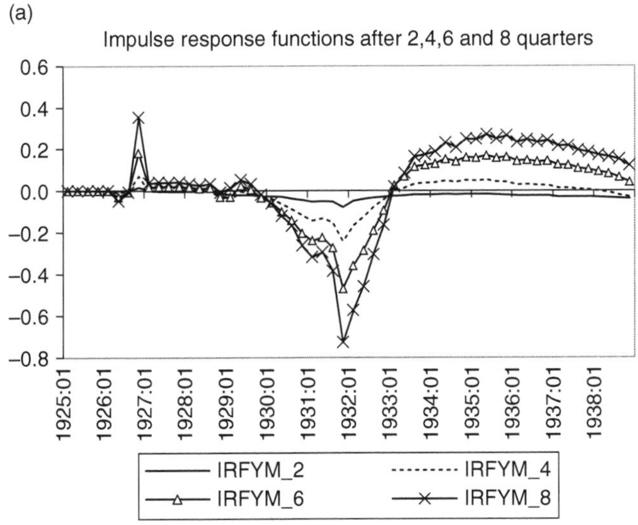

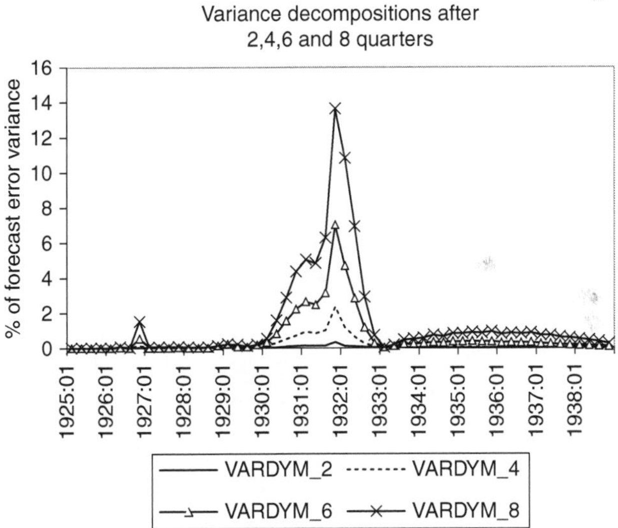

Fig. 4.1. The dynamic multiplier effects of money demand shocks on output in a time-varying VAR: output and prices assumed exogenous to money

$$\mathbf{x}_t = [1, y'_{t-1}, \ldots, y'_{t-p}]'$$

and let $\mathbf{u}_t$ be an $[n \cdot 1]$ vector of disturbance terms. Then, the i-th equation of a vector autoregression is:

$$y_{i,t} = \mathbf{x}_t^{'}\mathbf{b}_t + u_{i,t}$$

Here, the vector $\mathbf{b}_t = [\mathbf{c}'\boldsymbol{\beta}_t']'$ includes the vector of constants **c**, as well as the $[p \cdot 1]$ vector of coefficients $\boldsymbol{\beta}_t$, which links the variables of the system to their own lagged values in the VAR. $\boldsymbol{\beta}_t$ is our object of interest. We assume that this coefficient vector evolves according to the following state equation:

$$\boldsymbol{\beta}_t = \pi \bullet \boldsymbol{\beta}_{t-1} + (1-\pi) \bullet \overline{\boldsymbol{\beta}} + \mathrm{v}_t$$

where $\mathbf{v}_t$ is an i.i.d. disturbance term, and where $\overline{\boldsymbol{\beta}} = (0,1,0,\ldots 0)$ is the unit root prior in time series $\mathbf{y}_t$. The law of motion of these coefficients also depends on prior assumptions about parameter π. Setting the latter to zero, the coefficients would be stationary. Setting it to one, they follow a random walk.[1]

I obtain time-varying impulse response functions from these VARs, employing the standard Cholesky decomposition of the variance-covariance matrix. Figure 4.1 shows the responses of output to monetary shocks from a time-varying VAR that relates M1 to consumer prices, producer prices, and a quarterly series of gross domestic output (all data from Ritschl, 2002).

Figure 4.1 shows the results from under a standard ordering of money behind output and prices. Assuming—based on the evidence gathered in the previous section—that capital mobility was high, this ordering is also consistent with the implications of the Mundell–Fleming model, in which monetary policy must passively accommodate both nominal and real fluctuations under fixed exchange rates.

Up to 1929, the evidence from Figure 4.1 is precisely what the Mundell–Fleming paradigm would predict: for fixed exchange rates and high capital mobility, the money multiplier is zero, and so is its share in the variance explanation of output. Beginning with the German currency crisis of early 1929, however, things go awry: the measured money multiplier becomes increasingly negative, the more so the longer the lag after the initial shock. The decline is only reversed in late 1931. Beginning with the transition to a pure paper currency in early 1933, the multiplier turns into positive territory, suggesting moderate effects on output. The downward spike in the multiplier during the slump is mirrored by an increase in the variance explanation, as well as its subsequent fall.

This result may be an artefact of assuming money to be endogenous when it was not. Under looming debt constraints, inward capital mobility is reduced while outward capital mobility temporarily increases as foreign investors rush for the exit. The basic tenets of the Mundell–Fleming model then cannot apply, as money becomes temporarily exogenous to output. Figure 4.2 shows the results from going against the logic of the Mundell–Fleming model and assuming money to be exogenous to output. This ordering would reflect the prior belief that reserve flows under the Dawes and Young Plans responded to other things than German output and may themselves be causal for domestic adjustments.

[1] I adopt the standard choice of $\pi = 0.999$. Estimation is by Kalman filtering, using standard parameter choices for time-varying Bayesian VARs (Hamilton, 1994). All data are available at http://personal.lse.ac.uk/ritschl/interwargermanydata.html.

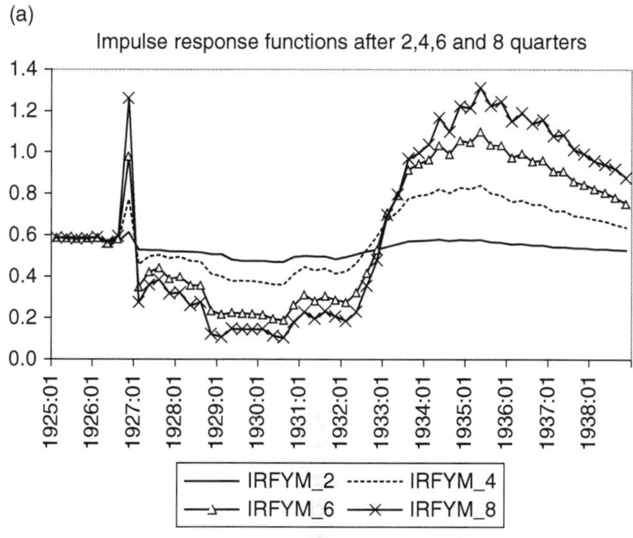

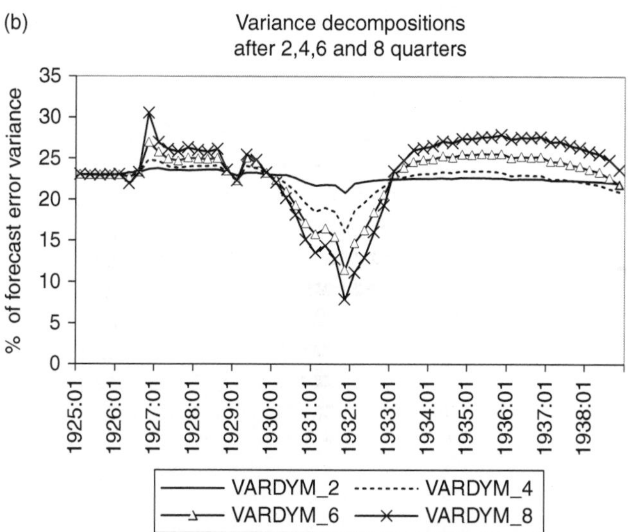

Fig. 4.2. The dynamic multiplier effects of money demand shocks on output in a time-varying VAR: money assumed exogenous to output and prices

Again, assuming money to be exogenous to output under a fixed exchange rate regime is not innocuous. In the absence of sovereign debt limits, both the Keynesian and the monetary approach to the transfer problem predict that cross-border capital movements ensure domestic currency is endogenous to domestic output (see Metzler, 1942 and Johnson, 1956, respectively). Conversely, if limits to borrowing abroad exist and debt levels approach these limits, inward capital movements and reserve flows become restricted and may cease altogether. This places an upper bound on the circulation of a currency that is subject to international reserve requirements. As a consequence, money becomes exogenous to output whenever the debt limit threatens to become binding.

Potentially, this could add explanatory power to the 'Golden Fetters' (Eichengreen, 1992) channel of crisis propagation under the interwar gold standard. The short-term responses of output to a monetary shock indeed seem quite robust over time. The forecast error decompositions on the right-hand side of Figure 4.1 suggest that slightly more than 20 per cent of the output variation would be explained by monetary shocks at a 6-month horizon. This is close to standard results for post-war evidence, (see e.g. Leeper et al., 1996; Bernanke and Mihov, 1998; Uhlig, 2005).

Time variation does affect the money/income relationship at longer horizons, though. Counter to expectation, the monetary transmission mechanism during the crisis became weaker, not stronger. After a peak in late 1926, the long-term relationship had weakened already in 1927, and even further in 1929, and was not to recover until 1932. Only then does the impulse response function recover the hump-shaped pattern familiar from post-war evidence, with responses reaching their maximum around two years after the shock.

The timing of the structural breaks suggested by the time-varying parameter structure is informative about the regime changes governing German monetary and balance-of-payments policies. The 1926 spike and subsequent decline in the responses, especially at longer intervals, coincide with the Reichsbank's intensified efforts to sterilize capital inflows. A further break in late 1928 marks the exit of foreign lenders from the German market, as well as the start of negotiations about the Young Plan. The next break is visible in the last quarter of 1930, after the last tranche of the Young Plan's stabilization loan to Germany was disbursed. The monetary multiplier at longer intervals recovers during 1932, surpassing its 1927 levels in the third quarter when the Young Plan was finally abandoned.

The weakness of the responses to a monetary shock during the slump is also reflected in the variance decompositions. Beginning in the spring of 1929, the variance explanation of output at longer horizons starts a precipitous decline, which continues to the last quarter of 1931, after the introduction of capital controls and Britain's departure from the gold standard.

The evidence in Figure 4.2 suggests that, during the contraction from 1929 to 1933, the money-output relationship was limited to the short-term impact. Further than that, the monetary transmission mechanism appears to have lost traction: at horizons larger than four quarters, money comes out as near-neutral. This effect is reversed in the recovery of the mid-1930s, in the environment of a low-inflation command economy with substantial financial repression and initially moderate money growth.

Several observations suggest themselves from the evidence gathered in these figures. First, results are extremely sensitive to the identification procedure, suggesting a fragile and unstable monetary transmission mechanism before 1933. Second, both exercises agree in assigning no active role to the money multiplier during the downturn after 1929. Third, the hiatus of the depression separates two distinct monetary policy regimes from each other, with low effects in the 1920s and arguably higher effects in the 1930s. These regimes are easily identifiable as the Dawes Plan, ended by the sudden stop in the balance of payments after 1928, and the transition to credit expansion in an autarkic economy beginning in 1933. The hiatus in between coincides with the Young Plan and its end in mid-1932. Solving the identification problem that sets the two estimates apart is beyond the scope of this chapter. But, despite their vast discrepancies in results, both specifications suggest that monetary policy during the Young Plan was not the dominant mechanism propagating the depression in Germany.

4.4. FISCAL POLICY: FROM RULES TO DISCRETION

Stabilization after the hyperinflation of 1923 was as much a fiscal as a monetary phenomenon, with a ban on the Reichsbank discounting treasury bills as a critical element (Sargent, 1982; Dornbusch, 1987). Fiscal policy was kept under close surveillance during the Dawes Plan of 1924. A reparations agent, Parker Gilbert, was installed in Berlin to effect the transfer of reparations into foreign exchange, and to report on German fiscal and monetary policy under the plan. As Germany's currency was shielded from reparations under transfer protection, his reports on Germany's progress towards increasing output, productivity, and, hence, her capacity to pay, were seen as critical for securing the inflow of funds from abroad. As a consequence, the central government budget—which the agent's office tracked closely—went from deficits during a mild recession in 1926 to surplus in the boom of 1927/28 (see Table 4.4). At the same time, however, lower level government budgets as well as the social insurance system remained in deficit.

In the aggregate, the public sector during the Dawes Plan never generated the fiscal surpluses required to pay for reparations. Table 4.4 permits a rough calculation of the fiscal sacrifice required to transfer reparations out of surpluses. Reparations amounted to less than 2.5 per cent of GDP, and in some years were much lower. The cost of generating fiscal surpluses to transfer reparations would nevertheless have been higher than that given the prevailing public sector deficits. Simply adding each year's fiscal surplus (i.e. subtracting the deficit) to reparations would place the total resource cost—including the elimination of the public deficits themselves—at 4–5 per cent of GDP during the 1920s. With ratios of public spending to GDP gradually approaching 30 per cent, this would have required a change of roughly 15 per cent in either public spending or tax revenues even if tax elasticities were zero.

While such adjustments would have been substantial, they were not outside the norm: as the data bear out, central government expenditure almost doubled between 1924 and 1929, fell by 20 per cent during the slump, and then grew fourfold from 1933 to 1938. The public sector share in GDP grew from 24 per cent in 1924 to 29 per cent in 1929, and continued to grow from 33 per cent in 1932 to 36 per cent in 1936, with a further jump to 42 per cent in 1938

However, given the political constraints on raising taxes in the presence of foreign reparation demands, the government found itself in a funding crisis as

Table 4.4. Key indicators of public expenditure (thousand mill. Reichsmarks, current values)

	Gov't Expenditure and Transfers		of which:	Surplus/Deficit			
	Central gov't	Public sector	Reparations	Central gov't	Public sector	GDP	CPI[1]
1924				0.77			
1925	5.38	16.92	1.08	−0.29	−0.52	71.15	141.9
1926	6.12	19.13	1.30	−0.78	−1.91	73.83	142.2
1927	6.55	21.93	1.71	0.01	−0.93	83.17	147.9
1928	6.87	23.77	2.16	0.15	−0.64	89.05	151.7
1929	7.75	26.05	1.96	−0.77	−2.23	89.25	154.0
1930	7.93	26.27	1.88	−0.16	−2.36	82.93	148.1
1931	6.52	22.71	0.99	0.36	−1.07	69.15	136.1
1932	5.75	18.91	0.18	0.13	−0.60	56.44	120.6
1933	6.49	19.84	0.15	−0.80	−0.78	57.72	118.0
1934	9.62	23.13	0.05	−3.41	−2.82	64.38	121.1
1935	11.85	25.08		−4.37	−3.22	71.75	123.0
1936	13.25	26.36		−3.52	−1.67	79.65	124.5
1937	18.62	32.06		−6.04	−3.61	89.11	125.1
1938	26.05	41.29		−9.46	−7.78	99.19	125.6

Notes: [1] 1913 = 100.
Sources: Statistisches Jahrbuch für das Deutsche Reich, various issues. German Federal Archive, Economics Ministry Collections, R7.

soon as the supply of foreign funds dried up. A major loan flotation in March 1929 failed after the news on the forthcoming Young Plan had reached the market. After that date, the government found itself essentially cut off from the credit market and relied on the central bank instead. The price to be paid for that was a rigid deflationary programme imposed and monitored by the bank. Except for the Young loan, which was internationally guaranteed, carried 7 per cent interest, and, hence, was well received by the market, Germany did not place a single bond issue on the market between early 1929 and mid-1934. During this time, the central government went through a succession of funding crises, being pushed into ever more severe deflationary measures in order to be able to roll over its short-term debt.

Stabilization of the central government budget was to some extent due to window dressing: as the data show, deficits persisted at lower level governments, and especially in the social security system. However, the budget squeeze is visible here as well. Exactly the reverse tendency becomes visible during the upswing of the 1930s: both the lower level budgets and the social security system went into surplus, while deficit were piling up in the central government account. As a consequence of these asymmetries, the share of public borrowing in GDP fluctuated markedly less during the 1930s than the central government deficits would suggest.

The extent to which the onset of the fiscal crisis in early 1929 affected Germany's borrowing dynamics is also borne out by time series evidence. To measure the effects of fiscal policy, I specify a time-varying VAR in output and central

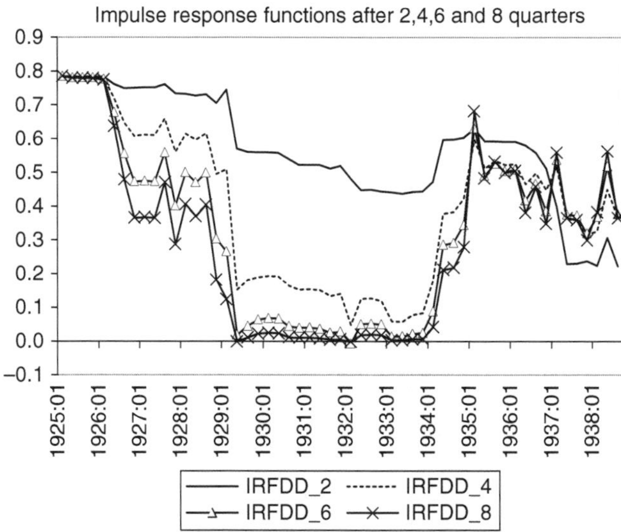

Fig. 4.3. The persistence of central government budget deficit shocks in a time-varying VAR

government deficits. To obtain the impulse response functions, shocks to these series enter a Cholesky decomposition in the same order. This helps to account for automatic stabilizers that affect the deficit contemporaneously with shocks to output. At semi-annual intervals, Figure 4.3 shows the impulse response function of deficits to their own impulse, i.e. the persistence of a deficit shock.

As the figure shows, the second quarter of 1929 marks a sudden regime change in fiscal policy: the persistence of deficit shocks at longer horizons drops to nearly zero, reflecting the pressure to swiftly restore budgetary in the face of a hardening credit constraint. Persistence recovers only during 1934, the year when military deficit spending began in earnest.

The same VAR also yields results on the dynamic multipliers of the central government's fiscal policy. Figure 4.4 shows the cumulative multipliers of a shock to central government budget deficits. Identifying fiscal policy solely through the deficit implicitly assumes the multipliers of spending shocks to be equal to those of taxation shocks. This comes at a cost, as the traditional Keynesian income–expenditure paradigm would predict that spending multipliers exceed tax multipliers. On the other hand, recent studies on fiscal multipliers (Bernanke and Mihov, 1998) have consistently found that responses to tax shocks exceed the multipliers of spending shocks, at least at longer horizons. Depending on the methodology applied, this discrepancy can be quite large (see Table 4.4).

The principal justification for this reduced form is that it implies a temporal Cholesky ordering: if both taxation and spending are a mixture of automatic and discretionary components, an ordering that places deficits after output emerges quite naturally, and the discretionary component of fiscal policy is identified without artificial assumptions about timing.

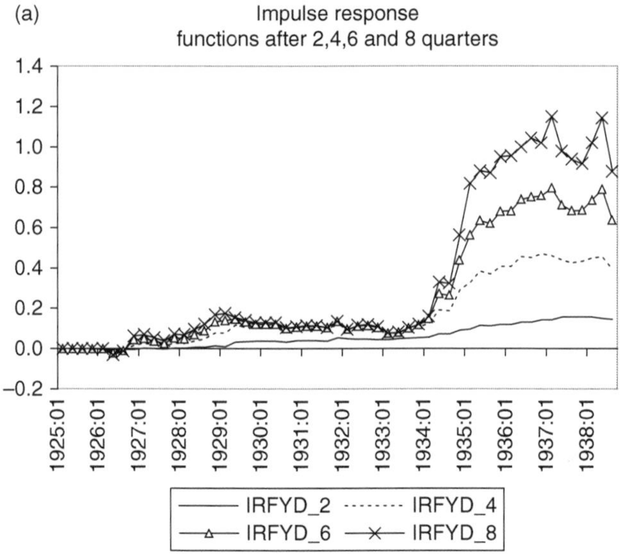

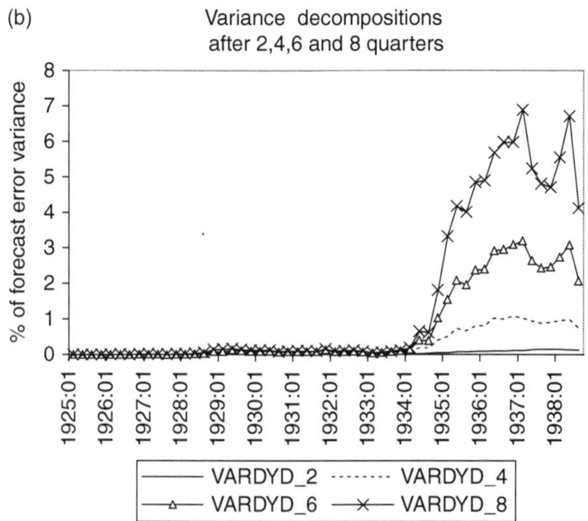

Fig. 4.4. The dynamic multiplier effects of central government budget deficits shocks on output in a time-varying VAR

Results for the multiplier of the discretionary component of the deficit are shown in Figure 4.4 for semi-annual intervals. As before, the dominant structural break occurs in 1934, when multipliers and explained variance go up sharply. Before that year, the multiplier effects of deficits are minuscule, as are the deficits themselves (see Table 4.3). After 1934, the variance decompositions suggest that fiscal deficits explain between 3 and 7 per cent of the forecast error variance in

Table 4.5. Multiplier effects of a public spending increase (results for Germany 1934–38 vs. estimates and calibrations for post-war data)

	1 quarter	4 quarters	8 quarters
I. Deficit financed spending shock			
Germany 1934–38	0.14*	0.42	0.97
Post-war data			
Blanchard and Perotti (2002)	0.9	0.55	0.65
(Simulation) anticipated	1.8	1.7	1.7 to 2.2
(Simulation) unanticipated	1.2	0.8	0.9
Mountford and Uhlig (2009)	0.44	0.42	0.67
Leeper et al. (2011)			
NK autarky, G non-traded	1.18	0.91	0.64**
Ilzetzki et al. (2010)			
Closed economy	0.11	0.6	0.9
II. Balanced budget spending shock			
Germany 1929–33	0.04*	0.10	0.12
Post-war data			
Blanchard and Perotti (2002)	0.2	−0.52	−0.67
(Simulation) anticipated	1 to 1.5	0.3 to 1	0.1 to 1.1
(Simulation) unanticipated	0.6	−0.1	0.4
Mountford and Uhlig (2009)	0.25	−0.79	−2.55
Ilzetzki et al. (2010)			
Fixed exchange rate	0.04	0.25	0.5
High debt/income ratio	0.06	0.06	−0.75

Notes: * 2 quarters. ** 10 quarters.

output, which is close to standard results from post-war evidence. Before that date, however, they indicate virtually no explanatory power for output at all.

That the lack of deficit spending before 1933 should have had such little effect on the German economy is not a foregone conclusion. As Table 4.3 bears out, budget cuts during 1930–32 reduced the central government's real expenditure by over 20 per cent; similar figures obtain for the public sector as a whole. Keynesian orthodoxy would predict a balanced budget cut of 4–6 per cent of 1929 GNP to reduce aggregate output and income by the same amount. By contrast, Figure 4.4 implies a multiplier of hardly more than 0.1, with a maximum at 0.17—i.e. of merely 17 *pfennigs* of GNP lost per 1 *Reichsmark* of public budget cuts.

Even these results still look pessimistic in the light of the post-war evidence gathered in Table 4.4. For a balanced budget variation, the multipliers found for US data (in the wake of Blanchard and Perotti, 2002) suggest the reverse effect: balanced budget cuts may have positive rather than negative effects on output at longer horizons. In contrast, international evidence collected by Ilzetzki et al., (2010) finds that, in economies operating a fixed exchange rate, fiscal shocks have small but generally positive effects on output. Even smaller but still mostly positive multiplier effects obtain for economies with high ratios of public debt to GDP. The results obtained in Figure 4.4 for Germany between 1929 and 1933 seem broadly consistent with this evidence.

As deficits grew in 1934, so does the deficit multiplier measured in Figure 4.4. The maximum multiplier of 0.97 is comparable to the Blanchard and Perotti (2002) estimates of deficit financed spending shocks, but builds up far more slowly. In this it is comparable to the temporal profile found by Mountford and Uhlig (2009) although it comes out somewhat higher. In Table 4.5 we also note the nearly perfect fit with the multipliers for closed economies found by Ilzetzki et al. (2010). Clearly, the effects of deficit spending in the German upswing after 1933 are very much in line with the post-war experience.

The effects of fiscal tightening have been the subject matter of intense debate also for the Great Recession after 2008. While a consensus on positive short-term effects of fiscal stimuli seems to have emerged (see Corsetti et al., 2009; Cwik and Wieland, 2010; Coenen et al., 2012), there is evidence casting doubt on the conclusion that by symmetry, austerity in the presence of high debt levels has contractionary effects (Alesina and Ardagna, 2010; Cochrane, 2011; Corsetti et al., 2010). Earlier research on episodes of fiscal austerity found mixed evidence but emphasized the possibility of favourable outcomes (see Alesina and Drazen, 1991; Bertola and Drazen, 1991).

By comparison, the evidence in Figure 4.4 points to an intermediate case: fiscal multipliers during the contraction period of 1929 to 1932 are small but still positive, indicating that austerity did contract economic activity, although probably not by as much as has commonly been taken for granted in the historical literature.

Drawing the results of this section together, the evidence shows how fiscal austerity during the slump after 1929 changed the time series characteristics. Fiscal shocks lost their persistence in mid-1929 when the first funding crisis occurred, and regained it when deficit spending began in 1934. Fiscal multipliers during the recession remained small overall. Multipliers increased again with the transition to exchange rate control and managed credit expansion. For both regimes, the multiplier estimates are in line with post-war evidence. Overall, these results assign a minor role to fiscal policy during the slump, but also suggest only a limited contribution to recovery after 1933.

4.5. THE WAGE CHANNEL OF CRISIS PROPAGATION

As a consequence of revolution in 1918, the German economy came to the reconstructed gold standard with a highly interventionist labour market regime. This included the 8-hour day, workplace councils, collective bargaining and mandatory state arbitration of labour disputes. Wage determination was soon a matter of party coalition politics, and arbitration by government officials became the rule (Feldman, 1993). Until 1929, wages increased substantially, and wage compression favoured unskilled workers (Bry, 1960). Still, output, and to a lesser extent employment, increased as well, as the economy continued to recover from the hyperinflation of the early 1920s.

As the data in Table 4.6 bear out, wages outstripped productivity growth during the late 1920s, leading to a substantial rise in unit labour cost. In spite of the drastic fall in output and employment during the subsequent slump, both real wages and productivity continued to grow. Again, however, wages increased faster. Only after 1934 was this tendency reversed, and unit labour cost gradually declined to the levels of the mid-1920s.

Table 4.6. Real wages and productivity (1925 = 100)

	Wages	Output	Employment	Unemployment (per cent)	Productivity	Unit Labour Cost
1925	100.0	100.0	100.0	4.0	100.0	100.0
1926	118.5	101.4	92.8	11.8	109.3	108.5
1927	121.3	111.8	101.0	7.1	110.7	109.6
1928	119.2	115.4	105.5	7.7	109.4	109.0
1929	127.0	113.6	103.4	10.4	109.9	115.6
1930	132.0	106.0	96.4	17.2	110.0	120.0
1931	142.2	93.8	83.5	25.5	112.3	126.5
1932	144.5	84.9	73.2	31.5	116.0	124.6
1933	149.7	91.2	75.3	27.2	121.1	123.7
1934	143.9	100.9	85.8	15.7	117.5	122.5
1935	140.9	113.2	92.2	12.1	122.8	114.8
1936	138.4	125.9	100.1	9.6	125.8	110.0
1937	135.4	140.0	107.8	5.0	129.8	104.2
1938	133.4	153.4	114.9	2.2	133.5	99.9

Source: Statistisches Jahrbuch für das Deutsche Reich, various issues; Ritschl (2002).

To identify regime changes that may have influenced the labour demand schedule, we employ the same time-varying VAR technique as before. In a setup that controls for output and ex-post real interest rates, the responses of labour demand to real wage shocks again reveal a regime dependent pattern (see Figure 4.5).[2]

At a 6-month horizon, the wage elasticity of labour demand remains more or less stable at values around -1, which conforms to theoretical priors and to earlier results for interwar Germany and Britain (Broadberry and Ritschl, 1995). At longer lags, the effects are again strongly regime dependent. From 1927 into early 1930, the labour demand schedule at longer horizons almost appears to break down. During the downturn, it recovers dramatically, suggesting strong and persistent effects of real wage shocks on labour demand. The schedule goes back to standard parameter values and loses its volatility during the recovery of the mid-1930s. A look at the variance decomposition suggests high explanatory power for wage shocks throughout; wage shocks during 1931/2 explain up to 65 per cent of the forecast error variance in output. This is gradually reduced as recovery sets in.

These results suggest that real wage rigidity—or more precisely, the continuing rise of unit wage cost in excess of productivity growth—was a major channel crisis propagation, consistent with findings of Borchardt (1990). Keeping real wages high through political arbitration had strong, pernicious effects on employment after 1929.

Prior to the depression, however, wages apparently did not affect employment very much. This anomaly coincides with the period of heavy capital inflows—of

[2] The variables included are (in this order of exogeneity in the Cholesky decomposition) quarterly GDP, commercial paper rates, non-agricultural total hours, and real wages per person employed. All data from Ritschl (2002, Appendix C.2).

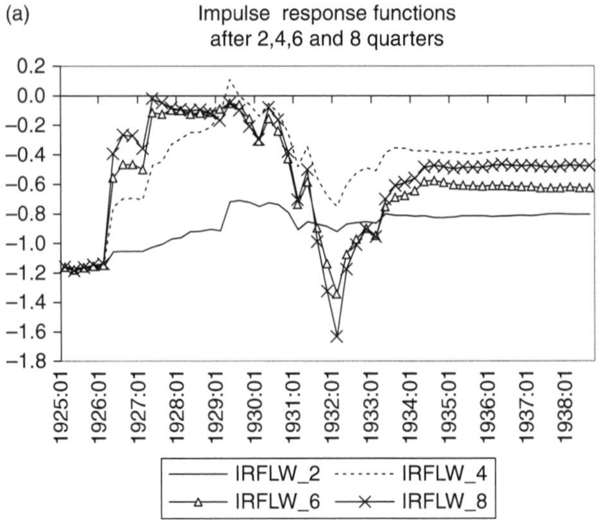

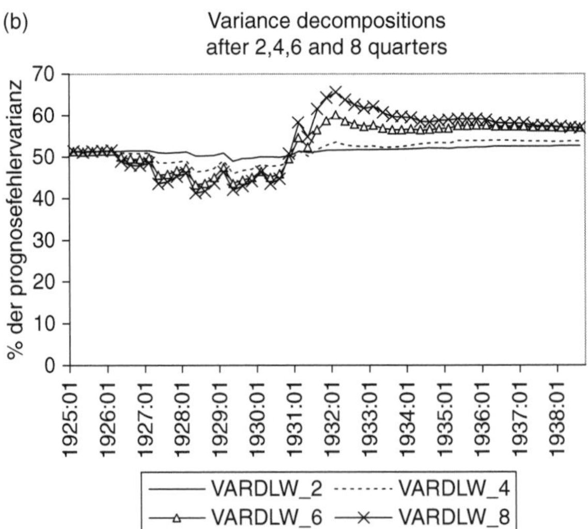

Fig. 4.5. The dynamic multiplier effects of real wage shocks on labour demand in a time-varying VAR

commercial credit until 1928 and of stabilization loans further until 1930—into the German economy. These inflows temporarily alleviated the wage pressure emanating from collective wage bargaining and arbitration. This would be consistent with findings that attribute little effect to wage pressure during the late 1920s (see e.g. Voth, 1995). As soon as the music stopped, however, adjustment set in rapidly, with detrimental consequences for employment.

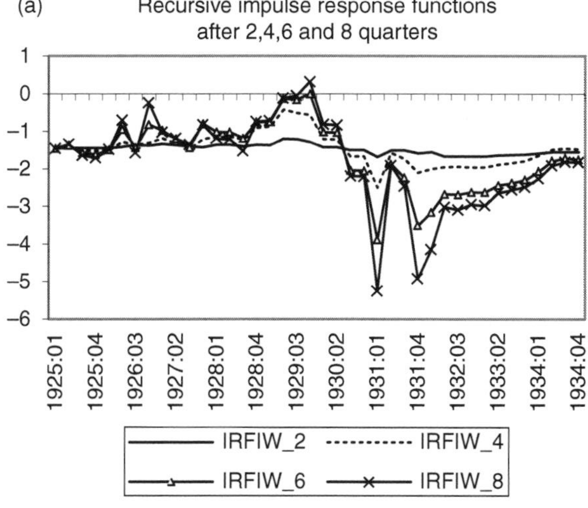

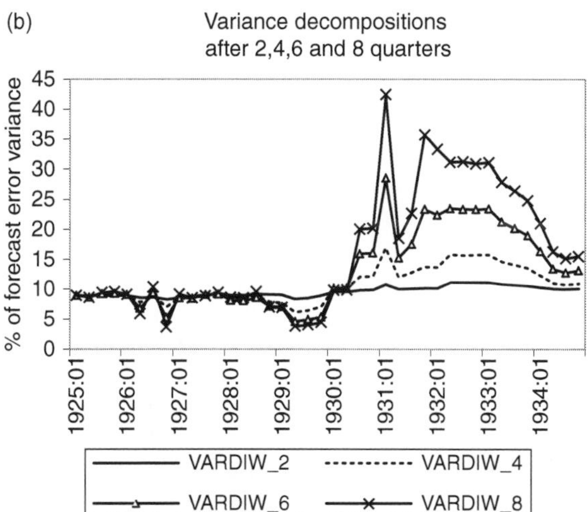

Fig. 4.6. The dynamic responses of planned investment to real wage shocks

Similar patterns become visible in the responses of investment activity to wages. Controlling for output and the cost of capital, the dynamic relationship between investment and wages until 1929 appears to be weak and ambiguous, with responses changing signs at longer horizons. After that, however, investment responded strongly and negatively to wage shocks at longer horizons. This effect persists until 1933 and only gradually weakens as recovery gets underway.

Figure 4.6 shows the wage elasticity of the demand for capital goods, measured by orders of factory equipment (data from VDMA, 1927; 1930). According to these results, wages seem to have little explanatory power for investment in the late 1920s (see on this Ritschl, 1994; Spoerer, 1994; Voth, 1994). However, this changes abruptly in early 1929; during the depression over 50 per cent of investment activity is explained by wage shocks at longer lags. This suggests a second wage channel of propagation of the depression in Germany, which goes beyond the labour market itself (consistent with a claim by Borchardt, 1980).

Drawing the results of this section together, wages come out as the predominant channel of crisis propagation in Germany during the depression. Wages appear to have affected economy activity in two ways: directly, going through the labour market, and indirectly, by their effects on the decision to invest. The wage channel provides what we could not find for monetary and even fiscal policy during the slump: a quantitatively important transmission mechanism that translated the sudden stop in the German current account after 1928 into a decline in output and employment.

4.6. CONCLUSIONS AND IMPLICATIONS FOR TODAY

Fiscal austerity programmes have a reputation for facing a Keynesian Laffer curve and thus be self-defeating. Potential dangers and pitfalls of this policy have been highlighted prominently during the Great Recession after 2008 (prominently by Krugman, 2008, in a fiery criticism of German plans to balance the budget after 2008). Germany's fiscal policy during the Great Depression of the 1930s was just such a policy: it was strictly deflationary, aimed to balance the budget, and followed many of the precepts implicit in the later Washington Consensus. Applied during a slump of catastrophic proportions, Germany's strategy of deflation has drawn the ire of commentators at all times.

This chapter has placed this policy in the context of Germany's mounting foreign debt crisis during 1929–31. German fiscal policy adhered to orthodox recipes, not so much out of misguided ideology but in an attempt to avoid defaulting on reparations. Transition from the earlier Dawes Plan with its lax payment conditions to the much stricter Young Plan had marked a sudden regime change in fiscal policy. From mid-1929 to late 1933, balancing the budget was the paramount fiscal priority. Success of this policy was mixed. While it reached the limited goal of averting outright default on reparations, it ultimately failed in its attempt to keep current on Germany's commercial foreign debt. There is general agreement that this course of action contributed to political radicalization. Political pressure to pay by creditors abroad and to default by voters at home put the government in the precarious position of an agent with two principals having diametrically opposed interests. The effects on the legitimacy of the Weimar Republic in the eyes of the population were detrimental.

This chapter has argued that the 1929 fiscal reversal in Germany came as a consequence of a sudden stop in the current account, following a pattern that closely resembles post-war sovereign debt crises. Cut off from foreign credit markets, the German government resorted to seeking a political stabilization loan as well as assistance from the central bank. Both came with a long laundry list of conditions, ranging from budget and wage cuts to reductions in administered prices; essentially the same conditionality that has been attached to recent relief programmes in southern Europe. Germany's deflationary policy is thus an early case of an international stabilization programme having run into trouble.

The quantitative evidence presented in this chapter suggests that, nevertheless, neither fiscal nor monetary policy were the principal mechanism of crisis propagation in Germany. Fiscal multipliers during the austerity phase were positive but low, which would be consistent with post-war evidence on balanced budget variations. The dominant channel of crisis transmission and propagation we found is real wage rigidity: though nominal wages did fall, producer prices declined faster, with direct effects on labour demand and indirect effects on investment. This highlights a fundamental dilemma of German deflationary policy, the inability to enforce wage cuts that would outpace price declines and thus result in real wage decline. As a consequence, real wages in Germany rose during the depression, as did unit labour cost.

The political economy of this phenomenon is not difficult to understand, and it gives reasons for concern. There is general agreement that unemployment after 1929 caused the rise of Nazi and communist votes and thus brought about the political collapse of the Weimar Republic. However, the mechanism linking the two does not appear to be as straightforward as early research (Frey and Weck, 1981; critiqued by Falter et al., 1986) would have it. Recent research suggests a potential for right wing extremism that had deep historical and cultural roots, although this would not itself explain the rise of the extremist vote since 1930 (Voigtlaender and Voth, 2012). Indeed, the increase in the Nazi vote came predominantly from the lower middle class worried about being thrown into unemployment and deprivation (King et al., 2008).

Similar destabilizing mechanisms might be threatening countries with weak institutions today. Governments confronted with a voter base susceptible to radicalization would find it politically expedient to eschew radical austerity measures. In a two-party system and its derivatives, participants might then play a waiting game, with each side attempting to place the onus on the other in a quick succession of unstable governments, thus postponing stabilization (Alesina and Drazen, 1991).

Germany's case is also instructive about the option of currency devaluation. Given that her debt was gold denominated, Germany opted for capital controls instead of open devaluation, a decision largely due to creditor pressure: US negotiators signalled to the Germans during 1931 that imposing capital controls would be more acceptable than open devaluation and default on the gold clauses in the loan contracts (Ritschl, 2002). Last, the German crisis provides lessons about the international repercussions of a large economy defaulting, including transatlantic feedbacks on the US economy (Ritschl and Sarferaz, 2010), the breakup of fixed exchange rate arrangements (Accominotti 2012) and the increase of protectionism.

In the light of these lessons, it is instructive to pursue the parallels between Germany's debt crisis in 1931 and the southern European debt crisis since 2009/10 a bit further. The first parallel is that the debtor country would adopt internal, fiscal devaluation instead of an open breakaway from the common monetary standard. This is all the more striking as the interwar gold standard was not a currency union: both the national currencies and the respective national payment systems continued to exist, enabling the member countries to exit at low transaction cost. The second parallel is the internal devaluation itself: Germany's policy of deflation between 1929 and 1932 is the quintessential economic history textbook example of a pre-Keynesian policy response to a recession, when in fact it was a policy of austerity in the face of a looming sovereign debt crisis. The third parallel is a government of technocrats, with only weak public support, installed to carry out austerity policies at the behest of the foreign creditor countries. In Germany, this arrangement eroded the support for democratic parties among voters and hastened social unrest, mass protests, and politically motivated violence—in 1932 alone, authorities counted 2,000 deaths in such incidents (Thamer, 1986). Violent mass protest against austerity measures in southern Europe has not been the norm but recent incidents suggest a potential for radicalization and societal disintegration. The fourth parallel is the failure of real wages to fall during the austerity period. In spite of emerging mass unemployment, real wages and unit labour costs continued to increase in Germany during 1929–32, a phenomenon that has been observed in the Mediterranean basin during the recent crisis as well (see e.g. EEAG, 2012). The last—potential—parallel is the breakup of the currency system by contagion. Germany itself, pressed but also incentivized by its creditors, responded to its own financial meltdown by financial repression and capital controls instead of devaluation. However, the knock-on effects of Germany's financial crisis on Britain's banking system seem to have been instrumental in Britain's departure from gold (Accominotti, 2012).

We do not have the counterfactual of what would happened had different policies toward the German crisis been pursued. Finding a feasible counterfactual was perhaps the biggest and most contentious issue of Weimar historiography in the 1980s and 1990s. The essence of the criticism was that Germany should have devalued openly and at an early stage, thus avoiding excessive fiscal contraction (Holtfrerich, 1982; Ferguson and Temin, 2003), while others have pointed out that given Germany's recent hyperinflation (Borchardt, 1979 and 1984), the actions of her foreign creditors (Ritschl, 2002), and the weakness of her national banking system (Schnabel, 2004), devaluation was not an easy game to play. Very similar counterfactuals have been popular in the current crisis of the European periphery. While it is too early to tell whether the analogy with interwar Germany will carry through, the indication again seems to be that creditor pressure and not the lack of economic insight is what might keep the debtor countries of southern Europe within the eurozone.

BIBLIOGRAPHY

Accominotti, O. (2012), 'London Merchant Banks, the Central European Panic, and the Sterling Crisis of 1931', *Journal of Economic History* 72, 1-43.

Alesina, A. (2011), 'Fiscal Policy after the Great Recession', *Barcelona GSE Lecture* XXI.

Alesina, A. and Ardagna, S. (2010), 'Large Changes in Fiscal Policy: Taxes versus Spending', in J. Brown (ed.), *Tax Policy and the Economy, Volume 24*. Chicago: Chicago University Press.

Alesina, A. and Drazen, A. (1991), 'Why Are Stabilizations Delayed?', *American Economic Review* 81, 1170–88.

Bernanke, B. and Mihov, L. (1998), 'Measuring Monetary Policy', *Quarterly Journal of Economics* 113, 869–902.

Bertola, G. and Drazen, A. (1991), 'Trigger Points and Budget Cuts: Explaining the Effects of Fiscal Austerity', *American Economic Review* 83, 11–26.

Blanchard, O. and Perotti R. (2002), 'An Empirical Characterization of the Dynamic Effects of Changes in Government Spending and Taxes on Output', *Quarterly Journal of Economics* 117, 1329–68.

Borchardt, K. (1979), 'Zwangslagen und Handlungsspielräume in der großen Wirtschaftskrise der frühen dreißiger Jahre', *Jahrbuch der Bayerischen Akademie der Wissenschaften*, 85–132.

Borchardt, K. (1980), 'Wirtschaftliche Ursachen des Scheiterns der Weimarer Republik', in K.-D. Erdmann and H. Schulze (eds), *Weimar, Selbstpreisgabe einer Demokratie: Eine Bilanz heute*. Düsseldorf: Droste, 211–49.

Borchardt, K. (1984), 'Could and Should Germany Have Followed Britain in Leaving the Gold Standard?', *Journal of European Economic History* 13, 471–98.

Borchardt, K. (1990), 'A Decade of Debate About Bruening's Economic Policy', in J. v. Kruedener (ed.), *Economic Crisis and Political Collapse. The Weimar Republic 1924–1933*. Oxford: Berg, 99–151.

Broadberry, S. and Ritschl, A. (1995), 'Real Wages, Productivity, and Unemployment in Britain and Germany during the 1920s', *Explorations in Economic History* 32, 327–49.

Bry, G. (1960), *Wages in Germany, 1871–1945*. Princeton: Princeton University Press.

Cochrane, J. (2011), 'Understanding Policy in the Great Recession: Some Unpleasant Fiscal Arithmetic', *European Economic Review* 55, 2–30.

Coenen, G., Straub, R., and Trabandt, M. (2012), 'Fiscal Policy and the Great Recession in the Euro Area', *American Economic Review* 102, 71–6.

Corsetti, G., Meier, A., and Mueller, G. (2009), 'Fiscal Stimulus with Spending Reversals', IMF Working Paper 09/106.

Corsetti, G., Kuester, K., Meier, A., and Müller, G. (2010), 'Debt Consolidation and the Effects of Fiscal Retrenchment in Deep Recessions', *American Economic Review* 100, 41–5.

Cwik, T. and Wieland, V. (2010), 'Government Spending Multipliers and Spillovers in the Euro Area', ECB Working Paper 1276.

Deutsche Bundesbank (1976), *Deutsches Geld-und Bankwesen in Zahlen, 1876–1975*. Frankfurt: Knapp.

Dornbusch, R. (1987), 'Lessons from the German Inflation Experience of the 1920s', in R. Dornbusch, S. Fischer, and J. Bossons (eds), *Macroeconomics and Finance: Essays in Honor of Franco Modigliani*. Cambridge: Cambridge University Press, 337–66.

Eaton, J., Gersovitz, M., and Stiglitz, J. (1986), 'The Pure Theory of Country Risk', *European Economic Review* 30, 481–513.

EEAG (2012), *The EEAG Report on the European Economy 2012*. Munich: CESifo.

Eichengreen, B. (1992), *Golden Fetters. The Gold Standard and the Great Depression 1919–1939*. Oxford: Oxford University Press.

Eichengreen, B. and Hausman, R. (1999), 'Exchange Rates and Financial Fragility', in Federal Reserve Bank of Kansas City (ed.) *New Challenges for Monetary Policy. A Symposium Sponsored by the Federal Reserve Bank of Kansas City, Jackson Hole, Wyoming, August 26-28, 1999*. Kansas City: Federal Reserve Bank of Kansas City, 329–68.

Falter, W., Lindenberger, T., and Schumann, S. (1986), *Wahlen und Abstimmungen in der Weimarer Republik. Materialien zum Wahlverhalten 1919–1932*. München: Beck.

Feinstein, C., Temin, P., and Toniolo, G. (1997), *The European Economy Between the Wars*. Oxford: Oxford University Press.

Feldman, G. (1993), *The Great Disorder. Politics, Economics, and Society in the German Inflation, 1914–1924*. Oxford: Oxford University Press.

Ferguson, N. (1998), *The Pity of War*. London: Penguin Press.

Ferguson, T. and Temin, P. (2003), 'Made in Germany: The Currency Crisis of 1931', *Research in Economic History* 31, 1–53.

Frey, B. and Weck, H. (1981), 'Hat Arbeitslosigkeit den Aufstieg des Nationalsozialismus bewirkt?', *Jahrbücher für Nationalökonomie und Statistik* 196, 1–31.

Gilbert, P. (1925–30), *Report of the Agent General for Reparation Payments*. Berlin: Agent General.

Hamilton, J. D. (1994), *Time Series Analysis*. Princeton: Princeton University Press.

Hardach, K. (1980), *The Political Economy of Germany in the 20th Century*. Berkeley: University of California Press.

Helbich, W. (1962), *Die Reparationen in der Ära Brüning: Zur Bedeutung des Young-Plans für die deutsche Politik 1930 bis 1932*. Berlin: Colloquium-Verlag.

Holtfrerich, C.-L. (1982), 'Alternativen zu Brünings Politik in der Weltwirtschaftskrise?', *Historische Zeitschrift* 235, 605–31.

Holtfrerich, C.-L. (1986), *The German Inflation*. New York: de Gruyter.

Holtfrerich, C.-L. (1990), 'Was the Policy of Deflation in Germany Unavoidable?', in Juergen v. Kruedener (ed.), *Economic Crisis and Political Collapse. The Weimar Republic 1924–1933*. Oxford: Berg, 63–80.

Ilzetzki, E., Mendoza, E., and Végh, C. (2010), 'How Big (Small?) are Fiscal Multipliers?', NBER Working Paper 16479.

James, H. (1985), *The Reichsbank and Public Finance in Germany, 1924–1933: A Study of the Politics of Economics during the Great Depression*. Frankfurt am Main: Knapp.

James, H. (1986), *The German Slump: Politics and Economics, 1924–1936*. Oxford: Clarendon Press.

Johnson, H. G. (1956), 'The Transfer Problem and Exchange Stability', *Journal of Political Economy* 64, 212–25.

Keynes, J. M. (1920), *The Economic Consequences of the Peace*. London: Macmillan.

Keynes, J. M. (1922), *A Revision of the Treaty*. London: Macmillan.

Keynes, J. M. (1926), 'Germany's Coming Problem', in C. Johnson (ed.), *The Collected Writings of John Maynard Keynes Vol. XVIII: Activities 1922–1932. The End of Reparations*. London: Macmillan, 271–7.

Keynes, J. M. (1929), 'The German Transfer Problem', *Economic Journal* 39, 1–7.

King, G., Rosen, O., Tanner, M., and Wagner, A. F. (2008), 'Ordinary Economic Voting Behavior in the Extraordinary Election of Adolf Hitler', *Journal of Economic History* 68, 951–96.

Klug, A. (1993), *The German Buybacks 1932–1939: A Cure for Overhang?* (Princeton Studies in International Finance). Princeton: Princeton University Press.

Krugman, P. (2008), 'The Economic Consequences of Herr Steinbrueck', *New York Times* 11 December 2008.

Leeper, E., Sims, C., and Zha, T. (1996), 'What Does Monetary Policy Do?', Brookings Papers on Economic Activity Series 2, 1–63.

Leeper, E., Traum, N., and Walker, T. (2011), 'Clearing Up the Fiscal Multiplier Morass', NBER Working Paper 17444.

Link, W. (1970), *Die amerikanische Stabilisierungspolitik in Deutschland 1921–32*. Düsseldorf: Droste.

Mantoux, E. (1946), *The Carthaginian Peace, or the Economic Consequences of Mr. Keynes*. London: Oxford University Press.

Marks, S. (1978), 'The Myth of Reparations', *Central European History* 11, 231–55.

McNeil, W. C. (1986), *American Money and the Weimar Republic*. New York: Columbia University Press.

Metzler, L. A. (1942), 'The Transfer Problem Reconsidered', *Journal of Political Economy* 50, 397–414.

Mountford, A. and Uhlig, H. (2009), 'What are the Effects of Fiscal Policy Shocks?', *Journal of Applied Econometrics* 24, 960–92.

Ohlin, B. (1929), 'The German Transfer Problem: A Discussion, I: Transfer Difficulties, Real and Imagined', *Economic Journal* 39, 172–78.

Ritschl, A. (1994), 'Goldene Jahre? Zu den Investitionen in der Weimarer Republik', *Zeitschrift für Wirtschafts- und Sozialwissenschaften* 114, 99–111.

Ritschl, A. (1996), 'Sustainability of High Public Debt: What the Historical Record Shows', *Swedish Economic Policy Review* 3, 175–98.

Ritschl, A. (2002), *Deutschlands Krise und Konjunktur, 1924–1934. Binnenkonjunktur, Auslandsverschuldung und Reparationsproblem zwischen Dawes-Plan und Transfersperre* (Beihefte des Jahrbuchs für Wirtschaftsgeschichte). Berlin: Akademie-Verlag.

Ritschl, A. and Sarferaz, S. (2010), 'Crisis? What Crisis: Currency vs Banking in the Financial Crisis of 1931', CEPR Discussion Paper 7610.

Romer, C. (2010), 'Back to a Better Normal: Unemployment and Growth in the Wake of the Great Recession', *Council of Economic Advisers: Speeches and Testimony.* <http://www.whitehouse.gov/administration/eop/cea/Back-to-a-Better-Normal>.

Rueff, J. (1929), 'Mr. Keynes' View on the Transfer Problem: A Criticism', *Economic Journal* 39, 388–99.

Sargent, T. (1982), 'The End of Four Big Inflations', in T. Sargent (ed.), *Rational Expectations and Inflation.* New York: Harper & Row.

Schnabel, I. (2004), 'The German Twin Crisis of 1931', *Journal of Economic History* 64, 822–71.

Schuker, S. (1976), *The End of French Predominance in Europe.* Chapel Hill: University of North Carolina Press.

Schuker, S. (1988), *American Reparations to Germany, 1924–1933.* Princeton: Princeton University Press.

Silverman, D. P. (1998), *Hitler's Economy. Nazi Work Creation Programs, 1933–1936.* Harvard: Harvard University Press.

Spoerer, M. (1994), 'German Net Investment and the Cumulative Real Wage Position, 1925–1929: On a Premature Burial of the Borchardt Debate', *Historical Social Research* 19, 26–41.

Thamer, H.-U. (1986), *Verführung und Gewalt: Deutschland 1933–1945* (Die Deutschen und ihre Nation). Berlin: Siedler.

Toniolo, G. (2005), *Central Bank Cooperation at the Bank of International Settlements, 1930–1973.* Cambridge: Cambridge University Press.

Uhlig, H. (2005), 'What are the Effects of Monetary Policy on Output?', *Journal of Monetary Economics* 52, 381–419.

VDMA (1927), *Statistisches Handbuch für die deutsche Maschinenindustrie 1927.* Berlin: VDMA.

VDMA (1930), *Statistisches Handbuch für die deutsche Maschinenindustrie 1930.* Berlin: VDMA.

Voigtlaender, N. and Voth H.-J. (2012), 'Persecution Perpetuated: The Medieval Origins of Anti-Semitic Violence in Nazi Germany', *Quarterly Journal of Economics.*

Voth, H.-J. (1994), 'Much Ado about Nothing? A Note on Investment and Wage Pressure in Weimar Germany, 1925–1929', *Historical Social Research* 19, 124–39.

Voth, H.-J. (1995), 'Did High Wages or High Interest Rates Bring down the Weimar Republic?', *Journal of Economic History* 55, 801–21.

5

Disintegration of the International Economy between the Wars

Forrest Capie

5.1. INTRODUCTION

The international economy that had prospered greatly in the 40 years before the First World War gradually disintegrated in the two decades following the war. By the end of the 1930s trade and capital flows had collapsed, the exchange-rate mechanism had been destroyed and a panoply of controls was in place. The late nineteenth century had been a period of considerable economic development and prosperity around the world. The international economy had become increasingly closely integrated through trade, capital flows, and the fixed exchange-rate regime that was the gold standard—in other words the first real period of globalization. Between 1870 and 1913 exports of the principal trading countries grew by around 6 per cent per annum. Foreign investment totalled £9.5 billion by 1914, the great bulk of it from Britain and France. Labour flows too were extraordinary with over 32 million people leaving Europe between 1881 and 1915, overwhelmingly to the United States.

The period was not without its tensions, some of them deriving from the process of globalization. In the last few years nationalism was on the rise and its economic manifestation, trade protection, had reappeared. Anti-immigration movements had sprung up (O'Rourke and Williamson, 1999).

The development was brought rather suddenly to an end in 1914 with the outbreak of war. What followed was the greatest turmoil imaginable. The economic consequences were manifold and the decades after the war reflected these difficulties. A long list of problems emerged, particularly for the international economy. The war had distorted trade patterns and capital flows, and put an end to migration; it left huge debts, resulted in the imposition of reparation payments, saw hyperinflation appear in several countries, and of course the break-up of the gold standard, at least for a time. In some ways the disintegration of the international economy began then. But the disintegration was not sudden. It was the consequence of the relentless build-up of difficulties that had their roots in the war or otherwise derived from war. In normal times with stability and growth the problems might have been manageable. But when the downturn in the US economy came at the end of the 1920s the problems were exacerbated and defensive domestic measures invariably intensified the problems.

Income slumped. Protectionism in all its manifestations spread. Trade collapsed as did capital flows. Debts were defaulted on. The exchange-rate system gradually crumbled. This chapter does not discuss the cause of the Great Depression, which is dealt with in other chapters. It takes the depression as a given.[1] Instead, it describes the disintegration in the world economy and attempts to draw some lesson from that experience. It pursues some obvious questions such as: what went wrong with trade policy? what exchange-rate regime was required? how might central banks have co operated? The system clearly had problems after the war but what brought about breakdown, and then how was depression transmitted internationally? And when it was, what were the responses in terms of exchange-rate regime, debt, and co operation?

We conclude that some lessons were learned such as those on protectionism, monetary and financial stability, and central bank cooperation. Some areas are less clear, such as exchange rates and asset prices. But while some lessons were absorbed into new institutional arrangements (as in GATT/WTO) these can be sorely tested/abandoned when serious crisis strikes.

5.2. INTERNATIONAL TRADE AND PAYMENTS

5.2.1. Trade

Following the huge disruption of the international economy in the war it should be no surprise to discover that the pattern of trade did not recover its nineteenth century shape nor did it grow at previous rates. During the war, the necessity of what would later be called import substitution meant that countries established some industries that would not otherwise have appeared, or not at least for some time, and sources of imports were diverted for shipping and security reasons. For example, when European exports to Latin America were interrupted on the outbreak of war, the US stepped in to take advantage. The marketing and distribution networks that they established were entrenched by the end of the war and the way back for the Europeans, further handicapped by the war, meant the situation was long lasting if not permanent.[2]

Complicating an examination of trade in the interwar years was the creation of new countries (for example, from the old Austro-Hungarian and other empires), the consolidation of other countries (in, for example, the newly founded Soviet Union), and the removal of still others from what was called the international economy. Thus, what was once intra-country trade now became international trade, or went the other way, or did not appear at all. All of these make

[1] There is still debate over whether the depression was inevitable. Bordo et al. (1993) argued that the Fed could and should have prevented the collapse in the money stock that was at the root of the collapse in the real economy.

[2] For a collection of some of the classic papers see Wood and Capie (2011).

comparison with previous periods difficult. That said, there is no mistaking the general trends of international trade between the wars.

The broad picture is quite well known. At the end of the 1920s (either 1928 or 1929) world trade in total was well above its 1913 levels. And that applied to all the sub-groups, from manufacturing to fuels and on to agricultural products. Manufacturing trade grew from an index of 100 in 1913 to 129 in 1929. There is a difference between food and commodities, but linked together as primary products they grew from 100 in 1913 to 138 in 1929. Cereals were up by 7 per cent, all food up by 36 per cent, agricultural raw materials up by 28 per cent, fuel by 73 per cent, and minerals by 55 per cent.

That picture changed dramatically between 1929 and 1937. Trade collapsed in the Great Depression after 1929 and then, in spite of some growth in some of the world economy after 1933, it did not recover in the remainder of the 1930s. Trade levels at the end of the 1930s were still below those of 1929. Every area of trade was affected. Continuing with the same index, trade in manufacturing fell from 129 in 1929 to 107 in 1937, in primary products to 109, in raw materials to 111. Only the numbers for fuel and minerals held up, being 171 and 151 respectively, though these are still slightly below their 1929 levels (Yates, 1959). All of that adds up to a disastrous performance in international trade across the period. Some countries were hit even harder, with primary producers who were heavily dependent on the US market suffering particularly.

The pattern of trade changed as well for reasons given at the outset—new producers and changed patterns of production—but also in part the changing pattern could be a result of protectionist measures. So, for example, Britain increasingly turned to the empire, giving preferential treatment to empire countries in the British market and expecting/demanding preferential treatment in their markets.

The most important factor at work in both the growth of the 1920s and the collapse in the 1930s was American economic growth. In the 1920s it was the chief positive element. By then clearly the largest economy in the world, it was growing strongly across the decade and primary producers of all kinds benefited enormously. But apart from that, after the initial period of post-war adjustment, there was reasonable growth in some other parts of the international economy. A factor militating against growth in trade was the protectionist tendency in commercial policies. The United States had a long history of protectionism through the nineteenth century and that carried on after the war. In 1922, the Fordney–McCumber Tariff introduced some of the highest tariffs ever. The British were also guilty, in spite of a long history of free trading, they also took some steps in the direction of protection soon after the war (safeguarding of industries legislation). There were also the problems associated with international payments (essentially floating exchange rates) to which we return below.

Yet, as noted, trade did grow through the 1920s. And, as also noted, that came to a dramatic end at the close of the decade. The principal cause of the collapse in trade was the collapse in US income, which fell by 35 per cent between 1929 and 1933, and US wealth collapsed too. One measure can be found in the stock market. The S&P90 index had peaked at 245 on 10 October 1929. Two weeks later it was at 165 and finally reached a low of 73 in June 1932. As the depression spread around the world, incomes and wealth tumbled in most places. Additionally, commercial policies turned viciously protectionist.

5.2.2. The capital account

The late nineteenth century had seen world trade thriving and huge flows of capital and of labour moving around the world. Britain was at the centre of the foreign investment in that period with investment spreading ever further afield. That came to an end with the war and, after the war, the US, having been a debtor in the late nineteenth century, emerged as the greatest creditor. In the 1920s it would lend, particularly to the Americas and to Europe, on a large scale. A criticism at the time and soon after was that the US carried out this investment with less care than it might—less attention to the nature of the investment taking place. Nevertheless, in the 1920s there were considerable flows of long-term investment around the world.

Additionally, in the opening years of the decade there was a good deal of monetary and exchange-rate chaos along with hyperinflation in much of central Europe. With continuing uncertainty attaching to exchange rates, there were the associated substantial short-term capital flows. And also affecting short-term flows were the differential interest rates with European and particularly German rates being well above those of the United States. But after these factors settled down in the mid-20s, with the clearer picture on the new gold standard emerging and the Dawes Plan agreed to sort German reparations, longer-term investment began to grow rapidly. Between 1924 and 1930 $10 billion flowed to Europe, of which $7 billion went to Germany. And at the same time a foreign loan boom developed in Latin America with an average of $300 million flowing each year in the mid/late 1920s (Marichal, 1989).

All of this came to an end at the end of the 1920s. There were several reasons. The first was the developing boom on the New York stock exchange. Not only was there a drying up of the funds to Europe and Latin America as funds poured into the New York market, but there was also a reversal as funds were withdrawn from these territories and redirected to the US. The second factor was the Great Depression itself. Following the American economic downturn, with trade collapsing, foreign borrowers were unable to earn sufficient to service and repay their loans.[3]

This was particularly striking in Latin America where many countries were heavily dependent on the US market and reliant on one or two products. Countries exporting sugar, coffee, wool, beef, copper, tin, and petroleum were especially badly hit. From 1929 these countries began to struggle to service their debts and by the end of 1931 gold reserves in Latin America were down by $1 billion. Reserves finally ran out and defaults or partial defaults followed. Bolivia was the first to impose a moratorium and was soon followed by Peru and Chile. The Dominican Republic followed and then the biggest borrower of all, Brazil, partially defaulted.

[3] An illustration of the effects can be found in the collapse of sovereign bond issues in New York. See Flandreau et al. (2009).

In 1932 more defaults followed, some partial. In 1933 countries defaulting included Columbia, Cuba, Guatemala, Panama, and Uruguay. And, indeed, the rest of the 1930s was taken up with renegotiation or readjustment of Latin American debt obligations.[4]

In Europe, some of the same effects could be seen and the repatriation of capital from some of the borrowers exposed the fragility of the banking systems and culminated in the central European banking crises. This was made worse by the political uncertainty. In 1930 German political instability frightened investors with a clear possibility of exchange-rate restrictions and a devaluation of the mark. In the September elections, the Nazis emerged as the second largest party in the Reichstag and capital flight quickly followed. The summer of 1931 saw the banking crisis in central Europe blow up. This was first seen in the collapse of the Creditanstalt in Austria in May 1931, and was quickly followed by the failure of the big Berlin bank, Danatbank, or Darmstadter und Nationalbank. The political upheaval that accompanied these events produced a huge capital flight. In July, the Brüning government introduced exchange controls and, in September, placed a standstill (the German Credit Agreement) on German short-term debts to overseas banks. The international debts of Austria and Hungary were subject to similar agreements.

In short, the abrupt cessation of the lending boom of the 1920s to Europe, and to Latin America at the end of that decade, was a calamitous event for the world economy. It contributed to the economic and political turmoil at the turn of the decade and produced further disastrous capital flight. The credit boom had turned to credit crunch.

5.2.3. Barriers to trade and capital flows

Once again, as for some of the other themes in the international economy, the threads of commercial protectionism can be picked up from towards the end of the nineteenth century. As economic rivalry grew so too did nationalism and along with that went its economic manifestation, trade protectionism. It may not be going too far to say that the tensions there contributed to the outbreak of the First World War. In the economic chaos following the war there were further examples of this, and protectionist measures were adopted widely. The British were among the earliest with the Safeguarding of Industries legislation (1921) supposedly to protect 'key industries' (Capie, 1985). The Americans, too, took emergency action with an Emergency Tariff Act in 1921 in part as a defensive measure against the Europeans who were showing signs of increasing barriers. They then introduced the Fordney–McCumber tariff in 1922 that raised the average rate of tariffs on dutiable goods by almost 50 per cent (Falkus, 1971). Other countries followed suit and the general mood was for increasing protection. The new countries of central Europe aiming to industrialize also

[4] See Eichengreen and Portes (1986); some of the debt obligations were eventually resolved in the 1950s.

adopted protection. While international conferences roundly condemned such sentiments and practices, domestic political pressures invariably triumphed.

Even before the Great Depression took hold properly, the Americans passed the Smoot–Hawley Tariff in 1930. The Act introduced the highest tariffs in American history. The direct impact is still debated, but they certainly encouraged others to move in that direction and did not help international relations (Eichengreen and Irwin, 2010). Perhaps more distressing for those seeking to keep the international economy on an even keel was Britain's reversal of almost 100 years of free trade policies. In late 1931 it introduced emergency 'Abnormal Import Duties' to protect itself from what it argued was dumping. Then, in early 1932, it introduced a general tariff covering most manufactured goods and some food and raw materials. These began at 10 per cent, were soon raised to 20 per cent, and in some cases 33.3 per cent. At Ottawa later in the year, it introduced Imperial Preference and a range of quotas on agricultural goods (Capie, 1985).

Subsequent to both these increases in protection came a raft of retaliatory protectionist policies in the rest of the world. Thirty nations immediately protested against Smoot–Hawley and many imposed countervailing duties. Some, such as Italy and Switzerland, boycotted American goods. In 1931 the French declared that retaliation was the basis of French policy. Germany was particularly aggrieved at the actions of the British and Americans, believing it had been singled out for adverse treatment, and it imposed an 'equalizing tariff'. In the course of 1932 it raised tariffs by 100 per cent. Tariff revisions also followed in Canada, Cuba, Mexico, Australia, and New Zealand. When tariffs proved insufficient to reduce imports to the extent desired other measures, such as quotas, were employed. Debate continues on the extent of the damage done by these but, coupled with the effect of falling income, they were responsible for a fall in trade between 1929 and 1932 of over 60 per cent in real terms. There was clearly a breakdown in international relations.

Barriers to trade took all forms. Tariffs were perhaps the favoured method, but quotas were extensive and outright prohibition was used. There were even invisible barriers to trade, and the Germans led the way with bilateral trading agreements.

And it was not only trade that was restricted. Payments were restricted by exchange controls. In the early 1930s scores of countries introduced such measures. They almost all devalued at the same time or soon thereafter. Restrictions on foreign lending were imposed by the United States, Great Britain, and Germany. These were among the most misguided of all the restrictive policies, but such was the mood of the time.

5.3. INTERNATIONAL MONETARY ARRANGEMENTS

It is impossible to understand the nature of the collapse of the international monetary system at the beginning of the 1930s without again outlining the problems the system developed in the course of the war and in the 1920s period of adjustment and stabilization. The gold standard had collapsed in the war. At the end of the war there was a clear desire on the part of all the principal participants to re-establish the standard and restore the world of pre-1914. But, at the end of the war, there were several inhibiting factors for the international monetary system. There had been a huge build-up of debt, both domestic and international. There was rapidly rising inflation in many countries, some of which would degenerate into hyperinflation. The consequences for exchange rates were catastrophic and long lasting. On top of the debt, but related, there came reparation payments imposed by the allies on the Germans.

Early attempts at some resolution of the interlinked problems could be found in international conferences at Brussels in 1920 and in Genoa in 1922 where a resolution was passed to pursue co-operation, but the French vetoed any attempt to re-open negotiation on the German reparation question.

The wrangling involved in the attempted resolution of the debt and reparation payments rumbled on for years. The scale of the problem was huge. Inter-allied war debt totalled $26.5 billion (roughly equal to twice British GDP). Most of this was owed to Britain and America. So, for example, France owed the United States approximately $4 billion and the United Kingdom $3 billion. Britain owed the United States $4.7 billion. The British were happy to settle with the US on the understanding that they would be paid by the French. But the French needed reparations payments from Germany in order to be able to do that. The reparations imposed on Germany totalled $33 billion, and most of that was to be paid to Britain and France. Reparations and debt could have been linked, and some netting out carried through, but the Americans, who were adamant that debts should be repaid, were equally resistant to the idea that they, the US, should be seen to be taking reparation payments from the Germans.

The problem had been made worse by the French invasion of the Ruhr in 1923. That was followed by the Dawes Plan for reparation payments in 1924 which, at least for a while, seemed to ease the process of payment. Further negotiations in the 1920s reduced these amounts and changed the way in which payment could be made.

A simplification of the problem in the 1920s that led on to the 1930s would be to say that American foreign investment in Europe, and principally Germany, was used in part to make reparation payments to the British and French and they in turn then repaid debt to the US. When American funds dried up at the end of the decade the game was up. European banks collapsed, Britain was forced off gold, and, as the Americans raised interest rates, their domestic economy floundered.

5.3.1. Floating exchange rates

In 1920 every important country had a depreciated and less than stable currency. During the war some stability had been given to the system with the Americans providing support to France and Britain to peg their currencies to the dollar at a slightly depreciated rate. But, at the end of the war, that support ended and a period of genuinely floating exchange rates followed. Only the US dollar remained convertible into gold. This period of floating in the first half of the 1920s was often used to suggest that floating rates were unsuccessful—too volatile and encouraged destabilizing speculation.[5] But, while it is true that rates were volatile, most countries were engaged in a variety of stabilization programmes—using mainly monetary and fiscal policies—the forecast consequences of which were bound to be translated into exchange-rate movements. In other words, the alternative interpretation was that it was policies that produced instability and the exchange rates reflected that (Freidman, 1953).

5.3.2. Return to gold

At any rate, the desire to restore the world of pre-1914 was powerful and in 1920 seemed absolutely necessary. The gold standard had provided a smooth means of adjustment for international trade, and payments and capital flows. Under it prices were stable, balances of payments were in equilibrium, and conditions for investors were ideal. It is not surprising that they wished to get back to that or something close to it.

The system had been lost in the war and inflation and instability followed. US prices doubled, as did the British. After the war, the Fed contracted sharply and brought the dollar down to within 40 per cent of its 1914 value. This was then something of a pattern, though with different countries having different levels to reach. The British soon embarked on a deflationary programme explicitly aimed at bringing prices down to within striking distance of those in the US. Some other countries were less ambitious.

Again across the world economy there were factors militating against the success. The world had changed dramatically. Whereas before the war the pain of adjustment was borne by the domestic economy, which meant in big part labour, that was no longer acceptable or possible in the newly unionized world of labour after the war. Equally, given the scale of the price rises and the impossibility of bringing them down to pre-war levels, there was insufficient gold in the world to support the system. And the problem was likely to intensify as growth was restored. More than that, the distribution of gold stocks had been badly disturbed, with large flows of gold moving to the US during the war and away from Europe.

At any rate, some countries tried to stabilize at pre-war levels (notably Britain, some Scandinavians, and the Netherlands) while those whose currencies had been wrecked in the hyperinflations introduced new currency units (in particular Germany and Austria), and others settled for something in between these (for example France and Italy who went back at rates of one-fifth and one-quarter of their 1914 levels, respectively).

Apart from the US and Britain, admittedly the leading two economies of the time, none of this was coordinated in any way. Each country pursued its own path to stability, often without much thought as to what was in line with other countries or appropriate for the changed international conditions. But, by the mid-1920s, most countries in the international economy had returned to gold in some form and an appearance of the old system had been restored.

[5] Nurkse (1944) is the main source of this kind of account. Much of the explanation derived from the experience of the French franc which was particularly volatile.

At least two further problems were present in the restored standard. One was the use of foreign exchange reserves. The second was the damage to confidence that had been done as a result of Britain's weakened position and the American reluctance to take on the role that Britain had performed so well before 1914. That left a gap in international leadership (Kindleberger, 1973).

Using foreign exchange in reserves had been done before 1914, but in the restored standard it was on a much greater scale and more widespread across countries. The danger that it carried was that doubts were likely to surround a currency where the backing was heavily foreign exchange, and in currencies of uncertain value as against a currency almost wholly backed by gold. It was not always clear what the backing was.

The gold shortage and mal-distribution alluded to above got worse in the second half of the 1920s. A prime reason was the undervalued French franc that gave the French a competitive advantage, a persistent current account surplus, and an accompanying large inflow of gold. This was then exacerbated by policies that effectively sterilized the inflows. France became the second largest holder of gold next to the United States. When the French decided, in 1927, to convert what foreign exchange they had into gold they endangered the whole system and had to modify their ambitions. Germany, too, was guilty, attracting gold flows with interest rates in excess of those prevailing elsewhere. And they also began to convert their foreign exchange holdings into gold.[6]

With the US reluctant to play that lead role, and international relations at a low ebb, there was little possibility of finding solutions to the problems.[7] Things were made worse by the perversity of the two largest and most dominant gold holders, France and America. America was the largest single holder of gold with almost 40 per cent of the world's supply. But more than that, it held gold reserves far in excess of that required by its own gold legislation. Then, in the late 1920s, the Federal Reserve made things even worse when it worried about the booming New York stock market and raised interest rates. That had the effect of pulling more funds into the US.

All of this meant that the problems the gold standard was designed to alleviate or remove had in fact worsened. France and America had growing balance of payments surpluses while others, such as Britain, had persistent deficits.

5.4. BREAKDOWN

It might almost seem redundant, given the above catalogue of problems, to describe how the system proceeded to implode. But there are several elements in the story that contributed to the disintegration, some of which are related but by no means all. And it should be said that the fact that one country's problems were on occasions followed by another country's does not always spell contagion. While there might be direct linkages through which contamination could travel, it

[6] For a wide ranging discussion of the role of gold see Temin (1989).

[7] The origins of these ideas can be found in Kindleberger (1973).

was also possible that actions of important participants could affect the behaviour of others through less easily seen means. The British, for example, had their own problems with their determination to return to the gold standard at the pre-war parity, and with London's declining international position. Given the loss of foreign assets it had suffered, together with its weakened trading position and burdened by debt, Britain struggled on several fronts. It was no longer able to influence capital flows in the way it could before the war and its reserves were even more depleted. On their own these might have been containable, but as part of the mix there was trouble.

Similar in many ways were the problems of banking in central Europe in the following limited sense. In Austria, the biggest bank in the country, the Creditanstalt bank, lost good business and kept bad on the break-up of the Austro-Hungarian empire. Then hyperinflation destroyed its capital. To make matters worse, it was poorly run. All of that might have been managed—solutions might have been found in some orderly wind-up—but when depression struck, the bank's reliance on foreign credits (foreign credits made up more than one-third of its total) meant that disaster loomed. The chaotic budgetary situation in Austria, and abuse of the bank by government, made matters impossible. The bank failed with widespread ramifications. (For a full account see Schubert, 1991).

Fears that these kinds of banking difficulties were prevalent in other parts of central Europe, and that international assistance was unlikely to be forthcoming, directed attention to other banks with potentially similar problems. The Austrian banking crisis was followed by bank runs in Hungary, Czechoslovakia, Romania, and Poland and spread to Germany and further afield. But whether or not these are examples of contagion is more difficult to establish. It can certainly be argued that circumstances in Germany were of a different kind and the problem of reparations was dominant. Then in 1931 the run on the banks went with a run on the currency.[8] The crisis also had the effect of freezing short-term assets of the Bank of England, and that raised doubts over the soundness of Britain's long-term loans abroad. It was a short step from there to investors wondering about the security of the pound/gold link. Speculation against the pound followed on a scale that was in the end decisive. Britain had to abandon the standard.

And, just as would be repeated in the 1960s, when one reserve currency was under attack the other was not far behind. As the pressure built on sterling in the second half of September so it also turned to the dollar. By the end of October, the Fed's gold holdings had fallen by $725 million—roughly 15 per cent of their total holdings—and that in spite of a sharp raising of the discount rate from 1.5 per cent to 3.5 per cent.

Separate from these events, but another calamity at the turn of the decade, was the failure of the US to maintain its recently acquired status as an international financial power. The war had badly damaged London's position as the dominant international financial centre. It had also allowed the US to engage in the kind of activity necessary for New York to establish itself as an international financial centre. The US was the leading economy and had emerged after the war as the leading international creditor. But before the dollar became an international

[8] For a full discussion of this as a twin crisis see Schnabel (2004).

currency, more was needed. The Fed began to fill the gap. Imitating the Bank of England's techniques, it began to purchase trade acceptances as part of its approach to smoothing interest rates. But there needed to be dollar-denominated trade acceptances to buy. That required American banks to transact abroad and that is what they did increasingly in the 1920s (Eichengreen, 2011). The war had been important in promoting US exports and American companies established themselves in other countries. On the other side, European credit dried up in the war and in particular British banks suffered. This allowed American international financial business to boom. In support of this business, the Federal Reserve Board encouraged its regional banks to buy acceptances for their own account. Gradually, foreign banks, both commercial and central, were attracted to the market. With British interest rates relatively high after the return to gold in 1925, American rates were attractive and New York business boomed. Not surprisingly, there was a learning process for the American banks and for some investors. Newcomers to the field lent overly enthusiastically and there was no shortage of takers as is usually the case in such circumstances. Once the depression began and trade collapsed, however, so too did international transactions. Long-term lending fell precipitously. Where the US had been lending at a rate of $1.2 billion per annum in the late 1920s, that dropped to virtually nothing—less than $1 million in 1932 (James, 2001).

Compounding the burden of debts in the interwar years was the phenomenon of deflation, something that characterized many countries in the 1920s and then worsened greatly in the depression. Irving Fisher argued at the time that this was a key element in explaining depression. He argued that, as individuals tried to escape the burden of debt, they in fact made it worse, 'the more debtors pay, the more they owe' (Fisher, 1933). The argument was that the process of liquidating debt leads to a fall in bank deposits, and hence to prices. Prices then fell faster than debt and real debt rose as did real interest rates.

5.4.1. Transmission of the depression

As we have shown, the chronology of the crisis between the wars is well known and agreed upon. After a certain degree of fiscal and exchange-rate stability had been achieved in the first half of the 1920s, a credit boom followed in the second half. Then, after the huge capital flows peaked in 1928 (Feinstein and Watson, 1995), credit contracted and sovereign bond issues collapsed (Flandreau et al., 2009). When the banking crises of central Europe followed in 1931, currency crises emerged quickly and severe repercussions were felt around the world. Thus, while the depression is usually seen as originating in the United States, there were serious problems elsewhere that produced weakening economic conditions. But how was depression transmitted from one region to another? There were two principal means by which depression might have been transmitted: exchange rates and financial inter-relatedness.

A central piece of exchange-rate theory is that, under fixed exchange rates, small countries import the monetary policy of the large or dominant country in the system. Flexible exchange rates, on the other hand, provide a cushion against an external shock and allow small countries the pursuit of independent monetary policy. A debate on the extent of this developed from the 1960s onwards based partly on the fact that domestic output and prices did not seem too different from their foreign counterparts under the flexible rates that were said to prevail after the abandonment of Bretton Woods at the beginning of the 1970s. The counter to this was that most countries did not follow independent monetary policies but rather resorted to some form of managed exchange rates.

But the evidence from the Great Depression lends greater support to the view that the gold standard, whatever its role in the onset of the depression, was certainly at fault in propagating the shock around the world. For example, in a specific test of the hypothesis, Choudhri and Kochin (1980) examined the experience of small European countries. Their conclusions were that the countries who stuck with fixed rates with the United States suffered similar contractions to those of the United States. Countries that maintained flexible rates enjoyed fairly stable output and prices, and those that adopted flexible rates in the middle of the depression escaped the worst of the contractions and recovered more quickly. They did not examine the British experience, but it would fit the last category of abandoning the fixed rate early—in September 1931. Britain was perhaps the only large country that escaped from depression. But, equally, US recovery dated from its leaving the gold standard in 1933 and the countries that stayed with gold remained in depression.

Separate evidence can be found, for example, on Spain where, amongst other things, a floating peseta protected the Spanish economy from the collapse taking place in most of the rest of the world. The mild recession Spain experienced appears to have been home-grown (Comin and Martin-Acena, 1985). These conclusions have recently been arrived at by different means (Schwartz and Castenada, 2011).

The exchange rate was not the only transmission mechanism. The recent financial crisis has reminded us that, even where floating rates were in place, some kinds of contagion also took place. One clear possibility lies in the interrelatedness of the financial sectors. It is clear that in central Europe in 1931 the close connections among the commercial banks were responsible in part for the spread of difficulties from one country to another. Allen and Moessner (2010) show the nature of the financial flows and the impact they had on the respective banking sectors. The UK's limited exposure has already been noted, as has the means of dealing with it.

As far as the impact of the European experience on the US goes, Richardson and van Horn (2011) have recently argued that the commercial banks in New York, together with the Federal Reserve Bank of New York, anticipated the European events and prepared themselves for possible consequences by building substantial reserves, and so prevented these particular problems from spreading to the US.

5.5. RESPONSES TO BREAKDOWN

At every turn there is evidence of the domestic–international interface. While trying to stay focused on the international aspects, it is impossible to escape the domestic. Many of the responses to international difficulties were taken on the domestic front. Some of the responses to trade have already been noted. Almost everywhere, regardless of the strength of the belief in free trade, domestic politics trumped any international considerations. Almost everywhere, there was resort to protectionist devices (that included subsidies to domestic production) in attempts at protecting domestic employment.

That was what dominated policy across the board, the attempt to protect the domestic economy. There was a range of responses on the payments side from debt rescheduling and restructuring through moratoria and standstill agreements to exchange-rate support in the form of exchange controls, currency blocs, and to the extreme version of the Schactian system in Germany. And finally there were the attempts at reviving international cooperation on the monetary front through the recently formed BIS (Bank for International Settlements).

5.5.1. The abandonment of gold

There are different ways of viewing the demise of the gold standard. Whether it should be seen either as a response to the difficulties in international finance at the time or as part of the disintegration of the system, about which little or nothing could be done, is an interesting question.

The facts are fairly simply set out. The main problems have already been described—a scarcity of, and a mal-distribution of, gold resulting in shortage of reserves—and when these are coupled with the lack of any international cooperation the strains produced prove unbearable for many. Gold reserves began falling sharply in the late 1920s. Some primary producers such as Argentina, Uruguay, and Australia were the first to go and they suspended the gold standard in December 1929. But it was after the British departure from the standard in September 1931 that collapse came. Britain had been at the centre of the system, the 'conductor of the orchestra', in the nineteenth century and when she went there was no way for others to survive. A wave of other suspensions followed almost immediately, many of them British empire countries or closely linked to the British market. Other countries followed in 1932, and the United States in 1933, while some others, such as Belgium and the Netherlands, hung on until 1935 and 1936. Strictly speaking, the French did not suspend the standard but devalued against gold in late 1936. The system was finished in the first half of the 1930s. It was no longer sustainable[9] (Aldcroft and Oliver, 1998).

From the present vantage point it might seem that there should be little surprise in this. With a better perspective we can see that monetary regimes seem to have relatively limited lives. But in the 1930s that must have looked considerably different. There had, after all, been an international economy for a fairly brief period, say from the late eighteenth century. Before that, trade had taken place since the beginning of time but without any sense of an international economy. It

[9] There is an abundance of explanations for the break up. Some of these focus more on political elements; in particular, for example, that democratic regimes were likely to abandon first (for one example see Wandschneider (2008); for a different, but not conflicting, view see Woolf (2008)).

was the rise of the nation state and national monies, and the need to coordinate these in some way, that brought something like a system into being. Commodity money had long been used in domestic and international payments, but it was only in the eighteenth and nineteenth centuries that gold and silver completely dominated. The emergence of the international gold standard for the first time provided what could reasonably be called an international monetary system. It was almost universally established. All the main countries joined and the others aspired to join. The late nineteenth century was then a period of globalization and growing economic development and prosperity. The gold standard stood unquestioned. It might have survived for very much longer than it did but for World War One. But the desire to restore it after the war rested on that belief in its worth and reflected the strength of feeling that the proper functioning of the international economic system depended on it. There then followed, as noted, a range of measures in order to restore the standard and ensure that the system could be maintained.

When the British exit came in September 1931 it triggered the end of the system. The suspension, '. . . more than any other event, symbolized the interwar gold standard's disintegration' (Eichengreen, 1996: 85). Some argue that Britain's suspension was a coldly rational decision taken by the monetary authorities to preserve domestic financial stability at the expense of the parity of the pound. So, for example, Eichengreen argues that the Bank of England's officials (not the Governor, who was indisposed) '. . . knew exactly what they were doing. They were consciously choosing the stability of the banks over the stability of sterling' (Eichengreen, 2011: 35; and see also Accominotti, 2011a). Leaving aside the question of whether these officials did know what they were doing, there are other questions that need answers. For example, what was there to save since the banks were stable; and what power did the bank have to act on its own?

Also, cold logic and rationality have not always come into it when questions such as these are confronted. And especially not by central banks, who have almost invariably favoured fixed exchange-rate regimes. And even less so by the Bank of England, which was also a powerful advocate of London as an/the international financial centre. The commitment to upholding the value of the currency was close to total. There are many examples of the same sort of thing in the post-World War Two world, where the several devaluations were the last desperate acts of despondent central banks.[10]

But it is worth spending a little longer on this question. For those familiar with the British banking system in the interwar years it may seem odd to talk of financial instability. If financial crises are best described as threats to the payments system (Schwartz, 1986) then there was no financial crisis in Britain between the wars. The commercial banks were completely stable. The big five banks were well diversified across the economy and performed well right through the 1920s and 1930s. Their profits moved with the cycle but since there was no serious downturn in Britain so there was no serious disruption to the banks' profits (Capie and Billings, 2001). By whatever measure used, the banks were sound and the payment system stable. If there had been a threat from some external shock that presented

[10] The belief in the euro is another case to which we shall return.

liquidity problems the solution was well understood and rehearsed. The Bank of England would behave as the lender of last resort and the gold standard temporarily suspended if need be, in a fashion that had long been used. These arrangements worked well in the nineteenth century and it came to be understood so much so that was no further need for suspensions. The banks were well behaved and there were ways of dealing with shocks (Capie, 2002a).

Some argue, however, that the merchant (investment) banks were exposed to the continental European banking crisis (see also Accominotti, 2011a). That is true, but two things need to be said. The merchant banks, while performing a key role for a financial centre in acceptance business, did not do the range of things they would later do and they were not deeply involved with the real economy. They had grown from financing international trade. Some of them (Kleinwort, Schroders, and, less so, Lazards), with their strong European connections, had quite large exposures to European business but others, such as Morgan Grenfell, had largely avoided private German business. In any case, these banks had only limited exposure to the English commercial banks. There was some exposure but it was limited and easily coped with.

And, as argued above, had the exposure presented difficulties to the commercial banks there were well-tested ways of dealing with that. It is true that the world had changed and the gold standard was no longer as secure as it had been. And it follows that the credibility that attached to the Bank's behaviour in the nineteenth century could no longer be taken for granted in the 1920s. Nevertheless, the case for contagion of this kind is surely weak. (For an overall assessment of the variables see Capie et al. (1986).)

In any event, after the break with gold it seemed there was little left to do but to let the pound find its own level. It dropped precipitously—by 30 per cent—in the next few months. Partly with the experience of the early 1920s still fresh in the minds of most countries, and with the perception of that experience as being poor, there was a general desire for stability in rates. As Nurkse put it, '. . . the monetary authorities in most countries had little or no desire for freely fluctuating exchanges'.[11] In Britain, the Exchange Equalization Account (EEA) was designed and announced in the budget of 1932 and was operating by 1 July 1932. The EEA was designed to dampen, or even eliminate, short-term fluctuations in the exchange rate even if the choice of the rate at which this was to be done was less clear. The operation of the account was opposite to that of the gold standard. Under the gold standard, adjustment took place by allowing capital flows to enter domestic credit directly, after which price changes would bring about the required correction to the external accounts. The EEA, on the other hand, was designed to prevent capital flows from affecting domestic credit. In other words insulation techniques were what were required. After the US left gold in 1933, it too established a stabilization fund the following year. Thus, while the rates were supposedly floating, there was little deviation in the sterling–dollar rate from 1933 to 1939. Other countries followed suit with their own stabilization funds. British empire countries tended to peg at some rate to the imperial power. And so emerged a set of managed rates. After the French devaluation of 1936, and the

[11] Nurkse, 1944: 122.

Tripartite Agreement (between US, UK, and France) of that year, the way was prepared for the Bretton Woods agreements of a few years later (Mundell, 2000).

5.5.2. Dealing with debt

Concurrent with these responses were others relating to debt. One approach was to default or restructure/reschedule and we have noted how that happened frequently in Latin America. In Europe the core problem was Germany, by far the biggest debtor. With the prospects for repayment bleak in May 1931, the U.S president, Hoover, proposed a one year moratorium on all reparation and war debts payments. The proposal was agreed on by the allies in July of that year. There were clear positives for Germany in that it immediately relieved pressure on their budget. But, more than that, it gave them the opportunity to negotiate the cancellation of reparation payments altogether. The moratorium discriminated in favour of commercial obligations, which disadvantaged France somewhat in relation to the US and so delayed the reaching of agreement. But, at the international conference in Lausanne the following year, agreements were struck that effectively brought reparation payments to an end.

Also, an agreement was reached to a standstill on the withdrawal of foreign credits from Germany. While these might look like moves in the desirable direction, there were, as is common, unintended consequences. In this case the smaller European countries were worst affected and began losing gold reserves. To off-set that, these countries sold sterling, and so put further pressure on sterling. But the September 1931 German Credit Agreement (the standstill) was then renewed annually from 1932 onwards. Approximately £54 million was initially due to British creditors, and one-third of that was to the clearing banks. Although the amounts for Britain were relatively small, the arrangements were seen by some as economic appeasement. But the British were inclined to go along with it for fear of something worse, such as complete moratorium (Billings and Capie, 2011).

5.5.3. Currency arrangements

All policy became domestic centred. There was a proposal in 1931 for an Austro-German customs union, only defeated because of opposition by the French. The British, too, considered turning the empire into a customs union. It went some way but achieved something less at the imperial conference held at Ottawa in 1932. A large number of agreements were struck between member countries favouring trade and capital flows including Britain's preferential treatment of empire goods in the British market. The guiding principle was Britain first, empire second, and foreigners last (Capie, 1985).

Countries were determined to avoid what they saw as the chaos of the early 1920s and employ controls. In the world of managed exchange rates, apart from the stabilization funds, which at least had a pretence of subtlety, other cruder techniques were employed. The crudest was the outright prevention of currency movement—exchange controls. A long list of countries introduced some forms of these from as early as 1931, and by the mid-1930s there were 34 countries with some form of these in place. By the end of the decade, around 30 per cent of world trade was conducted under exchange control (Capie, 2002b; Aldcroft and Oliver, 1998)

There also emerged currency blocs. The principal ones were the sterling area and the gold bloc, but there was also the Reichsmark bloc, and there were some parallel arrangements in the Americas with the US dollar. Even in the Far East there was something like a yen bloc. Sterling was by far the biggest, though, and extended beyond commonwealth countries to the Middle East, Scandinavia, and bits of Latin America. While there were no formal agreements, countries pegged their currencies to sterling and kept their reserves in sterling (and often in London). Not surprisingly, there was a measure of stability from these arrangements. The gold bloc was made up of those who were determined to hold to gold—principally France, Netherlands, Belgium, and Italy and one or two other smaller European countries. Most of these had amassed large gold reserves. These countries would, however, suffer from the depreciations that had taken place elsewhere, and it was only a matter of two or three years before they abandoned their position, in the process engaging in some 'competitive devaluation' or what later was called 'beggar-thy-neighbour' policies.

The most extreme exchange-rate measures could be found in Germany, where the principal device was bilateral exchange. Their recent experience of hyperinflation was still all too vivid so any policy that risked inflation was taboo. That meant that devaluation was out of the question and, indeed, the Brüning government pursued deflationary policies. With 6.5 million unemployed, and no foreign reserves, there was always the threat that if the Brüning government fell either a Bolshevik or Nazi terror would descend. Germany had already introduced exchange controls in July 1931. The standstill agreements had been predicated on Germany being able to run balance of payment surpluses. So Britain's departure from gold in September, along with all the countries which went with her, made this difficult and even impossible. Stronger measures were seen as necessary and, with Schacht reinstalled at the Reichsbank, a New Plan was indeed produced. The plan led to the bilateralization of trade, bilateral clearing with 25 countries. Different mark rates were developed for each currency. Export subsidies were added and imports squeezed dramatically.

5.5.4. Central bank cooperation

Amidst all these defensive devices there was one small exercise that at least had some semblance of desire for international monetary cooperation, and that was the creation of the Bank for International Settlements. The bank had its origins in the negotiations on debt and reparation payments. A proposal of the Young Committee handling these negotiations at the end of the 1920s eventually took form as a plan for the commercialization of German debt. When the bank was established in 1930 its main function was to administer the Young plan for reparations, but its statutes give its first objective as 'to promote the co operation of central banks'.[12]

[12] BIS Sixth Annual Report May 1936, p. 41.

It is not easy to define cooperation and more or less impossible to measure it. It has long been argued over and when some see evidence of it in action others completely fail to. When is a particular action cooperation and when self-interest possibly dressed up as cooperation? The BIS certainly provided a meeting place for the exchange of information and comparisons of the different conditions within which central banks were working. But that is some way short of carrying out agreed common actions in pursuit of a common goal, or coming to one another's support.[13] Nevertheless, the central banks met more or less monthly in Basle from the bank's inception. Clearly these early years could hardly have been worse for launching international cooperation in the face of such different and difficult domestic experiences.

In the summer of 1931, the BIS was powerless to prevent or even mitigate the collapse going on around it. And in the next few years it even dropped the section on central bank cooperation from its annual report, presumably on the grounds that there was little going on. At the world economic conference held in London in 1933 there had been a complete failure to promote any kind of cooperation on monetary matters.

Thus, although Bank of England governor, Montagu Norman, had done his bit to encourage central banking in the 1920s, and had some success working with Strong of the Fed on the restoration of the gold standard, the view of the Bank of England in the mid-1930s was that over the previous ten years cooperation had been negligible. As their leading spokesman on overseas matters, Siepman wrote:

> Ten years ago it seemed that Central Banking co-operation might become a factor of international importance . . . [By the mid-1930s] our business relations with other Central Banks had diminished to insignificant proportions and practical co-operation, whether directly or through the BIS was not a reality. This was due directly to our going off gold, which meant that the initiatives in monetary policy passed from the Bank to the Government; and monetary policy is the natural field of co-operation by Central Banks.[14]

5.6. LESSONS

In times of economic boom that usually precede a crisis, the mood tends to suggest that the world has changed; man's intelligence has finally cracked it, and a path to ever greater success has been embarked on. Anyone suggesting otherwise is seen as quaint. In times of crisis there is a sobering up and quite a widespread desire for drawing on the lessons of history. This is often talked about as if there was a manual containing these lessons that had been left neglected on the shelf and it was now time to pull it down and have a look. But the lessons of history are not so easily discerned, never mind agreed on, much less available in a form ready for acting on. For example, it is quite common still for it to be asserted that the Great Depression was caused by the stock market crash of October 1929. It followed the crash, but it was not caused by it. Such an event may be unfortunate

[13] See various papers in Borio et al. (2008).

[14] Quoted in Capie (2010: 163).

for investors and not helpful for the wider economy, but it was not the causal factor in the Great Depression. And even if an economic lesson is clear, trying to implement it in a new crisis is complicated by the prevailing politics.

That said, some lessons do seem to be reasonably clear and quite widely accepted; others are still debated. Those that most likely fit the first group are those on trade protection, on aspects of financial stability, on the need for independent monetary policy, and on the desirability of central bank cooperation. Those that are more contentious are likely to be the ones that relate to the exchange-rate regime, what should be done about sharp asset price rises, controls on international payments and the penalties for default.

5.6.1. Trade protection

It was widely agreed after the Second World War that a big lesson of the interwar years was the disastrous effects of trade barriers. And that was strongly supported by economic theory which demonstrated so convincingly the net gains when moving from no trade to trade, or from protection to freer trade. Surely something needed to be done that would limit such recourse to protection in the future. And it was done. Very soon after the war an agreement was struck to found an institution that would work toward ever-freer trade, the GATT (General Agreement on Tariffs and Trade). The United States, too, had become a convert to the principles and practice of free trade and undertook to do whatever it could to promote free trade. There was very little resistance to that stance. It seemed an obvious position to take.

Of course, in the aftermath of war and in the booming conditions for the world economy in the 1950s and 1960s (though some two-way causality was doubtless involved), ever greater free trade was achieved. But, in an early demonstration of the reversal or suspension of these views when the domestic economy came under pressure, as in the stagnation of the 1970s, protectionism returned.[15] Trade rounds began to be increasingly protracted and, at the time of writing, it seems that the latest round—the Doha round—is doomed.

So, in spite of trade protection being rejected by both theory and evidence, and of institutions designed and built to stop its spread, the real danger is always present that domestic politics will make it impossible to adhere to the lesson. That also happened in the 1930s when politicians would insist on being the greatest free-trader around but then go on to explain that current circumstances demanded they must support the moves to protection.

5.6.2. Monetary and financial stability

Another lesson of the period was that financial stability was a must. A robust financial system could withstand much of the pressure that came from other countries. Britain had long had financial stability, something that endured in the

[15] The IMF's index of protection started to rise and went on rising for several years.

1930s, and after World War Two it was taken for granted. But that was not true for many countries who had suffered severe instability between the wars.

Monetary historians have long appreciated the close connection between monetary and financial matters. But economists seemed to lose sight of this relationship. One of the remarkable things about the lead up to the recent crisis was that economists largely ignored the part the financial system played in the economy. For example, Mishkin of the Federal Reserve wrote, '. . . the 2007–09 financial crisis made it clear that the adverse effects of financial disruption on economic activity could be far worse than originally anticipated for advanced economies'. 'Financial frictions', he continued, 'should be front and centre in macroeconomic analysis; they could no longer be ignored in macro-econometric models that central banks used for forecasting and policy analysis.'[16]

The great lesson for monetary and financial stability was that central banks should stand ready in the face of a liquidity shock to provide the markets with the necessary liquidity. A panic finds the public rapidly converting assets into cash. The central bank should off-set that flight by whatever it takes to keep broad money growth stable. That is, to act as a lender of last resort. The banks need to hold the appropriate assets to allow this to work. The central bank does not supply capital to insolvent banks. It is unable to do that, not having the resources.

It was the Federal Reserve's great mistake not to supply liquidity at various points in 1930–33 that resulted in the collapse of so many banks and the money supply in the US. That lesson was learned and put into practice, for example, in the crash of 1987. There is a danger that it might be over-learned as seemed to be the case in the US in the 2000s when, at any hint of deflation, the Fed injected liquidity. That produced the easy money conditions that contributed to the asset price surge and collapse. But generally that lesson is well understood.

5.6.3. Independent monetary policy

A third lesson from the 1930s, and one that was later supported by theoretical developments in economics, is that in a crisis an independent monetary policy is essential. An independent monetary policy is not available to a small country in a fixed exchange-rate regime. In such a regime all the countries in the system are subject to the monetary policy of the dominant country. In the interwar years that meant the United States. Those countries that left the fixed exchange-rate regime that was the gold standard almost immediately began to recover. The key to the recovery was the monetary ease that was permitted. The clearest example of that was the United Kingdom, which left gold in 1931, and whose recovery was strong and evident from 1932 onwards. The years 1932–37 had the strongest growth of any such upswing in Britain's history. France was at the other end of the spectrum holding to gold for longest and experiencing the longest depression of all. The US left gold in 1933 and, without a conscious policy decision, found itself with rapid monetary growth and a strong recovery from 1933 onwards (Romer, 1993). Of

[16] Mishkin, 2011: 83.

course, refinements are always likely to be needed and one issue that has arisen is, in certain circumstances, how to get money into the hands of spenders.

5.6.4. Central bank cooperation

It seems obvious at one level that, when international problems emerge, some international discussion/agreement/cooperation should be desirable with possibilities for it being effective. In the 1920s and 1930s cooperation was desired but seldom achieved. It is true that Montagu Norman and Benjamin Strong worked together successfully in the reconstruction of the gold standard in the 1920s. But, outside the central banks' control, cooperation on war debts and reparations was less successful.

What might have been possible among central banks, if different personnel had been in place, would have been the persuasion of the Federal Reserve not to sterilize inflows of gold and, indeed, to draw on its more than sufficient reserves of gold to accommodate the liquidity needs of the economy after 1929. A depression could have been avoided.

The lesson was clear. It is a lesson that seems to have been picked up on after the Second World War and there are clear signs of it at work in the first half of the 1960s when the Bretton Woods arrangements were under pressure. But perhaps more encouraging was the degree of central bank cooperation in the recent crisis, with many central banks engaging in swaps that smoothed the liquidity squeezes of 2008–10 (Allen and Moessner, 2010).

While there would not be much disagreement over the lessons listed above, there is still far from full agreement on a number of other possibilities.

5.6.5. Exchange rates

One of the lessons that remains debated concerns the nature of the exchange-rate regime. In the interwar period it was concluded that floating rates in the 1920s had demonstrably failed. In the 1930s, when the link with gold was broken, rates were therefore managed as a substitute for fixed rates. That picture was reinforced by Ragnar Nurkse in his study for the League of Nations published in 1944. It was in big part the experience of the interwar years, and a hankering for some aspects of the gold standard that led to the fixed-rate system of Bretton Woods. But many would argue that the lesson was misconceived and a more satisfactory arrangement would have been a floating or flexible rate regime.

A related point concerns the supposed disciplinary benefits of a fixed-rate regime. It was sometimes argued that the gold standard imposed discipline on the conduct of monetary and fiscal policy in countries that were otherwise unable to impose it themselves. That was a reason given for returning to gold in the 1920s after the profligacy of war (albeit with understandable reason) and immediate post-war years. But, if a government cannot be trusted to maintain appropriate monetary and fiscal policies on its own, it is unlikely to be able to do it under a gold standard. Evidence for that could also be found in the experience of the gold standard in the nineteenth century in spite of a strong desire to conform. The reason for seeking discipline externally might well be political. While the proper course of action might be accepted as, say, fiscal stringency it might not be possible politically and so recourse to a fixed regime allows politicians to blame the need for discipline on external elements. That could explain why the British apparently failed to learn the lesson in 1972 when it joined the 'snake' and again when it joined the ERM in 1990. But the biggest lesson is surely for the euro. Countries were encouraged to join who lacked the capacity for implementing proper monetary and fiscal policy. Why would joining the euro change that? It did not, and, at the time of writing, the euro is suffering as a result and will undoubtedly not last in its current form.

5.6.6. Asset prices

An important criticism of the Federal Reserve as a cause of the Great Depression was its tightening of monetary conditions in 1928 in the face of the booming New York stock market. The result was to produce a steeper downturn in the economy than would have occurred. The question, then, is should central banks attempt to stabilize asset prices, of any kind? The most frequent answer is a rebuttal. If there were a rational boom in, say, house prices, based on a rational assessment of improving future prospects, we would not want it stopped. But if it were an irrational boom could monetary policy stop it? That does not mean that central banks should ignore asset prices. If asset prices contain information about future movements in the economy, they must at least be worth monitoring.

There is also an argument that when prices are rising at 'unsustainable' rates, the likelihood is of a sharp reversal. Yet the evidence that asset price bursts predict recession is not compelling. It seems that, on balance, the preferable policy is to let asset booms run their course but to ensure there is sufficient liquidity available in case of a price crash.

5.6.7. International payments

More obviously international is the question of exchange controls. Although exchange controls are demonstrably damaging, it is remarkable how quickly resort is made to them in times of crisis. The case for capital flows is powerful, with world savings being channelled to their most productive uses. And the case against restrictions is equally strong. Any kind of protection results in 'deadweight losses' and exchange controls are no exception. Furthermore, and much like any other kind of protectionist device, once introduced, they become difficult to remove and long outlast their original intention and their usefulness. That was the case in the 1930s. Exchange controls were a knee-jerk reaction to the exchange-rate pressures but they then lasted for decades, although the picture was complicated by the coming of the war at the end of the decade. Also, what may be presented as a short-term emergency measure, and a one-off policy, will likely be viewed differently in the markets.

The principal point to make is that there is never a need for such controls when the exchange rate is credible. It is when the exchange rate is unconvincing that attacks occur. As Robert Mundell expressed it, there is no such thing as a bad capital movement, only bad exchange-rate systems. (Mundell, 2000)

Yet at the end of the 1990s, at the time of the Asian crisis, they were again being discussed seriously and claims being made that where they had been introduced they were working satisfactorily in some Asian economies. And proposals for them have reappeared again in the recent crisis with serious commentators insisting that they have their uses. It is only for this reason that I have included them in this group of lessons over which there is continuing debate.

How should the recent crisis then be interpreted in the light of the experience of the 1930s?[17] It is always tempting to find parallels in previous episodes. But some find other crises better analogies. Sussmann and Yafeh (2012), for instance, view the current crisis in the mirror of the Baring crisis of 1890, whereas Neal (2012) strongly disagrees and suggests that LTCM (long-term capital management) of the 1990s is the better case. There are, of course, some similarities between today and the 1930s. One of the central ones is of unresolved imbalances of the 1920s ultimately producing the currency difficulties and crises of the early 1930s. Another is the abrupt reversal of capital flows and the liquidation of much international investment. In the 1930s, countries relying on foreign borrowing felt pressure immediately on their exchange rate and that in turn led to a damaged debt position. In the recent crisis there was a similar contraction in the flow of credit to emerging economies and a shrinkage of liquidity worldwide.

BIBLIOGRAPHY

Accominotti, O. (2011a), 'London Merchant Banks: The Central European Panic and the Sterling Crisis of 1931', *The Journal of Economic History*, 72, 1–43.

Accominotti, O. (2011b), 'Asymmetric Propagation of Financial Crises during the Great Depression', Unpublished Paper, London School of Economics.

Aldcroft, D. H. and Oliver, M. J. (1998), *Exchange rate regimes in the twentieth century*. Cheltenham: Edward Elgar.

Allen, W. A. and Moessner, R. (2010), 'Central Bank Co-operation and International Liquidity in the Financial Crisis of 2008–2009', BIS Working Paper 310.

Bank for International Settlements (1936), Annual Reports, available at <http://www.bis.org/publ/avpdf/1933>.

Billings, M. and Capie, F. (2011), 'Financial Crisis, Contagion, and the British Banking System Between the World Wars', *Business History*, 53(2), 193–215.

Bordo, M. and James, H. (2010), 'The Great Depression Analogy', *Financial History Review*, 17(2), 127–40.

Bordo, M. D., Choudri, E. U., and Schwartz, A. J. (1993), 'Could Stable Money have Averted the Great Contraction?', NBER Working Paper No. 4481 (October) (Reprinted in Capie and Wood, 2011).

Bordo, M. D., Choudhri, E. U., and Schwartz, A. J. (1999), 'Was Expansionary Monetary Policy Feasible During the Great Contraction? An Examination of the Gold Standard Constraint', NBER Working Paper, No. 7125 (May).

[17] There are many examples of this kind of exercise but a good one can be found in Bordo and James (2010).

Borio, C., Toniolo, G., and Clement, P. (2008) (eds), *Past and future of central bank co-operation*. New York: Cambridge University Press.

Capie, F. (1985), *Depression and Protectionism*. London: Allen and Unwin.

Capie, F. (2002a), 'The Emergence of the Bank of England as a Mature Central Bank', in D. Winch and P. K. O'Brien (eds), *The Political Economy of British Historical Experience*. 1688–1914. Oxford: for the British Academy by Oxford University Press.

Capie, F. (2002b), *Capital Controls: A 'Cure' Worse than the Problem?* London: Institute of Economic Affairs, Research monograph 56.

Capie, F. (2010), *The Bank of England: 1950s to 1979*. New York: Cambridge University Press.

Capie, F. and Billings, M. (2001), 'Profitability in English Banking in the Twentieth Century', *European Review of Economic History*, 5, 367–401.

Capie, F. and Wood, G. (eds), *The Great Depression*. London: Routledge.

Capie, F., Mills, T. C., and Wood, G. (1986), 'What Happened in 1931?', in F. Capie and G. Wood (eds), *Financial Crises and the World Banking System*. London: Macmillan.

Choudhri, E. U. and Kochin, L. E. (1980), 'The Exchange Rate and the International Transmission of Business Cycle Disturbances: Some Evidence from the Great Depression', *Journal of Money Credit and Banking*, 12(4), 3–26. (Reprinted in Capie and Wood, 2011).

Comin, F. and Martin-Acena, P. (1985), 'La Politica Monetaria y Fiscal Durante la Dictadura y la Segunda Republica', in *Papeles de Economia Espanola*, 20, 236–65.

Eichengreen, B. (1996), *Globalising Capital; A History of the International Monetary System*. Princeton: Princeton University Press.

Eichengreen, B. (2011), *Exorbitant Privilege; The Rise and Fall of the Dollar*. Oxford: Oxford University Press.

Eichengreen, B. and Irwin, D. (2010), 'The Slide to Protectionism in the Great Depression: Who Succumbed and Why', *The Journal of Economic History*, 70, 872–98

Eichengreen, B. and Portes, R. (1986), 'Debt and Default in the 1930s: Causes and Consequences', *European Economic Review*, 30, 599–640.

Falkus, M. E. (1971), 'United States Economic Policy and the 'Dollar Gap' of the 1920s', *The Economic History Review*, 24(4), 599–623.

Feinstein, C. H. and Watson, K. (1995), 'Private International Capital Flows in Europe in the Interwar Period', in C. H. Feinstein (ed.), *Banking, currency and finance in Europe between the wars*. Oxford: Clarendon Press.

Fisher, I. (1933), 'Booms and Depressions', *Econometrica*, 1(1), 337–57

Flandreau, M., Gaillard, N., and Packer, F. (2009), 'Ratings Performance, Regulation, and the Great Depression: Lessons from Foreign Government Securities', Centre for Economic Policy Research, Discussion Paper 7328.

Friedman, M. (1953), 'The Case for Flexible Exchange Rates', in *Essays in Positive Economics*. Chicago: University of Chicago Press, 157–203

James, H. (2001), *The End of Globalisation: Lessons from the Great Depression*. Cambridge, MA: Harvard University Press.

Kindleberger, C. (1973), *The World in Depression, 1929–1939*. London: Allen Lane.

Marichal, C. (1989), *A Century of Debt Crises in Latin America*. Princeton: Princeton University Press.

Mishkin, F. S. (2011), 'Monetary Policy Strategy: Lessons from the Crisis', in M. Jarocinski, F. Smets, and C. Thiman, (eds) *Approaches to Monetary Policy Revisited: Lessons from the Crisis*. ECB Sixth Central Banking Conference.

Moessner, R. and Allen, W. A. (2011), 'Banking Crises and the International Monetary System in the Great Depression and Now', *Financial History Review*, 18(1), 1–20.

Mundell, R. (2000), 'A Reconsideration of the Twentieth Century', *The American Economic Review*, 90(3), 327–40.

Neal, L. (2012), 'Comment on Sussman and Yafeh', Conference Reunion Cientifica Financial Crises in Historical Perspective, February, Madrid.

Nurkse, R. (with W. A. Brown) (1944), *International Currency Experience*. Princeton: League of Nations.

O'Rourke, K. H. and Williamson, J. (1999), *Globalization and History: The Evolution of a Nineteenth Century Atlantic Economy*. Cambridge, MA: MIT Press.

Richardson, G. and van Horn, P. (2011), 'When the Music Stopped: Trans-Atlantic Contagion during the Financial Crisis of 1931', NBER Working Paper No. 17437, September.

Romer, C. D. (1993), 'The Nation in Depression', *The Journal of Economic Perspectives*, 7(2), 19–39.

Schnabel, I. (2004), 'The German Twin Crises of 1931', *The Journal of Economic History*, 64(3), 822–71.

Schubert, A. (1991), *The Credit-Anstalt Crisis of 1931*. Cambridge: Cambridge University Press.

Schwartz, A. J. (1981), 'Understanding 1929–33', in K. Brunner (ed.), *The Great Depression Revisited*. Boston: Martinus Nijhoff Publishing.

Schwartz, A. J. (1986), 'Real and Pseudo-financial Crises', in F. Capie and G. Wood (eds), *Financial Crises and the World Banking System*. London: Macmillan.

Schwartz, P. and Castenada, J. (2011), 'The Great Depression in Spain (1929–1936): A Non-event', Unpublished paper.

Sussman, N. and Yafeh, Y. (2012), 'The Current Financial Crisis in Historical Perspective: A View from the Core'. Conference Reunion Cientifica Financial Crises in Historical Perspective, February, Madrid.

Temin, P. (1989), *Lessons from the Great Depression*. Cambridge, MA: MIT Press.

Wandschneider, K. (2008), 'The Stability of the Interwar Gold Standard: Did Politics Matter?', *The Journal of Economic History*, 68(1) 151–81.

Wood, G. and Capie, F. (2010) (eds), *The Great Depression*. London and Abingdon: Routledge.

Woolf, N. (2008), 'Scylla and Charybdis: Explaining Europe's Exit from Gold, January 1928–December 1936', *Explorations in Economic History*, 45(4) 383–401.

Yates, P. L. (1959), *Forty years of foreign trade*. London: Allen and Unwin.

6

The Political Lessons of Depression-era Banking Reform*

Charles W. Calomiris

6.I. INTRODUCTION

In the wake of the financial crisis of 2007–09, the United States and many other countries considered new legislation and regulation purportedly to respond to flaws in the financial system that were exposed by the crisis. Critics, however, have argued that the far-reaching legislative proposals drafted in the US Congress have failed to respond to the origins of the crisis, and instead have served other political purposes. For example, the more than 2,300 page legislation failed to address a major contributor to the housing finance boom-and-bust cycle at the heart of the crisis, namely the politically motivated government subsidization of mortgage risk in the financial system (Calomiris, 2008, 2009b and 2009c; Wallison and Calomiris, 2009). In fact, despite the financial collapse of the government-sponsored enterprises, Fannie Mae and Freddie Mac (now owned and controlled explicitly by the government), their importance has grown.

In this chapter, I argue that comprehensive regulatory reform passed in haste in the wake of a banking crisis is likely not to respond well to the problems that gave rise to the crisis. To illustrate why this is so, I consider the previous US attempt at comprehensive, post-crisis banking reforms in the 1930s. As in the reaction to the current crisis, the banking reforms of the 1930s not only failed to address the key structural problems that had caused the crisis, they actually reinforced those structural weaknesses. The central lesson of the 1930s reforms was that comprehensive, hasty, post-crisis reform initiatives maximize the potential for logrolling,

* This chapter was prepared for the conference, 'Lessons from the 1930s Great Depression for the Making of Economic Policy', sponsored by the Centre for Competitive Advantage in the Global Economy and the Oxford Review of Economic Policy, London, 16–17 April 2010. I thank Richard Grossman, Allan Meltzer, Larry Neal, the editors, and two anonymous referees for helpful comments.

which facilitates the enactment of ill-conceived ideas and special interest measures that otherwise would not have passed.

The economic contraction of the Great Depression in the United States (1929–33) was accompanied by a visible collapse of many US banks. According to the Federal Reserve Board (1943), the number of banks fell 39 per cent, from 24,633 in December 1929 to 15,015 in December 1933. The 9,096 banks that failed during the years 1930–33 tended to be small banks. Failed banks, as defined by the Federal Reserve (1943), represented 37 per cent of the banks in existence at the end of 1929, but the deposits of those failed banks (at their dates of failure) were only 14 per cent of the average level of bank deposits over the years 1930–33, and losses borne by depositors in failed banks were roughly US$1.3 billion, representing 2.7 per cent of the average amount of deposits in the banking system for the years 1930–33, and 2 per cent of average annual GNP for 1930–33.[1]

Although by current standards (summarized by Caprio and Klingebiel (1996) and reported in Beim and Calomiris (2001, chapter 7) and in Calomiris (2009a)), the Great Depression was not a very large bank insolvency crisis, it was more severe than the crises of most other countries (Grossman, 1994) and it was large by historical standards, even for the failure-prone US banking system. During the period 1873–1913, no year had seen losses to depositors in excess of 0.1 per cent of GNP. While the 1920s were a turbulent decade for agricultural states, many of which experienced comparable stress to that of the 1930s, the country as a whole did not see a national bank failure rate or depositor loss rate similar to that of the 1930s. The 5,712 banks that failed during the years 1921–29 had total deposits equal to $1.6 billion at the time of their failure, constituting 3.1 per cent of average total deposits in the banking system from 1921 to 1929. Losses to depositors for the period 1921–29 amounted to $565 million, which was 1 per cent of average deposits during the period 1921–29 and 0.6 per cent of average annual GNP.[2] Banks' abilities to avoid insolvency, including during the relatively severe episode of the Great Depression, reflected the intense and visible market discipline in the deposit market, which gave banks strong incentives to shore up their positions to avoid deposit outflows in response to loan losses. They did so by cutting lending, increasing reserves and Treasury securities holdings, and cutting dividends (Calomiris and Mason, 1997, 2003a; Calomiris and Wilson, 2004).

This chapter explores the principal regulatory changes in banking after the economic and financial collapse of 1930–33.[3] Presumably, any evaluation of the bank regulatory policy reaction to the Depression must first come to grips with the causes of the collapse of so many banks, in order to evaluate whether the policy responses addressed pre-existing weaknesses in the system. What did the Great Depression reveal about inherent flaws in the US banking system's structure and

[1] Deposits and failures are from the Federal Reserve Board's data in *Banking and Monetary Statistics: 1914–1941* (1943), using suspensions as the measures of failures. Nominal GNP is from the Census Bureau's *Historical Statistics of the United States* (US Bureau of the Census. 1970).

[2] Ibid.

[3] It is beyond the scope of this chapter to explore all the financial reforms of the 1930s. In particular, this chapter does not consider the motivations or consequences of securities markets regulations affecting the behaviour of dealers, exchanges, and mutual funds, including the creation of the Securities and Exchange Commission.

regulation? From the perspective of current scholarship, the two most obvious flaws in the structure of banking and in the operation of the central bank, which scholars have shown were particularly important in contributing to the severity of the Great Depression, were the US unit banking system (perpetuated by regulations that generally prohibited bank branching) and the central bank's adherence to the 'real bills doctrine'.

It should seem puzzling and ironic, therefore, that the three most important regulatory policy responses to the Great Depression—Regulation Q limits on bank interest payments, the exclusion of underwriting from depository banks, and the creation of federal deposit insurance—were consciously designed either to perpetuate unit banking (which was the conscious goal of the advocates of federal deposit insurance) or to facilitate continuing adherence to the real bills doctrine (the goal of Regulation Q and the separation of investment banking from commercial banking). In other words, the major bank regulatory 'reforms' of the 1930s consciously preserved and supported the two aspects of the pre-existing banking and central banking system that had done the most harm to the banking system and the economy in the 1930s.

How and why this happened is a fascinating tale that mixes misguided ideology and political intrigue, and one with important implications for understanding the risks that generally attend policy responses to financial crises, including the policy responses to the recent crisis that are being contemplated today. Before reviewing the regulatory reforms of the 1930s, it is useful to take a brief detour to understand the regulatory setting that existed prior to the Great Depression, and briefly review two peculiar aspects of the US financial system, namely its unit banking structure, and the dominant 'real bills' theory that guided its central banking.

6.2. THE HARMFUL PERSISTENCE OF UNIT BANKING

Despite some disagreement in the literature over the extent to which unwarranted panics or fundamental weaknesses precipitated bank failures in the 1930s, there is widespread agreement that the fragmented structure of the 'unit banking' system in the US was at the core of the systemic fragility of the system, for several reasons.[4] Unit banking made banks less diversified, and thus more exposed to location-specific shocks (such as agricultural price declines), as discussed by White (1983, 1984a) and Calomiris (1990, 1992, 2000). Unit banking made it harder for banks to coordinate their behaviour in the face of shocks at the regional or national level, thus making it more difficult to defuse liquidity crises (Calomiris and Gorton, 1991; Calomiris and Schweikart, 1991; Calomiris, 1989, 1990, 1992, 2000). Unit banking also made banks less competitive and less cost efficient, which made them less profitable as well.

[4] Comparisons of bank fragility across places and time clearly show that the US's unit banking structure resulted in greater propensities for bank failures. The Great Depression was just the latest in a long stream of evidence on that point (see Calomiris, 2000, Introduction and chapters 1–2).

None of this was news in the 1930s. US banks had demonstrated peculiar fragility relative to other banks in the world for many decades, both from the perspective of their greater propensity for failure, and the greater propensity of the system to suffer banking panics. The notion that unit banking was at the heart of the propensity for failure was recognized as common knowledge by the 1920s, when waves of bank failures swept through most agricultural producing areas of the country (Calomiris, 1992, 2000).

Indeed, many states had relaxed branching restrictions within their states in reaction to the banking distress of the 1920s. Fifteen states changed their regulations between 1920 and 1939 to allow expanded branching. The branching and consolidation movement was accelerating heading into the Great Depression, as shown in Table 6.1. Federal government adoption of deposit insurance and other policies, however, put an end to that trend for roughly 50 years (only four states relaxed their branching laws between 1939 and 1979). Eventually, the 1920s consolidation movement would be repeated and extended in the 1980s and 1990s. From 1979 to 1990, 15 states relaxed their branching restrictions. Bank distress related to the savings and loan (S&L) collapse in the late 1980s, agricultural bank failures in the early 1980s in the centre of the country, oil and gas related failures in Oklahoma and Texas, and commercial real estate losses in the late 1980s, all prompted the relaxation and elimination of branching restrictions at the state level. Banks operating national branching networks, as defined by

Table 6.1. Bank consolidation and branching, 1910–31

Year	Chapman Series	White Series	Fed Series	Branches
	Banks absorbed in mergers	Banks absorbed in mergers	Branch banks	
1910	128	–	292	548
1911	119	–	–	–
1912	128	–	–	–
1913	118	–	–	–
1914	143	–	–	–
1915	154	–	397	785
1916	134	–	–	–
1917	123	–	–	–
1918	125	–	–	–
1919	178	172	–	–
1920	183	184	530	1,281
1921	292	250	547	1,455
1922	340	311	610	1,801
1923	325	299	671	2,054
1924	352	341	706	2,297
1925	356	280	720	2,525
1926	429	348	744	2,703
1927	544	477	740	2,914
1928	507	455	775	3,138
1929	575	529	764	3,353
1930	698	627	751	3,522
1931	719	635	723	3,467

Source: Calomiris (2000: 57).

Correa (2008), rose from 10 per cent of the banking system's loans or deposits in around 1980 to more than 70 per cent of the system by the mid-1990s. Branching deregulation continued to gather force in the early 1990s, and ultimately at the national level, through the 1994 legislation permitting nationwide branching.

On prima facie grounds, given the bank failure experience of the 1930s, the decision not to permit branching and consolidation appears strange. Research has shown that the bank failures of the 1930s, like those of the 1920s, resulted from the inability of small, unit banks to withstand the severe fundamental shocks of the Depression (White, 1984a; Calomiris, 1990, 1992; Calomiris and Mason, 1997, 2003a). Moreover, even the banks that survived the Depression did so by contracting their lending supply dramatically to shore up their positions, which contributed greatly to the severity of the Depression, and the slow recovery from it during the 1930s (Fisher, 1933; Bernanke, 1983; Calomiris and Mason, 2003b; Calomiris and Wilson, 2004). Unit banking was a key influence on both the high US propensity for bank failure, and the propensity to suffer severe credit crunches; *ceteris paribus*, smaller banks were not only more likely to fail, but also tended to contract credit supply more dramatically (Calomiris, 1990, 1992, 2000; Calomiris and Mason 2003a, 2003b).

The decision to preserve unit banking in the 1930s, in spite of the evidence that it promoted bank fragility and credit crunches, echoed a similar decision made two decades earlier, at the time of the founding of the Federal Reserve System in 1913. Since the extinction of the prior US central bank, which was the Second Bank of the United States (the re-chartering of which was vetoed by Andrew Jackson in 1832), the US operated without a central bank until the creation of the Federal Reserve System in 1913.

The Fed's founding was a grand political compromise. After the panic of 1907, the National Monetary Commission (NMC) was established to recommend reforms to the American financial system in reaction to the peculiar US propensity for banking panics. The NMC published voluminous studies of other countries' banking systems, drawing attention in particular to the destabilizing role of America's unit banking system, in contrast to those of other countries. In particular, much attention was given to Canada's nationwide branching system, which avoided banking panics despite the absence of a central bank (the Bank of Canada was founded in 1935).

The unit structure of the banking system in the US was understood to be responsible for many problems that contributed to the peculiar instability of US banking. First, the barriers to entry implied by unit banking prevented productive competition among banks. Unit banks could only face competition from other unit banks, all of which faced high overhead costs that limited entry, especially in rural areas; low-overhead branching by banks headquartered elsewhere was prohibited. Barriers to competition allowed less profitable (more vulnerable) banks to survive during normal times, making bank failures more frequent during adverse times. The 1994 national legislation permitting nationwide branching in the US was associated with significant efficiency improvement resulting from the ability of successful branching banks to increase their share of the retail banking network (Lee, 2010). Carlson and Mitchener (2009) show that branching deregulation in California in the 1920s and 1930s substantially improved the efficiency of its banking system, even for surviving unit banks, which improved their performance as the result of intensified competition from branching banks.

Second, unit banking produced lack of diversification of loan risk within banks, as each bank's portfolio risk reflected the operations of its local economy. In agricultural areas, that meant that the income of banks was closely related to changes in the prices and harvests of one or two crops.

Third, unit banking inhibited financial integration across regions, which resulted in large differences in interest rates between the east and the west, and high seasonal volatility in liquidity risk. Seasonal swings in credit and liquidity risk in the banking system—visible in seasonal cycles in loan-to-reserve ratios, deposit-to-capital ratios, interest rates, and stock returns volatility (all of which peaked in the autumn and spring)—reflected primarily the harvesting cycle of the cotton crop (and, to a lesser extent, other crops). Crop planting and harvesting drove large seasonal swings in the demand for credit in agricultural areas in the autumn and the spring, which required seasonal transfers of funds, back and forth, twice a year, between New York and the periphery. In a branching system (e.g. Canada's, or the branching system of the antebellum south, or even the hybrid system of unit banks and the Second Bank of the United States from 1816 to 1832), branching banks internalized regional differences in credit demand within themselves and smoothed seasonal fluctuations in loan-to-reserve ratios, deposit-to-capital ratios, interest rates, and returns volatility. Branching systems thus limited the swings in credit and liquidity risk over the seasonal cycle, making banks less vulnerable to shocks. (For a review of recent studies, see Calomiris (2000, 2009a).)

Fourth, the lack of financial integration through branching encouraged peripheral banks to store their reserves in cities during low-demand seasons in the form of interbank balances. This 'pyramiding' of reserves in New York encouraged the use of interbank balances to fund securities market transactions (e.g. loans to brokers and dealers), which increased the vulnerability of the banking system to shocks originating in securities markets. For example, in the panic of 1857, shocks to western railroads' fortunes (related to political concerns over the future battle over the expansion of slavery into the west) created a run on New York banks, which led them to suspend convertibility, which, in turn, caused their correspondent banks in the periphery to suspend convertibility (Calomiris and Schweikart, 1991).

Fifth, when financial shocks occurred, it was virtually impossible for thousands of unit banks to coordinate their responses to those shocks via helpful collective action. Banks that belonged to clearing houses in major cities could coordinate to some extent within their cities—sometimes pooling their risks and resources to make markets in each other's liabilities to reduce liquidity risk by easing depositors' concerns about potential insolvency of any particular bank (see Gorton, 1985). In Indiana and Ohio during the antebellum period, self-regulating coalitions even operated effectively at the state level (Calomiris, 1989, 1990). But national shocks could not be stabilized by local action, and national action by a grand coalition of the nation's banks was not feasible. Cooperation within the banking system required mutual regulation and monitoring to prevent free riding. The physical ability to monitor was possible when banks were coincident (within a city, or within a country such as Canada, where a few banks operated branches alongside one another throughout the country). But tens of thousands of banks operating one-office banks throughout the US could not effectively establish credibly enforced rules to govern their behaviour. Thus, when adverse shocks hit the US banking system, it was not possible for banks to act collectively to mutual advantage (in contrast to the actions of the Canadian banks in the late nineteenth and early twentieth centuries, or the French banks during the Paris Bourse crisis of 1882, or the London clearing banks during the Barings failure in 1890).

Although there was not a consensus on precisely what weights to attach to each of these five aspects of unit banking for explaining the peculiar history of US banking instability and high failure propensity, all five problems pointed to unit banking as the ultimate source of banking instability. The obvious simple solution—to permit nationwide branch banking—was, however, a political non-starter.

As White (1984b), Calomiris (2000), and Calomiris and Ramirez (2010) show, political support for unit banking was not confined to unit bankers. The preservation of unit banking was one of the key campaign issues advocated by William Jennings Bryan (the candidate for both the Populist Party and the Democratic Party in the 1896 election, who was also an early advocate of federal deposit insurance). Why would the populist movement—a movement identified so strongly with agricultural interests—advocate unit banking, a banking regulation that resulted in fragile agricultural banks and expensive loans in rural areas? Why would a candidate who was so clearly interested in promoting the interests of agricultural debtors (the parties who would have most clearly benefited from Bryan's advocacy of currency devaluation via 'free silver' in 1896) also be advocating unit banking rules that raised the costs of credit to farmers?

Bryan's candidacy was not an isolated example. White (1984b) studies the 1923 Illinois referendum on relaxing branching restrictions, which resulted in the preservation of unit banking. Obviously, there were not enough Illinois voters who profited in any obvious way from preserving unit banking. Why, then, did the voters of Illinois want to preserve unit banking?

Calomiris (2000) and Calomiris and Ramirez (2010) show that the support for unit banking was strong in rural areas that had significant agricultural wealth in land, which were areas in which local farmers borrowed from unit bankers to finance their operations and land acquisition. But in areas of poorer farmers, there was little support for unit banking. That result holds both in the time series and in

Table 6.2. Rural wealth and branching restrictions

	States allowing some branching (1910)	States not allowing further branching (1910)
Rural per capita wealth (1900)		
Mean, all states	0.8	1.5
Median, all states	0.5	1.4
Mean, excluding south	1.4	1.7
Median, excluding south	1.2	1.8

Source: Calomiris (2000: 65.)

the cross-section. As Table 6.2 shows, as of 1900, states that supported unit banking had much higher rural wealth per capita. Calomiris (2000, chapter 1) also reviews changes in unit banking regulation over time. Agricultural distress (and reductions in rural wealth) is associated with declining support for unit banking. Indeed, the story of the expansion of the branching network of Bank of America within California illustrates that pattern well. When A. P. Giannini first applied for permission to expand his branching network into rural California, he was denied permission, owing to the opposition of rural unit bankers. But when agricultural distress arrived in those same areas a few years later, he was granted permission (James and James, 1954).

Calomiris (2000, chapter 1) and Calomiris and Ramirez (2010) argue that, by tying rural banks to one location, farmers limited the lending opportunities of banks in ways that increased the propensity of banks to lend to farmers in bad, but not disastrous, states of the world. Farmers were willing to pay for this 'loan insurance' in the form of higher interest rates on loans. Once disaster struck, however, both farm debtors and rural unit banks were ruined, and local support shifted towards permitting branching, which encouraged entry of new capital.

The founding of the Fed (like the creation of the Bank of the United States and the Second Bank of the United States before it) was a second-best economic solution to the deeper political problem of unit banking. The Fed smoothed the effects of seasonal and cyclical liquidity demands by making the supply of reserves more elastic via its new sources of reserves supply (the discount windows of the twelve Federal Reserve Banks). Importantly, the Federal Reserve Banks issued legal tender currency, which meant that the supply of riskless reserves was not limited by the inelastic stock of specie and other forms of currency. The Fed operated throughout the nation to smooth seasonal and cyclical demands for liquidity. The early history of the Fed indicates that it was quite successful in improving the elasticity of liquidity supply seasonally and cyclically (Miron, 1986; Bernstein et al., 2008).

The Federal Reserve System was an acceptable political solution to banking instability precisely because of the combination of structure, powers, and rules that it embodied, and because it did not attack unit banking interests. It was decentralized in structure, and thus did not run afoul of opponents of national consolidation of control. Even more important, it was an institutional embodiment of political balance. The Fed was not 'above it all' politically; rather, it combined in one organization the opposing interests that held sway over its existence. The political balancing act of the founding of the Fed gave important new powers and opportunities to agrarian interests (e.g. by permitting member banks to make real estate loans—an activity prohibited for national banks in the first 50 years of their existence), gave new opportunities for borrowing to member banks, and shared power over its rules and governance with the Executive and Legislative branches of the federal government, ensuring that all these parties had an interest in preserving the institution, and that none of them had much of a chance to hijack it for their own purposes. The Fed's charter was a credible commitment to the balanced interests that negotiated it because it would be difficult to change.

As Table 6.1 shows, bank consolidation and branching were gaining strength by the end of the 1920s, as the revealed superiority of branching for bank stability and profitability was leading to widespread relaxation of branching. Representative Henry Steagall of Alabama, who was the leading representative of the interests of unit bankers in Congress, saw federal deposit insurance protection of small banks as the last best hope of preventing competition and deregulation from ending the unit banking system.

Passing government deposit insurance as a salve for unit banking was not a new idea. Starting in the 1880s, there had been 150 attempts in Congress prior to 1933 to enact federal deposit insurance. Calomiris and White (1994) show that those attempts were championed by Congressional representatives of unit banking constituencies. Only once (in a proposed amendment to the Federal Reserve Act of 1913) did the idea of federal deposit insurance ever make it out of a Congressional banking committee.

Unit banking interests, however, had been successful in obtaining deposit insurance protection from a handful of state legislatures, in states where unit banking commanded strong support. As White (1983, 1985), Calomiris (1989, 1990, 1992, 2000), and Calomiris and White (1994) show, proposals to enact deposit insurance had been one of the key policy weapons used to defend unit bankers, and its use at the state level dates from the antebellum era.

In the early twentieth century, eight states had enacted deposit insurance systems for their state-chartered banks. All of these systems ended disastrously during the agricultural distress of the 1920s. The three states that operated long-lived mandatory deposit insurance systems for state-chartered banks (Nebraska, North Dakota, and South Dakota) suffered the most excessive risk taking in the agricultural states that rode the commodity price boom before the 1920s, and had by far the worst insolvency experience in the 1920s (Calomiris, 1990, 1992). That experience was common knowledge by the 1930s, which largely accounted for the fact that deposit insurance was almost universally understood by 1933 to be a source of excessive risk taking that had been responsible for the worst banking disasters of the 1920s (Calomiris, 1990, 1992; Flood, 1991; Calomiris and White, 1994). Henry Steagall would have his work cut out for him.

6.3. THE REAL BILLS DOCTRINE

Another primary contributor to the Great Depression was the failure of the Federal Reserve to prevent—through the implementation of expansionary monetary policy—the collapse of money, credit, income, prices, borrowers, and banks that occurred during 1929–33. That failure reflected more than just occasional misreading of the economy by the Fed, or the constraints of the gold standard (although it is also true that the Fed interpreted the preservation of the gold standard as sometimes requiring it to tighten monetary policy during the Depression). The intellectual foundations of the Fed's cyclical policy 'reaction function'—that is, the way the Fed targeted its open market operations and discount lending and advances in response to observable cyclical indicators—has been explored in detail by Wheelock (1991), Calomiris and Wheelock (1998), and Meltzer (2003). They show that adherence to the 'real bills doctrine' was at the heart of the failure of the Federal Reserve's desire to tighten monetary policy in 1929, and its failure to respond appropriately to the economic collapse of the Depression.

There are no living adherents to the real bills doctrine today of whom I am aware, and it conflicts sharply with all the dominant theories of monetary targeting that appear in textbooks or in today's central bank policy analyses. Nevertheless, this theory was of crucial importance in the policy architecture of the Federal Reserve System and in Fed policies in the first two decades of its existence.

According to the real bills doctrine, the Fed should accommodate cyclical demand for credit *related to trade*, but not variation in credit demand associated with securities lending, real estate lending, or industrial or consumer lending. The central bank, therefore, was emphatically not supposed to be in the business of targeting the growth of aggregate credit or money or economic activity or financial system health, but rather should see itself as ensuring that reasonable needs of trade finance were being met. There is no economic theory that supports the real bills doctrine, either as a theory of banking or as a theory of monetary policy. From the standpoint of banking theory, there is no obvious reason to believe that banks should be encouraged to engage solely or mainly in financing trade, rather than industrial finance, consumer finance, securities finance, or real estate finance; all credit supports economic activity and no type of credit is inherently more socially desirable than another. From the standpoint of currently accepted monetary theory, policy should focus on the targeting of interest rates, exchange rates, inflation, credit aggregates, and monetary aggregates, out of a desire to stabilize aggregate demand and/or inflation, and there is no recognized special connection between trade credit, per se, and aggregate demand or inflation.

The real bills doctrine played a central role in causing and worsening the Depression. In 1929, real bills thinking led the Fed to respond to the rise in the stock market with contractionary monetary policy and admonitions to member banks not to provide credit to the securities market. That policy was being publicly cheered on by real bills advocates in Congress—most notably, the premier proponent of the real bills doctrine in Congress, Senator Carter Glass (White, 1990). Throughout the Depression, in their attempt to follow the real bills doctrine, Fed officials focused on borrowed reserves of member banks and on the interest rates on bills and other instruments in the market. They regarded low nominal interest rates and low levels of borrowed reserves as indicative of loose credit conditions. That view, of course, was incorrect in the early 1930s. During a deflation, low nominal interest rates alongside severe deflation can imply high real interest rates. And, as the Depression led banks to scramble for cash (Calomiris and Wilson, 2004), cash was hoarded by banks and borrowed reserves fell, but these actually indicated contracting money and credit supply. Because the Fed's real bills philosophy argued against stabilizing securities markets, banks, or the economy, it led Fed officials to purposely ignore signals that the economy and the financial system was contracting during the early 1930s (Wheelock, 1991; Meltzer, 2003). Indeed, Meltzer (2003) points out that Fed officials were quite satisfied with their performance during the Depression, since they had adhered to principles rather than being distracted by what they saw as misguided desires to prevent economic and financial decline.

The real bills doctrine had many advocates, within and outside the Fed, including an influential Senator from Virginia, Carter Glass. Although Glass was not the chairman of the Senate banking committee, when Roosevelt took office he turned to Glass, who had been one of primary architects of the Federal Reserve Act of 1913 (which had passed Congress in 1913 as the 'Glass–Owen' bill) to formulate a regulatory response to the Depression. As he had done in 1912, Glass asked Parker Willis—one of the country's leading academic advocates of the real bills doctrine—to advise him on what should be done. Many of the Fed's initial architects, including Willis and Glass, had long harboured the view that the Fed had failed to fulfil its real bills ambitions, and they saw the 1930s as the opportunity to fix longstanding problems that would refocus the Fed on its real bills mission.

For example, bankers' acceptances—which real bills advocates hoped would become a dominant source of credit within the banking system—had not grown to be very important, despite the attempts to subsidize their use through Fed advances against them. The geographic breadth of the US, and its fragmented unit banking structure, made banks reluctant to discount bills over long distances (Calomiris, 2000, chapter 1); unlike in Great Britain, or the antebellum branching south, where bills thrived as a source of credit, they failed to become a large part of the US financial system, as real bills advocates had hoped.

Furthermore, real bills architects had hoped that the Regional Federal Reserve Banks would serve as independent sources of system-wide reserve management, thereby replacing the pyramiding of reserves in New York. Real bills advocates saw pyramiding as pernicious, since it encouraged the use of bank funding sources to finance speculative securities activities in New York banks during the seasons when credit demand was low in agricultural areas (summer and winter).

Real bills advocates in the 1930s wanted regulatory reform to focus on completing the unfinished business of restructuring the banking system—especially, reducing the connections between bank credit and securities lending and discouraging the pyramiding of reserves in New York. The intended solutions advocated by Carter Glass were the separation of commercial and investment banking, and the restriction on interest payments on deposits, especially interbank deposits. Limiting interest payments on interbank deposits would encourage banks to maintain higher reserves at the Fed rather than through the interbank market.[5]

6.4. THE RAPID AND LASTING REGULATORY POLICY RESPONSE OF THE 1930s

Despite the fact that restrictions on bank branching and adherence to the real bills doctrine had been two of the key contributors to the severity of the Depression, and despite the absence of evidence in support of the desirability of the three

[5] As White (1983) pointed out, the same objective could have been achieved by having the Federal Reserve Banks pay interest on reserves, which would have permitted them to compete with the interbank market, and would have avoided the distortion of prohibiting interest payments on deposits.

major banking reforms being proposed (Regulation Q, the separation of underwriting from commercial banking, and the creation of federal deposit insurance) regulatory reformers in Congress seeking to preserve unit banking or to enhance the operation of the real bills doctrine *successfully* passed all three of these initiatives into law. Not only did they succeed in doing so, the successful advocacy happened unusually quickly, in 1933, within a few months of President Roosevelt having taken office.

That policy response was more comprehensive, much faster, and more activist than in prior banking crises. Federal government interventions included both new short-term assistance measures for banks and other corporations, and major long-term alterations in bank regulation, which were adopted in the Banking Acts of 1933 and 1935.

In contrast, the policy responses to previous financial disasters had been slower, less dramatic, and had tended to encourage post-crisis relaxation of branching restrictions. During the antebellum era, the panics of 1837, 1839, and 1857 were quite dramatic events, and yet with the exception of changes in bank chartering laws at the state level, there was no significant policy response. Only one of the six banking panics (1873, 1884, 1890, 1893, 1896, and 1907) that occurred during the national banking era (1863–1913) produced a significant policy response, namely the panic of 1907.[6]

The bank regulatory response to the panic of 1907, however, was much less far-reaching and much more deliberate than the responses to the Depression. In the wake of the panic of 1907, the government passed the Aldrich–Vreeland Act of 1908 (a fairly modest reform that made it easier to expand the supply of national bank notes quickly during a liquidity crisis) and created the NMC of 1910. The NMC commissioned thousands of pages of serious research by the world's top scholars in the areas of money and banking about the causes of banking instability. That voluminous research ultimately led to the creation of the Federal Reserve System at the end of 1913. Recent work by Miron (1986) and Bernstein et al. (2008) suggests that Fed discounting was successful in reducing the seasonal volatility of financial markets.

It is worth emphasizing that the banking and central banking policy reactions to the Depression in 1933–35 were both more sudden and more wide-ranging than the reaction to the panic of 1907. The reactions included:

1. unprecedented government assistance programmes for banks in the form of government-funded preferred stock investments in banks by the Reconstruction Finance Corporation (RFC) beginning in November 1933 (Mason, 2001);
2. the restriction of interest payments on bank deposits, including the prohibition of interest payments on demand deposits (Regulation Q), as part of the Banking Act of 1933;

[6] For a review of these panic experiences, with special emphasis on the inadequacy of the fragmented financial system in preventing panics, see Sprague's (1910) and Wicker's (2000) accounts of all six events, Strouse's (1999, chapter 28) account of J. P. Morgan's interventions during the panic of 1907, Calomiris and Gorton (1991) on the common economic causes of the six panics, and Bruner and Carr (2007) on the panic of 1907.

3. the temporary, and then permanent, requirement of nationwide deposit insurance implemented in 1933 and made permanent in 1935, under the auspices of the newly created Federal Deposit Insurance Corporation (FDIC);
4. the Banking Act of 1933 prohibition of securities underwriting by depository institutions (the so-called 'Glass–Steagall' separation of commercial and investment banking);
5. the creation of new monetary powers for the executive branch, including the Thomas Amendment to the Agricultural Adjustment Act of 1933 (which allowed the president to require open market purchases by the Fed), the Gold Reserve Act of 1934 (which created the Exchange Stabilization Fund under the Treasury Department), and the Silver Purchase Act of 1934, all of which enhanced the Administration's ability to prevent Fed tightening; and
6. the restructuring of power within the Federal Reserve System in 1933 and 1935, which augmented and consolidated authority within the Federal Reserve Board over open market operations, discount rate setting, and reserve requirements (giving control over the setting of reserve requirements to the Fed) and removed the Secretary of the Treasury and the Comptroller of the Currency from the Federal Open Market Committee (FOMC).[7]

Although not all of these policy changes had a substantial impact on the banking system, many of them resulted in significant and lasting change. It took six decades to unwind Regulation Q limits on deposit interest, and only after those limits had produced the great disintermediation from banking that occurred in the 1960s and 1970s, as depositors sought higher rates of return in reaction to the accelerating inflation of that era and the limited nominal interest rates permitted under Regulation Q.

The prohibition of underwriting in commercial banks was unwound gradually beginning in 1987, as the result of Fed actions and Supreme Court decisions that permitted some underwriting at banks (Kaufman and Mote, 1990). Those actions reflected, inter alia, US bank regulators' observation of US and other banks' underwriting activities outside the US, which indicated little need for concern about risk or conflicts of interest. Regulators argued that the Glass–Steagall limitations served no legitimate purpose, but threatened to undermine US competitiveness by pushing banking activities abroad. Those deregulatory initiatives ultimately paved the way to full relaxation in 1999 as the result of the Gramm–Leach–Bliley Act.

FDIC deposit insurance has proved to be the most robust regulatory innovation of all. It has expanded over time and it seems unlikely that it will ever be repealed.

[7] One puzzling aspect of Carter Glass's actions in the 1930s was his support for the consolidation of authority within the Federal Reserve Board. Glass had always championed decentralization within the Fed system and had prided himself on preventing the centralization of banking policy in the original Federal Reserve Act. In private correspondence commenting on an earlier draft of this chapter, Allan Meltzer suggests a possible explanation for Glass's willingness to tolerate the centralization of authority in the 1930s: 'Glass was totally opposed to Strong and New York because they made the British loan and told him that real bills was unworkable as a regulatory device. The Board, especially Miller, stuck with real bills in the 1920s. Perhaps that is why Glass supported increased centralized power in the Board.'

Indeed, as the result of the private Certificate of Deposit Account Registry Service (CDARS) account swapping product, depositors can deposit tens of millions of dollars into a single bank account and obtain 100 per cent insurance on those funds.[8]

The bank regulatory changes of the 1930s had long lives even though they were not supported by any evidence presented at the time they were enacted, or in subsequent scholarly work, suggesting that these three initiatives were warranted by the experience of the Great Depression. Certainly, no one today would argue that the real bills doctrine (which, as noted above, was Carter Glass's primary motivation in his advocacy of Regulation Q and the prohibition of underwriting by commercial banks) was a legitimate motivation for Regulation Q or the prohibition of underwriting by commercial banks (or anything else).

Glass's real bills advocacy was not the only argument in favour of Regulation Q or the prohibition of underwriting by commercial banks. Some advocates of Regulation Q saw it as a means of raising the profits of banks by limiting competition among banks. And, some advocates of the prohibition of underwriting by commercial banks argued (i) that underwriting had destabilized banks by encouraging imprudent risks, and (ii) that underwriting created conflicts of interest within banks that engaged in both lending and underwriting. The Pecora Hearings drew attention to these alleged deficiencies, and channelled much public disapproval towards large banks and Wall Street. The popular disapproval of the big Wall Street banking establishment provided popular political support for a variety of regulatory reforms, including the prohibition of underwriting by commercial banks.

Benston (1989) provides a detailed critical review of the legislative decision-making process that led to the prohibition of underwriting by commercial banks, and argues that the decision was made without any credible evidence of the alleged problems. Furthermore, there is contrary evidence. With respect to the accusations claiming that underwriting weakened banks during the Depression, White (1986) finds that underwriting was a source of diversification that reduced banks' risks during the Depression.

Concerns were also voiced about conflicts of interest between commercial bank lending and underwriting. Some alleged that commercial banks as lenders had an incentive to exaggerate the quality of the securities they underwrote, to rid themselves of bad debtors. (Such allegations were part of the aggressive attack against banks during the Pecora Hearings of 1932, and which fuelled anger against large Wall Street banks.) These also have been shown to be without merit by recent econometric studies of the underwriting activities of commercial banks during the 1920s and early 1930s (Kroszner and Rajan, 1994; Puri, 1994).

The competition argument used to defend the enactment of Regulation Q—that bank weakness resulted from excessive competition during the Depression—has been contradicted by Carlson and Mitchener's (2009) work. They show

[8] CDARS is a private company that engages in deposit insurance limit arbitrage by arranging for interbank swapping of account balances to allow depositors to enjoy the convenience of full FDIC insurance on a virtually unlimited amount deposited within one account in one bank (which is swapped out within the CDARS network to meet the official deposit insurance limit of $250,000 per account).

that the insufficiency of competition that prevailed under unit banking weakened banks during the Depression by making them more vulnerable to local idiosyncratic shocks; more competition is associated with greater stability, not less.

And, of course, the widespread bank failure experience of the 1980s illustrated once again the destabilizing effects of unit banking, which finally was brought to an end by the branching deregulation of the last two decades of the twentieth century. Most ironically of all, deposit insurance, which was chosen as an alternative to branching deregulation in the 1930s, is the only lasting bank regulatory reform of the New Deal, despite the fact that it was opposed by the Roosevelt administration and the Fed, based on its chequered history during the 1920s. That negative opinion has been borne out by decades of experience and new research on the moral-hazard consequences of deposit insurance around the world in the past 30 years. Deposit insurance, and, more broadly, the generous safety nets that bail out depositors, creditors, and stockholders of banks, is now understood to be, on net, a destabilizing rather than stabilizing influence on banking systems around the world (Barth et al., 2006; Demirguc-Kunt et al., 2009; Calomiris, 2009a).

6.5. FALSE DIAGNOSES, BASED ON LITTLE EVIDENCE, ARE SUDDENLY EMBRACED

If the bank regulatory policy ideas of the 1930s were so bad, then how did reformers secure a quick consensus for such far-reaching reforms? The answer, as always, is a combination of influences, including powerful political influence by special interests, purposeful misstatements of facts and a lack of contradictory evidence at the time (which was hard to assemble, given the speed with which regulatory change occurred), and stubborn and sincere beliefs (about the desirability of prohibiting banks from engaging in underwriting, and about the benefits of limiting interest on deposits) by powerful and credible people such as Carter Glass that were hard to falsify in real time, even though they happened to be false.

The details of how Henry Steagall won inclusion of federal deposit insurance in the 1933 Act are particularly interesting. The full account is provided in Calomiris and White (1994). Contrary to popular misconceptions, deposit insurance did *not* win the day because it was part of a bail-out of the banking system, or a means to deal with systemic risk or widespread bank runs. In fact, Congress and the Administration refused to use deposit insurance to help resolve the bank runs and insolvencies of 1932–33. Deposit insurance only went into effect *after* the resolution of troubled banks had been handled through other means (through a combination of permanent closure of deeply insolvent banks, and RFC assistance for marginal ones).

Three key factors explain Steagall's success in passing deposit insurance:

1. As chairman of the banking committee in the House of Representatives, he had effective blocking power to prevent any banking reforms from passing. In their desire to respond aggressively to the financial crisis, Carter Glass and others were keen to implement Regulation Q and the separation of

investment banking from commercial banking, and Steagall, therefore, had bargaining power.

2. The Pecora Hearings had made large banks unpopular, and populist politicians such as Henry Steagall and Huey Long fed on that sentiment to argue in favour of support for small banks. Notwithstanding the merits of Glass's views on deposit insurance, the populists had won the debate with the public. As *Business Week* (12 April 1933) put it: 'Washington does not remember any issue on which the sentiment of the country has been so undivided or so emphatically expressed as upon this.'
3. Deposit insurance was passed as a temporary system, and one that covered very few deposits, which made it easier to win approval in Congress. In the future (at the next big legislative logrolling fest in 1935, and at other similar subsequent moments), advocates would have the opportunity to bargain further, and make coverage permanent and larger (Calomiris and White, 1994; White, 1998).

6.6. THE (HIDDEN) REALLOCATION OF MONETARY POWERS

Not only did the 1930s see a major restructuring of the rules governing the banking system in 1933 (Glass–Steagall, Regulation Q, FDIC insurance), there were also significant changes in powers regarding banking and monetary policy. These included the aforementioned creation of new monetary powers by the Treasury, the creation of new authority within the Fed, and the reallocation of decision-making authority over Fed policies in 1933 and 1935.

The list of policy changes may seem difficult to characterize, since some of the changes seem to enhance the Administration's power over central banking (the 1934 Acts, and the Thomas Amendment to the AAA), while other actions seem to increase Fed independence (the vesting of authority over reserve requirements within the Fed and the elimination of non-Fed officials from the FOMC). That ambiguity was intentional. The Administration pursued these reforms in order to increase its power and reduce Fed independence during the mid-1930s, while attempting to give the opposite impression to the public.

Treasury Secretary Morgenthau believed that he controlled Fed decision making through his ability credibly to threaten use of the Exchange Stabilization Fund and other levers of control over the money supply to reverse Fed actions, if necessary:

> the way the Federal Reserve Board is set up now they can suggest but have very little power to enforce their will . . . [The Treasury's] power has been the Stabilization Fund plus the many other funds that I have at my disposal and this power has kept the open market committee in line and afraid of me. (Blum, 1959: 352)

This loss in Fed independence in the mid-1930s (owing to pressures exerted outside of formal procedures governing policy) occurred in spite of new legislative powers given to the Fed in the Banking Act of 1935 (which consolidated power within the Board of Governors and gave the Board new authorities, including control of reserve requirements). Indeed, Morgenthau intimated in his diary that he supported the 1935 Act partly because it gave the appearance of enlarged power within the Fed, which would insulate him from responsibility 'if the financial situation should go sour', but also because he did not believe that the new powers of the Fed made a substantive difference to its power, given his ability to pressure the Fed to do his bidding.

Morgenthau, like Steagall and Glass, knew how to 'use the crisis' to his own advantage by manipulating public perceptions to his own purposes. That ability allowed him to accumulate more power with less responsibility. His forecasts were prescient; he cajoled the Fed successfully in March 1937 when he pressured the Fed into supporting bond prices, after threatening to intervene in the market if they did not. That threat was credible because the Treasury had more resources available under the law to increase the money supply than the Fed (with its limited balance sheet size) had to shrink it. The Fed capitulated to Morgenthau's demands (Calomiris and Wheelock, 1998: 40).

That trend away from Fed independence accelerated during the Second World War, as monetary policy took a back seat to the war effort (Calomiris and Wheelock, 1998; Meltzer, 2003). As the Fed emerged from the Second World War, however, the wartime growth that had occurred in its balance sheet gave the Fed new power—namely, the power to shrink its now massive balance sheet. In the mid-1930s, the Fed's balance sheet was no match for Secretary Morgenthau, who had more than enough resources to offset with expansion any attempt at contraction by the Fed. After the Second World War, that was not the case. This simple arithmetic of a credible threat to shrink underlay the 1951 Accord, whereby the Fed once again secured control over monetary policy.

6.7. THE POST-DEPRESSION LEGACY OF DEPOSIT INSURANCE

I have already noted that substantial costs have been attributed to Regulation Q and the separation of underwriting and lending during the post-Depression era. Regulation Q limits on deposit interest rates, combined with the high inflation of the late 1960s and 1970s, produced a massive financial disintermediation from the banking system as depositors sought higher returns from unregulated products (e.g. money market mutual funds, and commercial paper issued by finance companies). The separation of commercial banking from securities underwriting weakened US banks relative to foreign rivals that were not hamstrung by those limitations, which was the proximate cause of Chairman Greenspan's campaign to loosen those restrictions (Calomiris, 2000).

What about deposit insurance? To what extent can it be argued that deposit insurance—whatever its political motives—has been a positive contributor to systemic stability? Even though federal deposit insurance was not used in the 1930s to end bank runs or to assist failing banks, it is conceivable that its presence could have contributed to the financial stability that the US enjoyed in the 1950s and 1960s. While it is not possible to dismiss this possibility, there are several powerful arguments against it.

First, it is clear that deposit insurance is not necessary for banking stability. The experience of Canada prior to 1935—a branch banking system without even a central bank, which avoided financial panics—is illustrative of a broader pattern in historical banking. With the exception of the six US banking panics of the pre-First World War era, and four episodes of severe banking system insolvency outside the US that were linked to government subsidization of real estate expansion, banking crises (defined either as severe insolvency waves or disruptive banking panics), were virtually absent from the world in the 40 years prior to the First World War. A combination of branch banking and conservative central banking (defined as the willingness to provide liquidity support during crises, but not public bail-outs of insolvent banks) seems to have accounted for that favourable experience (see Calomiris, 2009a).

Second, there is little empirical support for the stabilizing role of deposit insurance. In theory, there are two offsetting potential influences from deposit insurance, one stabilizing, the other one destabilizing. The stabilizing influence is the reduction in liquidity risk resulting from the protection of depositors (i.e. the reduced risk that insured depositors would withdraw funds from banks that they believed were weak). The destabilizing influence of deposit insurance results from the increased tolerance for risk taking that occurs within protected banks. The greater tolerance for risk taking encourages greater risk taking and greater financial system volatility, either as the result of conscious risk taking by bankers—the so-called 'moral-hazard' problem—or as the result of undisciplined incompetence in risk management. In practice, the empirical literature on deposit insurance has concluded that deposit insurance tends to be destabilizing. That tendency is visible within and outside the US for the post-Depression period (see Demirguc-Kunt and Detragiache, 2000; Demirguc-Kunt et al., 2009; and Calomiris, 2009a).

Third, the macroeconomic stability of the US in the 1950s and 1960s is better explained by factors other than deposit insurance that were plausibly exogenous to the presence of deposit insurance. Measures of financial volatility (stock market returns volatility, interest rate volatility, inflation volatility) were all relatively low during that period. Furthermore, for large city banks in the US, deposit insurance offered very limited support against liquidity risk prior to the mid-1970s, since coverage was limited to small deposits. Banks in New York, in particular, had many large deposit accounts which were not covered by the limits in place prior to 1974. The limits rose from the $10,000 ceiling enacted in 1950 to $15,000 in 1966, and $20,000 in 1969. Despite their relatively unprotected status, there is no evidence suggesting that New York banks experienced runs or other severe problems owing to their higher liquidity risk from 1934 through the 1970s. The limit grew dramatically after 1974, when it was initially doubled to $40,000, to then more than doubled in 1980 at $100,000.

6.8. CONCLUSION

As policy makers today contemplate multiple and dramatic bank regulatory proposals in the wake of the subprime mortgage bust, it is useful to consider several aspects of the bank regulatory changes of the 1930s, which have useful lessons for policy makers today.

The central microeconomic cause of banking system fragility in the US, before, during, and after the Depression, was the unit banking structure of the US system. Not only was this unit banking structure not dismantled by 1930s regulatory reforms, the reforms of the 1930s intentionally halted the bank consolidation movement of the 1920s by offering new protection to unit banks in the form of federal deposit insurance (which came into play in 1934). Deposit insurance was correctly viewed at the time as a destabilizing influence and was opposed (privately) by virtually every financial authority of the time, including President Roosevelt. It succeeded politically because its advocates were masters of manipulating public opinion, and because their opponents were so eager to have their own (misguided, but sincerely motivated) reforms passed, that they were willing to compromise on deposit insurance.

The major banking reforms of the 1930s were justified by advocates as solutions to the problems that had plagued the banking system during the Depression, but financial historians have been virtually unanimous in disputing those claims. In the case of deposit insurance, there was never a credible empirical basis for believing that it was warranted, or that it would stabilize the banking system. Other 1930s banking reforms (separation of underwriting from lending, limits on deposit interest rates, and the changes in the structure of decision making in monetary policy) were unrelated to the shocks of the Depression; they were implemented in the 1930s because the banking shocks of the Depression created an 'up-for-grabs' environment that offered new opportunities for political entrepreneurs with longstanding agendas—especially advocates of the real bills doctrine—who couched their pre-existing agenda as a response to the Depression. (In the current environment, one can see a repetition of this phenomenon in Paul Volcker's current advocacy of his longstanding opposition to proprietary trading in banks, which had nothing whatsoever to do with the recent financial crisis—see Calomiris (2010a).)

Ironically, the primary motivations for the main bank regulatory reforms in the 1930s (Regulation Q, the separation of investment banking from commercial banking, and the creation of federal deposit insurance) were to preserve and enhance two of the most disastrous policies that contributed to the severity and depth of the Great Depression—unit banking and the real bills doctrine. Other regulatory changes, affecting the allocation of power between the Fed and the Treasury, were intended to reduce the independence of the Fed, while giving the opposite impression.

The ill-advised bank regulatory policies of the 1930s have had very long lives. Deposit insurance has grown from a temporary system designed to subsidize the risks of small unit banks to a permanent system that now covers virtually all deposits in the US. Statutory limitations on bank branching, which deposit insurance facilitated (by removing competitive pressures on small unit banks), were finally eliminated during the 1980s and 1990s, in reaction to widespread banking distress during the 1980s, culminating in free interstate branching after 1994. Limitations on interest rates for deposits have mainly been removed, but some still persist, and the removal did not begin until the 1980s. The separation of underwriting and lending activities was relaxed beginning in the late 1980s, and was repealed by the Gramm–Leach–Bliley Act of 1999. The structural changes in the Federal Reserve System passed in the 1930s remain in place, although subsequent events (the Second World War expansion of the Fed's balance sheet) set the stage for restoring Fed independence in the 1950s.

What are the lessons of the banking reforms of the 1930s for policy makers today? The overarching lesson is that the aftermath of crises are moments of high risk in public policy. The Great Depression provoked banking reform legislation that was quick, comprehensive, and unusually responsive to popular opinion. Each of these three aspects increases the risk that regulation will have adverse consequences. When regulation is passed quickly, there is little time to verify the empirical merits of the allegations that inspire it, which admits much mischief in the advocacy of regulation solutions to alleged causes of the crisis. Political entrepreneurs—Glass, Steagall, and Morgenthau in the 1930s—will take advantage of the opportunities to act quickly without having to justify the crackpot theories, special interests, or power plays that motivate them. Comprehensive regulation invites logrolling compromises that increase each political entrepreneur's ability to get the object of his desire by creating an unusually high tolerance for special interest measures or bad ideas in the interest of passing other measures. And when the public is engaged in the regulatory debate in such a heightened way, the technical issues of regulatory design can take a back seat to populist pressures for action on ideas that sound good to an angry public.

These three attributes—little deliberation, a comprehensive agenda, and an engaged public—which were so important during the bank regulatory debates following the Depression are not surprising in the wake of a banking crisis. Indeed, the recent crisis has provoked precisely the same sort of reaction. Public anger fuelled the perceived need to act quickly. Sensing the opportunity to pass landmark legislation, the Obama administration insisted on a comprehensive reform package, rather than a series of individual reform measures passed over time. Republican opposition to the Dodd–Frank bill invited political threats from Democrats to hold Republicans accountable in the autumn 2010 elections for a failure to respond to the public outcry for a bill. A poll by the Pew Trusts indicated overwhelming support by the public for doing something fast, and the opposition of several Republicans wilted in the electoral heat.

The Dodd–Frank Act has many flaws. It claims to reduce the chance of future bail-outs of large banks through the creation of a new resolution authority. Such an authority may make sense (Calomiris, 2010b), but the details of the authority as enacted (which extends FDIC resolution to non-banks and creates no credible barrier to unwarranted bail-outs) institutionalizes and broadens bail-out authority, making bail-outs more likely and placing no bounds on the ability of the FDIC to fully protect any holders of bank or non-bank debts.

Just as the Federal Reserve Act of 1913, and the Banking Acts of 1933 and 1935, did nothing to address the fundamental problem of unit banking, the Dodd–Frank Act does nothing to address one of the primary causes of the crisis—politically motivated government subsidization of mortgage risk in the financial system (Calomiris, 2008, 2009b and 2009C; Wallison and Calomiris, 2009). And, just as the banking crisis of the 1930s and the 1933 Act gave opportunity to unrealized objectives driven by advocates of the real bills doctrine, the Dodd–Frank Act contains reform proposals that are obviously unrelated to the crisis, but driven by the pet theories of influential people—most obviously, the Volcker Rule's proposed prohibition of proprietary trading (Calomiris, 2010a). Finally, just as the 1933 Act promoted special interest logrolling by Henry Steagall, the Dodd–Frank Act is full of special interest provisions (e.g. new outreach measures to expand banking services for the poor, and an unprecedented imposition of employment quotas for minorities and women on regulated financial institutions, to name only two). In all these respects, the Dodd–Frank Act has a great deal in common with the 1933 Act.

The ill-conceived banking legislation of the 1930s took very little time to pass, but a great deal of time to disappear, and its most robust element (deposit insurance) looks to be a permanent feature of the banking system going forward. This should be a cautionary tale for current reformers, but tales from the past are likely to have little effect. Politicians have their own agendas, especially when pursuing regulatory reforms in the wake of a crisis. Learning from history is not high on that list, and to financial historians, that is a scary thought.

BIBLIOGRAPHY

Barth, J., Caprio, Jr., G., and Levine, R. (2006), *Rethinking Bank Regulation: Till Angels Govern*. Cambridge: Cambridge University Press.

Beim, D. and Calomiris, C. W. (2001), *Emerging Financial Markets*. New York: McGraw Hill.

Benston, G. (1989), *The Separation of Commercial and Investment Banking: The Glass–Steagall Act Revisited and Reconsidered*. Norwell: Kluwer Academic Press.

Bernanke, B. S. (1983), 'Nonmonetary Effects of the Financial Crisis in the Propagation of the Great Depression', *American Economic Review*, 73(June), 257–76.

Bernstein, A., Hughson, E., and Weidenmier, M. D. (2008), 'Can a Lender of Last Resort Stabilize Financial Markets? Lessons from the Founding of the Fed', NBER Working Paper 14422.

Blum, J. M. (1959), *From the Morgenthau Diaries: Years of Crisis, 1928–1938*. Boston: Houghton Mifflin.

Bruner, R. F. and Carr, S. D. (2007), *The Panic of 1907: Lessons Learned from the Market's Perfect Storm*. Hoboken, NJ: John Wiley & Sons.

Calomiris, C. W. (1989), 'Deposit Insurance: Lessons from the Record', *Economic Perspectives*, Federal Reserve Bank of Chicago, May/June, 10–30.

Calomiris, C. W. (1990), 'Is Deposit Insurance Necessary? A Historical Perspective', *Journal of Economic History*, 50, 283–95.

Calomiris, C. W. (1992), 'Do Vulnerable Economies Need Deposit Insurance? Lessons from US Agriculture in the 1920s', in P. L. Brock (ed.), *If Texas Were Chile: A Primer on Bank Regulation*. San Francisco: The Sequoia Institute, 237–349, 450–8.

Calomiris, C. W. (2000), *US Bank Deregulation in Historical Perspective*. Cambridge: Cambridge University Press.

Calomiris, C. W. (2008), 'Statement before the Committee on Oversight and Government Reform, United States House of Representatives', 9 December, available at <http://www0.gsb.columbia.edu/faculty/ccalomiris/papers/CalomirisF&FTestimony2008.pdf>.

Calomiris, C. W. (2009a), 'Banking Crises and the Rules of the Game', Working Paper. New York: Columbia Business School.

Calomiris, C. W. (2009b), 'The Subprime Turmoil: What's Old, What's New, and What's Next', *Journal of Structured Finance*, 15(Spring), 6–52.

Calomiris, C. W. (2009c), 'Financial Innovation, Regulation, and Reform', *Cato Journal*, 29 (Winter), 65–92.

Calomiris, C. W. (2010a), 'The Volcker Rule: Unworkable and Unwise', *e21 Economic Policies for the 21st Century*, available at <https://www.economics21.org/commentary/volcker-rule-unworkable-and-unwise>.

Calomiris, C. W. (2010b), 'How To Fix the Resolution Problem of Large, Complex, Nonbank Financial Institutions', available at <http://www.economics21.org/commentary/how-fix-resolution-problem-large-complex-nonbank-financial-institutions>.

Calomiris, C. W. and Gorton, G. (1991), 'The Origins of Banking Panics: Models, Facts, and Bank Regulation', in R. G. Hubbard (ed.), *Financial Markets and Financial Crises*. Chicago, IL: University of Chicago Press, 107–73.

Calomiris, C. W. and Mason, J. R. (1997), 'Contagion and Bank Failures During the Great Depression: The June 1932 Chicago Banking Panic', *American Economic Review*, 87, 863–83.

Calomiris, C. W. and Mason, J. R. (2003a), 'Fundamentals, Panics and Bank Distress During the Depression', *American Economic Review*, 93, 1615–47.

Calomiris, C. W. and Mason, J. R. (2003b), 'Consequences of Bank Distress During the Great Depression', *American Economic Review*, 93, 937–47.

Calomiris, C. W. and Ramirez, C. (2010), 'The Political Economy of Bank Entry Restrictions: Theory and Evidence from the US in the 1920s', Working Paper.

Calomiris, C. W. and Schweikart, L. (1991), 'The Panic of 1857: Origins, Transmission, and Containment', *Journal of Economic History*, 51, 807–34.

Calomiris, C. W. and Wheelock, D. C. (1998), 'Was the Great Depression a Watershed for American Monetary Policy?', in M. D. Bordo, C. Goldin, and E. N. White (eds), *The Defining Moment: The Great Depression and the American Economy in the Twentieth Century*. Chicago, Ill.: University of Chicago Press, 23–66.

Calomiris, C. W. and White, E. N. (1994), 'The Origins of Federal Deposit Insurance', in C. Goldin and G. Libecap (eds), *The Regulated Economy: A Historical Approach to Political Economy*. Chicago, IL: University of Chicago Press, 145–88.

Calomiris, C. W. and Wilson, B. (2004), 'Bank Capital and Portfolio Management: The 1930s "Capital Crunch" and Scramble to Shed Risk', *Journal of Business*, 77, 421–55.

Caprio, G. and Klingebiel, D. (1996), 'Bank Insolvencies: Cross-country Experience', Working Paper No. 1620. Washington, DC: World Bank.

Carlson, M. and Mitchener, K. J. (2009), 'Branch Banking as a Device for Discipline: Competition and Bank Survivorship during the Great Depression', *Journal of Political Economy*, 117, 165–210.

Correa, R. (2008), 'Bank Integration and Financial Constraints: Evidence from US Firms', Working Paper, Board of Governors of the Federal Reserve System, March.

Demirguc-Kunt, A. and Detragiache, E. (2000), 'Does Deposit Insurance Increase Banking System Stability?', Conference Paper, The World Bank.

Demirguc-Kunt, A., Kane, E., and Laeven, L. (eds) (2009), *Deposit Insurance Around the World*. Cambridge, Mass.: MIT Press.

Federal Reserve Board (1943 [1976]), *Banking and Monetary Statistics: 1914–1941*. Washington: Board of Governors of the Federal Reserve System.

Fisher, I. (1933), 'The Debt-deflation Theory of Great Depressions', *Econometrica*, 1, 337–57.

Flood, M. (1991), 'The Great Deposit Insurance Debate', *Federal Reserve Bank of St. Louis Review*, 74(July–August), 51–77.

Gorton, G. (1985), 'Clearing Houses and the Origin of Central Banking in the United States', *Journal of Economic History*, 45, 277–83.

Grossman, R. S. (1994), 'The Shoe That Didn't Drop: Explaining Banking Stability During the Great Depression', *Journal of Economic History*, 54, 654–82.

James, M. and James, B. R. (1954), *Biography of a Bank: The Story of Bank of America NT&SA*. New York: Harper.

Kaufman, G. G. and Mote, L. (1990), 'Glass–Steagall: Repeal by Regulatory and Judicial Reinterpretation', *Banking Law Journal*, September–October, 388–421.

Kroszner, R. S. and Rajan, R. G. (1994), 'Is the Glass–Steagall Act Justified? A Study of the US Experience with Universal Banking Prior to 1933', *American Economic Review*, 84 (September), 810–32.

Lee, S. J. (2010), 'Performance Comparisons Across Merger Cohorts: The US Banking Industry after Branching Deregulation', Working Paper, Columbia University.

Mason, J. R. (2001), 'Do Lender of Last Resort Policies Matter? The Effects of Reconstruction Finance Corporation Assistance to Banks During the Great Depression', *Journal of Financial Services Research*, 20 September, 77–95.

Meltzer, A. H. (2003), *A History of the Federal Reserve, 1913–1951*. Chicago, Ill.: University of Chicago Press.

Miron, J. (1986), 'Financial Panics, the Seasonality of the Nominal Interest Rate, and the Founding of the Fed', *American Economic Review*, 76, 125–40.

Puri, M. (1994), 'The Long Term Default Performance of Bank Underwritten Securities Issues', *Journal of Banking and Finance*, 18, 397–481.

Sprague, O. M. W. (1910) [1977], *History of Crises Under the National Banking System*. New York: Augustus M. Kelley.

Strouse, J. (1999), *Morgan: American Financier*. New York: Random House.

US Bureau of the Census (1970), *Historical Statistics of the United States*, vol. I. Washington, DC: United States Census Bureau.

Wallison, P. J. and Calomiris, C. W. (2009), 'The Last Trillion-dollar Commitment: The Destruction of Fannie Mae and Freddie Mac', *Journal of Structured Finance*, 15(Spring): 71–80.

Wheelock, D. C. (1991), *The Strategy and Consistency of Federal Reserve Monetary Policy, 1924–1933*. Cambridge: Cambridge University Press.

White, E. N. (1983), *The Regulation and Reform of the American Banking System, 1900–1929*. Princeton, NJ: Princeton University Press.

White, E. N. (1984a), 'A Reinterpretation of the Banking Crisis of 1930', *Journal of Economic History*, 44, 119–38.

White, E. N. (1984b), 'Voting for Costly Regulation: Evidence from the Banking Referenda in Illinois, 1924', *Southern Economic Journal*, 51, 1084–98.

White, E. N. (1985), 'The Merger Movement in Banking, 1919–1933', *Journal of Economic History*, 45(June), 285–91.

White, E. N. (1986), 'Before the Glass–Steagall Act: An Analysis of the Investment Banking Activities of National Banks', *Explorations in Economic History*, 23(January), 33–55.

White, E. N. (1990), 'Carter Glass', in *The Encyclopedia of American Business History and Biography: 1913–1989*. Columbia, SC: Bruccoli Clark Layman, 157–64.

White, E. N. (1998), 'The Legacy of Deposit Insurance: The Growth, Spread, and Cost of Insuring Financial Intermediaries', in M. D. Bordo, C. Goldin, and E. N. White (eds), *The Defining Moment: The Great Depression and the American Economy in the Twentieth Century*. Chicago, Ill.: University of Chicago Press, 87–124.

Wicker, E. (2000), *Banking Panics of the Gilded Age*. Cambridge: Cambridge University Press.

7

The Banking Panics in the United States in the 1930s: Some Lessons for Today

Michael Bordo and John Landon-Lane

7.1. INTRODUCTION: THE FRIEDMAN AND SCHWARTZ HYPOTHESIS AND THE SUBSEQUENT DEBATE

In this chapter we raise and answer some questions about the recent financial crisis in light of the experience of the Great Depression of the 1930s. We ask what was similar and what different between now and then, and examine the implications of the 1930s banking panics for policy towards recent banking crises.

The Great Depression was by far the greatest economic event of the twentieth century and comparisons to it were rife during the recent Great Recession. Milton Friedman and Anna Schwartz's *A Monetary History of the United States 1867 to 1960* (1963) has long been viewed as the classic treatment of the Great Depression in the United States.[1] They labelled the downturn in the United States from August 1929 to March 1933 the Great Contraction. Since that event, a voluminous literature has debated its causes in the United States and its transmission around the world.

Friedman and Schwartz (1963) challenged the prevailing Keynesian view and attributed the Great Contraction from 1929 to 1933 to a collapse of the money supply by one-third, brought about by a failure of Federal Reserve policy. The story they tell begins with the Fed tightening policy in early 1928 to stem the Wall Street boom. Fed officials believing in the real bills doctrine were concerned that the asset-price boom would lead to inflation. The subsequent downturn beginning

[1] At the time, the consensus view was that the slump was a consequence of the speculative boom of the 1920s. The boom was regarded as a manifestation of deep-seated structural imbalances seen in overinvestment. Indeed, according to the Austrian view which prevailed in the interwar period, depressions were part of the normal operation of the business cycle. Policy prescriptions from this view included tight money, tight fiscal policy, and wage cuts to restore balance. Keynes (1936) rejected these prescriptions and the classical view that eventually a return to full employment would be achieved by falling wages and prices. He attributed the slump to a collapse of aggregate demand, especially private investment. His policy prescription was to use fiscal policy—both pump priming and massive government expenditures. In the post-Second World War era, Keynesian views dominated the economics profession and the explanation given for the depression emphasized different components of aggregate expenditure.

in August 1929 was soon followed by the stock market crash in October. Friedman and Schwartz, unlike Galbraith (1955), did not view the crash as the cause of the subsequent depression. They saw it as an exacerbating factor (whereby adverse expectations led the public to attempt to increase their liquidity) in the decline in activity in the first year of the Contraction.

The real problem arose with a series of four banking panics beginning in October 1930 and ending with Roosevelt's national banking holiday in March 1933. According to Friedman and Schwartz, the banking panics worked through the money multiplier to reduce the money stock (via a decrease in the public's deposit-to-currency ratio). The panic in turn reflected what Friedman and Schwartz called a 'contagion of fear' as the public, fearful of being last in line to convert their deposits into currency, staged runs on the banking system, leading to massive bank failures. In today's terms it would be a 'liquidity shock'. The collapse in money supply in turn led to a decline in spending and, in the face of nominal rigidities, especially of sticky money wages, a decline in employment and output. The process was aggravated by banks dumping their earning assets in a fire sale and by debt deflation. Both forces reduced the value of banks' collateral and weakened their balance sheets, in turn leading to weakening and insolvency of banks with initially sound assets.

According to Friedman and Schwartz, had the Fed acted as a proper lender-of-last-resort, as it was established to be in the Federal Reserve Act of 1913, then it would have offset the effects of the banking panics on the money stock and prevented the Great Contraction. Since the publication of *A Monetary History*, a voluminous literature has arisen over the issues whether the banking panics were really panics in the sense of illiquidity shocks or whether they reflected endogenous insolvency responses to a recession caused by other forces, such as a collapse of autonomous expenditures or productivity shocks. If the panics really reflected insolvency rather than liquidity shocks, then the case Friedman and Schwartz made that expansionary monetary policy could have avoided the Great Contraction would be considerably weakened.

Ben Bernanke, the current chairman of the Federal Reserve, also attributed the Great Contraction to monetary forces and especially the collapse of the banking system. However, he placed less emphasis on the effects via the quantity theory of money on spending as argued by Friedman and Schwartz, and more on the consequences of the collapse of the banking system in raising the cost of financial intermediation.

Thus the issue of whether illiquidity shocks triggering banking panics was at the heart of the Great Contraction is of crucial importance for the role of monetary policy in dealing with banking crises such as we recently witnessed. Indeed, in the crisis of 2007–08, the Bernanke Fed apparently learned the lesson from Friedman and Schwartz (Bernanke, 2002) by following expansionary monetary and credit policy and, to a large extent, prevented a repeat of the 1930s experience. Although there was not a classic Friedman and Schwartz banking panic in 2007–08, there was a panic in the shadow banking system and, unlike in the 1930s, many US banks deemed too big and too interconnected to fail were plagued with insolvency and were rescued by fiscal bail-outs.

In this chapter we revisit the debate over illiquidity versus insolvency in the Great Contraction. Section 7.2 discusses the recent debate and presents some econometric evidence that suggests that illiquidity shocks dominated in the banking panics in 1930 and 1931 while the last panic of 1933 was largely an insolvency event. In section 7.3 we examine why the US had so many bank failures and was so prone to banking failures in its history. Sections 7.4 and 7.5 compare the financial crises of the 1930s in the US to the crisis of 2007–08. Section 7.6 concludes with some lessons for policy.

7.2. THE RECENT DEBATE OVER US BANKING PANICS IN THE 1930s: ILLIQUIDITY VERSUS INSOLVENCY

In this section we survey recent literature on whether the clusters of bank failures that occurred between 1930 and 1933 were really panics in the sense of illiquidity shocks.[2] This has important implications for the causes of the Great Depression. If the clusters of bank failures were really panics, then it would support the original Friedman and Schwartz explanation. If the clusters of bank failures primarily reflected insolvency then other factors, such as a decline in autonomous expenditures or negative productivity shocks (Prescott, 1999), must explain the Great Contraction. We present some econometric evidence largely in support of the Friedman and Schwartz position.

Friedman and Schwartz viewed the banking panics as largely the consequence of illiquidity, especially in 1930–31. Their key evidence was a decline in the deposit–currency ratio, which lowered the money multiplier, money supply, and nominal spending. They describe the panic in the autumn of 1930 as leading to 'a contagion of fear' especially after the failure of the Bank of United States in New York City in December. They also discussed the effects of the initial banking panic leading to contagion by banks dumping their earning assets in a 'fire sale' in order to build up their reserves. This, in turn, led to the failure of otherwise solvent banks. Wicker (1996) disputes whether the 1930 panic and the spring 1931 Friedman and Schwartz panics were national in scope, but agrees with them that all four banking panics were liquidity shocks.

By contrast both Temin (1976) and White (1984), the latter using disaggregated data on a sample of national banks, argued that the original 1930 banking panic was not a liquidity event but a solvency event occurring in banks in agricultural regions in the south and the mid-west which had been weakened by the recession. These small unit banks came out of the 1920s in a fragile state, reflecting declining agricultural prices and oversupply after the First World War. As in Wicker (1980), they identify the locus of the crisis as the collapse, on 7 November 1930, of the Caldwell investment bank holding company of Nashville, Tennessee, a chain bank (in which one holding company had a controlling interest in a chain of banks), and its correspondent network across a half dozen states.

[2] Panics can arise because of exogenous illiquidity shocks in the context of the Diamond and Dybvig (1983) random withdrawals model, or in the context of asymmetric-information-induced runs and panics (Calomiris and Gorton, 1991).

Calomiris and Mason (2003), following the approach taken in Calomiris and Mason (1997) to analyse a local banking panic in Chicago in June 1932, use disaggregated data on all of the individual member banks of the Federal Reserve System to directly address the question of whether the clusters of banking failures of 1930–33 reflected illiquidity or insolvency. Based on a survival-duration model on 8,700 individual banks, they relate the timing of bank failures to various characteristics of the banks as well as to local, regional, and national shocks. They find that a list of fundamentals (including bank size, the presence of branch banking, net worth relative to assets as a measure of leverage, reliance on demand debt, market power, the value of the portfolio, loan quality, and the share of agriculture), as well as several macro variables, largely explains the timing of the bank failures. When they add into the regression as regressors the Friedman and Schwartz panic windows (or Wicker's amendments to them), they turn out to be of minimal significance. Thus they conclude that, with the exception of the 1933 banking panic, which, as Wicker (1996) argued, reflected a cumulative series of state bank suspensions in January and February leading to the national banking holiday on 6 March, illiquidity was inconsequential.

Richardson (2007) provides a new comprehensive data source on the reasons for bank suspensions from the archives of the Federal Reserve Board of Governors including all Fed member banks and non-member banks (both state and local) from August 1929 to just before the bank holiday in March 1933. He also distinguished between temporary and permanent suspensions. Based on answers to a questionnaire used by bank examiners after each bank suspension, Richardson put together a complete list of the causes of each suspension. The categories include: depositor runs, declining asset prices, the failure of correspondents, mergers, mismanagement, and defalcations. Richardson then classified each bank suspension into categories reflecting illiquidity, insolvency, or both. With these data he then constructed indices of illiquidity and insolvency. His data show that 60 per cent of the suspensions during the period reflected insolvency, 40 per cent illiquidity. Moreover, he shows that the ratio of illiquidity to insolvency spikes during the Friedman and Schwartz (and also Wicker) panic windows (see Figure 7.1). This evidence in some respects complements the Friedman and Schwartz and Wicker stories, and those of Temin and White. During the panics, illiquidity rises relative to insolvency; between the panics insolvency increases relative to illiquidity. Consistent with the Friedman and Schwartz stories, the panics were driven by illiquidity shocks seen in increased hoarding, but after the panics, in the face of deteriorating economic conditions, bank insolvencies continued to rise. This is consistent with the evidence of Temin and White. The failures continued through the contraction until the banking holiday of the week of 6 March 1933 (with the exception of the spring of 1932 while the Fed was temporarily engaged in open-market purchases).

Richardson (2006) backs up the illiquidity story with detailed evidence on the 1930 banking panic. As described in Wicker (1980), the failure of Caldwell and Co. in November was the signature event of this crisis. Richardson uses his new database to identify the cascade of failures through the correspondent bank networks based on the Caldwell banks. During this period, most small rural banks maintained deposits on reserve with larger city banks that, in turn, would clear their cheques through big city clearinghouses and/or the Federal Reserve

System. When Caldwell collapsed, so did the correspondent network. Moreover, Richardson and Troost (2009) clearly show that, when the tidal wave from Caldwell hit the banks of the state of Mississippi in December, the banks in the southern half of the state, under the jurisdiction of the Federal Reserve Bank of Atlanta, fared much better (had a lower failure rate) than those in the northern half, under the jurisdiction of the Federal Reserve Bank of St Louis. The Atlanta Fed followed Bagehot's Rule, discounting freely the securities of illiquid but solvent member banks. The St Louis Fed followed the real bills doctrine and was reluctant to open the discount-window to its member banks in trouble. This pattern holds up when the authors control for fundamentals using a framework like that in Calomiris and Mason (2003).[3]

Finally, Christiano et al. (2003) build a dynamic stochastic general equilibrium (DSGE) model of the Great Contraction, incorporating monetary and financial shocks. They find that the key propagation channels explaining the slump were the decline in the deposit–currency ratio, amplified by Bernanke et al.'s (1996) financial accelerator. The liquidity shock reduced funding for firms, lowering investment and firms' net worth. At the same time, the increased currency hoarding reduced consumption expenditure. Their simulations, like those of McCallum (1990) and Bordo et al. (1995) show that expansionary open-market purchases could have offset these shocks.

In sum, the debate over illiquidity versus insolvency in the failures of US banks hinges on the use of aggregate versus disaggregate data. Aggregate data tend to favour illiquidity and the presence of and importance of banking panics in creating the Great Contraction. Disaggregate data tend to focus on insolvency driven by the recession and to downplay the role of the panics in creating the Great Contraction. However, the recent, more comprehensive, data unearthed by Richardson, as well as the Christiano et al. model, suggest that the original Friedman and Schwartz story may well prevail.

7.2.1. Empirical evidence

In Bordo and Landon-Lane (2010) a vector autoregression (VAR) analysis of the determinants of bank failures is undertaken using the data of Richardson (2007). The VAR used includes the following six variables: bank failures/suspensions due to illiquidity; banks failures/suspensions due to insolvency; total bank failures/suspensions; the growth rate of money supply; the change in the unemployment rate; and the quality spread. The variables are ordered as listed above so that bank failures/suspensions will contemporaneously affect money, unemployment, and the quality spread.

The most important assumption is the ordering of the bank failures/suspensions due to illiquidity series before the bank failures/suspensions due to insolvency series in the VAR. In Richardson (2007) banks that fail or are suspended for

[3] Carlson (2008) shows that, during the panic, banks that would otherwise have merged with stronger banks rather than fail were prevented from doing so.

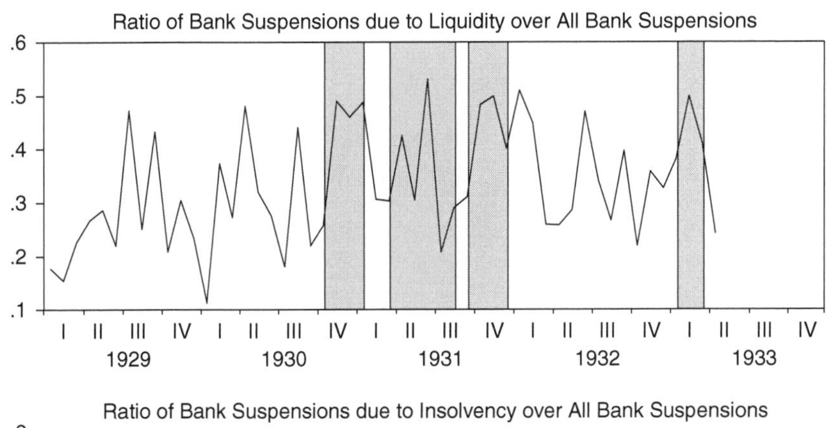

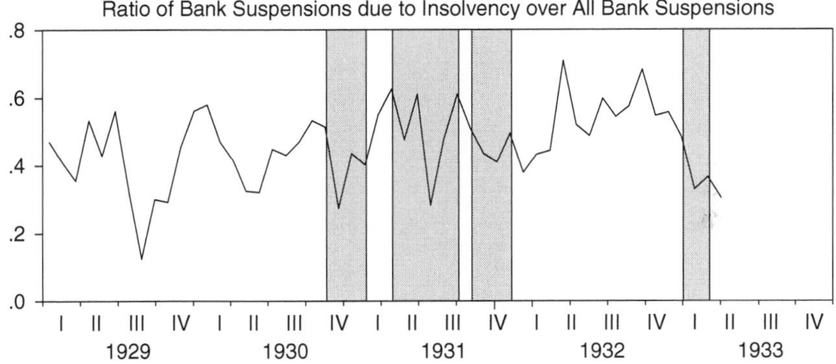

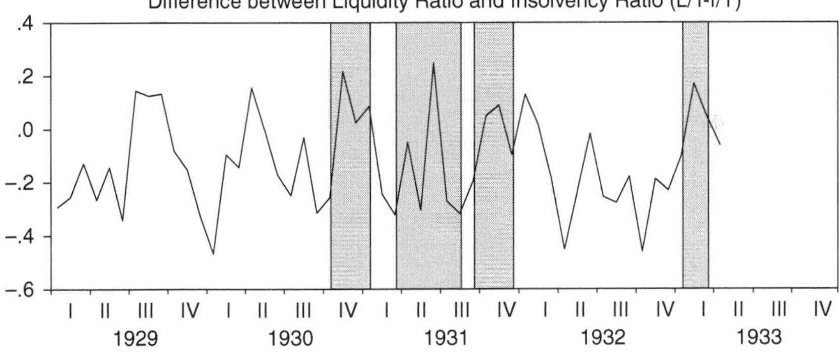

Fig. 7.1. Bank failures and suspensions

reasons of illiquidity are counted in the number of fails/suspensions due to liquidity, and banks that fail or are suspended due to insolvency are assigned to the number of fails/suspensions due to insolvency. It is possible to imagine a situation where a bank run (an illiquidity shock) may cause banks that are otherwise solvent to fail due to illiquidity. Insolvent banks may also be caught up in the bank run and therefore it is natural to think that bank failures due to illiquidity will contemporaneously affect banks failures/suspensions due to insolvency.[4]

The failure of insolvent banks would not immediately affect illiquid, but otherwise solvent, banks, at least in the short run. However, the solvency shock may also cause, through contagion, a run on otherwise healthy banks, especially if there was a run-up of closures of insolvent banks preceding the bank run. Our identifying assumption is that if the insolvency shock causes a bank run then this will happen with a time lag. That is, the identifying assumption is that the illiquidity shock might cause some insolvent banks to fail contemporaneously, whereas the insolvency shock will lead to failures due to illiquidity only with a lag. The final variable is total bank failures and is not exactly equal to the sum of the previous two bank failure series. This is because not all bank failures are attributed to illiquidity or insolvency, as noted in the previous paragraph.

The ordering we choose for the last three variables is the following: the first variable is the growth rate of the money supply; the second is the change in the unemployment rate; and the third is the quality spread. The triangular ordering we use implies, then, that each variable contemporaneously affects each variable ordered below it, but not any variable ordered above it in the vector. Thus, a change in the growth rate of money supply contemporaneously affects the change in unemployment and the quality spread, while the change in the unemployment rate contemporaneously affects the quality spread. These variables then affect bank failures/suspensions with a lag.

Thus, we identify six shocks in total that we interpret as follows: the first shock is the illiquidity shock; the second is the insolvency shock; while the third is a bank failure/suspension residual shock. It is the shock to banks failures/suspensions that cannot be attributed to either illiquidity or insolvency. The next three shocks are a money growth rate shock, an aggregate real shock to unemployment that is orthogonal to the money growth shock, and a shock to the quality spread that is orthogonal to all the previous shocks. We might consider this shock to be a credit shock. Note that we cannot, with this specification, identify supply or demand shocks for both the money shocks and aggregate real shocks.

The reduced form VAR is estimated using ordinary least squares with two lags of each variable in each equation. It was determined that the money supply and unemployment series were non-stationary, so that all variables enter the VAR in log-levels except for money supply and the unemployment rate which enter as first differences of the log-level. The sample period used (based on Richardson's data) finished in February 1933 and so does not include the period of the bank holiday starting on 6 March 1933.

The lag structure was determined using various information criteria and the standard sequential likelihood ratio tests. All information criteria and the sequential likelihood ratio test suggest two lags should be included. The results suggest that there are a large number of significant contemporaneous relationships between the variables. All coefficients are significant except for the effect of the illiquidity and insolvency shocks on the growth rate of money supply.

[4] These technically insolvent banks may still be operating owing to asymmetric information between depositors and bank operators.

Orthogonalized impulse response functions were computed, using the ordering described above, in order to determine the effect of the identified shocks on the variables of the system. It is clear from the results reported in Bordo and Landon-Lane (2010) that the illiquidity shock has a large and persistent effect on total bank failures/suspensions. The forecast error variance decompositions show that the illiquidity shock accounts for roughly 50 per cent of the forecast error, with the insolvency shock only accounting for 16 per cent. Thus, it appears that the illiquidity shock is very important for explaining total bank failures/suspensions. Money supply shocks also have an effect on total bank failures/suspensions. A positive shock to money growth has the effect of lowering bank failures/suspensions. This result is persistent and occurs for each of the bank failure/suspension series. The effect of money is especially strong and persistent for the bank failures/suspensions due to insolvency series. This result suggests that monetary policy aimed at increasing the growth rate of money may have helped to mitigate some of the bank failures/suspensions that occurred during the early 1930s. This result reinforces the views of McCallum (1990), Bordo et al. (1995), and Christiano et al. (2003).

The other impulse response functions, reported in Bordo and Landon-Lane (2010), support the identification assumption that bank failures/suspensions contemporaneously affect money, unemployment, and the quality spread, and that these three variables feed back into the bank failures/suspensions series with some lag. The illiquidity shock is seen to have a strong direct and indirect effect on total bank failures/suspensions due to insolvency, with the illiquidity shock affecting money supply, which in turn affects bank failures/suspensions due to insolvency.

The impulse response functions, together with the variance decompositions, show that the illiquidity shock is very important in explaining the bank failures/suspensions during the early 1930s. In order to determine if the illiquidity shocks played a role during the particular financial crisis windows identified by Friedman and Schwartz (1963), we now turn to historical decompositions. Figure 7.2 contains historical decompositions for the total bank failures/suspensions series. Each panel of Figure 7.2 contains a simulated total bank failures/suspensions series under the hypothesis that only one orthogonalized shock was driving the stochastic component of the data. Thus, the panel titled illiquidity shock shows the generated series if there was only an illiquidity shock.

The results of the historical decompositions clearly point to the illiquidity shock playing a significant role in the bank failures during the Friedman and Schwartz crisis windows. The most obvious case is during the first window from October 1930 to January 1931. Here the historical decomposition for the illiquidity series almost completely follows the actual data. The other shocks do not explain this first crisis window at all. For the next two crisis windows that take up most of 1931, the illiquidity shock does generate series that follow the actual series quite well. During these periods the money shock and the insolvency shock generate series that peak around the right time, but they do not generate series that closely follow the actual total bank failures/suspensions series. The only crisis window that the insolvency shock does predict well appears to be the final crisis of early 1933. In this case, it does appear that the financial crisis in 1933 is more an insolvency story than an illiquidity story.

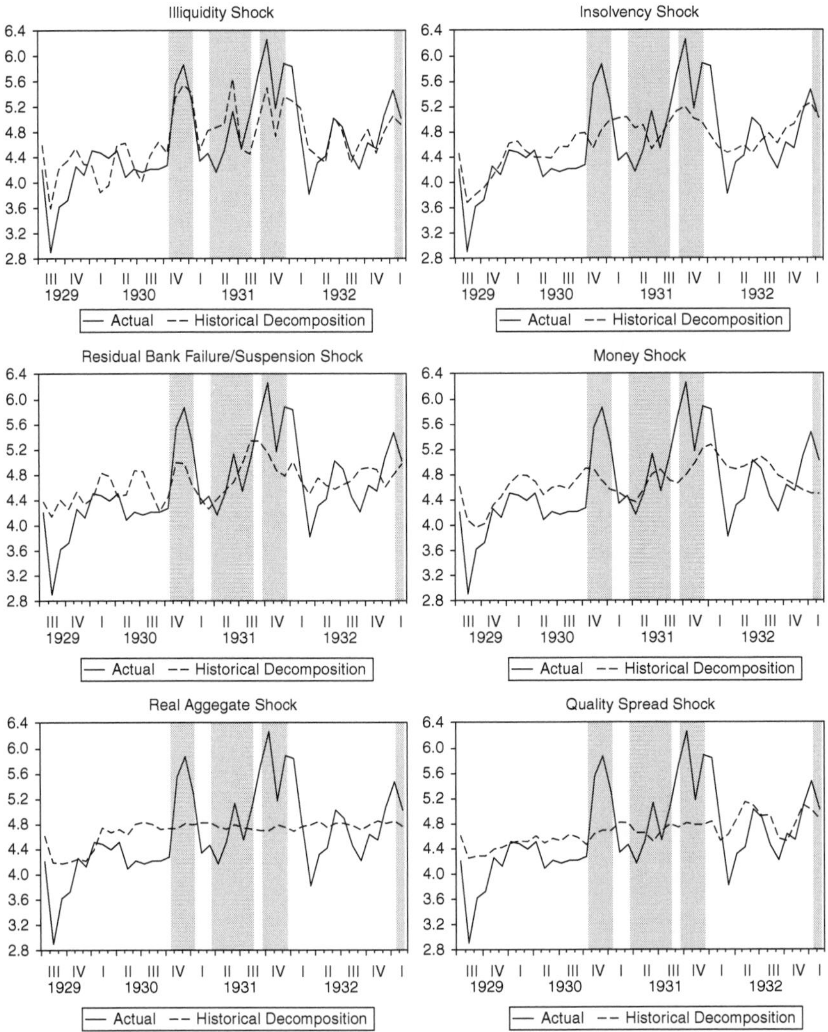

Fig. 7.2. Historical decompositions of total bank failures/suspensions

To summarize, we have estimated a VAR and used a triangular ordering to identify a set of shocks including illiquidity and insolvency shocks. The impulse response functions obtained from this orthogonalized VAR make sense and show that the illiquidity shock is an important shock for explaining the observed bank failures/suspensions series. Further, the historical decompositions show that the financial crises of late 1930 and all of 1931 are well modelled as illiquidity crises. The financial crisis of 1933 is better explained as an insolvency crisis.

Thus, the evidence suggests that the banking panics of the 1930s were largely a liquidity event which massive monetary expansion could have avoided. The key policy lesson from the 1930s experience is that central banks need to attach prominent importance to their role as lenders of last resort. As we discuss in sections 7.4 and 7.5, the Fed and other central banks learned this lesson well in the crisis of 2007–08.

7.3. WHY DID THE US HAVE SO MANY BANKING PANICS?

We have argued that the signature event in the US Great Contraction was the series of banking panics from 1930 to 1933. But this was nothing new in US financial history. From the early nineteenth century until 1914, the US had a banking panic every decade. There is a voluminous literature on US financial stability, and the lessons that come from that literature are that the high incidence of banking instability reflected two forces: unit banking and the absence of an effective lender-of-last-resort.

7.3.1. Unit banking

Fear of the concentration of economic power largely explains why states generally prohibited branch banking and why, since the demise of the Second Bank of the United States in 1836, there was until quite recently no interstate banking (White, 1983). Unit banks, because their portfolios were geographically constrained, were highly subject to local idiosyncratic shocks. Branching banks, especially those which extended across regions, can better diversify their portfolios and protect themselves against local/regional shocks.

A comparison between the experience of the US and Canadian banking systems makes the case (Bordo et al., 1996). The US, until the 1920s, has had predominantly unit banking and, until very recently, a prohibition on interstate banking. Canada, since the late nineteenth century, has had nationwide branch banking. Canada only adopted a central bank in 1934. The US established the Fed in 1914. Canada has had no banking panics since Confederation in 1867, the US has had nine. However, the Canadian chartered banks were always highly regulated and operated very much like a cartel under the guidance of the Canadian Bankers Association and the Department of Finance.

7.3.2. A lender-of-last-resort

From the demise of the Second Bank of the United States until the establishment of the Federal Reserve in 1914, the US had not had anything like a central bank to act as a lender-of-last-resort, into which the Bank of England had evolved during the nineteenth century (Bordo, 2007). Clearinghouses, established first in New York City in 1857 and other major cities later, on occasion acted as a lender-of-last-resort by pooling the resources of the members and issuing clearinghouse loan certificates as a substitute for scarce high-powered money reserves. However, on several prominent occasions before 1914, the clearinghouses did not allay panics (Timberlake, 2002). Panics were often ended in the national banking era by the suspension of convertibility of deposits into currency. Also the US Treasury on a few occasions performed lender-of-last-resort functions.

The Federal Reserve was established to serve (among other functions) as a lender-of-last-resort but, as documented in section 7.1, failed in its task between 1930 and 1933. Discount-window lending to member banks was at the prerogative of the individual Federal Reserve banks and, as discussed in section 7.2, some Reserve banks did not follow through. Moreover, until the establishment of the National Credit Corporation in 1931 (which became the Reconstruction Finance Corporation in 1932), there was no monetary authority to provide assistance to non-member banks (Wicker, 1996). Wicker effectively argues that the panics pre-1914 were always centred in the New York money market and then spread via the vagaries of the national banking system to the regions. The New York Fed, according to him, learned the lesson of the panics of the national banking system and did prevent panics from breaking out in New York City during the Great Contraction. But, as he argues, it did not develop the tools to deal with the regional banking panics which erupted in 1930 and 1931.

7.3.3. Recent evidence

There is considerable empirical evidence going back to the nineteenth century on the case linking unit banking to failures and panics (White, 1983). Cross-country regression evidence in Grossman (1994, 2010) finds that, during the 1930s, countries which had unit banking had a greater incidence of banking instability than those which did not. For the US, Wheelock (1995) finds, based on state- and county-level data, that states that allowed branching had lower bank failure rates than those which did not. However Carlson (2004) (also Calomiris and Mason, 2003) finds, based on a panel of individual banks, that state branch banks in the US were less likely to survive the banking panics. The reason Carlson gives is that, while state branch banks can diversify against idiosyncratic local shocks better than can unit banks, they were still exposed to the systemic shocks of the 1930s. He argues that branch banks used the diversification opportunities of branching to increase their returns but also followed more risky strategies such as holding lower reserves.

Carlson and Mitchener (2009) show, based on data on Californian banks in the 1930s (California was a state that allowed branch banking), that the entry of large branching networks, by improving the competitive environment, actually improved the survival probabilities of unit banks. They explain the divergent results between studies based on individual banks and those based on state- and county-level data by the argument that the US banking system would have been less fragile in the 1930s had states allowed more branching, not because branch banks would have been more diversified but because the system would have had more efficient banks.

The recent financial crisis, although not a classic banking panic, did exhibit a large number of bank failures (mostly in small banks, as in the past, although there were a few large ones such as Countrywide). Most of the bank failures were resolved by the Federal Deposit Insurance Corporation (FDIC) set up in the aftermath of the Great Contraction. So, again, some lessons were learned from the 1930s experience. However, unlike in the 1930s, as we discuss below, a number of very large banks, which became insolvent and were deemed too big and too interconnected to fail, were bailed out by massive capital injections and partial nationalization.

7.4. A COMPARISON OF THE FINANCIAL CRISIS IN THE US TO THE 2007–08 CRISIS

Many people have invoked the experience during the Great Contraction, and especially the banking crises of 1930–33, as a good comparison to the financial crisis and Great Recession of 2007–09. In several descriptive figures in this section we compare the behaviour of some key variables between the two events. We demarcate the crisis windows in the Great Contraction using Friedman and Schwartz's dates. For the recent period we use Gorton's (2010) characterization of the crisis as starting in the shadow bank repo market in August 2007 (dark grey shading) and then changing to a panic in the universal banks after Lehman failed in September 2007 (light grey shading). In most respects, e.g. the magnitude of the decline in real GDP and the rise in unemployment (see Figures 7.3 and 7.4), the two events are very different, but there are some parallels between recent events and the 1930s. In Figure 7.3, we report real GNP for the 1930s and for 2007–09, normalized to be 100 at the start of each period. It is quite clear that the contraction in late 2007 was mild (only about 5 per cent peak to trough) relative to the Great Contraction in the 1930s (roughly 35 per cent peak to trough). The same is clear for unemployment, which is depicted in Figure 7.4. Unemployment rose from near 0 per cent at the start of the Great Contraction to slightly over 25 per cent by the end of the contraction, whereas the rise in unemployment from 4 to 10 per cent for the most recent contraction is small in comparison.

As already discussed, the signature of the Great Contraction was a collapse in the money supply brought about by a collapse in the public's deposit–currency ratio, a decline in the banks deposit–reserve ratio, and a drop in the money multiplier (see Figures 7.5 to 7.7). In the recent crisis, M2 did not collapse; indeed, it increased, reflecting expansionary monetary policy. Moreover, the deposit–currency ratio did not collapse in the recent crisis, it rose. There were no runs on the commercial banks because depositors knew that their deposits were protected by federal deposit insurance, which was introduced in 1934 in reaction to the bank runs of the 1930s. The deposit–reserve ratio declined, reflecting an increase in banks' excess reserves induced by expansionary monetary policy, rather than a scramble for liquidity, as in the 1930s. The money multiplier declined in the recent crisis, largely explained by a massive expansion in the monetary base reflecting the Fed's doubling of its balance sheet in 2008. Moreover, although a few banks failed recently, they were minuscule relative to the 1930s, as were deposits in failed banks relative to total deposits (see Figure 7.8).[5]

[5] The large spike in 1933 largely represents the bank holiday of 6–10 March in which the entire nation's banks were closed and an army of examiners determined whether they were solvent or not. At

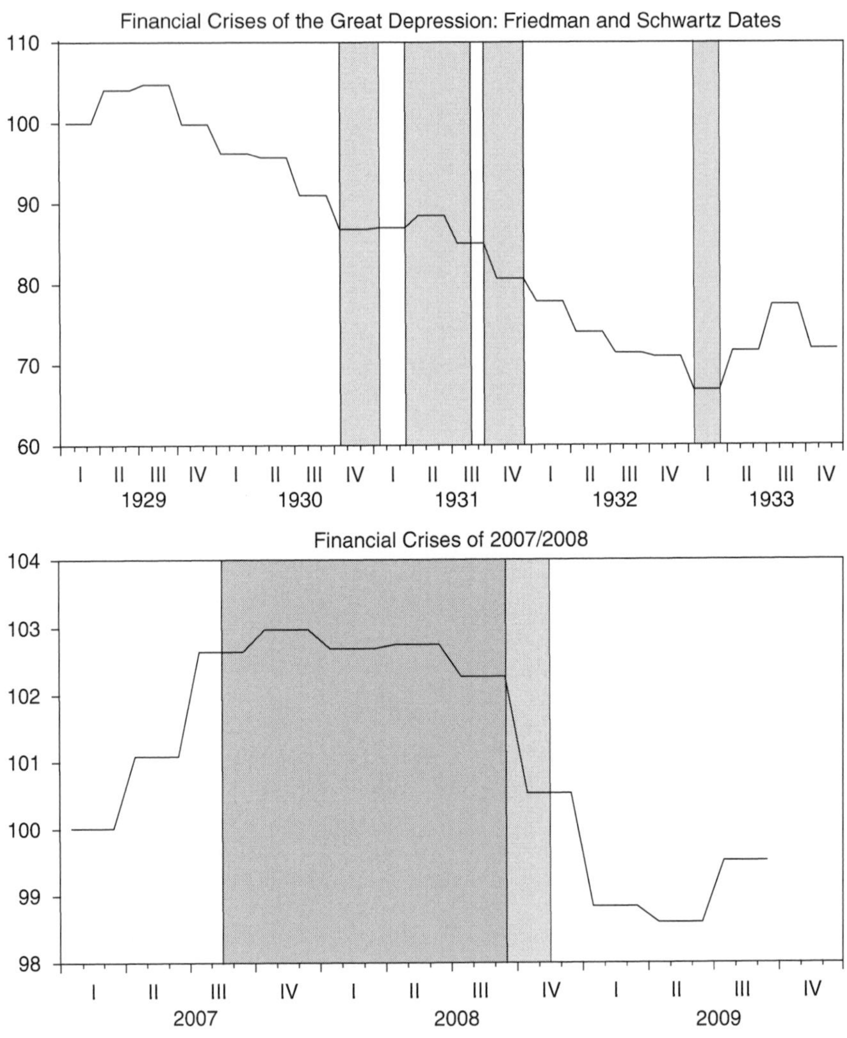

Fig. 7.3. Real GNP (quarterly data)

Thus, the recent financial crisis and recession did not constitute a pure Friedman and Schwartz money story. It was not driven by an old-fashioned contagious banking panic. But, as in 1930–33, there was a financial crisis. It reflected a run in August 2007 on the shadow banking system, which was not regulated by the

the end of the week, one-sixth of the nation's banks were closed. The relatively large spike in 2008 in the deposits in the failed banks series, reflected the failure and reorganization by the FDIC of Countrywide bank. Compared to the case in the 1930s failures, there were no insured depositor losses. With respect to the number of failed banks the current crisis was small with the maximum number of failed banks in the recent crisis being 25 compared with maximums 20 and 100 times greater during the banking crises of the 1930s.

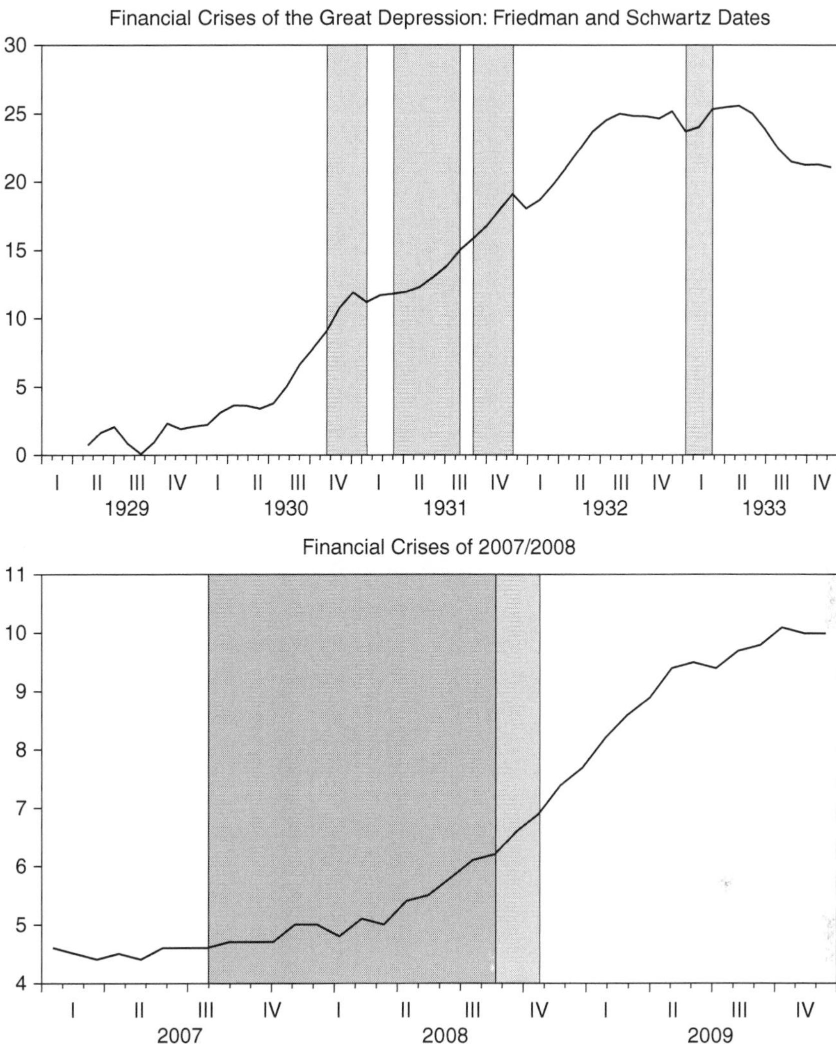

Fig. 7.4. Unemployment

central bank nor covered by the financial safety net. According to Eichengreen (2008), its rapid growth was a consequence of the repeal in 1999 of the Depression-era Glass–Steagall Act of 1935, which had separated commercial from investment banking. These institutions held much lower capital ratios than the traditional commercial banks and hence were considerably more prone to risk. When the crisis hit, they were forced to engage in major deleveraging, involving a fire sale of assets into a falling market, which, in turn, lowered the value of their assets and those of other financial institutions. A similar negative feedback loop occurred during the Great Contraction, according to Friedman and Schwartz.

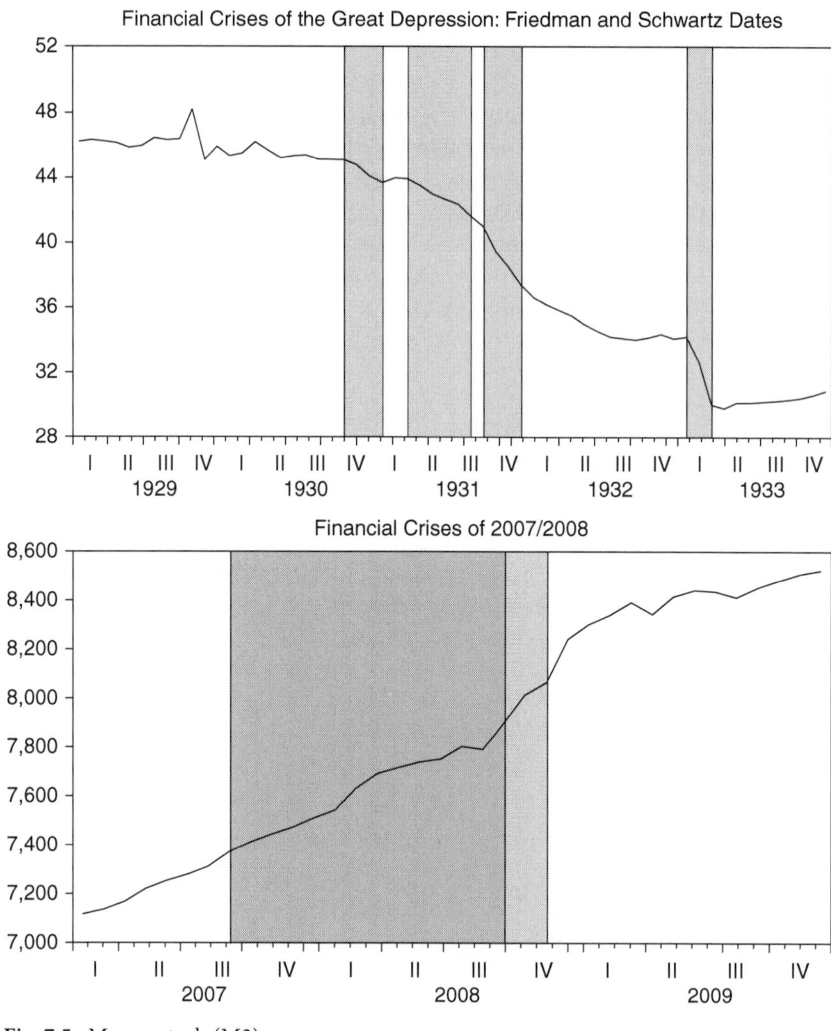

Fig. 7.5. Money stock (M2)

According to Gorton (2010), the crisis centred in the repo market (sale and repurchase agreements) which had been collateralized by opaque (subprime) mortgage-backed securities by which investment banks and some universal banks had been funded. The repo crisis continued through 2008 and then morphed into an investment/universal bank crisis after the failure of Lehman Brothers in September 2008. The crisis led to a credit crunch, which led to a serious, but, compared to the Great Contraction, not that serious, recession (see Figures 7.3 and 7.4). The recession was attenuated in 2009 by expansionary monetary and fiscal policy.

Finally, Figure 7.9 compares the Baa 10-year composite Treasury bond spread between the two historical episodes. This spread is often used as a measure of

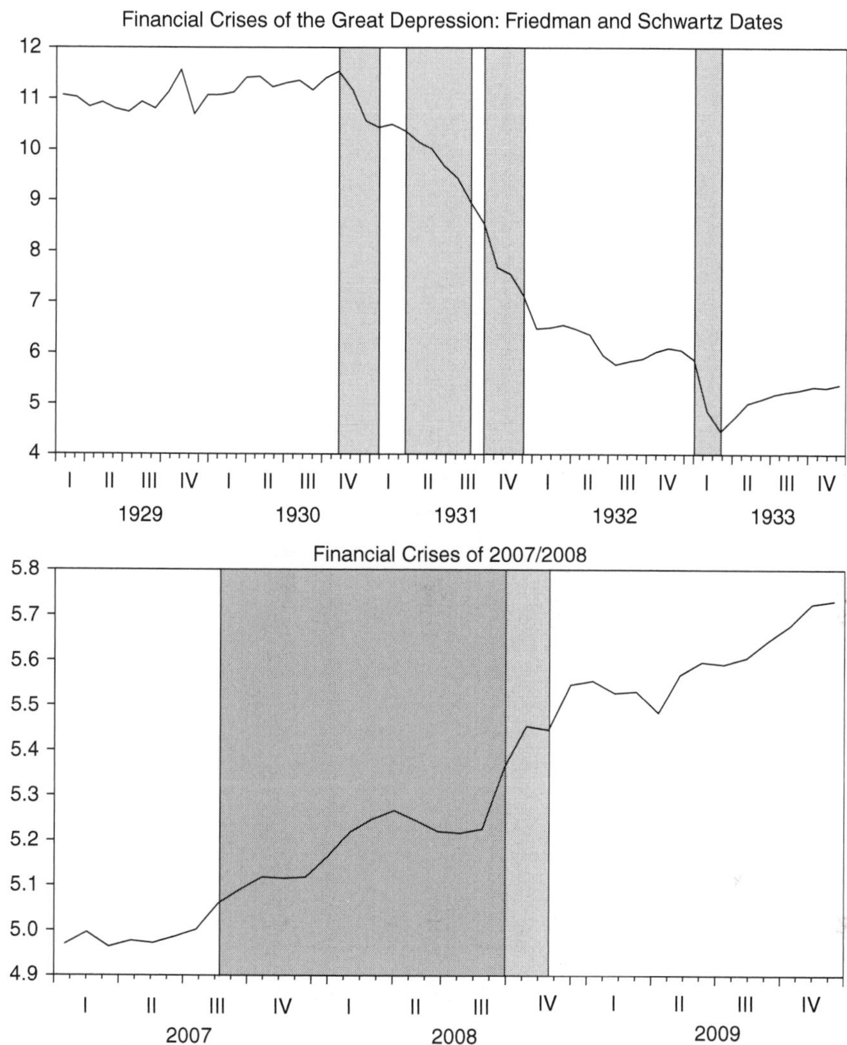

Fig. 7.6. Ratio of deposits to currency in circulation

credit market turmoil (Bordo and Haubrich, 2010). As can be seen, the spike in the spread in 2008 is not very different from that observed in the early 1930s.

7.5. THE RECENT CRISIS IN MORE DETAIL

The crisis occurred following two years of rising policy rates. Its causes include major changes in regulation, lax regulatory oversight, a relaxation of normal standards of prudent lending, and a period of abnormally low interest rates. The default on a significant fraction of subprime mortgages produced spillover effects

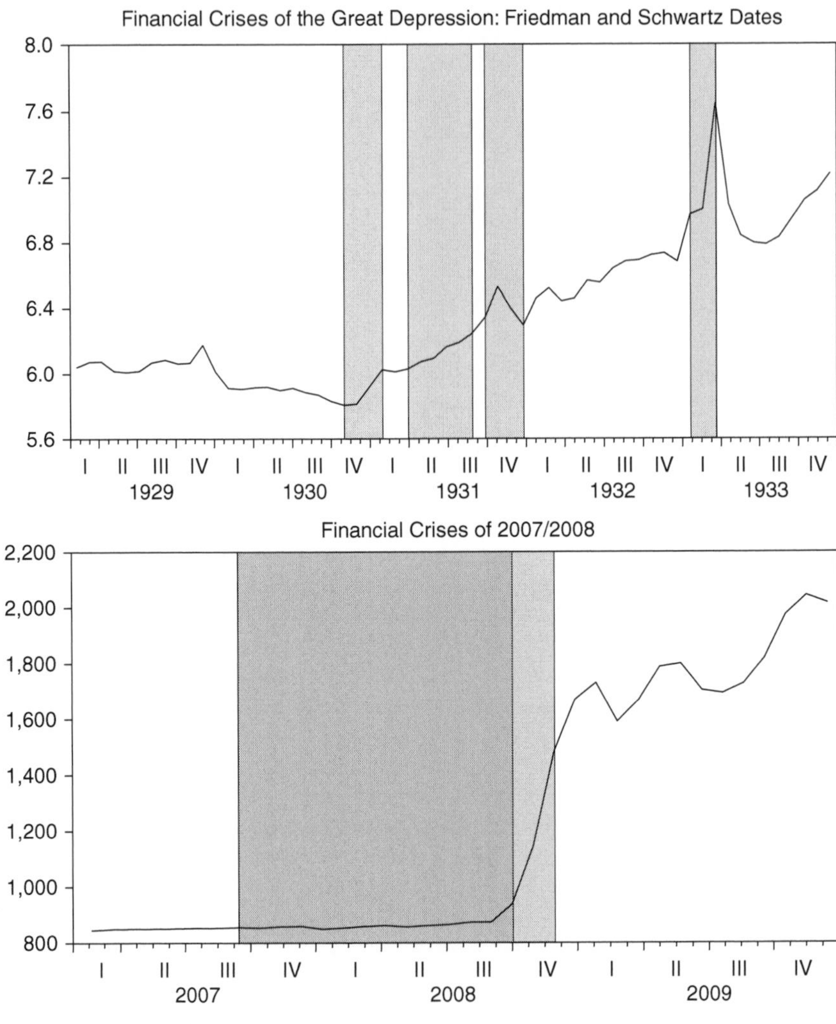

Fig. 7.7. Monetary base

around the world, via the securitized mortgage derivatives into which these mortgages were bundled, to the balance sheets of investment banks, hedge funds, and conduits (which are bank-owned but off their balance sheets) which intermediate between mortgage and other asset-backed commercial paper and long-term securities. The uncertainty about the value of the securities collateralized by these mortgages had the effect of spreading uncertainty about the soundness of loans for leveraged buy-outs through the financial system. All of this led to the freezing of the interbank lending market in August 2007 and substantial liquidity injections by the Fed and other central banks.

The Fed then both extended and expanded its discount-window facilities and cut the federal funds rate by 300 basis points. The crisis worsened in March 2008

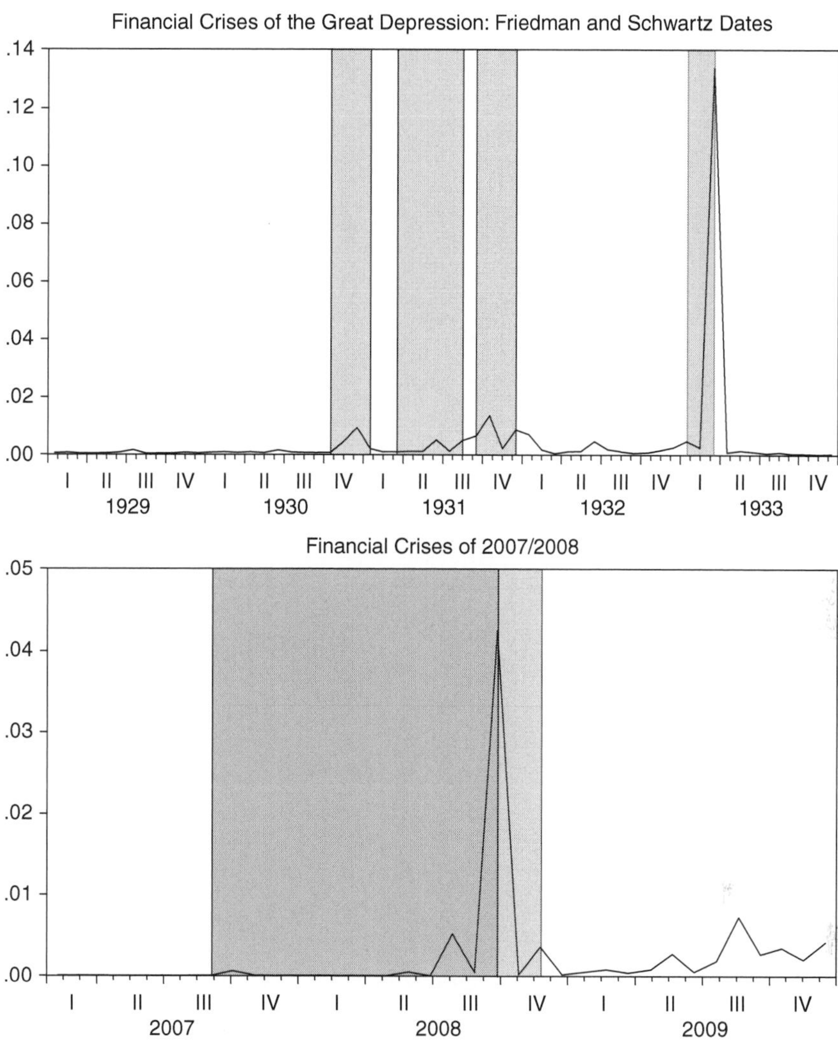

Fig. 7.8. Deposits in failed banks as a proportion of total deposits

with the rescue of Bear Stearns, an investment bank, by J. P. Morgan, backstopped by funds from the Federal Reserve. The rescue was justified on the grounds that the exposure of Bear Stearns to counterparties was so extensive that a worse crisis would follow if it were not bailed out. The March crisis also led to the creation of a number of new discount-window facilities whereby investment banks could access the window and which broadened the collateral acceptable for discounting. The next major event was a Federal Reserve–Treasury bail out and partial nationalization of the insolvent government-sponsored enterprises (GSEs), Fannie Mae and Freddie Mac, in July 2008, on the grounds that they were crucial to the functioning of the mortgage market.

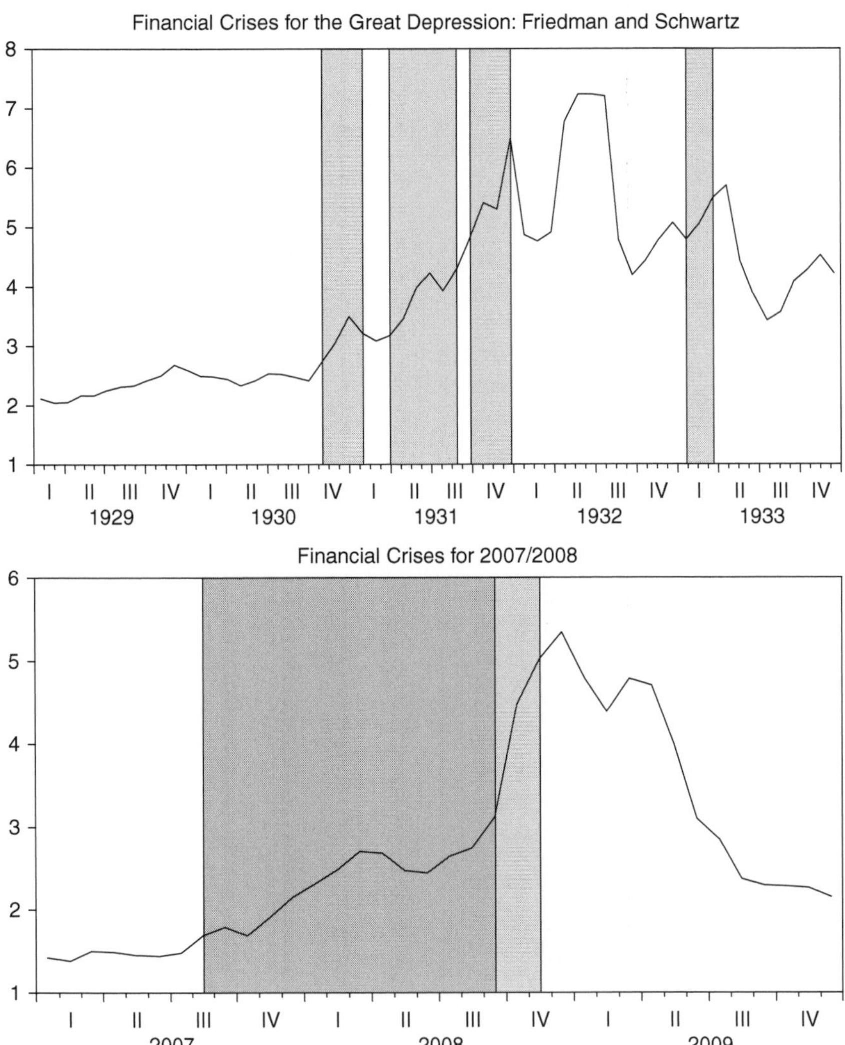

Fig. 7.9. Quality spread (Baa 10-year T-Bill)

Events took a turn for the worse in September 2008 when the Treasury and Fed allowed the investment bank, Lehman Brothers, to fail, in order to discourage the belief that all insolvent institutions would be saved, in an attempt to prevent moral hazard. It was argued that Lehman was both in worse shape and less exposed to counterparty risk than Bear Stearns. The next day, the authorities bailed out and nationalized the insurance giant AIG, fearing the systemic consequences for collateralized default swaps (insurance contracts on securities) if it were allowed to fail. The fall-out from the Lehman bankruptcy then turned the liquidity crisis into a fully fledged global credit crunch and stock market crash, as interbank lending effectively seized up on the fear that no banks were safe.

In the ensuing atmosphere of panic, along with Fed liquidity assistance to the commercial paper market and the extension of the safety net to money market mutual funds, the US Treasury sponsored its Troubled Asset Relief Plan (TARP), whereby $700 billion could be devoted to the purchase of heavily discounted mortgage-backed and other securities to remove them from the banks' balance sheets and restore bank lending. As it later turned out, most of the funds were used to recapitalize the banks.

In early October 2008, the crisis spread to Europe and to the emerging-market countries as the global interbank market ceased functioning. The UK authorities responded by pumping equity into British banks, guaranteeing all interbank deposits, and providing massive liquidity. The EU countries responded in kind. And on 13 October 2008, the US Treasury followed suit with a plan to inject $250 billion into the US banks, to provide insurance of senior interbank debt and unlimited deposit insurance for non-interest-bearing deposits. These actions ended the crisis. Expansionary Federal Reserve policy at the end of 2008, lowering the funds rate close to zero, was followed by a policy of quantitative easing; the open-market purchases of long-term Treasury bonds and mortgage-backed securities finally attenuated the recession by the summer of 2009.

Unlike the liquidity panics of the Great Contraction, the deepest problem facing the financial system was insolvency. This was only recognized by the Fed after the September 2008 crisis. The problem stemmed from the difficulty of pricing securities backed by a pool of assets, whether mortgage loans, student loans, commercial paper issues, or credit card receivables. Pricing securities based on a pool of assets is difficult because the quality of individual components of the pool varies and, unless each component is individually examined and evaluated, no accurate price of the security can be determined.

As a result, the credit market, confronted by financial firms whose portfolios were filled with securities of uncertain value—derivatives that were so complex the art of pricing them had not been mastered—was plagued by the inability to determine which firms were solvent and which were not. Lenders were unwilling to extend loans when they could not be sure that a borrower was creditworthy. This was a serious shortcoming of the securitization process that was responsible for the paralysis of the credit market.

Finally, another hallmark of the recent crisis which was not present in the Great Contraction, is that the Fed and other US monetary authorities engaged in a series of bail-outs of incipient and actual insolvent firms deemed too systemically connected to fail. These included Bear Stearns in March 2008, the GSEs in July, and AIG in September. Lehman Brothers had been allowed to fail in September on the grounds that it was both insolvent and not as systemically important as the others and, as was stated well after the event, the Fed did not have the legal authority to bail it out. The extension of the 'too big to fail' doctrine, which had begun in 1984 with the bail out of Continental Illinois bank, may be the source of future crises.

7.6. CONCLUSION: SOME POLICY LESSONS FROM HISTORY

In this chapter we have re-examined the issue of the role of the banking panics between 1930 and 1933 in creating the Great Contraction. We focused on the debate between those following the Friedman and Schwartz view, that the banking crises were illiquidity shocks, and those following the approach of Temin and others, who view the clusters of banking failures as not being liquidity-driven panics but insolvencies caused by the recession. Our survey of the evidence suggests that the banking crises did reflect contagious illiquidity, but also that endogenous insolvency was important between the panics. Bank failures, regardless of their genesis, contributed to the depression by reducing the money supply and by crippling the credit mechanism.

In Bordo and Landon-Lane (2010) we showed illiquidity played a major role in the financial crises of late 1930 and all 1931. We estimated a VAR and used a triangular ordering to identify a set of shocks including illiquidity and insolvency shocks. The impulse response functions obtained from this orthogonalized VAR make sense and show that the illiquidity shock is an important shock for explaining the observed bank failures/suspensions series. Further, the historical decompositions show that the financial crisis of late 1930 and all of 1931 are well modelled as illiquidity crises. The financial crisis of 1933 is better explained as an insolvency crisis.

The Federal Reserve learned the Friedman and Schwartz lesson from the banking panics of the 1930s of the importance of conducting expansionary open-market policy to meet all of the demands for liquidity (Bernanke, 2002). In the recent crisis, the Fed conducted highly expansionary monetary policy in the autumn of 2007 and from late 2008 to the present. Also, based on Bernanke's (1983) view that the banking collapse led to a failure of the credit-allocation mechanism, the Fed, in conjunction with the Treasury, developed a plethora of extensions to its discount-window referred to as credit policy (Goodfriend, 2009) to encompass virtually every kind of collateral in an attempt to unclog the blocked credit markets.

Some argue that, for the first three-quarters of 2008, Fed monetary policy was actually too tight, seen in a flattening of money growth and the monetary base and high real interest rates (Hetzel, 2009). Although the Fed's balance sheet surged, the effects on high-powered money were sterilized. This may have reflected concern that rising commodity prices at the time would spark inflationary expectations. By the end of the third quarter of 2008 the sterilization ceased, as evidenced by a doubling of the monetary base.

The Fed's credit policy involved providing credit directly to markets and firms that the Fed deemed most in need of liquidity, and exposed the Fed to the temptation to politicize its selection of the recipients of its credit (Schwartz, 2008). In addition, the Fed's balance sheet ballooned in 2008 and 2009 with the collateral of risky assets including those of non-banks. These assets were in part backed by the Treasury. The Fed also worked closely with the Treasury in the autumn of 2008 to stabilize the major banks with capital purchases and stress testing. Moreover, the purchase of mortgage-backed securities in 2009 (quantitative easing) combined monetary with fiscal policy. These actions, which many argue helped reduce the spreads and reopen the credit channels, impinged upon the Fed's independence and created problems for the Fed in the future (Bordo, 2010).

As discussed in section 7.5, the deepest problem of the recent crisis, however, was not illiquidity, as it was in the 1930s, but insolvency, and especially the fear of insolvency of counterparties. This has echoes in the correspondence-banking-induced panic of November 1930 (Richardson, 2006), but was very different from the 1930s. The too-big-to-fail doctrine, which had developed in the 1980s, ensured that the monetary authorities would bail out insolvent large financial firms which were deemed too interconnected to fail. This is a dramatic departure from the original Bagehot's Rule prescription to provide liquidity to illiquid but solvent banks. This new type of systemic risk (Tallman and Wicker, 2009) raises the spectre of moral hazard and future financial crises and future bail-outs.

7.6.1. Policies to prevent the next crisis

The crisis of 2007–08 had similarities to the 1930s experience in that there was a panic in the shadow banking system and the repo market in 2007, as argued by Gorton (2010), but also in investment banks and the universal banking system after Lehman failed in September 2008. But it was not a classic contagious banking panic. The decision to bail out large interconnected financial institutions in the autumn of 2008 does not have much resonance in the 1930s experience. The closest parallel from the 1930s was the Bank of United States, which failed in December 1930. It was one of the largest banks in the country, but it was insolvent and it was allowed to fail (Lucia, 1985).

A key concern from the bail-outs of 2008 is that, in the future, the too-big-to-fail doctrine will lead to excessive risk taking by such firms, and future crises and bail-outs. This was a major concern in the debate leading to the recent Dodd–Frank Wall Street Reform and Protection Act, passed in July 2010. The Act attempted to address the too-big-to-fail problem by establishing a Financial Stability Oversight Council made up of members from the Federal Reserve Board, The Treasury, the Securities and Exchange Commission, and a number of other financial agencies. The Council was charged with identifying and responding to emerging risks throughout the financial system. The Council would make recommendations to the Federal Reserve to impose increasingly strict rules for capital and leverage and other requirements to prevent banks from becoming too large and systemically exposed. It remains to be seen whether it will be effective in preventing future crises.

BIBLIOGRAPHY

Bernanke, B. (1983), 'Non Monetary Effects of the Financial Crisis in the Propagation of the Great Depression', *American Economic Review*, 73, 257–76.

Bernanke, B. (2002), 'On Milton's Ninetieth Birthday', speech given at the University of Chicago, 8 November.

Bernanke, B., Gilchrist, S., and Gertler, M. (1996), 'The Financial Accelerator and the Flight to Quality', *Review of Economics and Statistics*, 78(1), 1–15.

Bordo, M. D. (2007), 'The History of Monetary Policy', *New Palgrave Dictionary of Economics*, 2nd edn. New York: Palgrave Macmillan.

Bordo, M. D. (2010), 'The Federal Reserve: Independence Gained, Independence Lost . . .', Shadow Open Market Committee, 26 March.

Bordo, M. D. and Haubrich, J. (2010), 'Credit Crises, Money and Contractions: An Historical View', *Journal of Monetary Economics*, 57(1), 1–18.

Bordo, M. D. and Landon-Lane, J. S. (2010), 'The Lessons from the Banking Panics in the United States in the 1930s for the Financial Crisis of 2007–2008', NBER Working Paper No. 16365, September.

Bordo, M. D., Choudhri, E., and Schwartz, A. J. (1995), 'Could Stable Money Have Averted the Great Contraction?', *Economic Inquiry*, 33, 484–505.

Bordo, M. D., Redish, A., and Rockoff, H. (1996), 'The US Banking System from a Northern Exposure: Stability versus Efficiency', *Journal of Economic History*, 54(2), 325–41.

Calomiris, C. and Gorton, G. (1991), 'The Origins of Banking Panics: Models, Facts and Bank Regulation', in R. G. Hubbard (ed.), *Financial Markets and Financial Crises*. Chicago, Ill.: University of Chicago Press, 109–73.

Calomiris, C. and Mason, J. (1997), 'Contagion and Bank Failures During the Great Depression: The June 1932 Chicago Banking Panic', *American Economic Review*, 87(5): 863–83.

Calomiris, C. and Mason, J. (2003), 'Fundamentals, Panics and Bank Distress During the Depression', *American Economic Review*, 93(5), 1615–47.

Carlson, M. (2004), 'Are Branch Banks Better Survivors? Evidence from the Depression Era', *Economic Inquiry*, 42(1), 111–26.

Carlson, M. (2008), 'Alternatives for Distressed Banks and the Panics of the Great Depression', Finance and Economic Discussion Series. Washington, DC: Federal Reserve Board.

Carlson, M. and Mitchener, K. J. (2009), 'Branch Banking as a Device for Discipline: Competition and Bank Survivorship During the Great Depression', *Journal of Political Economy*, 117(2), 165–210.

Christiano, L., Motto, R., and Rostagno, M. (2003), 'The Great Depression and the Friedman and Schwartz Hypothesis', *Journal of Money, Credit and Banking*, 35, 1119–98.

Diamond, D. and Dybvig, P. (1983), 'Bank Runs, Deposit Insurance, and Liquidity', *Journal of Political Economy*, 91(3), 401–19.

Eichengreen, B. (2008), 'Origins and Responses to the Crisis', UC Berkeley, mimeo, October.

Friedman, M. and Schwartz, A. (1963), *A Monetary History of the United States 1867 to 1960*. Princeton, NJ: Princeton University Press.

Galbraith, J. K. (1955), *The Great Crash 1929*. London: Hamish Hamilton.

Goodfriend, M. (2009), 'Central Banking in the Credit Turmoil: An Assessment of Federal Reserve Practice', Bank of Japan Conference, May.

Gorton, G. (2010), 'Questions and Answers about the Financial Crisis', NBER Working Paper 15787, February.

Grossman, R. S. (1994), 'The Shoe that Didn't Drop: Explaining Banking Stability in the Great Depression', *Journal of Economic History*, 54, 654–82.

Grossman, R. S. (2010), *Unsettled Account: The Evolution of Banking in the Industrial World since 1800*. Princeton, NJ: Princeton University Press

Hetzel, R. (2009), 'Monetary Policy in the 2008–2009 Recession', *Federal Reserve Bank of Richmond Review*, 95(September), 201–33.

Keynes, J. M. (1936), *The General Theory of Employment, Interest and Money*. New York: Harcourt Brace.

Lucia, J. (1985), 'The Failure of the Bank of United States: A Reappraisal', *Explorations in Economic History*, 22(4), 402–11.

McCallum, B. (1990), 'Could a Monetary Base Rule have Prevented the Great Depression?', *Journal of Monetary Economics*, 26, 3–21.

Prescott, E. C. (1999), 'Some Observations on the Great Depression', *Federal Reserve Bank of Minneapolis Quarterly Review*, 23, 25–31.

Richardson, G. (2006), 'Correspondent Clearing and the Banking Panics of the Great depression', NBER Working Paper 12716, December.

Richardson, G. (2007), 'Categories and Causes of Bank Distress during the Great Depression, 1920–1935: The Illiquidity versus Solvency Debate Revisited', *Explorations in Economic History*, 44(4), 588–607.

Richardson, G. and Troost, W. (2009), 'Monetary Intervention Mitigated Banking Panics during the Great Depression: Quasi Experimental Evidence from the Federal Reserve District Border in Mississippi, 1929–1933', *Journal of Political Economy*, 117(6), 1031–72.

Schwartz, A. (2008), 'Origins of the Financial Market Crisis of 2008', Cato Conference, October.

Tallman, E. and Wicker, E. (2009), 'Banking and Financial Crises in the United States History: What Guidance Can History Offer Policy Makers?', Indiana University, mimeo.

Temin, P. (1976), *Did Monetary Forces Cause the Great Depression?*. New York: W. W. Norton.

Timberlake, R., Jr (2002), *Monetary Policy in the United States: An Intellectual and Institutional History*. Chicago, Ill.: University of Chicago Press.

Wheelock, D. (1995), 'Regulation, Market Structure and the Bank Failures of the Great Depression', *Federal Reserve Bank of St Louis Review*, 77, 27–38.

White, E. (1983), *The Regulation and Reform of the American Banking System, 1900–1929*. Princeton, NJ: Princeton University Press.

White, E. (1984), 'A Reinterpretation of the Banking Crisis of 1930', *Journal of Economic History*, 44, 119–38.

Wicker, E. (1980), 'A Reconsideration of the Causes of the Banking Panic of 1930', *Journal of Economic History*, 40, 571–83.

Wicker, E. (1996), *The Banking Panics of the Great Depression*. New York: Cambridge University Press.

8

Can Contractionary Fiscal Policy be Expansionary? Consolidation, Sustainability, and Fiscal Policy Impact in Britain in the 1930s*

Roger Middleton

> The national budget must be balanced. The public debt must be reduced; the arrogance of the authorities must be moderated and controlled. Payments to foreign governments must be reduced, if the nation does not want to go bankrupt. People must again learn to work, instead of living on public assistance (Cicero 55 BC).

8.1. INTRODUCTION

The Great Recession has rightly reawakened interest in the Great Depression. For Britain, which did not experience anything like the collapse of the real economy characteristic of the US and some continental European economies after 1929, the slump of the early 1930s was as much a political as a macroeconomic event. Indeed, it brought down a government (albeit a minority Labour administration) as a sterling and public finance crisis in the summer of 1931 erupted into a crisis of confidence in government itself, albeit one paradoxically that then brought about a transformation of the policy regime which, at a minimum, was permissive of economic recovery. To claim that this was as much a political as an economic crisis is not to understate British unemployment as an economic problem, nor to ignore its important role as an spur to the Keynesian revolution in theory and policy, but rather to direct attention to three aspects of the early 1930s which current circumstances suggest are worthy of re-examination in the context of the forces that shaped 1930s fiscal policy and what we know about policy impact. First, the issue of fiscal consolidation amidst a cyclical downturn, and more

* I thank the editors for helpful comments and Martin Earley, one of my PhD students, for allowing me to utilize his new, comprehensive dataset of British public social spending, 1830–1950.

particularly the infamous May committee report (HMSO, 1931a) and its predecessor, the Geddes 'axe'. Second, whether the expansionary fiscal contraction (EFC) hypothesis, which is now in vogue in certain quarters (so-called 'expansionary austerity'), might provide insights for further understanding this earlier age, and vice versa. And, third, debt dynamics and their implications for monetary and fiscal policy. Our starting point is perhaps novel: that British fiscal policy in the 1930s is a study of *twin* disappointments. In one tradition, of a Keynesian path (of deliberate deficit-finance) not trodden, and thus a slump prolonged and recovery delayed through deficient demand; and, in another, of the onward march of public expenditure, this despite the apparent dominance of an orthodox discourse on the imperative of containing Leviathan, which also prolonged the slump and delayed recovery but on more neo-classical, supply-side grounds, and especially the burden of personal/corporate taxation and labour market rigidities.

In the following, a companion to two recent survey papers on macroeconomic policy impact in interwar Britain (Middleton, 2010 and 2011), we offer a guide to how the British experience of 1929–39 may provide useful lessons for the present. Amidst the welter of comment on the present situation, the historical record has become, variously, a rhetorical weapon to be deployed or a knowledge base to be scoured for appropriate lessons. 'History' is here invoked typically in two distinctive senses. The first as a risk of repeating, or the prospect of avoiding, through policies unwisely or wisely chosen, a macroeconomic catastrophe of 1930s duration and depth; and the other as either the worst fiscal imprudence of any post-war British government, or the inevitable and justifiable consequence of a responsible government allowing the automatic stabilizers to operate to mitigate depressive impulses. Here, our stress must be on contingency and context, with the past duly scoured—but forensically so—for appropriate lessons with due acknowledgement of the very different circumstances of the present. Of these, the most important and most immediate relates to magnitudes.

Some key macroeconomic and fiscal indicators are given in Table 8.1 for the two recessions. It is immediately apparent that the cyclical downturn beginning in 2008 has had a very profound effect on the public finances, with public sector net borrowing (PSNB) rising from 2.3 per cent of GDP to a peak of 11.1 per cent between 2007/08 and 2009/10, at which point public sector net debt (PSND) was 60.3 per cent of GDP. The greater part of this deterioration was genuinely fiscal, rather than the cost of bank support (Holland et al., 2010, Figure 1), and this in the context of a labour market which, hitherto, has shown great resilience: ILO-definition unemployment only rising from 5.7 to 7.9 per cent between 2008–10 whilst real GDP fell 6.4 per cent from peak-to-trough between 2008.I and 2009. Moreover, as forecast by the Office for Budget Responsibility, the PSNB will still be at 2.5 per cent of GDP by 2014/15, this despite the very pronounced fiscal consolidation inaugurated by the outgoing Labour government and now intensified by the incumbent Conservative–Liberal Democratic coalition. By contrast, in the 1929–32 downturn—during which real GDP fell by a comparable amount, but unemployment, on the labour force measure (then contemporary statistics portrayed a much bleaker impression), more than doubled to 15.6 per cent—the government budget deficit, as then conventionally defined and publicly

Table 8.1. Macroeconomic and fiscal dynamics in two recessions: key indicators, 1929–33 and 2008–11

	A: 1929–33						B: 2008–11			
	Budget balance (B_c) as % of GDP [A]	Combined public authorities' budget balance (B_{GG}) as % of GDP [B]	Outstanding debt/GDP % [C]	Real GDP (1929 = 100) [D]	Labour force unemployment rate (%) [E]		PSNB as % of GDP [F]	PSND as % of GDP [G]	Real GDP (2007 = 100) (ONS ABMI) [H]	Labour force unemployment rate (%) (ONS LF2Q) [I]
1929/30	−0.3					2007/8	2.3	36.4		
1930/1	−0.6					2008/9	6.8	43.4		
1931/2	0.0					2009/10	11.0	53.0		
1932/3	−0.9					2010/11	9.6	60.3		
1929		−0.7	158.4	100.0	7.3	2007			100.0	5.4
1930		−1.4	159.2	99.2	11.2	2008			99.9	5.7
1931		−2.2	169.8	94.6	15.1	2009			95.1	7.6
1932		−0.5	173.6	94.7	15.6	2010			96.4	7.9
1933		0.5	179.2	97.7	14.1	2011 forecast [1]			97.6	7.9

Note: [1] NIESR forecast July 2011: Kirby and Whitworth (2011: Table 1).
Sources: A: Middleton (1985: Table 7.4); B: as Figure 8.8; C: as Figure 8.4; D: as Figure 8.1; E: Feinstein (1972: Table 65); [F–G]: Kirby and Whitworth (2011: Table 1); [H–I]: ONS StatBase.

debated (B_c)[1], only deteriorated from 0.3 to 0.9 per cent of GDP between 1929/30 and 1932/33 (at which point the debt-to-GDP ratio peaked at 179.2 per cent), whereas, even when under the imperative of rearmament (loan financed from 1937), the budget balance only moved from a surplus of 0.6 per cent in 1937/38 to a deficit of 4.9 per cent in 1939/40. We shall modify the interwar story somewhat in sections 8.3 and 8.4 when we use more modern data, fiscal concepts, and definitions of the public sector (series B_{GG} in Table 8.1, column B) but we will not change the historical significance of the present in terms of magnitudes. Current PSNB is unprecedented in peacetime, though that is far from being the case for PSND as a proportion of GDP.

The Federal Reserve chairman, an academic economist whose research was the Great Depression before he became a policy maker,[2] has recently identified four policy lessons from history: first, 'economic prosperity depends on financial stability'; second, 'policymakers must respond forcefully, creatively and decisively to severe financial crises'; third, 'international crises require an international response'; and, fourth, 'history is never a perfect guide' (Bernanke, 2010). He does not accord weights to these lessons, but we here signal from the outset of our analysis that, on the basis of what we now think we know about British policy in the 1930s, the major lessons are stronger as negatives than as positives: namely what should not be done in general as against what might be done, this largely situation specific. (This, of course, assumes we can surmount the epistemological problem of knowledge transfer.) I highlight also an immediate UK–US difference which relates to his first lesson, the primacy of financial stability. For Britain, there was domestic boom to break in 1929; no asset price bubble to unwind (this in the context of falling prices with consequent debt-deflation risks); and no domestic banking crisis (Billings and Capie, 2011). Consequently, relative to the US, the challenge for monetary policy would be different, as would the issue of business confidence fractured by the fragile real economy. Additionally, with respect to the fourth lesson, we might perhaps augment this: whilst 'history' provides no perfect lessons, the prior period that counts as history, the medium- and long-run forces that produced the historical 'episode', that is, the focus for lesson-drawing, need to be taken very seriously to understand what shaped policy. Policy path-dependence exists. Thus, whilst this chapter focuses on the period from the 1929 downturn to the eve of the Second World War, from the perspective of today's economist and policy maker needing to understand the specificity as well as possible knowledge transfer potential of this earlier key policy episode, considerable attention is necessarily given to the previous period. Without an appreciation of the fiscal significance of the First World War and its aftermath, including the first fiscal consolidation of the interwar period (the Geddes axe

[1] B_C represents the official (principally central government at this time) budget balance of ordinary and self-balancing revenue (T_c) less expenditure (G_c) as defined in Middleton (1985: 79–80). In section 8.4 we make adjustments to these aggregates, first to remove accounting convention curiosities and fiscal window-dressing of the time (to produce B, T, G), and, second, for cyclical factors, to derive constant employment budget measures (B^*, T^*, G^*). Additionally, we employ series which approximate to modern definitions of the public sector as general government, with B_{GG} the balance of total revenue (TR) less total public expenditure (TPE), with this data defined and derived from Middleton (1996: Appendix I).

[2] His major essays, solely and jointly-authored, are collected together in Bernanke (2000).

of 1922), it is very difficult to fully appreciate what shaped policy and conditioned policy impact in the 1930s, both in terms of the role and effectiveness of the policies pursued as well as the principal policy not adopted, namely the Keynesian solution of significant loan-financed public works to remedy mass unemployment.

One of the biggest questions, for both the 1930s and today, is that of policy makers (in)tolerance of debt, and the judgements made accordingly on whether the automatic stabilizers can be allowed to operate, or whether they should be overridden through discretionary adjustments to taxation and expenditure. In the 1930s, the British authorities not only eschewed the Keynesian solution but, from the outset, sought to override the automatic stabilizers. By contrast, for today's policy makers the key question has been about the desirable path for fiscal consolidation: neither too fast nor too deep, lest recovery be threatened; nor too slow and too shallow, lest the markets lose their tolerance for sovereign debt. Of course, since, to date, the Great Recession has not become a Great Depression, and, in particular, unemployment has not risen as much as feared initially, the question arises of whether it was policy makers' tolerance of the high levels of debt creation compelled by the massive budget deficits that prevented a slump. There is thus a clear counterfactual: an earlier fiscal consolidation, one which overrode the automatic stabilizers, would have produced a sharper and more prolonged downturn. Indeed, this was the rationale of the outgoing Labour government's position on fiscal consolidation, one maintained in relation to their opposition to the new Conservative-led coalition government's emergency June 2010 budget (and subsequent actions) which accelerated the path of consolidation and altered the balance between taxation and retrenchment. As today's policy makers grapple with this issue, the example of Britain in the 1930s is of major interest. Fiscal consolidation, involving both increased tax rates and expenditure retrenchment, was achieved (albeit quickly interrupted by the exigencies of rearmament) but arguably at the cost of enduring high unemployment. Similarly, the scepticism of many today towards the EFC hypothesis would seem to be vindicated by our exploration of this revival of neo-classical orthodoxy in the context of the 1930s.

The structure of this chapter is as follows. We start in section 8.2 with a survey in two parts of some stylized facts which conditioned policy priorities and responses, the first relating to the macroeconomy, and the second to the policy regime which, importantly, was very different from today. With this background, section 8.3 then examines interwar public finances using both contemporary and more modern data/definitions of the public sector. It considers the challenge posed by the new democratic politics for fiscal sustainability, examines the Geddes axe, and then interwar debt dynamics. The combined effect is to demonstrate the deep shadow cast by the First World War which created perceptions of a very narrow policy space with respect to monetary and fiscal policy, and all the more so in the early 1930s when a global Great Depression coincided with a domestic political crisis associated with responses to that depression. Our policy narrative and assessment then follows in section 8.4, with section 8.5 devoted to responses to the May committee's report, including how this might be viewed through an EFC lens. Section 8.6 provides an overall assessment and concludes with a summary of the lessons of Britain in the 1930s for today's economists and policy makers.

8.2. BRITAIN IN THE 1930s: SOME STYLIZED FACTS

8.2.1. The macroeconomy

Figure 8.1, which draws upon Maddison's global dataset, shows that, relative to the two biggest European economies and the US, the British downturn, as measured by real GDP, was the slightest, and its subsequent recovery the most impressive bar Germany, which followed a different political path. Indeed, and here the comparison is usually made with the US, the British economy did not experience a 'great depression' in any meaningful sense. Similarly, the UK recovery was of a very different order of magnitude with, relative to the US, greater scope to argue for the positive effects of government macroeconomic policies even if they did fall far short of what Keynes and other economic progressives considered desirable and deliverable.

Using annual national data, we calculate a peak-to-trough fall for the UK (1929–31) of 5.4 per cent and for the US (1929–33) 26.6 per cent, with the respective 1937 values being 16.4 per cent and 5.3 per cent above their 1929 levels.[3] Moreover, whilst unemployment was much higher in Britain in the 1920s than in the US, giving very different starting points for 1929, relatively, the UK record was much better after 1932 (Hatton and Thomas, 2010). UK income losses

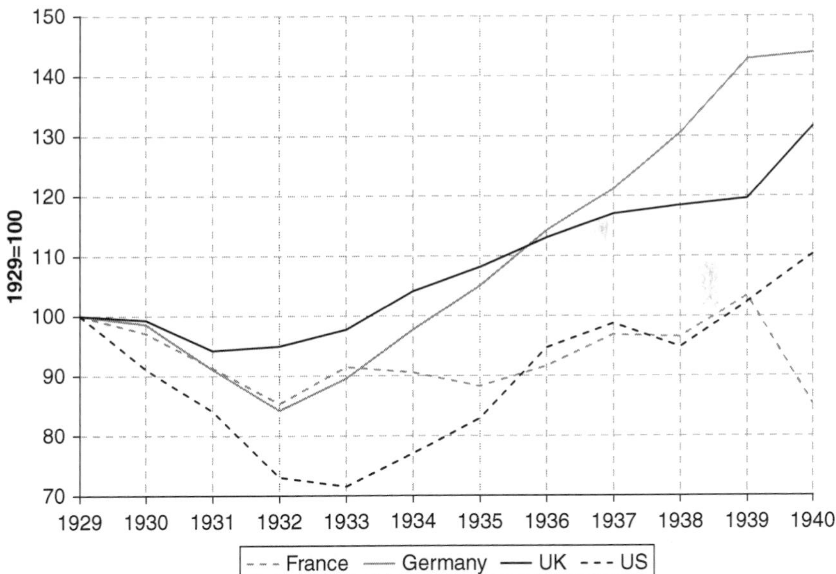

Fig. 8.1. Real GDP (1929 = 100), France, Germany, UK and US, 1929–40
Sources: Calculated from Maddison (2003: Tables 1b, 2b).

[3] UK: Sefton and Weale (1995: Table A3); US: Carter et al. (2006, III: series Ca9). Using quarterly GDP data, the UK turning-points were 1930, 1932, and 1938; using monthly data, January 1930, twin troughs September 1931/July 1932, and January 1938 (Mitchell et al., 2009: Tables 2A, 1A).

were thus very mild by this standard and there was a pronounced recovery after 1932. However, the UK output-employment elasticity was relatively high (Middleton, 1981: 277), such that the contraction phase of the real economy was manifest in a significant rise in unemployment and fall in employment. Labour force unemployment rose from an annual average of 1.5 million (7.3 per cent) in 1929 to 3.4 million (15.6 per cent) in 1932 and was still at 1.8 million (7.8 per cent) by 1937 (Feinstein, 1972: Table 57). The figures used by contemporaries, a by-production of the national insurance system which covered some 60 per cent of the labour force, gave much higher unemployment rates, peaking at 23.0 per cent in January 1933, a peak broadly comparable with the standard labour force measure for the US, but dwarfed by the widely cited non-farm labour force measure which signalled unemployment in excess of 30 per cent in 1932–33.

The rise in unemployment in Britain and the peak attained were thus far less significant than in the US. However, in addition to there being no boom to break in 1929, five issues are particularly important for the British story in comparative context:

1. Unemployment had high political salience even before the 1929 downturn as the 1920s has been widely perceived as one of economic underperformance (Pigou's (1947) 'Britain in the doldrums'); the June 1929 election had been dominated by unemployment and an early version of the Keynesian solution (Lloyd George's Liberal Party claim, 'We can conquer unemployment', comprising a £250 million two-year programme of loan-financed public works); and the 1929 downturn was not related to the breaking of a domestic boom.
2. The initial demand shock to the British economy was external, with export-sensitive employment leading at the upper turning point (Phelps Brown and Shackle, 1939: Diagram 3), whereas in the US depressive forces were internally generated, with employment data (Bernstein, 1987: 155–65) consistent with the Romer (1990) analysis that the 'great crash' quickly impacted on consumers' expenditure and thence employment.
3. Of the then large economies, the UK was the most open, and spectacularly so in relation to the US. The trade openness ratio (exports plus imports/GDP) was only 0.10 for the US but 0.42 for the UK.[4] Thus for the UK, but not for the US domestic economy, the international transmission mechanism of depressive impulses and a potential external constraint were essential elements of the macroeconomic circumstances to which policy makers had to respond.
4. With British central government expenditure at 25.2 per cent of GDP in 1932/33 as against 6.9 per cent for the US Federal government in 1932, the demand leverage of the former significantly exceeded that of the latter, with consequently much greater potential for stabilizing demand in Britain than the US *if* the British (highly centralized economic) authorities so chose (the

[4] Calculations: UK, from Sefton and Weale (1995, Table A.3); US, series Ca84, Ca87 and Ca88 from Carter et al. (2006, III).

figures for total public expenditure (TPE, both 1932) diverge less, being 27.9 per cent for Britain and 21.2 per cent for the US).[5]

5. Because of the characteristics of Britain's fiscal system (a high cyclical macro-marginal budget rate, a measure of the automatic stabilizing properties of Britain's budgetary system),[6] rising unemployment after 1929 quickly translated into a severe budgetary crisis. This peaked in the summer of 1931 and then, combined with a balance of payments crisis, resulted in the collapse of the Labour government and the advent of a (Conservative-dominated) national government for the remainder of the decade.

In these circumstances, it is not difficult to understand why mitigating the downturn and seeking to promote recovery became the policy issues that they did for both economic orthodoxy and heterodoxy. A closer examination of UK–US macroeconomic trends at a disaggregated level for three sub-periods (contraction, recovery, recession-rearmament) produces stunningly different results which must inform how we assess the relative policy space and potential efficacy of active fiscal and monetary policies, whether pre-Keynesian or Keynesian-inspired.

Starting with the respective contraction/depression phases, we have the scale factor in GDP losses that we have already noted. That said, in many ways it is the compositional story that is more interesting (Middleton, 2010: 418–20). The UK downturn was most evident in the fall in exports, whereas for the US, the dominant depressive impulses were the collapse of private consumption and investment (GDFCF). By contrast, in Britain consumers' expenditure rose and investment only fell slightly during the contraction phase. In both economies, nominal government expenditures rose slightly, but in the US this was dwarfed by the GDP loss. Importantly for Britain, the contraction phase saw a very marked deterioration in the current account balance of payments, which slipped from a surplus of 2 per cent of GDP in 1929 to a deficit of 2.4 per cent by 1931 (Middleton, 1996: Figure 7.8), contributing to the severity of the crisis of that year. This has important implications for the Keynesian counterfactual story, and it reaffirms our earlier point about the nascent external constraint confronting policy makers. Turning to the recovery phases, there is more similarity between the two national stories, but one important difference which draws our attention to a very probable differential monetary policy affect in Britain (with cheap money and housebuilding) as against the US. This is the failure of GDFCF, which in the US had, by 1937, only just reached its 1929 level, whereas in Britain it had attained its 1929 level during 1934 and, by 1937, would be nearly 27 per cent higher. We should note also for Britain the neutral affect on GDP of foreign trade during this phase. Lastly, on the final recession and pre-war recovery phases, there is much similarity between the two economies with government expenditures the

[5] UK: Middleton (1981: Table 5; 1996: Table AI.1); US: Carter et al. (2006, III: series Ca1; IV: series Ea14, Ea15).

[6] See Middleton (1981: 275–78). We lack similar research for the US, but we can presume that the Federal deficit was less responsive to income changes because of a lower welfare effort (thus lower unemployment benefits) and less progressive tax structure. This, together with the given that the Federal budget was a much lower proportion of GDP than the UK central government budget (Fishback, 2010), suggests much reduced automatic stabilizing properties relative to the UK.

dominant reflationary impulse. For Britain, this is essentially a rearmament-induced recovery; for the US this is not the case until 1941.

8.2.2. Policy regime and policy setting

One further stage of scene-setting is necessary if the policies of three generations ago are to be fully comprehended and genuine knowledge transfer made possible. Although possibly anachronistic, here we deploy the concept of policy regime as 'encompass[ing] the constraints or limits imposed by custom, institutions and nature on the ability of the monetary authorities to influence the evolution of macroeconomic aggregates' (Bordo and Schwartz, 1999: 151). This relates immediately to the monetary policy trilemma, that the authorities can attain only two out of three possible policy objectives simultaneously: exchange rate stability; free international capital mobility; and national monetary policy independence directed towards domestic goals (Obstfeld et al., 2005). Our account of the British policy regime draws upon Eichengreen (1992) in terms of the key role exercised by the gold standard as a commitment device for generating policy credibility about the implicit policy target of price stability and the explicit goal of maintaining the exchange rate; and, from a public choice perspective, upon Buchanan and Wagner (1977) on the role played by the nineteenth-century balanced budget rule in constraining Leviathan. In my own work (principally Middleton, 1996), I have tried to synthesis these approaches to generate an interlocking, nineteenth-century fiscal constitution which was carried forward after the First World War, was fatally disturbed by the events of 1929–31, and then did not survive the Second World War.

Comprising three elements—free trade, the minimal balanced budget rule (MBBR), and the gold standard—the traditional defences of the minimalist state, the nineteenth-century fiscal constitution provided the bedrock for British economic policy in the 1920s, and especially after 1925 when the return to the gold standard was secured at the pre-war parity. Freedom from political interference for trade, fiscal, and monetary policies was thus the explicit goal. However, this goal was more pronounced as rhetoric than as reality, and in particular:

1. Fiscal policy was assailed by constant pressure group lobbying. Churchill, as Chancellor of the Exchequer, used fiscal window-dressing to create the illusion of maintaining nominal balanced budgets, whilst in any case, the budget was no longer minimal. For the first time outside of war, a British government had real demand leverage, and, as we have seen, this was considerably greater than that available to the US Federal government.
2. Monetary policy, both before and during the period of the restored gold standard, saw severe tensions over interest rates (now highly politicized) between chancellors and the governor of the Bank of England, the infamous (and not just in central banking circles) Montagu Norman.

There were important differences in the policy regime between Britain and the US, and not just in relation to the greater fiscal leverage exercised by British central government. Policy institutions and preferences differed significantly, with British governance more centralized and its policy community less fragmented.

Additionally, in the cardinal choice of government or market, there was, in adversity, a growing British preference for the former. The two countries had very different pre-war and interwar policy trajectories. Above all, if chancellors were unencumbered by meddling or dissenting prime ministers and other senior Cabinet colleagues, as they were largely between 1929–37 (with first Philip Snowden and then Neville Chamberlain), their authority within the core executive was immense. Thus, at first sight, a determined British government could have a decisive economic impact if it so chose. Of course, and here we return to the Keynesian solution not adopted, in practice, successive British governments pursued a path that was neither that sought by economic progressives nor entirely that for which economic orthodoxy hankered (Middleton, 2004: 477–89).

Trade policies were the most distinctly different, with the dominant narrative being that the Smoot–Harley tariff contributed towards the US downturn becoming a global depression, whereas, for the UK, the formal abandonment of free trade (a temporary measure in November 1931, codified April 1932) is part of the standard explanatory set—albeit contested—for Britain's domestic economic recovery from 1932. For fiscal policy, there is obviously considerable overlap on the issue of the Keynesian solution, but as I show in section 8.3.1, in Britain there were strong pressures for public sector growth which were independent of the stabilization debate. On monetary policy the Federal Reserve System was new, relative to the Bank of England, and very differently structured, with—post Benjamin Strong—the US less committed to promoting international economic cooperation. There was no banking crisis in Britain, no burst asset price bubble, whereas in the US it would be impossible to explain monetary policy without starting with bank failures. Moreover, the very different economic experiences of the war impinged on the policy space, not least in terms of domestic and international indebtedness. Figure 8.2 charts the transformation of three key measures of debt dynamics (the ratios of government debt-to-GDP and debt interest to TPE and to GDP), with the Second World War and immediate post-war period shown as well as the First World War to illustrate the relatively greater fiscal significance of that first conflict. Given the significant price deflation between 1920–35 (see Figure 8.3), it is not difficult to see why debt management was to dominate both monetary and fiscal policy (Middleton, 1985: chapter 6; Foreman-Peck, 2002). Moreover, Figure 8.2 charts the combined public sector. For the central government budget, which was the focus of attention, debt service payments (which on contemporary conventions required a significant sinking fund) were appropriating at least 40 per cent of government expenditure from the early 1920s until 1930/31, at which point in extremis, first, the sinking fund was suspended and then cheap money delivered its substantial fiscal dividend (Middleton, 1985: Table 6.4).

Finally, exit from the gold standard was very different for the two countries: the US acted unilaterally in 1933, whereas Britain was forced to abandon gold in September 1931 as a toxic mix of budgetary and balance of payments crises morphed into a political crisis which made the status quo unsustainable. In the following nine months, there then occurred a reorientation of economic policy that impacted on each element of the monetary policy trilemma. It is this policy reorientation which is the dividing line for interwar British economic policy: between a macroeconomic policy passivity born of the gold standard

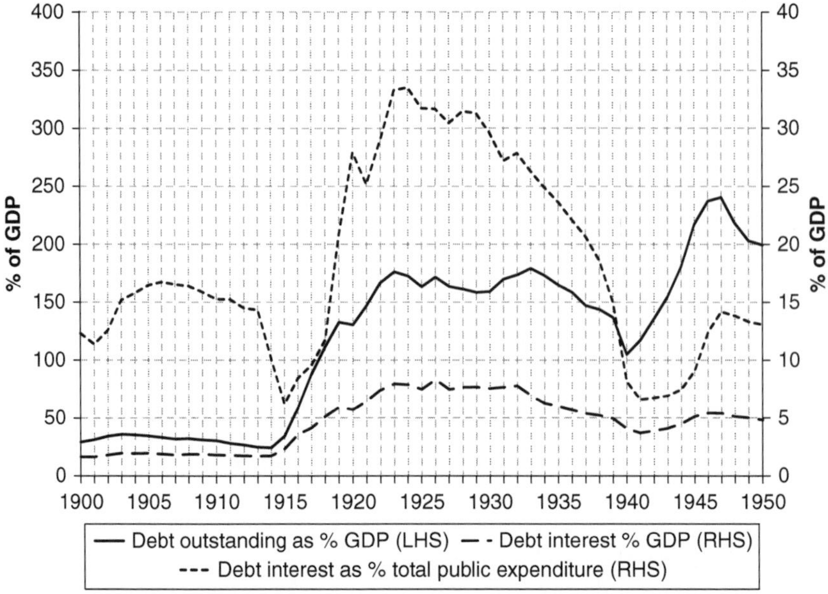

Fig. 8.2. UK: outstanding national debt, debt interest, and total public expenditure (% of GDP), 1900–50

Source: National debt outstanding at end of financial year: Mitchell (1988: 602–3); debt interest, total public expenditure and GDP: Middleton (1996: Table AI.1).

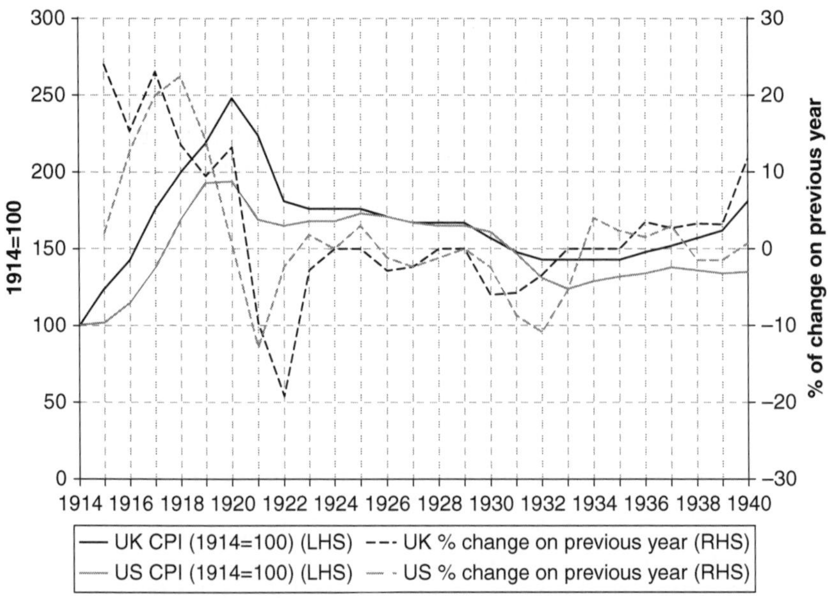

Fig. 8.3. Consumer Price Index (1914 = 100), UK and US, 1914–40

Source: Derived from Maddison (1991: Tables E2–4).

constraint, and a post-gold standard activism (albeit non-Keynesian) when freed from the 'golden fetter'. Moreover, Eichengreen and Sachs (1985) have argued, in what has become the orthodoxy, almost a stylized fact of the 1930s: those that left the gold standard early tended to be the first to recover in the 1930s. That said, a basic methodological problem has bedevilled all work on the impact of interwar macroeconomic policy, and especially post-September 1931 when sterling depreciation and policy reorientation brought, in sequence, a managed floating exchange rate; tariff protection for manufactures; 'cheap money' and regained monetary policy independence; and, after a longer lag, even a loosening of the fiscal stance. With a certain understatement, Solomou (1996: 112) writes that, such was the clustering of these momentous policy changes, that it is 'extremely difficult to distinguish individual policy impacts'.

8.3. INTERWAR PUBLIC FINANCES

The First World War transformed Britain's national debt and thus its public finances. However, debt dynamics are only one key to understanding interwar macroeconomic policy; another is the advent of democratic politics, for which there is long-established, cross-national evidence of an association with greater public expenditure, higher taxation, and deficit bias (Peters 1991; Lindert, 2004).[7]

8.3.1. Democratic politics and public expenditure

The fiscal trauma of the First World War should not obscure a pre-existing fiscal challenge, one which significantly predated the war but would come to maturity thereafter: that of containing pressures for public expenditure growth, and other governmental activities in the new environment of mass democracy, and all that this entailed for competition in the political market place. Certainly, relative to the US, Britain was in the vanguard of developing big government (Middleton 1996: chapter 3; 2004). Indeed, in the two decades before the First World War, there was considerable apprehension about the growth of TPE, though this had not as yet generated a crisis because of three mitigating factors. First, revenue growth (TR) kept pace (see Figure 8.4)—the product of tax innovation (especially the introduction of a progressive income tax, the potential of which was hardly tapped) and a growing economy—enabling debt to be repaid on a significant scale (Mallet, 1913: vii; Morgan, 1952: 89), such that, in 1913, debt outstanding as a percentage of GDP was at 24.8 per cent, a sixth lower than in 1900 (see Figure 8.2). Second, ideological innovation in the new political market place (especially so-called New Liberalism) depressed the hitherto dominant 'benefit' principle of taxation, permitting the principle of 'ability-to-pay' to take root and to give of its potential

[7] See Middleton, 1985: chapter 4; 1996: chapters 5 and 8. The most recent literature survey and empirical analysis of the pressures for public expenditure growth in Britain is Earley (2012); see also Aidt et al. (2010) for a rare demonstration that franchise extension in pre-war Britain plausibly also established new pressures for retrenchment.

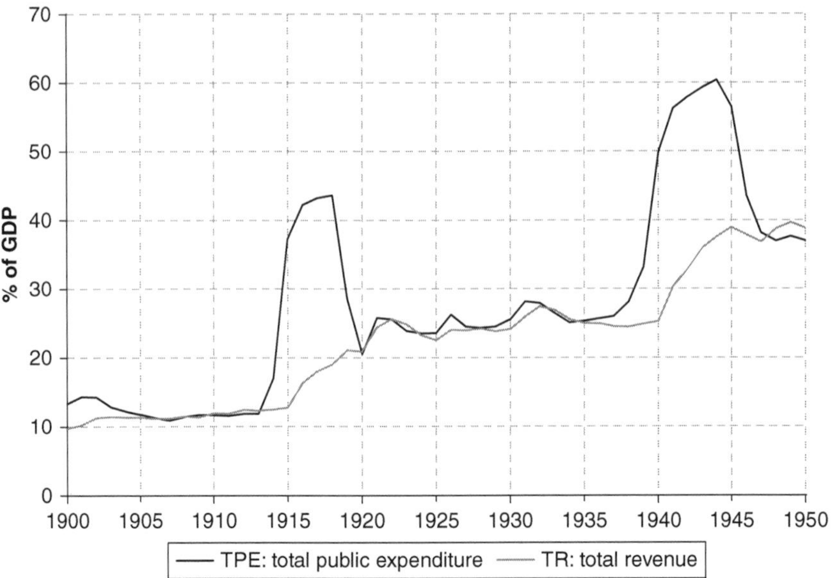

Fig. 8.4. Total public expenditure and total revenue (% of GDP), 1900–50
Source: Middleton (1996: Tables AI.1–AI.2).

once significant progression was introduced into the tax system (Middleton, 1996: 185–6). Third, the financial governance revolution of the second half of the nineteenth century (Peden, 2002) ensured that, even by modern standards of fiscal sustainability, there were in place robust institutions that disciplined the budgetary process and quantitative rules—not least the MBBR, part of the trinity of defences for maintaining the minimalist state—that set limits deemed prudent and politically acceptable. Figure 8.4 displays TPE and TR which are broadly stationary before the First World War once the effects of the Boer War are removed, these fiscal aggregates are defined on the same basis as the debt interest element displayed in Figure 8.2.

One of the principal tax innovators of the late nineteenth century, William Harcourt, Chancellor of the Exchequer 1892–95, lamented in his final budget that:

> There is a universal demand for more and more expenditure every year for every conceivable objective, all of them excellent objects, but all of them pursued absolutely without any regard to their cost. Besides these demands for additional expenditure . . . there are continual proposals to cut off first one and then another item of the public revenue. . . . in public administration you have to make your taxation keep pace with your profusion [but] economy (not only political economy) has become a lost art at the close of the century (cited in Mallet, 1913: 99–100).

Modern fiscal politics were thus well-established by 1914. Indeed, as is clear from a comparison of Figures 8.4 and 8.5, whilst TPE and TR are broadly stationary between 1900–13, public social spending was on a strong upward trend, and had been so since *c.* 1890. As Peacock and Wiseman (1967: 66) noted, there was an important change in attitude away from the primacy of retrenchment and instead

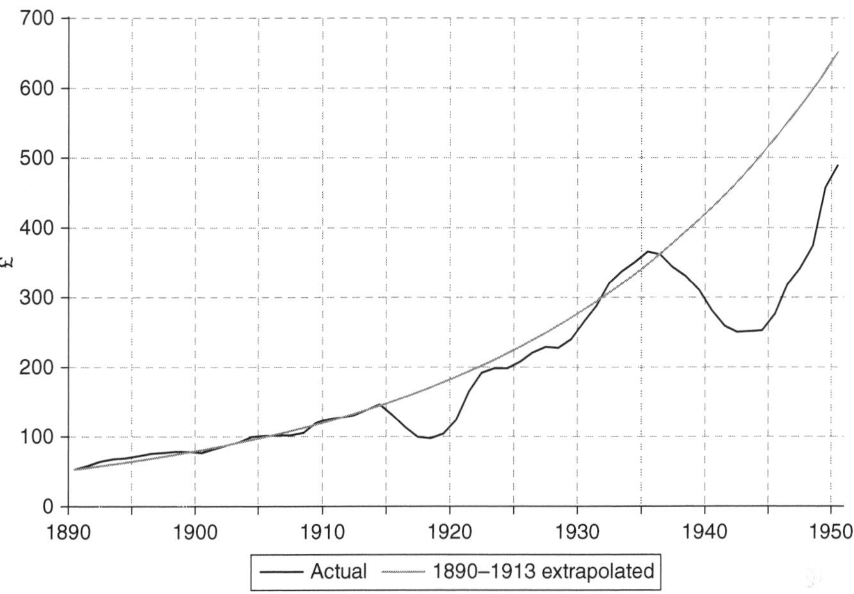

Fig. 8.5. Public social spending per capita at constant (2003) prices, 1890–1950, £
Sources: UK total public social spending: Earley (2012: series UKPSSTO); population: Officer (2011).

a shift towards taxable capacity as the effective constraint on government, this being a 'less concrete concept than retrenchment and hence a less severe curb—particularly in that it provided no similar check upon the upward displacement of expenditures by wars'. In the context of a rules versus discretion paradigm, the pre-First World War disposition to the former was being challenged, but the injury was not yet fatal. Indeed, the war saw the imposition of a new fiscal discipline: the so-called McKenna rule (named for the chancellor of 1915–16),[8] designed to set a framework for determining the proportion of additional wartime expenditure that must be tax-financed, with taxation thereby set at a level sufficient to provide for the future interest charge of the new debt and 'prudent' debt redemption path. Recently, the McKenna rule has been modelled by economists as a form of tax smoothing, one which resulted in an accelerated debt repayment path which depressed the interwar economy via higher taxation than would otherwise have been the case (Nason and Vahey, 2007). Whatever the macroeconomic consequences, the McKenna rule can be interpreted as a signal that there would be a peacetime return to balanced budgets. This, together with massive scale and the form of wartime borrowing (to an unprecedented extent dependent

[8] Nason and Vahey (2007) suggest a rather greater clarity for the rule than was conceived at the time. See, for example, Morgan (1952: 93), who labelled it 'one of the strangest principles ever laid down in the history of public finance', whilst Wormell (2000: 202–3) provides a provenance suggestive of only a retrospective status as a severe fiscal discipline.

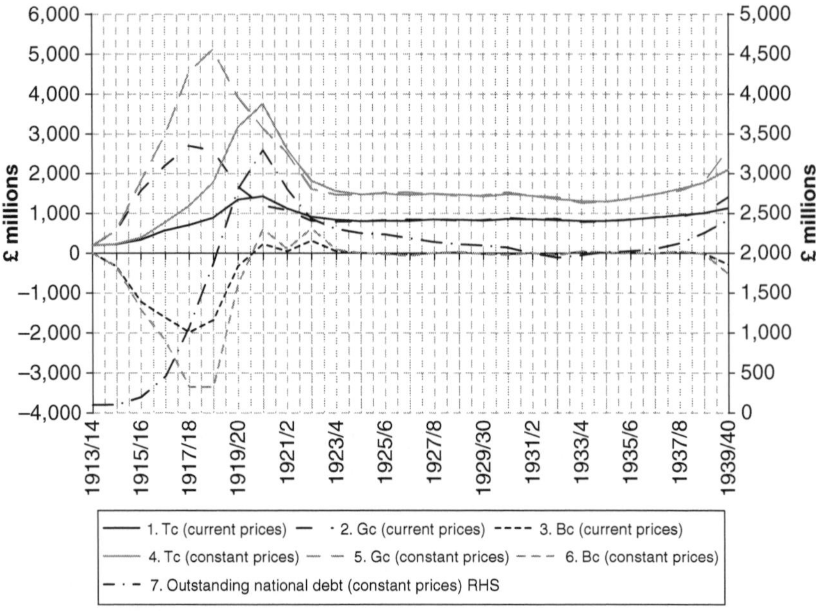

Fig. 8.6. Public finance aggregates, contemporary definitions, current and constant 1913/14 prices, 1913/14–1939/40, (£million)

Sources: *Statistical Abstracts of the United Kingdom*, 1922: 9; 1927:105; 1934: 135; 1937: 169; 1948: 213.

on short-term debt), ensured that, upon the war's end, it was imperative the Treasury re-establish firm financial control, as indeed must the Bank of England over market interest rates. Key contemporary public finance series for, as then defined, public expenditure (G_c), total revenue (T_c), and the budget balance (B_c) are given in Figure 8.6, shown both in nominal terms (series 1–3) and, to give a perspective on the war-induced transformation of the public finances, real values (series 4–6, 1913/14 prices). Additionally, also at constant prices, a seventh series (outstanding national debt) is shown to calibrate the consequences of heavy wartime deficit-finance and the subsequent peacetime budgetary struggle to counter deficit bias.

8.3.2. The Geddes 'axe' and the quest for budgetary stability

There is much debate about the macroeconomic consequences of the speedy re-establishment of the pre-war policy regime after the war. Ostensibly, little had changed from pre-war with official attitudes towards the desirable level of expenditure, taxation, the tax mix, and, above all, balancing budgets, appearing to have survived the war broadly intact, albeit that the M (Minimum) of MBBR was now a distant memory, and political realism dictated that it would so remain. Political consent for renewed fiscal orthodoxy reached a peak in 1922 with the so-called Geddes axe, the first fiscal consolidation between the wars, and 'one of the most controversial exercises in the reduction of public expenditure essayed by any modern British government' (McDonald, 1989: 643).[9] Charged by the Lloyd George-led, but Conservative-dominated, coalition government, this committee, appointed in August 1921, comprised solely leading businessmen—albeit that Geddes was one of the businessmen who had entered the wartime government as a minister—and was charged with securing economies of £100 million in projected 1922/23 'supply services' expenditure, this embracing the armed forces and civil categories of expenditure but not national debt charges. In the context of the time, £100 million represented 8.6 per cent of 1921/22 *ex ante* total expenditure as then defined (G_c), or some 2 per cent of *ex post* 1921 GDP.

The complex politics that brought about the Geddes committee, and what then transpired, are of sufficient interest today that the ESRC (Economic and Social Research Council) are currently funding a re-examination of this episode of 'public spending in hard times'.[10] What will be of particular interest is that, notwithstanding a membership and terms of reference which gave enormous latitude to impose rectitude, and, according to a close study by two accounting historians (Burrows and Cobbin, 2009: 200), undertaking the 'first whole-of-government review of an administration committed to the comprehensive social-welfare obligations associated with a modern state', the committee came up, by February 1922, with only £86.8 million of the £100 million, of which—predictably given this was a post-war retrenchment—the armed forces were to bear £70.3 million of economies (HMSO, 1922: 168–9). In turn, government then approved only £52 million of the committee's recommended total (Peden, 2002: 169), in effect only just over half the original target and thus amounting to no more than 1 per cent of GDP. This was intensely disappointing to those groups lobbying for retrenchment (McDonald, 1989: 672),[11] providing, of course, an undercurrent which would come to the fore once more in 1930–31 because, to balance the budget (B_c), chancellors increased taxation without a visible equivalent economy drive, that is until the May committee was appointed. Nonetheless, despite the fiscal disappointment, the Geddes axe served its political purpose. It prolonged the life of the coalition government, quite unlike the May report, which brought down the Labour administration, and resulted in a coalition government (Mowat, 1955: 382).

Interwar authorities on budgetary policy were more positive about the fiscal achievement, with Hicks (1938: 5) clear that 'through the activity of the Geddes Committee . . . the civil service was reduced to a peace-time footing, and by these means the budget was scaled down to more reasonable proportions'. What is of

[9] The Geddes axe has acquired a formidable reputation, but close inspection of the cuts and of the contemporary politics leads to the balanced judgement, here made by Cline (1974: 102), that 'where the Geddes axe cut was where the Treasury or the chancellor or any other vessel of orthodox economic views would have cut. There was nothing peculiarly philistine about the axe'.

[10] Comprising Christopher Hood, Carl Emmerson, and Ruth Dixon, this joint Oxford-IFS project has no substantive publications to date, but see <http://www.christopherhood.net/pdfs/public-spending-in-hard-times.pdf>, 09.08.11.

[11] Higgs' (1922) review of the three Geddes reports and associated official publications, also contains interesting material on the 'anti-waste movement' and the political leverage it exercised, including defeating a coalition candidate in a hitherto safe seat at a by-election in the summer of 1921. An interesting exercise would be to apply current political economy techniques (for example, Alesina et al., 2010) on the electoral consequences of large fiscal adjustments to interwar Britain.

importance about fiscal consolidation is its cumulative nature, as well as its beneficial consequences for interest rates, and thus the feedback loop to debt management costs (huge as we have seen) if it is deemed credible. On a simple analysis, were we to subtract £52 million from total government expenditure as then defined (G_c) from 1922/23 onwards, and then rebase at constant 1913/14 prices, the cumulative saving by end 1938/39 amounts to just over £0.5 billion, or well over two and a half times the 1913/14 budget. The Geddes consolidation applied to personnel and services (most very labour-intensive), making cuts in both, upon which it was able to take advantage of the declining official cost of living index. It also acted to curtail future commitments, especially unfunded superannuation, though the British civil servants' pension scheme remained non-contributory until 1972 (Burrows and Cobbin, 2009: 210). Additionally, and importantly, the Geddes axe had a parallel consolidation on the taxation side which found room, in the 1922 budget, for a reduction in the standard rate of income tax from 30 to 25 per cent, with the net effect being that, on the contemporary definition (B_c), a budget surplus was achieved until an unexpected deficit in 1925/26 occasioned another, much smaller, economy campaign. This aimed for supply service economies of £10–12 million per annum, but achieved cumulatively far short of this target. Nonetheless, 'the principal intention and effect of these efforts was to create an atmosphere of parsimony that would constrain future growth of expenditure, rather than to make actual reductions' (Peden, 2002: 207–8).

How might we view the Geddes axe in relation to what we know about more modern, successful fiscal consolidations? This question is separable into two parts: the macroeconomics, which connects to the EFC hypothesis which is considered in section 8.5, when we look more closely at the May committee, and the political economy, which we consider here.[12] First, from modern experience we know that there are key challenges associated with selecting the timing for initiating consolidation and the short-term conditions for its success. These include the opportunities provided by a sense of 'crisis', manifest in large deficits and high interest rates, and perceived by the public as an unsustainable situation; and that, to be successful, consolidation must be directed at current expenditure, with a large weight on social spending. Second, it is clear that countries with fiscal rules and targets/anchors with high transparency achieve better results in terms of magnitudes and duration. Above all, economic authorities that provide clarity are more likely to instil confidence and thus reap the reward (lower interest rates) of policy credibility. Third, it is more credible not to front-load fiscal adjustments unless there are urgent financing needs. This looks, fourth, towards the medium- and longer-term: of locking-in the gains made; and of containing the longer-term forces (as for example, an ageing population) of public expenditure growth and actions in the political marketplace which undermine the tax base.

With social expenditure identified as key, it is significant that defence bore the brunt of the Geddes axe. Nevertheless, a recent analysis by think-tank economists (Lilico et al., 2009: 29, 31)—one admittedly somewhat hidebound by having only a

[12] The literature is vast, but the following are useful on the political economy: Alesina et al. (1998); OECD (2007; 2010); Wagschal and Wenzelburger (2008), Lilico et al. (2009); and IMF (2010).

surface knowledge of the appropriate sources, and apparently little sense of the historiography—concluded that the 'Geddes cuts did not merely keep spending growth down, rather they actively reversed it' as 'the combination of financial pressure and the political threat of the Anti-Waste League forced the Cabinet into determined active cuts'. Overall, this study concluded:

> This action does appear to have been a success, in its own terms, in both the short and long runs. Spending was reduced very markedly and did not rise again for at least a decade. Even when it did start to rise again, the culture was such that spending cuts were proposed. Growth was considerably stronger subsequent to the consolidation than before it. The severe recession in the immediate aftermath of the Great War gave way to the 'roaring twenties' (Lilico et al., 2009).

No doubt this is the same 'roaring twenties' as the 1920s of Pigou's doldrums! One wonders also whether Lilico et al. have contemplated whether the 'severe' 1920–21 recession was, if not caused, then at least deepened, by the quantitatively more significant cuts in expenditure that preceded the Geddes axe (between 1918 and 1920 TPE fell from £2.287 to £1.229 billion, with the budget balance moving from a deficit of 24.6 per cent of GDP to a 0.4 per cent surplus—see Figure 8.4). Sarcasm and historiographical ignorance aside, this study makes insufficient allowance for the highly unusual, post-war, nature of this fiscal consolidation, the contemporaneous reconstitution of the UK constitution (which takes southern Ireland out of the financial accounts during 1922/23, but not instantly), and the longer-run context of TPE trends, and especially those for social expenditures where much welfare effort was provided at local level; some only in part wholly funded from central grants. Another recent analysis, the first ever comprehensive enumeration of public social spending on all spending programmes at all levels of government (see Figure 8.5), suggests that, in real terms, social expenditures in the 1920s regained their pre-war trend, recovering from the dislocation of the war, with any effect from the Geddes axe swamped by the rising burden of unemployment benefits which, of course, relates to macroeconomic underperformance. In short, a methodology dependent on a simplistic pre- and post-consolidation measurement of TPE, and expenditure programme growth rates independent of context and the endogeneity of the budget, will not take us very far.

Moving to my second point about successful fiscal consolidations, countering deficit bias through fiscal rules was, as we have seen, central to the political economy of Britain's public finance system. Though it had been severely battered by the war, the immediate post-war efforts to re-establish Treasury and parliamentary control (both *ex ante* and *ex post*) are all suggestive of policy credibility. The widespread discourse of discontent about Treasury 'candle-ends' speaks of their effectiveness. However, in the modern literature, conditions for successful consolidation include fiscal rules that are clear, transparent, and take account of the cycle, having sufficient flexibility to accommodate macroeconomic shocks. Arguably, the first criterion was satisfied; the second needs to be a little qualified (there was significant fiscal window-dressing; see Middleton, 1985: 80–3; Earley, 2012: chapter 3); but the third is problematic. Indeed, for Keynes, who, contrary to the opinion of constitutional economists (Buchanan and Wagner, 1977), did not favour long-term budget deficits, his key argument of the time was that the budget is endogenous and thus there are circumstances in which overriding the automatic stabilizers (a concept not then invented but intuitively understood) will depress demand further, thereby making longer-term budgetary equilibrium even more difficult to obtain. A successful fiscal consolidation involves attaining equilibrium between the interests and incentive structures of policy makers and economic agents who will need to adapt to consolidation and who, through the political marketplace, have scope for economic rents and political vetoes. By this standard, the Geddes axe was probably as much as could be achieved in the early 1920s, though I should also add that a successful fiscal consolidation ought not to involve microeconomic actions which undermine long-term growth potential. Here the accusation made at the time, that this was a 'rich person's economy drive', and, most particularly, as it related to state education, is relevant (Burrows and Cobbin, 2009: 214). On this aspect, as with the later May committee, *The Economist* for one was emphatic that this was false economy;[13] what we now know about human capital accumulation, and the supply-side dimension of Britain's interwar productivity performance, makes this even more important (Broadberry and Crafts, 1992).

Throughout the 1920s, official policy, in which the twin agencies of the Treasury and Bank of England were agreed on fundamental objectives, but not always on how to achieve them, was to seek an *ex ante* budget balance, (B_c) as then defined. This required strict expenditure control, significant debt repayment through a formal sinking fund, all in the hope that a combination of a revived economy and price stabilization would eventually permit tax reductions and lower interest rates. In practice, securing budgetary equilibrium was always difficult; long-term pressures for public expenditure growth were ineluctable, price deflation continued and, with the 1925 return to gold, the exchange rate was overvalued with predictable implications for monetary policy and the real economy. Some amelioration was obtained through tax reform, especially after successful business lobbying for rate relief, and a certain deviation from the fiscal rules became routine as successive chancellors succumbed to the temptations of fiscal window-dressing.

8.3.3. Debt dynamics

As I demonstrated in Figure 8.4, the early interwar period saw a very marked upwards shift in the debt interest/TPE ratio, peaking at 33.5 per cent (some 7.9 per cent of GDP) in 1924, just before Britain's return to the gold standard which locked it into a deflationary straightjacket until 1931 (Middleton 2011: 5–10). Debt did not just dominate interwar public finances, it swamped them. As is clear from Figure 8.7 on public sector budget balances, before the First World War, when the MBBR prevailed but was under pressure, the combined balance—of current plus capital accounts—was rarely in surplus but, bar the Boer War, the primary surplus (an important indicator in today's debate about debt dynamics and fiscal consolidation) was in healthy surplus, averaging 1.5 per cent of GDP between 1900–13. However, during the interwar period (1920–38), still a pre-Keynesian policy regime, the combined balance was only in surplus in five years, and, interestingly, two of these were 1933 and 1934—this a testament to the severe fiscal tightening of 1929–33. However, the current balance was positive in 15 out

[13] 'Stinting education', *The Economist*, 21 July 1934: 103–4.

of the 18 years, whilst the primary balance was positive *every* year, averaging 7.4 per cent of GDP for the period.

Judged both by contemporary standards, and by more modern experience with fiscal consolidations, this was an extraordinary debt management/amortization effort, though, as we shall see, the debt redemption path implied by the McKenna rule was, in periods of acute fiscal stress in the 1920s, subject to certain ad hoc adjustments and then, with the 1931 crisis, significantly downgraded. Even so, for Keynes and other economic progressives, the level of commitment to debt redemption imparted an unnecessarily deflationary bias to monetary and fiscal policies. Nonetheless, and this was reaffirmed by the influential Colwyn committee on national debt and taxation (HMSO, 1927: 330), it remained official opinion that the debt repayment path must be significant (with greater credibility when through formal sinking funds) as this 'provided the best means of maintaining confidence and keeping up the level of quotations of Government securities'. A trade-off between a low interest rate monetary policy and a less restrictive fiscal policy is thus at the heart of the interwar policy space.

This is all well-known amongst policy historians. However, what has not been explored hitherto is the implications of these debt dynamics for fiscal sustainability. A first step was made by Crafts and Fearon (2010: 310, n.11) who applied the standard formula for fiscal sustainability (**b**) to my data in Figures 8.2 and 8.7; this of the form: **b**>**d**(**r**-**g**), where **b** = primary surplus/GDP; **d** = outstanding national debt/GDP; **r** = real interest rate on government debt; and **g** = growth rate of real GDP. Using this standard formula, it follows that, for a given primary balance, the

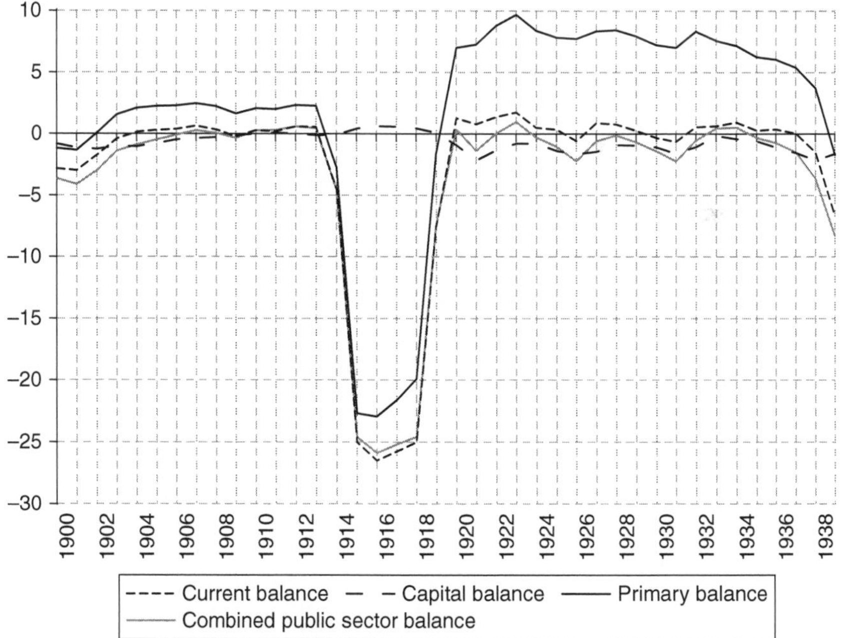

Fig. 8.7. Public sector budget balances, % of GDP, 1900–39

Source: Middleton (1996: Tables AI.1–AI.2).

debt/GDP ratio **d** declines so long as GDP growth **g** is higher than the interest rate **r**. The results are illuminating. For the late 1920s, were inflation to be at 0 per cent, then **b** would be 3.6 per cent, but were prices to fall by 5 per cent, **b** would rise to 12.1 per cent. In practice, **b** averaged 7.6 per cent between 1929–32 whilst consumer prices (see Figure 8.3) fell at an annual average rate of 5 per cent. Clearly **d** was enormously expanded, but this was also the case for other combatants: for example, proportionally the rise in debt was much greater for the US than for Britain.[14] The US did not experience heavy unemployment in the 1920s, nor did France, but the latter had very different price trends as the French government succumbed to the incentive to inflate its way out of its heavy war debt burden (Eichengreen, 1992: 113, 172–83). By contrast, Britain had a price deflation of variable intensity between 1920–35; and high **r** before 1932. Fortunately, notwithstanding the economic problems of the time, and widespread critique of policy, real GDP growth **g** was historically respectable on trend (1924–37) and this aided fiscal sustainability. Moreover, with the abandonment of gold, the substantial fall in **r**, and approximate price stability from 1932–35, and then gently rising prices, the necessary value for **b** fell sharply, to below 2 per cent later in the 1930s. However, the primary balance was still as high as 3.7 per cent of GDP in 1938, notwithstanding a now rapidly expanding deficit-financed rearmament programme. Viewed in the round, from the perspective of the modern fiscal sustainability literature, interwar governments achieved a level for **b** very much higher than appeared warranted by contemporary debt dynamics with consequent depressive effects on demand. Contemporaries, however, perceived their circumstances differently; thus did they calibrate their debt tolerance, and thus must we filter historical experience for any lessons for the present.

8.4. POLICY: NARRATIVE AND ASSESSMENT

After conducting a thorough literature review, Worswick (1984: 93) concluded emphatically: 'Spontaneous forces alone will not count for the recovery [of 1932–37]. Policy made important contributions.' Discounting a 'natural' recovery, and, in particular, following Dimsdale (1984: 102) that the fall in employment during the contraction phase and its recovery thereafter were largely accounted for on the demand side, we here follow Worswick, who, in identifying the proximate cause of the depression as a sharp decline in exports, quite naturally accorded the abandonment of gold and the ensuing depreciation of sterling as at minimum permissive of recovery. In the recovery phase, net export growth made no contribution to GDP growth, and we are thus looking to explain a recovery in domestic demand in terms of domestic policy.

Figures 8.3 and 8.7–8.9 provide the background for our policy narrative and the starting point for the assessment of policy effectiveness. Figure 8.3 charts UK and

[14] Total US national debt rose a factor of 21.4 times between 1914–20, reaching 33.2 per cent of GDP; for UK, the rise between 1913/14 and the 1919/20 peak was a rise of 11.2 times. US data: Carter et al. (2006, III: series Ca10; V: series Ea587); UK data: as Figure 8.4. See League of Nations (1934: 236–39) for comparative debt trends.

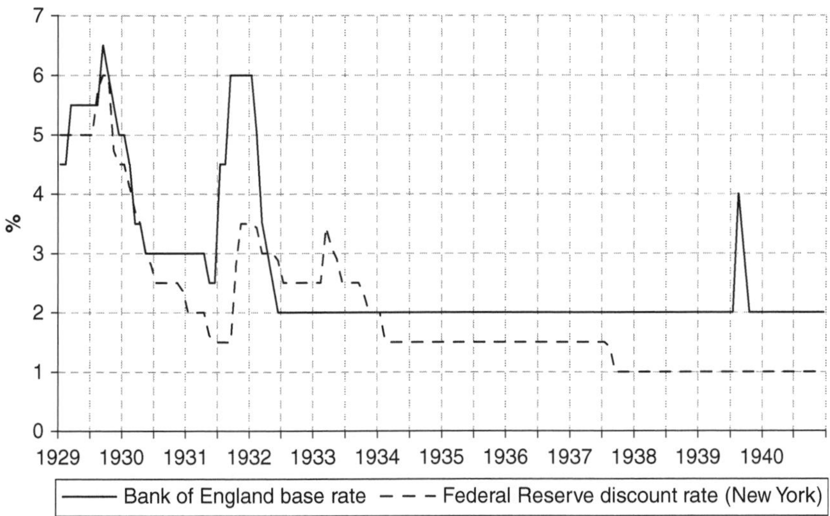

Fig. 8.8. Official interest rates, monthly averages: UK and US, 1929–40

Sources: UK: <http://www.bankofengland.co.uk/statistics/rates/baserate.xls>, 08.04.10; US: <http://www.nber.org/databases/macrohistory/contents/chapter13.html>, 08.04.10.

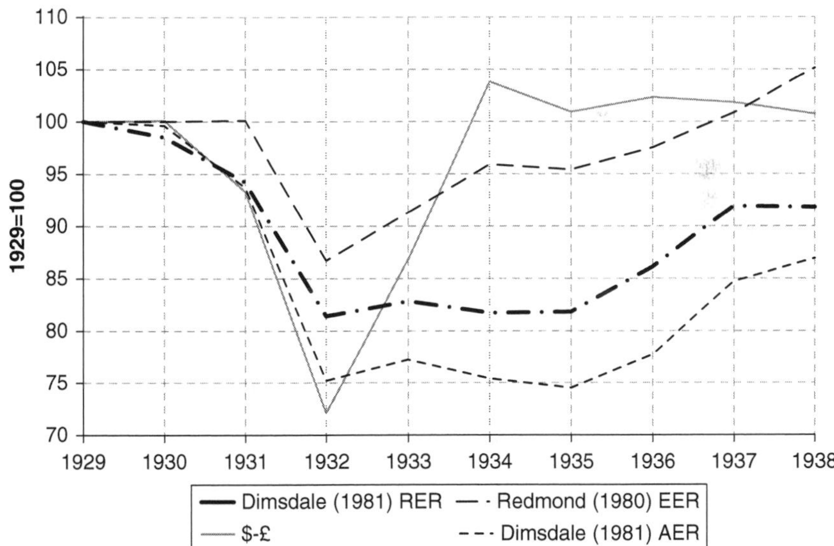

Fig. 8.9. Sterling exchange rates (1929 = 100), 1929–38

Source: Dimsdale (1981: Tables 3, 9).

US consumer prices, both as index numbers (1914 = 100) and as percentage change on the previous year; Figure 8.7 charts the combined public sector budget balances, including the primary balance; Figure 8.8 illustrates monthly movements in the two official interest rates, the Bank of England base rate and—since London perceived itself as a price taker during the gold standard era—the New York Federal Reserve discount rate; and Figure 8.9 illustrates the nominal $-£ and three effective exchange rate measures.

8.4.1. Monetary policy

Monetary policy divides relatively neatly at September 1931 when Britain was forced to abandon the gold standard, although two important considerations pertain in terms of policy space and the policy record. First, although pre-September 1931 monetary policy was often tighter than was desirable in light of the developing downturn, it is clear from the behaviour of the monetary aggregates and the policy record that the authorities were 'more focused on domestic objectives than on following the "rules of the [gold standard] game"', lowering the bank rate (from 6 per cent to 2.5 per cent between 1929 and 1931) and sterilizing the effects of gold outflows on the money supply (Howson, 1975: 43–4, 66–9; Bernanke, 2000: 151–2, Table 4.c). Second, the abandonment of gold coincided with a, temporary, substantial increase in bank rate (from 4.5 to 6 per cent). It was to take some months (an anxiety phase) before the authorities felt sufficiently confident to contemplate lower interest rates, a process greatly aided by tightening capital controls and financial turbulence elsewhere, which made London appear a relatively safe haven for highly mobile, short-term capital. Thus, the end of the golden fetter did not bring an immediate freedom of action, though the potential for reorientation was recognized from the outset (Howson, 1975: 79–89).[15]

For the beginning of our survey period there is a broad consensus that 'money played at best only a minor role in the economic depression of 1929–32'; and that, by abandoning gold, Britain 'dodged' the monetary collapse experienced by the US (Capie and Wood, 1994: 236, 242). Monetary policy independence, of course, did not exist with the gold standard. However, once a floating—indeed highly managed—exchange rate was secured and policy makers had recovered from the initial panic about inflation (fears that an uncontrollable depreciation of sterling would result in imported inflation, this being an added reason for quickly securing fiscal retrenchment to maintain confidence), the bank rate was reduced significantly (to 2 per cent) and was maintained thereafter (bar a short-lived spike associated with the onset of the war).

The standard questions asked about the role of monetary policy after September 1931 concern its effectiveness with respect to:

[15] There is a broad consensus amongst economic historians about interwar monetary policy, with little new work since the foundational studies of Moggridge (1972), Howson (1975), Sayers (1976) and Dimsdale (1981), though Nevin (1955) is still relevant, and especially for the impact of cheap money on the housing market and the cost of finance for industrial and commercial companies.

1. Exchange rate objectives.
2. The promotion of economic recovery through higher investment, and especially in the housing market.
3. The relaxation of the fiscal stance made possible by the significant reduction in the interest burden of the national debt.
4. The extent to which there was a trade-off between cheap money and greater fiscal activism.

Taking each in turn, beginning with exchange rate policy, this, after the anxiety phase of autumn/winter 1931, quickly and quietly evolved into a managed float of sterling designed, inter alia, to give some competitive edge to British exports without undue stress upon the geo-politics of international finance and of the British empire (Howson, 1980).

On the second point, the key question of the cheap money era, there have been a number of studies of the sensitivity of the components of interwar aggregate demand to interest rates. Broadberry's (1986: 64–5, 129, 131, 142–4) aggregate demand/supply model for interwar Britain, which has a monetary dimension though not a formal monetary sector, is widely cited on the effects of cheap money. He found a low interest elasticity for investment (-0.11 for non-housing and (long-run) −1.1 for housing) with the major effect of monetary policy transmitted via the external sector through the exchange rate, contributing to the 13 per cent depreciation of sterling between 1931–33 which raised output by about 3 per cent through the improvement in the balance of trade. Much, of course, has been claimed for the role of a housebuilding boom in the recovery of the 1930s, along with an older strand of structural change in industry (the 'old-new' industries debate) partly driven by rising real incomes over the depression period. Broadberry (1986: 25, 61) allocates about half the rise in housing investment 1931–33 to the advent of cheap money, with net investment in housing exceeding net total investment 1932–33. These broad parameters, of cheap money being most effective in the housing sector, are confirmed by Dimsdale and Horsewood (1995).

Similarly, from their review of the monetary data, Capie and Wood (1994: 246) confirmed that cheap money 'undoubtedly encouraged investment', and that whilst 'money was not central... to the recovery,... doubtless it was accommodating', though it should be noted that this, of course, is from the contested perspective that, in the long-run, monetary conditions do not determine real interest rates. We have, then, a positive role for cheap money (Dimsdale, 1984; Worswick, 1984): in terms of timing (coincident with the lower turning point in 1932) and significance, it impacted strongly on residential investment and supported the recovery of the industrial and commercial sector. Whilst money supply growth was not continuous over the recovery phase, relative to European competitors (many still fettered by the gold standard), it was undoubtedly helpful for recovery, and this notwithstanding the Treasury's 'funding complex' with respect to the floating debt which was in conflict with the cheap money policy, thereby lessening the fall in long-term interest rates (Howson, 1975: 95–103). The contrast with the US is twofold. First, the absence of banking crises; and, second, that in Britain the positive contribution of policy to the recovery was distributed between monetary and fiscal policy, whereas in the US little is claimed at best for fiscal policy and it is the monetary expansion that is highlighted (Romer, 1992).

Regarding the third question, it is arguable that further tax rises and/or retrenchment in expenditure were avoided in 1932/33 and, above all, 1933/34 because of the lessened debt charge on the budget: the reduction in total debt service including sinking funds between 1932/33 and 1933/34 was nearly 2.5 percentage points of GDP (see Figure 8.4). Without cheap money, the recovery could well have stalled. The fourth question, the trade-off, we defer until our treatment of fiscal policy and the Treasury view upon the (in)efficacy of long-financed public works. At this stage, all we need to report here is that key policy makers in the Treasury and Bank of England were certain that cheap money would be imperilled by an inappropriate setting of fiscal instruments.

8.4.2. Fiscal policy

Fiscal policy is both simple and incredibly complex to evaluate between the wars: apparently simple to comprehend, because the goals appear straightforward, in contrast with the pre-war observance of the MBBR. In practice, however, evaluation is incredibly complicated, as the period witnessed a complex of enormous pressures for expenditure growth, a budget now significantly enlarged from pre-war and highly cyclically sensitive, and all of this within the context of considerable macroeconomic instability and the pressures for the Keynesian solution which, importantly, predate the 1929 downturn.

The traditional view of fiscal policy in the 1930s is one of a rigid pursuit of orthodoxy (Richardson, 1967: 211–12), whereby the authorities sought an *ex post* budget balance and, if *ex ante* this was threatened by a macroeconomic shock, they were prepared to override the automatic stabilizers to regain budgetary equilibrium. On this view, fiscal orthodoxy equated to inherent macroeconomic policy destabilization. Policy makers set the budget, and the fiscal stance was assessed, in terms of the actual budget balance (for central, not general, government). As a summary measure of fiscal influence this is, of course, subject to the well-known problem, explored first for the US in Brown (1956), of the endogenity of the budget. Middleton (1981), whose results are in Figure 8.10, first adjusted the actual central government budget balance (B_c/Y) for the authorities' fiscal window-dressing to produce a new balance measure (B/Y) and then used a Brown (1956) type methodology to calculate a constant employment surplus measure (B^*/Y^*).[16] On this basis, fiscal policy was contractionary throughout the contraction phase and well beyond, though it did—via rearmament—impart a very significant stimulus which ensured that the 1937–38 recession was of short duration and that the economy was growing rapidly by the eve of the Second World War. Indeed, Thomas (1983: 571) argues 'the success of rearmament in creating employment, even at the top of the cycle, leads us to view the eschewment of fiscal policy in the thirties as a missed opportunity for the economy'.

[16] There has been debate about the appropriateness of this measure of fiscal policy (Middleton, 2011: 14–15).

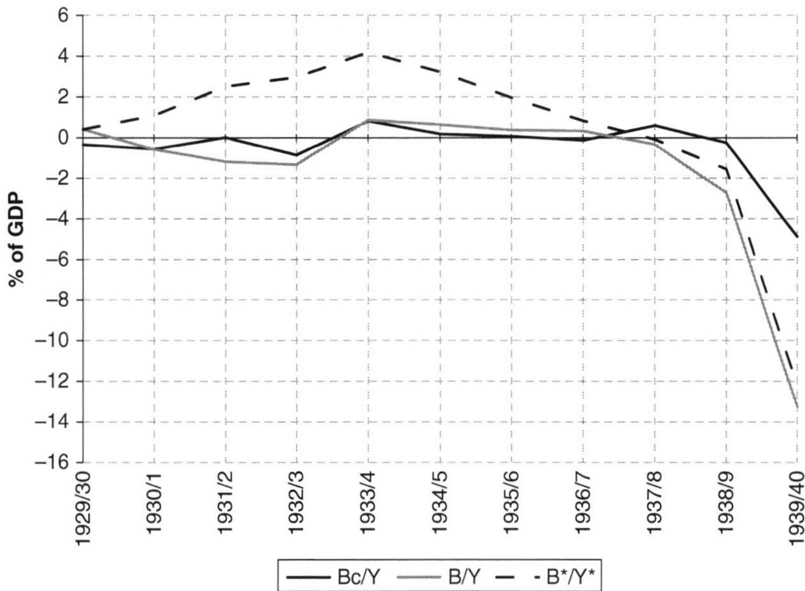

Fig. 8.10. Summary measures of fiscal stance, % of actual and constant employment GDP, 1929/30–1939/40

Source: Middleton (1981: Table 5).

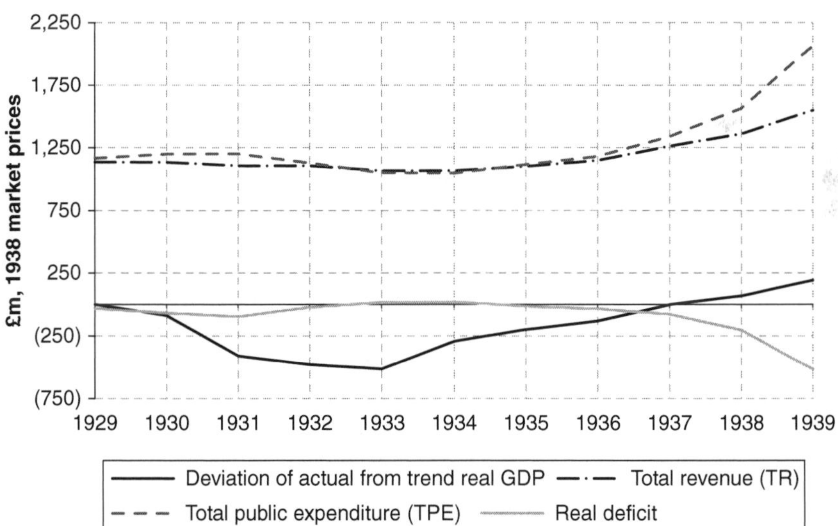

Fig. 8.11. GDP deviations, total public expenditure and total revenue, 1938 market prices, 1929–39

Sources: GDP: Feinstein (1972: Table 5); TPE and TR: Middleton (1996: Tables AI.1, AI.2) adjusted by GDP deflator, Feinstein (1972: Table 61).

The overall position can be demonstrated in a different fashion, conceptualized in Figure 8.11 to highlight the issue of scale (the smallness of the deficits in relation to the output gap) and to enable comparison with Fishback's (2010: Figure 4) identical presentation for US fiscal policy. The mildness of the output loss relative to the US is again immediately apparent, but what is new is the comparative stability of TPE and TR (both here measured at actual employment and for the combined public sector as against the central government accounts used for the fiscal stance debate discussed above), and especially in relation to the growing output gap to 1933 which amounted to over £510 million (nearly 11 per cent of 1929 GDP). Against this contraction, the public sector deficit was *reduced* by £50 million between 1929–33, although over 1929–31—the period in which the authorities attempted, but did not succeed fully, in overriding the automatic stabilizers—the actual deficit did widen. Nonetheless, this was only by 16 per cent of the 1931 output gap.

Finally, and again on the basis of data not cyclically adjusted, we can decompose both the expenditure and revenue sides of the combined public sector (see Table 8.2) to derive the following results about the path of fiscal policy. For the contraction phase, we note first that the combined public authorities' deficit fell from 0.7 to 0.5 per cent of GDP between 1929–32; the product of an increase in the expenditure ratio of 3.4 percentage points of GDP and the receipts ratio by 3.6 percentage points. For expenditures which could be considered to be exhaustive, or nearly so on the first round (current goods and services plus gross capital formation plus current grants to the personal sector), there was a rise of 3.3 percentage points, but against this must be set tax rises of 3.6 percentage points, with taxes on income rising slightly more than taxes on expenditure. The prevailing ethos amongst the interwar business community was that taxes on income were the most deflationary, and the US example suggests that further research is now needed on the supply-side effects of fiscal policy: how tax rates and tax structures impacted upon spending and investment. Looking at the recovery phase, 1932–37, the receipts ratio was reduced by five times more than the expenditure ratio, showing how difficult was fiscal consolidation on the expenditure side and how, with the recovery, taxes on income in particular could be relaxed. The beginnings of rearmament are also evident on the expenditure side. It is noteworthy that at the end of this phase there was a deficit of 1.5 per cent of GDP, this in the circumstances of a cyclical peak, whereas in the depth of the crisis the 1931 deficit had only been 2.3 per cent of GDP. Finally, the rearmament phase sees an unprecedented peacetime surge in expenditure on current goods and services, this financed by borrowing as the combined authorities' deficit was by 1939 some 8.3 per cent of GDP, making 1937–39 the most pronounced fiscal stimulus ever experienced by the British economy in peacetime.

8.5. EXPANSIONARY FISCAL CONTRACTION: THE MAY COMMITTEE

Those seeking lessons from the early 1930s for the present will find very instructive what can happen when the authorities override the automatic stabilizers. Additionally, the EFC hypothesis provides the potential for an enhanced

Table 8.2. Public sector accounts by economic classification, changes in % points of GDP at actual employment, 1929–39

A. Total public expenditure

	Current goods and services	Gross capital formation	Current grants to personal sector	Subsidies	Current grants paid abroad	Debt interest	Total
1929	9.2	2.6	4.4	0.5	0.1	7.7	24.5
1930	9.5	2.8	5.1	0.5	0.1	7.6	25.5
1931	10.2	3.3	6.5	0.5	0.1	7.7	28.2
1932	10.1	2.8	6.6	0.6	0.1	7.8	27.9
1933	10.1	2.2	6.4	0.7	0.1	7.0	26.5
1934	9.9	2.1	5.9	0.7	0.1	6.2	25.1
1935	10.2	2.4	5.8	0.8	0.1	6.0	25.3
1936	10.9	2.9	5.4	0.7	0.1	5.7	25.7
1937	11.7	3.3	5.0	0.6	0.1	5.4	26.0
1938	13.4	3.6	5.0	0.7	0.1	5.2	28.1
1939	19.8	2.9	4.5	0.8	0.3	5.0	33.2
Change (% points of GDP):							
1929–32	0.9	0.2	2.2	0.1	0.0	0.1	3.4
1932–73	1.6	0.5	−1.6	0.0	0.0	−2.4	−1.9
1937–39	8.1	−0.4	−0.5	0.2	0.1	−0.4	7.1

B. Total receipts

	Taxes on income	Taxes on expenditure	Taxes on capital	National insurance contributions	Gross trading surplus	Rent, interest and dividends	Current grants from abroad	Total
1929	6.2	10.6	1.7	1.7	1.1	2.0	0.5	23.8
1930	6.5	10.3	1.7	1.7	1.2	2.2	0.6	24.1
1931	7.5	11.0	1.7	1.9	1.3	2.1	0.5	25.9
1932	8.2	12.0	1.7	2.1	1.4	1.9	0.0	27.4
1933	7.3	12.1	2.0	2.1	1.5	1.9	0.0	26.9
1934	6.4	12.0	1.7	2.1	1.5	1.8	0.0	25.6
1935	6.0	11.8	1.8	2.1	1.4	1.8	0.0	25.0
1936	5.9	12.0	1.8	2.1	1.4	1.8	0.0	25.0
1937	6.2	11.6	1.8	2.0	1.3	1.7	0.0	24.5
1938	6.9	11.3	1.4	2.0	1.3	1.7	0.0	24.4
1939	7.4	11.5	1.3	1.8	1.3	1.6	0.0	24.9
Change (% points of GDP):								
1929–32	2.0	1.5	0.0	0.3	0.3	−0.1	−0.5	3.6
1932–37	2.1	−0.5	0.1	−0.1	0.0	−0.3	0.0	−2.9
1937–39	1.2	−0.1	−0.5	−0.2	−0.1	−0.1	0.0	0.3

Source: Derived from Middleton (1996: app. I).

perspective on, or at least an opportunity to revisit, the events surrounding the May committee and the macroeconomic consequences of the second major interwar fiscal consolidation. This also provides a natural connection to section 8.6 on the Keyensian path not trodden, where the maintenance of confidence was key.

8.5.1. Overriding the automatic stabilizers

To understand the, by Keynenain standards, fiscal contraction of 1929–33, three preliminary points are essential. First, policy must be grounded firmly in terms of contemporary parameters: it was the *actual* budget balance (B_c) which was the focus of contemporaries' attention and, in relation to earlier wartime and later post-1945 standards, the *ex post* deficits were *very* small in relation to GDP. Second, in the 1920s B_c also included—and was expected to include—a significant sinking fund for debt amortization. Third, as we saw in section 8.2.1, the headline contemporary public finance aggregates (T_c and G_c, and hence B_c) were significantly cyclically sensitive. In 1930/31 the cyclical macro-marginal budget rate was 0.440 (Middleton 1985: Table 7.3), comparable to the characteristics of the British fiscal system in the highly disturbed post-OPEC I era, although the ratio of autonomous expenditure to GDP was only half that of the 1970s (Ward and Neild, 1978: Table 3.6); a reflection of the much smaller public sector.

We start from the position that the 1929 downturn quickly and profoundly disturbed the fragile budgetary equilibrium. For the pre-crisis year of 1930/31, the authorities were facing a prospective deficit of £47.3 million (with G_c of £870.9 million), but after raising taxation and other measures in the April 1930 budget, in effect overriding the automatic stabilizers, they budgeted for a small surplus of £2.2 million. In the event, 1930/31 closed with a deficit of £23.2 million (Middleton, 1985: Table 6.2), but this was only 0.6 per cent of GDP. In the following year—the crisis year—the May committee report, published on 31 July 1931, forecast a deficit for 1932/33 of £120 million of expenditure over income, with this becoming the focus for what became the crisis that, on 24 August, brought down Labour and established a national government (the gold standard fell less than a month later). A prospective deficit of £120 million was viewed widely as enormous, requiring urgent action lest there be fatal injury to confidence and thence to the gold standard (Williamson 1992: 267–73).[17] A deficit of £120 million represented 3.1 per cent of 1931/32 GDP, a magnitude which would become routine during the Keynesian era of the 1950s and 1960s and, of course, in a year of extreme stress is small relative to deficits in Britain since 2007. Additionally, in

[17] *The Economist* ('A New Axe', 8 August 1931: 255) was initially a rare voice of balanced judgement, noting that the figure of £120 million 'rather seriously overpaints the gloom of the immediate budgetary prospect' because this was not the central government budget deficit per se as it included £40 million of prospective new borrowing on the Unemployment Insurance Fund that was not, on current accounting conventions, part of the government budget. Later, *The Economist* accepted the inevitability of very significant fiscal consolidation which, at the time of the emergency September budget, encompassed prospective *ex ante* deficits of £75 million for 1931/32 and £170 million for 1932/33 ('Balancing the Budget', 12 September 1931: 460). Additionally, within the Treasury some senior officials considered the May report's criteria for a balanced budget as excessively severe (Middleton, 1985: 113).

1930/31 and 1931/32, the balance of the British budget was closer to equilibrium than in the US, France, and Germany, and especially when the reported budget balances are credited with sinking fund payments. Indeed, when such an adjustment is made, Britain uniquely had a cumulative surplus, whereas the worst performer, the US, had a cumulative deficit amounting to 87 per cent of its 1929/30 revenue (Middleton, 1985: Table 6.8).[18] It was Britain's special position, and the perception at home and abroad of heavy British indebtedness, that dictated that it adhere more strictly to orthodox financial principles than were considered to be necessary elsewhere.

The emergency budget of September 1931 was the turning point for fiscal policy that decade. This made operational a significantly watered down version of the May report. Indeed, it bore a close resemblance to that which the outgoing Labour government had agreed, but which had been deemed insufficient by the financial community—domestic and international—and leading Conservative politicans.[19] The May committee had proposed a fiscal consolidation weighted at 80 per cent retrenchment (of which two-thirds would be cuts in unemployment benefits) and 20 per cent additional taxation, amounting to £120 million. The new government's budget made adjustments totalling £76 million for 1931/32, comprising additional taxation (£40.5 million), retrenchment (£22 million) and reduction in the sinking fund (£13.7 million) (Middleton, 1985: Table 6.2). Even if, as was then the convention, we count the sinking fund as expenditure, this gives fiscal consolidation which was now biased towards additional taxation (53 per cent); it also demonstrates that the national, unlike the Labour, government were able to operate with greater latitude in terms of their adherence to fiscal conventions (the sinking fund) and the extent of consolidation that would satisfy nervous markets. In short, in magnitude and in structure, this was a very different fiscal consolidation from that of the Geddes axe: it had a much briefer, smaller impact on TPE, so much so that, as early as March 1932, a senior Treasury official was informing the chancellor how limited was the room for tax remisison, assuming a recovery of economic activity, because of the onward march of public expenditure (Howson, 1975: 94–5). If a major criterion for a successful fiscal consolidation is that of lock in, of gains cumulatively secured, then the 1931 fiscal consolidation was unsuccessful. The 10 per cent cut in unemployment insurance benefit rates was maintained only for three years (Burns, 1941: Table IX); and whilst some of the associated eligibility measures (which cumulatively delivered a greater saving) endured somewhat longer, very quickly the continuing weight of unemployment and other pressures for social expenditure swamped the savings (Gilbert, 1970: 176–91).[20] Figure 8.5 confirms this limited policy space in the sense that real public social spending per capita grew unhindered until a peak in 1936, at which point rearmament interrupted the onward march as it had in 1914.

[18] See League of Nations (1933: chapter VI) for the impact of the global depression on the public finances of the major economies.

[19] Gilbert (1970: 176) estimates that economies implemented by the National government were just under £10 million less than those proposed by the outgoing Labour government, and over £25 million less than those recommended by the May committee.

[20] Using expenditure data from Burns (1941: Table VII) and insured unemployment data from HMSO (1971: Table 162) we calculate that, for Great Britain, the total cost of unemployment support per million insured unemployed (unemployment in parenthesis) rose on trend from £45.8 million (2.21 million) in 1930/31 to £59.9 million (1.813 million) in 1938/39.

For economists, the story of autumn 1931 is that of a tightening of the fiscal stance amidst a depression known to be deepening, but if we dig deeper into the mechanics of policy and what we know about policy makers' thinking, we arrive at a more nuanced picture. This was put very well by an historian who had no access to the offical papers (they were not released until the 1970s) but who could read the runes: 'The deflationary phase of the National government's policy was short-lived . . . [their] financial policies made the best of both worlds; they seemed sufficiently deflationary to restore confidence; they were in fact sufficiently inflationary to assist recovery by maintaining the purchasing power of the people' (Mowat, 1955: 455). Chancellors and their senior officials understood full well the undesirability of raising taxes in a depression; at least some appreciated the likely *net* adverse impact on purchasing power of cutting transfer payments; and a few may even have accepted the Keynesian logic that discretionary action to balance the budget by overriding the automatic stabilizers risked reducing GDP and thus making budgetary equilibrium more difficult to attain in practice—something Keynes (1931: 144–5) articulated for the first time convincingly during this crisis. Whatever their understanding, the reality for the policy space was that orthodoxy must be seen to prevail. That, covertly, the British Treasury had for some time been engaging in fiscal window-dressing (at times amounting to 1 per cent of GDP) to improve the *ex post* budget balance (B_c) suggests that they understood the dangers of overriding the automatic stabilizers, and that this device served the purpose of lessening the extent of fiscal tightening required in a depression to maintain a balanced budget. What light might the EFC hypothesis shed on how these events might be interpreted?

8.5.2. Expansionary fiscal contraction: now and then

The 1990s saw fiscal consolidation enter into the lexicon of the policy-making community, a decade which witnessed many consolidation exercises, some more successful than others, and considerable innovation in designing fiscal policy institutions and rules to counter deficit bias. The Great Recession has imparted a new urgency to the consolidation impulse as the macroeconomic downturn has eroded primary budget surpluses and led to a mushrooming of public debt/GDP ratios. One justification frequently articulated for such consolidations is that, far from consolidation deepening the downturn by undermining economic growth, only through deficit reduction, and in particular through expenditure consolidation, will the real economy revive. This is expansionary fiscal contraction: an oxymoron for some, but for others, whether consciously or not, reviving aspects of pre-Keynesian orthodoxy, the only viable economic route to a sustained economic revival and fiscal sustainability.

The germ of the EFC hypothesis—that of non-Keynesian and/or non-linear fiscal effects—can be found in long-standing post-war German views of fiscal policy and, later, in Feldstein's (1982) modelling of how public expenditure cuts may be expansionary if seen as indicative of future tax cuts. The EFC literature has since been developed for a range of countries which have experienced fiscal consolidations since the 1980s (Giavazzi and Pagano, 1990; Barry and Devereux, 2003; Afonso, 2010; and Ardagna, 2010). Early work examined small open economies burdened with large foreign debts, where a fiscal consolidation, through its impact on expectations of future taxation, resulted in growth in consumption and investment, i.e. crowding-in. Subsequent work has broadened the range of countries examined, the theoretical/econometric sophistication and the potential transmission mechanisms. To date, few have attempted to apply the EFC hypothesis to historical case studies, but there have been two exercises which include interwar Britain, though both remain unpublished, which may tell us something about peer reaction to this work.[21] Considine and Duffy (2007) examine 1930–31 (in order to cast light on Irish consolidation in the 1980s), but this study is flawed by the economists having limited knowledge of the relevant literature by economic historians, or indeed much about contemporary sources, whilst Chick and Pettifor (2010), an examination of the interwar period as part of a longer survey, is so clearly motivated more to understand current difficulties (the 'economic consequences of Mr Osborne' of its title) than the interwar period per se.

Even so, both studies require further comment. Considine and Duffy is not empirical work, but more an amateur history of economic thought which attempts to reconstruct thinking by leading British economists—who were part of the extended policy community in 1930–31—for the purpose of demonstrating that, for bastions of orthodoxy (Robbins and Pigou), as well as for leading exponents of a more progressive economics, which included some deficit-financing (Keynes and Stamp), there were well-specified circumstances in which they *all* accepted that a fiscal consolidation could improve consumer and/or investor confidence. This, of course, is a precondition for an EFC effect. In particular, they make much of Pigou's view (1950: 41) that 'if businessmen at home believe that the country is going to the dogs on account of extravagant consumption, an economy campaign may restore their confidence and so cause the demand schedule for investment to rise', upon which see Bretherton et al.'s (1941: 326) conjectures on why business opinion 'may defy rational analysis . . . but its importance is not lessened thereby'. However, in so doing they are too dependent on an uncritical reading of Howson and Winch's (1977) important study of the Economic Advisory Council (EAC), the source for the 1930–31 policy debate, and seem unaware that Pigou's late-career 'second thoughts' on his orthodox policy advocacy and fervent opposition to Keynes' *General theory* in the 1930s might be a problematic source. Nonetheless, in bringing the EAC and Pigou (1950) to wider notice amongst economists, Considine and Duffy provide an interesting perspective on the perceived role of expectations in 1930–31. However, what is unwarranted is their further conclusion that 'Pigou, Keynes and the [c]ommittee . . . had accepted the possibility of an EFC event before the events of 1931' with 'little disagreement on the importance of budgetary discipline for business confidence' (2007: 17, 19). This is a false reading of Keynes. Above all, it ignores the extraordinary efforts that he and others, even those of a more orthodox, conservative persuasion, were making to widen the policy space when constrained by the golden fetter. Of course, Keynes worried about business confidence and consequent investment decisions. What

[21] Additionally, Lilico et al. (2009) consider the May committee as a fiscal consolidation, using the same methodology that was applied to the Geddes axe.

was foremost in his thinking was the need to educate business opinion that there were circumstances in which their propensities to rectitude were self-defeating, this later embodied in a dictum, now recently rediscovered by opponents of EFC: 'Look after the unemployment, and the Budget will look after itself' (Keynes 1933a: 104; see Keynes 1931, an important contribution to that educational mission). Meanwhile, in 1930 the constraint of the gold standard precluded any direct fiscal activism beyond public works which the Labour government were already pursuing on an unprecedented scale (Middleton, 1983). Moreover, in seeking antecedents for EFC, Considine and Duffy commit a further sin of ahistoricism as they seem unaware that the traditional rationale for a balanced budget was blind to the business cycle with the maintenance of business confidence an imperative, not just for maintaining investment but also for low interest rates. In one sense, the hypothetical strategy of EFC is not really new at all. What are new are the concepts, tools, and data to explore the hypothesis.

Different concerns relate to Chick and Pettifor, who argue that fiscal consolidations weaken, not improve, the public finances, and that this was true of all of the episodes they studied for twentieth and early twenty-first century Britain, including what they label the 'great depression and the May committee, 1931–33'. The problems with this study are, first, methodological as their measure of public expenditure excludes transfers, and yet we know that reversing social expenditure growth is the linchpin of successful fiscal consolidations (and that this is where the onward march of public expenditure was focused). Second, the choice of data is not always appropriate, being, as with Considine and Duffy, indicative of trespass into unfamiliar terrains which can easily trap the unwary. Third, and most importantly, it is inconceivable that a complex phenomena such as fiscal consolidation can be adequately represented with the broad-brush measures of eight pairs of averages and a simple linear regression (Steele, 2011).

We are left, thus, with the potential of the May committee from an EFC perspective largely untapped, and all the more so as there is no one specification of the EFC and multiple potential foci (exchange rates, interest rates, expectations, and consumer and investor sentiment); all of which have great relevance to the very particular circumstances of interwar Britain and especially in 1931. That said, any discussion is necessarily hypothetical as conclusions about the theoretical scope for EFC must be grounded in both empirical reality and what we think we know about the effects of discretionary fiscal policy on aggregate demand. On the last of these, as put succinctly in a recent literature survey (Hebous, 2010: 674), '[e]conomic theory has offered more than one prediction depending on the characteristics of the economy under consideration': whether neo-classical or Keynesian, Ricardian or non-Ricardian consumers, a closed or open economy, and the genre of model—DSGE, VAR? The consequence, concluded Hebous, was that '[t]he theoretical debate seems not to reach a consensus due to a lack of persuasive empirical evidence [with] The crucial difficulty . . . the identification of the effects of the change in fiscal policy isolating all other effects'. To muddy the waters still further, the EFC hypothesis undoubtedly has ideological appeal for those for whom fiscal consolidation is part of a bigger, politically-inspired assault on big government, upon which Wren-Lewis (2011: R44–5) has recently written to condemn a Great Recession lengthened and deepened unnecessarily.

8.5.3. The May committee: fiscal consolidation and macroeconomic impact

Few financial reports for a British government can have been as closely studied at the time and since by historians and economists of every persuasion and specialism as that produced by the May committee. Yet, for all of that attention, it has had surprisingly little examination through the critical lenses of either accounting historians (as per Burrows and Cobbin, 2009, for Geddes), or public choice/constitutional economics, for whom the committee's strictures on how to contain pressures for expenditure growth and of renegotiating contracts amidst a price deflation would be of considerable interest (HMSO 1931a: 12–14, 220). Arguably, also, the focus given to the report and immediate events has been at the expense of considering the longer-term issues of expenditure control, how the May 'cuts' worked in practice and their presumed macroeconomic impact.

The macroeconomic effects of the 1930–32 fiscal tightening have not been much examined in detail. In particular, we know little about what we might call the pass through effects for the real economy of implementing the autumn 1931 fiscal consolidation.[22] The package adopted slightly favoured higher taxation over expenditure retrenchment (a ratio of 53 to 47 per cent). Of the tax rises, it was taxes on income, as against expenditure, which bore the main brunt, including a 2.5 point rise in the standard rate of income tax (to 25 per cent) and a 10 per cent surcharge on the supertax (which gave progression to the income tax), though there were additional reliefs for companies (there was no separate corporation tax at this time). The economic consequences of these tax changes are difficult to establish, and especially when income tax was actually paid in arrears. Nonetheless, we would, *ceteris paribus*, expect a depressive effect on incomes, spending, and thus employment, especially when we factor in the background of trend falling prices which impacted to raise the effective rate of the majority of taxes on expenditure, this the most important element of the tax base.

The likelihood of depressive effects becomes stronger as we examine the expenditure side. Of the £70 million of cuts planned for 1932/33, at least 15 per cent were planned public sector wage/salary cuts, a maximum of 34 per cent from cuts in expenditure on goods and services (current and capital), and 51 per cent from cuts in the net cost of the unemployment insurance scheme (combining reduced eligibility and benefit levels). The potential impact on consumer spending from salary and benefit cuts is relatively straightforward when such a high proportion of those affected were credit-constrained, but impossible to determine with precision when we lack key quarterly/monthly data. That said, we know that consumers' expenditure, having grown in the first two years of the contraction phase, now fell in 1932, but only by 0.6 per cent. We know further that a gross reduction in the purchasing power of the employed and insured unemployed of some £36 million at maximum was not even 1 per cent of 1931 consumers' expenditure (it is also, of course, dwarfed by the £100 million per annum public works programme proposed in 1929, and especially if multiplier effects are taken

[22] There is no one publication which combined all aspects of the fiscal consolidation, but see Hansard (1931), HMSO (1931a and b) and Middleton (1985: table 6.2).

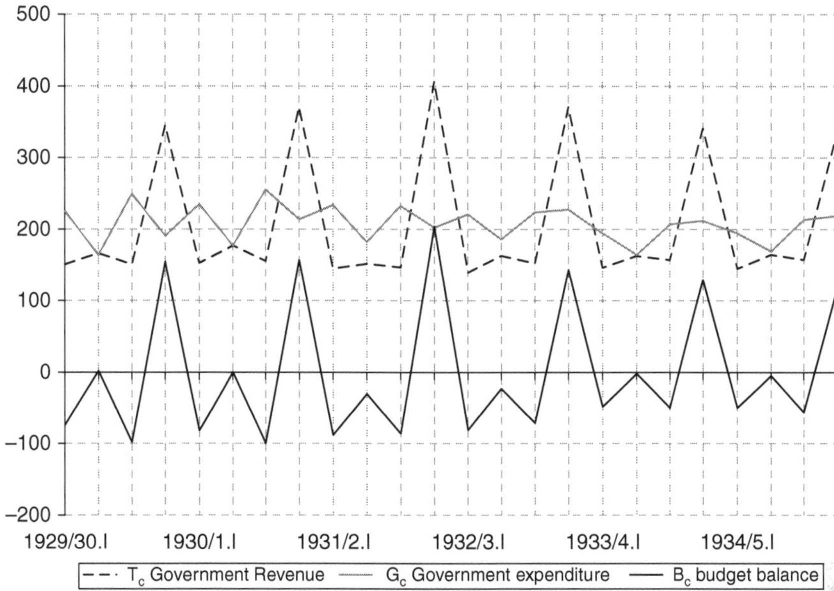

Fig. 8.12. Public finances, conventionally defined, quarterly, 1929/30–1934/35, £million

Source: *The Economist*, 1929–35, various.

into account). Moreover, the seasonally adjusted quarterly activity indices we have for this period all have industrial production as fluctuating but broadly trendless between 1931.III and1933.I, though employment and quarterly GDP data are less clearcut and might suggest a recovery in mid-1931 which was temporarily halted and did not resume until 1932.II or quarter III.[23] Even so, the key point is, however big the fiscal consolidation was as a political event, it was far less so in terms of macroeconomic impact. Furthermore, in relation to the modern literature on achieving successful fiscal reform (OECD, 2007), which emphasizes permanent expenditure cuts over increased taxation, the politics of the 1930s coalition government precluded what we now think to be the more robust consolidation path.

To make more progress with the macroeconomic effects, a quarterly econometric model would be desirable. This we lack, though we can reconstruct quarterly accounts for the conventional fiscal aggregates, T_c, G_c and B_c. Figure 8.12 depicts a highly stylized quarterly pattern for revenue, expenditure, and thus the budget balance on a financial year basis. Expenditure was broadly stable, as was revenue in the first three-quarters of the financial year, but in the final quarter (when, in the absence of a PAYE scheme, income—personal and corporate, the latter paid 18–24 months in arrears—tax fell due) there was always a huge surge in receipts, with Q.IV typically the only quarter in surplus (for once the characteristics of the fiscal system served to smooth revenue, but at the expense of company liquidity—Middleton 1985: 66). In 1931/32.IV (1932.I on a calendar year basis) the surplus

[23] Capie and Collins (1983: Tables 1.16, 1.36, 4.9) and Mitchell et al. (2009: Tables 1A, 2A).

was over £200 million, equivalent to over 18 per cent of quarterly GDP; a year later, 1933.I, the point at which unemployment peaked, the surplus was still as high as £140 million—equivalent to 13 per cent of GDP. We can speculate that for individuals and companies such sums, reflecting as they did earnings in more buoyant times, would have had a substantial depressing effect on spending, and thus on consumer and investment expectations.

Of course, central to the EFC hypothesis is that rational economic agents will judge the fiscal consolidation a credible regime shift, which presages a permanently lower path for government consumption and taxation, and thus they become more expansion minded with respect to consumption and planned investment. To produce these positive effects, the consolidation must be credible. If not, the expected conventional (Keynesian) negative aggregate demand effect might be expected. The premise is that non-linearities are present where a *large*—indicative of regime shift—and *persistent* change in fiscal policy is effected, as against the routine linear effects of fiscal policy during normal circumstances. For 1931 the evidence for credibility is strong, not least that a coalition government was able to gain market approval for a much smaller consolidation than had been recommended by the May committee, let alone the outgoing Labour government. A second test, of course, is that, within nine months of the forced abandonment of gold, the authorities were able to undertake a major debt consolidation and achieve permanently lower interest rates. Third, we know that across a broad swathe of orthodox opinion, both financial and political, there was a high level of approval for the 1931 crisis measures; that, following the October 1931 general election, which consolidated the new coalition government, sterling began to appreciate and there was a net flow of funds to London (Sayers, 1976, II: 420), and that gilt-edged prices rose more than 20 per cent in the nine months following gold's suspension (Nevin, 1955: 76). Nonetheless, what we cannot observe directly is consumer and investor opinion. Also, in the absence of a quarterly model, we lack the infrastructure to undertake the sort of VAR time-series event analysis, deriving from Blanchard and Perotti (2002), which some EFC studies have adopted to distinguish between normal and major policy actions.

What can be said, and here we reiterate that the actual fiscal adjustment of 1931/32 (whether Bc or B*/Y*) were small by post-war standards—as was the fiscal consolidation relative to those of the 1980s, and later upon which the EFC literature has focused—is that, if there was an EFC effect, it must be placed alongside what we now know about the 'normal event' fiscal policy multipliers. This, of course, touches on the much bigger topic of the Keynesian path not trodden, of its practicality as a policy option, and its possible macroeconomic impact (both expolored in Middleton, 2010: 433–6). The most recent econometric study, by Dimsdale and Horsewood (1995), which has both well-specified demand- and supply-sides, has received broad assent. They estimated higher values for the fiscal policy multiplier than an earlier generation of studies, and consequently were more optimistic about potential Keynesian solution effectiveness. Their simulations of the Keynes and Henderson 'We Can Conquer Unemployment' (1929) programme yielded a long-run multiplier of about 2.5, with the impact of the Keynesian solution stronger on output than employment. However, their results also raise questions about the sustainability of such counterfactual spending packages for the balance of payments in the context of a nascent external constraint amidst the depressed state of world trade. Dimsdale and Horsewood are clear that the output and employment rises 'would not have been undermined by crowding-out effects, because the feedback of a rise in interest rates turns out to be relatively weak' and that the Treasury view 'does not turn out to be a major obstacle to the effectiveness of the Henderson-Keynes proposals', but they do accept that 'the impact of crowding-out effects is somewhat greater when fiscal expansion is maintained over a decade' (1995: 391).

A deeper analysis of the 'Treasury view' on the futility of deficit-financed public works, with the special role played by psychological crowding-out (Middleton, 1985: chapter 8), would counsel even graver caution on the likely viability of the Keynesian solution. As we have seen, such were the debt dynamics that there was a constant risk that markets might require risk premia for new borrowing if they sensed major deviations from the path of accepted fiscal prudence in *peacetime.* As it was, with the sinking fund basically suspended from 1931/32, and the authorities placing so much emphasis on cheap money as the centrepiece of the recovery strategy, it was entirely logical to perceive a potential trade-off between an active monetary policy and untried Keynesian fiscal policies. Had orthodox financial opinion been convinced of the effectiveness of the Keynesian solution, financial and business opinion might have been different, but there was no such acceptance at this time nor any in immediate prospect. Moreover, as Wren-Lewis (2010: 78) shows for our current troubles, the point at which markets become spooked cannot be established a priori, and '[t]he key limit is not when a government will probably default, but when the possibility that it will default becomes significant enough for lenders to require a risk premium to offset this chance'. For Britain, in 1931–33 the risk of risk premia would not only have imperilled cheap money but also, via the debt dynamics, budgetary equilibrium, and thus the delicate balancing act that was the 1931/32 second budget and the 1932/3 'gamble' budget. Thus, however big the fiscal policy multiplier, given the size of the unemployment problem even before the 1929 demand shock, the fact that budget deficits would need to be sustained for a number of years inevitably posed the risk of higher interest rates, and thus crowding-out.

Where does this leave the EFC hypothesis? For the 1931 consolidation, as for Geddes, we lack the means for replicating modern studies. We lack also the appropriate indicators of consumer and business confidence and solid evidence of expectation formation though we have no shortage of 'mood music' from the spokesman of orthodox finance about the dangers of deviation towards the Keynesian solution. That said, the interwar period was no statistical desert (read carefully, *The Economist* provided contemporaries with much weekly data which could be usefully interpreted in this vein, as did the London and Cambridge Economic Service bulletins). We have good quantitative evidence on the growing preparedness of households, from late 1931 onwards, to undertake the expensive long-term commitment of a mortgage as well as additional hire-purchase obligations; and we do have the fruits of pioneering applied research from the Oxford economists' 'trade cycle' group of the mid–late 1930s, notably Meade and Andrews (1938) whose conclusions, drawn from extensive interviews with businessmen, have been much cited: that business investment was interest inelastic. Less cited, but potentially interesting, was the conclusion that businessmen '[w]ould take into account the psychological effect of a substantial rise in bank rate', even if 'normal changes have a very small effect': 'there is a tendency to regard such changes as analogous to a weather report, and as indications of the probable trend of trade' (1938: 15, 17, 29). We are thus back with the primacy of pre-Keynesian confidence; a phenomenon in which, as we saw with the required level of cuts in unemployment benefits necessary to satisfy orthodox opinion in August–September 1931, symbolism was important, but variably so according to perceptions of political risk.

8.6. CONCLUSIONS

Britain in the 1930s may well be a textbook example of monetary expansion made possible by fiscal conservatism. Alternatively, for many, it represents an exemplar of the dangers of, first, being a member of a fixed exchange regime in turbulent times; second, of then overriding the automatic stabilizers amidst a global downturn with a consequent deepening and lengthening of the depression; and, third, of ignoring the Keynesian solution of deliberate deficit-finance to eradicate deficient demand. What the interwar British experience does not appear to do is provide succour for the EFC hypothesis in current circumstances, though it has provided a useful vehicle for revisiting how confidence was understood in a pre-Keynesian world and for revealing much interesting material about the two fiscal consolidations of the period that are more visible in the historiography than as macroeconomic events. In the process, we have highlighted that the fiscal policy story of the 1930s is one of twin disappointments: of a Keynesian path not trodden, but also of a fiscal consolidation which was a major political but not a macroeconomic event.

The overall effectiveness of macroeconomic policy is difficult to evaluate since current policy objectives and targets are at variance with those of the 1930s. That said, within the limited role accorded fiscal policy as a stabilization instrument, it can be judged to have been successful because, with the exception of the 1931 crisis, fiscal operations provided a stable environment for business and permitted an expansionary monetary policy—conditions conducive to recovery, which, as we have seen, was very much more significant than that in the US. It is when fiscal policy is appraised with reference to modern objectives, those, of course, formulated and developed during the 1930s in response to the limitations and unsatisfactory macroeconomic impact of the existing policy, that its deficiencies and destabilizing characteristics become evident. It is a staple of the literature 'that recovery proceeded less strongly and rapidly than it would have done with more enlightened budgetary policies' (Winch, 1972: 218). This seems a general lesson of the 1930s, one recently confirmed by Almunia et al.'s (2010) cross-country study of 27 economies which identiifed small monetary policy effects, but very much more substantial potential for fiscal policy (short-run multipliers of 2.5; longer-run 1.2), potential not realized in most of their countries; '[w]here significant fiscal stimulus was provided, output and employment responded accordingly. Where monetary policy was loosened, recovery occurred sooner' (2010: 250). But, on the whole, fiscal policy was simply not used, it was not that it was ineffective.

Romer (2009) has identified six lessons from the US experience of the Great Depression:

1. small fiscal expansion has small effects;
2. monetary expansion is helpful even when interest rates are near zero;
3. beware of cutting back the stimulus too soon;
4. financial recovery and real recovery go together;
5. worldwide expansionary policy shares the burdens and benefits of recovery; and,
6. the Great Depression did eventually end (and would have ended earlier had there not been the 1937 policy-induced setback).

The British experience does not wholly map to these lessons as there was no banking crisis and no policy-induced setback (numbers 4 and 6). Additionally, the British case illustrates some more enduring lessons, not least that—as Keynes long argued—it is vital that a recession is never allowed to become a depression. Fortunately, in 2008–09 western policy makers appeared to understand this lesson, though not all appear to do so now in all countries, not least Britain. The critical role of the exchange rate regime is also confirmed by the British case, with the securing of a floating exchange rate widening the policy space at a critical juncture, upon which recovery hinged. The lesson here is obvious, though highly contextual. It also leads us back to Bernanke's fourth lesson, 'history is never a perfect guide'.

Lessons of a different sort are revealed by the British experience of overriding the automatic stabilizers and of fiscal consolidation. On the former, Keynes had argued at the time, and it has since been confirmed by recent econometric work (Dimsdale and Horsewood, 1995), that crowding-out was not a clear and present danger; instead, the authorities gambled on crowding-in when they overrode the automatic stabilizers. Given the high macro-marginal budget rate, this was a real gamble, and had it gone wrong the likely consequences would have been a vicious circle of an ever tighter fiscal stance which in depressing GDP made impossible *ex post* budget equilibrium. The gamble was that fiscal consolidation in 1931 would buy sufficient policy credibility to assuage orthodox opinion and boost business confidence, and it is important that it was motivated in part by the objective of defending the exchange rate. With gold's abandonment, a successful consolidation was even more important:[24]

> It is one thing to go off the gold standard with an unbalanced budget and uncontrolled inflation; it is quite another thing to take this measure, not because of internal financial difficulties, but because of excessive withdrawals of borrowed capital.

Had the 1931/32 financial year not closed with a budget surplus as then measured (B_c), and 1932/33 had a deficit which could be presented as manageable, given that recovery was now underway, the strategy could have failed and spectacularly so. Two further aspects of fiscal consolidation need highlighting. The first is the extent to which the 1931 crisis was exploited by those seeking to contain Leviathan and that, whatever the rhetoric, retrenchment did not translate into public sector

[24] Treasury press release, 20 September 1931 cited in Williamson (1992: 422).

job cuts. Nominal wage and salary cuts of 10–20 per cent were planned for the public sector, but not wholly delivered after a naval mutiny (Mowat, 1955: 403–6). However, public sector employment carried on growing, absolutely and relatively, although admittedly from a base very much smaller than today (in 1929, including the armed forces, public employment was 5 per cent of total employment, reaching 5.8 per cent by 1938 (Feinstein, 1972: Table 59)). As fiscal consolidation, the September 1931 package marked only a temporary halt to public expenditure growth (the Treasury knew this full well, being deeply concerned about the onward march of welfare spending), but, as we have seen, by modern standards the interwar authorities' conduct was exemplary. Setting the challenge of debt stabilization in the context of a cyclically unstable economy and a downward price trend, they attained a primary balance which never fell below +7.0 per cent of GDP between 1929–32; this at a point when the debt/GDP ratio averaged 165 per cent, whereas in 2009/10, at which point on the Maastricht definition the debt/GDP ratio was 68.2 per cent, the primary balance was −4.7 per cent of GDP (Barrell and Kirby, 2010: Table 3) and would have deteriorated sharply had not first Labour and then the coalition government accelerated the consolidation path.

In contemporary Britain, the commentariat and policy makers, informed economists less so, have been prone to seek lessons from the 1930s for the present. In part, this chapter has been motivated to show that such lessons are sparse and need careful calibration against the very different situation of 80 years ago. The economic lessons are either basically obvious or so situation-contingent as not to constitute useable knowledge for managing the Great Recession, whereas the political economy lessons are stronger and more generic. To secure big change requires a gamble with the real economy if fiscal consolidation becomes politically more appealing than the economic logic of stabilization.

BIBLIOGRAPHY

Afonso, A. (2010), 'Expansionary Fiscal Consolidations in Europe: New Evidence', *Applied Economic Letters*, 17(2), 105–9.

Aidt, T. S., Daunton, M. J., and Dutta, J. (2010), 'The Retrenchment Hypothesis and the Extension of the Franchise in England and Wales', *Economic Journal*, 120(6), 990–1020.

Alesina, A., Carloni, D., and Lecce, G. (2010), 'The Electoral Consequences of Large Fiscal Adjustments', Harvard University, mimeo, <http://scholar.harvard.edu/alesina/files/electoralconseqoflgefiscaladjust.pdf>, 17.08.11.

Alesina, A., Perotti, R., Tavares, J., Obstfeld, M., and Eichengreen, B. J. (1998), 'The Political Economy of Fiscal Adjustments', *Brookings Papers on Economic Activity*, (1), 197–266.

Almunia, M., Benetrix, A., Eichengreen, B. J., O'Rourke, K. H., and Rua, G. (2010), 'From Great Depression to Great Credit Crisis: Similarities, Differences and Lessons', *Economic Policy*, 25(2), 219–65.

Ardagna, S. (2010), 'Financial Markets' Behavior around Episodes of Large Changes in Fiscal Stance', *European Economic Review*, 53(2), 37–55.

Arndt, H. W. (1944), *The Economic Lessons of the Nineteen-Thirties*. London: Oxford University Press.

Barrell, R. and Kirby, S. (2010), 'UK Fiscal Prospects', *National Institute Economic Review*, 213(July), F66–F70.

Barry, F. and Devereux, M. B. (2003), 'Expansionary Fiscal Contraction: A Theoretical Exploration', *Journal of Macroeconomics*, 25(1), 1–23.

Bernanke, B. (2000), *Essays on the Great Depression*. Princeton, NJ: Princeton University Press.

Bernanke, B. (2010), 'Economic Policy: Lessons from History', Center for the Study of the Presidency and Congress, Washington, DC, 8 April, <http://www.federalreserve.gov/newsevents/speech/bernanke20100408a.htm>, 02.08.10.

Bernstein, M. A. (1987), *The Great Depression: Delayed Recovery and Economic Change in America, 1929–1939*. Cambridge: Cambridge University Press.

Billings, M. and Capie, F. H. (2011), 'Financial Crisis, Contagion and the British Banking System Between the Wars', *Business History*, 53(2), 193–215.

Blanchard, O. J. and Perotti, R. (2002), 'An Empirical Characterisation of the Dynamic Effects of Changes in Government Spending and Taxes on Output', *Quarterly Journal of Economics*, 117(4), 1329–68.

Bordo, M. D. and Schwartz, A. J. (1999), 'Monetary Regimes and Economic Performance: The Historical Record', in J. B. Taylor and M. Woodford (eds), *Handbook of Macroeconomics*. Amsterdam: Elsevier, vol. 1A, 149–234.

Bretherton, R. F., Burchardt, F. A., and Rutherford, R. S. G. (1941), *Public Investment and the Trade Cycle in Great Britain*. Oxford: Clarendon Press.

Broadberry, S. N. (1986), *The British Economy Between the Wars: A Macroeconomic Survey*. Oxford: Basil Blackwell.

Broadberry, S. N. and Crafts, N. F. R. (1992), 'Britain's Productivity Gap in the 1930s: Some Neglected Factors', *Journal of Economic History*, 52(3), 531–58.

Brown, E. C. (1956), 'Fiscal Policy in the 'Thirties: A Reappraisal', *American Economic Review*, 46(5), 857–79.

Buchanan, J. M. and Wagner, R. E. (1977), *Democracy in Deficit: The Political Legacy of Lord Keynes*. New York: Academic Press.

Burns, E. M. (1941), *British Unemployment Programs, 1920–1938*. Washington, DC: Committee on Social Security, Social Science Research Council.

Burrows, G. and Cobbin, P. (2009), 'Controlling Government Expenditure by External Review: The 1921–1922 "Geddes axe"', *Accounting History*, 14(3), 199–220.

Capie, F. H. and Collins, M. (1983), *The Inter-War British Economy: A Statistical Abstract*. Manchester: Manchester University Press.

Capie, F. H. and Wood, G. E. (1994), 'Money in the Economy, 1870–1939', in R. C. Floud and D. N. McCloskey (eds), *The Economic History of Britain since 1700*, 2nd edn. Cambridge: Cambridge University Press, vol. II, 217–46.

Carter, S. B., Gartner, S. S., Haines, M. R., Olmstead, A. L., Sutch, R., and Wright, G. (2006), *Historical Statistics of the United States: Earliest Times to the Present*, 5 vols. New York: Cambridge University Press.

Chick, V. and Pettifor, A. (2010), 'The Economic Consequences of Mr Osborne. Fiscal Consolidation: Lessons from a Century of Macro Economics', <http://www.debt.donatiuon.org>, 06.06.10.

Cline, P. K. (1974), 'Eric Geddes and the "Experiment" with Businessmen in Government, 1915–1922', in K. D. Brown (ed.), *Essays in Anti-Labour History: Responses to the Rise of Labour in Britain*. London: Macmillan, 74–104.

Considine, J. and Duffy, D. (2007), 'Tales of Expansionary Fiscal Contractions in two European Countries: Hindsight and Foresight', NUI Galway, Department of Economics Working Paper No. 120 <http://www.aran.library.nuigalway.ie/xmlui/handle/10379/1012>, 15.08.11.

Crafts, N. F. R. and Fearon, P. (2010), 'Lessons from the 1930s Great Depression', *Oxford Review of Economic Policy*, 26(3), 285–317.

Department of Employment and Productivity (1971), *British Labour Statistics: Historical Abstract, 1886–1968*. London: HMSO.

Dimsdale, N. H. (1981), 'British Monetary Policy and the Exchange Rate, 1920–1938', *Oxford Economic Papers*, n.s. 33(2, Supplement), 306–49.

Dimsdale, N. H. (1984), 'Employment and Real Wages in the Inter-war Period', *National Institute Economic Review*, 110(November), 94–103.

Dimsdale, N. H. and Horsewood, N. (1995), 'Fiscal Policy and Employment in Interwar Britain: Some Evidence from a New Model', *Oxford Economic Papers*, 47(3), 369–96.

Earley, M. F. (2012), 'Public Social and Welfare Spending in the UK, 1830–1950: Explanations from Data and Trends', PhD dissertation, University of Bristol.

Eichengreen, B. J. (1992), *Golden Fetters: The Gold Standard and the Great Depression, 1919–1939*. New York: Oxford University Press.

Eichengreen, B. J. and Sachs, J. (1985), 'Exchange Rates and Economic Recovery in the 1930s', *Journal of Economic History*, 45(4), 925–46.

Feinstein, C. H. (1972), *National Income, Expenditure and Output of the United Kingdom, 1855–1965*. Cambridge: Cambridge University Press.

Feldstein, M. S. (1982), 'Government Deficits and Aggregate Demand', *Journal of Monetary Economics*, 9(1), 1–20.

Fishback, P. V. (2010), 'US Monetary and Fiscal Policy in the 1930s', *Oxford Review of Economic Policy*, 26(3), 385–413.

Foreman-Peck, J. S. (2002), 'The Debt Constraint on British Economic Policy and Performance in the 1920s', in M. J. Oliver (ed.), *Studies in Economic and Social History: Essays in Honour of Derek H. Aldcroft*. Aldershot: Ashgate, 101–18.

Giavazzi, F. and Pagano, M. (1990), 'Can Severe Fiscal Contractions be Expansionary? Tales of Two Small European Countries', *NBER Macroeconomic Annual*, 5, 75–111.

Gilbert, B. B. (1970) *British Social Policy, 1914–1939*. London: Batsford.

Hansard (1931), 'Financial Statement by the Chancellor of the Exchequer', *Parliamentary Debates* (House of Commons), 5th ser. 256 (10 September), col. 297–313.

Hatton, T. J. (1987), 'The Outlines of a Keynesian Solution', in S. Glynn and A. E. Booth (eds), *The Road to Full Employment*. London: Allen & Unwin, 82–94.

Hatton, T. J. and Thomas, M. (2010), 'Labour Markets in the Interwar Period and Economic Recovery in the UK and the USA', *Oxford Review of Economic Policy*, 26(3), 463–85.

Hebous, S. (2010), 'The Effects of Discretionary Fiscal Policy on Macroeconomic Aggregates: A Reappraisal', *Journal of Economic Surveys*, 25(4), 674–707.

Hicks, U. K. (1938), *The Finance of British Government, 1920–1936*. Oxford: Oxford University Press.

Higgs, H. (1922), 'The Geddes Reports and the Budget', *Economic Journal*, 32(2), 251–64.

HMSO (1922), Committee on National Expenditure (Geddes Committee), *Third Report*, BPP 1922 (1589), ix, 287.

HMSO (1927), Committee on National Debt and Taxation (Colwyn Committee), *Report*, BPP 1927 (2800), xi, 371.

HMSO (1931a), Committee on National Expenditure (May Committee), *Report*, BPP 1930–1 (3920), xvi, 1.

HMSO (1931b), *Memorandum on the Measures Proposed by His Majesty's Government to Secure Reductions in National Expenditure*, BPP 1930–1 (3952), xviii, 371.

HMSO (1971), Department of Employment and Productivity, *British Labour Statistics: Historical Abstract, 1886–1968*. London: HMSO.

HMSO (2011), Office for Budget Responsibility, *Economic and Fiscal Outlook, March 2011*, BPP 2010–11 (8036).

Holland, D., Barrell, R., Fic, T., Hurst, I., Orazgani, A., and Whitworth, R. (2010), 'Decomposition of Fiscal Deterioration in the OECD', *National Institute Economic Review*, 213 (July), F13–F18.

Howson, S. K. (1975), *Domestic Monetary Management in Britain, 1919–38*. Cambridge: Cambridge University Press.

Howson, S. K. (1980), *Sterling's Managed Float: The Operation of the Exchange Equalisation Account, 1932–39*. Princeton, NJ: Princeton University Press.

Howson, S. K. and Winch, D. (1977), *The Economic Advisory Council, 1930–1939: A Study in Economic Advice during Depression and Recovery*. Cambridge: Cambridge University Press.

IMF (2010), *Strategies for Fiscal Consolidation in the Post-Crisis World*. Washington, DC: IMF Fiscal Affairs Department.

Kavanagh, D. and Cowley, P. (2010), *The British General Election of 2010*. London: Palgrave Macmillan.

Keynes, J. M. (1931), 'Some Consequences of the Economy Report', *New Statesman and Nation*, 15 August. Rep. in Keynes (1972), 141–45.

Keynes, J. M. (1933a), 'Spending and Saving: A Discussion Between Sir Josiah Stamp and J. M. Keynes', *The Listener*, 11 January. Rep. in D. E. Moggridge (2010) (ed.), *Keynes on the wireless: John Maynard Keynes*. London: Palgrave, 96–110.

Keynes, J. M. (1933b), *The Means to Prosperity*. Rep. in Keynes (1972), 335–66.

Keynes, J. M. (1972), *Collected Writings of John Maynard Keynes*, vol. IX: *Essays in Persuasion*. London: Macmillan.

Keynes, J. M. and Henderson, H. D. (1929), *Can Lloyd George Do It?—The Pledge Examined*. Rep. in Keynes (1972), 86–125.

Kirby, S. and Whitworth, R. (2011), 'Prospects for the UK Economy', *National Institute Economic Review*, 217(July), F46–F67.

Kitson, M. and Solomou, S. N. (1990), *Protectionism and Economic Revival: The British Interwar Economy*. Cambridge: Cambridge University Press.

League of Nations (1933), *World economic survey, 1932–33*. Geneva: League of Nations.

League of Nations (1934), *World economic survey, 1933–34*. Geneva: League of Nations.

Lilico, A., Holmes, E., and Sameen, H. (2009), *Controlling Spending and Government Deficits: Lessons from History and International Experience*. London: Policy Exchange.

Lindert, P. H. (2004), *Growing Public: Social Spending and Economic Growth since the Eighteenth Century*, 2 vols. Cambridge: Cambridge University Press.

Maddison, A. (1991), *Dynamic Forces in Capitalist Development: A Long-Run Comparative View*. Oxford: Oxford University Press.

Maddison, A. (2003), *The World Economy: Historical Statistics*. Paris: OECD.

Mallet, B. (1913), *British Budgets, 1887–1888 to 1912–1913*. London: Macmillan.

McDonald, A. (1989), 'The Geddes Committee and the Formulation of Public Expenditure Policy, 1921–1922', *Historical Journal*, 32(3), 643–74.

Meade, J. E. and Andrews, P. W. S. (1938), 'Summary of Replies to Questions on Effects of Interest Rates', *Oxford Economic Papers*, old ser., 1(1), 14–31.

Middleton, R. (1981), 'The Constant Employment Budget Balance and British Budgetary Policy, 1929–1939', *Economic History Review*, 2nd ser., 34(2), 266–86.

Middleton, R. (1982), 'The Treasury in the 1930s: Political and Administrative Constraints to Acceptance of the "New" Economics', *Oxford Economic Papers*, n.s., 34(1), 48–77.

Middleton, R. (1983), 'The Treasury and Public Investment: A Perspective on Interwar Economic Management', *Public Administration*, 61(4), 351–70.

Middleton, R. (1984), 'The Measurement of Fiscal Influence in Britain in the 1930s', *Economic History Review*, 2nd ser., 37(1), 103–106.

Middleton, R. (1985), *Towards the Managed Economy: Keynes, the Treasury and the Fiscal Policy Debate of the 1930s*. London: Methuen.

Middleton, R. (1996), *Government versus the Market: The Growth of the Public Sector, Economic Management and British Economic Performance, c.1890–1979*. Cheltenham and Brookfield, Vt.: Edward Elgar.

Middleton, R. (2004), 'Government and the Economy, 1860–1939', in R. C. Floud and P. A. Johnson (eds), *The Cambridge Economic History of Modern Britain*. Cambridge: Cambridge University Press, vol. II, 456–89.

Middleton, R. (2010), 'British Monetary and Fiscal Policy in the 1930s', *Oxford Review of Economic Policy*, 26(3), 414–41.

Middleton, R. (2011), 'Macroeconomic Policy in Britain between the Wars', *Economic History Review*, 64(V1), 1–31.

Mitchell, B. R. (1988), *British Historical Statistics*. Cambridge: Cambridge University Press.

Mitchell, J., Solomou, S. N., and Weale, M. R. (2009), 'Monthly and Quarterly GDP Estimate for Interwar Britain', National Institute of Economic and Social Research Discussion Paper No. 348.

Moggridge, D. E. (1972), *British Monetary Policy, 1924–1931: The Norman Conquest of $4.86*. Cambridge: Cambridge University Press.

Morgan, E.V. (1952), *Studies in British Financial Policy, 1914–1925*. London: Macmillan.

Mowat, C. L. (1955), *Britain between the Wars, 1918–1940*. London: Methuen.

Nason, J. M. and Vahey, S. P. (2007), 'The McKenna Rule and UK World War I Finance', *American Economic Review*, 97(2, Papers & Proceedings), 290–94.

Nevin, E. T. (1955), *The Mechanism of Cheap Money: A Study of British Monetary Policy, 1931–1939*. Cardiff: University of Wales Press.

Obstfeld, M., Shambaugh, J. C., and Taylor, A. M. (2005), 'The Trilemma in History: Tradeoffs among Exchange Rates, Monetary Policies and Capital Mobility', *Review of Economics and Statistics*, 87(3), 422–38.

OECD (2007), 'Fiscal Consolidation: Lessons from Past Experience', *Economic Outlook*, 81, 29–52.

OECD (2010), *Restoring Fiscal Sustainability: Lessons for the Public Sector*. Paris: OECD.

Officer, L. H. (2011), 'What was the UK GDP then?', MeasuringWorth <http://www.measuringworth.com/ukgdp/>, 22.08.11.

ONS (2010), 'Government Deficit and Debt under the Maastricht Treaty', *Statistical Bulletin*, 31 March, Office for National Statistics, <http://www.ons.gov.uk/ons/publications/index.html>.

Peacock, A. T. and Wiseman, J. (1967), *The Growth of Public Expenditure in the United Kingdom*, 2nd edn. London: George Allen & Unwin.

Peden, G. C. (2002), 'From Cheap Government to Efficient Government: The Political Economy of Public Expenditure in the United Kingdom, 1832–1914', in D. N. Winch and P. K. O'Brien (eds), *The Political Economy of British Economic Experience, 1688–1914*. Oxford: Oxford University Press, 351–80.

Peters, B. G. (1991), *The Politics of Taxation: A Comparative Perspective*. Oxford: Basil Blackwell.

Phelps Brown, E. H. and Shackle, G. L. S. (1939), 'British Economic Fluctuations, 1924–1938', *Oxford Economic Papers*, 2(1), 98–134.

Pigou, A. C. (1947), *Aspects of British Economic History, 1918–1925*. London: Macmillan.

Pigou, A. C. (1950), *Keynes's General Theory: A Retrospective View*. London: Macmillan.

Price, R. (2010), 'The Political Economy of Fiscal Consolidation', *OECD Economics Department Working Paper*, 776.

Redmond, J. (1980), 'An Indicator of the Effective Exchange Rate of the Pound in the Nineteen-Thirties', *Economic History Review*, 2nd ser., 33(1), 83–91.

Richardson, H. W. (1967), *Economic Recovery in Britain, 1929–39*. London: Weidenfeld & Nicolson.

Romer, C. D. (1990), 'The Great Crash and the Onset of the Great Depression', *Quarterly Journal of Economics*, 105(3), 597–624.

Romer, C. D. (1992), 'What Ended the Great Depression?', *Journal of Economic History*, 52(4): 757–84.

Romer, C. D. (2009), 'Lessons from the Great Depression for Economic Recovery in 2009,' Brookings Institution, 9 March, <http://www.brookings.edu/~/media/files/events/2009/0309_lessons/0309_ lessons_romer.pdf>, 13.08.10

Sayers, R. S. (1976), *The Bank of England, 1891–1944*, 3 vols. Cambridge: Cambridge University Press.

Sefton, J. and Weale, M. R. (1995), *Reconciliation of National Income and Expenditure: Balanced Estimates of National Income for the United Kingdom, 1920–1990*. Cambridge: Cambridge University Press.

Solomou, S. N. (1996), *Themes in Macroeconomic History: The UK Economy, 1919–1939*. Cambridge: Cambridge University Press.

Steele, G. R. (2011), 'Economic consequences', <http://www.lancs.ac.uk/staff/ecagrs/CP.pdf>, 15.08.11.

Thomas, M. (1983), 'Rearmament and Economic Recovery in the late 1930s', *Economic History Review*, 2nd ser., 36(4), 552–79.

Wagschal, U. and Wenzelburger, G. (2008), 'Roads to Success: Budget Consolidation in OECD Countries', *Journal of Public Policy*, 28(4), 309–39.

Ward, T. S. and Neild, R. R. (1978), *The Measurement and Reform of Budgetary Policy*. London: Heinemann.

Williamson, P. A. (1992), *National Crisis and National Government: British Politics, the Economy and Empire, 1926–1932*. Cambridge: Cambridge University Press.

Winch, D. N. (1972), *Economic and Policy: A Historical Study*, rev. edn. London: Fontana.

Wormell, J. (2000), *The Management of the National Debt of the United Kingdom, 1900–1932*. London: Routledge.

Worswick, G. D. N. (1984), 'The Sources of Recovery in the UK in the 1930s', *National Institute Economic Review*, 110(November), 85–93.

Wren-Lewis, S. (2010), 'Macroeconomic Policy in Light of the Credit Crunch: The Return of Counter-cyclical Fiscal Policy?', *Oxford Review of Economic Policy*, 26(1), 71–86.

Wren-Lewis, S. (2011), 'Lessons from Failure: Fiscal Policy, Indulgence and Ideology', *National Institute Economic Review*, 217(July), R31–R46.

9

US Monetary and Fiscal Policy in the 1930s

Price Fishback

9.I. INTRODUCTION

Economists and economic historians generally agree that the Federal Reserve (the Fed) made several major mistakes in conducting monetary policy between 1929 and 1937. It allowed the money supply to fall and did too little too late in trying to stave off the bank failures of the early 1930s. The Fed then reduced the money supply again by raising reserve requirements three times in 1936 and 1937 in a misguided attempt to prevent inflation by soaking up excess reserves. As a broad-brush explanation of the reasons for the Federal Reserve's choices, most scholars agree that its attempts to maintain the international gold standard between 1929 and 1933 explain a significant amount of why it followed its policy actions. Week-by-week accounts of the timing of bank failures and the Federal Reserve's policy moves, however, suggest a complex set of motives for the actions of the Fed and regional Reserve Banks that add a great deal more nuance to the story.

The largest debates about monetary policies during the 1930s arise over how effective they were in driving real GDP and unemployment. Nearly all agree that the Federal Reserve policy interacted with other negative shocks in ways that caused the Depression to deepen. The question remains, by how much? Estimates from a variety of models suggest that the impact of monetary policy explains a range of 20–70 per cent of the decline in real output between 1929 and 1933. Some scholars argue that the recovery that started in mid-1933 was driven by the Roosevelt administration's adoption of a new 'reflationary' policy regime that simultaneously freed the US from the 'golden fetters' of the gold standard, shifted to a looser monetary policy, and ramped up government spending just after the inauguration in 1933. The shock of a new policy dogma reversed deflationary expectations that contributed to most of the recovery. Later efforts by the Federal Reserve to combat potential inflation through increases in reserve requirements and cuts in federal spending signalled another policy regime change that contributed to the downturn of 1937–38.

How effective was fiscal policy? A nationwide Keynesian fiscal stimulus was never really attempted in the 1930s. During the Hoover presidency, Congress nearly doubled real federal spending and ramped up federal lending through the Reconstruction Finance Corporation (RFC). The Roosevelt congresses then spent nearly double the Hoover levels. But both administrations collected enough taxes in a variety of new forms to maintain relatively small deficits throughout the period. Relative to a Keynesian deficit target designed to return to full employment, the deficits were minuscule. State governments also ran deficits in the early 1930s and then expanded taxation and ran a surplus in the late 1930s. Even if fiscal deficits had been run, Romer's (1992) estimates of fiscal and monetary policy multipliers from 1921 and 1938 imply a weak effect of fiscal policy. Studies of the impact of government spending at the state, county, and city level suggest that the impact on real variables differed by programme. Public works and relief spending contributed to increases in economic activity, while the farm programmes were explicitly designed to reduce output. Preliminary estimates of the impact of net federal spending using annual data for 48 states between 1930 and 1940 suggest that a marginal increase of US$1 in net federal spending was associated with an increase of $1 to $1.50 in per capita personal income in the states.

The insistence upon raising tax rates during the 1930s also likely retarded growth. The Hawley–Smoot tariff of 1930 touched off a series of protectionist responses from other countries that cut world import activity by two-thirds by 1933. Increases in income tax rates, particularly spikes in the top marginal rates to 58 and 67 per cent, likely contributed to tax avoidance and inhibited economic activities at the top of the income distribution. A series of taxes on capital, dividends, and undistributed profits led to relatively small amounts of revenue at the cost of chilling some forms of investment activity. New excise taxes on bank cheques, motor vehicles, electricity, pipelines, gasoline, and communications likely slowed growth in the leading technological growth sectors in the economy. The new excise taxes, along with renewed collections on alcoholic beverages after the end of Prohibition, account for a significant part of the rise in tax revenues during the 1930s.

Modern policy makers have clearly sought to avoid making the macroeconomic policy mistakes of the 1930s. In contrast to the 1930s, the Federal Reserve, guided by the Depression scholar, Benjamin Bernanke, has flooded the banking system with liquidity since the autumn of 2008. The Bush and Obama administrations fought the downturn with tax rebates in 2008 and 2009. The Obama administration and the Democratic Congress pushed through a fiscal stimulus package that has driven the federal deficit near to 10 per cent of GDP, the largest peacetime deficit in American history.

On the microeconomic side, policy makers followed several strategies that mimic the activities of the RFC in the 1930s. Bernanke and Treasury secretaries, Henry Paulson and Timothy Geithner, orchestrated mergers, bailouts, and ownership stakes in major financial institutions to stave off anticipated financial disaster if an institution that was too big to fail went under. As the RFC did with the railroads and other industries, the Bush and Obama administrations made substantial loans to GM and Chrysler.

This chapter follows the path laid out in the introduction. I describe the monetary policies under the Hoover administration, discuss why the policies were chosen, describe the shift in monetary policy under Roosevelt, and then discuss extraordinary banking policies that set precedents for the bailouts, bank investments, and stress tests introduced in 2008 and 2009. I then address the modern versions of the debates over the causal impact of monetary policy with particular attention to dynamic structural general equilibrium modelling.

Following an examination of the fiscal policies of Hoover and Keynes in the light of Keynesian economics, I discuss estimates of the impact of federal spending on local economies, describe the supply-side aspects of the rise in tax rates, and conclude with further discussion of the lessons for the present from 1930s monetary and fiscal policy.

9.2. MONETARY POLICY UNDER THE HOOVER ADMINISTRATION

Nearly everybody agrees with Milton Friedman and Anna Schwartz (1963) that the Federal Reserve's monetary policy was misguided between 1929 and 1933. At the time, the Fed had two effective tools for influencing the money supply: open-market operations and the discount rate at which the Fed allowed member banks to borrow (or discount bills to the Fed) to meet reserve requirements. The open-market operations involved the purchase or sale of existing bonds. Reductions in the discount rate and purchases of bonds could be used to reduce the probability of bank failures in a panic and both contributed to increases in the money supply. Thus, if the Fed had focused on combating bank failures and unemployment within the US economy, the appropriate strategy was to lower the discount rate and purchase bonds.

Yet, the Federal Reserve also paid close attention to the international gold standard, which was essentially a promise that the Federal Reserve and US banks would pay out an ounce of gold for every $20.67 in Federal Reserve notes. To remain on the gold standard, the Federal Reserve was required to provide adequate US gold reserves to make this promise credible. If changes in the relative attractiveness of the dollar led the US supply of gold to fall below the appropriate level, the Fed was expected to take actions to make the dollar more attractive. At the time, the standard policies in response to gold outflows included raising the discount rate and selling (or at least reducing purchases of) existing bonds.

Table 9.1 shows the monthly movements, over the period from January 1929 to February 1933, of series representing two of the major dilemmas for monetary policy—the nominal volume of deposits in suspended banks and the change in the US gold stock. The table shows how specific measures of Federal Reserve activity were changing in response to these dilemmas, including changes in the Federal Reserve's holdings of US securities, the level of the New York Fed's discount rate, changes in the Fed's holdings of bills purchased, and changes in the member banks borrowing at the Fed. The bills purchased refer to short-term credit instruments, known as bankers' acceptances and trade acceptances, that Federal Reserve banks could purchase in the open market. These are the types of 'real bills' discussed in the 'real bills doctrine' described in section 9.3. At the founding of the Federal Reserve, changes in bills purchased were expected to be a major aspect of policy, as they were in England at the time. In the 1920s, however, open-market purchases and sales of US securities became the main source of adjustment and policy operations (Meltzer, 2003: 270).

Table 9.1. Monthly measures of key aspects of Federal Reserve policy and factors that might have influenced Federal Reserve Policy, January 1929–February 1933

Month/year	Value of banks deposits suspended ($m)	Change in gold stock in US ($m)	Change in Federal Reserve System's holdings of US securities ($m)	Change in bills bought by the Federal Reserve System ($m)	New York Federal Reserve Bank discount rate (% p.a.)	Change in member bank borrowing ($m)
January 1929	18.5	−14	−34	−9	5	−154
February 1929	24.1	26	−45	−88	5	30
March 1929	9.2	35	13	−120	5	80
April 1929	10.4	72	−32	−109	5	35
May 1929	15.6	41	−12	−11	5	−48
June 1929	25.4	23	26	−46	5	22
July 1929	60.8	17	−32	−24	5	118
August 1929	6.7	19	8	49	6	-53
September 1929	9.7	12	10	105	6	−74
October 1929	12.5	14	−11	108	6	−84
November 1929	22.3	−20	161	−41	4.5	68
December 1929	15.5	−82	131	24	4.5	−150
January 1930	26.5	9	39	−6	4.5	−302
February 1930	32.4	62	−5	−29	4	−123
March 1930	23.2	68	60	−39	3.5	−104
April 1930	31.9	68	−10	20	3.5	−43
May 1930	19.4	26	−1	−84	3	16
June 1930	57.9	18	42	−41	2.5	4
July 1930	29.8	−18	12	13	2.5	−25
August 1930	22.8	−16	16	−1	2.5	−12
September 1930	21.6	10	−2	44	2.5	−25
October 1930	19.7	24	5	−12	2.5	7
November 1930	179.9	36	−3	−1	2.5	25
December 1930	372.1	22	45	73	2	117
January 1931	75.7	50	3	−51	2	−85
February 1931	34.2	12	−44	−104	2	−37

Continued

Table 9.1. Continued

Month/year	Value of banks deposits suspended ($m)	Change in gold stock in US ($m)	Change in Federal Reserve System's holdings of US securities ($m)	Change in bills bought by the Federal Reserve System ($m)	New York Federal Reserve Bank discount rate (% p.a.)	Change in member bank borrowing ($m)
March 1931	34.3	42	1	21	2	−40
April 1931	41.7	29	−4	50	2	−21
May 1931	43.2	72	−1	−29	1.5	8
June 1931	190.5	158	11	−23	1.5	25
July 1931	40.7	−7	64	−42	1.5	−19
August 1931	180.0	46	38	56	1.5	53
September 1931	233.5	−254	24	124	1.5	58
October 1931	471.4	−449	−3	433	3.5	333
November 1931	67.9	122	−6	−132	3.5	82
December 1931	277.1	46	50	−220	3.5	79
January 1932	218.9	−45	−18	−119	3.5	54
February 1932	51.7	−62	−16	−70	3	20
March 1932	10.9	37	66	−46	3	−134
April 1932	31.6	−23	205	−53	3	−109
May 1932	34.4	−215	399	−11	3	−119
June 1932	132.7	−233	284	9	2.5	9
July 1932	48.7	55	121	10	2.5	28
August 1932	29.5	114	32	−23	2.5	−72
September 1932	13.5	105	−2	−3	2.5	−64
October 1932	20.1	71	3	0	2.5	−59
November 1932	43.3	76	0	0	2.5	−15
December 1932	70.9	173	3	0	2.5	−31
January 1933	133.1	40	−48	−2	2.5	−27
February 1933	62.2	−174	−2	70	2.5	52

Sources: All values except Fed discount rate are in millions of nominal dollars. Value of deposits suspended is from *Federal Reserve Bulletin* (September 1937: 909). Change in Federal Reserve System holdings of US securities, change in bills bought by the Fed, changes in member bank borrowing, and change in US gold stock come from *Federal Reserve Bulletin* (February 1930: 59; March 1931: 127; October 1931: 560; May 1932: 292; June 1932: 352; October 1932: 634; March 1933: 136; September 1933: 541; January 1934: 14). New York Federal Reserve discount rate is from Federal Reserve Board of Governors (1943: 493).

The Federal Reserve's attempts to slow the speculative boom in stocks contributed to slowing the money supply between 1928 and 1929. Soon after the recession started in August 1929, the Dow Jones stock index peaked in early September. For most of October the Fed had been selling US securities, but this policy changed swiftly when the Dow Jones index dropped 24 per cent on Monday 28 October and Black Tuesday, 29 October. The New York Fed responded immediately by purchasing $115m in US securities. Two days later the Federal Reserve Board agreed that it was the proper move. The entire Fed system purchased $157m in US securities during the last week of October, and then made net purchases (after subtracting sales of securities) of another $161m in November and $131m in December (see Table 9.1). The New York Fed lowered its discount rate from 6 to 5 per cent on 1 November and then to 4.5 per cent by 15 November, after the Dow dropped to roughly two-thirds of its 25 October level by 11 November (Meltzer, 2003: 284–8).

The Fed's response to bank failures over the next three years varied from crisis to crisis. Over most of the year 1930, the Fed made policy adjustments in response to gold flows and seasonal demands for credit. The spike in suspended bank deposits in November and December 1930, shown in Table 9.1, led the New York Fed to purchase $100m in US securities and $75m in bankers' acceptances between 30 November and 17 December. It then sold $50m in the middle of the month. The New York Fed then lowered its discount rate from 2.5 to 2 per cent (see Table 9.1) and purchased more than $100m in bankers' acceptances and $85m in US securities in the last week of December (Meltzer, 2003: 325). The rest of the regional Federal Reserve banks were leaning the other way, however, as the Fed systems' stock of US securities rose by only $45m in December (see Table 9.1) and the stock of acceptances rose by only $73m that month.

The Fed faced its ultimate dilemma between August and October of 1931 (see Table 9.1) when the volume of deposits suspended spiked again and a dramatic outflow of gold occurred after Britain left the gold standard in September 1931. Until October, the Fed's primary focus was international. During the first part of the summer, the Fed worried about a flight of gold out of eastern Europe and Germany into the US, associated with possible coups and the rise of Hitler. In response, the Fed participated in loans to banks in Hungary, the German Reichsbank, and the Austrian National Bank. In late July, the Fed approved a purchase of $125m in prime commercial bills guaranteed by the Bank of England to aid a crumbling situation in Britain. After Britain left the gold standard on 20 September, and gold started flowing out of the country, the Fed followed the standard responses. First, it purchased US securities, although the holdings of US securities changed very little relative to the changes in gold stocks or in bank suspensions during this period (see Table 9.1). The New York Fed then raised its discount rate from 1.5 to 2.5 per cent on 9 October and then to 3.5 per cent on 16 October (Meltzer, 2003: 332–48).

The memo for the Open Market Policy Committee (OMPC) meeting on 26 October finally focused more attention on the bank failures than the gold outflows, but this did not lead to much of a change in OMPC policy. The OMPC chose not to make any major open-market purchases of US securities. Instead, the OMPC recommended that member banks should be encouraged to lend to banks in difficulty and then rediscount those loans to the Federal Reserve System banks.

Most of the action was driven by the decisions of the member banks. Despite the higher discount rates in October, member banks sharply increased their borrowing at the Fed's discount window (see Table 9.1) and sold a large amount of bankers' acceptances to the Fed. Meltzer (2003: 348) argues that the Fed had done more to prop up the Bank of England in August and September than it did for the American banking system after Britain left gold.

The wave of bank failures over the summer led President Herbert Hoover to call for a new set of extraordinary measures outside the Federal Reserve. He met with bankers in October 1932 to establish the National Credit Corporation (NCC). The NCC was designed as a way for commercial banks to pool resources voluntarily to purchase marketable assets of insolvent banks and to provide alternative borrowing facilities for the banks based on assets that the Fed could not accept as collateral.

At the 30 November OMPC meeting, the committee members expressed satisfaction at their handling of the gold outflow. Essentially, they felt that they had stemmed the tide of the gold flow and meanwhile had done the right thing for the bank failures by lending a great deal at high discount rates, as seen in Table 9.1. They had not purchased securities to stave off the banking crisis, but seemed satisfied that that was the right course (Meltzer 2003: 348–9). They approved the capacity to purchase $200m in US securities in open-market operations but then sell them again in response to the seasonal demands for credit.

A new wave of bank suspensions hit in December 1931 and January 1932, but not much was done. The NCC made $155m in loans to 575 banks, but the volume of deposits suspended in December 1931 still reached $277m, the third highest monthly peak of the early 1930s. The Hoover administration started developing the plans for the RFC, which would become a government corporation with the authority to lend to banks and businesses, and the Glass–Steagall Act of 1932, which expanded the range of assets on which the Fed could provide credits to member banks. Despite the authority to make $200m in US security purchases, the Fed did not respond to the bank failures with purchases of US securities. Instead, it sought to time purchases to the passage of the RFC and the Glass–Steagall Act of 1932 (Meltzer, 2003: 357–61).

Finally, between February and June 1932, the Federal Reserve purchased slightly more than $1 billion in US government securities. Meanwhile, the RFC seemed to be much more active in trying to prevent bank failures by making $784m in loans to more than 4,000 banks between February and November of 1932.[1] Friedman and Schwartz (1963) argue that, had the $1 billion in open-market purchases of US securities been completed during the first wave of bank failures in late 1930, the move would have been effective in stemming the crisis in 1930 and stalling the drop in the money supply that followed. The economy would have been in a much better position when the next crises hit, or some of the later crises would have been prevented or softened significantly. In their view, the $1 billion purchase in 1932 was 'too little, too late'.

[1] See Mitchener and Mason (2010) and Mason (2001) for discussions of the effectiveness of the NCC and RFC in preventing bank failures.

After the major open-market purchases ended in the summer of 1932, Fed policy was relatively passive. When a new wave of bank failures hit in December 1932 and the first two months of 1933, the Fed did little. Meanwhile, President Hoover and President-elect Roosevelt could not come to an agreement on how to deal with the latest wave of suspensions of over 500 small banks between December and February. Hoover pressed Roosevelt to join him in developing a policy to counteract the bank failures, but he demanded that Roosevelt promise to stay on the gold standard and run a balanced budget. Roosevelt did not want to make such commitments or accept responsibility for a joint policy until he had actual authority. Meanwhile, state governments took action to prevent the failures, as 35 states declared bank holidays and the remaining states put strong restrictions on withdrawals (Meltzer, 2003: 379–80).

9.3. WHY WAS THE FEDERAL RESERVE SO RECALCITRANT?

A significant amount of the Fed's actions can be understood by examining its international role in defending the gold standard (Temin, 1989; Temin and Wigmore, 1990; Eichengreen, 1992). Until 1933, the Fed maintained a commitment to the international gold standard, a commitment that tied its hands to some degree. Even though the money supply and the economy was continuing to decline, outflows of gold, when Britain left the gold standard in 1931, and during the banking crisis in March of 1933, led the Fed to raise the discount rate. Once the US left the gold standard in 1933, it was freer to focus on domestic policy and the money supply.

Friedman and Schwartz argued that the Federal Reserve lacked the right type of strong leadership. Benjamin Strong, a powerful advocate for use of open-market purchases of US securities during recessions in the 1920s as the head of the New York Federal Reserve Bank, had died in 1928. Even though his replacement, George Harrison, and several others argued for expansive bond purchases at various times in the early 1930s, they were overridden by the rest of the Fed policy makers, who tended to hold the view that Fed interference would either prolong the problems or have little impact.

Not all agree that the Fed had changed directions with the death of Benjamin Strong. When Alan Meltzer (2003: 284–411) wrote his majestic history of the Federal Reserve System, he had access to many internal documents that had not been available to Friedman and Schwartz. He draws more nuanced conclusions about the internal policy debates within the Fed, as well as the attitudes of Strong's replacement, George Harrison. Between 1929 and 1933 the most common view held by the Fed policy makers was a combination of the 'real bills doctrine' and the Riefler–Burgess framework.[2] Under the real bills doctrine, increases in credit should be provided by the Federal Reserve by purchasing commercial bills of

[2] Winfield Riefler was an economist at the Federal Reserve Board and W. Randolph Burgess was at the New York bank.

exchange or bankers' acceptances because they arise from the financing of trade or production. The idea was that credit and output would expand together and thus not be inflationary. Credit expansion based on Fed purchases of government securities was considered to be speculative credit because no new production resulted. Real bills analysts wanted the member banks to initiate the demands for credit and to avoid having the Fed provide 'redundant' or 'speculative' credit (Meltzer, 2003: 263, 411).

The Riefler–Burgess framework:

> explained that banks were reluctant to borrow, borrowed only if reserves were deficient, and repaid promptly. To repay borrowing, banks called loans, raised lending rates, and sold government securities.... A rise in the discount rate lowered the level of member bank borrowing, reduced credit and money, and raised market interest rates (Meltzer, 2003: 161).

Meanwhile, open-market purchases of US securities supplied reserves and encouraged banks to repay borrowing, offer more loans, and reduce interest rates. Open-market sales drove banks to borrow, restrict lending, and raise interest rates. The doctrine suggested that the key variables to look at were member-bank borrowing and interest rates. If both were low, policy was easy. If the two were high, policy was tight. The cut point was $500m for borrowing (Meltzer, 2003: 734–5). Meltzer found that the Fed leaders spent very little time looking at the sharp decline in the money supply, although in late 1931 and 1932 they began to note signs of currency hoarding and the holding of excess reserves by banks.

There were disagreements among the members of the Board of Governors and the OMPC. At various times, one or more members advocated expansionary open-market purchases of US securities. Yet, in most situations there were always real bills and Riefler–Burgess advocates who saw low member-bank borrowing and low interest rates and felt that monetary policy was sufficiently easy. Several of the decision makers argued that prior attempts to promote recovery with open-market purchases of US securities had had little effect in the 1930s and had promoted speculation in the 1920s. Even during the $1 billion open-market purchase of US securities in 1932, some members of the OMPC were not fully on board. Most of the regional banks allowed the New York Fed to make most of the purchases. The members of the OMPC went ahead with the purchases in part because banks were already borrowing a great deal, so that Fed officials saw the purchases as a means of allowing the member banks to replace borrowing without promoting inflation. Further, Fed officials were worried that if they did not act, Congress might pass much more inflationary acts in the form of the First World War Veterans' Bonus and a new bill to expand the printing of greenbacks (Meltzer, 2003: 358–61).

One reason so many officials thought the policy was easy is that they did not adjust nominal interest rates for the high rate of deflation. Meltzer (2003: 411) finds no mention of officials adjusting the nominal rate for deflation and discussing the implications of a high real rate of interest. The Fed cut the nominal discount rate shown in Table 9.1 in 11 steps from 6 per cent in October 1929 to 1.5 per cent in 1931. But in that same time span, the Consumer Price Index inflation rate, shown in Figure 9.1, was near zero in 1929, and then became a deflation rate of −2.4 per cent in 1930 and −9 per cent in 1931. This meant that the

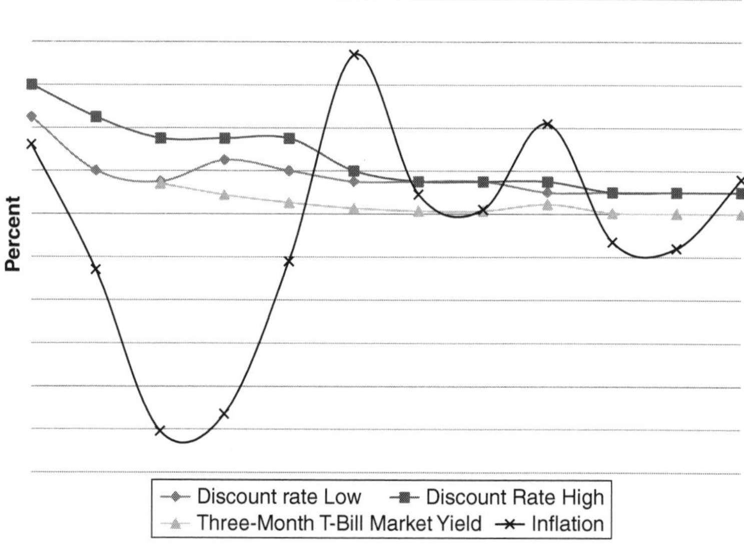

Fig. 9.1. Annual high and low Federal Reserve discount rates, 3-month Treasury bond market yield, and rate of inflation, 1929–1940

Sources: Federal Reserve Bank of New York discount rate low and high for year are series Cj113 and Cj114 from Wheelock (2006: 3–624); 3-month Treasury bill market yield is series Cj1232 from James and Sylla (2006: 3–822). Inflation is measured using the implicit price deflator from series F-5 in US Bureau of the Census (1975: 224).

ex post real discount rate, the discount rate minus the inflation rate, rose slightly from 4.5 to 4.77 per cent in 1930 and then jumped to 10.5 per cent in 1931. The Fed raised the discount rate back to 3.5 per cent in late 1931 to stem the outward flow of gold when Britain abandoned the gold standard. Then the Fed allowed it fall to 2.5 per cent for most of 1932. Yet, the 10 per cent deflation rate that year caused the real *ex post* discount rate to rise to 12.5 per cent. Even though low nominal interest rates led Fed officials to believe the monetary policy was easy, the effects of deflation drove the real interest rates to levels that were then two times as high as any real interest rate experienced in the US after 1933.

Brunner and Meltzer (1968) and Wicker (1966) argue that the Fed's policy objectives were similar in the 1920s and the early 1930s. Wheelock (1991) builds on their work by combining narrative discussions with time-series regressions to estimate the relationship between Federal Reserve policy tools and various economic targets. He then uses the regressions to identify the Fed's policy regimes and shows that the Fed responded to changes in domestic and international economic indicators in the 1930s with largely the same proportionate responses as they had in the 1920s.

Wheelock argues that the Fed policy makers did not realize that the same proportionate responses were not enough to offset the drastic downturn that was taking place. For example, the Federal Reserve and state bank regulators allowed an average of 630 banks per year to suspend operations between 1920 and 1929 because they believed them to be weaker banks that normally would not survive in a market economy. Analyses of individual bank failures in the 1920s and 1930s by Calomiris and Mason (2003) and Mitchener (2005) suggest that most of the failures in the early 1930s fit this pattern as well. As a result, many of the regional Federal Reserve banks felt comfortable in following the same lender-of-last-resort policies they had followed in the 1920s. The difference between the early 1930s and the 1920s was the sheer scale of the failures and the economy-wide problems. The number of banks fell from 25,000 to 17,800 between 1930 and 1933. The shares of deposits in suspended banks rose to 2 per cent in 1930, 4.5 per cent in 1931, 2.4 per cent in 1932, and 11 per cent in 1933. It was likely that the banks failing in the early 1930s, having already survived through the 1920s, were generally stronger, but they were hit by far worse circumstances in the 1930s as output dropped sharply in every state. Thus, the Federal Reserve policy rules were not enough to prevent failure owing to the extraordinary circumstances of the 1930s.[3]

9.4. MONETARY POLICY DURING THE ROOSEVELT ADMINISTRATION

After taking office on 4 March 1933, Roosevelt made sweeping changes. Within two months he had taken the US off the gold standard. The removal of the 'golden fetters' and the devaluation of the dollar, to $35 per ounce of gold, combined with political events in Europe to cause a flow of gold into America. The economy began to recover. This same pattern was repeated throughout the world. In country after country, as central banks sought to maintain the gold standard, their domestic economies continued to sink. As each left the gold standard, their economies rebounded (Temin and Wigmore, 1990; Eichengreen, 1992).

The New York Fed cut the discount rate from 3.5 to 3 per cent in early April. Eugene Black, the governor of the Atlanta Federal Reserve Bank, became the chairman of the Federal Reserve Board in May 1933. The Atlanta Fed was known for providing more liquidity during bank runs than most of the other regional Feds between 1930 and 1932 (Richardson and Troost, 2009). Under the new leadership, the Fed cut the discount rate again in May 1933, from 3 to 2.5 per cent. The rate in Figure 9.1 fell to 2 per cent by the end of the year, to 1.5 per cent in 1934, and then to 1 per cent in 1937, where it stayed for the rest of the decade. The rates stayed low in real terms as well. The highest *ex post* real rates occurred at around 2 and 3 per cent in the deflationary years of 1938 and 1939. In 1934, an inflation rate above 7 per cent led to a real discount rate of –6 per cent, while a 4 per cent inflation in 1937 led to a –2.5 per cent real rate. In terms of open-market operations, the Federal Reserve's holdings of securities were roughly steady around $2.5 billion dollars between 1934 and 1939 (Wheelock, 2006: 624–9).

[3] In some cases, increased state enforcement and monitoring activity actually made the situation worse for some banks. Richardson and Van Horn (2009) find that a change in monitoring activity by New York state banking officials may well have contributed to the failure of a number of banks in New York in the summer of 1932.

The Federal Reserve was given direct administrative control over the reserve requirements of member banks when it was reorganized under the Banking Act of 1935. Under the fractional reserve system, member banks were required to hold a share of deposits in reserve at the Federal Reserve. By 1935, the economy had been moving through two years of recovery. Real GDP growth was very rapid, in large part because the economy was starting from a base that was 36 per cent below the level in 1929. The number unemployed had dropped significantly, although they still composed over 15 per cent of the labour force. Noting that banks were holding large reserves above and beyond the required reserve requirements, the Fed began worrying about the possibility of inflation. If the banks started lending out their excess reserves, the Fed worried that the rise in the money supply would lead to rapid inflation that would halt the recovery. The Federal Reserve doubled the long-standing reserve requirements in three steps on 16 August 1936, 1 March 1937, and 1 May 1937. The Fed had not recognized that the banks were holding so many excess reserves to protect themselves against bank runs. The experience of the past decade had given the banks little confidence that the Fed would act as a lender of last resort. Therefore, the banks increased their reserves to make sure that they retained some excess reserves as a cushion. These changes were followed by a spike in unemployment to 19 per cent, and a decline in real GDP growth in 1937–38.[4]

9.5. EXTRAORDINARY BANKING POLICIES IN THE 1930s

Banking policy in the 1930s was not confined to the actions of the Federal Reserve. Precedents were set for Treasury Secretary Paulson to establish government ownership stakes in banks in 2008 and for Secretary Geithner to seek extra certifications of the quality of bank assets before allowing banks to buy back the government's ownership positions.

In February 1932, the Hoover administration established the RFC. Its first moves included making loans to 4,000 banks, railroads, credit unions, and mortgage loan companies to provide assets that would jump-start commercial lending. Among the most important programmes was the provision of loans to troubled banks to seek to provide them with enough liquidity to survive bank runs. Recent studies suggest that these initial loans were not successful because the RFC loans were given first priority over depositors and other lenders in situations where the bank failed. As a result, banks had to hold the assets that they could sell most easily to ensure repayment of the RFC loans. These assets could not then be used to repay depositors when the bank failed. When the RFC began to accept more risk by purchasing preferred stock in the troubled banks, it was more successful at staving off bank failures (Mason, 2001; Mitchener and Mason, 2010).

During a series of bank runs between October 1932 and March 1933, 30 states declared bank holidays and the remaining states put restrictions on deposits.

[4] This description is based on Friedman and Schwartz (1963) and Meltzer (2003). For a view that puts less emphasis on the Fed's role, see Romer (1992).

Under the national bank holiday, all banks and thrift institutions were temporarily closed. Government auditors were then sent in to evaluate the banks and allow them to reopen if they were sound. Conservators were appointed to improve the positions of the insolvent banks and the RFC was given the power to subscribe to stock issues from the reorganized banks. These seals of approval conferred on the reopened banks helped change expectations about the solvency of the bank system.[5]

9.6. THE CAUSAL IMPACT OF MONETARY POLICY

While the vast majority of economists agree that the Federal Reserve policies were flawed, there has been substantial debate about how much causal impact the monetary policies had on real GDP and unemployment. In *A Monetary History of the United States, 1867–1960*, Friedman and Schwartz (1963) saw the Great Depression as one of many episodes in which changes in the money supply strongly influenced the path of inflation and growth in real output, typically measured by real gross national product (GNP). The basic equation showing the multiplicative relationship between the money supply (M), velocity (V), the price level (P), and real output (Q) is

$$MV = PQ \tag{1}$$

The growth-rate version of the equation, with growth rates in lower-case letters is

$$m + v = p + q \tag{2}$$

These equations always hold in hindsight because velocity (V), the number of times the money supply turns over in the purchase of final goods and services, is calculated as the ratio of the money supply (M) to Nominal GNP (PQ).

In Friedman and Schwartz's monetarist model, the equation has analytical force because they argue that velocity moves in predictable ways. Thus, changes in the money supply will lead to changes in price (P) and real output (Q) in the same direction and the only question is how much of the change in the money supply is allocated to changes in price and real output. The annual growth-rate version of the variables in Figure 9.2 shows a strong visual relationship between the growth rate of the money supply and the growth in real GNP. The fit between M1 growth and the inflation rate is not so good for 1930, 1935, and 1936.

The strong correlations are consistent with the monetarist view, but correlation does not guarantee causation. The debates in the macroeconomic literature centre on the 'causal' impact of the monetary policy on real output. How much of the drop in real output between 1929 and 1933 was caused by the failure to loosen monetary policy? How much of the rise in output from 1933 to 1937 was attributable to the reflationary monetary policy, and how much of the drop in

[5] See Mitchener and Mason (2010) for more detail on these extraordinary policies.

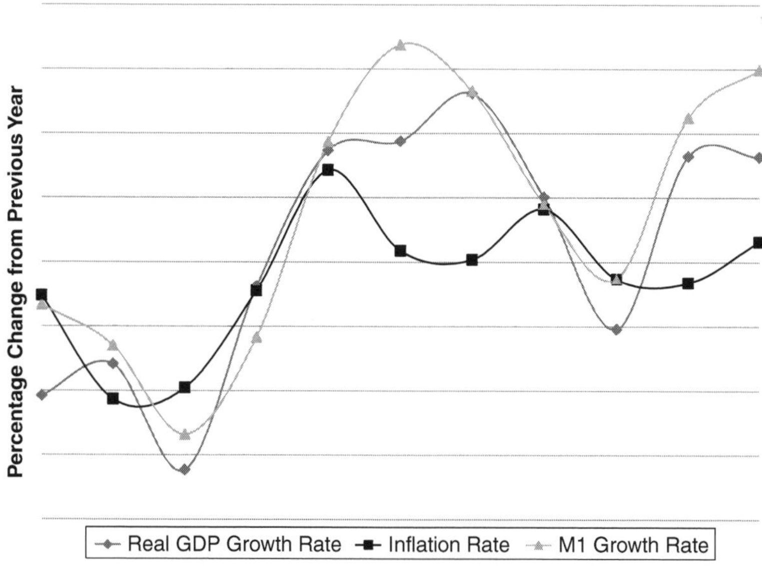

Fig. 9.2. Growth rates in real GDP, M1, and the price level, 1930–1940

Sources: Indices with 1929 = 100 were created based on GNP in 1958 prices and implicit price deflator (1958 = 100) from series F-3 and F-5 in US Bureau of the Census (1975: 224). The M1 measure of the money supply is series Cj42 from Anderson (2006: 3–604).

output from 1937 to 1938 was determined by the Fed's increases in reserve requirements?

Friedman and Schwartz argued that most of the changes in the measures of the money supply were caused by changes in monetary policy. On the other hand, macroeconomists of all stripes are aware that changes in real GDP can also cause changes in money-supply measures. Increases in income lead people to hold more money for transactions and as assets, and vice versa. Even though the velocity measure in the monetarist equation is seen as a money demand parameter, the money supply, prices, output, and velocity can all be seen as endogenous to the system, so that it is very difficult to sort out causality with ordinary least squares regressions. Keynesians, in particular, argued that the strong correlations between the money measures and real GDP were as likely to have been driven by a causal relationship that moved from a drop in output to a lower amount of money used in the economy. When Peter Temin (1976) asked, *Did Monetary Forces Cause the Great Depression?*, he argued strongly for unexplained drops in consumption as a primary cause of the Depression. There are plenty of other culprits that have been identified.

In the 1970s and 1980s numerous scholars debated the impact of the money supply using IS-LM frameworks to predict the impact of monetary policy on interest rates, prices, and output, and then provided empirical tests with the extant data. Since my charge in this chapter is to examine the scholarship of the past two decades, I cannot cover these debates adequately. Atack and Passell (1994) and Smiley (2002) provide readable surveys of the debates. Other excellent resources on past and current debates include Parker's (2002, 2007) interviews with the leading scholars of the Great Depression.

Rational-expectations economists argued that if enough people recognized that the changes in the demand they witnessed were on account of changes in the amount of money available, they would respond by changing price but not real output. Thus, people had to misestimate changes in monetary policy for changes in the demand for products to have a causal effect on real output and unemployment. This has led scholars to focus on expectations. For example, Hamilton (1987) argues that the impact of contractionary monetary policy that started in 1928 operated through unanticipated deflation and, after 1930, through the disruption of the real services of intermediation on the part of the financial sector as a consequence of banking panics. In Hamilton's (1987: 145) view, 'it would have been difficult to design a more contractionary policy than that adopted in January 1928'. As $307.8m dollars in gold flowed to France in 1928, the Federal Reserve raised the discount rate from 3.5 to 5 per cent, sold $393m in securities between December 1927 and July 1928, and cut its holdings of bankers' acceptances in half by raising its buying rates from 3 to 4.5 per cent. Despite Fed leaders' claims to the contrary, Hamilton is convinced the Fed was trying to slow the stock market boom. Meanwhile, the stock boom led to an increased demand for loans, and banks found it profitable to replace unborrowed reserves with borrowed reserves. Hamilton cites evidence that many policy makers did not anticipate deflation, that regression models with data from 1900 to 1940 fail to predict deflation, and that the deflation in commodity prices caught speculators by surprise.

More recently, real-business-cycle theorists have argued that a combination of large negative productivity shocks and ill-advised microeconomic policies designed to prop up wages and prices caused the downturn. Most recent tests of the impact of monetary policy in the Depression have been performed in the context of macroeconomic models based on microeconomic foundations. These dynamic stochastic general equilibrium (DSGE) models start with a dynamic scenario where representative households with infinite lives choose consumption and asset levels to maximize the expected utility of their long-run stream of consumption, subject to their anticipated long-run income stream. The firms that hire the household members maximize their expected stream of profits. There is typically a capital accumulation law for the economy.

The models then incorporate factors that would create inefficiencies in the operation of a competitive economy. Many modern scholars build on Keynes's emphasis on 'sticky wages' in the form of long-term labour contract provisions or government policies designed to promote high wages. Depression era policies include Hoover's jawboning with manufacturers to get them to maintain higher nominal wages and the Roosevelt administration's pressure to keep wages high while industry established its Codes of Competition on the National Industrial Recovery Act (Bordo et al., 2000; Chari et al., 2002, 2005; Cole and Ohanian, 2004; Eggertsson, 2008). Like Hamilton, Bernanke (1983) argues for a causal role for inefficiencies in credit markets caused by an increase in the cost of credit intermediation. In particular, unanticipated deflation may have caused lenders to see many previously sound borrowers as uncreditworthy. In the modern period, scholars add inefficiencies derived from sticky prices and some forms of regulation.

The scholars pick or estimate a set of parameters in the model that best fits a series of stylized facts about features of the economy. The model is then used to perform simulations to show how well the time paths associated with different policy regimes fit the actual Depression era data on real output, prices, investment, interest rates, and other variables of interest.

As one leading example, Bordo, Erceg, and Evans (2000) (henceforth known as BEE) develop a model with sticky wages to incorporate the common claim that manufacturing wages did not fall as much as people anticipated they should have during the Great Depression (Ohanian, 2009; Taylor, 2009). The BEE analysis finds that contractionary monetary shocks account for 50–70 per cent of the decline in real GNP between 1929 and the first quarter of 1933. They find a much weaker effect of expansionary monetary policy after the move off the gold standard in mid-1933. They argue that the expansionary monetary policy had much weaker effects because the National Industrial Recovery Act raised nominal wages in ways that limited production and hours worked.

Chari et al. (2002, 2005) re-examine the issue in the context of their 'wedges' model of the factors that lead to depressions. They use simulations to develop measures of three wedges: a labour wedge, an efficiency wedge, and an investment wedge. Their labour wedge includes the combination of sticky wages and monetary policy shocks analysed by BEE as well as the inefficiencies from National Recovery Administration (NRA) policies and failures to enforce antitrust described by Cole and Ohanian (2004). They describe the efficiency wedge as a result of poor government policy interacting with shocks. Finally, the investment wedge is associated with gaps between consumers' rates of substitution between current and future consumption and the marginal product of capital that might arise owing to agency costs (Bernanke and Gertler, 1989). This investment wedge might be associated with the types of extra costs of capital intermediation described by Bernanke (1983) for the Depression.

The wedge-model analysis tells a mixed story about the effect of monetary policy. The simulations from the model do not show as strong an effect for monetary policy as the BEE (2000) model does. The labour wedge, which incorporates the combination of monetary policy shocks and sticky wages analysed in the BEE model, accounts by itself for about half of the decline in real output from 1929 to 1933. Unlike the BEE model findings, the wedge model matches up well with the post-1933 period. The combination of efficiency and labour wedges together seem to fit the output data from 1929 to 1933 very closely. Meanwhile, the investment wedge, which might be associated with Bernanke's emphasis on the costs of credit intermediation related to bank failures, has very little explanatory power in the 1930s. Cole and Ohanian (2005: 32) argue that the BEE (2000) model overstates the impact of monetary policy because it includes only the sticky-wage monetary-policy shock channel and does not incorporate the other wedges included by Chari et al. (2005, 2002). Meanwhile, Cole and Ohanian (2005) analyse the experience of 17 countries during the Depression using a real-business-cycle model. They find that about one-third of the international Depression is accounted for by monetary shocks and two-thirds by productivity shocks.

Christiano et al. (2003) build a DSGE model to account for the Depression using data from the 1920s and 1930s. They argue that economic actors shifted their preferences in favour of more liquidity, which led them to shift away from holding time deposits to holding cash. They develop a monetary rule that would have called for a temporary increase in the money growth in periods after a negative shock. The rule could not call for money growth in the same period as the negative shock because short-term interest rates were near zero. The zero bound made contemporaneous money supply growth an ineffective policy tool. Their simulations suggest that this post-shock monetary growth response rule would have prevented about 80 per cent of the decline between 1929 and 1933 and improved the rate of the recovery. They also ran simulations of a monetary growth rule in which the growth rate was held constant over the period. The results suggest that following a consistent monetary growth rate rule would have done little to lessen the Depression. Finally, they do not find support for Friedman and Schwartz's claim that the Fed could have staved off most of the Depression by preventing the drop in M1 in 1930, seen in Figure 9.2.

Eggertsson (2008) builds another DSGE model based on the insights of Temin and Wigmore (1990). The scholars argue for a strong role for deflationary shocks as a major cause of the Great Depression. To turn the economy around, the Roosevelt administration and the Federal Reserve had to change course sharply with a combination of new policies that would lead to inflation. This shock to the public's expectations could cause the economy to recover.

To promote recovery and have a causal effect, it was not enough to announce new efforts by the Fed to raise the money supply. Interest rates on short-term Treasury bills were near zero and could go no lower. Further, the Fed's past actions meant that there were no guarantees that it would not reverse the policy in the future. Only a complete reversal of the policy dogma of the day would work as shock therapy to convince the public that future policy would no longer be deflationary. Expectations about future policy were the key. The move off the gold standard freed the Fed and the economy from the 'golden fetters' that had prevented an inflationary policy. The willingness to ramp up government spending signalled that the money supply would have to be raised further to monetize the new federal debt to be issued. Eugene Meyer, the new leader of the Fed, was known for his prior actions in combating bank failures.

The timing of changes in output fits the story. Seasonally adjusted industrial production spiked in April, May, June, and July, although it then declined in the latter half of the year. Real GNP returned to its 1929 peak in 1937. In Eggertsson's (2008) DSGE model, a continuation of the Hoover administration policies of small government, adherence to the gold standard, and balanced budgets would have implied that real income would have dropped from 30 per cent below the 1929 level in 1933 to 49 per cent below in 1937. The simulation with the new policy regime leads to a rise in real output that can account for as much as 80 per cent of the difference between the extremely low counterfactual prediction in output in 1937 and the actual output in that year.

Given that short-term nominal interest rates remained very close to the zero bound between 1933 and 1938, Eggertsson and Pugsley (2006) argue that they can use a similar DSGE model with low interest rates to explain why the US fell back into recession in 1937–38. They argue that the recession was the result of the public's perception that the Roosevelt administration was returning to a deflationary policy. Anybody paying attention might have thought so. The Fed raised reserve requirements in 1936 and 1937 and the federal government reduced government spending between fiscal years 1937 and 1938. Simulations from their model suggest that the sharp change to deflationary expectations driven by the new policies was a prime contributor to a GNP reduction of 9 per cent and a deflation of 11 per cent.

The most recent development in the study of the causal effects of monetary policy has been a focus on the impact of monetary policy on individual banks and the impact of bank failures on economic activity. Using state-level information and an instrumental variable strategy to control for endogeneity, Thomas Garrett and David Wheelock (2006) find that changes in per capita income had a strong positive correlation with bank failures across states in the 1920s.

Meanwhile, Richardson and Troost (2009) have used quasi-experimental techniques to examine the effects of different policy regimes followed by the Atlanta and the St Louis regional Federal Reserve banks in the state of Mississippi. Atlanta, which oversaw southern Mississippi, followed Bagehot's rule for banking panics. This meant acting quickly as a lender of last resort to provide liquidity to prevent solvent banks faced with deposit runs from failing and dragging healthy banks with them. St Louis, which oversaw northern Mississippi, followed the 'real bills' doctrine that the supply of credit should contract in recessions because less credit was required to sustain economic activity. During panics through July 1931, the St Louis Fed tended to limit lending and demanded extra collateral for loans.

Richardson and Troost (2009) use a variety of methods to ensure that banks in both Fed districts in Mississippi were similar on all dimensions, so that only differences in the Fed policies would lead to differences in bank failure rates. They show that, during the banking crisis of November 1930, bank failures rates were significantly higher under the St Louis Fed's tighter policy regime in northern Mississippi than under the Atlanta Fed's looser regime in southern Mississippi. When the St Louis Fed shifted to follow policies more consistent with the Atlanta Feds in mid-1931, the difference in failure rates went away. They then show a causal link to real measures of output by showing that declines in wholesale trade in Mississippi tend to follow closely behind a set of bank failures.

9.7. FEDERAL FISCAL POLICY: SPENDING AND TAXATION AT THE NATIONAL LEVEL

Nearly all of the discussion of macroeconomic policy by macroeconomists focuses on monetary policy because the Hoover and Roosevelt administrations ran relatively small deficits throughout the 1930s. Both administrations increased government spending. However, tax revenues also increased markedly during both administrations.

Most observers do not realize how much the Hoover administration increased government spending. One reason is that Hoover remained a staunch advocate for balanced budgets throughout his presidency. Unlike Roosevelt, Hoover did not trumpet spending increases through *new* work-relief programmes and public-works programmes. Instead, he expanded existing programmes by doubling federal highway spending and increasing the spending by the Army Corps of Engineers on rivers, harbours, and flood control by over 40 per cent.[6] Hoover dam, which was set in motion before the Depression hit, also contributed a great deal to enhanced public-works spending. The Hoover administration and Congress ramped up nominal federal expenditures (see Figure 9.3) by 52 per cent from $3.1 billion in fiscal year 1929, to $4.7 billion in 1932, and $4.6 billion in fiscal year 1933. After adjusting for the deflation in the early 1930s (see Figure 9.4), real government spending in the Hoover era peaked at over 88 per cent above the 1929 level in 1932 and 1933. (In these figures 1933 is considered a Hoover year because the spending and taxes are reported for a fiscal year that ran from July to June and Roosevelt's spending did not ramp up until July 1933.)

As the Hoover administration raised spending, tax revenues fell, and the federal budget fell into its first deficits since the First World War. The Hoover administration ran deficits because nominal and real tax revenues fell after 1930, largely because the economy was falling apart and despite Hoover's desire to maintain a balanced budget. Congress and the Hoover administration tried to reverse the drop in tax revenues, partly by a 'soak the rich' tax increase under the Revenue Act of 6 June 1932. Less than 10 per cent of households earned enough to pay income taxes throughout the 1930s because individuals with less than $2,000 in annual income and families of four with less than $5,000 were exempt. Those who were required to pay saw their tax rates jump sharply. For example, individuals earning between $2,000 and $3,000 per year saw their rates rise from 0.1 per cent to 2 per cent. The rate rose from 0.9 to 6 per cent for incomes from $10 to $15 thousand, and the top rate rose from 23.1 to 57 per cent for those earning over a million. Families of four did not pay taxes until their annual incomes reached $5,000. Those with incomes above $5,000 saw their rates rise across income categories in a similar fashion. The tax on corporations rose from 12 to 13.75 per cent (US Bureau of the Census, 1975: 1111; Revenue Act of 1932).

The rise in income tax rates did little to stem the drop in tax revenues because receipts from household and corporate income taxes and estate taxes fell 37 per cent from $1.1 billion to $780m between 1932 and 1933. The only reason total tax collections (shown in Figure 9.3) stayed roughly the same in 1932 and 1933 was an extra $311m in revenue delivered by the 1932 Revenue Act's new excise taxes on oil pipeline transfers, electricity, bank cheques, communications, and manufacturers—particularly motor vehicles, tyres, oil, and gasoline (US Bureau of the Census, 1975: 1107 and 1111; Commissioner of Internal Revenue, 1933: 14–15).

After Roosevelt's landslide win, the Roosevelt administration and the new Democratic Congress proceeded to raise annual nominal government spending (see Figure 9.3) by $2 billion to roughly $6.5 billion in both fiscal years 1934 and

[6] Nominal road spending under the Agriculture Department rose from $95m in 1929 to $207.2m in 1932, while spending on rivers and harbours rose from $83m in 1929 to $121m in 1931 to $118m in 1933 (US Bureau of the Census Statistical Abstract of the United States for the years 1931 (pp. 180–82), 1933 (pp. 165–67), 1934 (pp. 165–67); US Department of Treasury, 1931, pp. 435–42). In many cases the new Roosevelt agencies built roads and performed work on rivers, harbours, and flood control that could just as easily have been assigned to the highway departments and the Army Corps of Engineers.

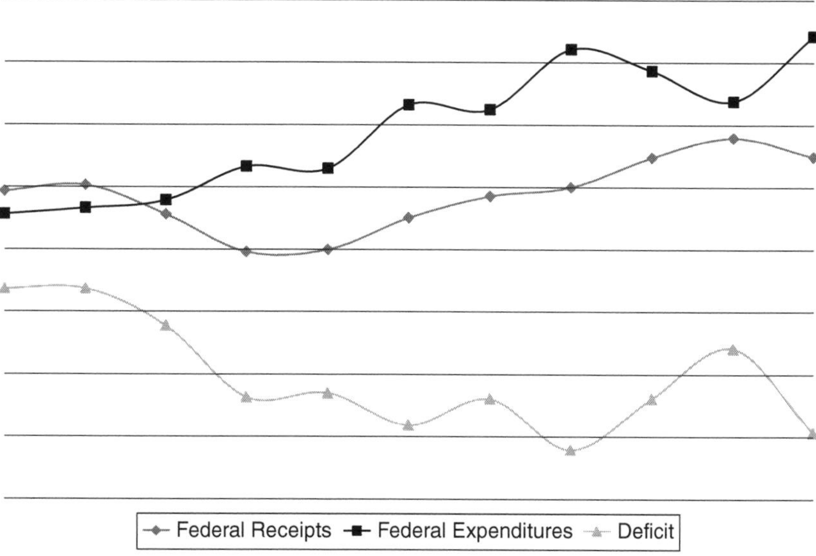

Fig. 9.3. Nominal federal government expenditures, revenues, and surplus/deficit in billions of dollars, 1929–39

Sources: Federal government expenditures, revenues, and surplus/deficit are series Ea584, Ea585, and Ea586 from Wallis (2006: 5-80 and 5-81).

1935, and then reached a temporary peak in 1936 at $8.4 billion. After a reduction to $6.8 billion over two years, the spending ramped up again to $8.8 billion in 1939. Yet, only the deficits of 1934, 1936, and 1939 (see Figures 9.3 and 9.4) are much larger than Hoover's 1932 and 1933 deficits.

Why? Tax receipts rose steadily from 1933 to 1938 before tailing off slightly (see Figure 9.3). Much of the rise reflects an increase in income tax and excise tax collections associated with the recovery. Income tax rates largely remained at the new higher levels. The Roosevelt administration readjusted the household income tax rates slightly in the Revenue Act of 1934 by lowering the rates paid by individuals earning between $2,000 and $20,000 per year by a few tenths of a per cent and raising them a few tenths for people earning between $20,000 and $1m, with similar adjustments for families. In the Revenue Act of 1936, the tax rate was raised from 31.4 to 33.4 per cent on individuals and families earning more than $100,000, and from 57.2 to 68 per cent for individuals and families with more than $1m in income. In fiscal years 1934 and 1935, the administration temporarily collected 23 and 16 per cent of its revenues from the Agricultural Adjustment Act (AAA) processing taxes used to pay farmers to take land out of production. By the time the AAA was declared unconstitutional in 1936, excise taxes on new alcohol sales after the end of Prohibition had risen to $505m, roughly 14 per cent of tax revenues (Commissioner of Internal Revenue, 1934: 76–7, 1935: 82–3, 1936; US Bureau of Census, 1975: 1107).

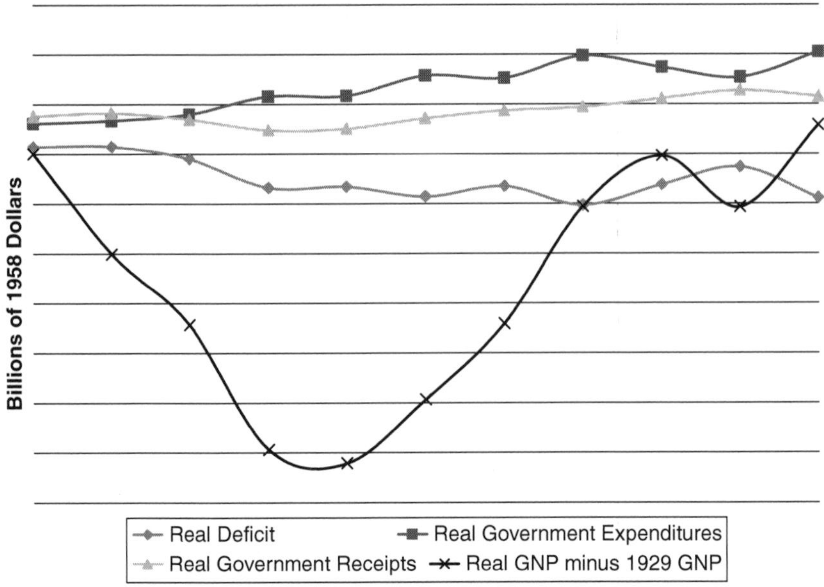

Fig. 9.4. GNP minus 1929 GNP, and federal expenditures, revenues, and budget surplus/deficit in billions of 1958 dollars, 1929–39

Sources: Federal government expenditures, revenues, and surplus/deficit are series Ea584, Ea585, and Ea586 from Wallis (2006: 5–80 and 5–81). Real GNP minus 1929 real GNP in 1958 prices is calculated from series F-3, and the implicit price deflator (1958 = 100) used to deflate the federal government data is series F-5; both are from US Bureau of the Census (1975: 224).

The Hoover and Roosevelt administrations ran deficits in most years, but economists do not consider them to be Keynesian stimulus attempts because the deficits were small relative to the economic declines during the 1930s. At the time, John Maynard Keynes was introducing his theories that the economy could be brought out of a low employment equilibrium by increasing government spending and lowering taxes and thus increasing government budget deficits (Keynes, 1964). Even though Roosevelt had ramped up spending, Keynes chastised him for not doing enough to stimulate the economy. In an open letter carried in several newspapers in December 1933, Keynes announced that more spending was not enough. Roosevelt needed to reduce taxes and run large federal budget deficits.[7] Writing in 1941, Alva Hansen, a major figure in aiding the diffusion of Keynesian thought in the economics profession, stated:

[7] In the *Los Angeles Times* on 31 December 1933, Keynes wrote: 'Thus, as the prime mover in the first stage of the technique of recovery, I lay overwhelming emphasis on the increase of national purchasing power resulting from governmental expenditure which is financed by loans and is not merely a transfer through taxation from existing incomes. Nothing else counts in comparison with this.' Barber (1996: 52, 83–4) discusses the relationship between Keynes and Roosevelt and the economic thinking of Roosevelt's Brains Trusters. Among Roosevelt's advisers, there were several who also argued for using government programmes as a stimulus, but they followed a different logical path for their arguments.

> Despite the fairly good showing made in the recovery up to 1937, the fact is that neither before nor since has the administration pursued a really positive expansionist program. . . . For the most part the federal government engaged in a salvaging program and not in a program of positive expansion (quoted in Brown, 1956: 866).

Brown (1956) and Peppers (1973) carefully examined whether the deficits were large enough to help the economy reach a target of full employment in a Keynesian model, and concluded that they fell well short. The magnitudes of the federal government spending and the federal deficits compared with the size of the income drop, shown in Figure 9.4, show why. The income drop is measured as the difference between real GNP (in 1958 dollars) in each year and the 1929 full-employment peak of $203.6 billion. The 1933 real GNP was $62.1 billion below its 1929 level in 1958 dollars, while the real budget deficit was only $2 billion. In 1934, a $5 billion dollar deficit was matched with a GNP shortfall of $49.3 billion; in 1935 the $4.5 billion dollar deficit was offsetting a $34.1 billion shortfall. The figures look strongest in 1936, when a $7.5 billion deficit was matched with a $10.6 billion GNP shortfall. Keynesians argue that budget deficits have multiplier effects. For such small deficits to have had any meaningful impact large enough for the economy to return to full employment, the multiplier effects would have had to have been much larger than the multiplier estimates of two proposed by the most ardent Keynesians.[8]

There still remains a question as to whether large federal deficits would have done much to increase real output and reduce unemployment. Romer (1992) estimated fiscal and monetary multipliers for the period using a simple equation where,

$$\textit{Output Change}_t = \beta_M\,(\textit{Monetary Change})_{t-1} + \beta_F(\textit{Fiscal Change})_{t-1} \qquad (3)$$

She argues for a year lag in the impact of policy and then picks two years where she could plausibly argue that monetary and fiscal policies were not designed to offset declines in the real economy. Romer picks output years 1921 and 1938 and thus policy years 1920 and 1937. In both cases she argues that Federal Reserve policy was independent and not focused on the economy. There was much less federal spending in 1937 than in 1936 because of the one-time payout of the veterans' bonus in 1936 over Roosevelt's veto. After plugging values in for these

[8] The extent to which fiscal policy is stimulative involves more complex calculations than the ones described here. Brown (1956) and Peppers (1973) find that the New Deal deficits were even less stimulative than the raw numbers shown here suggest. In fact, Peppers argues that Hoover was following more stimulative fiscal policies than Roosevelt. Any impact that the federal government deficits had in promoting recovery had to compete with the contractionary changes in state and local government budgets after 1933. Prior to 1933, state and local governments generally held nearly full responsibility for relief of the indigent and the unemployed. By 1933, state and local governments were overwhelmed by these and other responsibilities in the midst of a sharp decline in their revenues. A number were forced to run short-term deficits in the early 1930s. Yet, state constitutions generally require balanced year-to-year budgets. To repay the budget shortfalls, and also the debt issued during the early 1930s, state and local governments began raising taxes and establishing new taxes after 1933. The problem was further exacerbated when the federal government dumped responsibility for direct relief to 'unemployables' back on to the state and local governments in 1935, after two years of extensive spending. Thus, in the latter half of the 1930s, state and local governments were often running small surpluses.

two years, she finds a monetary multiplier of 0.823 that is much larger in magnitude than the fiscal multiplier of 0.233. Based on these calculations, the fiscal deficit would not have done much.

Eggertsson (2008) sees Roosevelt's shift to a fiscal deficit in 1933 as having large effects because it is part and parcel of the overall programme to reflate the economy by going off the gold standard and using more expansionary monetary policy. In his view, the deficit serves as a commitment device that helps to convince the public that the government will continue to run expansionary monetary policy to monetize the debt created. Thus, the deficit is a contributor to a change in expectations about future policy that will have large real effects. It is important to note, however, that Eggertsson's deficit arguments have to rely on the federal spending and deficit changes being part of a larger package with changes in Federal Reserve monetary policy. If spending more and running larger deficits were enough to reverse deflationary expectations by themselves, Hoover's doubling of spending and the presence of federal deficits in 1932 and 1933 should have helped boost the economy before Roosevelt was inaugurated.

9.8. FEDERAL SPENDING AND ITS IMPACT ON STATE AND LOCAL ECONOMIES

In the past few years there has been an explosion of work about New Deal spending policies that addresses the impact of the New Deal spending programmes at the state, local, and county level. One key insight of the papers is the importance of thinking about the purpose of the federal grants distributed and the terms on which they were distributed. For example, Fishback et al. (2005, 2006) find that public works and relief grants contributed to increases in economic activity and to net immigration into areas. Relief spending also contributed to reductions in crime rates and several death rates and contributed to returning birth rates to a more normal level (Fishback et al., 2007; Johnson et al., forthcoming). The public works and relief grants had such positive effects because they simultaneously provided employment, extra income, and public goods that raised productivity. Meanwhile, AAA farm payments had slightly negative effects. The AAA payments automatically had a crowding-out feature to them because they were designed to take agricultural land out of production in an attempt to lower output and raise farm prices nationally. The farmers who received the payments may have benefited, but this probably came at the expense of farm workers and croppers who lost employment or saw their wages decline owing to the drop in demand for labour.

A series of papers offer conflicting pictures of the impact of relief programmes on private employment in the 1930s. Studies of cross-sectional data using instrumental variable (IV) estimation by Fleck (1999) for county data in 1937 and 1940, and by Wallis and Benjamin (1981) using city data in 1934/35, suggest that areas with higher relief employment did not experience a reduction in private employment. On the other hand, studies using panel data sets, which allow the research to take advantage of variation across time within locations while controlling for nationwide shocks in different years, find some degree of crowding out that varies across time. In the early years of the decade when unemployment was at its peak, above 20 per cent, Matthews and Benjamin (1992) find that the addition of one work-relief job reduced private employment by about one-third of a job, while Neumann et al. (2010) find a slight positive effect of relief spending on private employment. After 1935, when unemployment rates fell below 20 per cent, both studies find that an additional work-relief job was associated with a reduction of up to nine-tenths of a private job.

Fishback and Kachanovskaya (2010) have recently estimated a New Deal fiscal multiplier at the state level. They examine the impact of net federal spending per capita (federal spending minus taxes) on state personal income per capita in an annual panel of states for the years 1930–40. In estimates that control for the endogeneity of the distribution of funds using state and year fixed effects and state-specific time trends, the results show a slight negative relationship between net federal spending and per capita income. They then add to the analysis an instrument for net federal spending that uses a combination of trends in spending outside the region and measures of swing voting. The multiplier estimates using the IV procedure with state and year effects range from 0.9 to 1.7, depending on how federal spending is defined. The multiplier for federal grants was 1.39 but only 0.9 when federal spending includes both grants and loans. When effects are estimated separately for AAA farm grants and non-AAA farm grants, the multiplier for the farm grants is –0.5 and the multiplier for non-AAA grants is 1.67. One thing to note is that these multipliers are for personal income, which includes transfer payments, and for government funds that include transfer payments; therefore, there is a strong initial effect because a dollar of transfers is automatically a dollar of income. Most macroeconomic estimates of multipliers focus on income measures and government purchases that eliminate transfer payments.

9.9. TAX RATES AND THE SUPPLY SIDE

The supply-side features of fiscal policy changes involving tax rates in the 1930s have not been investigated in great depth. Nearly all of the changes called for increased tax rates, which likely retarded the growth of the economy. The Hoover administration has been rightfully criticized for its attempts to raise tax rates. Although less than 10 per cent of households paid income taxes, the rise in income tax rates for households with more than $1m in earnings in 1932 was confiscatory and likely led to extensive tax avoidance. Given that the economy was falling further in 1932 and 1933, it is hard to sort out how much of the drops in income tax and estate tax collections was caused by the economy declining and how much was on account of tax avoidance. Some of the decline in the economy might well have been driven by the high rates (Piketty and Saez, 2003). The Roosevelt administration did little to reduce the tax rates in 1934 and then increased the top rate still higher in 1936.

Other new federal taxes created additional distortions. The new excise taxes on manufacturers established in the 1932 act contributed to inefficiencies in the economy. Lastrappes and Selgin (1997), for example, find that the 2-cent tax on cheques from 1932 to 1934 led households to shift significantly towards holding money in the form of currency rather than in the form of chequing accounts in banks. The National Industrial Recovery Act of 1933 instituted a tax on capital stock, dividends, and excess profits that was collected through the rest of the 1930s. These taxes typically led to the collection of roughly $100m to $150m in revenue, about 2–3 per cent of total federal receipts (Commissioner of Internal Revenue, 1934, 1935, 1936, 1937; Table 9.1). In 1936, the federal government added a surtax on profits not distributed as dividends. It rose progressively as a function of the percentage of earnings retained out of corporate income—from 7 per cent on the first 10 per cent retained, up to 27 per cent on retentions above 60 per cent of income. The surtax was reduced in 1938 and expired in December 1939. The undistributed profits tax delivered $145m in tax revenue in 1936 and $176m in 1937 (Calomiris and Hubbard, 1993).

Although the amounts of revenue collected were relatively small, all of these taxes likely led to distortions in investment spending. Calomiris and Hubbard (1993) studied the investment and cash-flow decisions of 273 publicly traded manufacturing firms. As might be expected, the share of income retained as earnings by companies fell from 23 per cent in 1935 to 15 per cent in 1936 and 1937. However, nearly one-quarter of the companies held enough earnings to pay the highest marginal rate of 27 per cent. These companies tended to be smaller firms in the fastest growing industries, who faced more difficulty in finding external financing. Thus, it appears that the undistributed profits tax led to significant distortions in investment decisions.

The final tax to consider is one that was clearly not designed to raise revenue. The Smoot–Hawley Tariff Act of 1930 raised taxes on imports substantially, on top of an earlier rise in 1922. The goal was to protect American manufacturers from competition from foreign imports. International trade was a small enough percentage of the American economy at the time that most economists ascribe the tariff a secondary role as a contributor to the Depression in the US. However, it had far worse implications at the international level. The Smoot–Hawley tariff was matched by a series of protectionist measures by countries throughout the world. As each nation tried to protect its home production interests through higher tariffs and restrictions on imports, world trade spiralled downwards. By 1933, the total imports for 75 countries had fallen to roughly one-third of the level seen in 1929 (Kindleberger, 1986).

The Roosevelt administration contributed to a recovery in world trade by relaxing these tariff barriers. The Reciprocal Trade Agreement (RTA) Act of 1934 freed the Roosevelt administration to sign a series of tariff-reduction agreements with key trading partners. Agreements with Canada, several South American countries, Britain, and key European trading partners loosened the trade restrictions markedly. As a result, American imports rose from a 20-year low in 1932–33 to an all-time high by 1940.[9]

[9] For historical comparisons of the impact of tariff rates, see Irwin (1998). Kindleberger (1986: 170) and Atack and Passell (1994: 602) describe the international trade developments in the 1930s.

9.10. CURRENT POLICY IN LIGHT OF 1930s POLICY

Nearly all agree that the Federal Reserve's monetary policy was disastrous in a variety of dimensions. The only disagreements relate to why the Federal Reserve followed the path it did and how large the causal effects were. On the fiscal side, the Hoover and Roosevelt administrations both increased federal spending, but tax revenues rose enough that they ran relatively small deficits. Since less than 10 per cent of households paid income taxes, most of the supply-side distortions came from the extraordinarily high tax rates of over 57 per cent paid by households with over $1m in income (roughly $16m in today's dollars) after 1932. The capital stock, dividend, and undistributed profits taxes contributed to distortions in investment decisions that have not been explored very fully. Meanwhile, the Smoot–Hawley tariff is largely considered to be a major mistake that greatly harmed world trade.

There is no doubt that the policies of the 1930s are influencing the policies developed during the financial meltdown of 2007–08 and the Great Recession of 2008–09. Federal Reserve Chairman Benjamin Bernanke has long been known for his work on the macroeconomics of the Great Depression. Bernanke and Treasury Secretaries Henry Paulson and Timothy Geithner have followed strategies that were the antithesis of Fed policy in the 1930s. The Federal Reserve of the 1930s did lower discount rates, but the high rates of deflation left real interest rates at double-digit levels not seen since. The Fed waited for three years, as unemployment rose above 10 per cent, then 16 per cent, and then 20 per cent, before making a large-scale open-market purchase of $1 billion. In contrast, Bernanke ran open-market operations that expanded liquidity and drove the federal funds rate close to zero before the unemployment rate passed 7 per cent in 2008. The Fed has continued the liquidity expansion by buying large amounts of mortgage-backed securities.

To prevent shocks from failures that they believed would topple the financial system, the Fed and Treasury tore pages out of the RFC playbook. They brokered mergers and bailouts of Bear Stearns, AIG, Fannie Mae, and Freddie Mac. They used Troubled Asset Relief Program (TARP) funds to take investment stakes and guarantee assets in banks, made loans to motor vehicle companies, and then developed stress tests of the banks similar to those of the 1933 bank holiday before allowing banks to buy out the government's interest. Given descriptions by the principals of how close to failure these institutions were, the monetary policy changes and emergency policies seem necessary and may well have staved off a financial meltdown that could have touched off a severe depression. We will never know for sure because so many events occurred in such a short timeframe that there is not enough variation to identify what the counterfactual would have been had the Fed and Treasury not acted.

It will take some more time before we see the actual cost of these moves, but the losses will likely be small relative to the reserves promised, and the government might even earn a profit on the transactions. There are two major issues to address associated with these moves. First, do we want the federal government so heavily involved in financing the economy? Fannie Mae and Freddie Mac, which were supposed to have been independent corporations since the 1970s, are now essentially government-owned enterprises that finance or guarantee the vast majority of new mortgage loans. Second, the bailouts and backing provided for the Great Recession have likely created moral-hazard problems, in which financial institutions take more risks in the future while anticipating another government bailout. Congress continues to struggle with this issue in trying to set regulations to ensure that no financial institutions are too big to fail. Arguments have been made to limit the size of commercial banks, or instead limit the types of investments, or even just leave the banks alone. It is a thorny issue and well-known economists have argued for each of the positions (Wessel, 2010).

On the fiscal side, Great Depression scholar, Christina Romer, was Obama's first head of the President's Council of Economic Advisors until August 2010. Here again, the Obama administration and the Democratic Congress have gone in the opposite direction from the Hoover and Roosevelt administrations. The new leaders built on a deficit that had been rising under George Bush by passing a sizeable fiscal stimulus package that raised the deficit to 9.6 per cent of GDP in 2009 from 3.3 per cent in 2008. Even after excluding the budget impact of TARP, the 2009 deficit was roughly 8.8 per cent of GDP.[10] The deficit for fiscal 2010 rose to 9 per cent of GDP and has fallen only slightly to 8.2 per cent of GDP in 2011. The US is flying blind with deficits of this size because previous experiments with large fiscal deficits have been of the order of 5–6 per cent of GDP.[11] In the case of the Reagan–Bush era of 1980–92, the economic logic underlying the deficits was an emphasis on the supply-side effects of lower tax rates on income.

Some think that the Second World War offers an example of a situation where fiscal stimulus worked. But the Second World War analogy is highly misleading for any discussion of a peacetime economy. The deficits were run during an all-out war, when 40 per cent of GDP was spent on munitions, the military made most of the allocation decisions in the economy, over 15 per cent of the workforce was in harm's way in the military, there were widespread wage and price controls, and rationing ruled the day. In essence, the Second World War deficit experience tells us more about fiscal stimulus in the Soviet Union's command economy during the Cold War than it does about the modern US mixed economy.

Even as an exercise in pure government spending, the current situation looks quite different from the Great Depression. A large share of federal government spending in the 1930s was spent on income maintenance programmes and work relief, and the federal government spending started at only 4 per cent of GDP at the start of the decade. With a much larger safety net already in place in the current era, federal spending has risen from 20 to 25 per cent of GDP. The most

[10] The bailouts and ownership stakes taken by the Treasury and Fed are not easily measured in the budget figures. Since the assets and ownership stakes have value, and many of the loans will likely be repaid, the actual Treasury costs could be quite low or the government could turn a profit. The listed federal outlays under the TARP in fiscal year 2009, 1 October 2008 to 30 September 2009, were $151 billion, which was about 1 per cent of GDP or roughly 10 per cent of the budget deficit. The outlay was substantially less than the earlier forecast outlay of $247 billion. The Obama administration predicts that the net cost to the Treasury will fall further once loans are repaid and assets resold. See Office of Management and Budget (2010: 152) for the actual 2009 figure and Office and Management and Budget (2009: 117) for the forecast. It is hard to see signs of the bail-out of Freddie Mac, Fannie Mae, and AIG in the budget figures.

[11] Deficit figures were downloaded on 11 June 2010 from the US Office of Management and Budget website, <www.whitehouse.gov/omb/budget/historicals/>.

famous programme of the 1930s, the Works Progress Administration (WPA), would not be acceptable today, because most people today receive unemployment insurance benefits that pay roughly the same share of income as the WPA did, but without the WPA's requirement that they work on construction or other projects to get the benefits.

There is no doubt that the Great Recession has been one of the two most serious post-war recessions. Unemployment rates were at 9 per cent or higher for 28 months between May 2009 and September 2011, and real GDP went through a year-long decline between the peak in the second quarter of 2008 and the trough in the second quarter of 2009. However, the Obama fiscal stimulus package in 2009 response seemed to be out of proportion to the problem, especially when the lost output and unemployment are compared with the Great Depression. The US in 2007 started at average GDP per capita levels that were five times higher than in 1929. Inflation rates are as low as they have ever been, and the US is not experiencing the large non-neutral deflation of the 1930s. By the time the fiscal stimulus package was passed in February 2009, the impending financial disaster of fall 2008 had largely passed. Real GDP turned upwards in the second quarter of 2009 before very much of the fiscal stimulus money had been passed out. By the first quarter of 2010 real GDP had reached 99.4 per cent of the GDP peak in second quarter 2008, and it is likely that more than half of the stimulus money had still not been distributed.

The major problem is that unemployment rates were roughly 10 per cent late in 2010 and early in 2011, yet only a small part of the stimulus money went towards expanded unemployment benefits. There are growing worries that the government expansion partially crowded out private activity. Many multiplier estimates are significantly less than one, implying that deficits lead to crowding out of private employment. The Obama fiscal stimulus programme of 2009 seemed to be the size of response a Keynesian would have called for in the Great Depression, while the changes in the size of the federal deficits during the Great Depression seem more like the changes we might expect policy makers to have made in response to the Great Recession of 2007–09.[12] Over 10 years, in response to unemployment rates ranging between 10 and 25 per cent, the Hoover and Roosevelt administrations raised the federal debt as a percentage of GDP by 28 percentage points, from 16 per cent in 1929 to 44 per cent in 1939. In response to unemployment rates rising from 5 to 10 per cent, the US government achieved a similar rise in the federal debt held by the public as a percentage of GDP in just three years, from 39 per cent at the end of 2007 to 72 per cent at the end of fiscal 2010. By the end of 2011 the debt share had risen to 78.6 per cent.[13]

As the recovery moved forward, macroeconomic policy makers have faced two major challenges. The huge amount of liquidity in the banking system has everybody anticipating a rise in inflation at some point, yet the recovery has been slow enough that inflation has not risen sharply despite multiple rounds of

[12] Unemployment figures were downloaded on 11 June 2010 from the Bureau of Labor Statistics website (<http://data.bls.gov/PDQ/servlet/SurveyOutputServlet> and real GDP was downloaded on the same date from the Bureau of Economic Analysis site (<www.bea.gov/national/nipaweb/TableView.asp?SelectedTable=6&FirstYear=2009&LastYear=2010&Freq=Qtr>).

[13] <www.treasurydirect.gov/govt/reports/pd/histdebt/histdebt_histo5.htm>.

'quantitative easing' by the Federal Reserve. Uncertainty about the recession, financial regulations, and the continued presence of toxic assets on the books of the banking sector have kept lending from expanding rapidly so far. The question still remains for the future: can the Fed effectively soak up this liquidity to prevent a raging inflation without causing the kind of second-dip recession that occurred in 1937 and 1938?

On the fiscal side, the deficit has risen markedly and the federal government still has not yet effectively addressed the long-run funding problems with the pay-as-you-go Social Security and Medicare programmes. Everybody expects the new health-care entitlements to add to those funding problems, particularly because Congress is currently trying to restore Medicare payments to doctors that were cut sharply in the health reform act to make the act look as though it would not add to the deficit. We know that budget deficits at 9 per cent of GDP are not sustainable.

So when will the US start dealing with these budget issues? After the recession of 2007–09, little was done for the next two years. Congress and the president failed to broker a budget cutting deal. In August 2011, the Budget Control Act was passed to force the issue. The Act established a super committee to identify $1.2 trillion in reductions in discretionary spending. By November of that year, the super committee had failed to come to an agreement on spending cuts and tax increases. This is supposed to trigger mandatory cuts across the board in discretionary spending in the 2013 fiscal year that began on 1 October. In the meantime, Congress has passed several temporary resolutions to continue funding the government so it will not shut down during the 2012 elections.

BIBLIOGRAPHY

Anderson, R. (2006), 'Monetary Aggregates', in S. Carter, S. G. Garner, M. R. Haines, A. L. Olmstead, R. Sutch, and G. Wright (eds), *Historical Statistics of the United States, Millennial Edition*, Vol. 3. New York: Cambridge University Press.

Atack, J. and Passell, P. (1994), *A New Economic View of American History from Colonial Times to 1940*, 2nd edn. New York: Norton and Company.

Barber, W. J. (1996), *Designs within Disorder: Franklin D. Roosevelt, the Economists, and the Shaping of American Economic Policy, 1933–1945*. New York: Cambridge University Press.

Bernanke, B. (1983), 'Non-monetary Effects of Financial Crisis in the Propagation of the Great Depression', *American Economic Review*, 73(3), 257–76.

Bernanke, B. and Gertler, P. (1989), 'Agency Costs, Net Worth, and Business Fluctuations', *American Economic Review*, 79(1), 14–31.

Bordo, M., Erceg, C., and Evans, C. L. (2000), 'Money, Sticky Wages, and the Great Depression', *American Economic Review*, 90(December), 1447–63.

Brown, E. C. (1956), 'Fiscal Policy in the Thirties: A Reappraisal', *American Economic Review*, 46(December), 857–79.

Brunner, K. and Meltzer, A. (1968), 'What Did We Learn from the Monetary Experience in the United States in the Great Depression', *Canadian Journal of Economics*, 1(May): 334–48.

Calomiris, C. and Hubbard, G. (1993), 'Internal Finance and Investment: Evidence from the Undistributed Profits Tax of 1936–1937', National Bureau of Economic Research Working Paper No. 4288, March.

Calomiris, C. and Mason, J. (2003), 'Fundamentals, Panics, and Bank Distress During the Depression', *American Economic Review*, 93(December), 1615–47.

Chari, V. V., Kehoe, P., and McGrattan, E. (2002), 'Accounting for the Great Depression', *American Economic Review Papers and Proceedings*, 92(May), 22–7.

Chari, V. V., Kehoe, P., and McGrattan, E. (2005), 'Business Cycle Accounting', Federal Reserve Bank of Minneapolis Research Department Staff Report 328, April.

Christiano, L., Motto, R., and Rostagno, M. (2003), *Journal of Money, Credit, and Banking*, 35(December), 1120–97.

Cole, H. and Ohanian, L. (2004), 'New Deal Policies and the Persistence of the Great Depression: A General Equilibrium Analysis', *Journal of Political Economy*, 112(August), 779–816.

Cole, H. and Ohanian, L. (2005), 'Deflation and the International Great Depression: A Productivity Puzzle', National Bureau of Economic Research Working Paper No. 11237.

Commissioner of Internal Revenue (1933; 1934; 1935; 1936; 1937), *Annual Report for the Year Ending June 30*. Washington, DC: Government Printing Office,.

Eggertsson, G. (2008), 'Great Expectations and the End of the Depression', *American Economic Review*, 98(4), 1476–516.

Eggertsson, G. and Pugsley, B. (2006), 'The Mistake of 1937: A General Equilibrium Analysis', *Monetary and Economic Studies*, 24(December), 1–41.

Eichengreen, B. (1992), *Golden Fetters: The Gold Standard and the Depression, 1919–1939*. New York: Oxford University Press.

Federal Reserve Board of Governors (1943), *Banking and Monetary Statistics, 1914–1941*. Washington, DC: Government Printing Office.

Federal Reserve Board of Governors (various years), *Federal Reserve Bulletin*. Washington, DC: Government Printing Office.

Fishback, P. V., Haines, M. R., and Kantor, S. (2007), 'Births, Deaths, and New Deal Relief During the Great Depression', *Review of Economics and Statistics*, 89(February), 1–14.

Fishback, P. V., Horrace, W., and Kantor, S. (2005), 'The Impact of New Deal Expenditures on Local Economic Activity: An Examination of Retail Sales, 1929–1939', *Journal of Economic History*, 65(March), 36–71.

Fishback, P. V., Horrace, W., and Kantor, S. (2006), 'Do Federal Programs Affect Internal Migration? The Impact of New Deal Expenditures on Mobility During the Great Depression', *Explorations in Economic History*, 43, 179–222.

Fishback, P. V. and Kachanovskaya, V. (2010), 'In Search of the New Deal Multiplier', working paper.

Fleck, R. (1999), 'The Marginal Effect of New Deal Relief Work on County-level Unemployment Statistics', *Journal of Economic History*, 59(September), 659–87.

Friedman, M. and Schwartz, A. (1963), *A Monetary History of the United States, 1867–1960*. Princeton, NJ: Princeton University Press.

Garrett, T. and Wheelock, D. (2006), 'Why Did Income Growth Vary Across States During the Great Depression', *Journal of Economic History*, 66, 456–66.

Geithner, T. (2010), *Written Testimony Before the US Senate Budget Committee*, 4 February, available at <http://budget.senate.gov/democratic/testimony/2010/TG_Budget%20Testimony_SBC.pdf>13 June 2010.

Hamilton, J. (1987), 'Monetary Factors in the Great Depression', *Journal of Monetary Economics*, 19, 145–69.

Irwin, D. (1998), 'Changes in US Tariffs: The Role of Import Prices and Commercial Policies', *American Economic Review*, 88(September), 1015–26.

James, J. and Sylla, R. (2006), 'Interest Rates and Yields', in S. Carter, S. G. Garner, M. R. Haines, A. L. Olmstead, R. Sutch, and G. Wright (eds), *Historical Statistics of the United States, Millennial Edition*, Vol. 3. New York: Cambridge University Press.

Johnson, R., Kantor, S., and Fishback, P. V. (forthcoming), 'Striking at the Roots of Crime: The Impact of Social Welfare Spending on Crime During the Great Depression', *Journal of Law and Economics.*

Keynes, J. M. (1964), *The General Theory of Employment, Interest, and Money.* New York: Harcourt, Brace and World Inc.

Kindleberger, C. (1986), *The World in Depression, 1929–1939*, revised edn. Berkeley, CA: University of California Press.

Lastrappes, W. and Selgin, G. (1997), 'The Check Tax: Fiscal Folly and the Great Monetary Contraction', *Journal of Economic History*, 57(December), 859–78.

Mason, J. (2001), 'Do Lenders of Last Resort Policies Matter? The Effects of the Reconstruction Finance Corporation Assistance to Banks During the Great Depression', *Journal of Financial Services Research*, 20(September), 77–95.

Matthews, K. and Benjamin, D. (1992), *US and UK Unemployment Between the Wars: A Doleful Story.* London: Institute of Economic Affairs.

Meltzer, A. (2003), *A History of the Federal Reserve, Volume I: 1913–1951.* Chicago, IL: University of Chicago Press.

Mitchener, K. (2005), 'Bank Supervision, Regulation, and Financial Instability during the Great Depression', *Journal of Economic History*, 65(March), 152–85.

Mitchener, K. and Mason, J. (2010), '"Blood and Treasure": Exiting the Great Depression and Lessons for Today', *Oxford Review of Economic Policy*, 26(3), 510–39.

Neumann, T., Fishback, P. V., and Kantor, S. (2010), 'The Dynamics of Relief Spending and the Private Urban Labor Market During the New Deal', *Journal of Economic History*, 70 (March), 195–220.

Office of Management and Budget (2009), 'A New Era of Responsibility: Renewing America's Promise', Washington, DC: US Government Printing Office, available at <http://www.gpoaccess.gov/usbudget/fy10/pdf/fy10-newera.pdf> 13 June 2010.

Office of Management and Budget (2009; 2010), *Budget of the US Government.* Washington, DC: US Government Printing Office, available at <http://www.gpo.gov/fdsys/browse/collectionGPO.action?collectionCode=BUDGET> 28 September 2012.

Ohanian, L. (2009), 'What or Who Started the Great Depression?', National Bureau of Economic Research Working Paper No. 15258, Cambridge, MA.

Parker, R. E. (2002), *Reflections on the Great Depression.* Northampton, MA: Edward Elgar.

Parker, R. E. (2007), *The Economics of the Great Depression: A Twenty-First Century Look Back at the Economics of the Interwar Era.* Northampton, MA: Edward Elgar.

Peppers, L. (1973), 'Full Employment Surplus Analysis and Structural Change: The 1930s', *Explorations in Economic History*, 10(Winter), 197–210.

Piketty, T. and Saez, E. (2003), 'Income Inequality in the United States, 1913–1998', *Quarterly Journal of Economics*, 118(February), 1–39.

Richardson, G. and Troost, W. (2009), 'Monetary Intervention Mitigated Panics During the Great Depression: Quasi-experimental Evidence from a Federal Reserve District Border, 1929–1933', *Journal of Political Economy*, 117(December), 1031–73.

Richardson, G. and Van Horn, P. (2009), 'Intensified Regulatory Scrutiny and Bank Distress in New York City During the Great Depression', *Journal of Economic History*, 69(June): 446–65.

Romer, C. D. (1992), 'What Ended the Great Depression?', *Journal of Economic History*, 52 (December). 757–84.

Smiley, G. (2002), *Rethinking the Great Depression: A New View of Its Causes and Consequences.* Chicago, IL: Ivan R. Dee.

Taylor, J. (2009), 'Work-sharing During the Great Depression: Did the "President's Reemployment Agreement" Promote Reemployment?', *Economica*, 78. 1–26.

Temin, P. (1976), *Did Monetary Forces Cause the Great Depression?.* New York: W. W. Norton.

Temin, P. (1989), *Lessons from the Great Depression*. Cambridge, MA: MIT Press.

Temin, P. and Wigmore, B. (1990), 'The End of One Big Deflation', *Explorations in Economic History*, 27(October). 483–502.

US Bureau of the Census (1975), *Historical Statistics of the United States, 1790 to the Present*. Washington, DC: Government Printing Office.

US Bureau of the Census (1931), *Statistical Abstract of the United States*. Washington, DC: Government Printing Office.

US Bureau of the Census (1933), *Statistical Abstract of the United States*. Washington, DC: Government Printing Office.

US Bureau of the Census (1934), *Statistical Abstract of the United States*. Washington, DC: Government Printing Office.

US Department of Treasury (1931), *Annual Report*. Washington, DC: Government Printing Office.

Wallis, J. (2006), 'Federal Government Finances', in S. Carter, S. G. Garner, M. R. Haines, A. L. Olmstead, R. Sutch, and G. Wright (eds), *Historical Statistics of the United States, Millennial Edition*, Vol. 5. New York: Cambridge University Press.

Wallis, J. and Benjamin, D. K. (1981), 'Public Relief and Private Employment in the Great Depression', *Journal of Economic History*, 41(March). 97–102.

Wessel, D. (2010), 'The "Too Big" Divide on Banks', *Wall Street Journal*, 10 June 2010, available at <http://online.wsj.com/article/SB10001424052748703890904575296430874218148.html?KEYWORDS=too+big+to+fail> 13 June 2010.

Wheelock, D. (1991), *The Strategy and Consistency of Federal Reserve Monetary Policy, 1924–1933*. New York: Cambridge University Press.

Wheelock, D. (2006), 'Monetary Policy', in S. Carter, S. G. Garner, M. R. Haines, A. L. Olmstead, R. Sutch, and G. Wright (eds), *Historical Statistics of the United States, Millennial Edition*, Vol. 3, New York, Cambridge University Press.

Wicker, E. (1966), *Federal Reserve Monetary Policy, 1917–1933*. New York: Random House.

10

What was New about the New Deal?

Price Fishback and John Joseph Wallis[1]

During the presidential election of 1932 Franklin Roosevelt promised a New Deal for the American people. By November 1932 unemployment rates had risen to more than 20 per cent and annual production of final goods and services had fallen nearly 28 per cent from the 1929 peak. The Hoover administration and Republican Congress had expanded federal outlays, added lending programmes, and called for voluntarism to combat the economic decline. Roosevelt won the election in a landslide and the Democrats took over both Houses of Congress. Meanwhile, the economy slid further. In their First Hundred Days, after Roosevelt took office in March 1933, the Democrats delivered a New Deal for the American economy. Over the next eight years the Roosevelt administration and Democratic Congresses continuously modified New Deal programmes and regulations. Some were eliminated, others ran for the length of the Depression and then disappeared, and still others established permanent programmes and precedents that remain in place today.

Scholars have sought in vain for an overarching unifying framework for the New Deal because the New Deal was not the implementation of an economic or political plan. The economics of the New Deal were not a Keynesian attempt to stimulate the economy. Keynes himself examined the fiscal structure in depth and argued that the spending increases were not examples of a Keynesian stimulus because taxes rose nearly as fast as spending; therefore, the deficits were nowhere near the size required to offset the economic decline. Federal budget outlays in real dollars rose 88 per cent under Hoover between 1929 and 1932, faster than the growth in the first three years under Roosevelt (although starting from a lower base). Budget deficits under Hoover look more Keynesian than Roosevelt's deficits, although likely not by Hoover's design.[2] Others argue that the New Deal was designed to raise prices to stimulate production and raise wages to help pay for the higher prices. The move off the gold standard, the National

[1] Price Fishback received research support for this chapter from National Science Foundation Grants SES-1061927 and SES-0921732. The opinions expressed in this chapter are our own and do not in any way represent the opinions and attitudes of the National Science Foundation. We would like to thank Charles Calomiris, Peter Fearon, and Alex Field for reading earlier drafts and providing valuable comments.

[2] See Keynes (1964 reprint), Brown (1956), Peppers (1973), and Fishback (2010).

Recovery Administration (NRA), the Agricultural Adjustment Administration (AAA), and the National Labor Relations Boards (NLRB) seemed to have this focus, but there were other areas of the New Deal that ran counter to these policies.

Roosevelt and the members of the New Deal coalition were pragmatists. Roosevelt certainly was not bothered by theoretical inconsistency. The focus was on solving specific problems and there were plenty of problems to solve with the depressed economy. Raymond Moley (1966: xviii), one of Roosevelt's original Brains Trust, wrote:

> For the New Deal was not of one piece. Nor was it the product of a single integrated plan. It was . . . a loose collection of many ideas—some new, most borrowed from the past—with plenty of improvisations and compromises. Those of us who participated were too busy for mature reflection or to create a system or an overall pattern.

In this chapter we hope to accomplish two goals. Raw experimentation does not offer a compelling or satisfying explanation for why the New Deal developed as it did, but any adequate explanation has to build from the reality that the early days of the New Deal were dominated by expediency and experiment. Experiment rarely proceeds *de novo* and one goal is to document which parts of the New Deal programmes picked up ideas that were being proposed and considered within the Hoover administration, which had been discussed in the 1910s and 1920s, and which programmes had a long tradition stretching back into the 19th century. The second goal is to understand why some programmes persisted and other programmes failed. In other words, we seek to provide the outline of an overarching explanation for the New Deal by looking at what lasted and what did not. This, admittedly, is not a very sophisticated approach, but it has the virtues of identifying the political constraints operating within the American political system and being a transparent explanatory technique.

Two distinctions are important to keep in mind. First, is the difference between fiscal and regulatory aspects of government programmes. Some programmes involved significant expenditures of funds, while others significantly affected the economy without involving large expenditures. Some programmes did both. Second, is the difference between national and federal programmes. National programmes were the distinct province of the national government which, in a historical irony, Americans still call the 'federal' government. Federal programmes were jointly funded and administered by national, state, and local governments. There was a marked tendency for regulatory programmes to be national programmes, while programmes with significant fiscal impacts were either federal programmes from the beginning or moved towards federal programmes if they persisted. The one big exception was the Old Age and Survivors Insurance (OASI) programme, which is the pension programme commonly known as Social Security today. When Roosevelt and the New Dealers wanted to spend lots of money, they had to operate in conjunction with state and local governments.

The New Deal programmes that built on existing national government programmes included providing funds for highways and roads; reclamation and irrigation; flood control and improved navigation; benefits to veterans; building of post offices and federal buildings; mortgage loans and emergency crop and feed loans for farmers; education; agricultural experimentation, extension, and advanced education; and national defence spending. Some of the activities went back to the 1790s. More funds were distributed in many of these programmes under both Hoover and Roosevelt. However, Hoover tended to do it within existing programmes, while Roosevelt often created new programmes or reorganized old ones in ways that emphasized that a New Deal programme was distributing a significant share of the funds. The federal government continued to regulate commercial banks and financial markets, but with a heavier hand than before. Some financial legislation gave new powers to the Treasury, which were sought as a means of undermining the monetary authority of the Federal Reserve System. As a result, the Fed lost power over monetary policy after 1933 and did not regain it until 1951 (Calomiris and Wheelock, 1998).

The New Deal programmes that built on the existing responsibilities of state and local governments were largest in the areas of relief of the unemployed and the poor. The New Deal created emergency programmes in which the federal government provided grants to state and local government to provide relief payments with and without work relief obligations. Under the Social Security Act of 1935, permanent matching grant programmes were established for three types of programmes that many states had already established, and administrative grants for state run unemployment insurance pools. To help the unemployed find work, the US created a National Employment Service that complemented or replaced state employment services in a number of states. In housing, the federal government built public housing projects; which a few cities had already done. As part of its emergency work relief and public works programmes, the federal government also began providing loans and grants for state and local public projects, like schools, parks, airports, and streets, in which it generally had not invested before. The Tennessee Valley Authority (TVA) originally began with building dams on the Tennessee River in line with the Army Corps of Engineers' emphasis on flood and navigation control, but they eventually gained the authority to own and operate electric utilities, as some states and cities had done with gas and electric utilities. The federal government set up deposit insurance nationwide even though the states that had experimented with deposit insurance in the 1920s had generally abandoned their programmes because they had been costly failures.

The truly *de novo* features of the New Deal came in several areas. The AAA began making rental and benefit payments to farmers to take land out of production after Hoover tried some minimal experimentation. The Commodity Credit Corporation created non-recourse loans that put a floor on farm prices for some commodities. The NRA created a framework for producers with some input from consumers and workers to set prices, quality, and wages in a large number of industries. The Home Owners' Loan Corporation bought over 1 million troubled mortgages and then modified the loans with new interest rates and repayment terms for the borrowers. The Farm Credit Administration began offering production loans and the Rural Electrification Administration offered loans to create cooperatives and build electricity lines in rural areas. The Social Security Administration provided administrative funds for state run unemployment insurance programmes and created a national programme for old age pensions based on contributions from workers.

The next section lays out the overall picture of fiscal developments during the New Deal, including the relationships between the national, state, and local governments. The sections that follow describe specific programmes in various areas of the New Deal. A lessons section and the conclusion draw together our views about what was new in the New Deal and why some of it survived.

10.1. THE STRUCTURE OF NEW DEAL FEDERALISM

The New Deal effected a political transformation in the structure of American government, changing its structure, function, and size. What stands out most prominently both in historical and contemporary debates over the New Deal is the growth of the national government, something Americans had steadfastly resisted for almost a century and a half. But fascination with the national government should not overshadow equally dramatic changes in the federal system of government. Fiscal and functional responsibilities were shuffled between national, state, and local governments in a way that set a new pattern for the structure of government that has persisted to the present. Part of what the New Deal did was truly new and part was built on precedents from earlier in the century or even from the Hoover administration. Understanding these patterns helps explain why Americans were willing to allow the national government to grow bigger.

Understanding how the New Deal patterns worked also provides an important lesson for the current economic and political crisis. After four years of attempting to deal with an unprecedented economic crisis through policies consistent with the existing framework of intergovernmental arrangements with some innovations by Hoover, the New Deal fundamentally altered those arrangements in a way that was both credible and durable. Europe, four years after the onset of a serious economic crisis, now faces a comparable political crisis involving precisely the same set of questions that faced the United States in 1933. How can the central government of a fiscal and monetary union expand its governance role to deal with the adverse consequences of an economic downturn without significantly, and perhaps unsustainably, reducing the sovereign independence of the member governments? While we neither suggest that the four year timing is determinative nor that the parallels between the United States in 1933 and Europe in 2012 are exact, there are interesting lessons to learn from the way that the New Deal dealt with the structure of America's federal union.

What was new about the New Deal mattered, because old patterns of relations between national, state, and local governments were politically much easier to work with and expand than completely new patterns. It is useful to distinguish national programmes, like defence, funded and administered solely by the national government, from federal programmes, like social welfare, funded and administered jointly by some combination of national, state, and local governments. Federal programmes had precedents going back before the federal highway programme began in 1916. The New Deal programmes with the largest fiscal impact in the 1930s were all federal programmes, funded and administered by a combination of national and state governments.[3] National programmes, in contrast, tended to be regulatory programmes with significant impacts on the economy and society, banking and financial reform for example, but much smaller fiscal impact on the national budget. This also followed an earlier pattern in which the national government developed responsibilities for important regulatory functions—railroads, antitrust, national banks, and food quality—that did not have large fiscal burdens.

The New Deal's impact on fiscal federalism in the US can be summarized by three important trends seen in Table 10.1. First, while total government grew during the New Deal, it did not grow faster relative to GDP in the 1930s than it had grown earlier in the 20th century. The ratio of total government spending at all levels to GDP nearly doubled between 1902 and 1927, and nearly doubled again between 1927 and 1940.[4] The public sector continued to grow in the 1930s, but not at an accelerating rate.

Second, the sharp increases in the national and state shares of government expenditure seen in Table 10.1 were new in the 1930s. Accepting that 1922, 1942, 1948, and 1952 are exceptional war or post-war years, the national share of public expenditure prior to 1934 was below 35 per cent, while, after 1952, it had risen to above 53 per cent. The local share, which had been above 50 before the 1930s, fell to 30 per cent or less, while the state share rose from less than 10 per cent in 1913 to 16 per cent in 1932 and to above 17 per cent after 1967.

National expenditures on cooperatively administered programmes accounted for more than the total increase in the Roosevelt administration's expenditures over the level of expenditures in the last year of the Hoover administration. These expenditures largely went to states, who passed some of the money on to local governments and spent the rest directly themselves. Although the national government increased its share of total government activity during the New Deal, by no measure was the state share of government activity reduced. The state government share of total government revenues from own sources rose from 16.4 per cent in 1927, to 21.7 per cent in 1934, to 28.2 per cent in 1940. The state share of total government expenditures rose from 13 per cent in 1927, to 16.8 per cent in 1934, and to 17.5 per cent in 1940 (the own expenditure shares are even higher).[5] All of the growth in the national shares came at the expense of local governments.

[3] Old Age and Survivors Insurance appears to be an exception because it was a purely national programme, but pensions were not distributed until 1940. Further, the large fiscal implications of OASI, which originally was to be funded largely by specific taxes, were not really foreseen until the late 1930s.

[4] We use 1927 because data for 1922 include relatively large interest expenditures incurred from the World War One debt that raised the national share that year. Even so, if we take the period from 1913 to 1922 and compare it to the period from 1922 to 1940, we get roughly the same effect.

[5] The reporting of intergovernmental grants differs in government reports of expenditures and revenues to avoid double counting the money. When the national government makes a grant to the local government, which then spends the money, the spending is reflected in the local government's spending but not in the national government's expenditures. On the revenue side, the grant money is assigned to the level of government that collects the taxes. Therefore, when the national government provides a grant to a local government, the national government revenues reflect the size of the grant, while the grant is not included in revenues for the local government. Thus, when the New Deal provided more intergovernmental grants, the national share of expenditures shown in Table 10.1 was

Table 10.1. Shares of government expenditure by level of government; total government expenditures as share of GDP; national grants to state and local governments as share of S&L revenue

Year	Share			Expenditures/	Grants/
	National (1)	State (2)	Local (3)	GDP (4)	S&L Rev (5)
1902	0.34	0.08	0.58	0.07	0.01
1913	0.30	0.09	0.61	0.08	0.01
1922	0.39	0.12	0.49	0.13	0.02
1927	0.30	0.13	0.57	0.12	0.01
1932	0.32	0.16	0.51	0.21	0.03
1934	0.39	0.17	0.44	0.19	0.10
1936	0.49	0.15	0.36	0.20	0.09
1938	0.43	0.17	0.39	0.21	0.06
1940	0.45	0.17	0.38	0.20	0.07
1942	0.76	0.08	0.16	0.28	0.06
1948	0.61	0.14	0.24	0.20	0.07
1952	0.69	0.11	0.20	0.28	0.07
1957	0.62	0.13	0.25	0.27	0.07
1962	0.60	0.14	0.26	0.30	0.10
1967	0.59	0.15	0.26	0.31	0.12
1972	0.52	0.18	0.30	0.32	0.14
1977	0.53	0.19	0.28	0.34	0.16
1982	0.58	0.17	0.25	0.38	0.14
1987	0.57	0.17	0.25	0.38	0.12
1992	0.54	0.20	0.26	0.39	0.13

Source: Calculated from information in Census of Governments, State and Local Financial Data, various years.

The reason for this is clear. National grants were given primarily to the states. Most of these grants offered incentives for state government to increase their own spending. Whether these incentives were explicit, like the strict matching provisions in the Social Security Act categorical relief programmes, or implicit as in Harry Hopkins' use of relief grants, they were real. Wallis (1984) found that, in the late 1930s, every dollar of national grants increased state expenditures from own revenues by US$0.31. At the same time, combined state and national grants actually reduced local government expenditures.

Where did these state revenues come from? In 1930, 16 states had individual income taxes, 17 had corporate income taxes, and none had a general sales tax. During the 1930s, 16 states added personal income taxes, 15 added corporate income taxes, and 24 created a sales tax. It is impossible to say whether these taxes were the result of New Deal grant programmes, since the majority of new state taxes were put in place in 1933 at the same time that the New Deal grant programmes were just getting under way. But one of the legacies of the New Deal was a much stronger state government sector with new and more flexible tax instruments.

smaller than the national share of revenues, while the local governments' share of expenditures were larger than their share of revenues.

Another way to see this is in the structure of state government programmes. In 1932, before New Deal relief programmes started up, only seven states had spent money for unemployment relief and had state relief agencies. By the end of 1933 all 48 states did. By 1939, all the states had approved unemployment insurance schemes, and almost all had approved OAA (Old Age Assistance), ADC (Aid to Dependent Children), and Aid to the Blind programmes in place. State highway boards were the result of the 1916 grants, but they too were still in place and would expand dramatically with the onset of the interstate highway programme in 1956. There is, then, no doubt that the programmes with the largest fiscal impact were federal programmes. Over time, the old age insurance part of Social Security would become an extremely important fiscal programme, but that was in the future in 1939.

Finally, the New Deal led to a dramatic expansion in the use of intergovernmental grants that became a fundamental feature of the fiscal structure of the country. Between 1902 and 1932 state and local governments' reliance on grants from the national government was minuscule, as the ratio of national grants to state and local revenues was between 0.01 and 0.03 in column 5 of Table 10.1. States and their local governments provided their own funding for the bulk of public services including public education, police protection, roads and sanitation, public welfare, and health and hospitals. Between 1932 and 1934 the shift to New Deal financing of relief spending sharply raised the ratio from 0.03 to 0.10. After World War Two, national grants to lower level governments became a more prominent feature of the federal fiscal system over the long run, as the ratio has been 0.10 or above since 1962.

The New Deal programmes with the largest effect on state and local governments, as well as the economy, were the relief programmes. This was not only the result of the large amount of funds expended for relief, but also because work relief programmes like the WPA (Works Progress Administration) made a significant contribution to a number of state and local functions through construction activity on schools, highways, parks, streets, sanitation, and natural resources. Understanding the relief programmes is central to understanding intergovernmental relations during the 1930s. These programmes had both major economic and psychological impacts. In fiscal 1934, the national government made over $2 billion in grants to state and local governments for relief, which in turn made more than $2 billion in relief grants to needy individuals and families. In 1933, $2 billion was 4 per cent of GNP.[6]

10.2. RELIEF AND POVERTY PROGRAMMES

During the 1930s, the federal government's relief efforts were new in two ways. The federal government, for the first time, actively distributed relief funds to

[6] Cross-country comparisons can be dicey, but Amenta (1998: 5) suggests that by 1938 the US governments were spending about 6.5 per cent of GDP on social welfare, a percentage substantially higher than in other major western countries. See Lindert (2004) to put these figures in long run historical perspective.

people outside the military, and the work relief programmes built many public works projects—schools, sanitation facilities, local roads—that would be run by state and local governments. Federal relief built on local relief activity that had been in place since colonial times and the state programmes that had developed during the Progressive Era. County, city, and town governments had provided for a mix of almshouses, poor farms, and 'outdoor' relief during the colonial period, following the English structure. The practice evolved and continued into the 1930s. During the late 19th century, there were periods when private non-profit groups like the Charitable Organizations Societies took over the operation of relief in some cities, and charitable donations expanded. The organizations later stepped out of operations and collected data on the provision of relief, and the shares of private and public spending on relief shifted back and forth for the next few decades. In the peak year of 1929, estimates from the state of Massachusetts suggest that public relief spending was roughly 1 per cent of Massachusetts state income and private relief spending approximately 2 per cent of income (Livingston, 2011).

Between 1929 and 1932, per capita spending on relief by state and local governments and private charities more than quadrupled in 114 cities, as the Depression drove increasing numbers of people onto relief. In 1932, the Hoover administration authorized $300 million in loans from the Reconstruction Finance Corporation (RFC) to cities around the country to help finance relief spending. Governors who applied for relief loans had to demonstrate that they had exhausted all means of raising revenue and propose worthy relief projects that would not otherwise be undertaken. The RFC loans were a bold move historically because the US federal system had long treated relief and labour issues as exclusively state and local issues. Originally, these loans were meant to be repaid at 3 per cent interest through reductions in future highway apportionments, but the RFC was allowed to write them off in 1938.[7] The RFC loans led several states to establish new relief administrations to organize relief at the state level.

With unemployment rates continuing at 25 per cent, the Roosevelt administration argued that America faced a national peacetime emergency and established the Federal Emergency Relief Administration (FERA) during the First Hundred Days. The FERA distributed federal money to the states, which in turn, distributed the funds to local officials, who administered payments to households 'in need'. The FERA programme offered either 'direct relief', which was straight cash payments, or 'work relief', which required a family member to work for the funds. The relief payment to a household was determined using a 'budgetary deficiency' principle. FERA relief workers and field agents measured the deficit between the family's actual income and a hypothetical minimum budget for a given family size. Actual relief benefits often did not fully cover the family's deficit because relief officials, faced with large case loads and limited funds, reduced benefits per household in order to provide relief for more families. The payments for FERA work relief jobs were designed to be income maintenance payments. Therefore, the FERA hourly 'earnings' were roughly half of the level

[7] For discussion of the RFC relief loans see Jones (1951: 178) and Fearon (2007: 39–49).

paid for jobs on Public Roads Administration (PRA) and Public Works Administration (PWA) projects.

To provide work relief for young people entering the workforce, the Civilian Conservation Corps (CCCR) provided work relief for young men and some young women between the ages of 16 and 24 from families eligible for relief. Most worked on natural resource conservation projects while living in camps run in a semi-military fashion by veterans. The pay was $1 per day, most of which was sent home to the workers' families. The CCCR had some problems with dropouts who did not like the semi-military organization, but a large share of the alumni of the camps considered them to be a life-changing experience that helped them develop the skills and attitudes necessary to become successful (Maher, 2008).

In November 1933, in the face of an expected onset of a rough winter with continuing high unemployment, the national government created the Civil Works Administration (CWA) to put people to work on public jobs immediately. By mid-December, the CWA employed 3.6 million people. The CWA hourly earnings matched public works earnings, but limited the number of hours per week that could be worked. About half of all CWA recipients were from existing relief programmes, and, after the CWA closed in March 1934, most of the workers were transferred back to FERA work relief programmes. Table 10.2 shows that, between July 1933 and July 1934, the FERA and the CWA distributed roughly $23.37 per person in 1930 dollars, or about 3.5 per cent of the 1929 peak in GDP per capita of $820 in 1930 dollars.

In 1935, the Roosevelt administration and Congress negotiated a redesigned relief programme that included an emergency relief component as well as a permanent national role in the welfare system. The Roosevelt administration gained much tighter control of the operation of emergency work relief by replacing the FERA with the WPA. State and local officials proposed projects and continued to identify who was eligible for relief based on household budget deficits. Then the federal WPA hired people from the certification rolls and paid them hourly earnings for a restricted number of hours per month. As with the FERA, the payments were for income maintenance and hourly earnings were roughly half those on PWA and PRA projects. To combat fears that private jobs would end quickly, the WPA assured people in many areas that they would be accepted back on work relief if they lost their private job. Even so, a significant percentage of workers stayed on work relief jobs for periods as long as a year and, in some cases, several years (Howard 1943; Margo, 1991, 1993). The FERA and WPA were temporary 'emergency' programmes that would end. Even though some members of the administration wished to make them a permanent feature of the economy, the WPA was phased out by the end of 1942.[8] Between fiscal years 1936 and 1939, the WPA spending in Table 10.2 averaged $16.52 per capita, roughly 2 per cent of 1929 per capita GDP.

[8] Howard (1943) describes WPA operation. For a good description of relief activity within a state, see Fearon (2007) for the state of Kansas. A large number of statistical studies analyse the political economy of the distribution of the New Deal relief funds, including most recently Fleck (1999a, 1999b, 2001a, 2008), Wallis (1987, 1991, 1998, and 2001) and Fishback et al. (2003), which summarizes results for a large number of studies of all New Deal programmes. See also Wright (1974).

Table 10.2. Average annual funds distributed by the federal government across states, by programme; in fiscal years of operation, in 1930 dollars per 1930 population

Category	Fiscal Years for programme between 1923–1939	New Deal acronym used in text	Level of government pre-New Deal	Annual Spending per 1930 Person in 1930$ during Years in Operation		
				Roosevelt 1934–1939	Hoover 1930–1933	Harding/ Coolidge 1923–1929
RELIEF GRANTS						
Civilian Conservation Corps	1934–1939	CCCR	State and Local	3.44	0.04	0.00
Civil Works Administration Work Grants	1934	CWA	State and Local	8.18	0.00	0.00
Federal Emergency Relief Administration Grant	1934–1935[a]	FERA	State and Local	15.19	0.00	0.00
Social Security Administration Public Assistance Grants	1936–1939	SSAPA	State and Local	1.91	0.00	0.00
Social Security Administration Administrative Assistance Grants	1936–1939	SSAAD	State and Local	1.44	0.00	0.00
Works Progress Administration Work Relief Grants	1936–1939	WPA	State and Local	16.52	0.00	0.00
US Employment Service	1934–1939	USES	State and Local	0.13	0.00	0.00
Vocational Education	1930–1939[b]	VE	Federal	0.13	0.08	n.a.s
AID TO VETERANS						
Soldiers and Sailors Homes	1923–1939	SSH	Federal	0.01	0.01	0.01
Veterans Administration Grants	1923–1939	VA	Federal	5.20	6.67	4.64
Adjusted Service Certificate Grants (Veterans' Bonus)	1936[c]	ASCG	Federal	33.84	0.00	0.00
Adjusted Service Certificate Loans	1927–1935[d]	ASCL	Federal	−1.35 in 1934 and 0.64 in 1935	3.74	0.22
Adjusted Service Certificate Loans Repayments	1936[e]		Federal	−16.14	0.00	0.00
Veterans Rehab Spending	1923–1930[r]	VR	Federal	n.a.s.	n.a.s	0.39
PUBLIC WORKS GRANTS						
Public Works Administration Federal Project Grants	1934–1939	PWAF	Federal	1.04	0.00	0.00
Public Works Administration Non-federal Project Grants	1934–1939	PWANF	State and Local	1.66	0.00	0.00
Tennessee Valley Authority spending	1934–1939	TVA	Federal	0.36	0.00	0.00

Continued

Table 10.2. Continued

Category	Fiscal Years for programme between 1923–1939	New Deal acronym used in text	Level of government pre-New Deal	Annual Spending per 1930 Person in 1930$ during Years in Operation		
				Roosevelt 1934–1939	Hoover 1930–1933	Harding/ Coolidge 1923–1929
State Highway Federal Aid (Public Roads Administration after 1933)	1923–1939	PRA	Federal	2.56	1.50	0.56
Public Housing Grants under the PWA	1935–1939	PWAH	Local	0.41	0.00	0.00
River and Harbour Grants Reported by the Army Corps of Engineers (not Relief or Public Works)	1923–1939	RH	Federal	1.21	1.01	0.59
Bureau of Reclamation Loans Reported by Bureau of Reclamation	1923–1939	REC	Federal	0.51	0.15	0.06
Public Building Administration Grants	1930–1939	PBA	Federal	0.40	0.84	n.a.
PUBLIC WORKS LOANS						
Public Works Administration loans for non-federal projects	1934–1939	PWANF	State and Local	0.83	0.00	0.00
US Housing Authority public housing loans	1939	USHA	Local	0.54	0.00	0.00
AGRICULTURAL GRANTS						
Agricultural Adjustment Administration Grants	1934–1939	AAA	None	4.66	0.00	0.00
Farm Security Administration Grants	1935–1939	FSA	None	0.52	0.00	0.00
Federal Surplus Commodity Corporation Grants	1938–1939	FSCC	None	1.00	0.00	0.00
Soil Conservation Service Grants	1934–1939	SCS	None	0.16	0.00	0.00
Agricultural Experiment Station Grants	1923–1939	AES	Federal	0.05	0.04	0.07
Agricultural Extension Works Grants	1923–1939	AEW	Federal	0.14	0.08	0.00
Colleges of Agricultural and Mechanical Grants	1923–1939	CAM	Federal	0.03	0.02	n.a.s
AGRICULTURAL LOANS						
Commodity Credit Corporation Loans	1934–1939f	CCCA	None	1.94	0.00	0.00
Disaster Loan Corporation Loans	1937–1939	DLC	Federal	0.05	0.00	0.00
Farm Credit Administration Emergency Crop and Feed Loans	1923–1939[g]	FCAEC	Federal	0.29	0.44	0.01
Farm Credit Administration Federal Land Bank Loans	1923–1939[g]	FCALB	Federal	3.62	0.80	1.02
Farm Credit Administration Production Credit Loans	1934–1939[g]	FCAPC	None	2.29	0.00	0.00

Joint Stock Bank Farm Mortgage Loans	1923–1932[g]	JSB	Federal	0.00	0.03	1.00
Farm Security Administration Loans	1936–1939	FSAL	None	0.82	0.00	0.00
Farm Tenant Purchase Loans	1938–1939	FTP	None	0.16	0.00	0.00
Rural Electrification Administration Loans	1936–1939	REA	None	0.30	0.00	0.00
MISCELLANEOUS						
Education Grants to States	1923–1939	ED	Federal, State and Local	0.17	0.10	0.09
National Guard Grants	1923–1939	NG	Federal	0.30	0.30	0.23
Home Owners' Loan Corporation Loans	1934–1936	HOLC	None	10.56	0.00	0.00
Reconstruction Finance Corporation Loans	1932–1939	RFC	Federal	3.50	9.84	0.00
HOLC and Treasury Loans	1934–1939	HOLCT	Federal	0.43	0.00	0.00
Federal Housing Administration: Value of Title I Repair and Reconstruction Loans Guaranteed by	1935–1939	FHAR	None	1.62	0.00	0.00
Federal Housing Administration: Value of Title II Non-farm Home Mortgage Loans Guaranteed	1935–1939	FHAM	None	3.58	0.00	0.00

Source: Based on data from Office of Government Reports, US Census Bureau, State Financial Statistics, US Treasury Department, Annual Reports. For details on the construction of the data see Fishback and Kachanovskaya (2011: Data Appendix). This is built up from a data set on grants and loans in each state and possibly understates total federal spending on each programme to the extent that there was no record of the state kept for that type of spending. Annual per capita income in 1930 dollars in 1929 was $820 based on series CA-11 and CA13 in Carter et al. (2006). There had always been some central aid to state and local governments, beginning with the national assumption of state debts in the 1790s. But intergovernmental grants in existence by 1900 were a small part of the public sector. They included textbooks for the blind (1879), agricultural experiment stations (1887), state soldiers homes (1888), resident instruction in land-grant colleges (1890), and irrigation (1894). These were followed by grants to state marine schools (1911), state and forestry operations (1911), the agricultural extension service (1914), vocational education (1917), and vocational rehabilitation (1920). But these programmes were, by 1920, overshadowed in fiscal terms by the highway construction grants begun in 1916. By 1922, $92 million of the $118 million in federal grants, or 78 per cent, were for highways. A maternity and infancy health plan was begun in 1921, which gave rise to the famous decision in Massachusetts vs. Mellon (262 US 447 (1923)) that conditional grants did not impinge on state sovereignty, since states were free to forgo the grants (Moehling and Thomasson, 2012). By 1930 there were 15 federal grant programmes to state and local government in operation, dominated by the highway construction grants. But they were still small in the aggregate; state grants to local governments were about five times as large as federal grants to state and local governments combined.

n.a.s. means not available separately.

n.a. means not available.

[a] The FERA spent a small share of its funds between July 1935 and March 1937 as programmes wound down.

[b] Vocational education information not available separately in 1920s so far.

[c] The ASC cash payments were distributed in June and July of 1936 and thus straddled the fiscal year.

[d] Loans for 1934 and 1935 reported separately because repayments of ASC loans outweighed new loans significantly nationwide. In 1935 new loans made outweighed repayments.

[e] When the ASC cash payments were made in June and July 1936, this amount per capita went to repaying ASC loans.

[f] CCC loans included loans not listed by state, so this understates amounts.

[g] These loans are reported for the calendar year.

The permanent components of the 1935 reforms were the most important. Care of the 'unemployable' poor was returned to local governments and termed 'general relief'. The Social Security Act created five big programmes. Four of them were federal programmes, administered and funded jointly by the national and state governments, and one was funded and administered solely by the national government.

The act created three categories of needs-based public assistance that had been established in several states prior to 1935. The 'categorical' relief programmes—Aid to the Blind, OAA, and ADC—were financed through closed end matching grants. States determined how much they would spend per case based on the budget deficiency principal, and the national government matched state spending up to a maximum amount per case. Matching grants were available to all states that passed enabling legislation that met certain administrative requirements. The state set the benefit levels and ran the programme. The matching grants generally increased the amount of aid available in the categories in states that already had programmes and led states without programmes to add them. ADC essentially took over from mothers' pension programmes that provided payments to widows with children and were present in 40 of 48 states in 1920 and 46 of 48 states by 1931. OAA replaced means tested old age programmes that were present in 10 of 48 states by 1929 and 28 of 48 states in 1934. OAA and the earlier state elderly programmes were truly means tested. Many states took liens on or ownership of the homes owned by recipients and then collected the amounts paid out in benefits when the person died before the heirs could receive their share of the value of the home. Aid to the Blind replaced similar programmes in 28 of 48 states as of August 1935 (Fishback and Thomasson, 2006). Within three years, most states had adopted the enabling legislation. The OAA programmes distributed about 80 per cent of the funds under the three public assistance programmes, as a large number of elderly were transferred off the general relief rolls and new elderly enrolled. In 1939, the states paid out about 0.65 per cent of 1929 GDP in public assistance benefits. Federal government grants for this purpose, in Table 10.2, averaged about $1.91 per capita in benefit payments and $1.44 in administrative payments.[9]

Another permanent element of the Social Security Act was national support for unemployment insurance. The national government collected a 3 per cent payroll tax from all workers in covered employment. Ninety per cent of the payroll taxes were paid into a separate reserve fund for each state. States could draw on their funds to pay benefits to unemployed workers. Prior to 1935, Wisconsin was the only state with an unemployment insurance programme, but it was still building up a reserve fund and had not yet started paying benefits. In order to participate in the programme, states had to pass the enabling legislation and then build their reserve fund for two years. By the end of 1938, 30 of 48 states were paying benefits totalling 0.36 per cent of 1929 peak GDP. The US unemployment insurance

[9] Information on the public assistance programmes is based on the payouts in the months of January, February, and March from Social Security Board. *Social Security Bulletin* (May 1939: 51). These were compared to an estimate of GDP, in 1929 dollars, in 1929 of $103.7 billion (series Ca10 from Carter et al., 2004) and then adjusted for inflation by the Consumer Price Index (1967 = 100) (US Census Bureau, 1975, series E-135: 210–11).

programmes differ from programmes in nearly all other countries in that they incorporate experience rating, which requires employers to make larger payments when their share of laid off workers is higher.[10]

The final component of the Social Security Act was a purely national programme, OASI. There was a loose precedent for the federal government's involvement in old age retirement pensions. The Civil War disability pension had expanded its eligibility requirements so broadly that the infirmities of old age were largely covered, so that a substantial share of the elderly in the north in the early 1900s were receiving federal military pensions. In the late 1930s, the OASI programme called for employers and workers to each pay taxes of 1 per cent of the worker's income up to a specified maximum each year. At retirement age the person then received monthly pension payments. Over the past 70 years, monthly pension payments have averaged about 40 per cent of the typical monthly earnings of workers at the time the pension was being paid. There were extensive debates over whether the system should run like an actuarially sound pension programme or insure a basic level of benefits. The original act split the difference but, by 1940, it became a pay-as-you-go programme. The long-term impact of Social Security has been enormous but its effects in the 1930s were limited to the impact of the new tax payments, which accounted for 5.6 per cent of internal federal tax revenue in fiscal year 1937. Benefits were not paid until 1940 (Commissioner of Internal Revenue, 1937: 75).

The final area of relief was veterans' benefits for disability relief and pensions, which had been the national government's responsibility since the nation's founding. Essentially, these were employment benefits for veterans who had worked in national defence. As seen in Table 10.2, annual payments for relief to state soldiers' and sailors' homes and veterans' administration payments in the 1930s had fallen from their peaks during the Hoover administration. The decline occurred in part because of drops in rehabilitation and retraining programmes for veterans who had fought in World War One.

The major exception came in the form of the Veterans' Bonus of 1936. In 1924, Congress provided for adjusted service certificates for World War One veterans that could be redeemed at face value 20 years after receipt. The amount to be paid was $1 for each day served in World War One inside the US, and $1.25 for each day overseas, and then the amount was multiplied by 1.25 to take into account the delay in payment. By the late 1920s, living veterans could borrow from the Veterans' Bureau against the certificates by accepting a lien on the value of the certificate. They could pay back the loan and receive the full certificate value upon maturity of the certificate in the 1940s or accept the amount left after interest was deducted. After Congress lowered the maximum interest on the loans to 4.5 per cent (and soon after to 3.5) and increased the amount that could be borrowed to half of the value of the adjusted service certificate on 27 February 1931, World War One veterans took out 2 million loans valued at $795 million within the next few months. Demanding that the full value of the certificates be paid without delay, groups of veterans marched on Washington in the summer of 1931 and again in the summer of 1932 when they set up camp near the Potomac. The

[10] This discussion is based on work by Baicker et al. (1998).

bloodshed that occurred when the army tried to clear the camp harmed President Hoover's re-election bid. Yet, Hoover and the Republican Congress refused to redeem the certificates early on the grounds that it would lead to higher taxes.

Veterans continued to lobby for early payment on the certificates and Congress passed the Veterans' Bonus Bill over President Roosevelt's veto in January 1936. The Veterans Administration (VA) received 3.3 million applications seeking cash settlements of $3.2 billion for settlement by 30 June 1936. The VA payout per person in the US, in Table 10.2, was $33.84 with $16.14 going to pay off the veterans' loans, and the remaining $17.70 in cash.[11]

A number of recent studies have addressed the impact of federal relief spending at the state and local level while controlling for a wide range of correlates, long-term features of each location, nationwide shocks that vary by year, and endogeneity bias. Relief spending had a number of salutary effects on measures of socioeconomic welfare. An injection of about $2 million in relief spending was associated with a reduction of one infant death, one suicide, 2.4 deaths from infectious disease, and one death from diarrhoea, while contributing to a rise in birth rates that returned to the long-term trend. A 10 per cent increase in work relief spending was associated with a 1.5 per cent reduction in property crime, although this is smaller than the 10 per cent reduction in crime associated with a 10 per cent rise in private employment. The expansion of benefits under the OAA programme allowed a larger share of elderly women to live on their own, while accounting for about half of the decline in the elderly workforce between 1930 and 1950, although it had no effect on reducing elderly mortality rates. Relief jobs and spending appear to have had little or no positive impact on private employment and, in some settings, appears to have crowded out some private employment even when unemployment rates remained above 14 per cent. Such crowding out also appears to have extended to private charitable spending. An additional dollar of New Deal spending reduced church charitable spending by about 29 per cent of the maximum to which it might have reduced.[12]

10.3. NATIONAL VERSUS STATE AND LOCAL DISCRETION OVER RELIEF SPENDING

Granting 2 to 4 per cent of GDP in relief funds each year during the New Deal was an unprecedented act of national government largesse, particularly because the

[11] See Administrator of Veterans' Affairs (1931: 10, 42–44; 1936: 1, 22–24). When the certificates were first issued, if the amount came to less than $50, they were paid in cash immediately, and the cash value of the certificate was paid out to heirs at the time of the veteran's death. Under the Bonus Bill of 1936, if veterans held the certificates for more than one year they could receive the face value plus 3 per cent interest per year until maturity on 15 June 1945. The three per cent interest rate was higher than the 2.5 returns on long term government bonds during that period.

[12] For the effects on birth and death rates see Fishback et al. (2007), the effects of old age assistance are measured in Balan-Cohen (2008), Costa (1999), Friedberg (1999), Parsons (1991), and Stoian and Fishback (2010). The crime effects are measured in Johnson et al. (2010). The impact on private employment is measured in Fleck (1999b), Wallis and Benjamin (1981), Neumann et al. (2010), and Benjamin and Mathews (1992). The charitable crowding out is from Gruber and Hungerman (2007).

grants created the possibility of unprecedented political patronage for the politicians in control of the money. How the political system evolved to both allocate and control the administration of relief funds was a central element of the New Deal. Before, the New Deal relief was funded and administered largely by local governments with some aid from state governments. The original FERA legislation made it clear that FERA was to restrict itself to making grants to state governments. Half of the original $500 million appropriation was to be allocated at the discretion of the national relief administrator on the basis of need, and half on a matching grant basis. By November of 1933, FERA head Harry Hopkins, had convinced Congress to drop the matching feature.[13] FERA promulgated an extensive set of regulations covering how the states were to administer relief programmes and all FERA grants were conditional on states meeting the regulations. Hopkins was able to enforce several simple and important regulations. For example, all relief funds had to be spent through public agencies. But FERA's ability to affect personnel policies and recipient selection criteria was limited. The agency's power was much greater in states where it played a larger fiscal role. As Williams (1939) noted, 'the ability to enforce these policies was much greater in states where the national contribution was larger'.[14] In extreme cases, the FERA legislation gave Hopkins the authority to 'federalize' relief and take over the administration of relief in a state. Hopkins federalized relief on seven occasions.[15] State governors were glad to get the national grants but were not happy to have Hopkins announce that grants would be reduced if the state government did not come up with a larger relief appropriation. State officials expressed their displeasure actively. Governor Davey of Ohio went to the extreme of swearing out an arrest warrant for Hopkins after he had charged Davey with using relief for political purposes.

The control Roosevelt and Hopkins had over the distribution of relief grants to the states strongly influenced the negotiations over which level of government would have discretion and control when the relief programmes were restructured for the long run in 1935. The compromise that emerged from the negotiations included the replacement of the FERA with the WPA to continue emergency relief and the long run programmes established by the Social Security Act of 1935. Aware that the FERA was an emergency programme designed to end after the emergency was over, Roosevelt and Hopkins established the Committee on Economic Security to work on a more permanent solution to the relief problem. In his state of the union address in January of 1935, Roosevelt announced that the national government 'must and will quit this business of relief', and he sent the Committee Report and proposed legislation to Congress. The proposal called for OAA, ADC, AB (Aid to the Blind), and UI (unemployment insurance) to be

[13] See Williams (1939: 181–90, 203–21). In the final analysis, it is clear that the original matching programme was relatively unimportant. Williams shows (1939: Table 6, p. 217) that the federal government's share of relief spending varied dramatically across states from a low of 39 per cent in Rhode Island to a high of 98 per cent in South Carolina.

[14] Quote is from Williams (1939). For a discussion of the rules and regulations, and their enforceability, see Williams (1939) and Wallis (1981).

[15] The logic of how Hopkins could use discretionary grants to pry more funds out of state governments is developed in Wallis (1981).

administered by a FERA-like agency in which the national relief administrator used discretion rather than matching grants to distribute fund.

The national relief administrator's discretionary control did not even make it through the first committee hearings in the House. In the Social Security bill that emerged from Congress, strong state control over OAA, ADC, AB, and UI was accomplished by tying the national government's fiscal hands through strict matching grant provisions. National grants were open ended, but grants per relief case were capped. The independent Social Security Board created by the bill had to approve each state's categorical programme, but there were strict limits on the Board's ability to interfere with the actual administration of the programmes. For example, the Board was explicitly forbidden from withholding grants because of personnel decisions at the state level. Given that general relief for the needy who did not fit these categories was left completely to state and local governments, control of the welfare system became as much a matter of state policy as of national policy. This return to state control was instituted despite the protests of social welfare professionals, who feared that returning control of relief to the states was just returning to the old system of political patronage and cronyism.[16]

In the negotiations over relief, the national government retained control over two programmes, the OASI pensions and the WPA emergency work relief agency that replaced the FERA. These programmes also contained important limits. The national government had very limited discretionary power over the OASI programme because individuals paid payroll taxes into the system and their benefits were fixed by formula. No matter where people lived during their working life or during retirement, their contributions and benefits were set by formula with no discretion on the part of the national government.

The one large relief programme where the national government still had a great deal of discretionary control was the WPA, which replaced the FERA as the emergency work relief programme. Hopkins did not have to work through the states to distribute funds and the national government paid WPA workers directly on the projects. The state and local governments had some role in proposing projects, identifying the eligibility of the relief workers, and in providing some funding. But there was no explicit matching formula and the amounts contributed by states varied widely (Howard, 1943: 734–5). It is clear from the congressional debates, however, that congressmen were willing to give the national government such discretionary power only because the WPA was an emergency agency that was expected to close down (Wallis, 1981 dissertation, and Wallis et al., 2006). In contrast, the permanent relief programmes created by the Social Security strictly limited the national government's discretion.

Understanding why the Social Security system was structured this way is critical to understanding the New Deal's legacy and position in the political and economic history of the century. With the addition of Medicaid and Medicare in 1967, the

[16] This story is told in a number of places. Brock (1988) and Bremer (1984) are very good on the details. The notion that returning relief to the states was an attempt to return control of the relief programmes to local economic elites is elaborated in Piven and Cloward (1971) and Block et al. (1987). For a reformulation of this hypothesis based on the interest of southern legislators, see Alston and Ferrie (1999).

Social Security system remains in place in an expanded form today. In 1992, outlays for social insurance, unemployment insurance, and public assistance were one-quarter of total government outlays at all levels. Medicaid was set up as a categorical assistance programme, with matching grants and state administration. Medicare was set up like old age insurance, with national administration and standards, but has gradually become a more federal programme as well.

The New Deal relief programmes initiated a pattern of cooperative intergovernmental activity with a distinctive bent: fiscal centralization and administrative decentralization. They continued the long running administrative decentralization of relief policies from colonial times, but added national government funding. Not only were New Deal programmes administered at the state level, but state governments possessed real decision making power. The states' decision making power in the long run increased closer to the pre-New Deal levels with the passage of the Social Security Act. The use of allocation formulas and matching provisions effectively eliminated the possibility that the national government would be able to use the discretionary allocation of funds across states to influence the administration of the OAA, AB, ADC, and UI programmes at the state level. Limitations on national administrative discretion were a necessary part of making the relief system politically sustainable over the long haul. The New Deal experience gives us strong confirmation of this conclusion. The crisis character of the early New Deal programmes resulted in the national government being granted extensive discretionary power. But that power was closely watched and eventually drastically curtailed. Further, this was not the outcome desired by social welfare advocates, who were the most vocal and well organized promoters of an expanded welfare system. They clearly wanted a more centralized programme.

The pattern of centralized finance and decentralized administration persists today. It is a central element in the interstate highway system, the structure of Medicare, the essential elements of welfare reform in the 1990s which gave states greater control over relief administration, and in the recent health care reforms embodied in the Affordable Care Act. The pattern of centralized finance and decentralized administration, particularly under a regime in which the discretionary control of the centralized government is strictly limited, affords one of the most important lessons for the current economic and political crises. The United States was unable to move very far away from the pattern. The Affordable Care Act is markedly 'federal'. The outcry over national government bailouts of private businesses, which involved a large amount of discretion on the part of national actors, far exceeds the outcry about the short run stimulus money that was transferred to the states. Opposition remains to deficit spending, not the allocation of spending to state and local governments. As the European crisis extends and deepens, however, it appears from some distance to involve precisely the opposite pattern. The EU is seeking to impose more inflexible fiscal and administrative rules on the member states while maintaining flexibility and discretion at the centre. At least, this is how negotiations over the recurring fiscal crises seem to be proceeding.

Harry Hopkins was a gifted administrator. Winston Churchill dubbed him 'Lord Root of the Matter' for his ability in negotiating and facilitating alliance arrangements during World War Two. Undoubtedly, he could have devised and administered a national welfare system that would have provided more assistance to the poor, unemployed, and needy at a lower fiscal cost than the system that emerged from the Social Security Act. But in a fiscal and political union such as the United States, locating excessive discretionary control at the centre is politically unsustainable, no matter what its policy effectiveness. This is a lesson of great importance for current crisis.

10.4. PUBLIC WORKS

Public works grants differed from relief grants in the operation and administration of the projects. About two-thirds of the funds distributed went to the types of projects that had long been run by the national government. The projects hired workers at full market wages, often through contractors who ran the projects. Administrators were not required to hire people eligible for relief, although it was encouraged. Under the Hoover presidency, the annual distribution of funds to state highways under the US Department of Agriculture (USDA) rose 167 per cent, rivers and harbours funds under the Army Corps of Engineers rose 152 per cent, and loans to the Reclamation Bureau for dams and irrigation projects rose 71 per cent. The reports at the time show that the increases were meant to be forms of stimulus.

The amounts distributed rose sharply again under the Roosevelt administration. But there was a difference in style. Where Hoover usually increased spending within existing programmes, Roosevelt had a flair for publicizing New Deal programmes that were renamed, reorganized, or new. The PRA took over the USDA highway programme. The PWA and the work relief projects provided grants for many river and harbour projects that were built under the direction of the Army Corps of Engineers. The Public Building Administration (PBA) took over the building of national buildings around the country. By the end of the 1930s, the PWA, PRA, PBA, US Housing Authority (USHA), and the WPA relief programme had been rolled into the Federal Works Agency (FWA). In 1942, the PWA and WPA emergency programmes were terminated and the PBA, USHA, and PRA duties were distributed to new agencies.[17]

There were three new features of the public works grants. The first was explicit grant and loan funding of state and local projects under the non-federal programme. The PWA was relatively slow to get started because its leader, Harold Ickes, wanted to focus on projects of high quality, but Table 10.2 shows that it distributed an annual per capita average of $1.04 for federal projects and $1.66 in grants and $0.83 in loans for the non-federal programmes. Second, during its first three years, the PWA spent an annual average of $0.41 per capita on a series of local public housing projects. In 1937, the USHA began providing loans for public housing projects. The third was the creation of the TVA. In most ways, the TVA was not new. It was a corporation set in motion to build dams along the Tennessee River, but these dams had been designed by the Army Corps of Engineers for flood control and to improve navigation of the rivers, and the Corps probably

[17] See Clarke (1996: 62–68) and Schlesinger (1958: 263–96).

would have built the dams relatively soon. The dams also produced hydro-electric power, and electric power became the primary emphasis of the TVA after 1935. The TVA became a new feature of national activity when it began buying up distribution lines and electric utilities, including many generating electricity with coal, and became the primary producer and distributor of electricity in the mid-south region. Some states and local governments had taken control of gas and electric utilities in the Progressive Era, but this was the first time the national government had stepped into the process.

In the Roosevelt administration's view, the public works and work relief programmes were not revolutionary. They were explicitly designed not to go beyond public sector functions. The projects were traditional government projects: building and maintaining public buildings, schools, parks, roads, sanitation facilities, dams, airports, and a variety of other public projects. Production of manufactured goods, creations of stores, and other private sector activities were off limits. The simultaneous goals were to put people back to work and build social overhead capital with hopes of stimulating the economy.

As with relief programmes, studies have examined the impact of combined spending on public works and relief on various aspects of the economy at the local level using similar sets of controls. The studies have generally combined public works and relief grants because they have found it difficult to find effective instrumental variables that can be used to identify the separate effects of the two programmes. The studies suggest that an additional dollar per capita of public works and relief spending during the period 1933 to 1939 in a county was associated with a rise in retail sales per capita of about 43 cents, which might have translated into a rise in per capita income of about 80 cents. A study of a panel of state information from 1930 through to 1940 suggests that a dollar increase in per capita public works and relief grants increased per capita income in the state by amounts ranging from \$0.9 to \$1.7, although none of the effects is statistically significantly different from one. This rise in income did not translate into increases in private employment in the states, as the coefficients on public works and relief grants were all negative. Higher public works and relief grants in a county served to stimulate in-migration into that county, even though there were a number of residency requirements that limited access to relief. One simulation suggests that the amount of internal migration in the US would have been lower by 15 percent had the public works and relief grants not been distributed. In-migration to cities, in turn, led to reductions in the number of weeks worked by the typical worker, greater difficulty in getting access to relief jobs, and out-migration by some workers.

Even though the TVA is credited with lowering the costs of electricity in the area, private firms had long been expanding electrification as well. A careful study of electric rates shows that the monthly bills for most TVA customers were the same as the bills for private utility customers. Only larger manufacturing operations received lower bills. Estimates of the TVA's impact suggest only small positive impacts on farm electrification and retail sales per capita. There may have been stronger effects on manufacturing activity.[18]

[18] The impact of public works and relief grants on retail sales and migration is estimated in Fishback et al. (2005 and 2006). The state level measures of the impact on per capita income and private

10.5. FARM PROGRAMMES

Farmers faced a dire situation in the early 1930s. The farm sector experienced a 'Golden Era' of farm prices in the early 1900s, followed by an expansion in demand during World War One. When Europe began producing again in the early 1920s, demand for American farm products declined, and the farm sector went through a difficult shakeout in the early 1920s. By the time the Depression hit, the farm sector had been in the doldrums for roughly a decade. The New Deal worked to aid farmers by continuing and expanding the national government's role in farm lending, and by seeking to raise farm prices by paying farmers to take land out of production and providing non-recourse loans that put a floor on farm prices.

Well before 1933, the national government had been heavily involved in providing networks of farm credit. Just before entering World War One, the national government passed legislation to fund farm mortgages through a federal land bank programme. The national government organized and provided starting capital to 12 federal land banks. They were authorized to extend loans with 5- to 40-year lengths through national farm loan association cooperative corporations organized by farmers. The membership of the cooperatives was made up exclusively of borrowers from the federal land banks. Each bank was liable for its own bond issues and the bond issues of the 11 other federal land banks. As of 1930, the federal land banks held about 12 per cent of the farm mortgage indebtedness in the US. The government also helped to organize a series of privately owned joint stock land banks that could make direct mortgage loans to farmers, while also providing capital to start intermediate credit banks to provide short run capital to farm lenders and cooperatives that faced short term liquidity constraints.[19]

By the early 1930s, a sizeable share of farmers had fallen behind on loan payments and become delinquent. In January 1932, the national government injected an additional $125 million into the federal land banks to expand credit availability. Even so, the real annual value of federal land bank loans declined from the 1920s into the early 1930s, as seen in Table 10.2. Meanwhile, loans from joint stock land banks declined to a trickle. In 1933, the Farm Credit Administration took over the administration of the federal land banks and the federal intermediate farm credit banks, and also gained authority to make direct loans to farmers, while the joint stock land banks were closed. The amount of annual mortgage lending to farmers thereafter more than quadrupled the amounts loaned in the early 1930s. Consequently, the national government was involved in more than half of farm mortgages by the mid-1930s.[20]

During the 1920s, Congress passed a series of acts to fund loans in specific areas where severe weather led to considerable crop damage. In 1933, the Farm Credit Administration took over the decision making and administration of these

employment are found in Fishback and Kachanovskaya (2011). The migration simulations are from Sorensen et al. (2011). The effects of internal migration are from Boustan et al. (2010). The effects of the TVA on farm electrification, retail sales and manufacturing are estimated by Kitchens (2011b); for a study of manufacturing productivity see Kline and Moretti (2011).

[19] Federal Farm Loan Board (1930: 2 and 12; 1932: 1–50).

[20] The paragraph is based on Halcrow, 1953: 342–43.

emergency credit loans. For the first time, it oversaw the development of a Production Credit Division, which authorized and provided initial capital stock to 12 production credit corporations, which made loans to production credit associations, each organized by 10 or more farmers in a mutual organization designed to make production loans for seed and machinery and production needs for farm animals. The credit associations could borrow from the Production Credit Corporation and had access to the intermediate farm credit banks.

The truly new farm programmes during the 1930s were the ones specifically designed to limit supply to the market and thus raise the farm/non-farm ratio of prices to levels seen during the Golden Era just prior to World War One. Farmers had protested their plight since the late 1800s and sought ways to limit output and raise prices. In both 1927 and 1928, their lobbying led Congress to pass versions of the McNary–Haugen bill designed to raise farm prices without supply controls, but each was vetoed by the president, Calvin Coolidge. In 1929, the Agricultural Marketing Act established the Federal Farm Board, with a revolving capital of $500 million, to work with cooperatives to market crops and limit the amount of surpluses that might have driven crop prices downward.[21] The New Deal response in 1933 was to create two new programmes: the AAA grant programme to pay farmers to take land out of production, and the Commodity Credit Corporation (CCCF) non-recourse loan programme to provide a floor on the prices received for certain farm commodities.

The centrepiece of the New Deal farm programme was the rental and benefit programme administered by the AAA. For specific crops, AAA offered production agreements to farmers that paid them to take land out of production. The funds for the programme originally came from a processing tax on farm output at the location where it was first processed; for example, a tax on ginned cotton. Farmers were not required to accept the agreements, but the AAA set attractive terms and actively marketed the programmes through county agents and local boards of farmers. In the tobacco and cotton programmes, national decision makers added a degree of coercion to the system by levying heavy taxes on any production beyond designated limits. As a result, the sign-up rates ranged between 70 and 95 per cent for most types of crops. In 1935, the Supreme Court found in *United States v. Butler* that the processing tax used to fund the AAA programme was unconstitutional. Farm interests who had warmed to the AAA pressed the Roosevelt administration to re-enact a similar programme that overcame the constitutional objections. Soon thereafter, a new AAA was established that made payments to curtail land use, adjust production, and conserve the soil under the Soil Conservation and Domestic Allotment Act of 1935 or 1936. The new AAA tried to add restrictions on output for nonparticipants.[22]

The other major New Deal attempt to raise farm prices was the Commodity Credit Corporation (CCCF). The CCCF loaned funds to farmers for crops at prices set at high target levels. If crop prices exceeded the target level when the

[21] Libecap (1998: 188–9) describes the development of farm programmes from 1870 to the present. For a long-term view of the farm programmes see Chapter 16.

[22] For a detailed description of the first three years of the AAA, see Nourse et al., (1937).

time came to repay the loan, the farmer would sell the crop on the market and repay the government loan. If crop prices were below the target, the farmer gave the crop to the government as payment on the loan. From the beginning, the CCCF set the target prices above market prices, so the CCCF programme operated as a price support programme.

The AAA and most loan programmes were primarily oriented toward large farmers, but also distributed smaller amounts of funds in programmes designed to eliminate areas of persistent rural poverty. The original FERA legislation called for aid to low income farmers in the form of relief, the Resettlement Administration moved some farmers to better land, and loans and grants from other programmes were provided to aid small family farms. These farm programmes were later transferred to the Farm Security Administration formed in 1937. Other smaller programmes were designed to aid farmers hit by droughts and hard times.[23]

The AAA and the CCCF were administered at multiple levels of government. The basic benefit payments per acre, the acreage allocations, were set for each crop at the national level. This made sense because the prices of AAA crops were largely determined in national markets with some variation around the prices on account of transportation costs. Meanwhile, the allocation of acreage reductions within states and the negotiations with individual farmers were administered by state and local boards of farmers with help from county extension agents. Under the initial law, the programme was funded by a processing tax on the commodity itself, tying overall funding to production throughout the country. After the AAA was declared unconstitutional in 1935, the programme was funded out of the general revenues. The AAA operations in the long run fit a picture of limited national discretion in the sense that the national rules were set for everybody producing the same crop, while deviations from the rules for specific groups were decided at a much lower administrative level.

Observers of the short term impact in mid-1930s were unsure whether the AAA payments to take land out of production were effective in raising prices. Several studies suggest that farmers took the lowest quality land out of production first and then found ways to raise the productivity on other acreage by using more fertilizers and adopting new technologies like tractors as labour-saving devices. Efforts to determine the AAA's impact have been confounded by the series of major climatic disasters, including droughts in some areas, floods in others, and the Dust Bowl, that coincided with the AAA's introduction and also contributed to drops in production and higher prices.[24]

Given that the programmes were mostly voluntary, the AAA probably benefited the farmers who accepted the production agreements. However, the AAA appears to have had adverse effect on the incomes of farm labourers, tenants, and sharecroppers because it led to declines in the demand for labour. Narratives and recent quantitative studies show that in cotton counties with more AAA cotton

[23] For more discussion of these types of programs, see Alston and Ferrie (1999) and Fearon (2007).

[24] See Libecap (1998: footnotes on p. 193) for discussion of weather versus AAA as a cause of reduced output. Some very preliminary examinations of cotton output at the county level suggest that he may be right. Whatley (1983), and Clarke (1994) discuss, and Sorensen et al. (2011) measure, the positive impact of the AAA on tractor diffusion.

spending, the number of black and white croppers declined by similar amounts, while the number of black managing share tenants declined more sharply than the number of white tenants. Infant mortality rates, which tend to be highest among low income people, were higher for both blacks and whites in southern counties with more AAA spending. Studies of per capita income at the state level, and retail sales and in-migration at the county level, show slight negative effects of AAA spending, consistent with a view that the positive benefits to the recipients of AAA funds were offset by losses among other members of rural society.[25]

On the positive side, the AAA's stimulus of out-migration of low income croppers and workers from poor areas appears to have had the side benefit of reducing malaria death rates (Barreca et al., 2011). Over the long term, the AAA had the positive effect of preventing later recurrences of the Dust Bowl of the 1930s. The dust storms developed in part because small farmers settled the areas and had little incentive to use farming techniques designed to prevent soil erosion because their farms were too small to get the benefits of erosion prevention. High winds and drought in the 1930s blew the loose soils into the sky. The post-1935 AAA encouraged the development of large farms and gave farmers incentives to prevent soil erosion, so that no Dust Bowl developed when wind and drought hit the area in the 1970s (Hansen and Libecap, 2004).

10.6. THE NATIONAL RECOVERY ADMINISTRATION AND PRESIDENT'S REEMPLOYMENT AGREEMENTS

Just as the New Deal sought to raise farm prices, it established a set of policies designed to raise industrial prices and wages. Since the early 1920s, industry associations facing declining demand and excess capacity, like coal mining, had lobbied Congress to develop institutions that would protect them from 'cut-throat competition'. During the Depression, the problems of excess capacity and falling demand hit most industries and lobbying for some government action accelerated. Meanwhile, both the Hoover and Roosevelt administrations sought to maintain demand by keeping wages high. Hoover met with industry leaders and asked them to voluntarily maintain hourly wage rates at a higher level (Rose, 2010).

The Roosevelt administration established the NRA in June of 1933. The NRA was intended to foster the collaboration of employers, workers, and consumers in each industry to establish 'fair codes of competition' governing minimum prices, quality standards, trade practices, wages, hours limits, and working conditions. Once an industry code was approved by the NRA, it legally bound all firms in the industry, even those not involved in writing the code. While waiting for the

[25] Alston (1981) describes a reduction in the demand for farm labour. The negative effects of the AAA on tenancy have been discussed by Alston and Ferrie (1999), Biles (1994: 39–43), Saloutos (1982) and Whatley (1983) and measured at the county level by Depew et al. (2012). The infant mortality effects of the AAA are found in Fishback et al. (2001). The slight negative effects of the AAA on state income are shown in Fishback and Kachanovskaya (2011) and the negative effects on in-migration and retail sales per capita are measured in Fishback et al. (2005, 2006).

codes to be written, a large number of firms signed President's Reemployment Agreements in the summer of 1933 that required them to raise wages, cut weekly hours, and try to increase the number of their employees. The administration advertised the NRA and PRAs by sponsoring parades, advertisements, and sending 1.5 million volunteers door-to-door with a goal of getting 20 million people to sign pledges that they would support NRA firms (Taylor, 2010). Within a year most industries had established codes. In many sectors, codes were largely written by the leaders of trade associations with some influence by consumers, because relatively few industries had a strong union presence. Many small firms complained that the codes favoured the large firms that were so prominent in writing them (Bellush, 1975).

Microeconomists who study the NRA bluntly describe the codes as cartel arrangements enforced by the national government. The codes violated the antitrust laws and could only be put in place because the national government shut down antitrust enforcement. Cartel theory suggests that the effectiveness of a cartel agreement is often reduced because firms have incentives to ignore the rules by lowering price and selling more output. In fact, industries with more diverse firms and products had trouble coming to agreement on the codes and enforcing them. Industries had more success with more complex codes that established restrictions on capacity, production quotas, and provided for data collection for monitoring. The extent to which cartels raised prices and lowered output depended heavily on these rules. Firms signalled that they were following the codes by displaying the Blue Eagle symbol of the NRA, but town gossip suggested that a number of violators were displaying the symbol just as prominently. The Supreme Court struck down the NRA as unconstitutional in the Schechter Poultry Case in 1935. Unlike the AAA, there was little support for re-enacting the NRA and the Roosevelt administration let it die.[26] A few industries, however, were able to re-implement some provisions of their codes through separate legislation.

Macroeconomists have split on the impact of the National Recovery Act and high wage policies. Several studies suggest that Hoover's jawboning to maintain hourly wage rates at 1929 levels contributed to higher unemployment in the early 1930s, although they differ on the size of the impact. Simulations from a structural model built to measure the impact of cartels and high wage policies and the absence of antitrust enforcement suggest that the recovery from 1933 to 1939 was slowed substantially by the NRA and New Deal labour policies. In contrast, other macroeconomists see the NRA and high wage labour policies as part of a package of policies that included the move off the gold standard, increases in national spending, and looser Federal Reserve policy designed to abruptly change expectations about future deflation. Their simulations suggest that the policy package's success in reversing deflation was the key to keeping GDP from declining even

[26] Bellush (1975) offers a good administrative history of the NRA. Alexander (1997) and Kline and Taylor (2008) show the effect of diversity on difficulties in agreeing on and enforcing codes. Kline and Taylor (2008) and Taylor (2007, 2010) analyse the impact of NRA codes and PRA agreements on prices and quantity in various industries.

more after 1933. These studies, however, do not isolate the impact of the NRA alone.[27]

One goal of the NRA was for labour to share in the economic profits generated by the codes. An industry-fixed effects analysis of monthly data by industry from 1927 through to 1937 shows that hourly wage rates were substantially higher, and employment somewhat higher, when the labour-oriented PRAs were in place, but hourly wages were only slightly higher and total employment lower during the periods covered by NRA codes. These benefits were offset by weekly hours worked that were low enough that weekly wages were lower (Taylor, 2011).

10.7. UNION POLICY AND MINIMUM WAGES

The NRA, and other laws passed in the 1930s, dramatically changed the landscape for unionization. Some states had passed laws outlawing yellow dog (non-union) contracts, stopping injunctions against union activity, and providing antitrust protection for unions, while other states had laws that made it more difficult to unionize. The Clayton Act of 1914 had exempted unions from antitrust laws. In 1932, Hoover and the Republican Congress approved the Norris–LaGuardia Act that stopped injunctions against peaceful union activity by federal courts, outlawed yellow dog contracts, and allowed workers to form unions without employer interference. Section 7a of the NIRA established standard language for codes giving workers the right to bargain collectively through the agent of their choice. After the NRA was declared unconstitutional, The National Labor Relations (Wagner) Act of 1935 reestablished the right of workers to collective bargain through their own representatives from section 7a of the NIRA. Up to that time, the 'at will' doctrine of employment followed by the courts allowed either the employer or the worker to terminate the employment relationship. Employers had the right to refuse to negotiate with union representatives and the right to refuse to recognize a union, even in cases where the vast majority of workers had unionized. Under New Deal legislation, workers acquired the right to vote on union representation. When a majority of workers voted in favour, the employer was required to recognize the union and enter into a collective bargaining agreement. In addition, employers could no longer establish company unions as alternatives to independent organizations. The NLRB was established to oversee union elections and the collective bargaining process. Union membership expanded rapidly through a mixture of union recognition strikes and union elections, particularly after the Wagner Act was declared constitutional in 1937. In some cases, both before and during the 1930s, when the press for union recognition met staunch resistance from employers, strikes turned violent.

[27] For discussions of Hoover's high wage policies, see Ohanian (2009) and Rose (2010). Cole and Ohanian (2004) developed the simulations that show a negative effect of the NRA. Building on work by Temin and Wigmore (1990), Eggertsson (2008) and (2012) developed the simulations for the package of programmes that included the NRA.

One benefit of the NLRB policies was to regularize the union recognition process and the incidence of violent strikes has diminished sharply since.[28]

The Fair Labor Standards Act (FLSA) of 1938 established the national government role in setting a national minimum wage, overtime requirements, and child labour restrictions. By this time, many states had limited child labour with specific child labour laws and school attendance laws and provided laws to limit work hours for women. During the Progressive Era, proponents of wage and hour limits for male workers had long been frustrated by court decisions preventing limits on male labour contracts. The FLSA was passed when a significant subset of employers joined with union leaders and reformers to set a minimum that was most often binding only in low wage industries in the south, while agricultural workers, domestic workers, and employers not involved in interstate commerce were exempted from the act. In the aftermath of the act, northern firms expanded employment while southern firms reduced employment in the textile industry, as southern firms shifted toward new mechanized production processes. In the lumber industry, war-related government purchases of lumber fuelled a large boom in lumber output, but employment grew much faster in the north than in the south, even though a majority of southern lumber firms dropped out of interstate commerce to become exempt from the FLSA (Seltzer, 1997).

10.8. THE RECONSTRUCTION FINANCE CORPORATION

As the Federal Reserve System allowed the money supply to decline in the early 1930s, the Hoover administration sought other ways to inject liquidity into the economy by forming the RFC in February 1932. The RFC was modelled after the War Finance Corporation of World War One. Its first moves included making loans to 4,000 banks, railroads, credit unions, and mortgage loan companies to provide assets that would jumpstart commercial lending. Among the most important programmes was the provision of loans to troubled banks in an attempt to provide them with enough liquidity to survive bank runs. Recent studies suggest that these initial loans were not successful because the RFC loans were given first priority over depositors and other lenders in situations where the bank failed. As a result, banks had to hold the assets that they could sell most easily to ensure repayment of the RFC loans. These assets could not then be used to repay depositors when the bank failed. When the RFC began to accept more risk by purchasing preferred stock in the troubled banks, it was more successful at staving off bank failures.

The RFC gave the Roosevelt administration enormous flexibility. It retained control of a large supply of funds that could be loaned out and had the authority to borrow still more funds without having to constantly return to Congress for new appropriations. As the loans were repaid, the RFC had new funds to loan out again. 'By the mid-1930s, the RFC was making loans to banks, savings

[28] For descriptions of the state laws see Fishback, Holmes, and Allen (2009). Freeman (1998) describes the New Deal Labor Legislation.

banks, building and loan associations, credit unions, railroads, industrial banks, farmers, commercial businesses, federal land banks, production credit associations, farm cooperatives, mortgage loan companies, insurance companies, school districts, and livestock credit corporations' (Olson 1998: 43–4) Perhaps even more importantly, the RFC became the banker to many of the New Deal programmes, providing loans and/or startup capital to the FERA, PWA, Home Owners' Loan Corporation (HOLC), FCA, the Federal Housing Administration (FHA), REA, and the WPA.[29]

The RFC's record at stimulating recovery is mixed. Hoover's original goal for the RFC to expand commercial credit to 1929 levels was not met until the end of the 1930s. For example, RFC loans to railroads and industries helped delay bankruptcies for businesses and railroads with conflicting effects. The delays gave financial institutions more time to dump their railroad bonds. However, the railroads receiving RFC support delayed expenditures on maintenance and capital improvements, while the ones who went through bankruptcy made these investments because they were necessary to attract the necessary capital for reorganization.

10.9. NON-FARM HOUSING FINANCE

Between the late 1920s and early 1930s the housing and mortgage markets fell apart after a large-scale boom in housing following World War One. Between 1930 and 1934, housing prices in a group of representative communities had fallen an average of 33 per cent, 20 per cent more than non-housing prices fell during the period (Wickens, 1941). The number of non-farm housing starts fell from over 750,000 in most years in the 1920s to around 100,000 in 1933 (Grebler et al., 1956: Table L-6). As incomes declined, hundreds of thousands of families fell behind on their mortgage payments. Many mortgages were interest-only 3- to 5-year mortgages with a balloon payment of the principal, typically about 50 to 60 per cent of the value of the house when the loan ended. Many balloon payments came due in 1932, 1933, and 1934. In normal times, the mortgages were routinely renewed, but in the early 1930s most mortgage lenders had seen sharp drops in the funds available to loan and thus sought full repayment. Many lenders modified the loans in hope of future repayment but each new wave of mortgages coming due, and drops in loan funds, led to sharp increases in foreclosures.[30]

Between 1932 and 1933, 28 states passed foreclosure moratoria to give borrowers more time to repay and/or to make foreclosures more costly, but the moratoria were a stop-gap solution that made the situation worse for lenders. In 1932,

[29] The descriptions in this section on the RFC are based on Olson (1998) and Jones (1939, 1951), who was the director of the RFC. The discussion of the RFC's impact on railroad investments is based on Mason and Schiffman 2004. The impact of the RFC on bank failures is discussed in Mason (2001) and Mason and Mitchener (2010).

[30] The information on the HOLC comes from Rose (2011), Courtemanche and Snowden (2011), Fishback et al. (2011), and Fishback et al. (2012).

Hoover and the Republican Congress set up a Federal Home Loan Board of 12 regional banks to make short term discount loans to lenders who were in good condition and needed short term loans to fix temporary mismatches between their loan funds and borrower demands for mortgages. But the banks focused on building and loan associations and largely ignored other mortgage lenders. Further, they only offered discount loans that were backed by mortgages that were in good condition and did little for lenders with large numbers of non-performnig loans.

During the First Hundred Days, the HOLC was created to help non-farm mortgage borrowers in trouble through 'no fault of their own'. The HOLC purchased over 1 million loans from lenders. The program had two parts. First, troubled mortgages were acquired from lenders who were given national government guaranteed bonds for all or part of the principle, interest, insurance, and tax payments outstanding. In essence, the HOLC swapped their highly liquid bonds for the 'toxic' mortgages on the lenders books.

The HOLC then restructured the loans for the borrowers. Most had to repay their full debt, but they received generous loan terms. The HOLC interest rate nationwide was 5 per cent when market rates on good loans were 6 to 8 per cent. The original loans were replaced by amortized 15-year loans with equal payments that fully retired the debt at the end. Thus, the borrowers with short interest-only balloon loans could spread their payments over an extended period of time. Borrowers with longer-term hybrid loans from building and loan associations no longer faced uncertainty about the number of payments required to fully pay off the loan. The HOLC also offered an option where the borrowers could pay only interest for the first three years and then switch to the long-term amortized loan. In 1939, the interest rate was lowered to 4.5 per cent.

The original loans had been high quality loans with borrowers borrowing at most 60 per cent of the value of the home—75 per cent if they took out a second mortgage with double the normal interest rate. However, the drops in income and housing prices during the Depression had turned them into troubled loans. The typical HOLC borrower was over two years behind on principal and tax payments at the time the HOLC refinanced. As a result, the HOLC ended up foreclosing on nearly 20 per cent of the refinanced loans by 1940.

Estimates suggest the HOLC had significant effects on home ownership and housing prices in the roughly 2,500 counties (out of 3,060) with fewer than 50,000 people. Non-farm home ownership rates in these counties fell from 45 to 40 per cent between 1930 and 1940. Had the HOLC not been in operation, they probably would have fallen to 37 per cent. Non-farm housing price in these counties fell by 37 per cent but possibly would have fallen by 47 per cent without the HOLC. The same studies find weaker effects for larger counties, but the methods used for identification of the effects in the smaller counties were not as effective in larger counties (Courtemanche and Snowden, 2011; and Fishback et al., 2011).

Congress expected the HOLC to be a money losing proposition. Official government estimates suggest that, after the HOLC was wound down in 1951, the mortgage purchase and refinance programme lost about $53 million, or 2.7 per cent of the $3 billion in loans made. This possibly understates the true size of the subsidy given to housing markets because the HOLC's interest costs were lower as HOLC bonds were guaranteed by the national government. Had the HOLC not received the national guarantee, their interest costs likely would have been 1 to 3 percent higher. Each additional 1 per cent in interest costs would have raised the subsidy by $300 million more.

The New Deal created a variety of other housing finance programmes that had much longer term rather than shorter term effects on the economy. In 1934, the Federal Housing Administration began providing mortgage guarantees to lenders for Repair and Reconstruction loans for one- to four-unit family housing. In 1935, the guarantees were expanded to cover mortgage loans. After both were in operation, they were guaranteeing values of new loans each year equal to about 0.74 per cent of 1929 peak GDP. The Federal Savings and Loan Insurance Corporation (FSLIC) was created to guarantee deposits at Savings and Loans (S&L), which became the dominant lenders for non-farm properties in the 1930s. In 1938, Fannie Mae (Federal National Mortgage Association) was created to establish a secondary market for mortgages by purchasing mortgages from lenders and giving them more loan funds to make more mortgage loans. Originally backed by the national government, Fannie was supposed to have become an independent corporation with no government guarantees in 1968. In the autumn of 2008, however, Fannie was taken over by the government when it sank into financial trouble.

10.10. FINANCIAL REGULATIONS

Large numbers of banks failed during the early 1930s. Difficulties in the banking sector erupted again in January and February of 1933. President Hoover and President-Elect Roosevelt jockeyed over how to deal with these issues, while most states declared bank holidays to ease the financial pressures on commercial banks. The day after Roosevelt was inaugurated, he declared a National Bank Holiday and government auditors set to work to determine the soundness of the banks. Once declared sound, banks reopened, while negotiations began to improve the soundness of weaker banks. Within a month, the pressure of the Federal Reserve to maintain the gold standard was eliminated when the US moved off the gold standard and the dollar was devalued.

Roosevelt's Bank Holiday and the RFC bank loans were temporary methods for solving problems with bank panics. The New Deal also created more permanent solutions, including a wide variety of regulations and the development of new financial institutions that are still with us today. The Securities and

Exchange Commission (SEC) was established to monitor stock markets, reporting requirements for firms issuing stock, insider trading, and to enforce imposing rules on market trades. In commercial banking, the Banking Act of 1933 restricted interest payments on demand deposits with Regulation Q and created the 'Glass–Steagall' wall between commercial banks and investment banks by prohibiting depository institutions from serving as underwriters for securities.

The New Deal banking legislation did little to resolve the problems with bank failures caused by bans on branch banking by a large number of states. This emphasis on unit banks led quite a few to suspend payments during the 1920s and 1930s when their communities hit hard times because they did not have a diversified range of assets. Experiments with deposit insurance by state governments to stem the tide of bank failures in the early 1900s had proved largely unsuccessful. Even so, the Roosevelt administration established the Federal Deposit Insurance Corporation (FDIC) and the FSLIC to provide national government insurance of deposits up to a set limit.[31]

10.11. THE NEW DEAL AND LESSONS FOR THE PRESENT FOR FEDERAL SYSTEMS

The New Deal developed a wide range of programmes and regulations designed to solve a multitude of perceived problems in the economy. The tinkering extended to many smaller programmes and regulations not discussed in our survey. What was truly new about the New Deal was the creation of the AAA farm programmes to pay farmers to take land out of production, the nationwide Social Security programme for American workers, the NRA's codes of competition, the HOLC's purchase and refinance of mortgage loans, and federal financing of farm production loans. The NRA was eliminated by Supreme Court decree and the HOLC ended by design, but the other programmes continue today. A significant share of New Deal activity involved the federal government becoming involved in regulations and spending programmes that had long been handled by state and local governments. Another significant share of New Deal spending and regulation continued activities in which the federal government was already involved. The latest innovations in New Deal research have included a significant number of quantitative assessments of the local impacts of the various programmes that offer insights into which programmes were successful and which were not.

The New Deal also had significant impact on the location of government activity within the federal structure of US governments in four ways. First, the

[31] White (1998), Mason and Mitchener (2010), and Calomiris (2010) provide summaries of New Deal banking policies. The studies of state deposit insurance and problems in the banking industry were performed by Alston et al. (1994), Wheelock (1992), White (1983), Calomiris and White (2000), and Richardson and Chung (2003).

New Deal largely strengthened the role of the federal and state governments at the expense of local governments. Second, the national government began to give grants to state and local governments to aid them in dealing with poverty and unemployment and the building of local public works. These programmes typically involved large fiscal expenditures and joint funding and administration by the national and state governments. Third, regulatory programmes that influenced economic activity but had little fiscal impact were more likely to be nationally administered. Fourth, the spending programmes that persisted and became permanent tended to limit the discretion of national programme administrators in ways that reduced the ability of the national administrator to treat states differently. If a programme did not limit national discretion at its inception, as in the relief programmes, the programme either evolved limits or it was eliminated. Giving national administrators long run discretion over the distribution of funds across states was a power that was deeply resisted in the 1930s, as it had been deeply resisted in American political history since the 1770s.[32]

Rules rather than discretion were the order of the day in both the fiscal and regulatory programmes. Regulatory programmes were not just national in being administered by the national government, they were national in the sense of applying equally to everyone. This need not have been the case, as was amply shown in the early days of the New Deal when emergency programmes did not treat everyone the same.

What lessons do we draw from this part of the New Deal experience for the current economic and political crises? Americans already know these lessons and they were reflected in the response to the crisis in 2008. Europeans are just now going through the pressures and conflicts that a major economic downturn creates for a federal fiscal, monetary, and political union. So far, they seem to be largely ignoring the New Deal lessons. The fiscal crisis of member states has been transmitted throughout the EU through the banking system, the currency union, and the extensive holdings of national member government debts in the private banks of other EU countries. Rescuing the finances of member states has raised a whole host of unresolved political issues about fiscal relations between the centre and the members. As of early 2012, it appeared that the EU was attempting to move towards changing their political union in a manner that creates rules for the member states and discretion for the centre. This is exactly the opposite of the long run American experience, where rules for the centre and discretion within the rules for the member states have been the common pattern.

[32] It is interesting to note that the Great Society programmes of the 1960s, in which the national government dealt directly with local governments, were quickly eliminated after Reagan and the Republicans captured the presidency and the senate, but the Great Society programmes that were jointly administered with the states, particularly Medicare, have persisted.

BIBLIOGRAPHY

Administrator of Veterans' Affairs (1931), *Annual Report.* Washington, DC: Government Printing Office.

Administrator of Veterans' Affairs (1936), *Annual Report.* Washington, DC: Government Printing Office.

Alexander, B. (1997), 'Failed Cooperation in Heterogeneous Industries under the National Recovery Administration', *Journal of Economic History*, 57 (June), 322–44.

Alexander, B. and Libecap, G. (2000), 'The Effect of Cost Heterogeneity in the Success and Failure of the New Deal's Agricultural and Industrial Programs', *Explorations in Economic History*, 37 (October), 370–400.

Alston, L. J. (1981), 'Tenure Choice in Southern Agriculture', *Explorations in Economic History* 18 (1981), 211–32.

Alston, L. J. and Ferrie, J. (1999), *Southern Paternalism and the American Welfare State.* New York: Cambridge University Press.

Alston, L. J., Grove, W., and Wheelock, D. (1994), 'Why Do Banks Fail: Evidence from the 1920s', *Explorations in Economic History* 31 (October), 409–31.

Amenta, E. (1998), *Bold Relief: Institutional Politics and the Origins of Modern American Social Policy.* Princeton, NJ: Princeton University Press.

Anderson, G. M. and Tollison, R. D. (1991), 'Congressional Influence and Patterns of New Deal Spending, 1933–1939', *Journal of Law and Economics*, 34 (April), 161–75.

Arrington, L. J. (1970), 'Western Agriculture and the New Deal', *Agricultural History*, 49 (October), 337–53.

Baicker, K., Goldin, C., and Katz, L. (1998), 'A Distinctive System: Origins and Impact of US Unemployment Compensation', in M. Bordo, C. Goldin, and E. N. White (eds), *The Defining Moment: The Great Depression and the American Economy in the Twentieth Century.* Chicago: Chicago University Press.

Balan-Cohen, A. (2008), 'The Effect on Elderly Mortality: Evidence from the Old Age Assistance Programs in the United States', Unpublished working paper. Tufts University.

Barreca, A., Fishback, P., and Kantor, S. (2011), 'Agricultural Policy, Migration, and Malaria in the US in the 1930s', National Bureau of Economic Research Working Paper No. 17526.

Bellush, B. (1975), *The Failure of the NRA.* New York: Norton.

Benjamin, D. and Mathews, K. G. P. (1992), *US and UK Unemployment Between the Wars: A Doleful Story.* London: Institute for Economic Affairs.

Biles, R. (1994), *The South and the New Deal.* Lexington, Ky.: University of Kentucky Press.

Block, F., Cloward, R. A., Ehrenrich, B., and Piven, F. F. (1987), *The Mean Season: The Attack on the Welfare State.* New York: Pantheon Books.

Boustan, L., Fishback, P., and Kantor, S. (2010), 'The Effect of Internal Migration on Local Labor Markets: American Cities During the Great Depression.' *Journal of Labor Economics*, 28 (October), 719–46.

Bremer, W. W. (1984), *Depression Winters: New York Social Workers and the New Deal.* Philadelphia: Temple University Press,.

Brock, W. R. (1988), *Welfare, Democracy, and the New Deal.* New York: Cambridge University Press.

Brown, E. C. (1956), 'Fiscal Policy in the 'Thirties: A Reappraisal', *American Economic Review*, 46 (December), 857–79.

Calomiris, C. (2010), 'The Political Lessons of Depression-era Banking Reform', *Oxford Review of Economic Policy.* 26 (Autumn), 540–60.

Calomiris, C. and Wheelock, D. (1998), 'Was the Great Depression a Watershed for American Monetary Policy?', in M. Bordo, C. Goldin, and E. White (eds), *The Defining*

Moment: The Great Depression and the American Economy in the Twentieth Century. Chicago: University of Chicago Press, 23–66.

Calomiris, C. and White, E. N. (2000), 'The Origins of Federal Deposit Insurance', in C. Calomiris, *US Bank Deregulation in Historical Perspective.* New York: Cambridge University Press.

Carter, S., Gartner, S. G., Haines, M. R., Olmstead, A. L., Sutch, R., and Wright, G. (2004), *Millennial Edition of the Historical Statistics of the United States.* New York: Cambridge University Press,.

Clarke, J. N. (1996), *Roosevelt's Warrior: Harold L. Ickes and the New Deal.* Baltimore: Johns Hopkins University Press.

Clarke, S. (1994), *Regulation and the Revolution in United States Farm Productivity.* New York: Cambridge University Press.

Cole, H. and Ohanian, L. (2004), 'New Deal Policies and the Persistence of the Great Depression: A General Equilibrium Analysis,' *Journal of Political Economy* 112 (August), 779–816.

Commissioner of Internal Revenue (1937), *Annual Report of the Commissioner of Internal Revenue for the Fiscal Year ended June 30, 1937.* Washington: DC: Government Printing Office.

Costa, D. L. (1999), 'A House of Her Own: Old Age Assistance and the Living Arrangements of Older Nonmarried Women', *Journal of Public Economics,* 72, 39–59.

Couch, J. and Shughart II, W. (1998), *The Political Economy of the New Deal.* New York: Edward Elgar.

Courtemanche, C. and Snowden, K. (2011), 'Repairing a Mortgage Crisis: HOLC Lending and Its Impact on Local Housing Markets', *Journal of Economic History* 71 (June), 307–37.

Depew, B., Fishback, P., and Rhode, P. (2012), 'New Deal or No Deal in the Cotton South: The Effect of the AAA on the Labor Structure in Agriculture'. Working paper, University of Arizona.

Eggertsson, G. (2008), 'Great Expectations and the End of the Depression', *American Economic Review* 98 (4), 1476–516.

Eggertsson, G. (2012), 'Was the New Deal Contractionary', *American Economic Review* 102 (February): 524–55.

Fearon, P. (2007), *Kansas in the Great Depression: Work Relief, the Dole, and Rehabilitation.* Columbia, Mo.: University of Missouri Press.

Federal Farm Loan Board (1930), *Annual Report of the Federal Farm Loan Board.* Washington, DC: Government Printing Office.

Federal Farm Loan Board (1932), *Annual Report of the Federal Farm Loan Board.* Washington, DC: Government Printing Office.

Fishback, P. (2010), 'Monetary and Fiscal Policy During the Great Depression', *Oxford Review of Economic Policy.* 26 (Autumn), 385–413.

Fishback, P. and Kachanovskaya, V. (2011), 'In Search of the Multiplier for Federal Spending in the States During the Great Depression', National Bureau of Economic Research Working Paper No. 16561.

Fishback, P. and Thomasson, M. (2006), 'Social Welfare: 1929 to the Present', in S. B. Carter, S. G. Gartner, M. R. Haines, A. L. Olmstead, R. Sutch, and G. Wright (eds), *Historical Statistics of the United States: Earliest Times to the Present, Millennial Edition.* New York: Cambridge University Press, 2-700–719.

Fishback, P., Haines, M. R., and Kantor, S. (2001), 'The Impact of the New Deal on Black and White Infant Mortality in the South', *Explorations in Economic History,* 38 (January), 93–122.

Fishback, P., Haines. M. R., and Kantor, S. (2007), 'Births, Deaths, and New Deal Relief During the Great Depression', *Review of Economics and Statistics,* 89 (February), 1–14.

Fishback, P., Holmes, R., and Allen, S. (2009), 'Lifting the Curse of Dimensionality: Measures of the Labor Legislation Climate in the States During the Progressive Era', *Labor History* 50 (August 2009), 313–46.

Fishback, P., Horrace, W., and Kantor, S. (2004), 'Did New Deal Grant Programs Stimulate Local Economies? A Study of Federal Grants and Retail Sales During the Great Depression', National Bureau of Economic Research Working Paper W8108

Fishback, P., Horrace, W., and Kantor, S. (2005), 'Did New Deal Grant Programs Stimulate Local Economies? A Study of Federal Grants and Retail Sales During the Great Depression', *The Journal of Economic History*, 65 (March), 36–71.

Fishback, P., Horrace, W., and Kantor, S. (2006), 'The Impact of New Deal Expenditures on Mobility During the Great Depression', *Explorations in Economic History*, 43 (April), 179–222.

Fishback, P., Kantor, S., and Wallis, J. (2003), 'Can the New Deal's Three R's Be Rehabilitated? A Program-by-Program, County-by-County Analysis', *Explorations in Economic History*, 40 (October), 278–307.

Fishback, P., Rose, J., and Snowden, K. (2012), 'HOLC: Fending off Foreclosures in the Great Depression', Unpublished Book Manuscript.

Fishback, P., Flores-Lagunes, A., Horrace, W., Kantor, S., and Treber, J. (2011), 'The Influence of the Home Owners' Loan Corporation on Housing Markets During the 1930s', *Review of Financial Studies*, 24 (July), 1782–813.

Fishback, P., Higgs, R., Libecap, G., Wallis, J., Engerman, S., Hummel, J., LaCroix, S., Margo, R., McGuire, R., Sylla, R., Alston, L., Ferrie, J., Guglielmo, M., Pasour, E. C. Jr., Rucker, R., and Troesken, W. (2007), *Government and the American Economy: A New History*. Chicago, Ill.: University of Chicago Press.

Fleck, R. (1999a), 'Electoral Incentives, Public Policy, and the New Deal Realignment', *Southern Economic Journal*, 63 (January), 377–404.

Fleck, R. (1999b), 'The Marginal Effect of New Deal Relief Work on County-Level Unemployment Statistics', *Journal of Economic History*, 59 (September), 659–87.

Fleck, R. (1999c), 'The Value of the Vote: A Model and Test of the Effects of Turnout on Distributive Policy', *Economic Inquiry*, 37 (October), 609–23.

Fleck, R. (2001a), 'Inter-party Competition, Intra-party Competition, and Distributive Policy: A Model and Test using New Deal Data', *Public Choice*, 108 (July), 77–100.

Fleck, R. (2001b), 'Population, Land, Economic Conditions, and the Allocation of New Deal Spending', *Explorations in Economic History*, 38 (April), 296–304.

Fleck, R. (2008), 'Voter Influence and Big Policy Change: The Positive Political Economy of the New Deal', *Journal of Political Economy*, 116, 1–37.

Freeman, R. (1998), 'Spurts In Union Growth: Defining Moments and Social Processes', in M. Bordo, C. Goldin, and E. N. White (eds), *The Defining Moment: The Great Depression and the American Economy in the Twentieth Century*. Chicago, Ill.: University of Chicago Press, 265–96.

Friedberg, L. (1999), 'The Effect of Old Age Assistance on Retirement', *Journal of Public Economics*, 71, 213–32.

Grebler, L., Blank, D. M., and Winnick, L. (1956), *Capital Formation in Residential Real Estate: Trends and Prospects*. Princeton, NJ: Princeton University Press.

Gruber, J. and Hungerman, D. (2007), 'Faith-Based Charity and Crowd Out During the Great Depression', *Journal of Public Economics*, 91, 1043–69.

Halcrow, H. G. (1953), *Agricultural Policy of the United States*. New York: Prentice-Hall Inc.

Hansen, Z. and Libecap, G. (2004), 'Small Farms, Externalities, and the Dust Bowl of the 1930s', *Journal of Political Economy*, 112 (June), 665–94.

Howard, D. S. (1943), *The WPA and Federal Relief Policy*. New York: Russell Sage Foundation.

Johnson, R., Fishback, P., and Kantor, S. (2010), 'Striking at the Roots of Crime: The Impact of Social Welfare Spending on Crime During the Great Depression', *Journal of Law and Economics*, 53 (November), 715–40.

Jones, J. H. (1939), *Reconstruction Finance Corporation Seven-Year Report to the President and the Congress of the United States, February 2, 1932 to February 2, 1939*. Reconstruction Finance Corporation pamphlet.

Jones, J. H. (with Edward Angly) (1951), *Fifty Billion Dollars: My Thirteen Years with the RFC (1932–1945)*. New York: The MacMillan Company.

Keynes, J. M. (1964), *The General Theory of Money, Interest, and Prices*. New York: A Harbinger Book, Harcourt, Brace and World Inc.

Kitchens, C. (2011a), 'A Dam Problem: TVA's Fight Against Malaria 1926–1951', Working Paper, University of Arizona.

Kitchens, C. (2011b), 'The Role of Publicly Provided Electricity in Economic Development: The Experience of the Tennessee Valley Authority, 1929–1955', Working Paper, University of Arizona.

Kline, P. and Taylor, J. (2008), 'Anatomy of a Cartel: The National Industrial Recovery Act of 1933 and the Compliance Crisis of 1934', *Research in Economic History*, 26, 235–71.

Kline, P. and Moretti, E. (2011), 'Can Public Investment Shift Regional Growth Equilibria? 100 Years of Evidence from the Tennessee Valley Authority', Unpublished Working Paper, University of California, Berkeley.

Kollmann, T. and Fishback. P. (2011), 'The New Deal, Race, and Home Ownership in the 1920s and 1930s', *American Economic Review Papers and Proceedings*, 101 (May), 366–70.

Libecap, G. (1998), 'The Great Depression and the Regulating State: Federal Government Regulation of Agriculture, 1884–1970', in M. Bordo, C. Goldin, and E. N. White (eds), *The Defining Moment: The Great Depression and the American Economy in the Twentieth Century*. Chicago: Chicago University Press.

Lindert, P. (2004), *Growing Public: Social Spending and Economic Growth Since the Eighteenth Century*. New York: Cambridge University Press.

Livingston, B. (2011), 'Interactions Between Private and Public Relief', PhD Dissertation, University of Arizona.

Maher, N. H. (2008), *Nature's New Deal: The Civilian Conservation Corp and the Roots of the American Environmental Movement*. New York: Oxford University Press.

Margo, R. (1991), 'The Microeconomics of Depression Unemployment', *Journal of Economic History*, 51 (June), 333–41.

Margo, R. (1993), 'Employment and Unemployment in the 1930s', *Journal of Economic Perspectives*, 7 (Spring), 41–59.

Mason, J. (2001), 'Do Lenders of Last Resort Policies Matter? The Effects of the Reconstruction Finance Corporation Assistance to Banks During the Great Depression', *Journal of Financial Services Research*, 20 (September), 77–95.

Mason, J. and Mitchener, K. (2010), '"Blood and Treasure": Exiting the Great Depression and Lessons for Today', *Oxford Review of Economic Policy*,. 26 (Autumn), 510–39.

Mason, J. and Schiffman, D. (2004), 'Too-Big-to-Fail, Government Bailouts, and Managerial Incentives: The Case of Reconstruction Finance Corporation Assistance to the Railroad Industry During the Great Depression', Working paper presented at the ASSA meetings in San Diego, CA, January.

Moley, R. (1966), *The First New Deal*. New York: Harcourt, Brace, and World.

Neumann, T., Fishback, P., and Kantor, S. (2010), 'The Dynamics of Relief Spending and the Private Urban Labor Market During the New Deal', *Journal of Economic History*, 70 (March), 195–220.

Nourse, E. G., Davis, J. S., and Black, J. D. (1937), *Three Years of the Agricultural Adjustment Administration*. Washington, DC: The Brookings Institution.

Ohanian, L. (2009), 'Who or What Started the Great Depression', *Journal of Economic Theory*, 144 (November), 2310–35.
Olson, J. S. (1998), *Saving Capitalism: The Reconstruction Finance Corporation and the New Deal.* Princeton, NJ: Princeton University Press.
Parsons, D. O. (1991), 'Male Retirement Behavior in the United States, 1930–1950', *Journal of Economic History*, 51, 657–74.
Peppers, L. (1973), 'Full Employment Surplus Analysis and Structural Change: The 1930s', *Explorations in Economic History*, 10 (Winter), 197–210.
Piven, F. F. and Cloward, R. A. (1971), *Regulating the Poor: The Functions of Public Welfare.* New York: Pantheon Books.
Reading, D. C. (1973), 'New Deal Activity and the States, 1933 to 1939', *Journal of Economic History*, 33 (December), 792–810.
Richardson, G. and Chung, C.-Y. (2003), 'Deposit Insurance in Developing Economies: Lessons from the Archives of the Board of Governors and the 1920s State Deposit-Insurance Experiments'. Paper presented at Cliometrics Conference in Raleigh, NC, May.
Rose, J. (2010), 'Hoover's Truce: Wage Rigidity in the Onset of the Great Depression', *Journal of Economic History*, 70 (December), 843–70.
Rose, J. (2011), 'The Incredible HOLC: Mortgage Relief During the Great Depression', *Journal of Money, Credit, and Banking*, 43 (September), 1073–107.
Saloutos, T. (1982), *The American Farmer and the New Deal.* Ames, Iowa: Iowa State University Press.
Schlesinger, A., Jr. (1958), *The Age of Roosevelt: The Coming of the New Deal.* Boston: Houghton-Mifflin.
Seltzer, A. J. (1997), 'The Effects of the Fair Labor Standards Act of 1938 on the Southern Seamless Hosiery and Lumber Industries', *Journal of Economic History*, 57 (June), 396–415.
Social Security Board (1939), 'Public Assistance Statistics for the United States, May, 1939', *Social Security Bulletin*, 2 (May).
Sorensen, T., Fishback, P., Kantor, S., and Rhode, P. (2011), 'The New Deal and the Diffusion of Tractors in the 1930s'. Working paper, University of Arizona.
Stecker, M. L. (1937), 'Intercity Differences in Cost of Living in March 1935, 59 Cities', *Works Progress Administration Research* Monography XII. Washington, DC: US Government Printing Office.
Stoian, A. and Fishback, P. (2010), 'Welfare Spending and Mortality Rates for the elderly Before the Social Security Era', *Explorations in Economic History*, 47 (January), 1–27.
Stromberg, D. (2004), 'Radio's Impact on Public Spending', *Quarterly Journal of Economics*, 119 (February), 189–221.
Taylor, J. (2007), 'Cartel Codes Attributes and Cartel Performance: An Industry-Level Analysis of the National Industrial Recovery Act', *Journal of Law and Economics*, 50 (August), 597–624.
Taylor, J. (2010), 'The Welfare Impact Of Collusion Under Various Industry Characteristics: A Panel Examination Of Efficient Cartel Theory', *The B.E. Journal of Economic Analysis & Policy*: Vol. 10: Issue 1, Article 97, 1–27.
Taylor, J. (2011), 'Work-Sharing During the Great Depression: Did the "President's Reemployment Agreement" Promote Reemployment?', *Economica*, 78, 133–58.
Temin, P. and Wigmore, B. (1990), 'The End of One Big Deflation', *Explorations in Economic History*, 27 (October), 483–502.
US Census Bureau (1975), *Historical Statistics of the United States: From Colonial Times to 1970.* Washington, DC: Government Printing Office.
Wallis, J. J. (1981), *Work Relief and Unemployment in the 1930s.* Unpublished PhD dissertation, University of Washington.

Wallis, J. J. (1984), 'The Birth of the Old Federalism: Financing the New Deal, 1932–1940', *Journal of Economic History*, 44 (March), 139–59.

Wallis, J. J. (1985), 'Why 1933? The Origins and Timing of National Government Growth, 1933–1940', *Research in Economic History*, 4, 1–51.

Wallis, J. J. (1987), 'Employment, Politics, and Economic Recovery During the Great Depression', *Review of Economics and Statistics*, 69 (August), 516–20.

Wallis, J. J. (1991), 'The Political Economy of New Deal Fiscal Federalism', *Economic Inquiry*, 39 (July), 510–24.

Wallis, J. J. (1998), 'The Political Economy of New Deal Spending Revisited, Again: With and Without Nevada', *Explorations in Economic History*, 35 (April), 140–70.

Wallis, J. J. (2001), 'The Political Economy of New Deal Spending, Yet Again: A Reply to Fleck', *Explorations in Economic History*, 38 (April), 305–14.

Wallis, J. J. and Benjamin, D. K. (1981), 'Public Relief and Private Employment in the Great Depression', *Journal of Economic History*, 41 (March), 97–102.

Wallis, J. J., Fishback, P.V., and Kantor, S. E. (2006), 'Politics, Relief, and Reform: Roosevelt's Efforts to Control Corruption and Manipulation During the New Deal', in E. Glaeser and C. Goldin, *Corruption and Reform*. NBER Volume. Chicago: University of Chicago Press.

Whatley, W. C. (1983), 'Labor for the Picking: The New Deal in the South', *Journal of Economic History*, 43 (December), 905–29.

Whatley, W. C. (1985), 'A History of Mechanization in the Cotton South: The Institutional Hypothesis', *The Quarterly Journal of Economics*, 100 (November), 1191–215.

Wheelock, D. (1992), 'Deposit Insurance and Bank Failures: New Evidence from the 1920s', *Economic Inquiry*, 30 (July), 530–43.

White, E. N. (1983), *The Regulation and Reform of the American Banking System: 1900–1929*. Princeton, NJ: Princeton University Press.

White, E. N. (1998), 'The Legacy of Deposit Insurance: The Growth, Spread, and Cost of Insuring Financial Intermediaries', in M. D. Bordo, C. Goldin, and E. N. White (eds), *The Defining Moment: The Great Depression and the American Economy in the Twentieth Century*. Chicago: University of Chicago Press, 87–121.

Wickens, D. (1941), *Residential Real Estate: Its Economic Position As Shown by Values, Rents, Family Incomes, Financing and Construction, Together with Estimates for All Real Estate*. New York: National Bureau of Economic Research.

Williams, E. A. (1939), *Federal Aid for Relief*. New York: AMS Press.

Wright, G. (1974), 'The Political Economy of New Deal Spending: An Econometric Analysis', *Review of Economics and Statistics*, 56 (February), 30–8.

11

Labour Markets in Recession and Recovery: The UK and the USA in the 1920s and 1930s

Timothy J. Hatton and Mark Thomas[1]

11.1. INTRODUCTION

The sharp and deep recession that followed the recent global financial crisis invites comparison with the Great Depression of the 1930s. Most of the initial focus in the literature has been on comparing the magnitude of the demand side shocks, and the strength and effectiveness of the policy response (Almunia et al., 2010). Attention has now turned firmly to the role of monetary and fiscal policies in speeding up or slowing down the recovery. Here too, historical comparisons are instructive (Crafts and Fearon, 2010). However, a sustained recovery depends not just on aggregate demand effects but also on how well the supply side responds. As the interwar period is famous above all for its persistently high unemployment, it is natural to look at the labour market response in that era.

In this chapter, we focus not only on the Great Depression of the 1930s but also on the 1920s, especially the early 1920s. The downturn of 1920–22 was short and sharp with an early recovery, while that of the 1929–31 was the prelude to a protracted period of high unemployment. Our approach is to compare the UK and the US in the two recoveries in the hope of gaining greater insight into the economic and institutional factors that were at work. For our underlying framework we draw on a literature that stresses the role of labour market institutions and their interactions with economic shocks as sources of labour market rigidity (Nickell, 1997; 2000; Blanchard and Wolfers, 2000; Layard et al., 2005).

We argue that, in the UK, the equilibrium unemployment rate shifted up in the 1920s (as compared with pre-World War One), with no further shift in the 1930s. By contrast, the US labour market behaved in the 1920s much as in the pre-World War One period, but equilibrium unemployment rose in the 1930s. Higher UK unemployment in the 1920s owed much to the evolution of labour market

[1] This chapter is a revised version of an earlier paper that was presented at the British Academy conference *Lessons from the 1930s Great Depression for the Making of Economic Policy*, and that subsequently appeared in the *Oxford Review of Economic Policy*, Vol. 26: 463–85. Special thanks are due for helpful comments from our discussant at the conference Chris Minns, to Price Fishback and Wendy Carlin, two anonymous referees, and to the editors, Nick Crafts and Peter Fearon.

institutions: the rise of trade unionism, the widening scope of collective bargaining, and the advent of a national system of unemployment insurance, as well as a sharp cut in working hours. These developments were either more muted or totally absent in the United States. In the 1930s there was little institutional change in the UK labour market, although some of the rigidities stemming from the 1920s remained. But policies under the New Deal led to growing labour market rigidity in the US. These included agreements on working hours and minimum wages and the introduction of relief projects. We then explore two potential causes of unemployment hysteresis: the spatial dispersion of unemployment and the rise of long-term unemployment. We suggest that the interaction of shocks and institutions caused the depression to persist in the late 1930s and we argue that high unemployment was ultimately brought to an end by the onset of the Second World War, with little help from equilibrating forces in the labour market. Finally we draw some comparisons between labour market conditions in the interwar period and in the current global recession.

11.2. UNEMPLOYMENT, WAGES, AND PRICES

The profiles of the unemployment rate in the UK and the US during the interwar period are generally well known. But it is worth extending the comparison back to the period before the First World War. Comparisons before and after the First World War are possible using the series provided by Boyer and Hatton (2002) for the UK and by Weir (1992) for the US.[2] These series are plotted in Figure 11.1. They illustrate that from 1890 to 1913 average unemployment rates were very similar in the two countries: 6.0 per cent for the UK and 5.7 per cent for the US. Movements in unemployment between the two countries were not highly synchronized—the correlation coefficient is only 0.2. But there are similarities in the short sharp recession of 1907–08 and the more protracted slump of the 1890s. However, the most important point to emerge is that until the 1920s the unemployment rate never exceeded 10 per cent in either country.

By contrast, average unemployment rates were substantially higher in the interwar period. For 1920–39 they averaged 10.5 per cent in the UK and 9.7 per cent in the US; the correlation between the two series is also stronger at 0.83. As Figure 11.1 shows, there was a sharp increase in unemployment between 1920 and 1921 which pushed the unemployment rate above 10 per cent in both countries. But then the histories diverge: while the US unemployment rate fell to levels resembling the pre-war average, the UK unemployment rate did not.[3] For our purposes, this is important because it is indicative of changes in the UK labour market that were not shared with the US. Unemployment rose steeply in both

[2] Although these are the best available time series, the methods of construction differ over time and between countries. The UK data are based on trade union unemployment rates before 1914 and on unemployment insurance statistics in the interwar period. The US data are based on estimates of employment and interpolated figures for the labour force.

[3] This is also reflected in the correlation between the two series, which is 0.49 for 1920–29 and 0.87 for 1929–38.

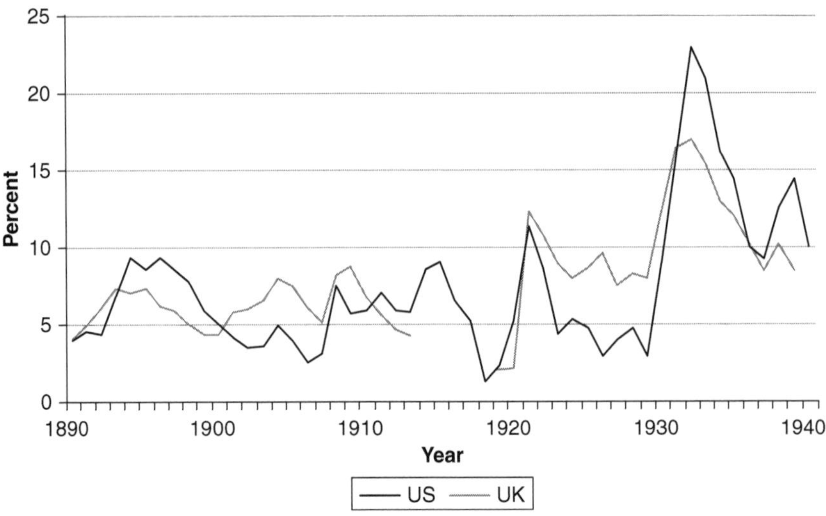

Fig. 11.1. Unemployment rates, 1890–1940

Sources: US: Weir (1992: 341–2); UK: Boyer and Hatton (2002: 667).

Notes: For the US in the 1930s relief workers are counted as employed.

countries after 1929 but the recession was much worse in the United States where the unemployment rate peaked at 23 per cent in 1932 as compared with 17 per cent in the UK. After that, unemployment then fell somewhat faster in the US than in Britain, reaching its lowest point in 1937 by which time the unemployment rate was 9.2 per cent, compared to 8.5 per cent in the UK.[4]

Annual inflation rates for prices and wages are displayed in Figures 11.2 and 11.3. For both countries, prices were fairly stable before 1914 with slightly more volatility in the US than in the UK. The First World War saw prices soar in both countries with peak inflation rates in excess of 20 per cent in 1917. This was followed by a severe deflation between 1920 and 1922, which saw the GDP deflators fall by nearly 25 per cent in both countries. Nominal wage rates followed a similar pattern. For the rest of the 1920s price and wage fluctuations in the UK were fairly mild with some upward drift at the end of the 1930s. In the US there were larger gyrations in the early 1930s with the price level falling by more that 20 per cent between 1929 and 1933, followed by milder fluctuations for the rest of the 1930s.

The causes and effects of fluctuations in wages and prices have been widely studied and we comment only briefly on the results. Multi-country studies of wage setting have generally found a degree of nominal inertia in wage setting (Newell and Symons 1988; Bernanke and Carey, 1996; Madsen, 2004). The consensus is that nominal inertia was somewhat greater for wages than for prices. Thus, a demand shock raised the real (product) wage, especially in the manufacturing

[4] The US figures, following Weir (1992), count relief workers as employed. If they are treated as unemployed, the unemployment rate peaks at 25 per cent in 1933 and reaches a low in 1937 of 14 per cent.

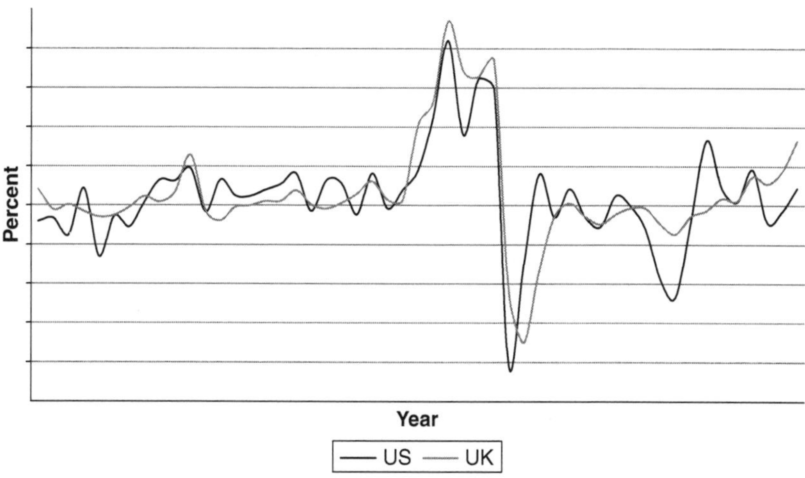

Fig. 11.2. Annual price inflation, 1890–1940

Sources: US: Balke and Gordon (1986: 782–3); UK: Feinstein (1972: T132–3).

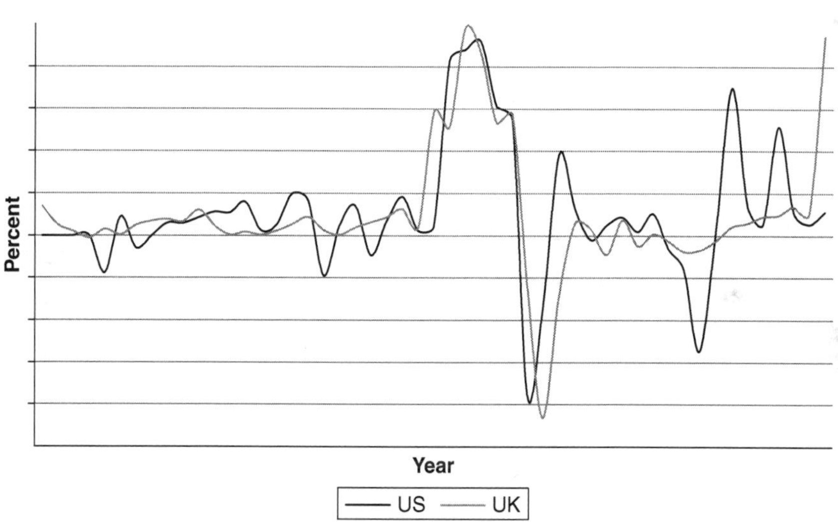

Fig. 11.3. Annual wage inflation, 1890–1940

Source: US: David and Solar (1977: 59); UK: Feinstein (1995: 263–6).

sector, and caused (or at least added to) the decline in employment in the early 1930s. Studies for the UK typically find that employment was negatively related to the real wage; the main difference among them being the degree to which other variables also mattered (Beenstock and Warburton, 1991; Dimsdale et al., 1989; Hatton, 1988b). Much of the research agenda on the US labour market of the 1930s has been directed at finding an explanation for the 'puzzling' positive correlation of unemployment and real wages (Jensen, 1989; O'Brien, 1989; Hanes, 2000; Cole and Ohanian, 2004; quote from Margo, 1993: 43).

Table 11.1. Unemployment in the UK and US 1891–1913 and 1920–39 (dependent variable: log U_t)

	UK	UK	US	US	Difference UK-US	Difference UK-US
Constant	0.59	0.84	0.77	0.72	−0.00	−0.01
	(3.7)	(4.7)	(4.3)	(4.3)	(0.1)	(0.1)
Log U_{t-1}	0.66	0.52	0.56	0.59	0.62	0.62
	(7.4)	(5.2)	(5.4)	(6.1)	(5.8)	(6.0)
$\Delta\Delta$Log P_t	−3.77		−1.86		−0.78	
	(6.5)		(3.0)		(0.9)	
$\Delta\Delta$Log W_t		−2.87		−2.08		−0.81
		(4.1)		(4.0)		(1.4)
Dummy 1921–1939	0.17	0.24	−0.14	−0.14	0.37	0.37
	(2.2)	(2.8)	(1.2)	(1.3)	(3.1)	(3.2)
Dummy 1930–1939	0.10	0.12	0.61	0.58	−0.51	−0.51
	(1.2)	(1.1)	(4.0)	(4.0)	(3.6)	(3.7)
Adj R^2	0.83	0.75	0.74	0.77	0.61	0.62
DW	1.62	1.93	1.52	1.32	1.85	1.86
No obs.	43	43	43	43	43	43

In Table 11.1, we analyse the unemployment rates observed in Figure 11.1 by relating them to price and wage changes using an inverted Phillips curve. The natural log of the unemployment rate is related to its own lagged value and to price or wage shocks as represented by the change in the relevant inflation rate. This can be derived from a model with nominal inertia in wage setting and a downward sloping labour demand curve (see Appendix at the end of this chapter). In the long run, this equation provides a version of the non-accelerating inflation rate of unemployment (NAIRU). The purpose here is to explore further the differences in unemployment behaviour in the 1920s and 1930s as compared with before the First World War. In each regression we introduce a dummy for 1921 to 1939 and another dummy for 1930–39. These two dummies, starting in the years following the cyclical peaks, are intended to capture shifts in the NAIRU. For both countries, the regressions are estimated over 1891 to 1939, omitting the years 1914 to 1919.

The first two regressions in Table 11.1 show that there is considerable persistence in the UK unemployment rate as reflected in the coefficient on the lagged dependent variable. Unemployment is negatively related to price or wage shocks and in both regressions there is a significant upward shift in the unemployment rate from 1921 onwards. Using the wage equation in the second column, this implies an increase in the NAIRU for the UK of about four percentage points, from 5.7 per cent to 9.5 per cent. The coefficient on the dummy for 1930–39 implies a further upward shift, but it is not significant. The same regressions for the US are shown in the third and fourth columns of the Table. There is about the same level of persistence in the unemployment rate as for the UK but somewhat smaller price and wage coefficients. By contrast with the UK, the coefficient for 1921 onwards is negative and not significant while the coefficient for the 1930–39 dummy is positive and significant. Using the wage equation, this implies a significant increase in the NAIRU of more than 12 percentage points, from 4.2 per cent to 16.9 per cent.[5]

The rise in average unemployment in the 1930s probably overestimates the increase in the NAIRU as both countries struggled to recover from the global shock. To the extent that the two countries experienced common shocks that are not accounted for in this simple model, this can be overcome by estimating in differences. In the fourth and fifth columns of Table 11.1, the dependent variable is the difference between the logs of the UK unemployment rate and the US unemployment rate, with the other variables treated similarly. The constant in these equations is very close to zero, indicating that there was essentially no difference before 1914. While lagged unemployment gives results that are similar to those in columns 1–4, differences in wage and price shocks are insignificant. In part, this reflects the fact that the shocks are correlated; the correlation coefficient over the estimation period is 0.7 for price shocks and 0.4 for wage shocks. The dummy for 1921 onwards is strongly positive, implying that the UK NAIRU shifted up relative to the US in the 1920s, while the dummy for the 1930s is negative, implying that this was (more than) reversed in the 1930s.

The regressions in Table 11.1 are illustrative rather than definitive. They are based on a simple model of the NAIRU that does not explicitly incorporate demand shocks or structural features of the labour market. Nonetheless, they confirm the differing evolution of average unemployment rates that can be seen in Figure 11.1. Its key implication is this: if we wish to identify the labour market forces that led to persistently high unemployment we should look at the 1920s in the UK and the 1930s in the US.

11.3. LABOUR MARKETS AND INSTITUTIONS IN THE 1920s

Between 1913 and the early 1920s there were radical changes in the UK labour market. Some of these developments had been in train since the 1890s but were sharply accelerated during and immediately after the First World War. To many contemporary observers, these changes placed upward pressure on wage rates and made them less flexible, so that negative demand shocks could be less easily accommodated. In 1927 A. C. Pigou wrote:

> In the post-war period... There is strong reason to believe that an important change has taken place in this respect; that, partly through direct state action, and partly through the added strength given to workpeople's organisations engaged in wage bargaining by the development of unemployment insurance, wage rates have, over a wide area, been set at a level which is too high... and that the very large percentage of unemployment which has prevailed during the whole of the last six years is due in considerable measure to this new factor in our economic life (Pigou, 1927: 355).

[5] As an alternative, the regressions for the US were estimated using the series that count relief workers as unemployed (Figure 11.4). The coefficients for the US 1930s dummy are larger (around 0.7 for the US alone and 0.6 for the UK–US difference) but are almost identical in other respects.

One key element was the growth of membership in trade unions. Trade union density increased sharply in the years before the war, from 12 per cent of the labour force in 1900 to 22 per cent in 1913. There were also important changes in the legal background to trade union action, most notably in the Trade Disputes Act of 1906 and the Trade Union Act of 1913. Unionization increased even more strongly over the war, to peak at 44 per cent in 1920 before declining to 26 per cent in 1929. As a result, union density in the 1920s was twice that of the pre-war decade. There were also qualitative changes, as unionism spread to less skilled workers in a widening range of industries and (increasingly unskilled) occupations. Not surprisingly, some observers have interpreted interwar wage setting in a formal framework of bargaining between employers and unions (Broadberry, 1986; Matthews, 1986).

The revolution in bargaining over pay was not simply one of numbers. The strength of unions in pay bargaining was also enhanced by the development of formal collective bargaining structures. In 1910, the Board of Trade recorded 1,696 collective agreements covering a total of 2.4 million workers, or 13 per cent of the labour force. Collective agreements were given a boost during the war by the establishment of wage councils, which were set up on the recommendation of the Whitley Reports (1917–18). In trades and occupations where there was insufficient organization among workers and employers for collective negotiation, the gap was filled by trade boards that set minimum wages. Established in four low paid sectors under the Trade Boards Act of 1909, their scope was radically expanded in the Trade Boards Act of 1918 and by 1921 there were 63 trade boards covering 3 million workers. The Trade Boards diminished in strength during the 1920s, but in 1935 there were still 47 trade boards covering 1.1 million workers.

Taken together, these forms of centralized wage setting machinery covered about half of the labour force in 1920, declining slightly to 44 per cent by 1937 (Thomas, 1992: 278). But their structure was very fragmented along industrial and occupational lines. Some observers have argued that wage rigidity is related to the degree of centralization in the bargaining structure and the degree of coordination in wage bargaining across sectors (Calmfors and Driffill, 1988; Soskice, 1990). When unions are strong, but the bargaining structure is fragmented and uncoordinated, individual wage bargains do not take into account the economy-wide effects of the bargains independently struck in each sector.[6] By contrast, with atomistic wage bargaining at the local or firm level, wage bargainers take into account the effect on employment of the high elasticity of demand faced by the individual firm in an industry. Thus potential job losses lead to moderation in wage claims. At the other extreme, when wage setting is coordinated through an encompassing institutional wage structure, a wage increase affects all firms equally. But centralized wage setters are more likely to take into account the economy-wide effects of their actions and therefore to coordinate on a set of wage bargains that would be consistent with high employment. The interwar system of

[6] This lack of coordination is illustrated by Keynes' comment a year before the general strike of 1926: 'Our export industries are suffering because they are the *first* to be asked to accept the 10 percent [wage] reduction. If *every one* was accepting a similar reduction at the same time, the cost of living would fall, so that the lower money wage would represent nearly the same real wage as before. But, in fact, there is no machinery for effecting a simultaneous reduction' (1931: 247).

collective bargaining in the UK seems to fall in the region of greater wage rigidity somewhere between the two extremes (Hatton, 1988a; Thomas, 1992).[7]

Perhaps the most controversial issue in the debate over unemployment in interwar Britain is the role of unemployment benefits. Until 1911 the only benefits available to the unemployed were from trade union benefit funds or from the Poor Law. Unemployment insurance, first introduced in a few cyclically sensitive sectors, was radically expanded in 1920–21. Coverage increased from 24 per cent of the labour force in 1920 to 63 per cent in 1921, and from 1921 to 1929 the average benefit to wage ratio for adult male workers was 45.6 per cent. In their controversial paper, Benjamin and Kochin (1979) argued that this reduced effective labour supply as workers chose to search longer or less intensively for jobs. However, microeconometric evidence on the incidence of unemployment has not been kind to this argument (Eichengreen, 1986; Hatton and Bailey, 2002). It seems more likely that unemployment insurance influenced the wage rates set in collective bargains by further reducing the weight placed on the consequences for unemployment. This is how its influence was seen by contemporaries, and it is a view that has received some support in econometric work on wage setting.

As noted in section 11.2, persistent unemployment is the outcome of the interaction between shocks and institutions. Most countries experienced a severe demand shock in 1920–21 but the UK also experienced a shock on the supply side. In an influential paper, Broadberry (1990) drew attention to the cut in the average weekly hours of industrial workers that took place in the second half of 1919. This cut of about 13 per cent in hours was not matched by a cut in the real weekly wage rate and thus labour productivity declined relative to the real wage. Thus, while economy-wide output per worker was the same in 1923 as in 1913, weekly earnings divided by the GDP deflator had increased by 13 per cent. The effect of a negative shock to productivity should have a transitory effect on unemployment which wears off as the real wage adjusts. The evidence suggests that the immediate effect of the productivity shock was to raise the unemployment rate by as much as three percentage points in 1922 but that the effect had largely disappeared by 1929 (Hatton, 2007: 486; Thomas, 1994: 338).

The United States in the early 1920s presents a very different picture. Union density was about ten per cent in the decade before the war, and, although it increased sharply to 17 per cent in 1921, by 1923 it was back almost to the pre-war level. The number and scope of collective agreements expanded, but again, much less dramatically than in the UK. In 1925, it was estimated that rather more than 5.5 million workers—or about 20 per cent of the non-farm labour force—were covered by specific wage agreements (Carr, 1925: 432). The national system of industrial relations established with the War Labor Board in 1918 was abolished a year later and nothing like it reappeared until the 1930s. Also, the permissive legal environment conferred by the Clayton Act of 1914 was reversed by Supreme Court decisions of 1921 and 1922 (Ebell and Ritschl, 2008). Above all, there was no system of unemployment insurance remotely like the one that emerged in the UK.

[7] As Soskice (1990) shows, the unemployment outcome will depend on workers' militancy and the bargaining strength of employers as well as on the overall level of aggregate demand. In a fixed exchange rate setting it will also depend on the level of employment that is consistent with balance of payments equilibrium.

On the other hand, working hours had been falling since the 1890s, a trend that accelerated between 1909 and 1919 when the working week in manufacturing fell by a little over ten per cent. The fall in hours occurred more gradually in the US than in Britain (though perhaps less smoothly than Whaples, 1990, suggests[8]) and it owed something both to increased militancy and to changes in state hours laws, as well as to organizational shifts within firms in response to technological opportunities. But, more importantly, it took place against the background of sustained growth in labour productivity and slower growth in labour supply, as immigration dried up during the war. Between 1913 and 1923, economy-wide output per worker increased by 11 per cent in the US, as compared with zero in the UK. And while the resumption of immigration provided a sharp boost to labour supply in 1920 (Vernon 1991: 576), it was quickly scotched with the introduction of the Emergency Quota in 1921.

11.4. LABOUR MARKETS IN THE 1930s

For the UK, developments in the 1930s run parallel to that of the US in the 1920s—essentially no change. Union density drifted mildly downwards in the early 1930s, before recovering to its 1929 level of 26 per cent by 1936, and, while there was some decline in the coverage of collective agreements, the essential structure of pay setting machinery remained unchanged. In 1931, there was a ten per cent cut in unemployment benefit, which was restored in 1934. But the fluctuation in unemployment during the 1930s was overwhelmingly due to aggregate demand shocks.

As is well known, demand side activism in the United States was largely a product of the New Deal. But there were significant developments on the supply side too. First and foremost was the National Industrial Recovery Act (NIRA) introduced in 1933, which guaranteed the right of workers to organize trade unions and banned non-union covenants (so-called yellow dog contracts). This led to a dramatic increase in collective bargaining coverage but only a modest increase in union density. Under the National Recovery Administration, codes were developed for 500 industrial sectors covering about 80 per cent of private non-agricultural employees. These codes fixed prices, set minimum wages, established maximum hours, and set minimum standards for working conditions. When the NIRA was declared unconstitutional in 1935, these measures were continued under the National Labor Relations Act (the Wagner Act), which gave more bargaining power to workers than had the NIRA and encouraged faster growth in unionism. In combination with a more aggressive grass roots movement among labour (Freeman, 1998), which had its most visible impact in

[8] Whaples's analysis is constrained by his sources, namely the Census of Manufactures, only available at five year intervals. Average 'normal' hours in manufacturing industries fell from 57.31 in 1909 to 55.51 in 1914 and 51.36 in 1919—a drop of 7.5 per cent over 1914/19 (1990: 394, n. 3). But evidence from industry-level analysis of hours shows falls of 7.6 per cent in cotton, 8.6 per cent in boot and shoes, and 9.2 per cent in iron and steel between 1918 and 1920, rather than being distributed evenly over the entire five-year period.

the formation of the Congress of Industrial Organizations (CIO) in 1936, a more militant organization than the American Federation of Labor (AFL), unionism grew rapidly. Between 1934 and 1939 union density increased from 11.5 per cent to 27.6 per cent.

In a pioneering study, Weinstein (1980) compared monthly movements in prices and hourly earnings in 1921–23 and 1933–35. He found that the total impact of the NIRA was to raise prices by 30 per cent and average nominal hourly earnings by over 70 per cent, increasing unemployment by about 6 per cent between 1933 and 1935. Other investigations have suggested that this overstates its effects on wages and prices. Using industry-level data (but not including the early 1920s), Bernanke (1986) argued that the effect of the NIRA was much more modest, raising real hourly earnings by no more than 10 per cent in any individual sector. In a detailed examination of work-sharing policies Taylor (2011) found that the cut in hours from 1933 to 1935 expanded employment by as much as 2.5 million in the covered sector, holding the real wage constant, but that this was largely offset by the effect on labour demand of the increase in hourly earnings. Using a two-sector dynamic general equilibrium model, Cole and Ohanian (2004) argue that the effect of New Deal-sponsored 'cartelisation' (including both the NIRA and the NLRB) was to raise the covered sector real wage by nearly 20 per cent between 1934 and 1939 and to increase the economy-wide unemployment rate by about 6 percentage points.

Of course, New Deal policies only came into effect after unemployment had reached its peak. By this time a significant real wage increase of around 16 per cent had already taken place as the sharp fall in the price level outpaced the more modest decline in wage rates. Indeed, there was almost no fall in hourly earnings in manufacturing until late in 1931 (Bordo et al., 2000; Hanes, 2000; O'Brien, 1989)—in contrast with the experience of the early 1920s. Accordingly, some observers have argued that Hoover's high wage policies produced effects that foreshadowed those of the New Deal.[9] Thus, even if the job losses caused directly by the advent of the New Deal were modest, it nevertheless had the effect of propping up the real wage at a time when the scale of unemployment suggests it should have been falling. Bordo et al. (2000: 1460) calculate that a normal recovery would have required a further 10–15 per cent fall in real wages, concluding that 'even if the NIRA only kept real wages from falling, such a policy would have significantly impeded recovery'.

The other important feature of the New Deal was the expansion of work relief programmes. These were administered through a sequence of different organizations, which were either run directly by the federal government or operated through state and local government, and some of which were targeted specifically to young workers.[10] In a controversial article, Darby (1976) argued that those who

[9] These policies include: Hoover's use of moral suasion to induce leading employers not to cut wage rates (Vedder and Galloway, 1993: 89–95; Rose, 2010); a series of court rulings, beginning in 1929, that supported union rights to organize (Ebell and Ritschl, 2008: 23–5); and subsequent supportive legislation embodied in the Davis–Bacon Act of 1931 and the Norris La Guardia Act of 1932 (Ohanian, 2009: 2316–18).

[10] Work relief programmes were established in 1930–32 but these were modest compared with what followed. The major relief programmes were operated under the Civil Works Administration

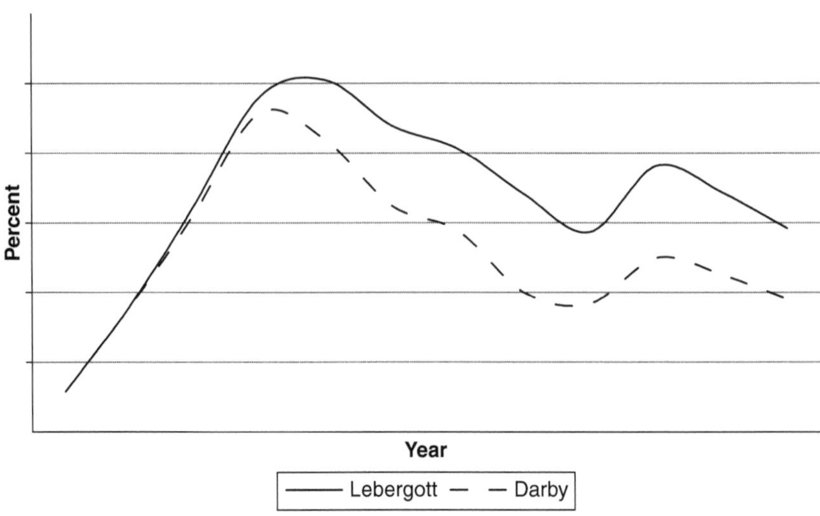

Fig. 11.4. US unemployment in the 1930s
Source: Smiley (1983: 488).

were on some form of work relief should be counted as employed rather than as unemployed (as in the standard BLS-Lebergott series). Those on work relief averaged 30 per cent of the unemployed between 1933 and 1940 and re-classifying them as employed makes the depression in the labour market look much milder (see Figure 11.4). Darby claimed that relief work crowded out private sector employment one for one, but a direct test of this hypothesis using aggregate time series data indicated that there was no crowding out (Kesselman and Savin, 1978).

Cross sectional analysis has been equally indecisive. Wallis and Benjamin (1981) found that relief spending had no effect on private sector wages and employment in 1934/35, while Fleck (1999) found that relief jobs had no effect on the numbers remaining jobless in 1937 and 1940. These results seem inconsistent with the finding that public works and relief spending had strong positive effects on local consumer demand (Fishback et al., 2005). However dynamic panel analysis at the city level offers some reconciliation. Using vector autoregression, Neumann et al. (2010) find that relief spending increased earnings and employment in the short run, but that the long run effect on employment was negative. In the long run, the creation of a relief job crowded out about one-half to two-thirds of a private sector job. And if relief jobs retained some workers in the labour force who would otherwise have withdrawn, then the overall effect on the jobless total may have been minimal (Fleck, 1999: 683; Fishback, 2007: 400).

Jensen (1989: 577) characterized those on work relief as 'the least skilled, the least employable'. This judgment is backed by Margo's (1991) analysis of the

(November 1933 to July 1934); the Federal Emergency Relief Administration (April 1934 to December 1935); and the Works Progress Administration (July 1935 to June 1943). Youth programmes were operated by the Civilian Conservation Corps (April 1933 to June 1943); and the National Youth Administration (January 1936 to May 1943).

individual characteristics of relief workers compared to the unemployed, as having 'even less schooling', and being drawn more consistently out of the ranks of the unskilled (50 per cent cited their regular jobs as unskilled labourer, compared to 25 per cent for the unemployed, and 11 per cent for those with jobs). Over time, those on work relief became even less employable, as their skills atrophied and their reputations became tarnished by association with federal support. In the words of one critic, 'The long years of unemployment which has been his lot since 1931 have naturally resulted in a deterioration of the little skill of which he was possessed' (Department of Labor, 1939: 810). In this light it is not surprising that relief workers seem to have exerted very little pressure in the competition for jobs.

11.5. THE INCIDENCE AND DYNAMICS OF UNEMPLOYMENT

One of the recurring themes in studies of the interwar labour market is that unemployment was very unevenly distributed. The incidence of unemployment varied widely by region, by industry, by occupation, and by skill level. For the UK, the most enduring impression of unemployment throughout the interwar period is the dramatic differences between industrial sectors. Not surprisingly some observers have interpreted the unemployment problem in interwar Britain as, in some sense, a structural problem (Booth and Glynn, 1975). In the 1920s, the highest unemployment rates (those over 10 per cent) among insured workers were concentrated largely in the great staple export industries (textiles, iron and steel, engineering and shipbuilding, coal) as well as the building trades. In the 1920s, their plight is often associated with the sterling overvaluation, but a modest devaluation would only have gone part of the way to reducing the wide variation in unemployment rates (Wolcott, 1993). These were the industries that suffered most in cyclical downturns even before the First World War and their position deteriorated further in the worldwide recession of the 1930s.

US unemployment in the 1930s was also marked by significant variation by age, skill, industry and, to a lesser extent than in the UK, by region. In March 1933, the highest unemployment rates were to be found in construction (at over 70 per cent), with manufacturing and transportation as heavily affected sectors (at around 40 per cent). Agriculture and services, perhaps unsurprisingly, had the lowest rates (around 15 per cent). The rank order remained the same throughout the 1930s, although the levels declined across the board (Margo, 1991: 334). Within manufacturing, Wallis (1989: 58) has noted that heavy industries and mining fared the worst during the early depression, compared to light industry and textiles. However, from the trough in 1933, heavy industry saw the fastest growth in employment (and was the only manufacturing sector with more jobs in 1937 than in 1929).

In the UK the staple industries were heavily concentrated by region and so the wide variance observed in industry unemployment rates translates into wide regional variations in unemployment. As Table 11.2 shows, in London and the southeast, the southwest, and the midlands, insured unemployment rates in

Table 11.2. Insured unemployment rates in UK regions

Region	1924	1929	1932	1936
London	9.0	5.6	13.5	7.2
Southeast	7.5	5.6	14.3	7.3
Southwest	9.1	8.1	17.1	9.4
Midlands	9.0	9.3	20.1	9.2
Northeast	10.9	13.7	28.5	16.8
Northwest	12.9	13.3	25.8	17.1
Scotland	12.4	12.1	27.7	18.7
Wales	8.6	19.3	36.5	29.4
N. Ireland	16.6	14.8	27.2	22.7
Variance	8.2	20.7	58.5	59.0
UK	10.3	10.4	22.1	13.1

Source: Booth and Glynn (1975: 619).

the late 1920s and late 1930s were not wildly higher than the national averages for the pre-1914 period. As the depression deepened in the 1930s, the variance of regional unemployment rates rose further as the absolute difference between unemployment rates in 'Inner Britain' and the 'Outer Regions' increased (Hatton, 1986). That raises the thorny question of why interregional mobility was so low despite official efforts to promote it. The most plausible explanation is that as workers were queuing for jobs at centrally negotiated rates, those that moved south merely swapped a position in the middle of a longer queue for one at the back of a shorter queue (Hatton, 2003).

While there was noticeable geographical variation in the employment impact of the Great Depression in the US, it was more muted than in the UK. Thus, the coefficient of variation (CV) of unemployment rates by region was only 0.19 in the US in 1940 (0.15 when the evening effects of work relief are included), compared to 0.35 in Britain in 1932, and 0.63 in 1936.[11] Even so, it is clear that some regions fared worse than others. In the early depression, employment held up best in the South Atlantic region and fell fastest in the Mountain states. The recovery rates show something of a rubber-band effect: the larger the decline between 1929 and 1933, the faster employment rebounded between 1933 and 1937. But there are two outlier regions—the Mountain states which rebounded more slowly and the South Atlantic region which expanded faster than predicted (a similar result obtains for 1933–40 relative to 1929–33). Some of this can be explained by the different industrial mixes in the regions, but Wallis (1989: 59) finds that about 60 per cent of the total regional variation in employment in the 1930s is still left unaccounted for. However, the local effects of bank failures and the differential regional impact of the NIRA codes, as well as the institutional aspects of the second New Deal, seem to have been fairly small (Rosenbloom and Sundstrom, 1999).

It is instructive also to look at unemployment dynamics. For the UK, analysis of the statistics stemming from the working of the labour exchanges and the

[11] The CV for US unemployment at the state-level for adult males in 1940 was 0.25 if relief workers are treated as employed and 0.24 if they are treated as unemployed; the CV for UK unemployment at the county level for all workers in 1937 was 0.49 (including women in the US data lowers the CV to 0.23 and 0.22 respectively).

unemployment insurance system yields a curious picture. On the one hand there was very high turnover in the labour market. During the 1930s the average monthly flow into jobs was equivalent to nearly two-fifths of the average number of wholly unemployed on the register.[12] On the other hand, the number of long-term unemployed (those continuously unemployed for at least a year) increased dramatically. This pattern has led some observers to describe the interwar labour market as 'bifurcated' (Thomas, 1988). This is because the probability of leaving unemployment declined very steeply with the duration of unemployment. In 1929, the probability of exit in the first week of unemployment was about 50 per cent but after a year of unemployment the weekly probability of exit was a mere 2 per cent (Hatton, 2003: 355). With the sharp increase in layoffs in the 1930s, the chances of re-employment declined for all the unemployed, and it was this that gave rise to the most sombre legacy of the depression: the host of long-term unemployed that persisted into the 1930s.

In Britain, long-term unemployment was probably less than 10 per cent of male unemployment in the 1920s, but it rose to exceed a quarter by 1936 (Crafts, 1987: 420). The incidence of long-term unemployment also fell very unevenly. It was much higher for men than for women; it declined with skill level; it increased with age; and it varied widely across industrial sectors. These differences are seen most clearly in the regional variations noted earlier. As Table 11.3 shows, even in 1932, the share of LTU in insured unemployment was low in the south and it was still fairly low four years later; but in the most hard hit regions it had risen to more than a third by 1936. Consistent with this, the average interrupted spell length of those on the register increased steeply from south to north and it increased substantially between 1932 and 1936. By contrast, the average unemployment duration of the typical new entrant into unemployment increased less steeply both in the cross section and over time.

Long-term unemployment rose even more sharply in the US during the 1930s. According to the Unemployment Census of 1930, only 2.6 per cent of the unemployed had been without work for more than a year. In Buffalo, a city that suffered more than most in the 1930s, long-term male unemployment soared: from 9 per cent of total unemployment in 1929, to 21 per cent in 1930, 43 per cent in 1931, 60 per cent in 1932, and 68 per cent in 1933 (Jensen, 1989: 564). By the mid-1930s, city surveys generally indicated very high proportions: 42 per cent in Springfield, Mass., over 60 per cent in Bridgeport, Conn. in early 1934 (Clarke, 1935), and 69 per cent in Philadelphia in 1935 (Palmer, 1937). As Table 11.4 shows, by the time of the 1940 Census, fully a third of those out of work had been unemployed for more than a year (the rates were lower for rural than urban places, while work relief had removed many of the hard-core jobless from the ranks of the unemployed). The regional pattern of long-term unemployment is again much more muted in the US than in the UK. The proportion of LTU was lower in the south and the west than in the north and the east, but the variation is comparatively small: the CV for the nine US regions is 0.23, relative to 0.50 for the

[12] For the US, monthly hirings by manufacturing firms accounted for about 6 per cent of the stock of unemployed in that sector in March 1933; by May 1938, the proportion had risen to 11.4 per cent.

Table 11.3. UK unemployment durations of insured men by region

	June 1932				June 1936			
Region	Unemp. Rate	Duration	Spell Length	Share LTU	Unemp. Rate	Duration	Spell Length	Share LTU
Great Britain	28.3	10.5	26.5	17.3	13.8	12.1	42.2	26.6
London	13.5	7.1	14.5	4.4	6.7	5.7	18.5	8.4
Southeast	14.3	6.4	14.1	3.8	5.4	6.0	18.7	8.5
Southwest	17.1	7.8	17.9	8.8	8.2	7.2	23.6	14.1
Midlands	20.1	9.0	25.5	14.6	9.8	10.5	39.7	23.1
Northeast	28.5	11.9	32.0	21.0	20.4	11.5	50.9	28.7
Northwest	25.8	10.3	29.1	18.3	17.2	13.2	46.1	27.2
Scotland	27.7	17.3	34.1	27.6	17.2	19.9	58.3	34.6
Wales	36.5	11.0	29.6	21.1	33.0	18.6	64.6	37.7

Source: Thomas (1988: 124).

Notes: Data refer to the insured unemployed only. Share LTU (long-term unemployed) is the proportion unemployed for more than a year; Duration is the average completed duration, in weeks, for a worker flowing into unemployment; Spell length is the average interrupted spell length of those on the register, in weeks.

Table 11.4. US unemployment durations for adult males by region, 1940

	exc. relief workers			inc. relief workers		
Region	Unemp Rate	Spell Length	Share LTU	Unemp Rate	Spell Length	Share LTU
United States	11.16	60.28	33.22	17.97	101.76	41.38
New England	11.56	55.55	32.45	17.67	99.65	41.75
Mid-Atlantic	15.27	73.69	42.11	19.98	97.19	46.46
East north central	10.51	66.05	35.10	17.44	124.04	46.02
West north central	11.31	58.43	30.00	20.25	118.08	41.67
South Atlantic	7.51	45.51	26.39	13.01	87.41	35.90
East south central	9.54	49.35	28.83	17.68	102.02	38.06
West south central	11.07	43.04	22.82	18.72	91.58	34.18
Mountain	13.14	44.21	23.40	23.06	95.84	33.00
Pacific	12.30	44.85	21.77	17.26	76.16	31.27

Source: Calculated from IPUMS 1 per cent sample of 1940 Census returns; excluding employers and self-employed.
Notes: Data refer to 16–65 year old males only. Relief workers are counted as employed in the first three columns and as unemployed in the final three columns. Variables defined as in Table 11.3.

UK regions in 1936. Once again, the work relief programmes further reduced regional variation (the CV falling to 0.14).[13]

The question has sometimes been raised as to whether the uneven distribution of unemployment hampered wage adjustment and contributed to persistence or hysteresis in unemployment rates during the 1930s. If wage adjustment in each region was determined by a convex Phillips curve, then increasing regional dispersion could add to wage pressure for a given national unemployment rate. However, the effect of regional unemployment variance on aggregate wage pressure seems weak. Another possibility is that leading wage bargains were set with reference to the industrial or regional labour markets where unemployment was lowest (Thomas and Stoney, 1971), although it is not clear why high unemployment regions per se should carry less weight in wage setting.

A more plausible explanation relates to long-term unemployment. If the LTU suffer a loss of motivation or an attrition of skills then they might be expected to exert less downward pressure on the wage. In an important paper, Crafts (1989) estimated quarterly wage adjustment equations for the UK using total unemployment and long-term unemployment as explanatory variables and found that the LTU exerted no downward pressure on wages. Similar results have been found for European unemployment in the post-war period (Layard et al., 2005; Llaudes, 2005). In the later 1930s, the LTU accounted for a quarter of male unemployment in the UK and upwards of a third in the US. Hence, wage pressure was

[13] The CV of long-term unemployment across states in 1940 is 0.32 if relief workers are treated as employed and 0.22 if they are treated as unemployed. It is not possible to calculate the dispersion of long-term unemployment at finer levels of disaggregation for the UK.

substantially higher than the total unemployment percentages would suggest—an effect that may have been exacerbated by regional imbalances, particularly in the UK.[14]

11.6. INSTITUTIONS AND SHOCKS

We have argued that labour market outcomes are the result of the interaction between shocks and institutions. While labour market institutions evolve from deeper long run causes, they are also shaped by shocks. Some observers see labour markets developing through a series of institutional stages where 'periods of stasis in the basic rules of the game were punctuated by episodes of rapid change' (Rosenbloom and Sundstrom, 2011: 5). While the underlying forces for change evolve slowly, economic or political shocks can provide the trigger for episodes of more rapid change. In both the US and the UK economies, the background fundamentals include the rise in the complexity of production processes with the concomitant increase in the size of firms and the bureaucratization of management (Jacoby, 2004) as well as the growing aspirations of workers based on rising real incomes, backed by increasing social organization and political voice.

The reaction of governments to changes in the labour market (and in society more generally) reflected two key elements. One was to cope with the rise of powerful economic interest groups by reconciling them through state intervention and regulation, with the aim of improving economic coordination and fostering more equal treatment (Wallis, 2010). Thus, to some degree, government activism was designed to stave off social and industrial unrest and preserve the smooth working of the capitalist system. The second was the gradual development of government sponsored insurance and protection against various contingencies. As Moss (2002: chapter 6) points out, the late nineteenth century saw the beginnings of a shift in the focus of government risk management polices from business security towards worker security. By the interwar period, the UK and the US were at different stages in this evolution, and, combined with differences in the nature and intensity of the shocks, this led to somewhat different policy reactions.

Between 1910 and 1920, the institutional structure of the UK labour market underwent dramatic change, but it was largely an acceleration of trends that were already under way. Unionism, especially among the unskilled, had been on the increase since the 1880s while collective bargaining arrangements grew in scope and centralization. Minimum wage legislation was first introduced in a very narrow range of occupations in 1909 while unemployment insurance was

[14] The figures in Tables 11.3 and 11.4 indicate that the share of long term unemployment increases roughly linearly with the unemployment rate. This means that the long term unemployment rate increases with the square of the overall unemployment rate in a region. Thus, the more unevenly distributed is unemployment, the higher the share of long term unemployment in the total. Calculations not reported here (but available from the authors on request) suggest that regional dispersion added about half a percentage point to the long term unemployment rate for the UK in the late 1930s and somewhat less for the US.

introduced on a modest scale in 1911.[15] During the war, tight labour markets, combined with growing militancy and industrial unrest, placed severe pressure on the government to produce formal wage setting arrangements in a wide range of industrial sectors. But, in the face of slow productivity growth, these more formal arrangements failed to deliver industrial peace until after the general strike of 1926. The rapid extension of unemployment insurance can be seen as a reaction to the implicit threat of insurrection against the background of the Russian revolution. Designed to replace the temporary out of work donation scheme, set up in 1918 to ease the transition to a peacetime economy, the unemployment insurance scheme was initially increased in scope and then augmented by a series of emergency measures throughout the 1920s that extended the coverage and the duration of benefit (Garside, 1990: 36–43).

In the United States, the First World War imposed similar pressures and, as already noted, it fuelled unionism and industrial militancy which called forth increasing public intervention. But these trends came to an abrupt halt as pressure eased and militancy finally collapsed in 1922 (Montgomery, 1987: Chapter 9). The reversal owed much to the fact that the effects of the war were shorter and less intense than in the UK, and there was no productivity setback. The wartime period also gave a fillip to growing pressure for social insurance of which workmen's compensation was the only tangible result. One of the chief impediments was the difficulty of promoting state-level legislation in the face of fierce competition between the states (Moss, 2002: 173–5). But the equilibrium that was underpinned by the benign conditions of the 1920s was overturned by the shock of the Great Depression. The policy of high wages and industrial collusion that began under Hoover, largely to avert the spread of unionism and industrial strife (Ohanian, 2009), was transformed into a new institutional structure under the New Deal. These reforms followed rather than led the economic downturn and some, such as the Social Security Act of 1935 and the Fair Labor Standards Act of 1938, only came into effect at the very end of the 1930s.

By contrast, the shock of 1929–1931 did not affect a fundamental reconsideration of the institutional arrangements governing the labour market in Britain, despite the identification by Pigou, Clay, and others that these were at the root of the high unemployment of the 1920s. Indeed, the very political pressures that underpinned the development of the ruling post-war institutional framework were intensified in the slump and ensured that any reforms would be limited at best.

Given the underlying imperatives for institutional change it may seem ironic that public intervention added to the unemployment burden. One reason is the lack of available alternatives. In the recent global recession, governments around the world have pursued active fiscal and monetary policies to stave off the worst effects of what appeared like another Great Depression. But, during the interwar period, adherence to the gold standard and to the economic policy regime that went with it precluded such immediate activism, even though it might have been

[15] The pre-war Liberal welfare reforms have also been interpreted as a means of preserving and enhancing the efficiency of the market system by achieving political consensus 'at a time of rising antagonism in the political and industrial world' (Harris, 1972: 365).

effective (Almunia et al., 2010). Despite growing recognition that unemployment was an industrial problem rather than an individual problem, the only tools available were direct market interventions. Because such interventions were novel, their likely effects were not as clearly understood as they are with the benefit of historical hindsight. Thus, although the effects of unemployment insurance, relief jobs, high wage policies, and support for collective bargaining were fiercely contested, carefully considered evidence-based policy was not possible.

The effects of different labour market institutions on the equilibrium rate of unemployment vary widely and they also depend on the structure of the labour market. Analyses of European labour markets in the 1980s and 1990s have found that the outcome for unemployment depends on interactions between institutions and not simply on adding up their individual effects. (Elmeskov et al., 1998; Belot and Van Ours, 2004). Thus, in the case of interwar Britain, the unemployment insurance system may have been more harmful in the presence of strong industry-level wage setting than otherwise (and vice versa). For the United States, the rise in real wages that took place in the early 1930s might have been less harmful in the long run if it had not been combined under the NIRA with the cartelization of large segments of industry.

However misplaced these measures may have been, the estimates of their contributions to the overall unemployment rate, either singly or in combination, are still highly uncertain. But once in place they almost certainly contributed to the *persistence* of unemployment. Before the First World War, and even into the interwar period, labour markets were relatively fluid with low job attachment, high labour turnover, and relatively short unemployment durations (Thomas, 1988; Jacoby and Sharma, 1992). But institutional change weakened these equilibrating forces and in the slump of the 1930s workers who were initially willing and able to work at the going wage queued for jobs while their skills and motivation atrophied. This in turn weakened wage pressure that might otherwise have hastened the recovery.

11.7. ENDING THE DEPRESSION

We have argued that a combination of shocks and institutions led, by the late 1930s, to equilibrium levels of unemployment that were significantly higher than before. That raises the question of what did bring the depression to an end. To many observers the answer is simple: the Second World War. However, not all agree. One view is that, in the absence of the recession of 1937–38, the recovery would have continued and unemployment would (eventually) have fallen to something resembling the 'normal' levels of the more distant past. In that case, the positive shock delivered by the onset of war simply speeded up the ongoing transition to low unemployment. The other view is that the US and UK economies had reached, or were approaching, labour market equilibrium in the later 1930s, even though unemployment remained comparatively high. In that case, the shift to low unemployment could be achieved only by a massive demand shock like war.

In the United States, output increased by a staggering 40 per cent between the depths of 1933 and the peak of 1937, and unemployment fell steeply (see Figure 11.4). The prevailing view is that this was driven largely by the demand side, particularly the monetary expansion that followed from the regime change of 1933 (Romer, 1992; Eggertsson, 2008). Nevertheless, equilibration on the supply side probably played some part: although wages and prices increased (largely because of NIRA and the Wagner Act), productivity grew especially strongly over the 1930s (Field, 2003). The downturn of 1937–38 was due to a radical shift in monetary policy—the sterilization of gold inflows and the doubling of banks' reserve requirements in 1936–37—as well as to a substantial fiscal tightening (Velde, 2009). The sharp recovery in 1938 can largely be accounted for by the reversal of these policies. Hence, over the range of unemployment rates down to about 10 per cent, the aggregate labour supply curve was highly elastic, and demand shocks had large employment effects. The question is whether, given more time, the labour market might have equilibrated at a substantially lower level of employment.

The US unemployment rate fell to just under 10 per cent in 1940 and then dropped to 6 per cent in 1941 before dipping below 2 per cent in 1943. Was there a 'natural' recovery up to 1941, before the full force of the war came into effect? Recent research suggests that monetary expansion up to 1940, and the subsequent fiscal expansion, were the driving forces rather than labour market equilibration (Vernon, 1994; Gordon and Krenn, 2010). Gordon and Krenn (2010) demonstrate that war-related expenditures gathered pace in 1940 rather than after the Japanese bombing of Pearl Harbour, as is sometimes supposed. Looking at contemporary reports, they find that labour shortages were not encountered until late 1941, by which time the unemployment rate was around 5 per cent. However, this was not an equilibrium unemployment rate. As Higgs (2006) shows, wage and price controls were introduced early in 1941, something that probably muted the inflation effects of an increasingly tight labour market.

A similar story can be told about the UK. The unemployment rate was 8.5 per cent in 1937 and, after a brief downturn, it rebounded to the same level in 1939. After that, the stock of unemployment fell steeply from 1.5 million in 1939 to 123,000 by mid-1942. Up to 1937, the fall in unemployment was driven by monetary and fiscal policies and by expanding world trade. The contribution of rearmament was larger and started earlier than it did in the US. Thomas (1983) shows that the direct and indirect effects of rearmament created a million jobs, accounting for more than four-fifths of the increase in civilian employment between 1935 and 1938. By the late 1930s there were reports of labour shortages that some have interpreted as capacity constraints, but the evidence is thin. However, by 1939 the labour market was tightening and, in advance of the imposition of controls, wage rates jumped sharply in 1940.

The experience in both countries suggests that, by the early stages of the war (early 1940 in the UK and mid-1941 in the US), unemployment rates were below what, for the 1930s, were equilibrium levels. In both countries, skilled workers, especially those in construction and engineering, had been fully mopped up, but there remained a residual of those who, in a peacetime setting, were virtually unemployable. How, then, did unemployment all but disappear in the months that followed? Clearly vast numbers were recruited into the armed forces (almost

11 million—20 per cent of the civilian labour force—in the US between 1940 and 1944). In the US, labour supply increased as youths and married women were added to the labour force (Long, 1944: Chapter 8). The expansion of civilian employment also included one and a half million men equally divided between those who would otherwise have retired and those 'of doubtful employability who had given up the search for a job after failing to measure up to the relatively rigid requirements of the pre-war labor market' (Eskin, 1944: 264). In order to facilitate re-employment, New Deal public employment programmes were adapted to provide vocational education and training for war-related industries. By February 1942, 3.3 million trainees had been through such programmes while almost as many received on-the-job training (Vatter, 1985: 43).

In the UK, more that 1.5 million men (equivalent to 7 per cent of the labour force) had been conscripted into the armed forces by the end of 1939. Some of these came from the ranks of the unemployed but only a few of the LTU found their way into the armed forces. More than half of the long-term-unemployed in May 1939 were aged 45 or over and therefore not eligible, and many others were not fit for active service. By early 1940 the unemployed consisted largely of labourers and older workers (George, 1940). Most of these were drawn into civilian or war-related employment, and by November 1940 only a very small residue of truly unemployables remained.[16] Besides the opening of opportunities for those who were previously considered unemployable, there was a series of active labour market policies that directed workers in ways that would have been almost inconceivable in peacetime (Reubens, 1945).

This analysis suggests that in both the UK and the US, the 'self correcting' labour market mechanism was so weak by the 1930s that, in the absence of positive shocks, it would not have driven the unemployment rate much below 10 per cent. The onset of war pushed unemployment below that level, but it was not until mass mobilization took hold that the hard core of unemployment was eliminated. It took a massive shock, combined with an equally radical shift in the institutional structure to finally jolt the labour market permanently out of its previous equilibrium.

11.8. THEN AND NOW

There is widespread agreement that the onset of the global financial crisis that began at the end of 2007 looked very much like the initial stages of the Great Depression in terms of its worldwide scope and the trajectories of key indicators such as stock prices, industrial production, and world trade. Although not as

[16] The number of long-term unemployed fell by half between April 1939 and May 1940. From July 1940, review panels were set up to evaluate those who remained unemployed with the aim of matching them to suitable employment or retraining. Of 152,000 men who were interviewed up to October 1940, more than three-quarters were found to be suitable for immediate employment. By that time 'hard core' unemployment was less that 100,000, and as one observer commented, 'large numbers of the so-called unemployables were being drawn back into the employment market under the constantly increasing pressure of war demands on the labour supply' (*International Labour Review*, 1942: 57).

severe as some expected, the fall in output has been the largest in the post-war period. For the UK, the decline of 6 per cent between the beginning of 2008 and the end of 2009 was comparable to that between 1929 and 1931. For the US, the 6 per cent drop in output was much smaller than the massive 14 per cent experienced between 1929 and 1931. The parallels between the 1930s and now raise the question of whether insights from the past are relevant for today—and in particular for fostering economic recovery. In this chapter we have argued that we need to look at the recession and recovery of the early 1920s as well as that of the early 1930s if we want to draw the right lessons from the interwar years. We also advocate an approach that has at its core the interaction between shocks and institutions.

One obvious insight from the interwar experience is that deep recessions are likely to trigger severe pressures on governments to intervene in order to avert unrest. In the interwar period those interventions focused largely on the supply side, on holding real wages up, and on mitigating the plight of the unemployed, rather than on stimulating aggregate demand. Following the global financial crisis, early and effective intervention on the demand side mitigated the scale of the demand shock. In the early stages of the recession, this averted pressures for extensive direct intervention in the labour market and it provided some justification (even among sceptics) for Keynesian style policies. But while a deeper recession was avoided, the deficit-reduction policies announced in 2010 and 2011 seem likely to delay economic recovery.

Fiscal and monetary policies on the scale witnessed in 2008/09 could not have been implemented in the interwar period, given the ideological and administrative constraints, but expectations effects did play a role in the recovery process. Leaving the gold standard, and abandoning the policy dogma that went with it, helped to end the downward spiral (Eichengreen and Sachs, 1985; Temin and Wigmore, 1990; Eggertsson, 2008). But these policy shifts did not come into effect until two years into the recession in the UK and nearly four years into the recession in the US. Nevertheless, monetary and fiscal policies had substantial effects during the interwar period, as illustrated by the experience of 1937–38, and even more demonstrably by the effects of rearmament. In the light of this evidence, it has been argued that earlier and larger-scale intervention on the demand side could have returned both economies to something resembling normal employment levels well before the war. Here we differ from other interpretations of the potential for recovery that focus entirely on the inadequacies of fiscal and monetary policies. Neither an earlier unshackling of the Golden Fetters nor a larger overall stimulus would have been enough unless institutional change in the labour market could have been averted in the case of the US or undone in the case of the UK.

Labour market institutions are probably more favourable to labour market recovery today than they were in the 1930s. In the UK the key institutional developments are the deregulation of wage bargaining that took place in the 1980s and, more recently, the various 'new deals' and welfare-to-work programmes aimed at enhancing labour market flexibility and reducing long-term benefit dependence. In the US, the renewal of Emergency Unemployment Compensation introduced in 2008, and other programmes introduced under the American Recovery and Reinvestment Act of 2009, may have marginally reduced search efficiency.[17] But there has been nothing resembling the institutional reforms that were introduced in the 1930s. Nevertheless, modern labour markets are less fluid than they were in the past and so a very rapid recovery like that of the early 1920s could not be expected.

In the current recession, UK unemployment rose from 5.4 per cent in early 2008 to 7.9 per cent three years later, while long-term unemployment increased from less than a quarter to more than a third of the total. In comparison to the interwar period, the labour market impact has been milder but there is likely to be greater persistence. However, in comparison to the more recent past (and in the absence of positive demand shocks) the signs for the UK are more encouraging. Although the rate of job loss was greater than in any other post-war recession, the rates of outflow from unemployment have held up remarkably well (Elsby et al., 2011). And there has been no outward shift in the relationship between unemployment and vacancies that would signal a decline in labour market efficiency. One reason may be that real wages have declined much more sharply, and this has helped to preserve employment more than in previous recessions (Martin, 2011).

In the US, the unemployment rate rose from 4.8 per cent at the beginning of 2008 to 9.7 per cent three years later. Hence, the labour market recession in the US has been far deeper although the shock to output has been similar. Elsby et al. (2010: 4) note that the unusually large decline in unemployment outflow rates has been accompanied by a record rise in long-term unemployment, which 'is likely to result in a persistent residue of LTU workers with relatively weak search effectiveness, depressing the strength of the recovery'. Accordingly, there is evidence that the unemployment–vacancies relationship has shifted outwards, implying some reduction in labour market efficiency.

Finally, when seeking insights from the past it is important to stress the differences as well as the similarities. Much of the discussion has now turned to how far deficit-reduction policies are slowing down the recovery and the obvious parallels are with the 1937–38 recession. As we have seen, rearmament was important in boosting the economy in the run up to the war, in the absence of strong equilibrating forces in the labour market. By contrast, in the present, no such stimulus is in sight but the combination of shocks and institutions is more benign and hence labour market equilibration should be stronger. In this regard, 1930s pessimism should not be carried over to the present and there is no reason to think that demand shocks on the scale of the early 1940s would be necessary for a full recovery.

A further issue is that of a slowdown in productivity growth. Productivity has sagged in recent recessions and then output has grown faster than labour input in the recovery (Gordon, 2010). In the current recession, productivity (per worker hour) has fallen much further in the UK than in the US, which has led some to the

[17] Emergency Unemployment Compensation introduced in June 2008 extended the duration of unemployment benefit from 26 to 53 weeks and was later renewed until March 2012. The American Recovery and Reinvestment Act of February 2009 included a variety of infrastructure projects and educational projects as well as subsidies for health care, homeownership, working tax credits and displaced worker support.

view that, especially in the UK, the output gap has not widened by as much as trend projections would otherwise suggest (Martin, 2011). Although in the 1930s, as now, there was a slowdown in capital accumulation, underlying productivity growth remained strong. In this respect, a parallel with the 1930s would be more apposite than one based on the UK productivity slump of 1919/20 or the productivity slowdown of the 1970s. In both these cases, and unlike the present, there were identifiable supply side shocks. As noted earlier, one reason for the UK productivity dip could be the decline in real wages—something that may mean a jobless recovery in the short run but an eventual return to low unemployment in the medium term.

11.9. CONCLUSION

The speed and extent of the economic recovery from a macroeconomic shock is conditioned both by the scale of the shock and by the structure of labour market institutions. The interwar experience can shed light on these issues because it witnessed large economic shocks and significant changes in labour market institutions. The Great Depression is aptly named. It was the worst depression since records began. But it is important to look at the 1920s as well as the 1930s.

In the early 1920s, the UK and the US experienced macroeconomic shocks, which seem to have been broadly similar in magnitude, and from which the US recovered rather better than the UK. We have argued that there was a distinct increase in the equilibrium unemployment rate in the UK in the 1920s associated with increased union militancy, the development of centralized but uncoordinated wage setting, and the advent of a national system of unemployment insurance. The UK recovery in the 1920s was also hampered by the sharp cut in working hours. By contrast, such institutional developments were largely absent in the US and the fall in working hours was more easily accommodated. The economic shock in the 1930s was more persistent and it was larger in the US than in the UK. In the UK the institutional structure established in the 1920s probably slowed the recovery, and its most important manifestation was the rise in long-term unemployment. In the US, the demand shock and the unemployment response was much larger. But New Deal legislation impeded labour market adjustment in the later 1930s.

What lessons should today's policy makers draw from the interwar experience? Clearly, one is to avoid labour market interventions that directly or indirectly reduce the resilience of the labour market, and thereby stifle the supply side contribution to recovery. Another is that the longer and the more severe are the new debt-driven austerity policies, the greater the risk of marginalizing sections of the workforce and creating a legacy of persistent unemployment, which only dramatic positive demand shocks can overcome.

APPENDIX

Nominal and Real Wage Rigidity and Unemployment

As noted in the text, the regressions that are presented in Table 11.1 reflect some combination of real wage rigidity and nominal inertia in wage setting. The derivation here follows the original formulation of Grubb et al. (1983), which has been followed by many others.

Here, lower case letters represent the log of a variable: w is the nominal wage, p is the price level, u is the unemployment rate, and q is productivity. The Phillips curve with nominal inertia can be written as:

$$\Delta w_t = a\Delta p_t + (1 - a)\Delta w_{t-1} - ab(u_t - u_0)$$

Where nominal inertia is captured by $a < 1$ and u_0 is the NAIRU. Price setting or, alternatively, labour demand is represented by:

$$\Delta p_t = \Delta w_t - \Delta q_t - c\Delta u_t$$

Substituting price setting into the Phillips curve to eliminate price change and putting unemployment on the left gives:

$$u_t = \frac{b}{b+c}u_o - \frac{1}{b+c}\Delta q_t + \frac{c}{b+c}u_{t-1} - \frac{1-a}{a(b+c)}\Delta\Delta w_t$$

For zero productivity growth (or where productivity growth appears directly in the Phillips curve), a constant rate of wage change and a constant unemployment rate, unemployment will be at the NAIRU: $u_t = u_{t-1} = u_0$. Here real wage rigidity defined by $1/b$ and nominal wage rigidity defined by $(1—a)/ab$ are not directly identified. But clearly the larger is the coefficient on lagged unemployment the greater is real wage rigidity and the larger is the coefficient on $\Delta\Delta w$, the greater is nominal wage rigidity.

Eliminating the wage gives a slightly more complex expression in terms of price change:

$$u_t = \frac{ab}{ab+c}u_o - \frac{1}{ab+c}\Delta q_t + \frac{c}{ab+c}u_{t-1} - \frac{1-a}{ab+c}\Delta\Delta p_t + \frac{1-a}{ab+c}\Delta q_{t-1} + \frac{(1-a)c}{ab+c}\Delta u_{t-1}$$

As before, for constant growth rates of productivity and prices, and a constant unemployment rate, unemployment is at the NAIRU, u_0.

BIBLIOGRAPHY

Almunia, M., Bénétrix, A., Eichengreen, B., O'Rourke, K. H., and Rua, G. (2010), 'From Great Depression to Great Credit Crisis: Similarities, Differences and Lessons', *Economic Policy*, 25, 219–65.

Balke, N. S. and Gordon, R. J. (1986), 'Historical Data', in R. J. Gordon (ed.), *The American Business Cycle: Continuity and Change*. Chicago: NBER, University of Chicago Press.

Beenstock, M. and Warburton, P. (1991), 'The Market for Labor in Interwar Britain', *Explorations in Economic History*, 28, 287–308.

Belot, M. V. and Van Ours, J. C. (2004), 'Does the Recent Success of some OECD Countries in Lowering their Unemployment Rates Lie in the Clever Design of their Labour Market Reforms?', *Oxford Economic Papers*, 56, 621–42.

Benjamin, D. K. and Kochin, L. A. (1979), 'Searching for an Explanation of Unemployment in Interwar Britain', *Journal of Political Economy*, 87, 441–78.

Bernanke, B. S. (1986), 'Employment, Hours, and Earnings in the Depression: An Analysis of Eight Manufacturing Industries', *American Economic Review*, March 76 (1), 82–109.

Bernanke, B. S. and Carey, K. (1996), 'Nominal Wage Stickiness and Aggregate Supply in the Great Depression', *Quarterly Journal of Economics*, 111, 853–83.

Blanchard, O. and Wolfers, J. (2000), 'The Role of Shocks and Institutions in the Rise of European Unemployment: The Aggregate Evidence', *Economic Journal*, 110, C1–33.

Booth, A. E. and Glynn, S. (1975), 'Unemployment in the Interwar Period: A Multiple Problem', *Journal of Contemporary History*, 10, 611–37.

Bordo, M., Erceg, C. J., and Evans, C. L. (2000), 'Money, Sticky Wages, and the Great Depression', *American Economic Review*, 90, 1447–63.

Boyer, G. R. and Hatton, T. J. (2002), 'New Estimates of British Unemployment, 1870–1913', *Journal of Economic History*, 62, 643–75.

Broadberry, S. N. (1986), 'Aggregate Supply in Interwar Britain', *Economic Journal*, 96, 467–81.

Broadberry, S. N. (1990), 'The Emergence of Mass Unemployment: Explaining Macroeconomic Trends in Britain during the Trans-World War I Period', *Economic History Review* 43, 272–82.

Calmfors, L. and Driffill J. (1988), 'Bargaining Structure, Corporatism and Macroeconomic Performance', *Economic Policy*, 6, 13–61.

Carr, E. B. (1925), 'The Use of Cost-of-Living Figures in Wage Adjustments', *Department of Labor Bulletin*, 369. Washington DC: Government Printing Office.

Clark, F. M. (1935), 'Unemployment Survey of Bridgeport, Conn., 1934', *Monthly Labor Review*, 40 March, 626–45.

Cole, H. L. and Ohanian, L. E. (2004), 'New Deal Policies and the Persistence of the Great Depression: A General Equilibrium Analysis', *Journal of Political Economy*, 112, 779–816.

Crafts, N. F. R. (1987), 'Long-Term Unemployment in Britain in the 1930s', *Economic History Review*, 40, 418–32.

Crafts, N. F. R. (1989), 'Long-Term Unemployment and the Wage Equation in Britain, 1925–1939', *Economica*, 56, 247–54.

Crafts, N. F. R. and Fearon, P. (2010), 'Lessons from the 1930s Great Depression', *Oxford Review of Economic Policy*, 26, 285–317.

Darby, M. R. (1976), 'Three-and-a-half Million US Employees have been Mislaid, or an Explanation of Unemployment, 1934–1941', *Journal of Political Economy*, 84, 1–16.

David, P. A. and Solar, P. (1977), 'A Bicentenary Contribution to the History of the Cost of Living in America', *Research in Economic History*, 2, 1–80.

Department of Labor (1939), 'Duration of Public Relief in Milwaukee County', *Monthly Labor Review*, 48 April, 809–12.

Dimsdale, N. H., Nickell, S. J., and Horsewood, N. (1989), 'Real Wages and Unemployment in Britain during the 1930s', *Economic Journal*, 99, 271–92.

Ebell, M. and Ritschl A. (2008), 'Real Origins of the Great Depression: Monopoly Power, Unions and the American Business Cycle in the 1920s', London School of Economics CEP Discussion Paper 876.

Eggertsson, G. B. (2008), 'Great Expectations and the End of the Great Depression', *American Economic Review*, 98, 1476–516.

Eichengreen, B. (1986), 'Unemployment in Interwar Britain: Dole or Doldrums?', *Oxford Economic Papers*, 39, 597–623.

Eichengreen, B. and Sachs, J. (1985), 'Exchange Rates and Economic Recovery in the 1930s', *Journal of Economic History*, 45, 925–46.

Elmeskov, J., Martin, J. P., and Scarpetta, S. (1998), 'Key Lessons for Labour Market Reforms, Evidence from OECD Countries' Experiences', *Swedish Economic Policy Review*, 5, 205–52.

Elsby, M. L., Hobijn, B., and Şahin, A. (2010), 'The Labor Market in the Great Recession', *Brookings Papers in Economic Activity*, Spring, 1–48.

Elsby, M. L., Smith, J. C., and Wadsworth, J. (2011), 'The Role of Worker Flows in the Dynamics and Distribution of UK Unemployment', *Oxford Review of Economic Policy*, 27, 338–63.

Eskin, L. (1944), 'Sources of Wartime Labor in the United States', *Monthly Labor Review*, 44, 264–78.

Feinstein, C. H. (1972), *National Income, Expenditure and Output of the United Kingdom, 1855–1965*. Cambridge: Cambridge University Press.

Feinstein, C. H. (1995), 'Changes in Nominal Wages, the Cost of Living, and Real Wages in the United Kingdom over Two Centuries, 1780–1990', in P. Scholliers and V. Zamagni (eds), *Labour's Reward*. Aldershot: Edward Elgar.

Field, A. (2003), 'The Most Technologically Progressive Decade of the Century', *American Economic Review*, 93, 1399–413.

Fishback, P. V. (2007), 'The New Deal', in P. V. Fishback (ed.), *Government and the American Economy: A New History*. Chicago: University of Chicago Press.

Fishback, P. V., Horrace, W., and Kantor, S. (2005), 'Did New Deal Grant Programs Stimulate Local Economies? A Study of Federal Grants and Retail Sales during the Great Depression', *Journal of Economic History*, 65, 36–71.

Fleck, R. K. (1999), 'The Marginal Effect of New Deal Relief Work on County-Level Unemployment Statistics', *Journal of Economic History*, 59, 659–87.

Freeman, R. B. (1998), 'Spurts in Union Growth: Defining Moments and Social Processes', in M. D. Bordo, C. Goldin, and E. N. White (eds), *The Defining Moment: The Great Depression and the American Economy in the Twentieth Century*. Chicago: University of Chicago Press.

Garside, W. R. (1990), *British Unemployment 1919–1939: A Case Study in Public Policy*. Cambridge: Cambridge University Press.

George, C. O. (1940), 'Comment on R. D. G. Allen (The Unemployment Situation at the Outbreak of War)', *Journal of the Royal Statistical Society*, 103, 211–13.

Gordon, R. J. (2010),'Okun's Law, Productivity Innovations and Conundrums in Business Cycle Dating', *American Economic Review*, 100, 11–15.

Gordon, R. J. and Krenn, R. (2010), 'The End of the Great Depression 1939–41: VAR Insight on Policy Contributions and Fiscal Multipliers', Northwestern University, unpublished paper.

Gregg, P. and Wadsworth, J. (2010), 'The UK Labour Market and the 2008–09 Recession', *National Institute Economic Review*, 212, R61–72.

Grubb, D. B., Jackman, R., and Layard, R. (1983), 'Wage Rigidity and Unemployment in OECD Countries', *European Economic Review*, 21 (1–2), 11–39.

Hanes, C. (2000), 'Nominal Wage Rigidity and Industry Characteristics in the Downturns of 1893, 1929, and 1981', *American Economic Review*, 90, 1432–46.

Harris, J. (1972), *Unemployment and Politics: A Study in English Social Policy, 1886–1914*. Oxford: Clarendon Press.

Hatton, T. J. (1986), 'Structural Aspects of Unemployment in Britain between the World Wars', *Research in Economic History*, 10, 55–92.

Hatton, T. J. (1988a), 'Institutional Change and Wage Rigidity in the UK, 1880-1985', *Oxford Review of Economic Policy*, 4, 74–86.

Hatton, T. J. (1988b), 'A Quarterly Model of the Labour Market in Interwar Britain', *Oxford Bulletin of Economics and Statistics*, 50, 1–26.

Hatton, T. J. (2003), 'Unemployment and the Labour Market, 1870–1939', in R. C. Floud and P. A. Johnson (eds), *The Cambridge Economic History of Modern Britain*. Cambridge: Cambridge University Press.

Hatton, T. J. (2007), 'Can Productivity Growth Explain the NAIRU? Long Run Evidence from Britain, 1870–1999', *Economica*, 74, 475–91.

Hatton, T. J. and Bailey R. E (2002), 'Unemployment Incidence in Interwar London', *Economica*, 69, 631–54.

Higgs, R. J. (2006), *Depression, War, and Cold War: Studies in Political Economy*. New York: Oxford University Press.

International Labour Office (1942), 'The Impact of War on Long Term Unemployment in Great Britain', *International Labour Review*, 45, 44–63.

Jacoby, S. M. (2004), *Employing Bureaucracy: Managers, Unions, and the Transformation of Work in the Twentieth Century*, Revised Edition. Mahwah, NJ: Erlbaum Associates.

Jacoby, S. M. and Sharma, S. (1992), 'Employment Duration and Industrial Labor Mobility in the United States 1880–1980', *Journal of Economic History*, 52, 161–79.

Jensen, R. (1989), 'The Causes and Cures of Unemployment in the Great Depression', *Journal of Interdisciplinary History*, 19, 553–83.

Kesselman, J. R. and Savin, N. E. (1978), 'Three-and-a-half Million Workers Never Were Lost', *Economic Inquiry*, 16, 205–25.

Keynes, J. M. (1931), *Essays in Persuasion*. London: Macmillan.

Layard, R., Nickell, S. J., and Jackman, R. (2005), *Unemployment, Macroeconomic Performance and the Labour Market* (2nd edn). Oxford: Oxford University Press.

Llaudes, R. (2005), 'The Phillips Curve and Long-term Unemployment', Frankfurt: ECB Working Paper no. 441.

Long, C. D. (1944), *The Labor Force in Wartime America*. New York: National Bureau of Economic Research.

Madsen, J. B. (2004), 'Price and Wage Stickiness during the Great Depression', *European Review of Economic History*, 8, 263–95.

Margo, R. A. (1991), 'The Microeconomics of Depression Unemployment', *Journal of Economic History*, 51, 333–41.

Margo, R. A. (1993), 'Employment and Unemployment in the 1930s', *Journal of Economic Perspectives*, 7, 41–59.

Martin, B. (2011), 'Is the British Economy Supply Constrained? A Critique of Productivity Pessimism', UK-IRC Report: University of Cambridge, available at <http://www.cbr.cam.ac.uk/pdf/BM_Report.pdf>.

Matthews, K. G. P. (1986), *The Interwar Economy: An Equilibrium Analysis*. Aldershot: Gower.

Montgomery, D. (1987), *The Fall of the House of Labor: The Workplace, the State, and American Labor Activism, 1865–1925*. New York: Cambridge University Press.

Moss, D. A. (2002), *When All Else Fails: Government as the Ultimate Risk Manager*. Cambridge MA: Harvard University Press.

Neumann, T. C., Fishback, P. V., and Kantor, S. (2010), 'The Dynamics of Relief Spending and the Private Urban Labour Market during the New Deal', *Journal of Economic History*, 70, 195–220.

Newell, A. and Symons, J. S. V. (1988), 'The Macroeconomics of the Interwar Years: International Comparisons', in B. Eichengreen and T. J. Hatton (eds), *Interwar Unemployment in International Perspective*. Dordrecht and Boston: Martinus-Nijhoff, 61–96.

Nickell, S. J. (1997), 'Unemployment and Labor Market Rigidities: Europe versus North America', *Journal of Economic Perspectives*, 11, 55–74.

Nickell, S. J. (1998), 'Unemployment: Questions and Some Answers', *Economic Journal*, 108, 802–16.

Nickell, S. J. (2000), 'Institutions and the Workings of the Labour Market', in H. de Largentaye, P.-A. Muet, J.-F. Richard, and J. E. Stiglitz (eds), *Governance, Equity and Global Markets: Proceedings of the Annual Bank Conference on Development Economics in Europe*. Paris: La Documentation Française.

O'Brien, A. P. (1989), 'A Behavioral Explanation for Nominal Wage Rigidity during the Great Depression', *Quarterly Journal of Economics*, 104, 719–35.

Ohanian, L. E. (2009), 'What—or Who—Started the Great Depression?', *Journal of Economic Theory*, 144, 2310–35.

Palmer, G. L. (1937), *Recent Trends in Employment and Unemployment in Philadelphia*. Philadelphia: University of Pennsylvania.

Pigou, A. C. (1927), 'Wage Policy and Unemployment', *Economic Journal*, 37, 355–68.

Reinhart, C. M. and Reinhart, V. R. (2009), 'When the North Last Headed South: Revisiting the 1930s', *Brookings Papers in Economic Activity*, Fall, 251–72.

Reubens, B. C. (1945), 'Unemployment in Wartime Britain', *Quarterly Journal of Economics*, 59, 206–36.

Romer, C. (1992), 'What Ended the Great Depression?', *Journal of Economic History*, 52, 757–84.

Rose, J. D. (2010), 'Hoover's Truce: Wage Rigidity in the Onset of the Great Depression', *Journal of Economic History*, 70, 843–70.

Rosenbloom, J. L. and Sundstrom, W. A. (1999), 'The Sources of Regional Variation in the Severity of the Great Depression: Evidence from US Manufacturing, 1919–1937', *Journal of Economic History*, 59, 714–47.

Rosenbloom, J. L. and Sundstrom, W. A. (2011), 'Labor-Market Regimes in US Economic History', in P. W. Rhode, J. L. Rosenbloom, and D. F. Weiman (eds), *Economic Evolution and Revolutions in Historical Time*. Stanford, CA: Stanford University Press.

Smiley, G. (1983), 'Recent Unemployment Rate Estimates for the 1920s and 1930s', *Journal of Economic History*, 43, 487–93.

Soskice, D. (1990), 'Wage Determination: The Changing Role of Institutions in Advanced Industrialized Countries', *Oxford Review of Economic Policy*, 6, 36–61.

Taylor, J. E. (2011), 'Work-sharing During the Great Depression: Did the "President's Reemployment Agreement" Promote Reemployment?', *Economica*, 78(309) January, 133–58.

Temin, P. and Wigmore, B. A. (1990), 'The End of One Big Deflation', *Explorations in Economic History*, 27, 483–502.

Thomas, M. (1983), 'Rearmament and Economic Recovery in the Late 1930s', *Economic History Review*, 36, 552–79.

Thomas, M. (1988), 'Labour Market Structure and the Nature of Unemployment in Interwar Britain', in B. Eichengreen and T. J. Hatton (eds), *Interwar Unemployment in International Perspective*. Dordrecht: Kluwer.

Thomas, M. (1992), 'Institutional Rigidity in the British Labour Market, 1870–1939: A Comparative Perspective', in S. N. Broadberry and N. F. R. Crafts (eds), *Britain in the International Economy, 1870–1939*. Cambridge: Cambridge University Press.

Thomas, M. (1994), 'The Macro-economics of the Inter-war Years', in R. Floud and D. N. McCloskey, *The Economic History of Britain since 1700, volume 2: 1860–1939*. Cambridge: Cambridge University Press.

Thomas, R. L. and Stoney, P. J. M. (1971), 'Unemployment Dispersion as a Determinant of Wage Inflation in the UK 1925–66', *Manchester School*, 39, 83–116.

Vatter, H. G. (1985), *The US Economy in World War II.* New York: Columbia University Press.

Vedder, R. K. and Galloway, L. E. (1993), *Out of Work: Unemployment and Government in Twentieth Century America.* New York: Holmes and Meier.

Velde, F. R. (2009), 'The Recession of 1937—A Cautionary Tale', *Economic Perspectives*, 33, 16–37.

Vernon, J. R. (1991), 'The 1920–21 Deflation: the Role of Aggregate Supply', *Economic Inquiry*, 29, 572–80.

Vernon, J. R. (1994), 'World War II Fiscal Policies and the End of the Great Depression', *Journal of Economic History*, 54, 850–68.

Wallis, J. J. (1989), 'Employment in the Great Depression: New Data and New Hypotheses', *Explorations in Economic History*, 26, 45–72.

Wallis, J. J. (2010), 'Lessons from the Political Economy of the New Deal', *Oxford Review of Economic Policy*, 26, 442–62.

Wallis, J. J. and Benjamin, D. K. (1981), 'Public Relief and Private Employment in the Great Depression', *Journal of Economic History*, 41, 97–102.

Weinstein, M. (1980), *Recovery and Redistribution under the NIRA.* Amsterdam: North Holland.

Weir, D. R. (1992), 'A Century of US Unemployment, 1890–1990: Revised Estimates and Evidence for Stabilization', *Research in Economic History*, 14, 301–46.

Whaples, R. (1990), 'Winning the Eight-Hour Day, 1909–1919', *Journal of Economic History*, 50, 393–406.

Wolcott, S. (1993), 'Keynes vs. Churchill: Sterling Overvaluation and British Unemployment in the Twenties', *Journal of Economic History*, 53, 601–28.

12

Economic Growth and Recovery in the United States: 1919–1941

Alexander J. Field

12.1. INTRODUCTION

This chapter has two main sections and an appendix. The first section provides an overview of what lay behind record productivity growth in the US economy between 1929 and 1941. The second considers the role of rigidities and other negative supply conditions in worsening the downturn and slowing recovery. While I argue consistently that the overarching explanation of the Great Depression will and should continue to emphasize a collapse and slow revival of the growth of aggregate demand, I spend relatively little time on what drives this since these issues are dealt with in detail elsewhere in the volume. The chapter instead concentrates on the aggregate supply side—both the broad array of positive shocks that I argue propelled potential and, eventually, actual output forward, and the negative conditions which, in interaction with aggregate demand, may have increased the size of the output gap and prolonged its persistence. An appendix offers detail discussion and updated calculations of productivity growth rates for the critical period from 1929 to 1941.

12.2. GROWTH AND CYCLES

Economic growth and business cycles are two of macroeconomists' central concerns. In principle, this should be no less true in studies of the Great Depression. Yet for perhaps understandable reasons, the preponderance of academic scholarship has focused on the persistent output gap and high unemployment that marked the 1930s. In other words, it has focused on cycles.

This chapter examines the years 1929–41 in the United States with a focus on the growth of actual and potential output during this period as well as the expansion and contraction of the output gap—the difference between actual and potential.[1]

[1] Potential output, sometimes referred to as natural or full employment output, is the highest level of output sustainable without so stimulating the economy through monetary and/or fiscal policy that

A principal theme is that potential, and, eventually, actual output rose very rapidly over this 12 year period, almost entirely as the consequence of the growth of total factor productivity.[2] It was this growth that made possible the successful prosecution of the Second World War as well as what Walt Rostow (1960) called the age of high mass consumption that followed. In other words, I argue that the infrastructural, organizational, and technological foundations of the golden age (1948–73) were already largely in place by 1941. This contrasts with the standard narrative which suggests that the war somehow magically transformed the doom and gloom of the Depression years, so that, like a phoenix rising from the ashes, the US suddenly, in 1948, stands a colossus astride the world economy. Given that the United States was involved in the war for less than four years, with full scale war mobilization lasting perhaps sixteen months, this narrative warrants re-examination.

The Depression years were disastrous from the standpoint of capacity utilization, and I do not mean to downplay any of this. Bank failures and financial crisis were associated with an 87 per cent decline in real gross private domestic investment between 1929 and 1932. Construction spending never recovered from its 1920s peaks until after the war. 1929 vehicle production was not reattained until 1949. The Dow Jones Industrial Index dropped 89 per cent from its August 1929 peak to its trough in July of 1932, with many of the twentieth century's largest one day *increases* occurring during that volatile and sickening slide. Real GDP declined more than 27 per cent and unemployment rose from 3.2 per cent in 1929 to 25 per cent in 1933, while consumption declined 18 per cent in real terms. Double digit unemployment for more than a decade represented a terrible waste of human and other resources, and untold hardship for the millions of people out of work.[3]

And yet the Depression years were also a triumph of American ingenuity, inventiveness, and hard work. Fuelled by an explosion of research and development, government infrastructure investment, and creative response to adversity, scientific, technological, and organizational advance expanded the capabilities—

an acceleration of the inflation rate ensues. Generally speaking, when one is below potential, that is, in the presence of an output gap, an increase in nominal income will result mostly in increases in output and employment. As an economy approaches potential from below, additional stimulus begins to be experienced as price increases rather than output growth. With labour and physical capital now in short supply, inflation accelerates and, in the face of further increase in aggregate demand, growth in output and employment will stall.

[2] Total factor productivity (TFP) is the ratio of output to a combined measure of capital and labour input. Labour productivity, in contrast, is the ratio of output to the number of workers or worker hours. The growth of TFP is the difference between the growth of output and a weighted average of the growth of inputs, with the weights corresponding to the shares of the two factors in national income. For the Depression years, the precise weights don't matter much, because neither labour nor private sector physical capital inputs grew noticeably between 1929 and 1941. Thus, all of the substantial output growth between these years can be attributed to an increase in total factor productivity. For details, see Field (2011: introduction and appendix), as well as the appendix to this chapter.

[3] Investment, consumption, and output data are from <http://www.bea.gov>, National Income and Product Accounts, Table 1.1.3, accessed 22 January 2012. The unemployment data are from Lebergott (1964). Construction data are from Carter et al, (2006), series Dc262. For the Dow Jones Industrial Index, see: <http://stockcharts.com/freecharts/historical/djia19201940.html>.

the potential output—of the economy.[4] What I have called the country's Great Leap Forward (Field, 2011) helped the United States win the war and set the stage for a quarter century of post-war prosperity. It is part of the explanation, along with wartime destruction in other countries, for why the US loomed so large in the world economy in 1948, and high post-war growth rates in Europe and Japan represented, in part, catch up to a frontier that had been pushed out in the United States during the 1930s (Abramovitz, 1986).

This expansion in potential and, when demand conditions permitted, actual output was fuelled by several tributaries. The first was the maturing of a privately funded research and development system that had begun with Thomas Edison in Menlo Park, New Jersey. Then, as now, most private sector R&D was conducted in manufacturing, and we have good data on activity in this sector because of surveys conducted by the National Research Council in 1927, 1933, and 1940. R&D employment, which stood at 6,274 in 1927 had, by 1933, after four of the worst years of the Depression, climbed to 10,918. In 1940, after another seven years of double digit unemployment, that number stood at 27,777. Data on the number of labs established, and actual spending, paint a similar picture, with particularly dramatic increases after 1935 (Mowery and Rosenberg, 2000: 814; Field, 2011: 56, Table 2.4).

A second tributary reflected spillovers from the government funded build out of the surface road network. The US produced more than four million passenger vehicles in 1929, a level of production not reached again for twenty years (Carter et al., 2006, series Df343). By the second half of the decade the growth of vehicle registrations had outrun the capabilities of the road infrastructure. A strong political coalition pressed for better roads. Farmers wanted them, complaining that their French counterparts moved grain at half the cost over a superior surfaced road network, while American agriculturists faced the equivalent of a mud tax. Bicyclists wanted them, car owners and car makers and suppliers to the auto industry (plate glass makers, tyre makers, steel makers) wanted them, as did the petroleum, asphalt, and motel industries. Truckers wanted them, as did, perhaps surprisingly, railroads, which saw themselves as evolving a symbiotic relationship with truckers in which they (the railroads) would be the senior partners (Paxson, 1946; Finch, 1992; Goddard, 1994).

But the location of a national road network was a contentious business, because it would mean (as did the building of the interstates three decades later) the making and breaking of many local communities. State highway departments had to reach agreement with each other and the federal authorities over what routes would be national. By November of 1926 a treaty had been negotiated, its terms reflected in the publication of a detailed map showing the proposed US route system. The country then started building or improving streets, highways, bridges, and tunnels, and if one just looks at the data for such expenditures, it is hard to tell that the country had a depression (there were moderate declines in spending,

[4] The full dimensions of that expansion were first appreciated when war planners, in particular Simon Kuznets, began, after Pearl Harbor, to reckon how much guns and butter the US economy could produce, and were not fully revealed until the massive fiscal and monetary stimulus associated with the Second World War closed the remaining output gap.

relative to the late 1920s, in 1933, 1934, and 1935).[5] By 1941, the US route system was complete, and, because of its growth, productivity in transportation (both trucking and railroads) as well as wholesale and retail distribution had risen dramatically (Field, 2006, 2011: chapter 2).

Finally, some sectors, like railroads, benefited from the kick in the rear of adversity that generated creative responses. In the 1920s, railroads had been able to solve their problems essentially by throwing money at them. But, in the 1930s, access to cheap 50-year mortgage money dried up, and by the middle of the decade roads responsible for more than a third of first track mileage were in receivership (Schiffman, 2003). Rationalization, including major advances in freight interchange, meant big gains in efficiency. Progress toward unlimited freight interchange began with gauge standardization in the 1880s and continued during the First World War when, as troops operated the rail system, the government pressed for standardization of equipment and operating procedures. The US had a national rail network, but it consisted of individual lines owned and operated by private firms. The question of what happened when, for example a freight car went into 'foreign' territory had important economic consequences. Was it necessary to break cargo? Could a car delivering outside of its system pick up a new load for the return trip in a competitor's region? If locomotives or rolling stock broke down, could they be repaired in a foreign yard?

Developing uniform procedures and tariffs governing interline transactions allowed huge efficiency gains. The number of employees, locomotives, freight cars, and passenger cars each dropped by a quarter or a third between 1929 and 1941. Yet revenue freight ton miles in 1941 were slightly higher than in 1929, and passenger miles were almost as high. These ratios translated into very significant productivity gains (Stover, 1997; Field, 2011: chapter 12, 2012).

It is natural to ask, given the coincidence of the greatest economic depression and the most rapid productivity growth of the twentieth century, whether there is a necessary connection between depression and rapid productivity growth. There is no simple answer. Much of the coincidence reflects serendipity. A number of technological paradigms were ripe for exploitation at the time, and a good deal of what happened would have happened without the Depression. If it were true that economic downturns laid the foundations for higher productivity growth in the future, we could console those out of work with the thought that their sacrifices were laying the foundation for a better tomorrow. To argue thus would, however, be both cruel and largely unjustified, because the response of economic organizations to adversity, like that of individuals, varies greatly. Some sectors did respond in ways that generated persisting benefits, and for the 1930s the railroad sector is the poster child for this style of argument, providing the best support for Richard Posner's suggestion that depressions may have a silver lining (Posner, 2009). There is anecdotal evidence that this dynamic may also have affected parts of the manufacturing sector.[6]

[5] See Carter et al. (2006), series Dc371.

[6] 'In the automobile industry particularly, but in other manufacturing industries as well, improvements in plant layout appear to have been greatly stimulated by the depression, with resulting better continuity of the flow of work and savings in direct and supervisory labor, equipment, floor space, and inventories' (Weintraub, 1939: 26).

Technological change during the 1930s involved both product and process innovations: the development, introduction, and refinement of dramatic new products, as well as more mundane changes in how they were made or services delivered, that cumulatively and in the aggregate made a big difference. Some Depression era advance involved refinements of products already available in the 1920s (automobiles and mechanical refrigerators are examples). In other instances (nylon a case in point), entirely new materials and products made from them were both developed and rolled out during the Depression years. Finally, research and development restocked the larder for the post-war period, by replenishing the storehouse of only partially or minimally exploited innovations, such as television.

In the latter category, Philo T. Farnsworth's development of what would be the signature new consumer product of the post-war period was financed during the 1930s by San Francisco venture capital. After a lengthy patent dispute, in which Farnsworth prevailed, television was introduced to the public by RCA at the 1939–40 New York World's Fair, at the same time as commercial broadcasts began. Although production and diffusion was interrupted by the war, take-up was extremely rapid beginning in the late 1940s, as is typical for new entertainment as opposed to labour saving consumer appliances (Bowden and Offer, 1994; Field, 2010b).

Advances in aeronautical innovation impacted a nascent industry during the Depression at the same time as they laid the foundation for war production as well as the post-war aviation sector. In 1936, Donald Douglas introduced the DC3—arguably the world's most famous and successful aircraft (it had a starring role in the closing scenes of the movie Casablanca, alongside Humphrey Bogart and Claude Rains). Over 16,000 were produced, including over 10,000 C-47s—a military version with strengthened floor and cargo doors, built during the war. Several hundred are still in operation. A reflection of the state of aeronautical advance during the 1930s (as well as the relatively short period of US involvement in the war) is this: all US aircraft that saw major service operation in World War Two were already on the drawing boards ('substantially designed') in December of 1941 (Galbraith, 1967: 22).

Other products, developed and rolled out during the Depression, achieved high penetration before the war began. In 1928 the DuPont Corporation lured Wallace Caruthers away from his laboratory at Harvard to Delaware, where he began to develop blockbuster new materials including neoprene and nylon. The company introduced nylon stockings to a ravenous female population on 15 May 1940, selling almost 5 million pairs the first day, and 63 million pairs the first year, before production was diverted towards parachutes and mosquito netting for the Pacific campaigns. Caruthers unfortunately did not live to see any of this. Suffering from depression of a different kind, he committed suicide in 1937 (Hermes, 1996).

The 1930s also saw major refinement of products already available to a limited audience in the 1920s. During the 1930s, mechanical refrigerators moved from a 'bleeding edge' product to a mass production and mass consumption item. In the 1920s, if you asked members of an American household whether they had refrigeration, and they answered affirmatively, it usually meant they had an icebox—literally. A huge infrastructure supported an industry that cut frozen water from northern lakes and ponds during the winter, stored the product in insulated warehouses, and distributed it throughout the year.

Entrepreneurs commercialized two systems of mechanical refrigeration for homes during the 1920s. The first, powered by gas, silent and involving no moving parts, was arguably the superior technology (the Servel Corporation continued to manufacture these into the 1950s). The other, whose descendants cool our food today, involved mechanical compressors driven by an electric motor. Electric utilities were involved in marketing the new product, and favoured the latter technology. But they did not push home refrigeration hard until the 1930s.

During the 1920s, both types of refrigerators were boutique products, produced by hundreds of small companies, and achieving low penetration. The appliances were prone to breakdown and required a great deal of after sales service. Although mechanical refrigeration was available, by the end of the decade, it was in use in only a small fraction, perhaps 3 per cent, of American households (Tobey, 1996: 17–19).

In addition to questions of reliability, the state of wiring in American households placed serious obstacles to diffusion. By the end of the 1920s a large fraction of urban US households were 'electrified'. What this typically meant, however, was that there was one light fixture in the ceiling of each room and perhaps one wall or 'utility' outlet per room. The outlets and the electrical feed could handle a floor lamp or a small radio, but the heavier loads demanded by refrigerators or washing machines would almost certainly blow a fuse.

By 1941, many houses had upgraded wiring, mechanical refrigerators were much more reliable, and with experience and mass production, their cost had come down. By 1940, 44 per cent of US households had mechanical refrigeration: 56 per cent of urban households, 39 per cent of rural non-farm households, and 15 per cent of farm households (US Bureau of the Census *Statistical Abstract of the United States, 1948*: 813, Table 914). This diffusion is a concrete manifestation of the fact that if you kept your job during the Depression, your real hourly wages went up, and quite dramatically, rising at a rate equal to or exceeding what occurred in the post-war period.

In contrast with mechanical refrigerators, automobiles had achieved mass market status in the 1920s, with registrations increasing from 6.7 million to 23.1 million over the decade. Because of the Depression and the war, car production did not reattain its 1929 peak until 1949. US car makers nevertheless produced 33.3 million passenger vehicles during the twelve years of the Depression (1930–41 inclusive), slightly more than the 32.7 million manufactured during the eleven years 1919–29. Registrations grew by 6.5 million (Carter et al., 2006: series Df340, Df343). Stated another way, there was enough automobile production during the Depression to replace every car registered in 1929 at least once, as well as add millions to the stock of those on the road by the time the war began.

And the cars were much improved. Radios, heaters, and four wheel hydraulic brakes were now standard. Automatic transmission, power steering, and more powerful engines became options. Tyres moved from the narrow profile high pressure products of the 1920s—reflecting the birth of the automobile in the bicycle industry—to the low pressure balloon tyres upon which most of us roll today. Vehicles were streamlined and more aerodynamic, with headlights and trunks (boots) incorporated into the body rather than add-ons. Raff and Trachtenberg (1997) see the decade of the 1930s as the last in which major innovations in vehicle design took place.

Although the absolute numbers were smaller, the percentage increase in truck and bus production and registrations was even larger. Truck registrations grew from 3.5 million in 1929 to 5.2 million in 1941, and bus registrations almost quadrupled, from 34,000 in 1929 to 120,000 in 1941. Combined truck and bus production between 1929 and 1941 inclusive totalled 7.5 million, as compared with 4.9 million between 1919 and 1929 inclusive (Carter et al., 2006: series Df341, Df342, and Df345). As was the case for automobiles, there was enough production during the Depression to replace every truck and bus on the road in 1929 at least once, and add millions more to the transportation system. These newer vehicles were, on average, larger, more powerful, and more reliable.

Although perhaps less visible to the consumer, the 1930s were also a great age of process and materials innovations. There were big improvements in thermal efficiency, as well as gains based on the exploitation of square–cube relationships in the construction of, for example, larger boilers. In 1941, US output of electricity was 87 per cent above its 1929 level, driven largely by improvements in productivity, as well as government expansion of hydropower. The bulk of the industry, however, relied then, as it does today, on fossil fuel to drive steam turbines. Here, topping techniques used the steam from high pressure boilers to heat lower pressure boilers. Topping raised capacity by 40 to 90 per cent with no increase in fuel costs or labour. More generally, throughout industry, exhaust gasses from stacks were used to preheat air to improve combustion, preheat materials for subsequent fabrication, or generate steam (Weintraub, 1939: 20).

Improvements in thermal efficiency also benefited from attention to low cost, but often high payoff, investments in insulation. Similarly, modest investments in instrumentation yielded big efficiency gains, facilitating automatic process control, which lengthened the life of equipment, and reduced downtime and maintenance costs. The cost of instruments was often trivial compared to the improvements in capital and labour productivity they enabled. In the 1920s, cracking units in petroleum refining needed to be cleaned every four to five days. Instrumentation cut this to every one or two months. Hand controlled boilers required rebricking every three months; instrument controls eliminated the need to do so entirely. Engineers and chemists also made great progress in finding new uses for solid and liquid by-products, thus performing the alchemy of turning industrial excrement into gold.

Machinery became larger, which often resulted in scale economies. Industrial locomotives sold between 1932 and 1936 averaged 11.4 tons, versus 7.4 tons between 1924 and 1927. The capacity of a power shovel rose from 1.73 cubic yards in 1920–23, to 1.90 in 1924–27, to 2.51 in 1928–31, to 3.28 cubic yards in 1932–36. Square–cube relationships meant that capital and operating costs per unit of output dropped when capacity increased. This dynamic could also be observed in electric power generating units as well as in the spiral conveyer screws used to move materials in flour mills (Weintraub, 1939: 17).

Advances in chemical engineering and the use of new materials made contributions as well. Better treatments extended the life of wooden railroad ties from eight to twenty years. Quick drying lacquers reduced the time needed to paint a car from more than three weeks in the early 1920s to a few hours, with consequent reductions in inventory costs. Stainless steel reduced oxidization on railway cars, while chrome plating lengthened the lives of tools and moving parts. Carbon steel blades had to be removed and resharpened after cutting 60 feet of plastic. A tungsten carbon alloy blade could cut 10,000 feet without refitting. Substituting plastics for wood or metal parts saved in fuel, fabrication, and capital costs (Weintraub, 1939: 21, 23).

The 1930s also saw the tail end of the revolution in factory layout and design that had produced such extraordinary TFP gains in manufacturing between 1919 and 1929 (over 5 per cent per year). That revolution involved replacing systems for distributing power internally within a factory. Nineteenth-century systems were mechanical, relying on leather belts and mechanical shafts and gears to move power from a prime mover, usually either a steam engine or a water wheel. The canonical nineteenth-century brick factory building was four or five stories tall. Multi-story buildings represented an engineering solution to the problem, given the energy losses from friction in mechanical power distribution, of minimizing the sum of runs from the central power source. Since many of the new factory towns were on greenfield sites, building up was rarely dictated by high land values.

In a process that gathered momentum in the second decade of the twentieth century, and continued at an accelerated pace during the 1920s, businesses replaced mechanical systems with networks of electrical wire and small individual electric motors. The transition removed a straightjacket from factory design. Twentieth-century factories are typically one or two stories, with skylights to improve lighting and ventilation, as well as overhead systems for moving sub-assemblies or power tools. Even without a new building, ripping out the shafts and belts produced immediate and large gains. Under the old system there was prime real estate directly under the shafts—but much of the rest of the floor space was low value—used for storage or otherwise wasted. With electric wiring and small electric motors, space could be used much more efficiently (Field, 2011: chapter 2; Devine, 1983). And freed finally from the dirt, grime, and lubricating oils dripping from overhead shafts, factories could become much cleaner.

By 1929, roughly three-quarters of US industrial capacity had already experienced this transition,[7] with results reflected in strong TFP growth across all two digit manufacturing industries (Field, 2011: 52–3, Table 2.2). This transition could propel manufacturing TFP to permanently higher levels but, as the Solow growth model reminds us, could not permanently increase growth rates. Still, as the 1930s began, there was some juice left in this fruit. In 1933, for example, Cadillac consolidated production of drive trains from four floors onto one, leaving the other three available for other uses. In 1934, Packard cut in half its floor space

[7] Within manufacturing, electric motor horsepower more than doubled between 1919 and 1929, from 15.613 million in 1919 to 33.844 million, and increased further to 45.291 million in 1939 (this includes motors driven by purchased electricity as well as those that used electricity generated onsite). Other power used directly in production in 1929 included 9.157 million horsepower from steam engines, 1.203 million from internal combustion engines, and 1.557 million from hydroturbines and water wheels. Manufacturing also exploited 7.410 million of steam turbine horsepower, but most of this was probably used for onsite generation of electricity rather than directly in the production of motive power. Bringing these numbers together, we can conclude that, in 1929, 33.844 million out of a total of 45.761 million horsepower used directly to produce motive power (74 per cent) was provided by electric motors. This slightly underestimates that share since most of the hydroturbines (included in the data with water wheels) were probably also used for onsite electricity generation rather than directly for motive power (US Bureau of the Census, *Statistical Abstract of the United States, 1948*: 828, Table 927).

requirements per unit of output, freeing an entire building, and similar improvements were reported by Westinghouse and Western Electric. And by rearranging machinery in a linear pattern and changing the way materials were handled, the textile industry garnered high rates of productivity growth during a period in which spinning and weaving technology remained largely unchanged. In other industries, electrically driven conveyer belts saved labour, but also saved capital through the elimination of waste, reduction of spoilage, and shortening of time in process (Weintraub, 1939: 24–25).

Nevertheless, as the gains in manufacturing from this source waned, TFP growth in the sector would inevitably weaken. And indeed, manufacturing TFP growth declined by almost half, comparing 1929–41 with 1919–29, although remaining world class by any standard of comparison other than the 1920s (Field, 2011: 54, Table 2.3). An important question is what kept it from falling further. The answer is to be found in the remarkable development of a privately funded R&D system, some of whose contributions we have already discussed.

In the 1920s, almost all (about four-fifths) of the 2 per cent per year TFP growth in the private non-farm economy is attributable to the 5 per cent per year sectoral growth in manufacturing (Field, 2011: 69 Table 2.10). It is true that the manufacturing share of national income grew in the 1930s, but since its TFP growth rate was declining, it is obvious that the explanation for a higher private non-farm economy (PNE) TFP growth rate in the 1930s must be found in part in other sectors.

The other major source, as noted, was spillovers in transportation and distribution resulting from the build-out of the surface road network. High rates of productivity growth in trucking, railroad transportation, and trade, weighted by their sectoral shares, in the aggregate made a contribution to PNE TFP growth in the 1930s roughly equal in magnitude to that of manufacturing. Railway productivity soared, in part because of institutional and organizational changes involving freight interchange, but also because the paving and extension of the road network solved a critical peak load problem that had plagued the system in prior decades.

Railways depended on surface roads to move merchandise the final mile to households, but many of these roads were impassable because of snow or mud during much of the year. Thus, the demand for freight cars exceeded capacity for four months of the year, while the system had to carry excess capacity for the remainder. Road improvements largely solved this problem. The developing symbiotic relationship with the flexible and rapidly growing trucking system meant that railways performed much better in the Second as opposed to the First World War, when they were taken over and operated by government troops. Another contributor to better performance during 1941–45 was that it was a two front war—in the Pacific as well as the Atlantic—thus solving the backhaul (east to west) problem that had bedevilled the system in 1917 and 1918. The trucking industry, in turn, grew very rapidly, experiencing high rates of productivity advance. Together, these improvements allowed big gains in efficiency in wholesale and retail trade (Goddard, 1994; Field, 2003, 2011: chapter 2).

By 1941, the US route system was complete, and the beginnings of a network of controlled access highways could be seen in the Pennsylvania Turnpike and the Pasadena Freeway. Although the almost exclusively two lane US route system would eventually be overshadowed by the Interstate system begun fifteen years later, at the time the US system represented a huge improvement over what it replaced, both in the engineering standards to which it was built and in the simple fact, in many parts of the country, that it was paved.

These developments, and others like them, underlie what we see in aggregate measures of output and productivity. A rough measure of the technological and organizational progressivity of an era is how much more rapidly output grows than a weighted average of the growth of labour and physical capital (structures and equipment). That difference, or residual, represents the growth of total factor productivity. The basic arithmetic of growth accounting over the twelve years of the Depression is fairly simple. In the PNE, which excludes agriculture and government but covers almost everything else—about three-quarters of GDP—labour hours grew not at all between 1929 and 1941, and the private sector capital stock remained also, in the aggregate, basically unchanged. Yet real output in 1941 was between 33 and 38 per cent higher (the difference depends upon whether or not we use the newer chained index estimates of output—see the appendix). The result is a TFP growth rate of between 2.3 and 2.5 per cent per year in the PNE.

These rates of increase are before a cyclical adjustment. Since at least the end of the nineteenth century, TFP growth has been pro-cyclical, which means it tends to fall when the output gap rises, and increases as a recession ends (Field, 2010a). Ideally, to abstract from these cyclical influences, we would measure from business cycle peak to business cycle peak. This is not entirely possible for the Depression because, although 1929 can be considered a peak, the unemployment rate in 1941 was still 9.9 per cent. If we use chained index estimates of output, and make a cyclical adjustment as described in the appendix, both TFP and labour productivity growth approach 3 per cent per year across the Depression years. Since private sector input growth was effectively absent, *all* of the growth in output was on account of TFP advance. And since there was virtually no capital deepening, almost all of the growth in output per hour (labour productivity) can also be attributed to TFP growth.

Output growth in the vicinity of 3 per cent per year between 1929 and 1941 is not, per se, unusual. The long run 'speed limit' for the US since at least the end of the Civil War has been a little over 3 per cent per year. But in other periods much of that is due to input growth. What is unusual about the Depression experience, from a growth accounting perspective, is that almost all is attributable to TFP advance.

12.3. THE OUTPUT GAP

The increase of potential (and, as the output gap closed, actual) output across the Depression years was quite high, with most of the gain, especially in the former, driven by record breaking TFP advance. At the same time, the 1930s were distinguished by high unemployment and a very poor record of capacity utilization, particularly between 1929 and 1933. In this section, I consider three related issues. First, the causes of the rising unemployment and sharp decline in output between 1929 and 1933. Second, the failure of the output gap to close completely

Table 12.1. Annual growth rates of TFP, labour, and capital productivity, private non-farm economy, United States, 1869–2010, including a cyclical adjustment for 1941

	TFP	Output/ Hour	Output/Adjusted Hour[b]	Output/Unit Capital Input	Capital/ Labour[c]
1869/78–1892[a]	1.95	2.36	1.89	0.28	2.08
1892–1906	1.11	1.66	1.48	0.15	1.51
1906–1919	1.12	1.89	1.63	−0.16	2.05
1919–1929	**2.02**	**2.27**	**2.33**	**1.09**	**1.18**
1929–1941	**2.97**	**2.92**	**2.78**	**3.56**	**−0.63**
1941–1948	2.08	2.54	2.32	1.36	1.28
1948–1973	1.88	2.75	2.64	0.16	2.59
1973–1989	0.36	1.28	1.06	−1.25	2.53
1989–2000	0.79	2.07	1.57	−0.91	2.98
2000–2007	1.40	2.60	2.26	−0.51	3.11
2007–2010	0.72	2.72	2.10	−1.91	4.63
1995–2005	1.46	2.92	2.62	−0.78	3.70
2005–2010	0.59	2.15	1.58	−1.30	3.45

[a] Kendrick includes annual index numbers in levels going back to 1889, and then index numbers for the ten year periods 1879–88 and 1869–78. One way to calculate growth rates leading up to the 1892 business cycle peak would be to centre the 1869–78 observation on 1873.5 and simply calculate a continuously compounded growth rate. This yields 2.38 per cent per year. But this estimate is too high because 1873.5—indeed the whole period of post civil war adjustment—is not a business cycle peak, and this procedure will bias upwards a TFP calculation since we will measure from a trough to a business cycle peak. An alternate procedure is to run a regression through the logged values of 1879–88 (centred on 1873.5), 1879–88 (centred on 1883.5), and annual observations from 1889–1907. This returns a trend growth rate over the entire period of 1.59 per cent per year. To be consistent with the estimate of 1.59 per cent per year from 1869–78 to 1907, we need a trend growth rate of 1.95 per cent per year between 1869–78 and 1892. That is, TFP growth of 1.95 per cent from 1873.5 to 1892, and 1.11 per cent thereafter, is consistent with 1.59 per cent per year over the whole period.

[b] Output per adjusted hour uses an hours index that has been augmented to reflect changes in labour quality or composition. In creating this index, different categories of labour are weighted by their sectoral wage rates. TFP calculations are made using the adjusted hours series. For details on the cyclical adjustment for 1941, please see the appendix.

[c] Rates of capital deepening are approximately equal to the difference between the growth rate of capital productivity and the growth rate of labour productivity.

Sources: 1869–1929: Kendrick (1961, Table A-XXIII). The unadjusted data are from the column headed output per man hour, the adjusted data from the column headed output per unit of labour input. Capital Productivity is output per unit of capital input.

1929–1948: See appendix.

1948–1989, Bureau of Labour Statistics, 'Net Multifactor Productivity and Costs, 1948–2002' (1 February 2005).

1989–2010: ⟨http://www.bls.gov⟩. Data are drawn from the multifactor productivity section of the website, accessed on 22 February 2012. Output per adjusted hour is real value added in the private non-farm business sector divided by labour input, which includes the compositional adjustments.

until 1942, in spite of strong growth between 1933 and 1937 and again between 1938 and 1941. And finally, the causes of the sharp recession of 1937–38.

In the 1930s, John Maynard Keynes developed a mordant and compelling critique of the then (and again, until relatively recently) dominant view that the normal tendency of an economy, free from interference from unions, business cartels, or government, is toward full employment. If the views against which Keynesian thinking was (and sometimes still is) opposed are correct, we do not really need the concepts of full employment or an output gap. Employment is always, in a sense, 'full', and the distinction between voluntary and involuntary unemployment moot. Lower employment to population ratios can be attributed to individuals' dynamic reallocation of labour supply over the life cycle. An economy tends automatically to produce at potential, and the only meaningful way we can speak of an output gap is as a measure of the difference between what the economy is actually producing and what it could produce absent the deleterious interventions of governments or unions.[8]

When the economic downturn began in 2008, the stream of modern macroeconomics developing out of the real business cycle tradition unfortunately had very little constructive contribution to policy discussions. Faced with a developing financial crisis, and potentially catastrophic decline in aggregate demand, policy makers in the United States pulled out their intermediate macroeconomics textbooks, dusted off their IS-LM analysis, and began to calculate how large multipliers might be and what kind of fiscal and monetary stimulus was needed to avoid disaster. The experience of countries such as Britain where, ironically, policymaking was less influenced by Keynesian thinking, and indeed often operated in antagonism to its tenets, provides additional evidence that the framework Keynes developed for thinking about the performance of an economy in the short run remains as relevant as ever. Political constraints limited the size of the fiscal response in the United States. These constraints were, however, even more severe in Britain, which weathered a downturn whose depth and duration was comparatively worse than that in the United States.

The best overarching explanation for the Depression continues to be that it resulted from a collapse and slow revival of aggregate demand. To make this argument in its starkest form, we lack a plausible explanation of how potential output could have fallen so much between 1929 and 1933. There is little evidence that a large fraction of the US labour force decided between 1929 and 1933 voluntarily to reallocate its labour supply to subsequent years, or that Henry Ford suddenly forgot how to run an assembly line, or that a substantial portion of the population fell prey to a mysterious virus, or that war destroyed a major portion of the country's capital stock. All such hypotheticals would indeed have lowered potential output, but nothing remotely comparable occurred during this time frame.

To say that the Depression was principally caused by a decline and then slow revival in the growth of nominal income does not, however, preclude attention to supply-side conditions with which this interacted. In particular, we can ask to what degree obstacles on the supply side may have worsened the downturn or provided obstructions to revival, and to what degree these were the consequence of government action.

There is a venerable tradition in macroeconomic and monetary theory focused on whether or not money is 'neutral' in the short as well as the long run, that is, whether it can have real effects on output and employment. The way the question is typically posed reflects acceptance of a key premise in Milton Friedman's monetary framework (1971), the proposition that the demand to hold cash

[8] Writers within this tradition have remained somewhat ambivalent about the role of cartels or monopolies. Many dismiss their possible effects in limiting output and employment as of little empirical significance (Harberger, 1954), and are therefore sceptical of the value of antitrust policy. This attitude seems to soften considerably, however, when, as in the case of the National Industrial Recovery Act, it is the government that may be responsible for the cartelization. In such instances, combinations in restraint of trade are seen as quite damaging.

(money) is a stable function of a limited number of variables, and moreover, that there is little interest elasticity to the demand for money. Friedman's work provided much of the intellectual underpinning for attempts by central banks in the late 1970s and early 1980s to adopt constant growth rate of the money supply rules.

Such rules, and monetarism as a coherent intellectual philosophy, have been largely abandoned today and replaced with an operational emphasis on interest rate targeting, influenced by some version of the Taylor rule.[9] One of the reasons for the demise of monetarism as a guide to policy is that the demand for money or near monies has in fact proven to be quite unstable, subject, particularly in times of uncertainty or financial instability, to large perturbations based on sudden increases in the demand for liquidity, as well as flexibility in the face of changes in nominal interest rates.

A broader and more encompassing way of framing questions of neutrality is to ask whether fluctuations in *nominal income* are neutral in both the short and long run. Nominal income (GDP) is the product of real income or output and the GDP deflator. It is also arithmetically the product of the stock of money and the income velocity of money, with velocity defined as nominal income divided by the money stock. The money stock, in turn can be understood as the monetary base (high powered money), as M1, or as whatever aggregate one chooses, as long as income velocity is defined in a corresponding manner.

Nominal income and its growth fluctuate, as Friedman emphasized, because the level or growth rates of nominal money change. But they can also fluctuate because of changes in velocity, which can be due to perturbations in the demand to hold money, or particular forms of cash, as well as changes in fiscal variables (government tax and spending programmes) or changes in private sector spending propensities, especially those associated with the acquisition of investment goods (structures or equipment) and consumer durables.[10] Friedman's neutrality question, redefined, becomes whether, when for any of the reasons described above, nominal income falls, or its rate of growth decelerates, this has real effects on output and employment, and, if so, how large they are. Rigidities and/or negative changes on the supply side can make a difference in terms of the size of such effects.

Here it can be useful to partition these supply-side conditions into two categories: those that could in principle be overcome, either temporarily or permanently, by reversing the decline or slow growth of nominal income, and those that could not. For example, downwardly inflexible wages would not contribute significantly to an output decline in the absence of nominal income decline. In contrast, a

[9] The Taylor rule, developed by John Taylor of Stanford University, attempts to capture how central banks do, and perhaps should, respond to their dual mandates of controlling inflation and fostering full employment. Taylor posited that central bankers aspire to 2 per cent inflation (the ideal would be no inflation, but given that this is an imperfect business, they prefer a 2 percentage point buffer to reduce the likelihood of undershooting, which could yield deflation—which can also have deleterious consequences). Assuming a long run real interest rate of about 2.5 per cent, their base target is 4.5 per cent nominal, increased in the presence of higher than desired inflation, decreased in the presence of a persisting output gap.

[10] Only when velocity is invariant do questions of monetary and nominal income neutrality become the same.

negative aggregate supply shock that caused a third of the population and labour force to become permanently incapacitated, or a sudden, overnight change in workers' preferences in favour of leisure over work, or work five years from now versus work this year, could not be overcome, in terms of their effects on real output, simply by higher nominal income growth. The problem of lower real output in these latter cases would not be that there has been a widening of the output gap, but rather that potential output had, in a real sense, actually declined.

In terms of developments in the latter category, however, there is, as noted, no smoking gun on the supply side that can explain the rise of the unemployment rate from 3.2 per cent in 1929 to 25 per cent in 1933 and the 27 per cent decline in real output between these years. This cannot plausibly be attributed to a rise in the natural rate of unemployment because of changes in the demographic composition of the labour force, or increases in the attractiveness of living on the dole, or civil war, or some sudden collective amnesia about how to manufacture steel. That is why, in discussing the Depression, we talk in terms of an increase in the output gap. It is why we describe most of that unemployment as involuntary.[11] And it is why we continue to explore the role of changes in spending propensities, liquidity shocks, bank failures, inadequate Federal Reserve response, and other factors in bringing this about.

Distinguishing between these categories of supply conditions can matter when we move into discussions of proximate and ultimate cause. Suppose, for example, we believe that Irving Fisher's debt deflation mechanism is important in prolonging depressions. Obviously, without a deflationary impulse, debt deflation could not operate. But equally obviously, that mechanism depends on a system of borrowing and lending in which interest payments are fixed in nominal terms. In an imagined world of fully indexed debt contracts, the results for the economy would differ. In this case, however, it is still appropriate to describe the downturn as being caused by the shock to nominal income, not the absence of indexed loan contracts. The potential output of the economy would not rise with the introduction of fully indexed loan contracts (although its vulnerabilities to recessions might decline).

Similarly, if institutional changes have increased the downward inflexibility of money wages, and output falls in the face of a deflationary demand shock, it is appropriate to say that the output loss has been caused by the demand shock, not the absence of a completely flexible nominal wage system in which the spot price of labour rose and fell with demand conditions as does the price of wheat. The introduction of a regime of more downwardly flexible money wages would not

[11] Thus, while I am broadly sympathetic to many of the conclusions of Hatton and Thomas (2013), I find implausible their suggestion that the NAIRU (non-accelerating inflation rate of unemployment) rose 12 percentage points, from 4.2 to 16.9 per cent in the US during the Depression. Every period of elevated unemployment in the United States has brought forth a literature suggesting that this has been caused by a rise in the NAIRU. For the 1970s see, for example, Tobin (1977). I am receptive to the argument that the NAIRU may temporarily rise as the consequence of an economic downturn hysteresis due to atrophying of labour market attachment among the long term unemployed. But I am sceptical when large increases in the unemployment rate are attributed after the fact to rises in the NAIRU, that is, when the causal roles are reversed.

mean that the potential output of the economy had actually risen, nor would downward inflexibilities mean that it had fallen.[12]

In a series of papers, Lee Ohanian (2003, 2009), sometimes in collaboration with his co-author, Harold Cole (Cole and Ohanian, 2000, 2002, 2004), has argued that government-induced negative supply shocks explain much of the Depression's depth and duration. Although the specific culprits and particular emphases have differed as this research programme has developed, three policies have borne the brunt of the blame. First, a meeting organized by President Hoover in November of 1929 in which the president encouraged manufacturers to hold the line against nominal wage cuts in the face of what was then anticipated as a likely recession. Second, the passage in 1933 of the National Industrial Recovery Act. And third, the passage of the Wagner Act establishing the National Labour Relations Board in 1935, providing a more favourable environment for union organizing.[13]

If the Cole and Ohanian papers have a common thread, it is the claim that the main explanation for the Depression is not that nominal income was too low, but that wages were too high. In particular, they argue, between 1929 and 1933 (or at least through 1931), jawboning by Hoover kept nominal wages from falling. After 1933, New Deal policies not only kept them from falling, but caused them to rise. In both instances, policy actions allegedly made the Depression worse.[14]

The evidence indicates, however, that wages were not downwardly inflexible, even between 1929 and 1931. In *Historical Statistics of the United States*, there are two main series covering hourly wages during the Depression, one for unskilled workers, and one for production workers. Figures 12.1 and 12.2 present these, along with the CPI (consumer price index), and their ratio, which measures real wages. Let us begin with the evidence for unskilled workers.

Nominal wages fell in 1930, 1931, and 1932, for a total decline of approximately 18 per cent. Almost all of that loss was recovered between 1933 and 1934, after which nominal wages rose modestly before jumping again between 1936 and 1937. They then grew modestly through 1940, increasing sharply between 1940 and 1941. While nominal wages fell between 1929 and 1932, output declined dramatically, and while nominal wages grew, after 1933, output rose dramatically.

It is true that the CPI fell further than nominal wages during the worst years of the Depression. This meant that if you managed to keep your job and your hours, your real standard of living actually improved slightly between 1929 and 1933. Real wages then began to rise very sharply after 1933, along with economic recovery, as a large output gap began to close. Perhaps the suggestion is that if nominal wages had fallen even further, real wages could have declined, and the Depression thus avoided.

[12] Except in the sense that even in a dynamic economy with positive but low inflation, the flexibility might facilitate sectoral readjustment.

[13] Cole and Ohanian's work is part of a larger body of work intent on blaming recessions on government action. Other examples include Jude Wanniski's (1978) attribution of the Depression to the Smoot–Hawley tariff, or Robert Higgs' emphasis on the second New Deal, especially the work of the Temporary National Economic Committee, often interpreted as hostile to big business, as well as the more aggressive enforcement of antitrust policy.

[14] I interpret their argument in terms of nominal wages, because that is all an employer can set; real wages can only be known after the fact.

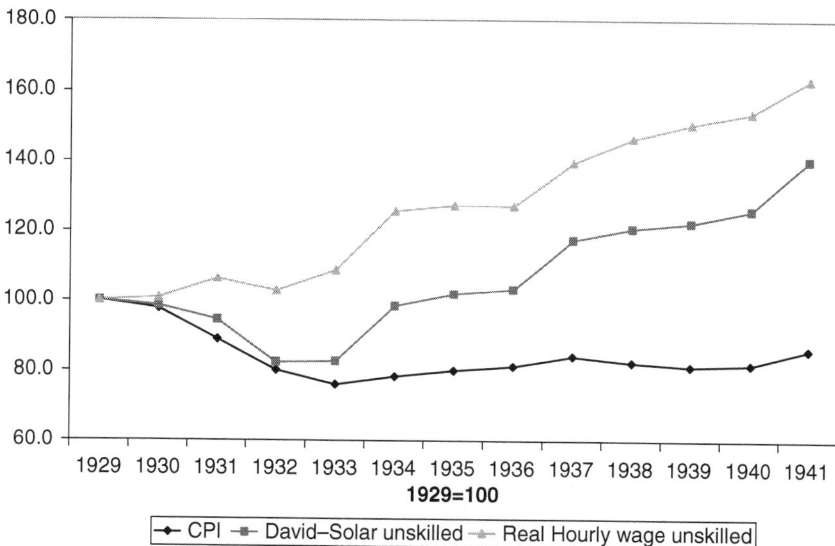

Fig. 12.1. Real hourly wages of unskilled workers, United States, 1929–41
Sources: Carter et al., 2006: Series Ba4218 and Cc1-2.

Is this likely? In answering this question, Fisher's analysis is relevant. During the seven years of rough CPI constancy between 1922 and 1929, much debt had been contracted based on the expectation of continued price stability. When prices plummeted between 1929 and 1933, real interest rates on existing and newly issued debt soared, even as nominal rates dropped. It is hard to see how a more severe deflationary impulse would have ameliorated this dynamic. Indeed, it would likely have made it worse.

Cole and Ohanian are, however, sceptical that the standard explanations of nominal income decline—bank failures, the absence of adequate Fed response, high real interest rates, and disruptions to the credit machinery—had much to do with the downturn. In support of this view, they cite the rise in the loan to output ratio between 1929 and 1932 as evidence that loanable funds were actually quite abundant during these years (Ohanian, 2003: 1212).

This, however, misinterprets what was actually happening during a period in which prices were falling and hundreds, indeed thousands, of banks were failing. Since most loan obligations were fixed in nominal terms, with deflation we would expect this ratio to have risen even if there had been no new loans to be had at any price after 1929. The numerator would have declined moderately as existing loans ran off, but the denominator would likely have been dropping even more rapidly (nominal GDP declined 46 per cent between 1929 and 1933).[15] The trend in this ratio is simply reflective of the operation of Fisher's debt deflation mechanism: the real burden of debt rose with unanticipated deflation. The rise in the burden of debt, and the increase in its value for those to whom it was owed, is consistent with

[15] <http://www.bea.gov>, NIPA Table 1.1.5.

the fact that despite loan defaults, bond interest was the only category of income to capital to rise between 1929 and 1933 (Field, 2011: 269).

The data on wages for production workers paint a very similar story. These numbers are perhaps even more relevant for the Ohanian argument, since they pertain to workers who would presumably have been most affected by restraint on the part of the captains of industry upon whom Hoover was, allegedly, effectively leaning. Here we see nominal wages dropping 10 per cent between 1929 and 1931, the period most emphasized in Ohanian's analysis, and 21 per cent between 1929 and 1933.

Neither of these series suggests that nominal wages were downwardly inflexible. Ohanian may wish that wages had fallen more, or suspect that absent Hoover, they would have fallen more. It is, however, questionable whether a faster rate of nominal wage decline would have lessened the cumulative output loss between 1929 and 1933, particularly in a world of non-indexed loan contracts and interest rates that cannot go below zero. There is, moreover, some question whether Hoover's jawboning had any significant effect on the course of nominal wages. Rose (2010) finds no evidence that industry attendance at the December 1929 conference affected the timing of reductions in nominal wages.

With respect to the 1933–41 period, our analysis can be somewhat more nuanced. We can grant the Cole–Ohanian premise that New Deal policies and legislation played a role in raising both nominal and real wages. But we should also take exception to their characterization of the recovery from 1933 as 'weak' (Ohanian, 2003: 1205). Post 1933 recovery, particularly between 1933 and 1937 (which includes the period of the NRA (National Recovery Administration)), was in fact extraordinarily strong, with rapid rises in output, employment, and income to capital as well as labour. The stock market increased by a factor of five from its trough in 1932 to its peak in 1937. Growth in real output was also strong from 1938–41, following the Wagner Act and big increases in unionization, although stock market gains were lower. Overall, output, wages, and income to capital all grew very rapidly between 1929 and 1941, and particularly between 1933 and 1941. We should not be surprised by this coincidence, since national income accounting identities tell us that the sum of income flows must approximately equal the flow of output.

How exceptional was this growth? In 1937 real output was 43 per cent higher than it had been in 1933 (NIPA, Table 1.1.6). Over those four years the economy grew at a continuously compounded rate approaching 9 per cent per year. Real output in 1941 was 91 per cent higher than in 1933—almost twice as high—a continuously compounded rate of growth of 8 per cent per year over a period that included the sharp recession of 1937–38. It is of course true that the output gap was not finally closed until 1942, which is why Ohanian can use, as evidence of weak recovery, the observation that output in 1939 was 'below trend'.

The proximate cause of recovery after 1933 was revival in the growth of aggregate demand; the particular contributors to this are discussed elsewhere in this volume. One important factor was the removal of the straightjacket on monetary growth resulting from the abandonment of the gold standard. Policy measures ended the deflation, allowing real interest rates to decline, and investment, output, and employment to begin growing again. But backstage, as the drama of this revival unfolded, potential output grew by leaps and bounds,

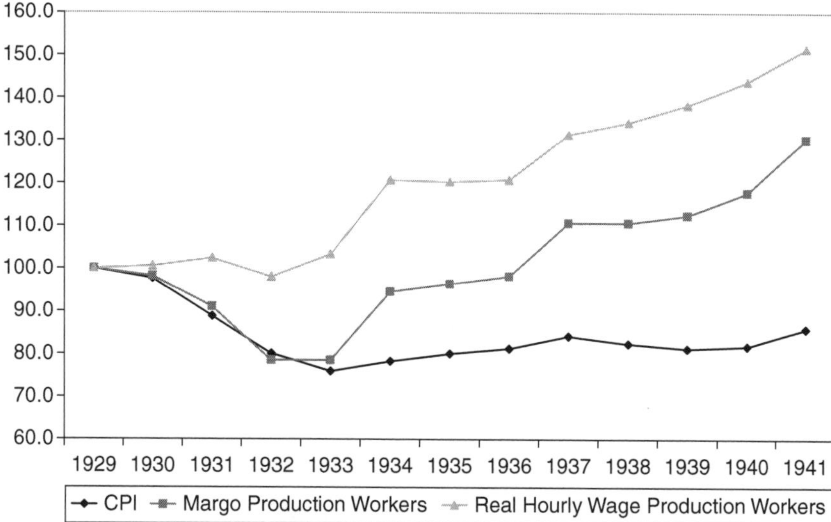

Fig. 12.2. Real hourly wages of production workers, United States, 1929–41
Sources: Carter et al., 2006: Series Ba4361 and Cc1-2.

helping to sustain an output gap that did not close completely until after the US entered the war. Its persistence can partly be attributed to supply-side obstacles to recovery in sectors such as construction (see below in this section). But it was also the case that productivity advance, which reduced the inputs required to produce a given output, contributed to slower employment growth. Concerns with technological unemployment were widespread during the Depression and, although in a well managed economy these should not be an issue over the longer run, worries about the effects of innovation on job growth had a basis over the short to medium term.[16]

There is no historical necessity that labour will share, or share proportionately in productivity gains. Institutions, politics, and culture matter. To take an extreme case, in a slave system, improvements will devolve almost entirely to the benefit of the owning class. Slave prices may be bid up, perhaps providing some additional incentives for better housing, food, and medical care, but most of the gains go to the owners. 'Free' labour markets are not all of one kind, and can be governed by quite different legal and institutional rules affecting, for example, how easy it is for labour to organize and bargain collectively.

Twentieth-century evidence suggests that there is a range of correspondence between wages and productivity—both levels and rates of growth—that can allow

[16] Capital also suffered from (or enjoyed) technological unemployment. With strong rises in capital productivity, the need for (and demand for) investment spending beyond that needed to replace worn out building and equipment was attenuated. Along with the effects of obstacles to renewed residential housing construction, this resulted in increases in gross private domestic investment that were lower than they otherwise might have been. Even after 1933, weak private capital formation hindered, from the aggregate demand side, a closing of the output gap.

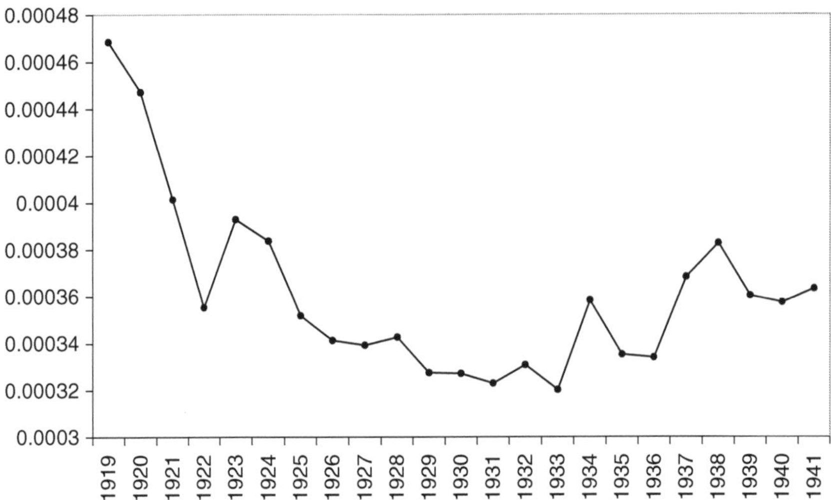

Fig. 12.3. Ratio of real hourly production worker wage to manufacturing productivity, United States, 1919–41

Source: Carter et al., 2006: Series Ba4361; Kendrick, 1961: 465–6 Table D-2.

full employment, the accumulation of physical and human capital, and healthy economic growth. In the 1960s, for example, as governments and companies in the United States and Europe dealt with strong organized labour movements, a consensus emerged that a workable course of action was to agree—at the national level, if possible—that wage gains would rise roughly alongside productivity gains. That incomes policy was considered within the realm of political discourse testifies to the fact that, under different circumstances, wage gains might or might not keep up with productivity gains, or might exceed them.

Cole and Ohanian do not dispute that productivity rose sharply, particularly after 1933. But they emphasize that wages rose faster, arguing (2002: 30) that the ratio of wages to productivity between 1929 and 1939 increased in the United States by 25 per cent, and implying that the New Deal policies that allowed labour to reap a disproportionate share of productivity gains were an impediment to full recovery. A look at Figures 12.1 and 12.2, in conjunction with Table 12.1, does indeed show that wages increased even faster than measures of productivity.

But the rise in this ratio has to be understood in the context of what had transpired in the 1920s. The 1920s were a period of high and rising income inequality, leading to levels rivalled only by what we have been experiencing in the most recent decade. If we look at the ratio of the real hourly wage of production workers to Kendrick's estimate of output per hour in manufacturing across the entire interwar period, we place in perspective the increase in the ratio to which Cole and Ohanian call our attention (see Figure 12.3). What we see is that, in terms of real hourly wages, labour shared hardly at all in the very large productivity gains in manufacturing during the 1920s. Workers did benefit from relatively full employment, which sustained household income, and increased opportunities for buying on credit allowed consumption to rise. It is nevertheless fair to say that capital reaped almost all of the gains from productivity growth in the 1920s.

This underscores the political dimension of Hoover's November 1929 meeting. A concern about labour peace was understandable, since the insult of widespread unemployment was about to be added to the injury of having received in the 1920s, in the form of increments to real hourly wages, a very small share of the preceding decade's productivity gains. This was understood at the time, if not precisely in these terms. As Hoover argued in 1931, '[w]ages during Prosperity went nowhere near so high, comparatively, as commodity prices, business profits and dividends; therefore they should not come down with the general decline' (*Time*, 13 April 1931, cited in Ohanian, 2009: 16). Following a decade in which labour reaped virtually none of the gains from prosperity, the economy in 1929 was poised to go into a devastating depression, in spite of wages then prevailing that were low in comparison with what they would have been had labour shared in the 1920s gains. Cole and Ohanian's criticism seems to be that Hoover did not do more to insure that real wages declined even further relative to productivity levels.

Before leaving Cole and Ohanian, it is worth mentioning a notable paper that recently appeared in the *Journal of Economic History*, because it goes to the heart of the real business cycle approach that informs their work. Inklaar et al. (2011) apply a methodology pioneered by Basu et al. (2006) which extracts from the Solow productivity measures that portion due to systematic pro-cyclicality. Because of the inability of the private sector as a whole to get rid of physical capital in a downturn, and thus avoid ongoing depreciation and holding costs, the economy tends to experience short run increasing returns to scale as the output gap closes (see Field, 2010a).[17] This is different from saying that the economy is subject to long run increasing returns to scale. What it means is that, while TFP really does go down (or experiences a reduced rate of growth) during a recession, this is not because of technological regress.

If we 'purify' measures of TFP by removing these cyclical effects, we can then test whether there is any discernible short run relationship between purified TFP and input levels, a key prediction of the RBC approach. Inklaar et al. (2011) show that for US manufacturing between 1919 and 1939 there is none. Their work is consistent with the view that the pro-cyclicality of TFP is principally driven by aggregate demand fluctuations, which, as one goes into recession, cause declines in output that are greater than the reduction of inputs, especially those associated with physical capital, particularly structures. By and large, observed TFP pro-cyclicality is the consequence of business cycles, not their cause.

Although it is doubtful that Hoover's and Roosevelt's labour market policies were responsible for much of the Depression, there were supply-side problems standing in the way of full recovery. Perhaps most important was the legacy of premature subdivision and fractionated land ownership that resulted from the

[17] Voluntary labour hoarding is the more typical explanation for pro-cylical productivity. It is clearly relevant in some instances—particularly in early stages of a downturn where it may not be clear how long the recession will last. But I question the persistence and generality of the phenomenon, emphasizing instead the involuntary dynamic with respect to physical capital as the more fundamental and general cause. See also Field (2010c).

uncontrolled land boom of the 1920s. I discuss the details of this at length in Field (1992); see also Field (2011: chapter 11). Neither commercial nor residential construction reattained its 1920s peaks until after the war, although commercial came back somewhat more robustly than residential. The slow revival of commercial construction is partly attributable to capital saving innovation that made more efficient use of floor space, particularly in manufacturing. The obstacles to increased residential construction were different. They included large transactions costs associated with tracking down owners of record, clearing up tax liens, and paying mortgage obligations on properties comprising failed 1920s subdivisions, many of which had been poorly designed from the standpoint of automobile transportation.[18] If we are searching for supply-side obstacles to full employment, their contribution to the collapse and slow revival of spending on residential construction is a stronger candidate.

The idea that construction held the key to understanding incomplete recovery is not novel, and was widely shared by economists both before and after the war. As Kenneth Roose, writing in 1954, said,

> ... many believed construction bore a heavy responsibility for the low level of economic activity in the 1930s. This belief was held by analysts with widely differing theoretical approaches to the recession and business fluctuations in general. Thus the National City Bank of New York, *The Economist*, and [Alvin] Hansen attached importance to the weakness of the building industry ... [Hansen] concluded "It is in this area that one finds the explanation for the incomplete recovery of the thirties" (1954: 14).

In Field (2011: 271), I calculate that the low level of residential and, to a lesser degree, non-residential construction spending relative to a 1920s baseline was responsible for approximately half of the output gap remaining at the local peak in 1937. Had potential output grown at its long term rate of approximately 3 per cent per year, it would have increased from \$87.2 billion (I take 1929 actual as potential) to \$110.9 billion in 1937 dollars. This can be compared with actual 1937 output of \$91.9 billion; the difference is the output gap. Had residential and non-residential construction spending each retained the rough equality with equipment spending characteristic of the 1920s, there would have been an additional \$5.8 billion of gross private domestic investment in 1937 dollars.

Based on the ratio of changes in real output to changes in the sum of the components of autonomous planned spending, I estimate a multiplier of 1.78 for the period 1933 through to 1937 (Field, 2011: 240, Table 10. 1).[19] This additional construction spending would, therefore, have brought actual output to \$102.2 billion, bridging roughly half the distance between actual and potential in 1937. Had exports and consumer durables been at their 1929 levels, output would have been another \$2 billion higher, getting us to \$104.2 billion. The remainder of the gap

[18] It is the absence of zoning and land use regulation, the result of inadequate rather than excessive regulation, that lies at the heart of this supply-side legacy of the 1920s for the 1930s.

[19] Keynesian multipliers, to the degree that they estimate the impact of changes in autonomous spending on real output and employment, have their greatest relevance when an economy is in recession or depression, and there is slack labour and capital available to produce additional output. This was surely one of the instances in which we should expect crowding out.

could have been closed by an additional injection of less than $4 billion in government or private infrastructure or equipment spending.

The final issue to consider concerns the causes of the sharp recession between 1937 and 1938. Here again, the overarching contributor is likely to have been a contraction in the growth of nominal income. The role of increases in reserve requirements, emphasized by Friedman and Schwartz (1963) has recently been questioned (Calomiris et al., 2011). Excess reserves were so large at the time that even the higher requirements were not binding. Irwin (2011) has emphasized the empirical significance of the Treasury's gold sterilization policy in restraining the growth of the money supply. But there is a problem with this argument. We can agree that absent sterilization, high powered money would have grown faster. But if Calomiris et al. are right, and reserve requirements were not binding, banks might well simply have held more excess reserves. For these reasons, and although its impact has been questioned by Romer (1992: 776), fiscal policy seems a better candidate if we are to emphasize a role for aggregate demand in explaining the downturn. There can be little doubt that comparing 1937 with the previous year, the fiscal posture changed from one of expansion associated with veterans' bonus payments, to contraction, associated with the introduction of payroll taxes to finance the new social security system as well as lower government spending on goods and services (NIPA, Table 1.1.6).

That said, other factors were also operative. Joshua Hausman (2011) has argued that the traditional emphasis on monetary and fiscal policy short-changes supply-side factors, in particular those affecting the motor vehicle industry. He notes that the coefficient of variation of changes in state-level private non-farm employment during the recession of 1937–38 was approximately twice what it was in other severe recessions, including 1929–33 and 2007–09. This was the consequence of particularly steep declines in manufacturing employment in states within which the auto industry was concentrated, such as Michigan, Ohio, and Indiana.

Hausman's story is that car production was hit by a negative supply shock in the form of the unionization of GM and Chrysler and higher raw material costs, leading to price increases in 1938. These increases were anticipated, leading to a shift forward of car sales to the 1937 model year at the expense of 1938 model year purchases. Motor vehicle and parts sales fell more than a third during this recession.

Christina Romer (1992: 763) raises some doubts about this argument, noting that producer prices fell 9.4 per cent. But as Hausman points out, car prices rose, and that is where the big employment losses were. Romer also argues that construction expenditures fell in late 1937, and that interest rates spiked, suggesting clear evidence of monetary tightening. The annual construction data do not seem to be consistent with this story. An index of overall construction contracts awarded (1923–25 = 100) rose from 55 in 1936, to 59 in 1937, to 64 in 1938, to 72 in 1939 (US Bureau of the Census, *Statistical Abstract of the United States, 1941*: 945, Table 929). Housing units starts (in thousands) rose from 304.2 in 1936, to 332.4 in 1937, to 399.3 in 1938 (Carter et al., 2006: Series Dc510). Residential investment, which declines in almost all recessions, actually increased slightly across this downturn, although of course, as already noted, it remained quite depressed relative to what had prevailed in the 1920s, and the monthly data do show some effect of the recession.[20] Still, the somewhat anomalous behaviour of residential construction during the 1937–38 downturn suggests that this was not entirely a garden variety recession, such as 1982, in which slowed growth in aggregate demand accounted for almost everything. As for interest rates, the annual data show declines across the board, comparing 1938 with 1937, rather than the spike posited by Romer (Carter et al., 2006: Series Cj1224 and 1231). Nor do the monthly data on short term rates show any evidence of monetary stringency in the fall of 1937 or winter of 1938 (*Banking and Monetary Statistics 1914–1941*: 451, 464, Tables 120, 125).

Finally, we can mention Robert Higgs's argument that the downturn after 1937 is attributable to the second New Deal, and Roosevelt's adoption of more vigorous antitrust enforcement, the Temporary National Economic Committee hearings, and more populist rhetoric (Higgs, 1997). Supposedly owners of capital went on a capital strike, refusing to invest because of their dislike of Roosevelt or concerns about insecure property rights. There is no doubt that a segment of the electorate hated Roosevelt, although there is little evidence their animosity was worse in 1937 than it had been in 1933. The facts are that owners of capital did much better under Roosevelt than they did under Hoover. And, after falling dramatically in 1938, real gross private domestic investment in 1939 exceeded 1936 levels, and in 1940 exceeded the 1937 peak. These data are hardly consistent with the notion of a 'capital strike' during Roosevelt's second term (USDC, NIPA, Table 1.1.6). And again, the biggest shortfalls remained in residential construction spending. One might have expected the effect of regime uncertainty, or Roosevelt hatred, to have been more apparent, for example, in producer durables spending.

Higgs and Ohanian are, of course, part of a continuing tradition aimed at fixing the responsibility for business cycles on government. That tradition includes Jude Wanniski's 1978 attempt to attribute the Great Depression entirely to the passage of the Smoot–Hawley tariff. The unifying theme in this literature is that depressions are the result of government intervention in the workings of the 'free market' system. There is no doubt that some of the policies discussed did have the potential to generate efficiency losses. But arguments that might make sense if economies always operated at potential often cease to hold in a world where output gaps are a real and continuing problem. In Economics 1, students are taught that there's no such thing as a free lunch, that everything has an opportunity cost, that if you want more guns you have to have less butter. Such pieties simply do not apply when, in a recession, one is operating well within the production possibility frontier.

Thus, in principle, David Ricardo was right: tariffs reduce global welfare and output by impeding the international division of labour. But in a world of slack resources, such damage may be small, and by redirecting purchasing power towards import competing domestic producers, tariffs during recessions may actually have a mildly stimulative effect (Eichengreen and Sachs, 1985). And whereas the theory of monopoly suggests that the policies of the NRA, which

[20] Monthly data on the value of construction contracts awarded in 37 states suggest a roughly half year slowdown running from September of 1927 through to February 1938 (US Bureau of the Census *Statistical Abstract of the United States, 1941*: 945 Table 928).

encouraged cartelization and wage and price increases, could have reduced output and damaged consumer welfare, in the presence of deflation and large scale unemployment they may have done the reverse, by helping to break the back of deflationary expectations (Eggertsson, 2008).

Finally, note that while Cole and Ohanian attack the NRA for fostering monopoly, Higgs criticizes the second New Deal for trying aggressively to restrict it. One can either take the view that the efficiency losses from monopoly are small, in which case one might conclude that the concerns about the NIRA are misplaced, or one can take the opposite view, which would undercut Higgs' position. But one cannot consistently endorse both Higgs and Ohanian unless one believes that the fostering of monopolies is necessarily damaging when done by governments but not so when done by private enterprise.

The facts of economic performance in the United States between 1929 and 1941 have not changed, but many of the same issues continue to be relitigated in the literature. Much of the 'new' focus on negative government-induced supply shocks represents an attempt to refocus attention away from the gap between actual and potential output and towards efficiency losses associated with different kinds of government intervention. In 1977, James Tobin, surveying a related set of arguments concerning economic policy and performance in the 1970s, opined that '[i]t takes a heap of Harberger triangles to fill an Okun gap' (Tobin, 1977: 468). Tobin meant that the welfare losses from tariffs, taxes, and other government regulations were often small compared to those associated with operating an economy below capacity in the case of the Depression for more than a decade.

12.4. CONCLUSION

Although our emphasis in understanding the depth and duration of the Depression will and should continue to be on aggregate demand, more attention to aggregate supply is welcome and overdue. The dominant story here is of a broad array of positive shocks that caused potential, and, as the output gap closed, actual, output to grow rapidly between 1929 and 1941. In contrast, research associated with the real business cycle tradition has emphasized negative shocks resulting from deleterious actions by government and unions. These, it is argued, help account for the duration of the downturn. Although the Flint sit down strike and other labour disturbances likely played a role in the decline of output and employment during the 1937–38 recession, the influence of labour policy in prolonging the Depression has been exaggerated. Much of what happened rectified in part the unbalanced distribution of gains from productivity growth during the 1920s. The resulting moderation in inequality, which became especially apparent after the war, persisted through the 1970s and, as the post-war experience suggests, should not have posed an obstacle to full recovery in the late 1930s had there been adequate growth in nominal income. Obstacles on the supply side did play a role, but the impediments to the revival of residential construction, reflecting the hangover from the 1920s boom, were more important.

What lessons can we draw for the twenty first century? From the standpoint of long run growth the most compelling question is whether there is necessarily a silver lining to recession in the form of a productivity windfall. It is a question, unfortunately, without a clear answer. Productivity growth was unusually strong across the worst downturn in US experience, but this coincidence was in part an historical accident. Preliminary data indicate modest TFP growth from 2005 or 2007 up through 2010, although labour productivity growth after 2007 has been stronger (see Table 12.1). These data are, however, subject to revision, and we do not yet know how much of this may reflect cyclical influences. Part of the more robust growth in output per hour is the consequence of a rapid rise in the capital-labour ratio attributable to slow employment growth. As the output gap closes labour productivity growth may experience retardation unless compensated for by strong TFP advance. Even in the event the longer term TFP trajectory turns out to be favourable, it will be difficult to assess whether much or any of it can be attributed to the recession per se.

Considering shorter term supply-side effects, in both instances legacies from the boom retarded recovery, and in both instances construction was implicated. But the mechanisms differed. In post-war housing booms, including the saving and loan boomlet of the late 1980s as well as the more severe cycle of the 2000s, zoning and land use regulation ameliorated the problems of premature subdivision, without, of course, preventing overbuilding. Thus, the physical and some of the legal obstacles to recovery are today less severe than they were during the Depression, a positive contribution of government regulation, albeit at the local level, to macroeconomic stability. This contribution was offset, nevertheless, by the deterioration of effective regulatory efforts in the financial sector, and the financial wreckage from the prior construction boom remains worse in the 2010s than it was in the 1930s, which suffered more from the legacy of a highly leveraged stock market boom (see Field, 2011: chapter 10, 2013).

This chapter has focused attention largely on the supply side. As far as aggregate demand is concerned it is fair to say that, in both instances, the cumulative output gap could have been less had more aggressive government action counteracted the persisting shortfalls in nominal income growth resulting from weak private investment spending, as well, to a lesser degree, from cutbacks in household spending on consumer durables. Monetary policy, at least subsequent to 2008, gets better marks in the more recent episode than during the Depression, although fiscal policy stimulus, particularly on the expenditure side, could have been stronger in both instances. The rapid closing of the remaining output gap in 1942 makes this point effectively for the Great Depression. And contrary to political claims that the 2009 stimulus programme (the American Recovery and Reinvestment Act) did not work, its main defect was simply that it was too small. Without it, the unemployment rate would have been as much as two percentage points higher.[21]

[21] Congressional Budget Office, 2011. A larger stimulus might have devoted more funds to revenue sharing with state and local governments, which faced plummeting tax revenues on account of the downturn, without much of an option of running deficits. While real federal spending increased 14 per cent between 2007.4 and 2011.4, real state and local spending fell 7 per cent over the same period (NIPA Table 1.1.6, accessed 21 February 2012). Because state and local spending was higher in the aggregate than federal spending on goods and services (74 per cent higher in 2007.4), these changes were largely although not entirely offsetting.

APPENDIX: PRODUCTIVITY GROWTH IN THE UNITED STATES: 1929–1948

This appendix describes the calculations underlying the Table 12.1 productivity estimates for the US PNE over the intervals 1929–41 and 1941–48. The raw materials are series on output, capital, and hours. In calculations in Field (2011) and earlier work, all three of these series are drawn from Kendrick (1961). The updated numbers reported in this chapter are based on newer series for output and capital and show stronger gains in productivity growth for these periods than those reported earlier. The output series is based on the latest chained index estimates from the National Income and Product Accounts (NIPA) tables provided by the Bureau of Economic Analysis (BEA). This series grows more rapidly than that used by Kendrick, and is the principal reason the productivity growth rates reported here are higher. The capital stock series is drawn from the fixed asset portion of the BEA website, and differs slightly from what Kendrick used. The labour hours series is the same as that used by Kendrick in 1961; it has not been updated in the half century since he published.

The substitution of the newer output and capital series yields an unadjusted PNE TFP growth rate of 2.54 per cent per year between 1929 and 1941, which can be compared with an unadjusted 2.31 per cent per year, calculated directly from Table A-XXIII of Kendrick (1961). With a cyclical adjustment, the newer estimate rises to 2.97 per cent per year, as compared with a cyclically adjusted 2.78 per cent reported earlier (Field, 2011: 43, 100). Most of the difference between these two sets of growth rates is attributable to the faster growth of the chained index output series.

Chained indexes try to resolve the fundamentally unresolvable differences between Paasche and Laspeyres quantity indices by taking a geometric average of the growth rates from one year to the next calculated using each type of index, and then creating a linked series. Chained index methods are better for calculating the growth of aggregates over time than the older procedures of sticking with base period prices for a number of years, and then switching to a new base year. The problem with this approach is that every time a new base year is introduced, the calculated growth of aggregates changes, requiring us, in a sense, to rewrite periodically our economic history even though the underlying data are not changing.

Although chained index methods are better for measuring the growth of aggregates over time, they are not as useful for estimating the relative shares of components of the aggregates, since these shares, if calculated using the same procedures, will not necessarily continue to sum to the aggregates year after year. Since measures of TFP growth involve relationships between the growth of aggregates, however, it is appropriate to ask how the use of series not

Without the stimulus, the decline in state and local revenue, and thus expenditures, would have been even greater, and one would have also lacked the benefits of federal infrastructural spending as well as the weaker support for consumption provided by the tax reductions included in the American Recovery and Reinvestment Act and such programmes as 'cash for clunkers'. By 2011.4, state and local spending was 46 per cent higher than federal spending (NIPA Table 1.1.5, accessed 21 February 2012).

available to Kendrick in 1961 affects the quantitative narrative. I begin with the Bureau of Economic Analysis National Income and Product Accounts (BEA NIPA) Table 1.1.6, available at <http://www.bea.gov/>, which gives chained index estimates of annual GDP going back to 1929.

The aggregate used in Table 12.1 is the PNE, a subset of the national economy excluding agriculture and government. The logic of excluding these two sectors from studies of long term productivity growth is that the value of much of the former (government product) is set at its cost of production, precluding by convention any productivity improvement. And output in the latter sector—agriculture—is often affected by supply shocks (floods, hailstorms, temperature changes) that have little to do with improvements in efficiency. Because of these exclusions, I need to adjust downward the annual levels of real GDP from NIPA Table 1.1.6 so that they correspond roughly to the PNE.

Kendrick (1961: 298–300, Table A-III) provides annual estimates not only for GDP but also for government and farm product separately. I subtract the latter two subtotals from the former to get estimates of the PNE in 1929 dollars, and use the ratios of the PNE to GDP in the Kendrick data to adjust the BEA NIPA Table 1.1.6 numbers for the entire economy to approximate those for the PNE. According to the chain weighted series, 1941 GDP was 39.8 per cent higher than the comparable 1929 figure (2.79 per cent growth per year). Using the PNE/GDP ratio from Kendrick as described above to calculate PNE levels for the chained index series, I estimate that real output in the PNE was 37.7 per cent higher in 1941 than in 1929 (2.67 per cent growth per year).

I then go to the BEA Fixed Asset Table 2.1 for levels of private fixed assets (structures and equipment) during the period 1929–41. Since Kendrick provides estimates of the capital stock for the private domestic economy (1961: 334–7, Table A-XXII; this includes farm output) as well as for the PNE (1961: 338–40, Table A-XXIII), I use the ratio of the latter to the former to adjust the BEA private fixed asset data to get estimates of private non-farm chained index capital. This series grows very slightly rather than, as had been the case with Kendrick's, declining very slightly between 1929 and 1941. Kendrick had PNE capital about 1.6 per cent lower in 1941 than 1929, while the newer BEA series with the adjustment to approximate fixed capital in the PNE shows a small increase (1.5 per cent) over the 12 year period. Substituting the newer capital series for the one used by Kendrick will slightly reduce calculated TFP growth by slightly increasing the growth of the combined input measure. In the calculations that follow, however, this effect will be more than swamped by the substantially higher growth in output using chained indexes.

I then proceed to calculate revised indexes of TFP levels (A) for 1929, 1941 and 1948. The assumed functional specification of the production function is Cobb–Douglas, with constant returns to scale:

$$Y = AK^{\beta}N^{1-\beta}$$

Y = real output
N = labour hours
K = capital input

Rearranging, we have

$$A = Y/(K^{\beta}N^{1-\beta})$$

Using lower case letters to represent continuously compounded growth rates, we have a version of the fundamental growth accounting equation. This equation tells us that TFP growth (a) is the difference between output growth (y) and a weighted average of capital (k) and labour (n) growth.

$$a = y - \beta k - (1 - \beta)n$$

β, the elasticity of output with respect to capital, as well as capital's share, is assumed to be 0.25, and that of labour, $(1 - \beta)$, 0.75. These are the shares Kendrick assumed for 1929–37 (Kendrick, 1961: 285, Table A-10). He used an even smaller capital share (0.23) for 1937–48, but I am assuming most of the small drop in the share occurred after the start of the war, and to keep matters simple, use 0.25 for the entire 1929–41 period. As already noted, because the growth of labour and capital input both remain close to zero between 1929 and 1941, changes in these weights will make almost no difference in calculated TFP growth rates.

The PNE TFP levels resulting from these calculations show TFP 35.7 per cent higher in 1941 than in 1929 (2.54 per cent growth per year). Recall that real output in the PNE was 37.7 per cent higher (2.67 per cent growth per year). Once again, almost all of the growth in output can be attributed to TFP growth, not growth in inputs conventionally measured. This is not surprising. Since we are using the same series for labour hours input as did Kendrick, and the capital input series has received only a slight upward adjustment, combined private sector input growth over the 12 year period is still very close to zero.

This estimate of 2.54 per cent per year PNE TFP growth is before a cyclical adjustment. The adjustment is based on a regression of differences in logs of annual levels of TFP ($\Delta\ln(TFP)$) on a constant and the change in the unemployment rate in percentage points for the period 1929–41. The coefficient on the constant term (0.0306, or 3.06 per cent per year) provides a rough gauge of the trend growth rate of total factor productivity across the Depression years. The coefficient on the change in the unemployment rate (−0.0084, or −0.84 percentage points) estimates how much the PNE TFP growth rate tended to decline (rise) if the unemployment rate increased (decreased) one percentage point.[22] The econometric specification assumes that fluctuations in the unemployment rate (and, implicitly, the output gap) during this period are driven primarily by fluctuations in aggregate demand; the hypothesis maintained is that TFP procyclicality is almost entirely a consequence of business cycles, rather than their cause (see the main body of the chapter). The regression results are as follows (t statistics in parentheses).

Dep. Var.	Years	n	Constant	ΔUR	R^2
Δln(TFP)	1929–41	12	0.0306	−0 .0084	0.617
			(3.34)	(−4.01)	

[22] That coefficient is remarkably stable across the entire period 1890–2004, even though trend growth rates have varied substantially. See Field (2010a).

One way to cyclically adjust would simply be to replace the 2.54 per cent with the 3.06 per cent coefficient on the constant in the above regression. I use a related procedure that yields something very close to this. Since unemployment in 1941 was still 9.9 per cent, I ask, in light of the cyclicality coefficient, what the level of TFP in 1941 would have been had unemployment in that year been what it was in 1948 (3.8 per cent). Based on the regression results, the natural log of the 1941 level of TFP would have been 0.0512 higher (−6.1 *−0 .0084) had unemployment in 1941 been at the 1948 rate of 3.8 per cent. That also implies that the difference in the log level from any earlier year would have been 0.0512 higher. Dividing by 12, this would mean an additional 0.427 percentage points per year added to the continuously compounded growth rate measured from 1929 to 1941.[23] Thus, with a cyclical adjustment, the TFP growth rate for the PNE rises from 2.54 per cent per year to 2.97 per cent per year. This is the rate reported for 1929–41 in Table 12.1.

The cyclical adjustment strengthens my argument about the magnitude of a Great Leap Forward between 1929 and 1941. But it is not essential for the narrative since the dominance of that period stands out even without the adjustment, and, for that matter, even with the somewhat lower unadjusted TFP rate calculated directly from Kendrick. No other period in US economic history exhibits a comparable rate of growth of total factor productivity.

With the cyclically adjusted level for 1941, we can now also calculate 1941–48 TFP growth, which comes in at 2.08 per cent per year, close to estimates for the golden age (1948–73), higher than that reported in Field (2011: 43), but still almost a third below the estimated rate of growth for 1929–41.

Let us consider now how the use of the chained index numbers affects other productivity measures. Using chained index output and capital, labour productivity (output per hour in the PNE), grew 38 per cent between 1929 and 1941 (2.68 per cent per year). Output per adjusted hour (adjusted hours take into account possible changes in labour quality) was 35.7 per cent higher (2.54 per cent growth per year). Because Kendrick's implied measure of labour quality grows slightly over the Depression years, output per adjusted hour growth is slightly lower than growth in output per unadjusted (raw) hours.

These growth rates are before a cyclical adjustment. Specifying the appropriate counterfactual here is trickier than with TFP. We know that labour productivity growth is also pro-cyclical, although not as strongly so as is TFP (Field, 2010a). We also know, from a rearrangement of the fundamental growth accounting equation, that labour productivity growth is equal to the sum of TFP growth and capital's share times the rate of capital deepening:

$$y - n = a + \beta(k - n)$$

This equation tells us that labour productivity growth (y−n) is affected by two influences in principle distinct: technological and organization innovation (reflected in the (a) term), and increases in the ratio of physical capital to labour, or capital deepening, reflected in the (k−n) expression. Capital deepening results when an economy allocates part of its annual GDP to produce buildings and

[23] With the cyclical adjustment, the 1941 level of TFP would have been 42.8 per cent higher than in 1929, as compared with the actual 35.7 per cent higher.

equipment. So long as gross private domestic investment exceeds depreciation (the annual wear and tear on the existing stock), the physical capital stock will grow, and when it grows faster than labour or labour hours, the ratio of physical capital to labour increases. We say that capital has deepened (k − n is positive), and on this account alone, output per hour should rise. A road construction crew using heavy construction equipment should, for example, be able to move more cubic metres of earth per hour than a crew using pick axes and shovels. The transition from digging with shovels to digging with backhoes requires capital accumulation, and its contribution to growth in output per hour is at least conceptually distinct from a technological or organizational innovation that adds to a nation's book of available blueprints.

We have already calculated that, with the chained index output and capital numbers, and under a counterfactual in which 1941 unemployment was 3.8 per cent rather than the actual 9.9 per cent, the rate of growth of TFP between 1929 and 1941 would have been 2.97 rather than 2.54 per cent per year (0.43 percentage points per year higher). Since TFP growth is one of two key influences on labour productivity growth, this cyclical adjustment to TFP, by itself, would contribute a similar bump to growth in output per hour. But we also know that capital tends to 'shallow' in a recovery: the growth of the capital–labour ratio, and quite possibly its level, decline as one approaches potential output from below (in the short run, the denominator (labour) grows faster than the numerator (capital)). Capital shallowing weakens labour productivity growth during a recovery, partially counterbalancing the positive influence of pro-cyclical TFP. From a growth accounting perspective, this counterbalance is the main explanation for why labour productivity growth is more weakly pro-cyclical than TFP growth.

From a regression of the change in the natural log of the capital–labour ratio on a constant, and the change in the unemployment rate over the entire 1890–2004 period, we can estimate the cyclicality coefficient for the capital–labour ratio at 0.0151: roughly speaking, K/N declines by 1.5 per cent for each one percentage point decline in the unemployment rate (Field, 2010a).

Dep. Var	Years	n	Constant	ΔUR	R^2
Δln(K/N)	1890–2004	114	0.0163	0.0151	0.741
			(7.53)	(16.70)	

Had the unemployment rate been 6.1 percentage points lower in 1941, we can posit that the natural log of K/N would have been lower in that year by 0.092 (−6.1*0.0151 = −0.092). Dividing this by 12, we conclude that this would have lowered the continuously compounded growth rate of the capital–labour ratio (K/N) between 1929 and 1941 by −0.77 percentage points per year per year. Since the contribution of capital deepening to labour productivity growth is weighted by capital's share, this would have reduced the growth rate of labour productivity by 0.77*0.25 = 0.19 percentage points per year.

Summing the effect of the hypothetically higher TFP growth rate (0.43 percentage points per year) and the effect of the hypothetically lower (negative) growth rate of the capital–labour ratio (−0.19 percentage points per year), we conclude that the appropriate cyclical adjustment for the labour productivity growth rate between 1929 and 1941 is 0.24 percentage points per year (0.43–0.19). Adding this to our initial estimate of the growth of (actual) output per adjusted labour hour, we reach a cyclically adjusted rate of growth of output per hour of 2.92 per cent per year. Using the hours series that has been adjusted for improvements in labour quality we get, using the new output series, a cyclically adjusted rate of growth of 2.78 per cent.

This is a striking result, since it tells us that the growth of output per hour between 1929 and 1941 was at least as high as it was across the quarter century generally viewed as the golden age of US living standard improvements (1948–73). It is important contextually in understanding the discussion in the second part of this chapter about the growth of real wages during the Depression.

Finally, let us consider how the introduction of these two new series affects calculations of capital productivity (output per unit of capital). Using the new capital and output series, adjusted as described to correspond with the PNE, we have output per unit of capital rising 35.6 per cent between 1929 and 1941 (2.54 per cent per year). This is once again before a cyclical adjustment. We know that capital productivity is very strongly pro-cyclical (and indeed it is this pro-cyclicality, even more than the weaker pro-cyclicality of labour productivity, that in an accounting sense, drives TFP's strong pro-cyclicality). The regression below, for the period 1890–2004, shows that, while there is no long term trend in capital productivity (the constant term is approximately 0, confirming one of Nicholas Kaldor's stylized facts about economic growth), a one percentage point decline in the unemployment rate typically adds about 2 per cent to that year's growth in output per unit of capital (Field, 2010a). This pro-cyclicality is because, when an economy comes out of a recession, output grows much faster than physical capital.[24]

Dep. Var.	Years	n	Constant	ΔUR	R^2
Δln(Y/K)	1890–2004	114	0.002	−0.0200	0.654
			(0.0061)	(−14.52)	

Since the counterfactual we have been exploring involves 1941 unemployment at 1948 levels (3.8 per cent), which is a 6.1 percentage point difference from actual, this suggests that had 1941 been at or close to potential, the natural log of 1941 capital productivity would have been 0.122 higher that year. Dividing by 12, that would have added 1.01 percentage points to the continuously compounded growth rate of capital productivity between 1929 and 1941, yielding a cyclically adjusted rate of growth of 3.56 per cent per year. A check on the reasonableness of this calculation can be made through another rearrangement of the fundamental growth accounting equation, which tells us that TFP growth must be equal to a weighted average of capital productivity and labour productivity growth. (To persuade yourself of this, multiply out, eliminate the βy terms which cancel out, and rearrange the remaining terms).

[24] I am approximating the service flow from the capital stock by assuming that it is proportional to the stock. For mechanical machinery, depreciation can be affected by hours of operation or start-stop cycles. But mechanical machinery is a small fraction of the fixed asset stock, the bulk of which consists of structures. For the canonical physical capital good—a building—the rate at which a roof wears out, or exterior paint oxidizes, is almost entirely independent of how full or empty it is, or how rapidly goods and people move through it. For further discussion of this approximation, see Field, 2010a,c.

$$a = \beta(y - k) + (1 - \beta)(y - n)$$

Noting that the relevant labour input series in both Kendrick's and my revised calculation is adjusted hours (adjusted for labour quality growth), we can deduce an implied rate of capital productivity advance (y − k) consistent with our estimates of TFP and labour productivity advance. Since we have already calculated cyclically adjusted estimates for a and y − n, these numbers are easily backed out. For the 1929–41 period, this comes in at 3.54 per cent per year, very close to what we arrive at using the cyclicality coefficient from the 1890–2004 regression.

Output, both actual and potential, grew substantially between 1929 and 1941 with only minimal increases in private sector physical capital, which is to say that the capital to output ratio declined, since the output to capital ratio rose. There are other periods in US economic history in which labour productivity grew as rapidly as during the Great Depression. There is none in which this was true for capital productivity. The uniqueness of this development is brought into strong relief when we remind ourselves that there is no long run upward trend for capital productivity.

Making an upward adjustment to the 1941 level of the output to capital ratio will of course raise the 1929–41 growth rates, and reduce the growth rate for 1941–48. In this case, the cyclical adjustment lowers capital productivity growth between 1941 and 1948 from 3.07 per cent per year (using the unadjusted level of capital productivity in 1941) to 1.34 per cent (using the adjusted level). As a check, the calculation using the formula above relating TFP growth, labour productivity growth, and capital productivity growth comes in at 1.36 per cent.

As already discussed in describing the cyclical adjustment for 1941 labour productivity, a cyclically adjusted level for the 1941 capital–labour ratio is based on a regression of the log difference of the capital–labour ratio on a constant and the change in the unemployment rate in percentage points. The regression shows that the capital–labour ratio has risen over the long run at about 1.6 per cent per year, but there has also been strong cyclical variation. In particular, as an economy recovers, labour input grows much more rapidly than capital input so the capital–labour ratio falls. Without a cyclical adjustment, the capital–labour ratio in the PNE rises very slightly (0.14 per cent per year) between 1929 and 1941. We have already calculated that had the 1941 unemployment rate been 3.8 per cent, the natural log of the 1941 capital–labour ratio would have been 0.092 lower, which would have reduced the annual growth rate of the ratio by 0.77 percentage points per year, yielding a cyclically adjusted growth rate of −0.63 per cent per year. With a cyclical adjustment, the ratio then grows at a rate of 1.28 per cent per year between 1941 and 1948. We can check on the reasonableness of these calculations by observing that the difference between the rate of labour productivity growth and capital productivity growth should yield the rate of capital deepening:

$$y - n - (y - k) = k - n$$

To summarize, the pivotal number in all of these calculations is the TFP growth rate for the PNE. Using output, hours, and capital input from Kendrick (1961), TFP growth is 2.31 per cent per year, continuously compounded (with a cyclical adjustment: 2.78 per cent per year). Using the same hours series, but the newer chain weighted output series and the chain weighted capital stock series, we get

2.54 per cent per year. A cyclical adjustment raises this to 2.97 per cent per year. These cyclically adjusted growth rates approximate, using the different data series as described, what TFP growth between 1929 and 1941 would have looked like had there been no remaining output gap in 1941. A TFP growth rate approaching 3 per cent per year is unmatched in any comparable period of US economic growth, and can be decomposed into a rate of labour productivity growth equal to or exceeding that realized during the golden age, combined with a rate of capital productivity growth far exceeding that in any other period.

Several concerns might be raised about the conclusion, to borrow from the title of my 2003 *American Economic Review* article, that the 1930s were indeed 'the most technologically progressive decade of the century'. First, could some of the high rate of TFP growth be due to the ramp up in military spending prior to US entry into the war in December of 1941? Only in the sense that, as noted, TFP growth displays strong pro-cyclicality, and increased military spending prior to the war accelerated the closing of the output gap through traditional aggregate demand mechanisms. Thus the actual growth rate of TFP between 1940 and 1941 is affected by the narrowing of the output gap associated with war preparations. But what is relevant here is not the growth in TFP from 1940 to 1941, but rather the growth as measured from 1929 to 1941, preferably adjusted to account for the cyclicality of TFP.

Still, is it possible that the military build-up prior to Pearl Harbor not only helped close the output gap, but also augmented potential output? One must keep in mind the relative magnitude of what happened before the US entered the war. It is true that military manpower and spending, including Lend Lease, grew dramatically from 1939 to 1941. For example, men in uniform almost tripled, from 600,000 to 1.8 million. But this is dwarfed by maximum military manpower in 1944 of over 12 million. The US was effectively demilitarized during the 1930s, and military disbursements to the end of 1941 were less than 5 per cent of what would be expended cumulatively between 1939 and 1945 (Field, 2003). The United States was not fully mobilized for war until sometime in mid-1942. Given these timelines, there is far too little opportunity for cumulative output and learning by doing in war-related production to have generated technological and organizational spillovers with enduring impact on the economy's potential output (Field, 2011: chapter 3). Thus, it is unlikely that the measure of the TFP trend growth rate between 1929 and 1941 is influenced by the military build-up.

A second concern is whether or to what degree TFP growth might be based on improvements in human capital or labour quality. As can be seen from the second column of Table 12.1, which shows the growth of adjusted labour productivity, the overall growth of labour quality was modest during the Depression years, and thus the numbers for output per hour and output per adjusted hour growth are quite similar. Human capital mattered, but the contributions of the rather small number (in comparison with the total labour force) of workers in R&D labs was probably more important than any general upward trend in the quality of labour. And whatever the position one takes on the empirical relevance of selective retention of higher quality labour in economic downturns (Margo, 1991), this is simply not relevant for comparisons between the years 1929 and 1941. Although private sector hours were effectively unchanged, because of a reduction in hours per person, there were actually 11 per cent more persons employed in the latter year than in 1929 (Kendrick, 1961). Any effect of selective retention that might have been in play between 1929 and 1933 would have been more than reversed by the rapid growth of the economy and the increase in persons employed between 1933 and 1937 and again between 1938 and 1941.

A third concern involves the extent to which these calculations overlook the influence of public sector infrastructural investments. Are we, for example, simply seeing a statistical artefact, the effect of the substitution of publicly owned street and highway capital for privately owned railway capital? Including economically relevant public capital, which, unlike private sector capital, did grow over the Depression, will, of course, reduce the calculated TFP growth rate, because combined input growth will be positive and higher. Recalculating TFP growth rates for the last three-quarters of the twentieth century using an augmented capital input series that includes economically relevant public sector capital does, as expected, show the Depression years with TFP growth rates that are lower than those calculated using private sector capital alone. But this dynamic affects other periods as well, and 1929–41 still stands out as exhibiting significantly higher TFP growth than the 1920s or any of the post-war periods (Field, 2003, 2011).

BIBLIOGRAPHY

Abramovitz, M. (1986), 'Catching Up, Forging Ahead, and Falling Behind', *Journal of Economic History*, 46 (June), 385–406.

Basu, S., Fernald, J. G., and Kimball, M. S. (2006), 'Are Technology Improvements Contractionary?', *American Economic Review*, 96, 418–48.

Board of Governors of the Federal Reserve System (1941), *Banking and Monetary Statistics, 1914–1941*. Washington: Government Printing Office, available at <http://www.fraser.stlouisfed.org/publication/?pid=38>.

Bowden, S. and Offer, A. (1994), 'Household Appliances and the Use of Time: The United States and Britain since the 1920s', *Economic History Review*, 47 (November), 725–48.

US Department of Commerce, Bureau of Economic Analysis, 'National Income And Product Accounts Tables' (NIPA), available at <http://www.bea.gov/iTable/iTable.cfm?ReqID=9&step=1>.

Calomiris, C. W., Mason, J. R., and Wheelock, D. C. (2011), 'Did Doubling Reserve Requirements Cause the Recession of 1937–1938? A Microeconomic Approach', St Louis Fed Working Paper 2011-002A, available at <http://www.research.stlouisfed.org/wp/2011/2011-002.pdf>.

Carter, S. B., Gartner, S. S., Haines, M. R., Olmstead, A. L., Sutch, R., and Wright, G. (eds) (2006), *Historical Statistics of the United States, Millennial Edition*. New York: Cambridge University Press.

Cole, H. and Ohanian, L. (2000), 'Re-Examining the Contributions of Money and Banking Shocks to the US Great Depression', NBER Macroeconomics Annual.

Cole, H. and Ohanian, L. (2002), 'The US and UK Great Depressions through the Lens of Neoclassical Growth Theory', *American Economic Review*, 92 (May), 28–33.

Cole, H. and Ohanian, L. (2004), 'New Deal Policies and the Persistence of the Great Depression: A General Equilibrium Analysis', *Journal of Political Economy*, 112 (August), 779–816.

Congressional Budget Office (2011), 'Estimated Impact of the American Recovery and Reinvestment Act on Employment and Economic Output from April 2011 Through

June 2011 (August)', available at <http://www.cbo.gov/ftpdocs/123xx/doc12385/08-24-ARRA.pdf>.

Devine, W. (1983), 'From Shafts to Wires: Historical Perspectives on Electrification', *Journal of Economic History*, 43 (June), 347–72.

Eggertsson, G. (2008), 'Great Expectations and the End of the Depression', *American Economic Review*, 98 (4), 1476–516.

Eichengreen, B. and Sachs, J. (1985), 'Exchange Rates and Economic Recovery in the 1930s', *Journal of Economic History*, 45 (December), 925–46.

Field, A. J. (1985), 'On the Unimportance of Machinery', *Explorations in Economic History*, 22 (October), 378–401.

Field, A. J. (1992), 'Uncontrolled Land Development and the Duration of the Depression in the United States', *Journal of Economic History*, 52 (December), 785–805.

Field, A. J. (2003), 'The Most Technologically Progressive Decade of the Century', *American Economic Review*, 93 (September), 1399–413.

Field, A. J. (2006), 'Technological Change and US Economic Growth in the Interwar Years', *Journal of Economic History*, 66 (March), 203–36.

Field, A. J. (2008), 'The Impact of the Second World War on US Productivity Growth', *Economic History Review*, 61 (August), 672–94.

Field, A. J. (2010a), 'The Procyclical Behavior of Total Factor Productivity in the United States, 1890–2004', *Journal of Economic History*, 70 (June), 326–50.

Field, A. J. (2010b), 'What can we learn from the Carousel of Progress?', paper delivered at the CEPR-CREI conference 'Concucopia Quantified' at Universitat Pompeu Fabra, Barcelona, Spain, 21–22 May 2010.

Field, A. J. (2010c), 'Should Capital Input Receive a Utilization Adjustment?' (working paper).

Field, A. J. (2011), *A Great Leap Forward: 1930s Depression and US Economic Growth*. New Haven: Yale University Press.

Field, A. J. (2012), 'The Adversity/Hysteresis Effect: Depression Era Productivity Growth in the US Rail Sector', in J. Lerner and S. Stern (eds), *The Rate and Direction of Inventive Activity*. Chicago: University of Chicago Press for NBER.

Field, A. J. (2013), 'The Interwar Housing Cycle in the Light of 2001–2011: A Comparative Historical Approach', in P. Fishback, K. Snowden, and E. White (eds), *Housing and Mortgage Markets in Historical Perspective*. Chicago: University of Chicago Press for NBER.

Finch, C. (1992), *Highways to Heaven: The AUTObiography of America*. New York: Harper Collins.

Fisher, I. (1933), 'The Debt Deflation Theory of Great Depressions', *Econometrica*, 1 (October), 337–57.

Friedman, M. (1971), *A Theoretical Framework for Monetary Analysis*. New York: Columbia University Press for NBER.

Friedman, M. and Schwartz, A. (1963), *A Monetary History of the United States*. Princeton: Princeton University Press.

Galbraith, J. K. (1967), *The New Industrial State*. Boston: Houghton Mifflin.

Goddard, S. B. (1994), *Getting There: The Epic Struggle Between Road and Rail in the Twentieth Century*. New York: Basic Books.

Harberger, A. (1954), 'Monopoly and Resource Allocation', *American Economic Review*, 44 (May), 77–87.

Hatton, T. and Thomas, M. (2013), 'Labour Markets in Recession and Recovery: The UK and the USA in the 1920s and 1930s'. This volume.

Hausman, J. (2011), 'What was Bad for GM was Bad for America: The Automobile Industry and the 1937–38 Recession', Working Paper, University of California at Berkeley (December).

Hermes, M. E. (1996), *Enough for One Lifetime: Wallace Caruthers, Inventor of Nylon*. Washington, DC: American Chemical Society and Chemical Heritage Society.

Higgs, R. (1997), 'Regime Uncertainty: Why the Great Depression Lasted So Long and Why Prosperity Resumed after the War', *The Independent Review*, 1 (Spring), 561–90.

Inklaar, R., de Jong, H., and Gouma, R. (2011), 'Did Technology Shocks Drive the Great Depression? Explaining Cyclical Productivity Movements in US Manufacturing, 1919–1939', *Journal of Economic History*, 71 (December), 827–58.

Irwin, D. A. (2011), 'Gold Sterilization and the Recession of 1937–38', NBER Working Paper 17595 (November).

Kaldor, N. (1961), 'Capital Accumulation and Economic Growth', in F. A. Lutz and D. C. Hague (eds), *The Theory of Capital*. New York: St. Martin's Press.

Kendrick, J. (1961), *Productivity Trends in the United States*. Princeton: Princeton University Press.

Lebergott, S. (1964), *Manpower in Economic Growth: The American Record Since 1800*. New York: McGraw Hill.

Lebergott, S. (1996), *Pursuing Happiness: American Consumers in the Twentieth Century*. Princeton: Princeton University Press.

Margo, R. (1991), 'The Microeconomics of Depression Unemployment', *Journal of Economic History*, 51 (June), 331–41.

Mowery, D. and Rosenberg, N. (2000), 'Twentieth Century Technological Change', in S. Engerman and R. Gallman (eds), *The Cambridge Economic History of the United States*, volume III. Cambridge: Cambridge University Press, 803–926.

Ohanian, L. (2003), 'Liquidity Shocks and the Great Depression: Comment on "The Great Depression and the Friedman-Schwartz Hypothesis" by Lawrence Christiano, Roberto Motto, and Massimo Rostagno', *Journal of Money, Credit, and Banking*, 35 (December), 1205–15.

Ohanian, L. (2009), 'What—or Who—Started the Great Depression?', NBER Working Paper 15258 (August).

Paxson, F. L. (1946), 'The Highway Movement, 1916–1935', *American Historical Review*, 51 (January), 236–53.

Posner, R. (2009), *A Failure of Capitalism: The Crisis of '08 and the Descent into Depression*. Cambridge: Harvard University Press.

Raff, D. and Trachtenberg, M. (1997), 'Quality Adjusted Prices for the American Automobile Industry: 1906–1940', in T. F. Bresnahan and R. J. Gordon, *The Economics of New Goods*. Chicago: University of Chicago Press, 71–108.

Romer, C. (1992), 'What Ended the Great Depression?', *Journal of Economic History*, 52 (December), 757–84.

Roose, K. D. (1954), *The Economics of Recession and Revival*. New Haven: Yale University Press.

Rose, J. (2010), 'Hoover's Truce: Wage Rigidity in the Onset of the Great Depression', *Journal of Economic History*, 70 (December), 843–70.

Rostow, W. W. (1960), *The Stages of Economic Growth: A Non-Communist Manifesto*. Cambridge: Cambridge University Press.

Schiffman, D. A. (2003), 'Shattered Rails, Financial Fragility, and Railroad Operations in the Great Depression', *Journal of Economic History*, 63, 802–25.

Solow, R. J. (1957), 'Technical Change and the Aggregate Production Function', *Review of Economics and Statistics*, 39 (August), 312–20.

Stover, J. F. (1997), *American Railroads*, Second edition. Chicago: University of Chicago Press.

Tobey, R. C. (1996), *Technology as Freedom: the New Deal and the Electrical Modernization of the American Home*. Berkeley: University of California Press.

Tobin, J. (1977), 'How dead is Keynes?', *Economic Inquiry*, 40 (October), 459–68.

United States Bureau of the Census (1941), *Statistical Abstract of the United States, 1941*. Washington: Government Printing Office, available at <http://www.census.gov/compendia/statab/past_years.html>.

United States Bureau of the Census (1949), *Statistical Abstract of the United States, 1948*. Washington: Government Printing Office, available at <http://www.census.gov/compendia/statab/past_years.html>.

United States Department of Commerce, Bureau of Economic Analysis (2012), National Income and Product Account tables, available at <http://www.bea.gov>.

Wanniski, J. (1978), *The Way The World Works*. New York: Basic Books.

Weintraub, D. (1939), 'Effects of Current and Prospective Technological Developments upon Capital Formation', *American Economic Review*, 29 (March), 15–32.

13

'Blood and Treasure': Exiting the Great Depression and Lessons for Today

Kris James Mitchener and Joseph R. Mason[1]

13.1. INTRODUCTION

US policy making during the current financial and economic crisis has consciously been shaped to avoid the mistakes of the 1930s and prevent a meltdown as severe as the Great Depression. The Federal Reserve (the Fed) therefore quickly dropped interest rates to their lower bound, provided liquidity support to financial markets that were malfunctioning, and capital support to financial institutions that were suffering both illiquidity and insolvency problems. The Obama administration carried out a massive fiscal stimulus and extended many of the credit- and capital-support programmes initiated by the Treasury Department in the last few months of the Bush administration.[2]

Of course, aggressive approaches aimed at preventing tail outcomes can be expensive, and those costs have had measurable consequences on long-run budget projections for countries that chose to combat the recession with policies similar to those that the US has pursued. As a result, policy makers worldwide are keenly aware of the need for a prompt and timely exit from the fiscal and monetary stimulus programmes that have, so far, been judged favourably as useful in avoiding deeper financial and economic ruin (Del Negro et al., 2009). Beginning in 2009, economists began calling on government officials to define their 'exit strategy'. In the present context, however, the term was never adequately defined. We propose that an exit strategy is: a movement back to institutional conditions associated with steady-state growth, including stable inflation and broadly non-interventionist credit- and capital-market policies.

Although avoiding the policy *mistakes* of the 1930s helped define how American policy makers responded to the 2007–08 financial crisis and ensuing

[1] This chapter was originally prepared for the British Academy conference, 'Lessons from the 1930s Great Depression for the Making of Economic Policy', 16–17 April 2010 in London. We thank Mark Carlson, Marcus Miller, Jonathan Rose, two anonymous referees, and conference participants for useful suggestions and comments. Mitchener acknowledges the financial support of the Hoover Institution while in residence as a National Fellow, 2009–10.

[2] For an example of how the Depression has defined policymaking, see Romer (2009).

recession, policy applications to the recovery phase are less well understood. We draw on the experience of the US in the 1930s to shed light on exit strategies, and describe how policy responses to the deflation and banking crises of the 1930s coloured the exit policy debate after the Great Depression. We show that a full exit from the Great Depression, defined as the point at which interventionist credit- and capital-market policies and institutions were wound down, did not occur in the 1930s. Indeed, it took until the 1950s for this to occur and for the Federal Reserve to regain its independence and return unfettered to its longer-run objectives.

The rest of this chapter proceeds as follows. Section 13.2 clarifies how exit strategies applied to normal recessions may differ from those applied to financial crises and develops some preliminary ideas about applying the idea of 'exit' to the 1930s. The next two sections of the chapter discuss the monetary policy responses to the Great Depression and introduce the distinction between monetary and bank policy instruments that are typically employed in recoveries. Section 13.5 reviews the story of the exit from those policies in the Great Depression, suggesting that exit to any significant degree only occurred in the 1950s, not the 1930s. Section 13.6 then organizes the components of monetary and bank policy into a functional taxonomy that helps clarify exactly what needs exiting and draws parallels to the present financial crisis and recession. Based on this taxonomy we propose a metric that might help policy makers understand how to time exits. Section 13.7 concludes.

13.2. EXIT STRATEGIES: DISTINGUISHING GARDEN-VARIETY RECESSIONS FROM THOSE ACCOMPANIED BY FINANCIAL CRISES

In the military (the sphere in which the term originated), 'exit strategies' are defined in terms of minimizing the loss of blood (lives) and treasure (equipment). To extend this metaphor to economic policy making and apply it to the 1930s, we need to define the function that policy makers are minimizing as well as the shift in policy from an unfavourable policy environment

Most central banks have an explicit or implicit long-run inflation target as well as a target rate of growth for the economy's output (usually equal to potential GDP). Since many central banks carry out expansionary monetary policy to counteract the effects of falling aggregate demand on equilibrium output and unemployment, policy makers will eventually turn course and raise rates as the economy recovers. The challenge is to time the rate increase optimally. If rates are increased too late, the cost is inflation. If rates are increased too quickly or sharply, the cost can be lost output, higher unemployment, and the potential of a 'double dip' recession. Hence, central bankers attempt to minimize inflation and exit a low-interest-rate policy stance without generating further unemployment or losses in output, i.e. more 'blood' and lost 'treasure'. The present policy stance of loose monetary and fiscal policy is seen as unfavourable in the long run (or at least not optimal) in the sense that, if it were maintained, it would eventually generate unsustainable public budget deficits and inflation.

We argue, however, that it is important to make the distinction between 'exits' from garden-variety recessions and those that are accompanied by financial crises. There is emerging evidence that recessions accompanied by financial distress tend to be deeper and longer (most recently, Claessens et al., 2008; Reinhart and Rogoff, 2009). Hence, the present medley of expansionary policies was implemented to protect against extremely severe losses in output and unemployment, and potentially large declines in prices, that are thought to come with recessions accompanied by financial crises. At least with respect to central bank policy making (the focus of this chapter), we view this distinction as important.[3] All business cycles, regardless of their origins, eventually require central bankers to shift their concerns from the short run to the medium run and long run, but deeper and longer downturns often result in more drastic interventions and hence the necessity to think more explicitly about exit strategies.

Monetary policy exit from garden-variety recessions typically involves simply raising the short-term policy instrument (i.e. the Fed funds rate) to a more neutral position in order to satisfy a long-run inflation target. During financial crises, however, the central bank's role as a lender of last resort (LOLR) is often invoked. In many cases, acting as an LOLR not only changes a central bank's balance sheet, but it also transforms the operation of financial markets so that the LOLR begins to take on roles typically played by financial institutions. Hence, an exit strategy from a financial crisis entails more than planning on how to return to medium-term and long-term objectives for inflation: it also requires the central bank to make decisions about how and when to cede its emergency role as a banker back to the markets.

Moreover, exit strategies from recessions accompanied by financial crises often involve both monetary and fiscal policy components, which can sometimes overlap (particularly in applications of industrial policy and bail-out policy). Our discussion of fiscal policy will be limited to how it affects financial markets, i.e. what we will refer to as bank policy.[4] We feel that bank policy is different from traditional fiscal policy because the public barometers of economic activity; for instance reduced jobless claims, are not as clear-cut for ramping down the fiscal stimulus to the financial sector, while the personal rewards of distributing capital and directing investment can be large. Rather, as we discuss in detail throughout the chapter, fiscal stimuli to the financial sector are attractive to politicians and policy makers for a variety of reasons, but may ultimately prove risky to the prospects for long-term economic growth.

In sum, the complexity of monetary and bank policy as well as the political attractiveness of allocating capital and credit make exit a tricky business. Monetary and bank policy exit requires the rare combination of both good economic

[3] One could also examine exits from fiscal policy, but changes in the deficit GDP ratio in the mid-1930s were small and in some years contractionary, so there is little to discuss with respect to the period of interest.

[4] Complicating matters further, the fiscal stimulus to financial institutions can come from either the federal or the central-bank budgets. We do not distinguish between the two as many of the programmes in the Great Depression were duplicated across the two sources of funding, and we feel the policy lessons established here generalize regardless of the source of the fiscal funding.

judgement and the political will to wind down or liquidate institutions that were created to combat a crisis. In some cases, the lack of both of those conditions has led to the continued reliance on short-term stimulus policies long after the crisis and recession has subsided.

In many cases, policies aimed at economic recovery in the short run can prove disruptive in the long run. This has been seen in developing countries. For example, policies aimed at generating inflation, devaluing exchange rates, subsidizing credit, or even nationalizing strategic industries can have stabilizing benefits in the short run, but can be destructive in the long term if they set the stage for crony capitalism, or, worse, kleptocracy. It is easy in times of financial distress for central banks to lose their independence, where the support of credit and financial markets makes central banks into organs of the state that allocate credit for political reasons.

As described above, before delving into the details of the 1930s, we make three initial observations about exit strategies based on our definition. First, stimulus can turn out to be problematic if it leads central banks to veer too far away from independence and towards government credit policy. Indeed, in the case of the 1930s, there is evidence that the Fed became a hostage to the US Department of Treasury. Second, the political economy of exit will likely be challenging: agencies created during a crisis may not wither because they have champions within government who stand to gain electorally or personally, or because too much uncertainty over the path of the economy remains. The Reconstruction Finance Corporation (RFC) is an example of an agency that served short-term benefits, but continued to provide credit to private firms long after the distress of the 1930s had ended. This leads us to our final observation. A full exit from the Great Depression, where institutions were wound down and the central bank regained its independence, did not occur in the 1930s—significant exit took until the 1950s, and still left behind a legacy of stimulus institutions such as Fannie Mae, the Federal Housing Administration (FHA), and the Small Business Administration that, it can be argued, were never truly unwound.

13.3. MONETARY POLICY: MOVING FROM SHORT-TERM STIMULUS BACK TO THE STEADY STATE IN THE 1930S

13.3.1. Monetary expansion?

One of the most noteworthy contractionary periods in US central banking history began in the late 1920s with the open-market sales of the Fed in 1928, which lasted through to 1929, as well as increases in the discount rate in 1929, both of which were aimed at dampening stock-market speculation. These moves were followed by another hike in the discount rate in 1931, in response to Britain's departure from the gold standard. Since the path-breaking study by Friedman and Schwartz (1963), it has been known that monetary policy mistakes cost the US economy dearly in the early 1930s.[5] The Fed's inability or unwillingness to prevent the collapse of monetary aggregates after banks began to fail was a glaring error (Friedman and Schwartz, 1963), and its failure to act as an LOLR is widely believed to have helped turn the recession into a depression. Constrained by adherence to the gold standard, Eichengreen (1992) and Temin (1989) further argue that the Fed could not prevent banks from failing so long as it remained committed to staying on the fixed exchange-rate system of the interwar period. Matters were made worse by other policies, including presidential candidates from both parties campaigning on balanced budgets in 1932, and protectionist trade policy that helped foster a global collapse in trade.

It was not until the US abandoned the gold standard in April 1933, four years after the downturn started, that monetary policy shifted course and the money supply began to expand dramatically (Eichengreen and Sachs, 1985; Temin, 1989; Eichengreen, 1992). After the dollar was devalued, output in the US then grew at an average rate of 8 per cent per annum from 1933 to 1937.

On 5 April 1933, the government outlawed the holding of gold domestically, and on 18 April, it announced that the Treasury would no longer issue licences to export gold.[6] By making the dollar inconvertible into gold, these actions effectively ended US participation in the gold standard. Gold began to flow into the US thereafter. Political instability in Europe, beginning in the mid-1930s, and the lower value of the dollar (a 60 per cent decline by January 1934) provided the source of the gold inflow and the means for increasing the money supply.

Critically, the gold inflows were not sterilized by the US Treasury and passed directly into the money supply. Treasury carried out purchases of gold and silver, which they believed would raise gold prices and prices in general, thus reflating the economy. The rapid increase in money growth rates generated inflation expectations (Eggertsson, 2008) and lowered real rates of borrowing, in turn increasing expenditure on interest-sensitive goods, such as plant and equipment, consumer durables, and construction.

By our definition, however, we would not consider mere reversals of ill-advised contractionary policy as constituting an 'exit strategy'. An exit strategy requires decisions that lead to the discontinuation of all manner of policies that emphasize short-run expansion over long-run steady-state growth. In a typical recession, an exit, therefore, constitutes a strategy aimed at returning to the medium- and long-run monetary targets for inflation and growth, like the one embodied in a central bank reaction function, such as the Taylor Rule.

Moreover, central bank policies that proved detrimental to recovery continued well past 1933. Growth stopped again in 1937–38 due to further policy mistakes Output growth then resumed at a rate of roughly 10 per cent per year between 1938 and 1941.[7] The Fed would have had to undertake a coordinated

[5] In addition to the aforementioned mistakes, the Fed began to carry out expansionary open-market purchases in the spring of 1932, but they turned out to be short-lived (Friedman and Schwartz, 1963).

[6] Congress authorized abrogation of the gold clause in public and private contracts on 5 June.

[7] Romer (1992) attributes the observed recovery of the real economy to large gold inflows, which led to a dramatic expansion in the money supply and low or negative real interest rates through to the end of the decade. Prices and wages did not fully adjust to higher levels, so that the real money supply (M1)

expansionary policy strategy before it could be properly said to have embarked upon an exit strategy.

13.3.2. Regional conflicts and Fed policy making in the 1930s

Lester Chandler describes Federal Reserve System officials during the early 1930s as holding 'sharply conflicting views concerning the System's responsibilities, its proper objectives, its powers, and the effects of its policies on the economy' (Chandler, 1971: 129). This divisiveness was fostered by the general wording of the Federal Reserve Act, which 'practically assured a maximum amount of conflict and controversy within the System' (Chandler, 1971: 6). The polar extremes in the philosophical debate were held by the Federal Reserve Banks of New York and Chicago, whose respective geographic domains were impacted quite differently by the early banking crises during 1929–31 (Mason, 2010).

The Federal Reserve Bank of New York was a leading advocate within the system of using monetary policy to control the economy. However, the Federal Reserve Bank of New York's overzealous attempts to take a leadership role in such matters during a period of centralization of power at the Federal Reserve Board led to the alienation of the Board and the Banks.

Governor McDougal of the Federal Reserve Bank of Chicago took the opposite view with respect to using monetary policy for economic stabilization. McDougal first challenged the Federal Reserve Bank of New York's strong desire to control monetary policy at the June 1916 Governors' Conference. By 1927, McDougal objected to the easy-money policy of the New York Federal Reserve Bank, which had been implemented to promote central bank cooperation internationally; the Board of Governors responded by mandating the Chicago Fed to reduce its discount rate (Friedman and Schwartz, 1963; Wicker, 1966; Chandler, 1971).

McDougal felt that domestic, and more important, local economic conditions should take precedence over international considerations. In July 1930, the Midwestern reserve banks firmly opposed the Federal Reserve Bank of New York's requests for an open-market purchase programme.[8] McDougal remained adamantly opposed to open-market purchases throughout the crises of 1931, after which many of the other Federal Reserve Banks throughout the country began to share the belief that further open-market purchases would simply cause reserves to accumulate in reserve-centre banks. Other Federal Reserve Banks soon realized that, as regional banking crises progressed, reserve city banks were seeking liquidity by calling loans and investing in short-term government

grew by 27 per cent from the end of 1933 to the end of 1936, and by 56 per cent from December 1937 to December 1942. The growth in monetary aggregates does not appear to take place through demand-induced changes in the money multiplier as the deposit–currency ratio is fairly stable through the mid-1930s and into the first years of the 1940s. This suggests growth occurred as a result of increases in high-powered money.

[8] O. M. Attebury, deputy governor at St Louis, opined that 'conditions in the Eighth District provided no justification for further open market purchases'. See Friedman and Schwartz (1963: 373fn).

securities. Open-market purchases, therefore, simply served to push the yields on such securities lower.

Figures 13.1 and 13.2, from Mason (2010), show that the shift in bank portfolios into government notes and bills began much earlier in the Chicago Federal Reserve District than elsewhere. The Federal Reserve Bank of New York's attempts to instigate a more active programme of open-market purchases waned in late 1932 as banks in that district began to accumulate large amounts of short-term government paper, while the hoarding of governments in the St Louis District was less pronounced over this period. Figure 13.1 shows that banks in the Minneapolis District on aggregate held over 10 per cent more than the system average of their portfolios in investments until the end of 1930, when they began to divest heavily. Figure 13.2 suggests that the disinvestment of Minneapolis District banks was a result of an early panic, when levels of governments were drawn far below the Federal Reserve System average over 1931 and 1932. The massive flight to quality resulted in a precipitous decline in yields on notes and bills during this period, with negative yields resulting in late 1932 (Friedman and Schwartz, 1963; Chandler, 1971; Epstein and Ferguson, 1984).

The policy of the Federal Reserve Bank of Chicago was that it was better to leave the eligible securities in the banks so that they could be used as collateral on loans, furthering credit expansion and preventing extreme declines in yields. McDougal was not against providing liquidity to bankers, rather he argued that, 'on general principles, he preferred to see the banks borrowing to secure funds' (Friedman and Schwartz, 1963). By early 1932, Governor Harrison of the Federal Reserve

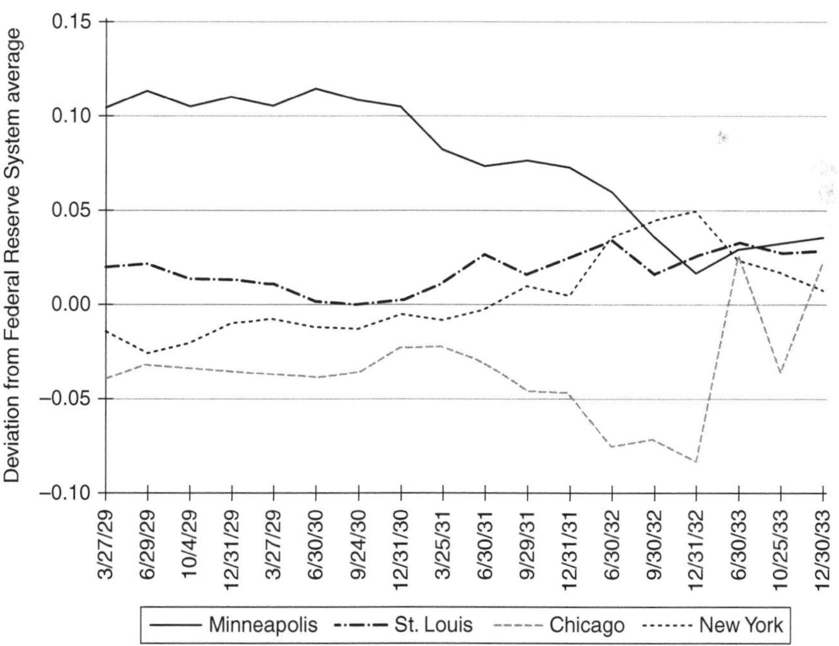

Fig. 13.1. Ratio of investments to loans and investments, 1929–33

Source: Mason (2010).

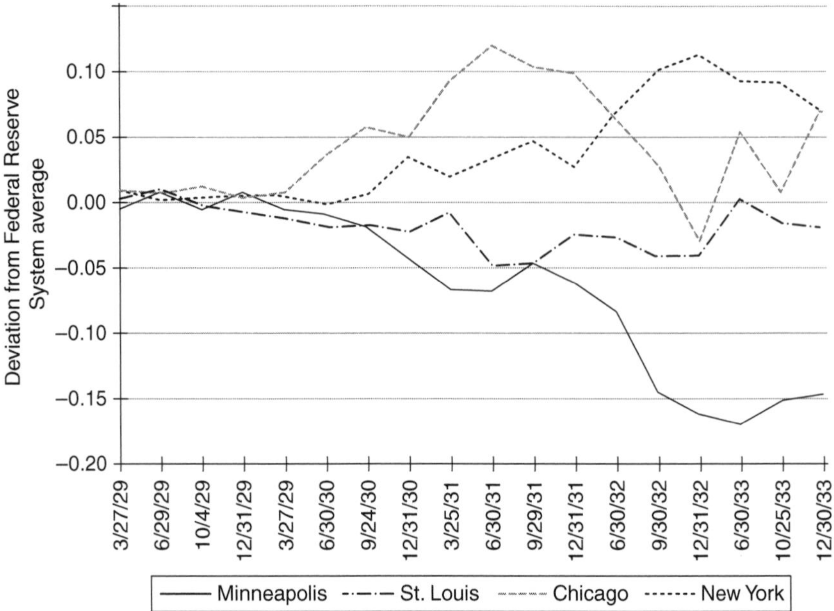

Fig. 13.2. Ratio of bills and notes to total investments, 1929–33
Source: Mason (2010).

Bank of New York was forced to admit that banks' 'attitudes had changed gradually since the last year in the face of the shrinkage in values', and that 'banks were much more interested in avoiding possible losses than in augmenting their current income' through an expansion of the supply of credit (quoted in Friedman and Schwartz, 1963: 380–5). This was as close as the Federal Reserve Bank of New York would come to disavowing its belief that monetary policy was an adequate stabilization tool for all economic crises.

The lack of agreement within the Fed carried over to the regional Federal Reserve Banks' relationship with the Board as well as their relationship with the executive branch of the government. Indeed, until the Banking Act of 1935, which placed the Board at the centre, differences between the Board and the regional banks may have contributed to the general passivity in Fed policy making in the 1930s. The Fed's decision to increase reserve requirements in 1936–37 in many ways stands out because it was otherwise inactive during the 1930s. In the first part of the decade, the Fed's failure to act as an LOLR resulted in the collapse of the banking system. And after 1932, the Fed took a back seat to the Treasury and initiatives proposed by Congress and the Roosevelt administration.[9] The profits from the 1934 revaluation of gold went to establish the Exchange Stabilization Fund, and Treasury threatened to use this fund to carry out open-market operations if the Fed did not go along with its efforts to expand the monetary base,

[9] Meltzer (2003) also suggests that passivity may have resulted from the widespread belief among the Federal Reserve Board and its staff that monetary policy was impotent.

keep real interest rates low or negative, and reflate the economy through gold purchases. Hence, the Fed did not drive policy decisions in the exit from the Depression. As a result, the institutions and policies created to combat the financial crisis and revive bank lending were largely programmes initiated by Congress and the Roosevelt administration. We now turn our focus to these.

13.4. BANK AND CREDIT POLICY

Although it is not as widely discussed as conventional monetary policy, bank and credit policies are central to understanding exit strategies from financial crises, such as the current crisis and the Great Depression. This section describes the institutional changes that constituted bank and credit policy in response to the economic decline of the early 1930s. We discuss the better-known policies (the banking holidays, capital assistance programmes to banks through the RFC, and federal deposit insurance) as well as programmes and policies that have received less attention, but nevertheless shaped the exit from the Great Depression, including loan support to railroads and corporations.

13.4.1. The National Credit Corporation

International influences, such as the failure of the Creditanstalt in Austria and the British departure from gold, exacerbated the banking situation in 1931. By late in that year, the frequency and severity of regional banking crises in the US were increasing rapidly; however, the Federal Reserve continued to direct its policies at maintaining its nominal anchor, even at the cost of reducing liquidity in an already unstable domestic banking system through discount rate increases.

For many banks, reduced depositor confidence forced bankers to maintain liquidity. Epstein and Ferguson (1984) describe how banks shifted their portfolios out of loans and into short-term assets, especially government securities, in order to maintain high levels of liquidity from October 1929 to March 1933. Despite high reserve ratios, continuous pressure on banks caused levels of liquid assets, in even the largest banks in the US, to decline to precariously low levels in 1932. Increasingly, the federal government was pressured to respond to requests by banks and the public to do something to mitigate the effects of the crisis (*Commercial and Financial Chronicle*, 11 February 1933: 936, 939; Wigmore, 1985).

In September 1931, President Hoover met with Eugene Meyer, chairman of the Federal Reserve Board and former board member of the War Finance Corporation (WFC), to propose a private corporation that would provide emergency funds to stem liquidity crises: the National Credit Corporation (NCC). Membership in the corporation was to be voluntary and the funding would come from the bankers themselves, with the government providing only legal recognition of the organization. Hoover's proposal was met with restrained enthusiasm, however (Olson, 1977: 25).

The NCC was formally organized on 13 October 1931, endorsed by the American Bankers Association and, later, the Investment Bankers Association.

Participating banks were required to subscribe to an amount of NCC notes, not less than 2 per cent 'of their respective net demand and time deposits'. The corporation was to consist of many regional subsidiaries that would oversee lending in their respective districts, and banks would only be liable for losses incurred from the lending activities in their own districts (Miller, 1931: 53–6).

The NCC, however, failed to provide broad enough assistance to stimulate a national recovery. It lacked the authority to lend to the railroads (in which many banks had invested) and small country banks, which were often most in need of funds but usually lacked funds to contribute the 2 per cent subscription required for NCC membership. Additionally, the NCC provided no assistance to life insurance companies, savings banks, building and loan associations, and a host of other financial institutions that held the same sorts of frozen assets as commercial banks (Olson, 1977: 30–2). By November 1931, it became apparent to Hoover that the NCC was a failure, and he made plans to introduce the necessary legislation for a reincarnation of the WFC when Congress reconvened.

As a result of the impending legislation, the NCC lent over $140m in January and February of 1932, compared with only $10m in October and November of 1931 (Olson, 1977: 29–30; Olson, 1988: 10).

13.4.2. The Reconstruction Finance Corporation and Federal Reserve loans

Ideological differences between Chicago and New York City bankers determined the boundaries for the legislative debate over the structure of the proposed RFC. The central points of concern for the Chicago bankers were the eligibility of liberal classes of collateral for loans to illiquid and closed banks. Meanwhile, New York bankers still felt that problems in the banking system stemmed from undue credit contraction, and that there was no reason to lend to closed or even illiquid banks, much less take illiquid collateral for security.

The resulting bill was a compromise. Congress did not even consider the radical idea of recapitalizing banks as suggested by some Midwestern bankers, and it placed limits on the amount of loans that could be used to pay off deposits of closed banks. Beyond this, however, the bill only stipulated that loans be priced so as not to crowd out private investment and to be 'adequately secured'. The new institution was thus given powers broad enough to meet the demands of Midwestern bankers, in that it stood ready to assume the risk of loss—and the losses—of banks and depositors (Ebersole, 1933: 467; Friedman and Schwartz, 1963: 303, 309; Olson, 1977: 47–55).

The RFC opened on 2 February 1932, and initially attempted to reduce bank failures by infusing the system with liquidity through a policy of making loans to those which cannot otherwise secure credit. The RFC sold capital worth $500m—which amounted to roughly 8.8 per cent of bank capital or 1.4 per cent of bank assets as of 30 June 1932—all subscribed by the United States of America and held by the Secretary of the Treasury. The corporation was authorized to issue notes, debentures, bonds, or other such obligations in an amount not exceeding three times its subscribed capital. These additional obligations could be sold to the public or the Treasury of the United States. The amount of subscribed capital was increased several times during the 1930s as the responsibilities of the RFC mushroomed.

The RFC was empowered to make loans to a variety of financial institutions as well as railroads, a decision that addressed the two main concerns of the erstwhile opponents of the NCC. But initial RFC lending policies were conservative to a fault. The RFC had authority to extend maturities to three years; however, its practice was to set maturities on its loans at less than six months so that it could exert greater control over borrowers. The Board of Directors of the RFC, which included the Secretary of the Treasury, the Governor of the Federal Reserve Board, and the Farm Loan Commissioner as *ex officio* members, set loan interest rates at 6 per cent, well above the market rate, to ensure that RFC financing would not drive out private alternatives. Additionally, the RFC often took a bank's most liquid assets as security for loans, increasing the risk of default on remaining bank debt and undermining the stabilizing effect of assistance. These policies surely limited the effectiveness of the RFC in its first year of operation and, some argued, may have hastened failures among vulnerable banks.

The RFC authorized $238m in loans during the first two months of operation, $160m of which went to banks and trust companies (James, 1938). Bank suspensions fell from 342 in January, to 119 in February, and to 45 in March. However, the declining number of bank failures during this period may provide a somewhat misleading measure of the effectiveness of the RFC. Problem banks received forbearance, but not necessarily salvation. Of the more than $1billion lent to banks prior to the March 1933 banking holiday, nearly 70 per cent went to banks borrowing more than once, and 15 per cent to banks borrowing more than five times. The most conspicuous episodes of such behaviour took place in Nevada and Michigan, two states which were hit especially hard during the banking of late 1932 and early 1933 (RFC, 1932; Olson, 1977; Doti and Schweikert, 1991).

13.4.3. Bank holidays and licensing programmes

Few were surprised when President Roosevelt imposed a nationwide 3-day moratorium on banking upon his inauguration, on 6 March 1933. By 3 March 1933, more than 5,500 banks with combined deposits of over $3billion had already suspended operations and only a handful of states were left without some sort of restrictions on banking. By 5 March, all 48 states and the District of Columbia had imposed various types of moratoria on banking within their borders (Jones, 1951; Kennedy, 1973; Olson, 1977).

Hence, even before the US went off gold, the Roosevelt administration took action to stop the fear and panic that was gripping the nation over the continued failure of banks and mounting evidence of fraud in the industry arising from the Pecora hearings.[10] This cooling-off period prevented depositors from

[10] At the time, the Pecora hearings sought to lay blame at the doorstep of Wall Street, but as we and others have emphasized, much of the blame lies with poor policy making, including that carried out by the Federal Reserve.

withdrawing their funds and gave examiners breathing room to sort out solvent banks from insolvent ones.

In order to restore confidence in the banking system, Roosevelt then signed the Emergency Banking Act of 9 March 1933, which authorized the US Secretary of the Treasury and state banking departments to issue licences to banks that were declared solvent, reorganize and support banks through the RFC, and close the rest.[11] The plan for reopening banks was described by Roosevelt in his fireside chat on 12 March: licensed banks in Federal Reserve cities would open on 13 March, and if these proceeded in an orderly fashion, it would be followed by banks opening in the 250 cities with clearinghouses on 14 March. And assuming all went well with the second round of openings, the remaining licensed banks would be allowed to open on 15 March. At the end of the day on 15 March, nearly 70 per cent of the 18,390 banks in operation on 3 March had reopened, including 5,038 of the existing 6,816 Federal Reserve member banks (Olson, 1988: 65–6).

Still, that left thousands of banks closed pending further investigation. The process to reopen those banks proceeded much more slowly. Some 1,300 additional banks were authorized by the Fed to reopen between June 1933 and December 1936, and roughly 3,900 never reopened (Board of Governors, 1943: 16). There were also wide differences in the rate of openings across regions since some state banking authorities permitted all banks to be reopened simultaneously. As a result, credit availability also varied widely after 1933. The RFC used new powers granted to it through the Emergency Banking Act and aided marginally solvent institutions through recapitalization and the application of liberal accounting standards.

13.4.4. Restructuring the RFC

The majority of Roosevelt's Emergency Banking Act consisted of legislation left over from the Hoover administration. Title I of the Emergency Banking Act formally legitimized Roosevelt's power under the Trading with the Enemy Act of 1917 to declare a national banking holiday. Title II, also known as the Bank Conservation Act, enabled conservators to be appointed to national banks that were deemed unsound by federal examiners. Title III granted the RFC permission to purchase a special class of preferred stock with full voting rights in any 'national banking association or any state bank or trust company in need of funds for capital purposes in connection with the organization or reorganization of such association' (Olson, 1977: 107).

The preferred stock of banks that was purchased by the RFC paid dividends of 6 per cent per annum, and was senior to all other stock upon liquidation of the firm. All other dividends were limited to a specified maximum, and additional retained earnings were devoted to a preferred stock retirement fund. The RFC's preferred stock was not subject to double-liability requirements, could be resold to the

[11] An executive order dated 10 March 1933 commanded the Secretary of the Treasury to 'license any member of the Federal Reserve System which could obtain endorsement of its soundness from its district Reserve bank; state banking authorities could reopen non-member banks at their discretion' (Kennedy, 1973: 180).

public at the discretion of the RFC, and carried voting rights that were often used to direct the institution towards solvency and profitability.

The RFC was prohibited from purchasing more than 49 per cent of the total outstanding voting stock in any one bank; however, it often owned the largest voting bloc in commercial banks. Thus, the RFC had effective control of many of the institutions in which it had investments. In several situations, the RFC used this control to replace officers and significantly alter the business practices of the institution.[12]

13.4.5. Federal Deposit Insurance and RFC support of reopened banks

The Glass–Steagall Act of June 1933 provided various reforms with respect to branch banking, securities affiliates, and deposit insurance. Most significantly, the Act strove to strengthen confidence in the banking industry through the provision of deposit insurance on a national level.[13]

Early deposit insurance schemes proved inadequate as a direct result of their inability to diversify beyond some tightly constrained geographic area and provisions which encouraged moral hazard. The new Federal Deposit Insurance Corporation (FDIC) intended to combat these shortcomings with a comprehensive nationwide system. In so doing, however, the plan relied strongly upon the membership of all the nation's banks. All Federal Reserve member banks were required to subscribe to the FDIC, and non-member banks were allowed to join if they could prove solvency before the date the programme took effect, 1 January 1934 (Jones, 1951; Calomiris and White, 1994; Wheelock and Kumbhakar, 1994).

During his fireside chats, Roosevelt promised the public that only solvent banks would reopen after the holiday. However, in examiners' haste to open as many banks as possible, they sometimes overestimated the value of bank assets. Thus, by June 1933, the RFC was not only busy trying to reopen banks, but also assisting those shaky banks that slipped past examiners. Jones (1951: 27) estimated that over 5,000 banks that reopened after the holiday 'required considerable added capital to make them sound'. The RFC and the Federal Reserve realized that the unsound nature of these banks precluded FDIC membership on 1 January 1934, but Roosevelt wanted them to join on that date to ensure public confidence in the system (Burns, 1974: 121).

The RFC could exert considerable influence over banks that had not reopened since the bank holiday. These banks often took on assistance packages of preferred stock investments and loans rather readily, as these measures were necessary if the bank was to continue operations. The unsound banks that had already reopened,

[12] The earliest and most prominent intervention was that involving Continental Illinois National Bank of Chicago. However, other prominent banks were assured that the situation at Continental Illinois was on account of a combination of various unusual circumstances, and would not be repeated without due cause.

[13] It should be noted that deposit insurance was only one possible reform path for improving financial stability. Indeed, it was also the product of intensive lobbying by small banks, which feared that other possible reforms could include deregulating bank entry and permitting widespread branch banking.

however, presented Roosevelt and the RFC with a significant problem. Open banks were reluctant to participate in the preferred stock programme because they thought RFC assistance signalled their unsound condition to the public. The RFC had little power to force these banks to participate.

In September 1933, Jesse Jones, Chairman of the RFC, addressed the American Bankers Association in Chicago and rebuked bankers for their reluctance to participate in the preferred stock programme, and strongly urged all the leading banks in the US to sell preferred stock to the RFC 'so that depositors would not be induced to switch out of . . . banks when [recipients'] names were published'. The appeal to the American Bankers Association convention seemed to have had some impact on the bankers, and the number of applications received daily at the RFC increased substantially. Eventually, nearly all the banks sold stock to the RFC, although several sold only small amounts and immediately repaid them (Jones, 1951; Burns, 1974; Wigmore, 1985). Mason (2001b) established, however, that the stigma that many were worried about was unwarranted. Moreover, recent historical studies of the phenomenon typically misstate which transactions were made public and when, confounding the problem further. Nonetheless, Mason (2001b) suggests that since the RFC only granted assistance to reasonably sound institutions, there is no reason to believe that such assistance was accompanied by the type of stigma feared by many (see also Schwartz, 1992).

In response to a backlog of assistance applications, on 23 October 1933 the RFC created the Non-Member Preferred Stock Board to handle the most delicate cases: more than 2,500 non-Federal Reserve member banks whose financial positions were still unverified by the Federal Reserve or the Secretary of the Treasury. At the same time, dividend and interest rates were lowered to 4 per cent, inspiring even more banks to participate in RFC programmes (Olson, 1988: 79). By November 1933, RFC applications were being sorted in a manner of triage. Banks 'whose assets appeared to equal 90 per cent of their total deposits and other liabilities exclusive of capital' were urged to seek private buyers for their stock, believing that otherwise the RFC could end up owning a sizable portion of the banking industry. Banks which could not meet these requirements were put in what Jones (1951: 28) refers to as the 'hospital', awaiting the arrangement of more complex assistance packages.

On 15 December 1933, more than 2,000 open banks were still in the RFC hospital and unopened. With only two weeks until the deadline for FDIC membership, the RFC began to seek quick solutions to gain membership for these banks and avoid another crisis of confidence. After a fruitless appeal to the Senate Committee on Banking and Currency, it sought to soften the deadline. On 28 December, Jones met with Secretary of the Treasury Morgenthau to propose a compromise: if Morgenthau would certify the hospitalized banks as solvent, Jones guaranteed they would be so within six months. The hospitalized banks were thus recapitalized in a more orderly fashion than otherwise would have occurred, and another possible crisis of confidence was avoided (Jones, 1951: 28–30). 'On January 1 Walter Cummings announced that the FDIC had accepted 13,423 banks as members and had rejected only 141' (Olson, 1988: 81).

By March 1934, the RFC had purchased preferred stock in nearly half the commercial banks in the US (Jones, 1951). By June 1935, these RFC investments made up 'more than one third of all outstanding capital in the entire [US] banking system' (Olson, 1988: 82).

13.4.6. RFC assistance to non-bank firms

Between 1932 and 1937, the RFC experimented with a wide variety of programmes aimed at resolving systemic distress. It did so by attempting to stimulate credit and capital-market activity by acting as an LOLR, not only recapitalizing the banking industry, but providing direct credit and capital to commercial and industrial enterprises.

13.4.6.1. Loans to railroads

The railroad loan programme served two purposes over the life of the RFC. When the RFC began operations, the railroad loan programme's objective was to augment directly the financial intermediary loan programme. After 1933, the railroad loan programme shifted its objective to become a means to stabilize general business activity and maintain employment.

Federal and state governments had recapitalized or otherwise bailed out weak railroads since the late nineteenth century. Because of this implicit bail-out provision, nearly all railroad bonds were rated AAA. As the stock of US government securities was retired during the 1920s, banks and other financial intermediaries increasingly relied upon railroad bonds as safe and liquid investments that were a close substitute for reserves. But when railroads were not bailed out in the early 1930s, the value of railroad bonds fell precipitously. In theory, therefore, helping out railroads through an RFC lending programme could increase the value of bank assets and stimulate credit activity, relieving the perceived credit stringency and pulling the economy out of the debt deflation spiral.

Rather than pricing themselves out of the relevant market as with loans to financial intermediaries, between 1932 and 1935 the RFC actually priced themselves *into* the market for railroad loans by setting rates below even benchmark common stock yields. As with the loans to financial institutions, railroad loans were set at 6 per cent in 1932, 5.5 per cent in 1933, and 5 per cent in 1934 and beyond. Moody's common railroad stock yields over this period were more than 7 per cent in 1932 and almost 6 per cent in 1933 and 1934. During 1935 and after, common railroad stock yields were below RFC rates. RFC debt was therefore cheaper than a typical railroad equity issue between 1932 and 1934.

From February 1932 to October 1933, most RFC railroad loans paid the interest and principal on existing debt. Between November 1933 and October 1934, the most popular use of RFC loans was to pay off the principal on short-term debt. Both these types of loans directly helped preserve the value of railroad securities and thereby aided banks (Mason and Schiffman, 2003).

Between February 1932 and October 1933 the RFC also dedicated a substantial amount of resources towards purchasing equipment trust certificates, that is, debt instruments for the purchase of operating equipment such as locomotives and freight cars and secured by the same. The purchase of equipment trust certificates maintained business activity and employment in ancillary industries. As it later turned out, support to this sector significantly smoothed production of railroad equipment on the eve of a high-demand period during the Second World War (Mason and Schiffman, 2003).

The incentive to finance with RFC debt rather than equity, and the moral hazard implications of less-than-secured lending to railroads mandated under the RFC Act, soon placed RFC capital at risk. The RFC was forced into litigation to recover loan proceeds in large-scale, widely publicized bankruptcy proceedings involving railway companies. Since RFC railroad loans were not 'fully secured' under the original statute, many of the first loans that went to railroads failed shortly thereafter. Perverse incentives existed whereby railroads could borrow from the RFC to pay favoured creditors and investors in full before defaulting. More importantly, since railroad capital levels were not regulated, and rates on railroad loans (unlike those on RFC loans to financial intermediaries) were favourable, railroads had an incentive to borrow from the RFC to finance new public-market capital issues, which could then be used to replace private debt (sometimes held primarily by insiders) with a mix of equity and RFC debt.

Once RFC officials recognized this problem, they began pushing for changes in the original statute. In June 1933, the RFC Act was amended so that the agency could no longer make a loan to any railroad or railway that was in need of financial reorganization in the public interest. In 1935, as policy makers became further convinced of the long-term nature of the economic downturn, the RFC railroad loan programme was further restricted to those applicants 'who could demonstrate the fundamental soundness of their financial position and their ability to survive a reasonably prolonged period of depression' (Spero, 1939: 2).

From November 1934 until October 1936, the principal purpose of RFC assistance shifted from commercial banks to repurchasing railroad securities in order to reduce railroad leverage ratios. In January 1935, the agency was further empowered to purchase and guarantee directly the general obligations of railroads and railways (Spero, 1939). As a result, RFC railroad loans, which were initially used to pay down debt and finance equipment purchases, were eventually used as a substitute for railroad capital. The extension of the RFC's powers suggests that policy makers within the Roosevelt administration believed that the Depression might last much longer. The operations of the agency furthered this changing view of reality since it moved to providing long-term capital (or debentures) rather than short-term secured debt.

Even with strict conditions, RFC loans to railroads simply prolonged impending bankruptcy: 'Prices of railroad bonds moved generally downward, intensifying the economic, banking, and credit difficulties' (Spero 1939: 143). Like the RFC's loans to banks, 'the underlying problems of the railroads—declining revenue, increased competition, and burdensome debt structures—were left untouched' (Olson, 1972: 181).

13.4.6.2. Loans to commercial and industrial enterprises

Preferred stock stabilized the banking sector, but as long as banks were primarily concerned with default risk as perceived by depositors, they were unwilling to undertake new lending. RFC officials and other policy makers nevertheless believed that an ample supply of business credit was the key to unwinding the debt–deflation spiral that was central to the economic downturn. In June 1934, the RFC and Federal Reserve therefore began making commercial and industrial (C&I) loans directly to businesses in order to relieve the credit stringency and expand economic activity.

The legislation passed in June 1934 allowed the RFC to make C&I loans with maturities:

> up to five years provided the applicant was sound, could supply adequate collateral, and could not get credit at banks. Loans could be advanced for working capital rather than equity or fixed capital, but could not exceed $500,000 per customer or be used to pay off existing indebtedness (Olson, 1972: 274).

In addition, the same section of the act that granted direct C&I loan authority to the RFC also amended the Federal Reserve Act to give equal authority to the Federal Reserve System for making C&I loans (Walk, 1937: 62). The legislation 'allowed the RFC to loan up to $300,000,000 and the Federal Reserve Banks up to $280,000,000'—of the $280m authorized to the Federal Reserve Banks, half was funded by their own surplus, and half by the Treasury (Walk, 1937: 65). Any future extensions of the $280m limit would be funded in the same manner.

Like the railroad and preferred stock programmes, the assistance to C&I firms enabled the RFC to have 'a profound influence upon policies and organizations of borrowers to insure soundness of their equity' (Sullivan, 1951: 7). As long as any portion of a C&I loan remained outstanding, no dividends could be paid by any corporate borrower nor could distribution or withdrawal be made by a partnership or individual borrower without the RFC's consent (Walk, 1937).

In order to conserve capital and reintroduce banks into business credit arrangements, the RFC and Federal Reserve developed cooperative credit arrangements with banks by purchasing participations in C&I loans rather than originating the loans exclusively (Olson, 1972). Most of the RFC C&I assistance authorized after 1934 therefore took the form of loan participations with firms' existing banks (Agnew, 1945).

These loan programmes had the capacity to make up a substantial portion of C&I lending during the early to mid-1930s, but they ended up having limited impact. At the end of 1937, the RFC had only authorized about $140m in its C&I loan programme and the Fed about $150m (Mason, 2001a). In 1935, Hardy and Viner concluded that 'efforts to relieve [credit] stringency through direct lending on the part of the Federal Reserve Bank of Chicago and the Chicago agency of the Reconstruction Finance Corporation have so far had a negligible effect on the general state of credit' (Hardy and Viner, 1935). In a later study, Kimmel reached similar conclusions for the entire period, 1933–38:

> both the demand for loans and the soundness of [C&I] borrowers was not what [RFC officials] expected. By September [1934], the Corporation had authorized only 100 business loans totaling $8,000,000. Less than $400,000 had been disbursed. Either because of inadequate security, insolvency, excessive indebtedness, or lack of potential earning power, the RFC rejected the majority of applications. But the apparent lack of demand for credit by business provided the RFC with its greatest surprise. It was a direct contradiction of what both [the Hoover and Roosevelt] administrations had told the country since 1931 (Olson 1972: 277).

In fact, policy makers and RFC officials discovered what banks knew all along: aggregate credit stringency did not exist. C&I firms often did not want loans because consumption was stagnant. RFC C&I lending, preferred stock, or other assistance to the corporate sector offered limited assistance in fostering aggregate demand. Indeed, total bank lending remained below its 1921 levels until the 1940s, when fiscal programmes stimulated by wartime production resuscitated economic activity.

13.5. UNWINDING THE EXPANSIONARY POLICIES OF THE 1930S

Hindered by the opposing objectives of restoring budget discipline but maintaining programmes for political objectives, unwinding monetary and bank credit facilities proved difficult. Policy makers in the 1930s thus waffled on exit—ultimately putting it off until after the Second World War.

The RFC provides a vivid example of the difficulty in winding down emergency programmes and policies. In 1934, Secretary of the Treasury Morgenthau successfully pressured the RFC to reduce assistance in order to help balance the budget, but was pressured by the railroad industry to hold off. By the beginning of 1935, with the economic expansion well under way, President Roosevelt and Morgenthau 'were adamant about reducing the budget deficit' and liquidating the RFC (Olson, 1988: 180). But by March 1934, the RFC had purchased preferred stock in nearly half the commercial banks in the United States (Jones, 1951). By June 1935, these RFC investments made up 'more than one third of all outstanding capital in the entire [US] banking system' (Olson, 1988: 82). At the peak, the RFC had outstanding loans of some $1.5billion (about $25billion in today's dollars).

Responding to political pressure, the RFC refused new applications for preferred stock and capital note purchases on 15 July 1935, and by November Jesse Jones announced to the American Bankers' Association that 'the bank emergency was over' (Olson, 1988: 181). Banks that had sold preferred stock to the RFC to help reduce the alleged stigma associated with RFC capital injections were the first to repurchase their equity. By the end of 1935, banks had repurchased nearly $100m of their preferred stock and capital notes.

In early 1936, the largest banks had retired their preferred stock and by July of that same year, the amount of RFC assistance outstanding had fallen by almost 35 per cent from its December 1934 peak. Over half of this decline occurred during the first six months of 1936. To the administration's delight, these repayments added $239m in revenue to the 1936 budget (a response that has a similar flavour to the Treasury touting the repayment of TARP (Troubled Asset Relief Program) money by banks today). They were even more delighted when Jones informed them that fiscal year 1937 would net another $700m by 'slowing down the pace of [RFC] loans and not providing funds to other government agencies' (Olson, 1988: 182).

Of course, any exit of a programme cannot be successful if the crisis is ongoing. In fact, that appears to be what happened with RFC programmes. While much of the academic debate over bank reserves treats the subject in isolation, to ignore the broader impacts of bank and monetary policy at the time is to see only a portion of the problem. In reality, debates over bank reserves, which relate both to credit policy and monetary policy, make far more sense in the context of the entirety of policies in place at the time.

As the RFC began to exit, some policy makers became increasingly concerned about the growing quantity of reserves that banks were accumulating above and beyond what was required by the Fed. Some even felt that those reserves could be a harbinger for higher inflation rates in the future. Meltzer (2003) suggests that Fed officials worried that the build-up in reserves would reignite the asset-price bubble of the late 1920s, and that lowering excess reserves would encourage discount-window borrowing and therefore allow the Fed to regulate borrowed reserves and therefore inflation. Romer (1992: 765) suggests that the Fed doubled the reserve requirements for banks between August 1936 and May 1937 because it was 'concerned about the high level of excess reserves in 1936 and wanted to turn them into required reserves'. As a result, banks responded by lending even less than previously, so that their reserves were still higher than the new required levels. Interestingly, none of those explanations takes into account the fact that RFC capital and credit were being drained from the banking system from 1934 onwards.

Nonetheless, Friedman and Schwartz (1963) suggest the increase in reserve requirements decreased the money supply because banks wanted to hold excess reserves (i.e. they were eschewing risk). Reserve policy therefore further contracted the money supply because it misunderstood the bankers' motivation. It is clear, therefore, that reserves were tied to monetary policy making, but some policy makers also believed that the large accumulation by commercial banks signalled continued weakness in the economy, either a lack of demand from businesses or an unwillingness to lend to new investment projects by the banks.

The dearth of lending clouded policy makers' ability to make a clear call as to when to remove key programmes supporting banks and credit. As a consequence, the RFC's C&I credit and capital programmes were rekindled and continued to provide business finance during the late 1930s and into the Second World War. The RFC was then used to combat the recession following the war. It continued with credit programmes through 1953, when the agency was finally liquidated amid charges of influence peddling and corruption. The liberal practices that became the key to effective government credit programmes during the early 1930s were, in the end, a detriment to sound management.[14]

The Federal Reserve's secondary role that had come about in the 1930s continued into the 1940s, and early 1950s. Despite the passage of the Banking Act of 1935 (which removed the Treasury Secretary and the Comptroller of the Currency as *ex officio* members of the Federal Open Market Committee (FOMC)), the

[14] The legacy of its operations lives on through spin-off agencies still in existence today, such as the Federal National Mortgage Association, the Export–Import Bank, the Commodity Credit Corporation, and the Small Business Administration (McGowen, 1977: 3, 11).

growth of the Treasury's balance sheet in the 1930s (through the Exchange Stabilization Fund and the Thomas Amendment) had made the Fed a tool of Treasury policy. This compromised the Fed's independence and challenged its ability to commit to a return to long-run targets that would be consistent with the modern-day central bank objectives of low and stable inflation and growth at potential GDP. The Fed's balance sheet continued to grow enormously during the Second World War through the issuance of government debt, and continued thereafter in efforts to combat the ensuing recession.

Fed independence was not obtained until the accord of 4 March 1951. At about the same time as Congress was shutting down the RFC, the Federal Reserve and Treasury entered the famous accord to divorce operations, allowing the Federal Reserve to target interest rates without concern for Treasury borrowing costs as it had almost since its inception (see, for instance, Hetzel and Leach, 2001). The accord provided the necessary break from strategies that might otherwise have led to alternative paths for the US economy, perhaps including either debt deflation (as in Japan in the 2000s) or crony capitalism (as in many developing countries).

13.6. POLICY IMPLICATIONS

Having reviewed the institutions and policies of the 1930s, we now suggest a framework for viewing them in terms of 'an exit strategy' from a financial crisis. We first define the 'three Rs' of emergency support: (i) provide *resources* for growth; (ii) *reallocate* financial industry assets; and (iii) *resolve* failed institutions. The three Rs mix monetary and bank policy in a way that provides comprehensive support to the economy during times of economic and financial distress.

Note that the three Rs constitute short-term emergency response measures that can be generalized to any financial crisis. In our discussion, we sidestep the messier process of regulatory reform in response to financial crises for two reasons. First, regulatory reform is often specifically related to 'fighting the last war'. Optimal regulation may need to do more than this, such as enable regulators to supervise new financial technologies, those that often cause shocks to the real economy. Second, (political influences notwithstanding) regulatory reform can wait until steady-state growth is regained. Evolving experience based on the present crisis as well as that from the implementation of Basel I during the 1991 recession suggests that regulatory reform might be best delayed until economic growth is somewhat less than 'unusually uncertain' (as Ben Bernanke characterized it in 2010), at which point the disruption to business activity can be better borne by short-term economic growth.

Since delaying exit is often justified for political reasons, we next suggest a metric for timing the shift from short-run to long-run objectives—one that blends the dual objectives of monetary and bank policy—in order to insulate the process from potentially economically harmful (and politically motivated) delay. We contend that having a policy target that relates directly to the distress can help guide long-term decision making and defend seemingly costly (in the short run) policy reversals that result in a return to steady-state conditions.

13.6.1. Provide *resources* for growth

13.6.1.1. Go easy on accounting measures

In the wake of financial crises, regulators commonly augment loans and capital with accounting forbearance. As is the case today, this was an important component to the recovery policy of the Great Depression. According to Simonson and Hemple (1993), the Comptroller of the Currency (and later the FDIC) and the Federal Reserve disagreed over accounting forbearance in the 1930s. On the one hand, the Office of the Comptroller of the Currency (OCC) and FDIC desired strict financial cut-offs in order to protect bank creditors, particularly depositors. On the other, the Federal Reserve wanted to smooth market effects on bank values, reducing the impact of the Depression upon banks in a more subjective manner (see also Jones, 1940). To some extent, the strategy was born of necessity because the true value of assets was unknown in the wake of the financial crisis.

For an example of what we mean, we again turn to the history of the RFC. The seemingly simple task of restricting credit programmes to sound institutions proved difficult to implement in practice because the RFC often evaluated firm solvency and soundness on the basis of future market expectations or favourable environmental conditions that were (and still are) impossible to quantify. A similar approach was applied in 1990–92, when supervisors practised widespread accounting forbearance (Simonson and Hemple, 1993). And, today, banks may be overvaluing assets on a strictly accounting basis, most plausibly with the tacit collusion of their regulators (Huizinga and Laeven, 2009). If financial crises elicit this regulatory forbearance, how can the costs of such behaviour be limited? Based on the 1930s, RFC programmes often took a measure of control over institutions to assuage junior creditors and nurse firms to profitability and recovery over the long run, both helping to ensure the success of the programmes and stemming the moral hazard of forbearance.

13.6.1.2. Subsidize earnings through low interest rates

Whereas in the standard view lower real interest rates serve to boost new investment in a recession, a newer strand of the literature suggests that low rates also aid banks in the wake of a financial crisis. Low interest rates effectively subsidize bank earnings by allowing them to borrow cheaply while investing at high post-crisis returns. This can be particularly useful in a post-financial crisis environment, when bank capital is scarce, because retained earnings are often the only available source of funding to rebuild bank capital. Since banks derive a preponderance of their funding from individual deposits, the arrangement can be thought of as a transfer from current depositors to bank profits (see, for instance, Henry, 2010).

13.6.1.3. Promote investment

When fear replaces greed and markets seize up, the federal government may provide direct lending in order to keep the economy from collapsing further. Whether through facilities such as the RFC or by directing banks how to allocate funds, governments routinely employ programmes and policies to create credit and stimulate new investment.

Some variations on the theme involve directly bailing out large firms and sectors. Today, we call them 'systemically important'. In the Great Depression, the RFC specifically targeted banks and railroads. Those programmes have obvious parallels with the $750billion TARP and the $17.4billion federal bail-out of US auto companies, Chrysler and Ford, in the wake of the 2008 financial crisis.

In the Great Depression, many offshoots of the RFC and related entities, including the Export–Import Bank, the Federal National Mortgage Association, and the Home Owner's Loan Corporation, also played a role in promoting investment during the Great Depression (Rose, 2010). That said, RFC assistance to banks and other assistance provided directly to bank borrowers, such as Home Owner's Loan Corporation loans, have been found to be substitutes in efforts to shore up bank conditions (see, for instance, Mason 2001a). Hence, there is a wide variety of policy choices in this realm.

Politicians, however, tend to favour such programmes most strongly when they can distribute the proceeds to key constituents. Allegations of favouritism and lending to big business were commonplace even with the RFC. Incentive problems with directed credit programmes appear insensitive to place as well as period. For example, Krueger and Yoo (2001) show that, in developing Korea in the 1990s, resources were channelled in large part to value-destroying large firms. Thus, while such programmes are believed to be crucial to restoring confidence and aiding recovery, they can potentially disrupt long-term growth.

13.6.2. *Reallocate* financial assets

13.6.2.1. Maintain credit supply commensurate with credit demand

Several studies of credit activity concluded that the perceived credit stringency during the 1930s may, in fact, have been a lack of demand for business credit rather than a lack of supply (see Hardy and Viner (1935) and, later, Kimmel (1939)). The RFC initially focused on a conservative strategy of primarily extending fully secured, short-term credit at penalty rates to banks, much as an LOLR would do; however, those RFC programmes were soon broadened in scope to recapitalize the banking sector and make loans to a broad base of C&I enterprises.

The idea was that, while regulators cannot control loan demand, they can at least push out money and therefore loan supply in the hope that the market will equilibrate at a higher level of lending. In modern banking literature, however, theories of credit rationing such as that of Stiglitz and Weiss (1981), which incorporate a bank loan supply curve that turns down when increased risk outweighs return, suggest that a higher equilibrium level of lending may not arise until preferences affecting the downward bending portion of the supply curve are resolved. The means to resolve such preference shifts is typically the same as resolving asymmetric information problems—whether through a bank holiday, quarantining assets in a bad bank, or other certification exercise. Nonetheless, it is important to ensure capital remains adequate to extend supply to meet demand when such asymmetries are resolved.

13.6.2.2. Prevent disintermediation and preserve lending relationships

Bernanke (1983) sought to identify a credit channel that could explain the propagation of the Great Depression beyond Friedman and Schwartz's (1963) classic account of a decline in monetary aggregates. He focused on the loss of information and credit 'disintermediation' when banks failed. He surmised that as 'a matter of theory, the duration of the credit effects . . . depends on the amount of time it takes to (1) establish new or revive old channels of credit flow after a major disruption and (2) rehabilitate insolvent debtors'. The difficult and slow adjustment of these two factors supports Bernanke's argument for the persistence of non-monetary effects.

Bank regulators can ensure that sufficient capital remains in place to 'establish new or revive old channels of credit flow', particularly for solvent borrowers unaffected by the larger macroeconomic movements (Bernanke, 1983). Such policy seeks prospectively to maintain resources for a nascent recovery, given the lack of credit demand. Hardy and Viner (1935) and Kimmel (1939) both concluded, in part, that businesses had largely declined to apply for credit and certainly had little desire to expand investment in the Depression.

13.6.2.3. Provide bank capital and reserves to fuel charge-offs

More pointedly, banks in the Depression allocated substantial resources to writing down loans and re-provisioning reserves for potential withdrawals. The stresses on capital and reserves resulting from both write-downs and withdrawals, even at healthy institutions, can be debilitating. Hence, bank policy usually focuses on providing additional sources of both capital and reserves to mitigate the effects.

In the bank capital crunches of both the 1930s and 1990–91, financial institutions suffering from large losses raised virtually no new equity capital (Calomiris and Wilson, 2004). Financial economists attribute the lack of new equity offerings by banks in response to large losses to adverse-selection problems that result from asymmetric information. Any bank trying to issue equity at a time when potentially large hidden losses remain unidentified will experience a large decline in its stock price since the market infers that the offering institution may have unusually high losses that it wants to share with new investors. The ensuing price pressure would therefore dilute a stock offering and thus destroy value for existing shareholders (see Calomiris, 2008).

In the 1930s, as well as today, contemporaries also complained about banks piling up reserves well above and beyond the Fed's requirements. In the 1930s, the Fed became increasingly concerned that excess reserves in the commercial banking system would ignite inflation. Fed officials at that time viewed an increase in reserves as indicating a potential for credit expansion and viewed them as economically unnecessary ('redundant surplus' in Meltzer's (2003) terminology).

Member banks had built up more than $3.6billion in excess reserves by October 1935 (an amount that exceeded the size of the Fed's open-market portfolio), $1.6billion of which had been accumulated since March of that same year. In March 1935, the Fed issued a memorandum in which it described this accumulation, but ruled out using open-market sales to absorb the excess reserves for two reasons. First, it worried that it would cut short the economic recovery that was taking place by putting too much emphasis on the dangers of inflation. Second, it did not believe it could carry out this action on its own and without the support of the Treasury, since that agency could offset the Fed's actions by using its stabilization fund or by issuing paper money under the Thomas Amendment (Meltzer, 2003).

Moreover, if monetary restraint was not coordinated with Treasury to reduce the budget deficit, it would result in higher rates of financing for new sales of US government debt. By October 1933, the Fed had already decided that it would have to coordinate its policy with the Treasury; it decided that the best way to drain off the excess reserves without simultaneously tightening credit was to raise the reserve requirements for member banks. They believed that the effects of increasing required reserves depended on the distribution of excess reserves by type of bank and by the location of bank (Meltzer, 2003).

Still, an understanding of reserve dynamics is substantially lacking. Despite its beliefs that the reserves were excessive, it does not appear to be the case that the Fed commissioned a study to understand why banks held such large reserves. Was the problem a lack of demand for new loans (Cargill and Mayer, 2006) or was it banks acting with increased risk aversion in response to the waves of panics and widespread bank failures (Friedman and Schwartz, 1963)? Alternatively, it could be that researchers have focused too strongly on reserves instead of 'near reserves'—which could include government debt and other short-term highly liquid financial instruments that evolved during the period—and that the series of the combination of the two is largely invariant.

Regardless, it appears the Fed likely overestimated lending potential, putting it at more than 20 times excess reserves. In its view, the huge volume of excess reserves was a 'serious menace' and inflationary threat. This belief led to its fateful decision to vote for increases in reserve requirements, beginning in 1936.

Today, as in the Great Depression, therefore, there appear to be two concerns. One is that excess reserves indicate that banks are not lending when they should be; therefore, the economy is not growing as much as it should via new investment spending. A second concern is that the reserves will eventually come back into the system and that will drive up prices and inflation. Without an answer informed by systematic economic research, however, the debate over which is more important continues to rage.

13.6.3. *Resolve* failed institutions

In resolving failed institutions, three factors are important. First, regulators need to address asymmetric information problems that cause financial panics. After stabilizing the system, regulators can then resolve insolvent institutions. During the resolution process, means by which trustees can return at least partial recoveries to investors (particularly depositors) before having to wait for the final liquidation can help smooth consumption and return investable funds to the public sooner than would otherwise be the case, spurring recovery. We discuss each of these in turn.

13.6.3.1. *Quarantine bad banks to alleviate asymmetric information*

Crisis responses are commonly accompanied by some form of certification or quarantine of the toxic assets that are the source of asymmetric information. In the Great Depression, Roosevelt's bank holiday and the licensing process that ensued fulfilled this function. The recent Supervisory Capital Assessment Program (SCAP) was interpreted by some to be a similar effort.

The bank holiday of 1933, accompanied by the commitment to deposit insurance, resolved asymmetric information among depositors in the Great Depression.[15] In the present-day SCAP application, however, the failure to resolve obviously insolvent bank holding companies, or even publish the results of the audit, was interpreted by some as a failure to resolve the asymmetric information problems among financial institutions. Many policy makers dismissed the need to resolve the fundamental asymmetric information, feeling that the after-the-fact capital subsidies were sufficient to do so. The success of the approach remains to be seen.

In the meantime, however, it is important to remember that, while asymmetric information shocks may not be the cause of the lion's share of the decline, they can substantially prolong business-cycle persistence. Without adequate information on financial institution conditions, depositors and investors fled banks and refused to put their money into alternative investments. Hence, businesses were starved of funds and investment and economic growth underperformed (Calomiris and Mason, 1997).

13.6.3.2. *Improve resolution technology in order to get cash to creditors*

Prior to the Great Depression, bank regulators could only close banks and liquidate the assets, paying creditors as the liquidation proceeded. Hence, trustees during the 1930s would sell assets at fire-sale prices just to help creditors. To remedy that shortcoming, in October 1933, the RFC established the Deposit Liquidation Board in order to provide an orderly liquidation of bank assets. The Board was technically an extension of the executive branch, although it was funded by and worked very closely with, the RFC.

Even before the Deposit Liquidation Board, however, bank regulators looked for more creative means of resolution during the 1930s. One approach was a 'Spokane sale'. A cross between reorganization and liquidation, bank assets were sold in bulk to an existing bank or a company established exclusively for their liquidation, after which the proceeds would be used to pay at least a proportion of creditors. 'After the sale and distribution, a receiver could liquidate the old bank and collect stock assessments.' A bank was thus liquidated in a Spokane sale, but depositors received their funds in a more timely manner than otherwise (Kennedy, 1973: 193–5).

[15] While the Great Depression process may (and probably did) suffer from a lack of certainty—some assets could not be verified in the short time allotted—remaining banks were the target of a commitment by the government to have largely 'gotten it right'. Indeed, open banks were subsidized where necessary in order to gain access to federal deposit insurance when the FDIC opened for business in January 1934.

Banks in a relatively better condition had another alternative. They could seek a 'creditor waiver', which restructured debt to levels commensurate with assets. In order to maintain bank operations in the short term, the RFC typically lent funds to give banks time to 'eliminate that portion of liabilities which exceeded assets'. Usually such adjustment was made by 'persuading banks' creditors to sign waivers of a percentage of their deposits or other claims', which also acted as a show of good faith from debt holders to the RFC (Kennedy, 1973: 190–3; see also Upham and Lamke, 1934: 124–41). Once the balance of assets and liabilities was re-established, preferred stock was then purchased in these banks to provide a better capital foundation for the firm (Upham and Lamke, 1934; Kennedy, 1973).

The Emergency Banking Act gave resolution authorities the legal means to carry out a conservatorship rather than a liquidation (receivership). This enabled a bank to be restructured and continue as a going concern. Conservatorship gave regulators the authority to enter into capital correction procedures, where banks simply needed an increased capital buffer. Often such cases were resolved with the provision of long-term capital through RFC-preferred stock purchases. Sometimes, as with Continental Illinois Bank and Trust Company, the RFC imposed its voting rights to reorganize the bank's management as well, although such actions were rare. By the end of 1937, the RFC had authorized just under $1.2billion to receivers, liquidating agents, and conservators of banks and trust companies, compared to just over $1.3billion to open banks.

Recently, policy makers have sought improved resolution technologies, including what is referred to as banks that are 'systematically important' or 'too big to fail'. It seems every large crisis necessitates improvements in resolution and bankruptcy provisions, and the present crisis is therefore no exception.

13.6.4. The goldilocks problem: avoid fire sales, but sell assets in a timely manner

Balancing the speed of bank liquidations with recoveries to creditors (particularly depositors) is important. Faster liquidations get money to creditors sooner, but more careful consideration can often substantially increase recovery rates. The RFC loans and, later, the FDIC therefore played two important roles. First, loans and deposit insurance reduce the depth and persistence of business downturns by 'maintaining depositors' access to funds—even in the presence of depositor losses or haircuts (amounts failed-bank depositors may concede as a moral hazard penalty)—so that those funds can be reinvested quickly and efficiently in the financial sector' (Anari et al., 2005). Second—and less recognized—the RFC loans and the FDIC arguably allowed for a more careful liquidation of failed-bank assets and limited fire sales. Since creditors were not clamouring for liquidity, trustees and liquidating agents could shop for the best price for failed-bank assets; this supported asset prices and benefited creditors in the failed enterprise.

Anari et al. (2005) show that it is important to get recoveries to creditors in a timely manner. They show that a sizable portion of liquidated bank assets persisted well into the late 1930s and hypothesize that the drag on consumption and investment resulting from the resolution delay played a substantial role in business-cycle persistence. Cangemi et al. (2010) show a similar (though slightly less important, economically) role for defaulted corporate debt, where investor coupons are cut off during defaults that may last several years, during which time the losses attributable to bondholders (and therefore bond values and prices) are highly uncertain, resulting in substantial and persistent illiquidity.

As a result, responses to many financial crises since the Great Depression have often included a role for asset management companies, which can mitigate asset-price volatility by liquidating bank assets at a controlled and reasonable rate. Using these companies is thought to reduce the effects of asset-market overhang (Kaufman and Seelig, 2000; Klingebiel, 2000; Bergoeing et al., 2002; Kehoe and Prescott, 2002; Mason, 2005). The Resolution Trust Corporation is widely credited (rightly or wrongly) for successfully mitigating asset-price declines in the US, especially in the real estate sector, and thereby reducing business-cycle persistence in the late 1980s and early 1990s.

Of course, this does not rule out alternative ways of achieving a similar objective; for example, if the Fed had been able to generate some inflation, it may have at least stopped asset prices from declining further. Japan offers a contrasting example, where the 'Heisei Malaise' has dragged on for two decades. These observations suggest that there exists an important, often-overlooked, macroeconomic role for the deposit insurer. Beyond its microeconomic objective of making depositors whole, the deposit insurer can work as asset liquidator and, in conjunction with a central bank that is focused on generating inflationary expectations, alleviate banking distress.

13.6.5. Incorporating resolution rates in the determination of policy exits

In terms of the 'three Rs' taxonomy presented above, exit conditions for resolution and reallocation—that is, bank policy—are largely organic: once failed banks are resolved and loans get reallocated, the work is done. That does not mean the process happens quickly. It takes some banks 20 years or more to be resolved. It may nevertheless be possible to use economic information on the state of the resolution process to guide the exit strategy.

We propose, therefore, that bank and non-bank resolutions can be used to parameterize less quantifiable monetary and bank policies when traditional monetary targets are rendered inoperable or highly suspect as the result of extraordinary monetary policy measures to combat a financial crisis (zero interest-rate policies, quantitative easing policies, etc.). That is, the need for credit stimulus should end when failed intermediaries are resolved and positive net present value credits are reallocated to solvent lenders.

We suggest that it is feasible to parameterize both the degree of stimulus and the exit by targeting a money supply analogue, particularly one that represents the degree of distress and the depletion of monetary resources as a direct result of the crisis. In the Great Depression, for instance, deposit accounts rendered inaccessible by bank failures could no longer be counted in M1, resulting in a severe

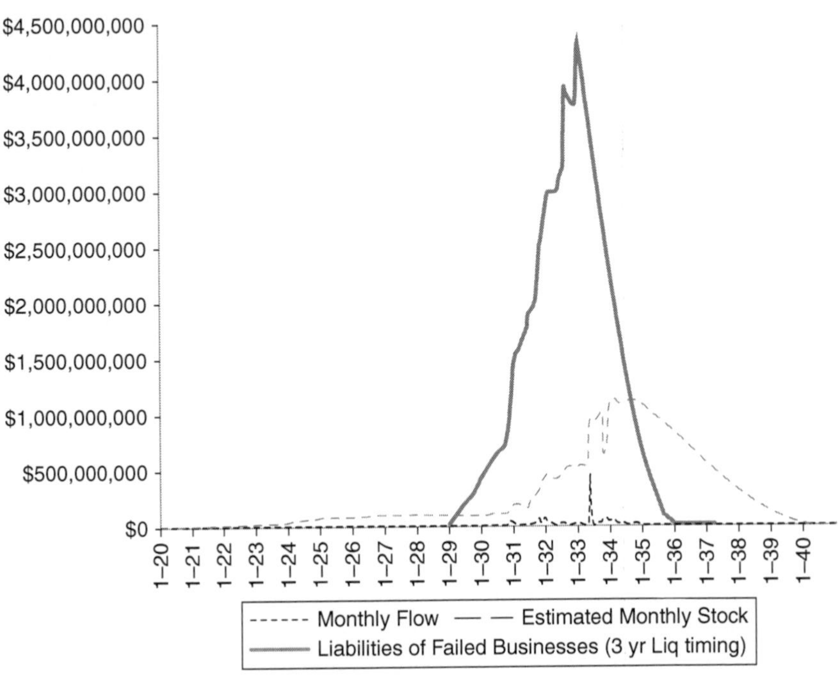

Fig. 13.3. National bank and commercial failures and liquidations, 1920–40

Sources: Dun and Bradstreet; Anari et al. (2005).

decline in the money supply. As a result, Anari et al. (2005) find that the stock of deposits in closed banks had an effect on economic growth similar in magnitude to the decline of M1, and that the depressing effect lasted well into the late 1930s. Rockoff (1993) suggests a similar relationship.

Nonetheless, given that persistent downturns associated with financial crises have remained a fixture of business cycles even after the advent of deposit insurance, there must be an additional dynamic. An exit strategy parameterization ought also to account for other defaulted or otherwise 'forcibly altered' financial contracts, so that liquidity and wealth effects associated with an economic downturn are factored in explicitly.

Even a brief view of the size of such effects shows they can be substantial. Figure 13.3 adds Dun and Bradstreet's monthly series on the liabilities of failed businesses to the Anari et al. (2005) graph of the stock of deposits in failed banks. The graph uses Dun and Bradstreet's data for 1929–33 and conservatively assumes a 3-year, straight-line liquidation of the liabilities of failed businesses (hypothesizing that business assets suffer less asymmetric information than bank assets, and therefore should sell sooner) and no loss.[16]

[16] There already exists a literature on wealth effects of depositor recoveries (see, for instance, the discussion of wealth effects in Friedman and Schwartz, 1963). Average pay-outs for national banks were about $0.56 per dollar of deposits. Corporate recoveries are usually assumed to be about $0.40 per dollar of face value.

While one can argue that corporate investors expect less liquidity than bank depositors, the effect makes that resulting from bank deposits in the Great Depression look minuscule, by comparison. It is immediately apparent that the stock of liabilities of failed businesses dwarfs even that of the stock of failed-bank assets in liquidation, which itself dwarfs the previously investigated flow of failed-bank assets, including the famous spike of March 1933 arising from the bank holiday (which peaked at just under $3.3trillion but only for roughly a week, in duration).

Cangemi et al. (2010) show that the drivers of corporate bond defaults are the same as those that delay bank liquidation, even if the defaults eventually recover at a lower loss rate than in full liquidation. From the perspective of business-cycle persistence, those corporate defaults also deprive investors of substantial liquidity and marketability until the uncertainty about default resolution timing and ultimate losses is resolved. Mason (2005) and Cangemi et al. (2010) suggest that the determinants of resolution delays can be derived from a real options model, where low discount rates and high expected upside volatility can delay recovery. Such results, however, have yet to be incorporated into business-cycle dynamics. Anari et al. (2005), Mason (2005), and Cangemi et al. (2010), therefore suggest that incorporating such delays into a theory of business-cycle persistence can be a meaningful empirical approach to measuring the practical impact of work such as Kiyotaki and Moore (1997) and others.

This preliminary evidence suggests that it is the disruptive effects of such failures and reallocations of credit and value that monetary and bank policy seeks to offset in a recession. Information on the speed of the resolution process can therefore provide an alternative signal as to when exit from emergency policies should be initiated or accelerated. By utilizing the resolution of failed banks and firms as a policy target, it may therefore be possible to return to long-run objectives without inciting another bubble or irritating the endogenous cycle of liquidation, which we suggest is a primary source of business-cycle persistence.

13.7. SUMMARY AND CONCLUSIONS

While concerns about expeditious exit are warranted, they must be weighed against the fact that, in the heat of a crisis, there is no certainty about where an economy is in the cycle. If there is one lesson that seems readily apparent from the 1930s, it is that taking the patient off life support too early can lead to another bout of illness. The current global economy still faces anaemic growth in output, exceptionally high unemployment, a banking system that is hampered by new bank failures every week, trillions of dollars of bank assets in resolution, and shaky sovereign borrowers seeking lines of support from more solvent countries.

Some might argue that applying lessons from the 1930s on when to remove stimulative monetary policy is muddled, in part because of the different trajectory of prices then in comparison to now. The US economy of the 1930s suffered severe deflation. Producer prices fell by more 40 per cent between 1929 and 1932. In response, the Roosevelt administration was focused on ending deflation and expectations that prices would continue to decline and opposing those (including bankers) who still blamed the depression on inflation. Their goal was to change the monetary regime, and install a very inflationary monetary one (Eggertsson, 2008; Temin and Wigmore, 1990). The Fed, however, was concerned that the growing volume of bank reserves would reignite inflation. It took pre-emptive action against inflation beginning in 1936 by doubling reserve requirements (Meltzer, 2003). Friedman and Schwartz (1963) argue that the result was a short and severe recession in 1937–38: output declined by roughly 10 per cent and unemployment returned to around 20 per cent. Recovery resumed after the Fed removed these rate increases and Treasury reversed course on a decision it had made in 1936 to sterilize large gold inflows (an action which had reduced high-powered money).

Perhaps the Fed has already applied the lesson from the 1930s regarding the movement of prices in two ways: (i) it used accommodative monetary policy to prevent deflation from happening in the first place and (ii) it appears to have recognized the possibility that removing policies that were used to combat a financial crisis too quickly can lead to a policy-induced recession (as in 1937–38) and therefore has moved with measured steps in unwinding its programmes. Indeed, in its August 2010 policy meeting, the FOMC decided to continue purchasing government securities in the wake of soft economic data.

That said, it is less clear how the present-day Fed is approaching credit policies. One theme that emerges from our analysis is that there is a troubling lack of knowledge regarding bank behaviour then and now. In both periods, it is not fully understood how to get financial institutions to lend again after a crisis. In both periods, banks built up 'excess reserves' and reduced their lending. It may be optimal for banks to do this in the wake of a financial crisis (too few positive net present value projects to invest in, a desire to recapitalize at the equivalent or higher level relative to assets, or heightened risk aversion), but it complicates the central bank's decision to remove itself from credit markets and return banking activities to markets. We suggest that the Fed would have a better sense of what to do today if we knew more about why banks failed to lend in the 1930s, why they held these reserves, and what their potential effects are on the path of prices. Hence, this may be a fruitful area for future research on the Great Depression.

But while prompt intervention probably avoided a deeper recession, there are arguments that such intervention heightened moral hazard by not allowing Schumpeterian 'creative destruction' or a 'Minsky moment' to occur, or at the very least failing credibly to resolve the asymmetric information about financial losses that caused the crisis in the first place.

Recessions often shift policy makers towards focusing on short-term solutions in efforts to stimulate economic activity. When recessions are exacerbated by financial crises, policy makers often respond by creating new institutions or facilities for restoring credit and stabilizing the financial system or by taking on functions that, in normal times, are carried out by markets, adopting what we call bank policy, to augment traditional monetary and fiscal policy.

Once in place, policies that augment credit, subsidize earnings, provide accounting forbearance, or raise investment are devilishly difficult to remove in a way that preserves appropriate exit timing without significant push back from politicians, who often benefit from distributing the spoils. Central banks are at the centre of these arrangements. They have to remain vigilant about returning the economy to its long-run path, even in the face of the political consequences, or they risk losing their independence and their ability credibly to manage macroeconomic growth and inflation, and fiat exchange rates.

The policy uncertainty created by the inexorable political debates over exit, as well as the possibility of central bank capture, creates its own problems. It is hard for businesses to make investments on the basis of expansionary government programmes that could expire overnight. Like the hidden story of the Thrift Crisis—in which the repeal of the 1981 Economic Recovery Tax Act (which allowed business to write off 40 per cent of real estate project losses in the first year) via the 1986 Tax Reform Act only five years later left businesses unexpectedly to absorb high losses—the tangle of massive uncoordinated stimulative economic policies could very well extend the present crisis or cause a new one shortly down the road. It is hard to argue that uncertainty about exit policy, therefore, does not taint business decision making in today's economic environment.

More subtly, however, if the political risk of 'exit' constrains recovery, prompt intervention can potentially prolong a recession even as it reduces its depth. The ultimate accounting exercise as to whether policy makers reduced the severity of any given recession likely needs to net out the potential costs of prolonging it.

BIBLIOGRAPHY

Agnew, R. L. (1945), 'Loans to Financial Institutions by the Reconstruction Finance Corporation', University of Nebraska, Masters Thesis.

Anari, A., Kolari, J., and Mason, J. R. (2005), 'Bank Asset Liquidation and the Propagation of the Great Depression', *Journal of Money, Credit, and Banking*, 37(4), 753–73.

Bergoeing, R., Kehoe, P. J., and Soto, R. (2002), 'A Decade Lost and Found: Mexico and Chile in the 1980s', *Review of Economic Dynamics*, 5, 166–205.

Bernanke, B. S. (1983), 'Non-monetary Effects of the Financial Crisis in the Propagation of the Great Depression', *American Economic Review*, 73(June), 257–76.

Board of Governors Federal Reserve System (1943), *Banking and Monetary Statistics, 1914–1941*. Washington, DC: National Capital Press.

Burns, H. M. (1974), *The American Banking Industry and New Deal Banking Reforms, 1933–1935*. Westport, CT: Greenwood Press.

Calomiris, C. W. (2008), 'The Subprime Turmoil: What's Old, What's New, and What's Next', paper prepared for presentation at the Federal Reserve Bank of Kansas City's Symposium, 'Maintaining Stability in a Changing Financial System', Jackson Hole, Wyoming, 5 August.

Calomiris, C. W. and Mason, J. R. (1997), 'Contagion and Bank Failures During the Great Depression: The June 1932 Chicago Banking Panic', *American Economic Review*, 87 (December), 863–83.

Calomiris, C. W. and White, E. N. (1994), 'The Origins of Federal Deposit Insurance', in C. Goldin and G. Libecap (eds), *The Regulated Economy: A Historical Approach to Political Economy*. Chicago, IL: University of Chicago Press, 145–88.

Calomiris, C. W. and Wilson, B. (2004), 'Bank Capital and Portfolio Management: The 1930s "Capital Crunch" and Scramble to Shed Risk', *Journal of Business*, 77(July), 421–56.

Cangemi, R., Mason, J., and Pagano, M. (2012), 'How Much of a Haircut? Options-Based Structural Modeling of Defaulted Bond Recovery Rates', *Journal of Financial Intermediation*, 21(3), 473–506.

Cargill, T. F., and Mayer, T. (2006), 'The Effect of Changes in Reserve Requirements during the 1930s: The Evidence from Non-member Banks', *Journal of Economic History*, 66 (June), 417–32.

Chandler, L. V. (1971), *American Monetary Policy, 1928–1941*. New York: Harper & Row.

Claessens, S., Kose, M. A., and Terrones, M. E. (2008), 'What Happens During Recessions, Crunches and Busts?', IMF Working Paper No. 08-274, December.

Del Negro, M., Eggertsson, G., Ferrero, A., and Kiyotaki, N. (2009), 'The Great Escape? A Quantitative Evaluation of the Fed's Nonstandard Policies', New York Federal Reserve Bank Working Paper, December.

Doti, L. P., and Schweikert, L. (1991), *Banking in the American West: From the Gold Rush to Deregulation*. Norman, OK: University of Oklahoma Press.

Ebersole, J. F. (1933), 'One Year of the Reconstruction Finance Corporation', *Quarterly Journal of Economics*, 47(May), 563–83.

Eggertsson, G. (2008), 'Great Expectations and the End of the Depression', *American Economic Review*, 98(4), 1476–516.

Eichengreen, B. (1992), *Golden Fetters: The Gold Standard and the Great Depression, 1919–1939*. New York: Oxford University Press.

Eichengreen, B. and Sachs, J. (1985), 'Exchange Rates and Economic Recovery in the 1930s', *Journal of Economic History*, 45(4), 925–46.

Epstein, G. and Ferguson, T. (1984), 'Monetary Policy, Loan Liquidation, and Industrial Conflict: The Federal Reserve and the Open Market Operations of 1932', *Journal of Economic History*, 44(4), 957–83.

Friedman, M., and Schwartz, A. (1963), *A Monetary History of the United States, 1867–1960*, Princeton, NJ: Princeton University Press.

Hardy, C. O. and Viner, J. (1935), *Report on the Availability of Bank Credit in the Seventh Federal Reserve District*. Washington, DC: US Government Printing Office.

Henry, D. (2010), 'The Government's $56 Billion Gift to Banks', *Bloomberg Businessweek*, 4 February.

Hetzel, R. L. and Leach, R. F. (2001), 'The Treasury–Fed Accord: A New Narrative Account', *Federal Reserve Bank of Richmond Economic Quarterly*, 87(1), 33–55.

Huizinga, H. and Laeven, L. (2009), 'Accounting Discretion and the Reliability of Banks' Financial Accounts: Evidence from the US Mortgage Crisis', IMF Working Paper, June.

James, C. F. (1938), *The Growth of Chicago Banks*. New York: Harper & Brothers.

Jones, H. (1940), 'An Appraisal of the Rules and Procedures of Bank Supervision, 1929–39', *Journal of Political Economy*, 48(April), 183–98.

Jones, J. H. (1951), *Fifty Billion Dollars: My Thirteen Years with the RFC* (1932–1945). New York: Macmillan Company.

Kaufman, G. G. and Seelig, S. A. (2000), 'Treatment of Depositors at Failed Banks: Implications for the Severity of Banking Crisis, Systematic Risk, and Too-big-to-fail', Working Paper presented at the annual meetings of the Financial Management Association, Seattle, WA.

Kehoe, T. and Prescott, E. C. (2002), 'Great Depressions of the 20th Century', *Review of Economic Dynamics*, 5, 1–18.

Kennedy, S. E. (1973), *The Banking Crisis of 1933*. Lexington, KY: University Press of Kentucky.

Kimmel, L. H. (1939), *The Availability of Bank Credit, 1933–1938*. New York: National Industrial Conference Board.

Kiyotaki, N. and Moore, J. (1997), 'Credit Cycles', *Journal of Political Economy*, 105(April), 211–48.

Klingebiel, D. (2000), 'The Use of Asset Management Companies in the Resolution of Banking Crises: Cross-country Experiences', Washington, DC: World Bank, Research Working Paper Number 2284.

Krueger, A. O. and Yoo, J. (2001), 'Chaebol Capitalism and the Currency-Financial Crisis in Korea', NBER Conference on Currency Crises Prevention, Islamorada, Florida, January.

McGowen, J. C. (1977), *The Reconstruction Finance Corporation: Some Historical Perspective*. St Louis: Washington University.

Mason, J. R. (2001a), 'Do Lender of Last Resort Policies Matter? The Effects of Reconstruction Finance Corporation Assistance to Banks During the Great Depression', *Journal of Financial Services Research*, 20(September), 77–95.

Mason, J. R. (2001b), 'Reconstruction Finance Corporation Assistance to Financial Institutions and Commercial & Industrial Enterprise in the US Great Depression, 1932–1937', in S. Claessens, S. Djankov, and A. Mody (eds), *Resolution of Financial Distress*. Washington, DC: World Bank Press, 167–204.

Mason, J. R. (2005), 'A Real Options Approach to Bankruptcy Costs: Evidence from Failed Commercial Banks during the 1990s', *Journal of Business*, 79(3), 1523–53.

Mason, J. R. (2010), 'The Evolution of the Reconstruction Finance Corporation as a Lender of Last Resort in the Great Depression', in R. E. Wright (ed.), *Bailouts and Government Rescues*. New York: SSRC/Columbia University Press, 70–107.

Mason, J. R. and Schiffman, D. (2003), 'Too-big-to-fail, Government Bailouts, and Managerial Incentives: The Case of Reconstruction Finance Corporation Assistance to the Railroad Industry during the Great Depression', in B. E. Gup (ed.), *Too-Big-To-Fail: Policies and Practices in Government Bailouts*. Westport, CT: Greenwood Press, 49–75.

Meltzer, A. (2003), *A History of the Federal Reserve*. Chicago, IL: University of Chicago Press.

Miller, J. (1931), 'The National Credit Corporation', *Investment Banking*, 2, 2 December, 55–7.

Olson, J. S. (1972), *From Depression to Defense: The Reconstruction Finance Corporation: 1932–1940*. dissertation, State University of New York at Stony Brook.

Olson, J. S. (1977), *Herbert Hoover and the Reconstruction Finance Corporation, 1931–1933*. Ames, IA: Iowa State University Press.

Olson, J. S. (1988), *Saving Capitalism*. Princeton, NJ: Princeton University Press.

Reinhart, C. M. and Rogoff, K. (2009), 'The Aftermath of Financial Crises', *American Economic Review*, 99(May), 466–72.

RFC (1932), *RFC Circular*, No. 4, Reconstruction Finance Corporation. Washington, DC: US Government Printing Office.

Rockoff, H. (1993), 'The Meaning of Money in the Great Depression', NBER Historical Paper No. 52.

Romer, C. D. (1992), 'What Ended the Great Depression?', *Journal of Economic History*, 52 (4), 757–84.

Romer, C. D. (2009), 'Lessons from the Great Depression for Economic Recovery in 2009', Policy Speech at the Brookings Institution, 9 March, available at <http://www.brookings.edu/~/media/Files/events/2009/0309_lessons/0309_lessons_romer.pdf>.

Rose, J. D. (2010), 'The Incredible HOLC? Mortgage Relief during the Great Depression', Working Paper, Board of Governors of the Federal Reserve System, 15 January.

Schwartz, A. J. (1992), 'The Misuse of the Fed's Discount Window', *Federal Reserve Bank of St Louis Review*, 74(5), 58–69.

Simonson, D. G. and Hemple, G. H. (1993), 'Banking Lessons From the Past: The 1938 Regulatory Agreement Interpreted', *Journal of Financial Services Research*, 7(3), 249–67.

Spero, H. (1939), *Reconstruction Finance Corporation Loans to Railroads, 1932–1937*. New York: Bankers Publishing Company.

Stiglitz, J. and Weiss, A. (1981), 'Credit Rationing in Markets with Imperfect Information', *American Economic Review*, 71(3), 393–410.

Sullivan, F. J. (1951), 'Reconstruction Finance Corporation and Corporate Financial Policy', George Washington University, thesis.

Temin, P. (1989), *Lessons from the Great Depression*. Cambridge, MA: MIT Press.

Temin, P. and Wigmore, B. (1990), 'The End of One Big Deflation', *Explorations in Economic History*, 27(October), 483–502.

Upham, C. B. and Lamke, E. (1934), *Closed and Distressed Banks: A Study in Public Administration*. Washington, DC: The Brookings Institution.

Walk, E. G. (1937), 'Loans of Federal Agencies and their Relationship to the Capital Market', University of Pennsylvania, dissertation.

Wheelock, D. C. and Kumbhakar, S. C. (1994), '"The Slack Banker Dances": Deposit Insurance and Risk Taking in the Banking Collapse of the 1920s', *Explorations in Economic History*, 31(July), 357–75.

Wicker, E. (1966), *Federal Reserve Monetary Policy 1917–1933*. New York: Random House.

Wigmore, B. A. (1985), *The Crash and its Aftermath; A History of Security Markets in the United States, 1929–1933*. Westport, CT: Greenwood Press.

14

Fetters of Gold and Paper

Barry Eichengreen and Peter Temin

We are lucky to have avoided another catastrophe like the Great Depression in 2008–09, mainly by virtue of the aggressive use of monetary and fiscal policies by governments and central banks. However, the world economy, and the European economy in particular, are still experiencing many difficulties. As in the Great Depression, European countries are now grappling with a second round of problems stemming from the equivalent of fixed exchange rates in the form of the euro. Fixed exchange rates and their 21st century equivalent, the European monetary union, facilitate business and communication in good times, we are reminded, but they intensify problems when times are bad. In effect, the gold standard and the euro share the attributes of the young lady described by the American poet and author, Henry Wadsworth Longfellow (1807–82):

> There was a little girl, who had a little curl
> Right in the middle of her forehead,
> And when she was good, she was very, very good,
> But when she was bad she was horrid.

We describe in this chapter how fixed exchange rates display this same dual character, why the gold standard and, even more, the euro are extreme forms of fixed exchange rates, and how these policies had their most potent effects in the worst peaceful economic periods in modern times. We do not ask or attempt to answer whether widespread adoption of the gold standard in the mid-1920s and the creation of the euro in 1999 were mistakes.[1] The economic historian's taste for counterfactual history notwithstanding, the question is ahistorical: both decisions reflected deep-seated historical processes that unfolded over long periods of time: a set of gold standard conventions and a mentality that flowered in the 19th century, allowing the gold standard to be seen as the normal basis for international monetary affairs; and a process of European integration that came into flower in the fertile seedbed that was the second half of the 20th century as economic and financial integration—culminating in the creation of a single European currency—came to be seen as the ultimate guarantor against the resumption of the kind of hostilities that had riven the European continent in the first half of the

[1] This kind of counterfactual history has its place, but not here.

century. We take these historical circumstances as given and ask how they could have been and, in the latter case, might now be managed better. We ask in particular whether they could and can be managed to prevent economic disaster.

The gold standard was characterized by the free flow of gold between countries, the maintenance of fixed values of national currencies in terms of gold and therefore each other, and the absence of an international coordinating organization. Together, these arrangements created an asymmetry between countries experiencing balance of payments deficits and surpluses. There was a penalty for running out of reserves and being unable to maintain the fixed value of the currency but no penalty, aside from forgone interest, for accumulating gold. The adjustment mechanism for deficit countries was deflation rather than devaluation, that is, a change in domestic prices and incomes instead of a change in the exchange rate.[2]

This last point—the conscious decision to opt for deflation over devaluation—can be seen clearly in contemporary views in the depths of the Great Depression. Lionel Robbins argued that 'a greater flexibility of wage rates would considerably reduce unemployment' (Robbins, 1934). He applied this view to the Depression: 'If it had not been for the prevalence of the view that wage rates must at all costs be maintained in order to maintain the purchasing power of the consumer, the violence of the present depression and the magnitude of the unemployment which has accompanied it would have been considerably less' (Robbins, 1934). Robbins had the wit to acknowledge that this was a 'hard saying' and to insist that the entire range of prices and costs, including prices of outstanding stocks of debt—and not just wages—needed to be flexible for his happy result to obtain. But these caveats did not moderate his prescription; they simply exposed the depth of his conviction that internal deflation was the only way to deal with a fall in demand (Robbins, 1934: 186).[3] Mario Draghi, the president of the European Central Bank (ECB), made eerily similar statements more recently. When asked of internal devaluation and fiscal consolidation in 2011, '. . . these austerity programs are very harsh. Don't you think that some countries are in effect in a debtor's prison?' he responded with Robbins-like bluntness: 'Do you see any alternative?'[4]

The gold standard was preserved by an ideology dictating that only under extreme conditions could a fixed exchange rate be unfixed. The euro has gone one step further by eliminating national currencies and fostering the development of an ideology where, for better or worse, first the creation and now the survival of the euro is central to the success of the post-World War Two European project. As a result, unilateral modification of the policy regime is more difficult even than under the gold standard. While it is conceivable under current circumstances that a member of the euro area could opt to reintroduce its national currency and depreciate it against the euro, there is no provision for doing so in the Lisbon

[2] Dam, 1982. For more details and documentation on the following argument about the gold standard and the Great Depression, see Eichengreen and Sachs, 1985; Temin, 1989; Eichengreen, 1992; Eichengreen and Temin, 2000.

[3] Later he regarded this view as a 'fundamental misconception'.

[4] FT interview transcript: Mario Draghi (19 December 2011), <http://www.ft.com>.

Treaty or the European Union's (EU) other founding documents.[5] It is conceivable, of course, that an incumbent member of the euro area and the EU might choose to disregard its treaty obligations. But, even then, if the decision to reintroduce the national currency and convert all the financial assets and liabilities of residents into that unit was not done instantly, a period of extreme financial instability would almost certainly ensue as investors withdrew their money from the domestic banking and financial system en masse, creating what one of us has called 'the mother of all financial crises' (Eichengreen 2010). This spectre raises the question whether the operation can be done at all, parliamentary democracies not being in the business of taking decisions overnight. And, if it cannot, the question is what to do instead.

14.1. THE GOLD STANDARD

Keynes had no doubt about the impulse that initiated the Great Depression. He said in mid-1931 that in 'the fall of investment . . . I find—and I find without any doubt or reserves whatsoever—the whole of the explanation of the present state of affairs' (Keynes 1931: 349–51).[6] We follow Keynes, but take the argument a step further. The tight monetary and fiscal policies of the late 1920s that induced investment to fall were because of the adherence of policy makers to the ideology and policy dictates of the gold standard. Choices in the years around 1930 were informed by a worldview according to which maintenance of the gold standard was a key prerequisite for prosperity. As a result, monetary and fiscal authorities pursued restrictive policies when hindsight leaves no doubt that expansionary policies were appropriate. In practice, however, no pressure to adopt expansionary policies was felt by authorities with the freedom to do so.

We refer to the ideology determining these actions as the policy *regime* that dictated a stable reaction to events. It was well known to contemporary observers. Both policy makers and individuals affected by their actions operated within this regime. When they thought of possible actions, they contemplated options within this regime, that is to say, within the framework of the gold standard. Alternatives outside the regime were not taken seriously by policy makers, investors, or consumers.[7] They were interpreted as aberrations from the stable gold standard regime. In previous work we have labelled this policy regime the 'gold standard *mentalité*' (Eichengreen and Temin, 2000).

The gold standard was revived after World War One in an effort to extend the stability and prosperity of the great Victorian boom (Wolf, this volume). The

[5] The treaty contains an obscure provision providing for the possibility that a member might withdraw from the EU, which would presumably entail abandoning the euro (although not necessarily, since a number of non-EU members such as Montenegro utilize the euro). But withdrawing from the EU is an extreme step that even financially-distressed member states would hesitate to take.

[6] His interest—like that of his modern-day followers and critics—was in the propagating mechanism, and he consequently did not examine more closely his candidate for the shock.

[7] Thus, while Keynes had famously opposed Winston Churchill's decision to put sterling back on the gold standard at the pre-war parity in 1925, once the decision was taken he took the gold standard as a given—as an immutable constraint on policy. For more on this, see below in this section.

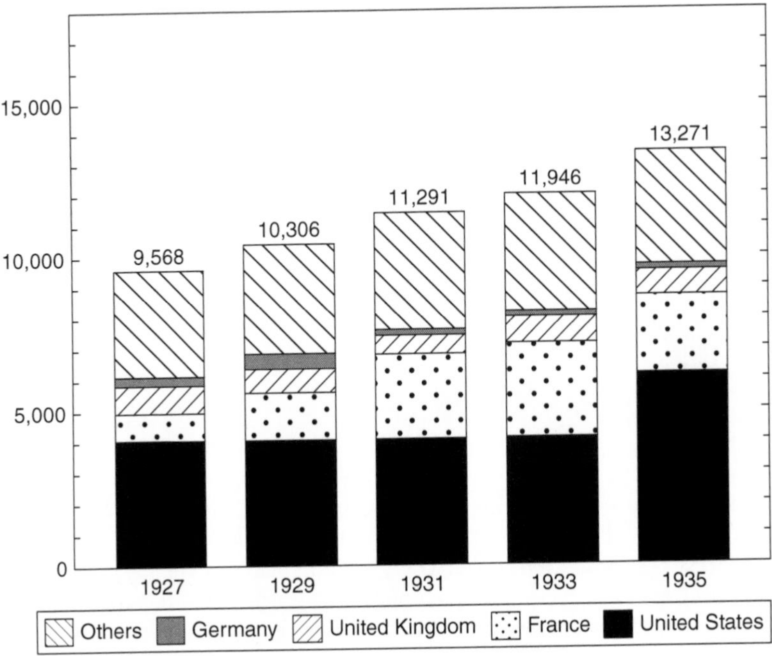

Fig. 14.1. International distribution of gold reserves, 1927–1935
Source: Hardy (1936: 92–3).

leading industrial countries went back on gold, many at pre-war levels.[8] Yet within a few years, the asymmetry of the gold standard made its maintenance impossible. We show this evolution by analysing in turn the four major countries: the United States, United Kingdom, France, and Germany.

Their experience is encapsulated by Figure 14.1, which shows world gold reserves for several interwar dates, divided into those of the four major countries and the residual. The bars show that total reserves rose continuously from 1927 to 1935. The bottom (black) bars show that US gold reserves jumped dramatically after 1933. The next (speckled) bars show that France's gold reserves rose continuously from 1927 to 1933 after which they declined. The United Kingdom and Germany never had reserves near as large, and German gold reserves in any case vanished in 1931. The evolution of gold reserves, starting with their scarcity in the UK and Germany, drove the economic fortunes of these countries in the Depression years.

While we speak today of the interwar period as a distinct epoch, contemporaries in the 1920s knew only that the world had changed as a result of the Great War. Trade patterns had shifted because European agriculture was largely out of commission during the war, causing other regions to permanently expand production, and because the United States had established a commercial beachhead

[8] Some, like France, went back to gold at significantly devalued exchange rates, which will be important to our story.

in Latin America in the period when trans-Atlantic commerce was disrupted. The financial positions of countries changed even more dramatically as the combatants dissipated their capital stocks and financial reserves by fighting one another. The pattern of international settlements was further complicated by the reparations imposed on Germany, the war debts owed to the United States by Britain and France, and loans by the US to back Germany.

Inflation during the war also put strain on the gold standard. Compared to the pre-1913 period, prices relative to the value of gold reserves were higher in the 1920s. This created a deflationary bias that aggravated the pressure for deficit countries to reduce prices (Johnson, 1998; Mundell, 2000).

The United States never went off gold during World War One. On the contrary, the Federal Reserve Act that went into operation in 1914 limited the cash reserves of the US central bank to gold and lawful money. It required reserve banks to hold gold equal to 40 per cent of the value of Federal Reserve notes issued, not merely Federal Reserve notes in circulation. This effectively raised the gold backing requirement for the note circulation by a quarter, from 40 to 50 per cent. This provision was designed to assure the public that Federal Reserve notes were fully backed with gold and real bills. If eligible securities fell short of 40 per cent of notes issued to reserve banks, the shortfall had to be covered with additional gold. Additional gold equal to 35 per cent of deposits placed with the reserve banks also had to be maintained.

The United States in the 1920s thus became a sink for the gold reserves of the rest of the world. Despite accumulating nearly 40 per cent of global gold reserves by the end of the decade, the Fed's free gold—the amount left over after statutory requirements were subtracted—was relatively small. As a result, the Fed had only limited scope for engaging in expansionary open market operations, producing a worry that the restrictions would bind precisely when the need for such operations was greatest. In a recession, when lending opportunities evaporated, member banks would use their available liquidity to pay back their borrowings from the Fed. As the Fed's rediscounts of member bank paper declined, so would its eligible securities, increasing the required gold cover and further reducing the scope for expansionary open market operations.

Scholars debate exactly when and how tightly these constraints bound (Eichengreen, 1992; Hsieh and Romer, 2006). But the important point is not when the free gold constraint bound from a technical point of view or whether it could, in principle, have been circumvented, but whether its presence, in conjunction with the *mentalité* of the time, inhibited the tendency to adopt more expansionary policies. For example, the Federal Reserve's expansionary open market operations in the summer of 1932, analyzed by Hsieh and Romer, came in the aftermath of its stunning support of the gold standard the previous autumn, when the Fed jacked up interest rates in the teeth of a ferocious slump. No investor could doubt the Fed's commitment to maintaining the gold standard in 1932, even if at the moment it was not up against that constraint.

France also accumulated gold in the run-up to the Depression. In the first half of the 1920s, the political left and right had engaged in a protracted struggle over who would bear the burden of taxation. The fragmentation of the polity, attributable in part to the system of proportional representation under which members of the Chamber of Deputies were elected, heightened the difficulty of resolving the dispute. Reluctance to compromise was reinforced by the reparations tangle—for to raise taxes was to admit the unrealism of the nation's reparations demands and reduce the pressure on Germany to pay. The longer the stalemate persisted, the further the franc depreciated, and the more perilous the financial situation became.

France's crisis had two phases. In the first, the war of attrition over taxes and public spending produced a string of budget deficits that could be financed only by money creation. Inflation and currency depreciation were outgrowths of this budgetary deadlock. By 1924, the situation had deteriorated so alarmingly that the politicians, to avert disaster, saw no choice but to compromise. The *Bloc National*, the governing coalition of centre-right parties, led from January 1922 by Raymond Poincaré, succeeded in increasing taxes—mainly turnover and excise duties—by 20 per cent. The budget swung into balance, inaugurating a period of financial stability.

In the second phase of the crisis, from mid-1924 through to mid-1926, the dispute over taxation provoked a series of sharp bond market sell-offs despite the fact that the budget was broadly balanced. Each time it appeared that the burden of taxes might be shifted from workers to rentiers, the latter refused to renew their maturing treasury bills, forcing the authorities to print money to refund the principal. Monetization produced inflation, depreciation, and a deepening crisis. When the financial chaos became intolerable, the left-wing Chamber again accepted the leadership of Poincaré, whose opposition to economic radicalism was beyond question. Poincaré's accession to power is popularly credited with reassuring investors, even though, as revealed by the earlier episode of financial instability that he had also overseen, it was not his personal reputation that mattered. Instead, his return to office at a time of left-wing control of the Chamber signalled wider recognition of the need for political compromise.

It would appear that the fiscal crisis had come to an end. Yet in 1925–26 the exchange rate resumed its depreciation, even more rapidly than before. The franc fell from 19 to the dollar at the beginning of 1925, to 27 at year's end, and to more than 41 at the height of the crisis in July 1926. At this point, it was not so much current as future policies that concerned investors. A desperate Parliament granted Poincaré full powers of decree to take unilateral financial action, effectively removing financial decision making from the political arena. To buttress the budgetary position, Poincaré imposed increased indirect taxes and spending reductions. The magnitude of these measures has been the subject of some exaggeration, perhaps because of the dramatic return to financial stability that accompanied their adoption. France then stabilized the franc at the low level that had resulted from the inflation. This decision to restore the franc's gold standard parity, de facto in 1926 and de jure in 1928, was designed to signal that the new policy regime was permanent.

This combination of policies—fiscal tightening in conjunction with one last devaluation—can be understood as a way of making stabilization politically tolerable. It allowed Poincaré to cut domestic demand as needed for budget balance while goosing export demand as a way of avoiding a more painful post-stabilization recession (Eichengreen and Wyplosz, 1988). But the strategy had implications not just for France but also for the larger international system. As a result of the low value at which the franc was stabilized, French exports were rendered artificially competitive. France accumulated gold at a rapid rate after 1927, as shown in Figure 14.1.[9]

The entire experience created fear of inflation and an association in the popular mind—and the mind of policy makers—between high inflation and suspension of the gold standard. In the absence of the golden anchor, it was concluded, destabilizing speculation could overturn even fundamentally stable policies. The gold standard and stability became all but synonymous in the collective mind, as did fiat money and speculation-induced instability. Come the 1930s, France remained even more wedded than other countries to the gold standard *mentalité*.

Although Britain did not experience a comparable inflation, debate over how to apportion the costs of stabilization took place there as well. Workers felt that they already had paid enough during the Great War. After its defeat in 1924, the Labour Party adopted a programme of 'socialism now', which meant a minimum wage and state-provided family allowances legitimated by the workers' contribution to the war effort. Allowances were required because the reduction in costs required for the restoration of gold payments at the pre-war parity was threatening to reduce wages. For defenders of the gold standard, the problem was not that wages would fall, of course; the danger was that they would not. The growth of trade unionism, the provision of unemployment benefits, and the existence of minimum wages for unskilled workers in industries where trade boards had been established immediately before or during the war all worked to slow downward wage adjustment. The danger in this setting was that deflation would worsen the lot of the workers by both lowering wages and producing unemployment.

The wage issue was particularly contentious in the coal industry, a hotbed of labour activism. The demand for coal received a boost in 1923–24 when Ruhr supplies were disrupted by the French occupation. For the miners, these were favourable circumstances, and the agreement they negotiated guaranteed a minimum wage. But when the conflict on the continent went into remission, the demand for British coal fell, and the agreement collapsed.

The Conservative prime minister, Stanley Baldwin, repeated the mantra of the gold standard: men would have 'to face a reduction in wages' to put the coal industry on its feet.[10] This, of course, was just one way of putting industry on its feet, but it was the only way open under the gold standard, alternatives involving higher prices and lower exchange rates being inadmissible.[11] Countries on the gold standard could not devalue or allow the demand for exports to determine the exchange rate. They could not expand the money supply to stimulate domestic

[9] One is reminded of the modern debate over expansionary fiscal consolidation. France, like Ireland and the Netherlands in the 1980s, and Finland in the 1990s, was able to balance the budget without experiencing a severe recession because it could depreciate the exchange rate and crowd in exports (an option not available to members of the euro area like Greece). But as a large country, its policy had adverse systemic implications not shared by those of the small northern European countries in the 1980s and 1990s.

[10] Baldwin was quoted in the newspaper as saying, '[a]ll the workers of this country have got to take reductions in wages to help put industry on its feet', but this more inclusive statement was denied by the government. Middlemas and Barnes, 1969: 387.

[11] Keynes famously had argued for a lower exchange rate in 1924–25, but his was a voice in the wilderness. And once the pre-war parity was restored, he too took it as a given.

demand, for doing so would push up prices, provoke gold exports, and weaken the currency. The only way of reducing prices was to reduce production costs, the largest of which was labour.

The Royal Commission on the Coal Industry, chaired by a Liberal, Sir Herbert Samuel, insisted that wages had to be lowered. The mine owners based their wage offer on the commission's recommendation, insisting on lower wages and longer hours. From labour's point of view, pushing down wages reduced the purchasing power of the employed and implied job losses insofar as the mechanism for depressing wages was further restriction of demand. And union leaders did not share the central bankers' apocalyptic vision of a world of managed money. They were not sufficiently secure to trade current sacrifices for purported future gains. They had contributed to the war effort and now expected recompense.

The result was not just a coal strike but a general strike, which ended in defeat for labour, further hardening the unions' opposition to the constraints of the gold standard. Ultimately, that opposition would weaken both the Conservative government (defeated in 1929) and Britain's commitment to the gold standard (abandoned in 1931). The Treasury sought to defuse this conflict in the late 1920s by asserting that the 'rationalization' of industry, rather than wage reductions, was a better way of cutting labour costs, and even enlisted the Bank of England in its rationalization efforts (Tolliday, 1987). But the gold standard mantra of lowering costs remained clear.

Montagu Norman, the governor of the Bank, was so eager to maintain the pressure on the British economy and on wages that he refused to expand the money supply even on those relatively rare occasions when he had excess gold, such as in the aftermath of the 1925 stabilization. Norman hid his excess gold in an account at the Federal Reserve Bank of New York where it was not visible to outsiders.[12] The excess of gold had dissipated by late 1928, but Norman still understated the Bank of England's gold reserve in order to keep the pressure for deflation on (Garrett, 1995).

Germany represented the other side of the French coin. Balancing the budget and stabilizing the currency might be seen as admissions that the government's obligations did not exceed its financial capacity—that the Reich could afford to pay reparations after all. The incentive to inflate preceded France and Belgium's invasion of the Ruhr, but foreign occupation of Germany's industrial heartland provided ample justification for running the printing presses full out. Hyperinflation, though an effective weapon in the diplomatic battle with Paris, grew increasingly disruptive to the operation of the German economy. As inflation ran out of control, its main effects came to be aggravating uncertainty and demoralizing consumers. Industrial production went into decline, and influential industrialists like Hugo Stinnes swung toward compromise, accommodation, and exchange rate stabilization (Feldman, 1997). In 1924, these shifts in sentiment allowed stability to be re-established under the provisions of the Dawes Plan, a key component of which was stabilizing the mark with the aid of a massive loan from the United States.

[12] Sayers (1976: 3, 349–54), however, could see the excess gold in retrospect without difficulty.

The sanctimonious quality of the restored gold standard is evident in the missions sent by the US government to help Weimar. S. Parker Gilbert, the Agent-General for Reparation Payments appointed under the Dawes Commission, was clear that he saw the means for doing so as preserving the gold standard at all costs. As he explained, '[t]he Experts' Plan thus established a protected system, which was intended to safeguard the German exchange against the danger of instability through excessive reparations transfers'.[13] There was no need in Gilbert's view to do more than assert the link between a stable exchange and a stable economy.

14.2. THE GREAT DEPRESSION

Like the Baring Crisis and the Great War, the Great Depression was a shock to this happy world. It started out as a rather unexceptional economic contraction, first in Germany and then in the United States. This unexceptional downturn then was converted into the Great Depression by the actions of central banks and governments, notably in their failure to stem the wave of currency and banking crises in the summer and autumn of 1931. Economic policies did not alleviate the Depression; if anything, they served to intensify it. Actions that worked well in more prosperous times had damaging results when economies contracted in the early 1930s.

Policies were perverse because they were formulated to preserve the gold standard, not to stabilize output and employment. Central bankers thought that maintenance of the gold standard would, in time, restore employment while attempts to increase employment directly would fail. The collapse of output and prices, and the loss of savings as banks closed in the early 1930s, were precisely what the gold standard promised to prevent. Reconciling outcomes with expectations consequently required interpreting these exceptional events in unexceptional terms. Where the crisis was most severe, blame was laid on the authorities' failure to embrace the gold standard *mentalité*. The Federal Reserve and the Bank of England, it was alleged, had succumbed to the lure of managed money. Having refused to defer to the rules of gold standard, they had committed abuses of credit, sterilized gold flows and prevented them from exerting their normal stabilizing influence on credit conditions. This, in turn, prevented prices and costs from adjusting.

This was the view that prevailed in Washington DC and in the regional branches of the Federal Reserve System. As unemployment spiralled upward, Lynn P. Talley of the Federal Reserve Bank of Dallas wrote to George Harrison of the New York Fed that his directors were not 'inclined to countenance much interference with economic trends through artificial methods' (Friedman and Schwartz, 1963: 372). Treasury Secretary Andrew Mellon famously advised President Hoover that the only way to restore the economy to a sustainable footing was to 'liquidate labor, liquidate stocks, liquidate the farmers, liquidate real estate . . .

[13] Gilbert, 1925–1930, 10 December 1927: 172.

purge the rottenness out of the system... People will work harder' (Hoover, 1951–52: 3, 30). Those espousing the puritanical strand of gold standard dogma grew more strident as unemployment rose. Hoover himself regarded the gold standard as little short of a sacred formula. Any deviation he dismissed as collectivism, an all-embracing label for economic and social decay.

Members of the British Committee on Finance and Industry (the Macmillan Committee), reporting in the summer of 1931, were prepared to entertain the heresy of a tariff before recommending that the gold standard be abandoned. Even internationalist politicians like the Labour prime minister, Ramsay MacDonald, were prepared to turn their backs on nearly a century of free trade before jeopardizing sterling's hallowed status (Boyce, 1987; Williamson, 1992). Keynes, the committee's leading intellectual light, had opposed Britain's return to gold at the pre-war parity in 1925, arguing that the proper target for monetary policy was internal price stability rather than exchange rate stability, but once the decision was made he reconciled himself to it (Moggridge, 1969; Clarke, 1988). He was unwilling to recommend going off gold in 1930, seeing it as the linchpin of the international financial system and essential for financial stability, but his desperation grew as the Depression deepened. He 'was willing to try anything—a tariff, quotas, a national treaty on wages, profits and rents, foreign lending restrictions—anything except suspending the gold standard, which was too drastic to contemplate' (Boyce, 1987: 293).

Weimar Germany's chancellor, Brüning, decided for domestic political reasons to denounce reparations and proclaim that Germany had paid all that it could in 1931. The *Notverordung* that Hindenburg signed on 5 June and was published, together with an accompanying manifesto, the next day, stunned not only Germany but also the world. German newspapers had been speculating since 25 May that Brüning was likely to ask for some sort of relief from reparations. The French government had drawn the inevitable conclusions; suspicions that Germany might postpone reparations transfers had been circulating for some time. Young Plan loans fell sharply on 28 May on the rumour that the German government was contemplating a reparations moratorium, as shown in Figure 14.2.

The distinction that Brüning and other German officials planned to highlight outside of Germany—that the official announcement did not formally repudiate reparations or invoke the Young Plan's provisions for postponing payments—no longer mattered by the time of publication. The manifesto's sensational references to tributary payments and intolerable reparation obligations, and its provocative language about a people's capacity for suffering having reached its limits, spoke loudly to investors in and out of Germany. It was read everywhere as heralding a broader German inability to make international payments, not least because it was accompanied by official denials that Germany would soon be forced to suspend payments on both reparations and private debts. As investors converted Reichsmark deposits into gold, the Reichsbank's gold cover suddenly began to look dangerously thin (Ferguson and Temin, 2003).

Reichsbank gold reserves did not fall in March when the customs union was announced. Neither did they fall after the Austrian Creditanstalt collapsed—indeed, both Reichsbank gold and total foreign exchange reserves rose all through the month of May, though the entries for 30 May probably reflect a final payment that the government received as part of a deal struck in 1929 for a match

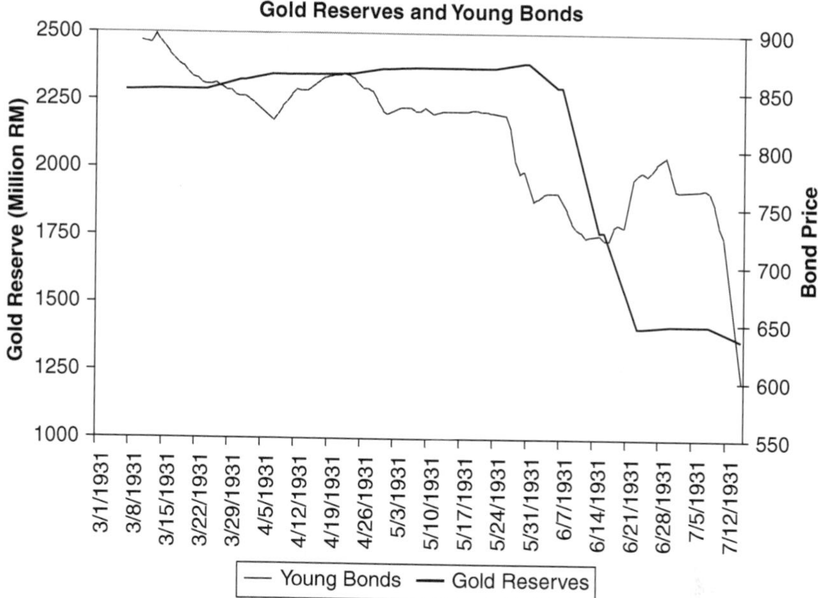

Fig. 14.2. Reichsbank gold reserves and Young Plan bond prices in Paris 1 April to 12 July 1931

Source: Temin, 2008.

monopoly. In the two weeks after 6 June, Reichsbank gold reserves fell by 40 per cent, before stabilizing briefly at 60 per cent of their previous level as it became clear that the Reichstag would not overturn the *Notverordung*. Figure 14.2 shows how German gold reserves fell off a cliff. Brüning was forced to control trading in the mark, but in a stunning example of the hold of the deflationary gold standard *mentalité*, he did not use either monetary or fiscal policy in an effort to stabilize the German economy.

The speculative attack spread next to Britain, forcing the Bank of England to abandon free trading in gold and float the pound in September. As in Germany, the Bank of England did not make use of its increased monetary policy autonomy to expand the economy for another six months.

Even in these extreme circumstances, then, the gold standard *mentalité* was not abandoned. Its rhetoric was deflation, and its policy was one of inaction. The Federal Reserve System, inferring from low interest rates and excess bank reserves that no panic was in sight, pursued a policy of inaction. But when there was a threat to the US commitment to gold in October 1931, it responded by raising interest rates and driving the country deeper into depression.

In this environment, supplies of money and credit depended on the quantity of gold and foreign exchange convertible into gold in the hands of central banks. As uncertainty mounted about the stability of key currencies, and hence about the future price at which they might be converted into gold, central banks liquidated their foreign balances and scrambled to replace them with gold. The share of foreign exchange in global monetary reserves fell from 37 per cent at the end of

1928 to a mere 11 per cent by the end of 1931 (Nurkse, 1944: Appendix A). But there was only so much gold to go around. Central banks jacked up interest rates in a desperate effort to obtain it, destabilizing commercial banks and depressing prices, production, and employment. Bank closures disrupted the provision of credit to households and firms, forcing the former to cut their consumption and the latter to curtail production. Deflation further raised the burden of outstanding debt, forcing debtors to curtail their spending yet again in the effort to maintain their credit worthiness. As the gold exchange standard collapsed back into a pure gold-based system, markets were destabilized as never before.

Sustaining the gold standard required a stomach for harsh medicine, as true believers incessantly reiterated. But deflation that once might have elicited mute acceptance now provoked hunger marches and mass demonstrations. In Germany, the Communist-led Reich Committee of the Unemployed took to the streets in December 1929 before those streets were taken over by the Nazis. The British National Unemployed Workers' Movement staged demonstrations. Farm workers in California and motor vehicle workers in Michigan clashed with police; the Bonus Army of veterans, who camped out in Washington in 1932 to get their bonus, had their tents in 'Hooverville' set on fire by the army. Hunger and despair which had once led to alienation from politics and disenchantment with political parties now led workers to organize and voice their objections. Even Conservative governments, intellectually committed to deflationary measures, hesitated to stay the course for fear of inciting a political backlash (Eichengreen and Jeanne, 2000).

These national policies also had cross-border repercussions—in economists' terminology, 'externalities'. When the United States jacked up interest rates in October 1931 to defend the dollar's gold parity—the sharpest such increase in the short history of the Federal Reserve System—it drained gold from other countries, and ratcheted up the pressure on their central banks. When, in 1933, France did likewise, it intensified the deflationary pressure on other members of the so-called gold bloc. Had there been a policy regime where countries acknowledged their interdependence and acted on it—where they sought to internalize the externalities in question—things might have been different. While it was impossible for one country acting alone to cut interest rates in order to counter deflation, since doing so would cause gold losses and jeopardize gold convertibility, several countries acting together would have been able to do so, since 'my interest rate cuts would cause me to lose gold but your interest rate cuts would cause me to gain it' (Eichengreen, 1984). But this kind of cooperation was not part of the policy regime. Efforts to arrange it at, inter alia, the London World Economic Conference of 1933, went nowhere.

Similarly, emergency financial assistance to counter threats to financial stability in individual countries—Austria in May 1931 being the prototypical example—came to naught. The effort to arrange a Bank for International Settlements loan in response to the Creditanstalt crisis was torpedoed by France, angry that Austria and Germany were engaged in customs union negotiations in violation of the provisions of the Versailles Treaty, and that Germany was building pocket battle ships. Domestic politics got in the way of international financial cooperation. In the fertile environment that was the gold standard *mentalité*, what started as a threat to one bank was allowed to mutate into a threat to the international financial system and the world economy.

14.3. FROM THE GOLD STANDARD TO THE EURO

We are reliving this painful experience in the aftermath of the financial crisis of 2008–09. The gold standard is gone, but it has been replaced by more recent adoption of fixed exchange rates and, in Europe, monetary union and by the same *mentalité* of deflation, motivated now by government debt and deficits. The crisis of 2008–09 was stopped in part by government assumption of private bank debts. The result was a massive increase in public debt, coming on top of the usual growth in fiscal deficits from recession, which Reinhart and Rogoff (2009) showed are like puddles after the rain.

While the euro is not the same as the gold standard, the parallels are there. Adopting the euro, like adopting the gold standard, was meant to be a credible commitment; indeed that commitment was absolute rather than contingent. Countries could, and did, leave the gold standard during wars without antagonizing investors, but countries cannot temporarily abandon the euro in times of crisis.[14] There is no provision in the Treaty of Lisbon for a participating country to withdraw or for 'a holiday from the euro'.[15] Procedures by which a member state adopting the euro might reintroduce its own national currency were not even alluded to, much less detailed. This reflects a political logic: European leaders wanted their new monetary union to appear irreversible. This approach also has an economic logic: escape clauses providing for exit might become destabilizing if investors began to bet on their activation. Since the expectations they engendered could become self-fulfilling, it was thought better not to lift the lid on this Pandora's Box.

The euro area did not simply follow the gold standard; it also followed the Bretton Woods System created after World War Two. The importance of this interlude for our story is not the Bretton Woods System itself, but rather the wartime negotiations that led to it. Keynes in particular had come to realize the pernicious influence of the gold standard as it operated in the interwar years. He acknowledged that deflating in response to a loss of reserves was not only harmful for the country in question, but also had the external effect of depressing economic activity in other countries—leading to the race to the bottom seen in the Great Depression (Vines, 2003).

Keynes sought to avoid a similar outcome in the post-war world. He wanted to avoid the conditions, shown in Figure 14.1, where asymmetries in the operation of the international system imparted a chronic deflationary bias. He therefore proposed a clearing union that would oversee the distribution of international reserves. The essence of his plan was that surplus countries would be obligated to curtail their imbalances in more or less the same way that deficit countries were obliged to curtail their imbalances under the gold standard. These plans did not come to fruition because of the conflict between the US and Britain, as expressed in the conflict between Keynes and Harry Dexter White. Keynes did not want Britain to be forced into continued austerity like that of the interwar years; White did not want to give the UK a free ride after the war. Harking back to the gold

[14] Martin Feldstein (2010) suggested otherwise, but this does not make it so.

[15] See note 5.

standard, White advocated using monetary restraints to keep excessively expansive countries in line; Keynes implied that fiscal policy would work better in a setting of low interest rates—anticipating a fateful gap in the architecture of the euro area. The issues were not resolved, and they were largely forgotten by the architects of the euro (Skidelsky, 2000; Vines, 2003).

The euro area differed from the gold standard in that it talked the talk but did not walk the walk of international cooperation. There was awareness that fiscal and financial policies were a matter of common concern, and that coordinated adjustments, in which countries in chronic surplus expanded while countries in chronic deficit did the opposite, were desirable. But the area's various mechanisms for coordination, the Stability and Growth Pact, the Excessive Deficit Procedure, and the Broad Economic Policy Guidelines, were honoured mainly in the breach. Representatives of Europe's national governments went to Brussels to discuss them, after which they went home and did more or less as they pleased. Like the Pope, the European Commission had no army. While national politicians spoke the language of cooperation, they were mainly concerned with the reaction of their domestic constituents when taking actual decisions. In Greece, deficit spending and government debts were allowed to grow. In Germany, meanwhile, there was nothing to prevent a chronic deflationary bias. For a time, this preference in one country for deficits, combined with a preference in the other for surpluses, seemed like a happy symbiosis—just as it had in the second half of the 1920s. But this did not mean that this situation was any more sustainable than its predecessor 80 years before.

Another thing the euro area lacked when it entered its crisis was an emergency financing facility to provide adjustment assistance to countries in exceptional financial difficulty. In 1931, as we have seen, when the international system began coming apart, there was an unsuccessful attempt to arrange an international loan for Austria through the Bank for International Settlements. When in 2010 it became necessary to arrange an emergency loan for Greece, there was no analogous organization suitable for arranging a loan for a euro area country. Some suggested that responsibility should be assigned to the International Monetary Fund. Others objected that Greece's tragedy was Europe's own affair; bringing in the International Monetary Fund (IMF) would be a little bit like having an international organization bail out California. Unable to decide, Europe in the end had it both ways—the Greek bailout was financed jointly by the IMF and the EU, with supervision provided by 'the troika' of the Fund, the European Commission, and the ECB—which did little to reassure the markets.

There is now belated acknowledgment of the need for an emergency facility to lend to countries in distress. Europe has responded by creating first a temporary mechanism, the European Financial Stability Facility (EFSF), and designing a permanent successor, the European Stability Mechanism (ESM), slated to come into operation in 2012. But both mechanisms remain thinly capitalized, and schemes to leverage them—in the case of the EFSF, to attract private funding or investments by Asian sovereign wealth funds—have not met with much success. An underpowered rescue mechanism is better than no rescue mechanism, but not much better.

In the absence of effective international cooperation, and an adequate adjustment mechanism, the only option available to countries that had now inherited unsustainably heavy debts and lost the confidence of investors was internal deflation. Interwar experience should have served as a caution that sharp deflation of wages and prices was not easy. And, inevitably, not everyone's wages and prices fell at the same time or to the same extent. In addition, deflation redistributed income from debtors to creditors, whose assets, if they escaped restructuring, became more valuable rather than less. In Britain in the 1920s, the struggle over the distributional consequences of deflation had centred on burden sharing between capital and labour. In the more recent euro crisis, there were conflicts along similar lines, for example over whether Irish taxpayers should be required to continue to shoulder the burden of servicing bank bonds (responsibility for which was assumed by their government) when everyone else's incomes were being cut. In other cases the struggle was between current workers and retirees, actual or current, where the latter resisted the tightening rules for pension eligibility, or between different groups of workers: unionized truck drivers benefiting from strict work rules, accountants benefiting from barriers to entry to the occupation, and public-sector workers who had seen their relative wages rise handsomely in the previous decade and now saw the prospect of dramatic cuts.

When the Great Depression struck, and the constraints of the gold standard left austerity and deflation as the only permissible policy response, the hopeful view, associated with Austrian economics à la Robbins and other liquidationists, was that, if only deflation was allowed to run its course without interference, the economy would mount a spontaneous recovery. The lesson of the 1930s, of course, is the opposite. Spontaneous recovery is the product of a vivid imagination in the circumstances of depression; actual recovery requires freeing up policy instruments, whether through abandonment of external constraints or effective international coordination, and taking forceful policy action. In the current episode, we have heard similar neo-Austrian tales of 'expansionary fiscal consolidation', the idea that with sharp fiscal consolidation that put budgets on a solid footing there would be not only spontaneous recovery but immediate spontaneous recovery.[16] Recent data and analysis speak equally clearly about the empirical validity of this view; they speak against it (Guajardo et al., 2011).

While the Great Depression was, at one level, a balance of payments crisis, it was also a banking crisis, as banks were allowed to underwrite risky securities, increase their leverage, and incur foreign exposures, but were then inadequately backstopped when the crisis hit. The crisis of the euro is similarly, at one level, essentially a big banking crisis. Excessive leverage and reckless recourse to the interbank market were what allowed the liabilities of the Irish banking system to grow so large, ultimately resulting in the migration of such weighty obligations onto the government's balance sheet. For every reckless borrower there is a reckless lender, and the French and German banks were allowed to accumulate dangerous exposures to southern European sovereign debt—indeed they were encouraged to do so by the low risk weights attached to sovereign securities under the Basel II capital adequacy accord (Jablecki and Machaj, 2011). While the EU may operate under the so-called principle of subsidiary, where only national

[16] See for example Alesina and Ardagna (1998).

policies without significant cross-border repercussions devolve from the level of the union to that of the nation state, banking—where cross-border implications are especially powerful—was delegated to national supervisors and regulators, all common sense to the contrary. For the euro area to end up with a banking crisis, a sovereign debt crisis, and a balance of payments crisis all at the same time, a considerable amount of history and common sense had to be forgotten.

14.4. FETTERS OF GOLD AND PAPER

As we write, Europe's crisis remains far from resolution. The EU has created an emergency lending facility for lending to governments, as noted in the preceding section, but hesitates to use it more than sparingly. The ECB has reiterated its reluctance to provide support for governments undertaking internal adjustments by, inter alia, intervening in the secondary market for government bonds so as to place an effective ceiling on yields. Austerity is the prescription for budget balance, while internal devaluation is seen as a panacea for restoring internal competitiveness. The 21st century equivalent of the gold standard *mentalité* dominates across much of Europe—certainly in Germany. This counsels inaction on the part of central banks—or on the part of a specific central bank, the ECB. Just as the gold standard *mentalité* dictated that central banks should operate under rules rather than discretion—they should act to maintain a minimum level between their gold reserves and eligible liabilities, as required by their gold standard statutes, rather than intervening as lenders of last resort—the ECB's statute, which states that the ECB should not directly finance governments, and, more importantly, the 'stability culture' through whose lens that statute is interpreted, dictates that the ECB should mechanically follow an inflation targeting rule rather than prioritizing its responsibility for the stability of the European economy.[17]

The moralistic aspect of the current regime or *mentalité*, echoing the attitudes that prevailed in the 1920s, is evident in the statements of European monetary officials. Aficionados of Andrew Mellon's description of liquidationism will recognize the response of Bundesbank president, Jens Weidenmann, to suggestions that the ECB should ramp up its government bond purchases. This, he commented, 'is like an alcoholic saying that I need to get a bottle tonight... Starting tomorrow I will be clean and abide by the rules, but I need a bottle tonight. I don't think it is sensible to give the alcoholic the bottle. He won't have an incentive to solve the problem'.[18] The crisis of the euro is framed, notably in certain northern European countries, as a crisis of profligacy where southern European governments, having chronically lived beyond their means, now need to reform. That several of them in fact ran balanced budgets or even surpluses prior to the onset of the crisis does not figure in this debate. That their subsequent

[17] An early recognition of this dilemma—would the ECB act as a normal central bank or simply conceive of itself as executing a monetary rule—is Folkerts-Landau and Garber (1992).

[18] Reuters (2011: 1).

budget deficits resulted in large from the migration of bad bank debts onto government balance sheets, suggesting that the problem lay in the inadequate regulation of banks and financial markets rather than inadequate fiscal restraint, is almost entirely missing from the story as it is told in tabloid newspapers.

The role of the ECB and the governments of Europe's strong countries has been to keep up the pressure for the crisis countries to raise taxes, cut public spending, and reduce wages and costs. The ECB has intervened in government bond markets just enough to prevent their collapse but not enough to relieve the pressure on national polities. One cannot help but be reminded of Montagu Norman's efforts to disguise the extent of British gold reserves in 1928 as a way of keeping the pressure on for internal devaluation. The problem with economic policy brinkmanship, of course, is that the economy can be pushed over the brink if internal devaluation proves difficult, growth suffers, and public support for policies of austerity dissipates. Austerity that slows growth and raises the level of bad loans may push the banking system to the brink and create a vicious spiral between weak public finances and weak banks, the first of which leads to the latter and then feeds back to the former. Austerity that slows growth and raises the level of unemployment can push the political system to the brink and create a vicious spiral between weak public finances and weak governments which lack the support necessary to stay the course. Britain learned the first lesson the hard way in 1931, when the deepening crisis led to the German standstill and, in turn, the insolvency of some of London's most important merchant banks (Accominotti, 2010). It learned the second one when the Depression led to the fall of the Labour government. Germany, of course, learned the same lessons even more painfully, in the form of a full-blown banking crisis and the collapse of democracy.

Moreover, the members of the euro area seem to have magically forgotten the lesson that Keynes sought to emphasize at Bretton Woods: that the strategy of internal devaluation, even if feasible in a single country, can be suicidal if adopted collectively. Expenditure restraint and cost cutting that enhances external competitiveness does so in part by shifting the burden of adjustment onto neighbouring countries. In Europe, we see the entire collection of EU countries—not just the crisis countries but also the eurozone's strong members and non-eurozone countries, like the UK—simultaneously engaged in fiscal consolidation and internal devaluation without regard to the cross-border repercussions of their policies or any awareness of their collective fallacy of composition. German policy makers prescribe internal devaluation to their southern European neighbours without recalling that the last ten years of competitive devaluation in Germany, even while it brought down that country's high unemployment, contributed directly to the competitive difficulties of its neighbours. Southern Europe may have spent the better part of the last decade running current account deficits, spending more than it produced, but someone had to be on the other side of that equation, running surpluses and producing more than it spent. The identity of that someone, in no small part, was, of course, Germany. And now that southern European countries are compelled to implement painful policies of austerity, there is no reasoned discussion of the need for measures of fiscal stimulus in northern Europe—of income tax cuts to stimulate household spending or investment tax credits to encourage corporate investment. Lack of symmetry remains a problem for the euro area, just as it was a problem for the gold standard.

As noted, the interwar gold standard was laid low by a *mentalité* that enabled the operation of two vicious circles: between internal devaluation and financial stability and between internal devaluation and political stability. We have noted the first vicious circle in the 1930s as a cautionary tale for the present.

One potentially positive development is that the ECB took steps to break the first of these vicious circles. In December 2011, it committed to providing unlimited liquidity to euro area banks for as long as 36 months against a growing range of collateral. Not just in the German and Austrian cases in 1931, but also the US case in 1933, doubts about the solvency of governments and the stability of exchange rates were allowed to undermine confidence in the banks, leading to capital flight that in turn weakened the financial condition of governments and the reserve position of central banks, collapsing the entire edifice. Sceptics about the staying power of the euro have similarly warned that the prospect of involuntary debt restructuring and the reintroduction of national currencies in Greece and, conceivably, other European countries might lead to flight by depositors and runs on banks in a similar self-fulfilling prophecy.

That the ECB has committed to providing European banks with essentially guaranteed funding against a wide range of collateral, essentially breaks this vicious spiral, assuming, that is, that the central bank lives up to its promise. But the ECB has relatively little power as a supervisor, and its president, Draghi, still talks like a deflationist—despite his dramatic intervention to arrest the burgeoning panic in December 2011. Whether the ECB will remain willing to provide cheap liquidity to distressed banks indefinitely, in the absence of a European authority with the power to require those banks to raise additional capital where necessary and otherwise repair their broken balance sheets, remains to be seen. Some steps are now being taken to enhance the authority of the European Banking Authority, the EU's nascent supervisor. Whether they prove effective and inspire sufficient confidence on the part of the ECB, or whether 1930s-style worries about moral hazard re-emerge, only time will tell.

The second vicious circle arises from the prospect that policies of austerity and deflation designed to restore budget balance and internal competitiveness will only deliver recessions that cause government revenues to undershoot, requiring yet additional tax increases and public spending cuts, seemingly without end. As voters feel the pain in the form of unemployment, but see no benefit in terms of enhanced prospects for economic growth, popular and political support for the governments committed to the policy status quo continues to dissipate, while support grows for extremist anti-system parties. The link between the gold standard and the Brüning recession, on the one hand, and the rise of the Nazis in the 1930s on the other is less than mechanical, but it is there. If Europe's current governments fail to deliver growth, it is not clear what kind of governments will come next. But it is safe to predict that their successors will be less committed to fiscal consolidation as a panacea. Not just financial stability but also political stability could conceivably be the casualty.

BIBLIOGRAPHY

Accominotti, O. (2010), 'London Merchant Banks, the Central European Panic, and the Sterling Crisis of 1931,' unpublished manuscript.

Alesina, A. and Ardagna, S. (1998), 'Tales of Fiscal Adjustment,' *Economic Policy*, 27, 489–545.

Boyce, R. (1987), *British Capitalism at the Crossroads, 1919–1932*. Cambridge: Cambridge University Press.

Calvo, G., Leiderman, L., and Reinhart, C. (1993), 'Capital Inflows and Real Exchange Rate Appreciation in Latin America,' *IMF Staff Papers* 40, 1, 108–51.

Clarke, P. (1988), *The Keynesian Revolution in the Making, 1924–1936*. Oxford: Clarendon Press.

Committee on Finance and Industry (1931), *Report*. London: HMSO.

Dam, K. W. (1982), *The Rules of the Game: Reform and Evolution in the International Monetary System*. Chicago: University of Chicago Press.

Eichengreen, B. (1984), 'Central Bank Cooperation under the Interwar Gold Standard', *Explorations in Economic History* 21, 1, 64–87.

Eichengreen, B. (1992), *Golden Fetters: The Gold Standard and the Great Depression, 1919–1939*. New York: Oxford University Press.

Eichengreen, B. (2010), 'The Breakup of the Euro Area', in A. Alesina and F. Givazzi (eds), *Europe and the Euro*. Chicago, University of Chicago Press, 11–56.

Eichengreen, B. and Jeanne, O. (2000), 'Currency Crisis and Unemployment: Sterling in 1931,' in P. Krugman (ed.), *Currency Crises*. Chicago: University of Chicago Press, 7–46.

Eichengreen, B. and Sachs, J. (1985), 'Exchange Rates and Economic Recovery in the 1930s', *Journal of Economic History*, 45, 4 (December), 925–46.

Eichengreen, B. and Temin, P. (2000), 'The Gold Standard and the Great Depression', *Contemporary European History*, 9, 2 (July), 183–207.

Eichengreen, B. and Wyplosz, C. (1988), 'The Economic Consequences of the Franc Poincaré,' in E. Helpman, A. Razin, and E. Sadka (eds), *Economic Effects of Government Expenditure*. Cambridge, MA: MIT Press, 257–86.

Feldman, G. (1997), *The Great Disorder: Politics, Economics and Society in the German Hyperinflation, 1914–1924*. New York: Oxford University Press.

Feldstein, M. (2010), 'Let Greece Take a Euro Holiday,' *Financial Times* (16 February), <http://www.ft.com>.

Ferguson, T. and Temin, P. (2003), 'Made in Germany: The German Currency Crisis of 1931,' *Research in Economic History*, 21, 1–53.

Fishlow, A. (1985), 'Lessons from the Past: Capital Markets during the 19th Century and the Interwar Years,' *International Organization*, 39, 3, 383–439.

Folkerts-Landau, D. and Garber, P. (1992), 'The European Central Bank: A Central Bank or a Monetary Policy Rule?' NBER Working Paper no. 4016 (March).

Friedman, M. and Schwartz, A. (1963), *A Monetary History of the United States, 1860–1963*. Princeton: Princeton University Press.

Garrett, J. R. (1995), 'Monetary Policy and Expectations: Market-Control Techniques and the Bank of England, 1925–1931', *Journal of Economic History*, 55, 3 (September), 612–36.

Gilbert, S. P. (1925–30), *Report of the Agent-General for Reparations Payments*, Berlin: Office for Reparation Payments.

Guajardo, J., Leigh, D., and Pescatori, A. (2011), 'Expansionary Austerity: New International Evidence,' IMF Working Paper no.11/158 (July).

Hardy, C. (1951–52), *Is There Enough Gold*? Washington, DC: Brookings Institution, 1936.

Hoover, H. (1952), *The Memoirs of Herbert Hoover: The Great Depression, 1929–1941*, 3 Vols. New York: Macmillan.

Hsieh, C-T, and Romer, C. D. (2006), 'Was the Federal Reserve Constrained by the Gold Standard during the Great Depression? Evidence from the 1932 Open Market Purchase Program', *Journal of Economic History*, 66, 1(March), 140–76.

Jablecki, J. and Machaj, M. (2011), 'A Regulated Meltdown: The Basel Rules and Banks' Leverage', in J. Friedman (ed.), *What Caused the Financial Crisis*. Philadelphia: University of Pennsylvania Press, 200–27.

Johnson, C. (1998), *Gold, France and the Great Depression*. New Haven: Yale University Press.

Keynes, J. M. (1973), 'An Economic Analysis of Unemployment (Harris Lectures), 1931', reprinted in D. Moggridge (ed.), *The Collective Writings of John Maynard Keynes*. London: Macmillan.

League of Nations (1935), *World Economic Survey, 1934/35*. Geneva: League of Nations.

Middlemas, K. and Barnes J. (1969), *Baldwin: A Biography*. London: Macmillan.

Moggridge, D. (1969), *The Return to Gold, 1925: The Formulation of Economic Policy and its Critics*. Cambridge: Cambridge University Press.

Mundell, R. A. (2000), 'A Reconsideration of the Twentieth Century,' *American Economic Review*, 90 (June), 327–40.

Nurkse, R. (1944), *International Currency Experience*. Geneva: League of Nations.

Reinhart, C. M. and Rogoff, K. S. (2009), *This Time is Different: Eight Centuries of Financial Folly*. Princeton: Princeton University Press.

Reuters (2011), 'ECB's Weidman Opposes Boosting Bond Buys', *Reuters* (14 December), <http://www.reuters.com>.

Robbins, L. (1934), *The Great Depression*. London: Macmillan.

Sayers, R. S. (1976), *The Bank of England, 1891–1944*. Cambridge: Cambridge University Press.

Skidelsky, R. (2000), *John Maynard Keynes, 1937–1946: Fighting for Britain*. London: Macmillan.

Temin, P. (1989), *Lessons from the Great Depression*. Cambridge, MA.: MIT Press.

Temin, P. (2008), 'The German Crisis of 1931: Evidence and Tradition,' *Cliometrica*, 2 (April), 5–17.

Tolliday, S. (1987), *Business, Banking and Politics: The Case of British Steel 1918–1939*. Cambridge, MA: Harvard University Press.

Vines, D. (2003), 'John Maynard Keynes, 1937–1946: The Creation of International Macroeconomics' (Review essay on Skidelsky, 2000), *Economic Journal*, 113 (June), F3380–61.

Williamson, P. (1992), *National Crisis and National Government: British Politics, the Economy and the Empire, 1926–1932*. Cambridge: Cambridge University Press.

Wolf, M. (2011), 'Creditors can Huff but They Need Debtors,' *Financial Times*, 2 November.

Index

Printed and bound by CPI Group (UK) Ltd, Croydon, CR0 4YY

DISCARDED
CONCORDIA UNIV. LIBRARY
CONCORDIA UNIVERSITY LIBRARY
MONTREAL